OXFORD PAPERBACK REFERENCE

Handbook of the World

Peter Stalker is a writer, based in Oxford, who works as a consultant to many UN agencies. He is a former editor of the annual *Human Development Report*, which is produced by the United Nations Development Programme, and has written several books on international labour migration for the International Labour Organization. His website is at www.pstalker.com.

Oxford Paperback Reference

Abbreviations
ABC of Music
Accounting
Archaeology*
Architecture
Art and Artists
Art Terms*
Astronomy
Bible
Biology
British Women Writers
Buddhism*
Business
Card Games
Chemistry
Christian Church
Classical Literature
Classical Mythology*
Colour Medical Dictionary
Colour Science Dictionary
Computing
Dance*
Dates
Earth Sciences
Ecology
Economics
Engineering*
English Etymology
English Folklore*
English Grammar
English Language
English Literature
English Place-Names
Euphemisms
Film*
Finance and Banking
First Names
Food and Nutrition
Fowler's Modern English Usage
Geography
Handbook of the World
Humorous Quotations
Irish Literature
Jewish Religion
Kings and Queens*
King's English
Law
Linguistics
Literary Terms
Mathematics
Medical Dictionary
Medicines
Modern Design*
Modern Quotations
Modern Slang
Music
Nursing
Opera
Paperback Encyclopedia
Philosophy
Physics
Plant-Lore
Plant Sciences
Political Biography
Political Quotations
Politics
Popes
Proverbs
Psychology*
Quotations
Sailing Terms
Saints
Science
Scientists
Shakespeare
Ships and the Sea
Sociology
Statistics*
Superstitions
Theatre
Twentieth-Century Art
Twentieth-Century Poetry
Twentieth-Century World History
Weather Facts
Who's Who in Opera
Who's Who in the Twentieth Century
Word Games
World History
World Mythology
World Religion
Writers' Dictionary
Zoology

* *forthcoming*

Handbook of the World

PETER STALKER

OXFORD
UNIVERSITY PRESS

OXFORD
UNIVERSITY PRESS

Great Clarendon Street, Oxford OX2 6DP

Oxford University Press is a department of the University of Oxford. It furthers the University's objective of excellence in research, scholarship, and education by publishing worldwide in

Oxford New York

Athens Auckland Bangkok Bogotá Buenos Aires Calcutta Cape Town Chennai Dar es Salaam Delhi Florence Hong Kong Istanbul Karachi Kuala Lumpur Madrid Melbourne Mexico City Mumbai Nairobi Paris São Paulo Shanghai Singapore Taipei Tokyo Toronto Warsaw

with associated companies in Berlin Ibadan

Published in the United States by Oxford University Press Inc., New York

First published 2000

British Library Cataloguing in Publication Data
Data available

Library of Congress Cataloging in Publication Data
Data available

ISBN 0-19-280093-0

3 5 7 9 10 8 6 4 2

Printed in Great Britain by
Cox & Wyman Ltd.
Reading, Berkshire

Preface

In an era of globalization the nation-state seems anachronistic. Huge quantities of data, funds, and consumer products are rushing around the world contemptuous of national borders. People too are travelling more rapidly and casually than ever before. So the principle of organizing the world according to a specific group of people occupying a designated part of the earth's surface seems increasingly old-fashioned. Do we really need all these countries?

It seems we do. Indeed, the nation-state appears to be in remarkably vigorous health. Not only do we have far more states, they have been reproducing ever more rapidly. In the first half of the twentieth century, new states materialized at the rate of around one per year. Between 1950 and 1990 the rate was over two. In the 1990s, new states appeared on average at a rate of almost three per year.

In large part, this has been a process of fragmentation. Many groups and people now believe that the only way to protect their interests and establish a more cohesive national identity is to secede and to create a state of their own, however minuscule. Ultimately, they are chasing a myth. No country of whatever size or type conforms to the ideal model of the nation-state—a well-defined territory that forms the homeland of a single people united by a common history, language, and culture. All states are home to more than one nation; all nations are dispersed across more than one state.

In one sense, globalization actually makes it easier to form new states. Cross-national groupings such as the EU, for example, or agencies of the UN, now offer many more facilities. So smaller states can now contract out difficult functions—like defence, or pensions management, or disaster relief. And transnational corporations will be only too happy to print the banknotes, manage the customs service or run the prisons, for a suitable fee. Rather than disappearing, therefore, the nation-state is merely taking a more modern form.

Certainly, the UN is becoming an increasingly popular club. In 1945, the UN was founded with 45 members. In 2000, with the arrival of Tuvalu, its membership should swell to 189, and many others are surely on the way. In the longer term, a membership of 300 or even 400 is not impossible.

This makes the world a more interesting place, but also more confusing. The average newspaper reader might once have been satisfied to identify the vast land mass of the Soviet Union, say, on a globe,without being too curious about its component parts. Now the headlines can raise more awkward questions. Where is Tajikistan, or Turkmenistan? And where, for that matter, did Tuvalu come from, or Kiribati? Citizens of these countries are in no doubt. People who live further away may be less sure.

The *Handbook of the World* offers some help—a compact digest of the economic and political situation in 230 countries. The treatment is inevitably sketchy, and destined to be left further and further behind by the rapid march of events. But a tenuous and fleeting grasp may be better than none.

Inevitably, too, the perspective is a personal one. The data and events included here accord with some globally accepted priorities and concerns. But the selection and the treatment inevitably reflect my own interests and inclinations.

I am grateful to Yusuf Bangura, John Black, and John Connell, who reviewed some of the material at an early stage. All errors and misconceptions that remain, however, are entirely my own work.

For the names of countries I have used the conventional short form in the title rather than the official name. Thus the Libyan Arab Jamarhiya is referred to as Libya, and the Republic of Korea as South Korea. Most countries are covered in two pages. If each profile were weighted for population size, then a page for Nauru, say would imply 120,000 pages for China. Nevertheless, as a gesture to proportionality, the largest countries, with populations of over 100 million, are accorded a generous three pages, and the smallest, which are collected together at the end of the book, only half a page. This arrangement may seem strange and arbitrary. To that extent at least, the *Handbook*'s contents are appropriate to its subject.

Introduction

Each country has an accompanying box summarizing some of the more significant data. Such information, here and elsewhere, should be treated with caution. Many countries do not collect data in a consistent and comprehensive fashion. The size and distribution of population, for example, can be considered politically sensitive and thus subject to manipulation.

Less reliable still are the estimates on such issues as language, ethnic group structure, and religion. These take little account of the fact, for example, that many people speak a number of languages. People can also profess multiple and overlapping ethnic identities, and while for some people such matters are central to their lives, for others they may be of scant significance. Nevertheless these issues can have political consequences so some indication, however approximate, can be useful. In each case the data are for the latest available year. Where a figure is quoted in dollars, this refers to US dollars.

Sources of information

Economic and social data have been taken from various editions of the UNDP *Human Development Report,* the ILO *World Employment Report*, and the *World Bank World Development Report*. Also useful have been the national *Human Development Reports* prepared locally for individual countries. For consistency, most of the estimates for ethnic structures and language come from the *CIA World Factbook.*

More recent political developments have been traced through a number of printed publications. These include principally: the *Economist*, the *Economist Intelligence Unit* country reports, the *Far Eastern Economic Review*, the *Financial Times*, the *Guardian,* and the *New Internationalist.*

Of the sources available on the internet, among the most useful ones have been: *OneWorld Online* (oneworld.org); *Africa News* (africanews.org); *Pacific Islands Report* (pidp.ewc.hawaii.edu); and Wilfried Derkson's electoral web site (agora.it/elections).

Terms used in the text

This book is intended for the general reader so tries to avoid most jargon. It may be useful, however, to indicate the usage of some of the terms that crop up regularly.

Gross Domestic Product (GDP). This is the total value of all the goods and services produced in a country. This can then be allocated to different forms of activity—agriculture, industry, and services, say—to give an indication of the structure of the economy.

Gross National Product (GNP). This is similar to GDP but adds to it the net income from abroad—from overseas investments, say. The GNP is thus equivalent to a country's total income. Dividing this by the population, to give the GNP per capita, gives an indication of how rich or poor a country is.

Human development. This is an all-encompassing view of human well-being, that takes into account not just income but many other issues such as health and standards of education.

Human development index (HDI). This is an attempt to measure human development. It combines data on income, educational attainment, and life expectancy into a single composite figure. This can then be used to rank countries in order of success. Not all countries can provide sufficient data to do this. The 2000 *Human Development Report* from the United Nations Development Programme was able to rank 174 countries—Canada was at the top; Sierra Leone at the bottom.

Poverty rate. This is the proportion of people living on less than $1 per day. Strictly speaking, this is only 'income poverty'. There are also broader measures of 'human poverty' that indicate a lack of basic services.

Purchasing power parity (PPP). If you compare the per capita GDP or GNP between different countries using the standard exchange rate to convert the local currency into US dollars you can get a misleading result. This is because the cost of living is lower in some countries than others. Purchasing power parity takes into account the real purchasing power of the local currency. So comparisons of GNP as $PPP give a better indication of relative national incomes.

Contents

Smaller countries

Indicator tables

Afghanistan

Afghanistan's rigid Islamic regime has driven it into international isolation

Land area: *652,000 sq. km.*
Population: *26 million—urban 20%*
Capital city: *Kabul, 1.2 million*
People: *Pashtun 38%, Tajik 25%, Hazara 19%, Uzbek 6%, other, 12%*
Language: *Pashtu 35%, Afghan Persian 50%, Turkic languages 11%. other, 4%*
Religion: *Muslim*
Government: *Islamic state*
Life expectancy: *45 years*
GNP per capita: *$250*
Currency: *Afghani*
Major exports: *Opium, fruits, carpets*

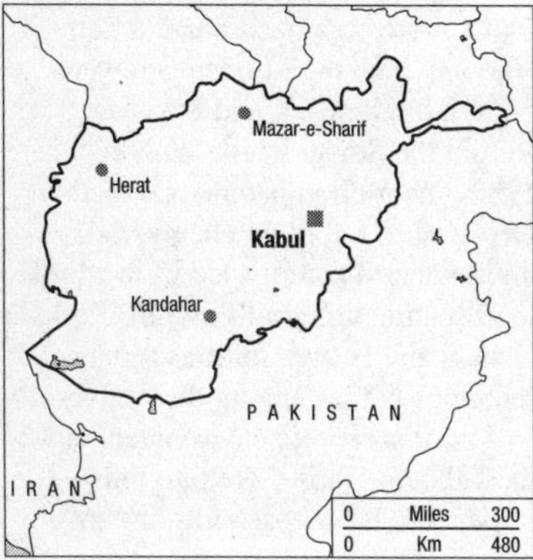

Afghanistan is a largely mountainous country: more than half the territory is above 2,000 metres. Its central highlands are the western end of the Himalayan chain and include the Hindu Kush mountain range. The richest and most intensively cultivated agricultural land is in the lowland plains of the north. The land to the south and south-west is mostly desert or semi-desert.

The main ethnic group in Afghanistan are the Pashtun. They live throughout the country, but particularly in the south and east. Though they are the dominant group, the Pashtun are by no means homogenous and there have been frequent conflicts between different tribes and sub-tribes. The second largest group are Tajiks. Not organized on tribal lines, they are found mainly in the north-east and the west, particularly in the capital, Kabul, where they have made up most of the educated élite. The third main group, and among the poorest, are the Hazara, who live in the central highlands or as labourers or servants in Kabul.

Other groups include Uzbeks and Turkmen, descendants of refugees from the former Soviet Union who live in the northern plain. Almost all Afghans are Muslims, predominantly Sunni.

Population estimates are only approximate. Since 1979, at least a million people have been killed, and millions more have become refugees, the majority of whom are in Pakistan. Levels of human development in Afghanistan were never high. Even in 1979, health services covered only one-quarter of the population—and most facilities were in Kabul.

Since then, hospitals and health centres have been destroyed and many medical workers have fled. Most parts of the country lack access to clean water, adequate sanitation, and sufficient food. Infant mortality has soared to 30% or more.

Education too is in a grim state. Most qualified teachers have left the country. The current regime, the Taliban, closed most of the remaining girls' schools when they took power in 1989— though at the end of 1999 they permitted a few new ones to open.

Women have always led restricted lives, and cannot be seen in public unless covered head to foot by their blue chaderei. International aid helps many people to survive. At times the regime has had conflicts with the few aid agencies that remain, particularly over their employment of women. But, threatened with a total withdrawal of aid, the Taliban have now allowed some Afghan women to work with the aid agencies.

Most people were involved in subsistence agriculture, raising livestock or growing crops on irrigated land—chiefly wheat, corn, and rice. But incessant conflict has undermined food production and also destroyed most industry and infrastructure. The only thriving activity seems to be various forms of illicit trade, or the cultivation of opium in the north-east to be shipped to the Central Asian republics to the north. Local warlords make a good income by taxing such trade and even the austere Taliban administration seems to regard the cultivation of the opium poppy as a necessary evil.

Warlords exploit the opium trade

Political power has never been highly centralized in Afghanistan. Political allegiances have been based more on region or tribe or on occupational group. The most recent conflicts date from 1978, when Soviet-supported communists seized power in a military coup and attempted a series of radical reforms. Crucially, this included an attack on Islam and provoked widespread tribal revolts that threatened the regime. The Soviet Union, fearful of an Islamic republic on its doorstep, from 1979 sent in more than 100,000 troops to fight the rebels—the Mujahideen (holy warriors).

Localized rebellions then exploded into a more organized jihad, a holy war, in which the Mujahideen were backed by the USA and Pakistan. Before the Soviet Union withdrew in 1989, one million people had died. Deprived of a foreign enemy, the now highly-armed factions led by warlords representing different Pashtun, Tajik, Uzbek, and Hazara militias fought ferocious battles among themselves.

Into this chaotic environment came the Taliban. 'Talibs' are religious students in Islamic schools and their movement had its roots in Pashtun refugee camps in Pakistan. Well organized, and probably armed by Pakistan, by September 1996 they had swept aside the Mujahideen warlords, seized Kabul, and imposed their authoritarian combination of rural Pashtun values and Islamic fundamentalism.

Since then, Afghanistan has been more stable. The Taliban control around 90% of the country though are still fighting the forces of Ahmad Shah Massoud, the remnants of the regime they displaced.

In October 1999, the UN imposed economic sanctions because Afghanistan was harbouring Osama bin Laden, an Islamic militant leader whom the USA wants to try for terrorism.

By early 2000, following a bumper crop of opium that had filled the warlords' coffers, the violence seemed to be escalating again.

Albania

One of the most isolated of the former communist states, Albania remains poor and lawless

Land area: *29,000 sq. km.*
Population: *3 million—urban 37%*
Capital city: *Tiranë, 0.3 million*
People: *Albanian*
Language: *Albanian 95%, Greek 3%, other 2%*
Religion: *Muslim 70%, Albanian Orthodox 20%, Roman Catholic 10%.*
Government: *Republic*
Life expectancy: *73 years*
GNP per capita: *$PPP 1,120*
Currency: *Lek*
Major exports: *Metals, electricity*

Though Albania is a coastal country, not much of its territory is at sea level. Mountains make up more than two-thirds of the land area: north, west, and south—highest in the north and centre; lower in the south where they merge with the mountains of northern Greece. Even the coastal plain in the west and centre of the country is scattered with hills.

Most Albanians live in the coastal plain and are one of Europe's more homogenous populations—a product partly of the country's physical isolation. Nevertheless there are some language differences, since there are two dialects of Albanian. Most people in the north speak Gheg while those in the south, along with Albanians in Kosovar, speak Tosk.

Albania previously had very rapid population growth. The communist regime promoted fertility and in the 1980s achieved population growth of more than 2% per year. Following the collapse of communism, the birth rate plummeted as many people left the country in search of work. Between 1990 and 1997 around 40% of the population aged 19-40 emigrated, chiefly to Italy, former Yugoslavia, and Greece.

More than 350,000 Albanians are thought to be overseas—most of them living and working illegally. Remittances from overseas workers also provide most of the country's foreign exchange—$476 million in 1996. Because of the way Albania's borders were delineated in 1921 many ethnic Albanians also finished up in neighbouring countries: around 2 million live in the Kosovo region of Yugoslavia and hundreds of thousands in Macedonia.

Living standards were low during the communist era but subsequent economic collapse and social chaos have seen standards slip further. In 1995, more than 80% of people lived below the poverty line.

More than half of GDP comes from agriculture, though despite extensive terracing only around one-quarter of the country is suitable for arable farming. By 1994, the collective farms had been dismantled and almost all land had been returned to private hands. Privatization boosted the output of grains, maize, and vegetables. But irrigation is limited, technology primitive, and productivity low.

Albanian manufacturing industry collapsed when exposed to world markets and subsequent bouts of rioting looted factories of what equipment remained. Nevertheless, given political stability, Albania's relatively educated and low-waged workers could prove attractive to investors for production of low-tech products like garments and footwear.

Prospects for the mining industry are reasonable. Albania was at one point the world's third largest producer of chrome ore and has significant deposits of other minerals such as copper. But the mines too are sorely in need of investment.

For forty years until his death in 1985, Albania was in the grip of the repressive, and steadily more isolated, regime of Enver Hoxha. When the communist system collapsed, two main parties emerged. The first was the reformed communist party, now called the Socialist Party (SP). The second was the right-wing Democratic Party of Albania (DP).

Naive investors caught by pyramid schemes

Elections for the People's Assembly in 1992 resulted in a convincing victory for the DP, which used its majority to elect Sali Berisha as president. Berisha pushed through a number of economic reforms but his government became steadily more corrupt and repressive, persecuting former communists, and muzzling the press and the courts. Berisha and the DP also won the 1996 elections—though the opposition protested that these were fraudulent.

Albania's economic reforms had made the country feel more prosperous and this, combined with remittances, had tempted unsophisticated investors to sink their money into fraudulent financial 'pyramid' schemes. When these schemes collapsed spectacularly at the end of 1996 around half the population lost their savings. This provoked widespread riots and an insurrection that required the intervention of an Italian-led peacekeeping force. It also led to the collapse of the DP government, which had been linked to bogus schemes.

The ensuing 1997 election was won by the SP. The new government was initially led by an old SP politician, Fatos Nano, but after accusations that he colluded in the murder of a DP politician he was replaced as prime minister early in 1998 by Pandeli Majko.

The Kosovo war in 1999 thrust Albania into the international spotlight—and caused 450,000 refugees to flood into the country. Fortunately most of these now seem to have returned. But at the same time the emergency aid also dried up.

Albania still gets international aid, but development is slow and corruption is rife. In October 1999, Majko resigned to be replaced by Ilir Meta, who was more favoured by Fatos Nano, who had returned as SP leader. At the end of 1999, the two parties remained at loggerheads while the country around them became ever more lawless.

Algeria

Algeria has been racked by violence for more than a decade—but peace may now be returning

Land area: *2,382,000 sq. km.*
Population: *30 million—urban 58%*
Capital city: *Algiers, 4 million*
People: *Arab-Berber*
Language: *Arabic, Berber*
Religion: *Muslim*
Government: *Republic*
Life expectancy: *69 years*
GNP per capita: *$PPP 4,380*
Currency: *Algerian dinar*
Major exports: *Oil, gas*

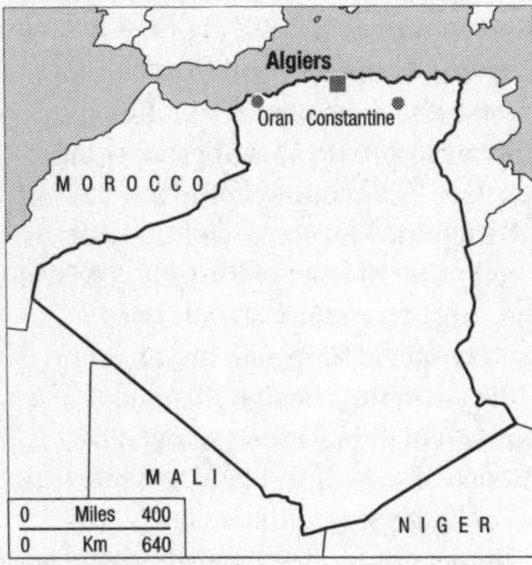

Algeria has a narrow coastal plain which is regularly broken by parts of the Atlas range of mountains which run across the country from east to west and between which there are high plateaux. To the south, the mountains give way to the arid, sandy expanse of the Sahara that accounts for around 90% of the territory.

Most Algerians, 90% of whom live in the coastal region, are of mixed Arab and Berber descent and are Sunni Muslims. But around one-fifth of the population, particularly in the Kabylia region, consider themselves to be Berber rather than Arab and have protested against official efforts at 'Arabization'. In response, the government is to give official recognition to the Berber language.

Algeria's rapid development after independence in 1962 was based on huge reserves of hydrocarbons in the Sahara. Initially the emphasis was on oil extraction, and Algeria still produces around 1% of the world's oil and has five refineries. But in recent decades the balance has now swung in favour of natural gas of which there is a huge field at Hassi R'Mel, 500 kilometres south of Algiers. Gas now makes up 80% of hydrocarbon production. Most is pumped to Europe through two trans-Mediterranean pipelines: one via Morocco to Spain; the other via Tunisia to Italy.

Algeria also has extensive reserves of iron ore as well as smaller deposits of other metals. In the past, mining has been fairly neglected, but the government is now keen to develop the mining industry by inviting foreign investment for extracting phosphorus, gold, and diamonds.

In the 1970s, Algeria used its oil revenues to finance industrialization in a number of other sectors, including steel, vehicles, and cement. Almost all of this was state-owned, and remains so, although there have been efforts to attract foreign partners in oil, gas, and other industries. As a result, most people in formal employment work for the state.

By 1999, most state enterprises were working far below capacity and making heavy losses, and the government came under pressure from the IMF to lay off more than 100,000 workers. This added to an increasing employment crisis: around two-fifths of the workforce are unemployed or underemployed.

Only a small proportion of the land, mostly in the coastal plains and valleys, is suitable for agriculture, which employs around 15% of the workforce. The country does grow cereals, but for many foods it depends on imports.

Algeria waged a long and bitter war for independence from France. In the decades following independence in 1962, political life in Algeria was dominated by the only legal party, the Front de libération national (FLN). Development initially took the form of state socialism but this started to unravel in the mid-1980s with the fall in oil prices, and the government started to liberalize the economy.

From 1988, the younger generation became increasingly resentful of the FLN's grip on power and protested at its austerity measures. The president, Colonel Chadli Benjedid, responded in 1989 with a new constitution that legalized other parties. Radical Islamic groups took full advantage, and in 1990 the Front Islamique du Salut (FIS) gained control of local government in most major cities. Then in 1992 they looked like taking power nationally. After the first round of voting in the parliamentary elections, the FIS took 188 of the 231 seats.

Radical Islamic groups win an election

Faced with the prospect of an Islamic government, the military leadership stepped in, cancelled the election, suspended parliament, and forced Benjedid to resign. This provoked a ferocious backlash. The armed wing of the FIS, the Islamic Salvation Army, targeted not just the military but most other secular groups. The government, led by a series of army appointees, responded in kind and armed village militias unleashed carnage on a horrific scale. The AIS agreed a truce in 1997, but the fighting continued with some of the worst atrocities now committed by other loosely organized groups: the Groupe Islamique Armée, and the 'Group for Preaching and Combát' as well as by the army. By 1999, the war had cost more than 80,000 lives.

Prospects for peace improved in 1999 with the election of Algeria's first civilian president, Abdelaziz Bouteflika. In July 1999, he launched a 'civil accord' initiative that offered a complete or partial amnesty to all those who had not been involved in killings and rapes. This plan was approved by a referendum and was accepted by the AIS though the two other groups are still fighting.

According to the government, 80% of the militants had surrendered early in 2000 when the amnesty expired. There have, however, been protests from the victims that the amnesty has become too broad and that too many guilty people are going free.

Life in Algiers is closer to normal than for a long time. Many of the barriers and sandbags remain in the streets, though more people are venturing out of their homes. In the rural areas, however, the killing continues.

More worryingly, there seems little sign of any real political resolution—or that the army will withdraw permanently from politics.

Angola

Angola's long and agonizing civil war, financed by oil and diamonds, continues with no end in sight

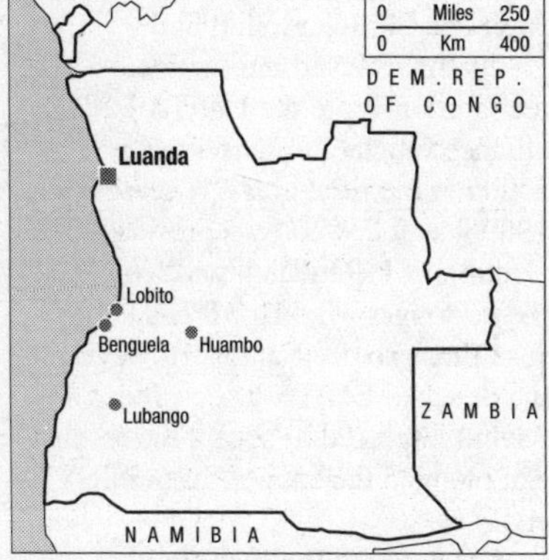

Land area: *1,247,000 sq. km.*
Population: *12 million—urban 33%*
Capital city: *Luanda, 2.2 million*
People: *Ovimbundu 37%, Mbundu 25%, Bakongo 13%, other 25%*
Language: *Portuguese, Bantu, and others*
Religion: *Indigenous beliefs 47%, Roman Catholic 38%, Protestant 15%*
Government: *Republic*
Life expectancy: *47 years*
GNP per capita: *$PPP 840*
Currency: *Kwanza*
Major exports: *Oil, diamonds, gas*

Angola has a dry coastal plain which is at its broadest in the north where it extends up to 200 kilometres inland. From this plain the territory rises through a number of escarpments to highlands that reach 2,600 metres. Beyond the highlands is a vast plateau that covers around two-thirds of the country. The population is concentrated in and around the highlands.

The largest ethnic group are the Ovimbundu, who are to be found mostly in the central highlands as well as in the coastal towns. The second largest are the Mbundu, who live more along the coast and in the north and north-west; they tend to be the most urbanized and many speak only Portuguese. The third group, the Bakongo, are also to be found in the north, as well as in neighbouring countries.

Decades of civil war have devastated a potentially rich country. At least half a million people have been killed in the fighting, and the disruption to food supplies and health services is killing many more. More than 40% of children are malnourished. In many parts of Angola the health system has ceased to function, added to which is the largely unmeasured devastation caused by HIV/AIDS. The war has also destroyed much of the education system. Although some schools that closed during the mid-1990s have now reopened, attendance is low.

Most people struggle to survive from subsistence agriculture. The land in the fertile highlands allows for ample food crops of cassava, beans, maize, millet, and sorghum. Since the mid-1980s, there have been good harvests during occasional lulls in the fighting, but the country is heavily dependent on food aid. The north-west of Angola used also to be a major coffee producer, though the output of this and other cash crops like sisal and cotton has declined steeply. Long-term prospects will also be severely affected by the legacy of landmines—estimated in 1998 at around 6 million.

Though agriculture has been

devastated by the war, two other areas of economic activity have been less affected: oil extraction, which funds the government; and diamond mining, which funds the rebel UNITA army.

Oil was first produced in 1955 and Angola has become Sub-Saharan Africa's largest exporter after Nigeria. Vast new offshore areas continue to be discovered. In 1999, total reserves were 10 billion barrels. Although current production is fairly modest, new discoveries are likely to double output by 2005. The national oil company Sonangol has joint ventures with many companies, the largest being with Chevron. Since the oil is offshore it is not affected by the fighting, and because Angola is not a member of OPEC the country can export as much as it likes. Oil accounts for half the GDP and more than 90% of exports, and for 75% of locally generated government revenue.

Angola's offshore oil is not affected by the war

Angola is also one of the world's largest diamond producers. These alluvial deposits are spread over large areas, much of which are controlled by UNITA which in 1997 mined about half the $1 billion-worth of output—the rest being produced officially by foreign companies in better defended areas or by illegal operations.

Angola's civil war started even before independence in 1975. There were three main independence movements. The Movimento Popular de Libertação de Angola (MPLA), was more urban-based and Marxist and had Soviet and Cuban support. The União Nacional para a Independencia Total de Angola (UNITA) was supported by the Ovimbundu in the rural areas and had the backing in particular of South Africa. A third group, the Frente Nacional de Libertação de Angola (FNLA), represented the Bakongo in the north.

The MPLA took control of Luanda when the Portuguese left and gradually achieved international recognition while the UNITA-FNLA alliance fought a bitter rearguard action in the rural areas. A ceasefire in 1989 was followed by a presidential election in 1992 which was won by the no-longer-Marxist MPLA led by José Eduardo dos Santos. However, the defeated UNITA leader, Jonas Savimbi, refused to accept the result and plunged the country back into civil war.

Another fragile peace was established in 1994, offering Savimbi the vice-presidency. But UNITA re-armed and war erupted again in 1998. A war that started with some ideological basis had long since degenerated into a struggle for power and money. By mid-1999 the MPLA, with oil money, controlled about 70% of the population but UNITA, which despite UN sanctions since 1993 has earned more than $4 billion from diamond sales, had 70% of the territory, and Angola was sinking deeper into chaos and starvation.

Early in 2000, President dos Santos announced that there would be presidential and parliamentary elections in 2001, which would be the first since 1992. This prospect has encouraged some of the small opposition parties. There have also been street protests against steep rises in the cost of living.

Argentina

Economic reforms have accelerated growth, but economic and social stability remain elusive

__Land area:__ 2,767,000 sq. km.
__Population:__ 36 million—urban 89%
__Capital city:__ Buenos Aires, 10 million
__People:__ White 85%, mestizo, Indian, and others 15%
__Language:__ Spanish
__Religion:__ Roman Catholic
__Government:__ Republic
__Life expectancy:__ 73 years
__GNP per capita:__ $PPP 10,200
__Currency:__ Peso
__Major exports:__ Oil, cereals, processed food, vegetable oil

To the west, Argentina is bounded by the southernmost section of the Andes, but most of the country is a vast plain that descends gradually eastwards to sea level. The north-eastern part of this plain includes semi-tropical forests and Argentina's section of the arid Gran Chaco region, and to the south lies the semi-desert tableland of Patagonia. But it is the rich agricultural area of the central plain, the pampas, that is home to two-thirds of the population.

Argentines are of European descent, predominantly Italian. The country was originally settled by the Spanish who optimistically named it 'land of silver'. In fact, the territory had few precious metals though good prospects for agriculture. The largest wave of immigration, from the 1880s to the early years of the 20th century, brought people to work on the farms and ranches of the pampas. Around half were Italian, and most of the rest Spanish, though there were also Welsh who settled in Patagonia, as well as English investors and managers who developed many of the roads and railways. There are now few descendants of the original Indian inhabitants.

During its peak years of immigration Argentina was among the ten richest countries in the world and a land of immense promise. But long decades of political upheaval and social stagnation have stifled development. Today, around 20% of the population live below the poverty line and unemployment is around 15%. There are also stark contrasts in wealth between those living in the poorest regions of the far north and those in cities such as Cordoba or Buenos Aires.

In many ways, Argentina still has great potential. It has rich agricultural resources. Cattle ranching, the basis of its early wealth, still provides substantial export income and beef remains a mainstay of the diet—Argentines eat three times as much beef per person as Europeans. In recent years the fertile soils of the pampas have also permitted a rapid increase in cereal and oilseed exports.

By 1996, however, the major export was oil. In the past, oil production was largely for local use, but between 1990 and 1996 extraction increased by nearly 60%, and 40% of output was exported. The major trading partner is Brazil—a relationship fostered by the creation in 1991 of the free-trade area Mercosur.

Argentina is also a major manufacturer. The opening up of the economy in the 1980s and 1990s boosted productivity, and output has increased substantially. The food industry, for example, was previously the preserve of family firms but has gradually been penetrated by multinationals such as Nabisco or Cadbury-Schweppes.

The most radical free-market reforms started from 1989. Previously, the country had been plagued by bouts of hyperinflation. To fight this tendency, the peso was in future to be pegged to the dollar and made freely convertible. Other reforms included privatizing banks and the national airline. This encouraged foreign investors and delivered price stability and growth but also exposed Argentina to the fluctuations of the international capital markets.

Historically Argentina's politics has been dominated by 'caudillos', strongmen. One of the most significant was General Juan Peron. Peron was a populist, who, with the support of his charismatic wife, Evita, took over as president in 1946. He worked closely with the strong labour unions and nationalized many industries, rising to semi-mythical status in Argentina's history, and the Peronist party is still a force.

The legacy of Juan Peron and Evita

Peron's overthrow in 1955 launched Argentina on three decades of economic and political instability punctuated by military coups. One of the most violent periods followed a coup in 1976 when the military government launched the 'dirty war' against leftist guerrillas. This resulted in widespread torture and murder, with up to 30,000 'disappeared'—and a legacy of bitterness that still echoes through Argentina's politics.

But the military made a fatal miscalculation in its 1982 invasion of the Malvinas Islands ruled by the British as the Falklands. The British responded by sending a task force which retook the islands, a crushing defeat which effectively put paid to the era of military rule. The new presidency of Raul Alfonsín helped to re-establish democracy but he was replaced in 1989 by Carlos Menem.

Menem was a Peronist but rapidly set about dismantling Peron's statist legacy. His free-market policies ushered in a period of rapid economic growth—though at immense social cost as older people struggled to come to terms with a 'dollarized' economy.

The Peronists lost the 1999 presidential election to Fernando de la Rua of the Radical Party at the head of a coalition called the Alliance. He is a less flamboyant character than Menem and has promised to try and build consensus. With the country's economy in poor shape, he will need all the friends he can get. Total production fell by 3% in 1999, though the government is optimistic and forecasting a return to strong growth in 2000.

Armenia

Armenia is a poor and landlocked country with a worldwide diaspora and a distinctive culture

Land area: *30,000 sq. km.*
Population: *4 million—urban 69%*
Capital city: *Yerevan, 1.2 million*
People: *Armenian 93%, Azeri 3%, Russian 2%, other 2%*
Language *: Armenian 96%, Russian 2%*
Religion: *Armenian Orthodox*
Government: *Republic*
Life expectancy: *71 years*
GNP per capita: *$PPP 2,260*
Currency: *Dram*
Major exports: *Jewellery, manufactured goods*

Occupying the north-western part of the Armenian Highlands, Armenia is almost entirely mountainous: the average elevation of 1,800 metres. The landscape is spectacular, with rushing rivers, deep valleys, and many lakes—the largest of which is Lake Sevana. The land can also be violent. The country is dotted with extinct volcanoes, and an earthquake in 1988 killed more than 25,000 people. But the country has few resources in terms of energy or minerals, and much of Armenia's land and water is heavily polluted.

Armenia is one of the world's oldest civilizations and its territory once extended from the Mediterranean in the west to the Caspian Sea in the east. Centuries of conquest and occupation have, however, shrunk it to more modest boundaries. Even within these the population is fairly concentrated. Two-thirds of Armenians live in towns and cities, with the greatest numbers in the Ararat plain along the south-western border with Turkey. There is also an extensive Armenian diaspora. Around 1.5 million ethnic Armenians live in other republics of the former Soviet Union and 2.5 million more are scattered around the world. Recent wars have also generated around 250,000 ethnic Armenian refugees.

Armenia's distinctive culture also survived through the Soviet era. Ethnically the country is very homogenous. Most people are Christians—members of the Armenian Orthodox Church, and the Armenian language has retained its own distinctive alphabet.

The Soviet era did however transform Armenia into an industrial economy. Around 40% of the population work in industry or construction—much of it in defence-related manufacturing. After the collapse of the Soviet Union, many of these markets disappeared and the relatively inefficient heavy industries suffered a steep decline. One of the more productive areas remains precious stones and gem cutting—based on skilled and low-cost labour, though often using imported diamonds. Other healthier industries in recent years include energy, telecoms, and chemicals. Gold mining has also benefited from new flows of foreign investment.

Armenia's steep terrain does not make for much productive agriculture and the country has to import a high proportion of its grains and dairy products. Nevertheless, agriculture still employs around two-fifths of the population, working largely on irrigated land in the Ararat plain where the main crops include potatoes, grapes, and tobacco. The country's agriculture was boosted by land reform in the 1990s, and most agricultural land is now in private hands.

Economic reform has been fairly slow. A privatization programme started in 1994 but by mid-1997 it had only privatized around 10% of enterprises. The economy, which had shrunk dramatically in the early 1990s, only started to grow again in 1994. This drove even more people into the informal sector which is thought to account for around half of GDP.

Armenia itself became independent in 1991. The new president was the leader of the Pan-Armenian National Movement, Levon Ter-Petrosian, who was elected on a platform of modest reform. Since then political developments have been shaped by the dispute over the Nagorno-Karabakh region of Azerbaijan, which is inhabited by ethnic Armenians. When in 1992, Nagorno-Karabakh declared its independence, Armenia supplied it with weapons and eventually invaded. Since Armenia's soldiers had previously been among the élite of the Soviet Army, they easily overcame the Azerbaijanis and in 1993 seized around 20% of Azerbaijan—including Nagorno-Karabakh. A cease-fire was agreed in 1994 but Armenian troops remain in place.

The dispute over Nagorno-Karabakh

Ter-Petrosian seemed likely to be around for a long time. A new constitution in 1995 had reinforced his powers in what was already a fairly authoritarian regime and he was re-elected in 1996 in a partially rigged election. But in 1997 he made the fatal mistake of softening the line on Nagorno-Karabakh by proposing modest troop withdrawals. This was aimed at placating Turkey, an ally of Azerbaijan which was blockading Armenia. This outraged nationalist sentiment and helped provoke mass defections from the Pan-Armenian National Movement to the opposition, and in early 1998 forced Ter-Petrosian to resign.

The ensuing presidential election in April 1998 was won by his ex-prime minister Robert Kocharian, also an ex-leader of Nagorno-Karabakh—which may make him less likely to negotiate, or more likely since he could do so from a position of greater strength.

On the domestic front, popular discontent with the government took a violent turn in October 1999 when a group of armed nationalists stormed Armenia's parliament building. In a burst of gunfire they killed the prime minister along with seven other people. Though there were fears that this might be linked to a coup attempt this seems to have been an isolated incident.

Australia

Australia has been establishing stronger links with Asia—and trying, unsuccessfully, to shake off the British monarchy

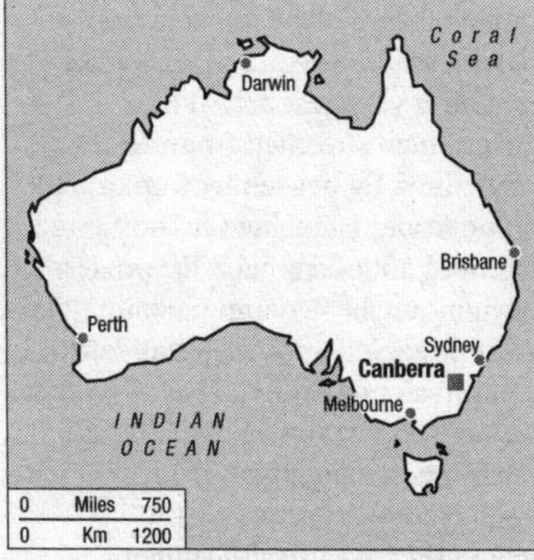

Land area: *7,713,000 sq. km.*
Population: *19 million—urban 85%*
Capital city: *Canberra, 309,000*
People: *Caucasian 92%, Asian 7%, Aboriginal and other 1%*
Language: *English*
Religion: *Anglican 26%, Roman Catholic 28%, other Christian 24%, other 22%*
Government: *Constitutional monarchy*
Life expectancy: *71 years*
GNP per capita: *$PPP 20,130*
Currency: *Australian dollar*
Major exports: *Minerals, agricultural products, manufactures*

Australia's landmass—which can be viewed as the world's largest island—is dominated by a vast and largely empty interior of arid plains and plateaux, known as the outback. The most significant mountainous area is the Great Dividing Range, which runs down the east of the country, separating the outback from the coastal plain, re-emerging further south as the island of Tasmania. Most people are concentrated in the more fertile coastal areas, particularly in the east, south-east, and west.

Australia's population has been shaped by a long and continuing process of immigration: one-quarter of the current population were born overseas. Until the mid-1960s the government had a 'white Australia' policy which ensured that immigration was largely from Europe and particularly from the British Isles.

Since then, it has cast its net wider, seeking the people with the highest skills. This, combined with refugee flows, has tilted the balance in favour of Asia, which in 1998-99 accounted for more than one-third of the 143,000 new immigrants. Even so, the largest single source of immigrants is New Zealand.

Immigration is giving Australia an increasingly diverse population, but its most distinctive ethnic group are the original inhabitants—a quarter of a million Aborigines. They are the most marginalized part of Australian society—the majority living in desperate poverty, either in reserves in the outback or in squalid urban settlements. In recent decades they have become more assertive—and have had notable clashes with the mining companies who exploit their ancestral lands.

Australia's economy is dominated by service industries that account for more than two-thirds of GDP and employment. The largest employer is the retail sector, but many others work in catering—which also involves feeding more than 4 million tourists who arrive each year. Manufacturing has declined significantly. Until the

1990s, many Australian producers were protected by high tariffs, but now that most of these have been cut output has fallen and in 1997 manufacturing employed only 12% of the workforce.

Australia remains a major producer and exporter of raw materials. Its extensive mineral wealth includes iron, aluminium, uranium, zinc, nickel, and lead. It also has gold and diamonds, as well as abundant energy sources in the form of coal, oil, and gas. For many minerals, Australia is the world's leading exporter. Mineral rights are generally vested in the Crown or in individual states which receive royalties from mining companies. But land title has become increasingly contentious; Aboriginal communities are demanding either a veto over mineral development or a share of the profits.

Aboriginal communities demand their rights

Much of the territory is arid, but Australia also has rich agricultural land. Agriculture has become a less significant part of the economy but it still generates around one-quarter of exports—chiefly from wool, cereals, meat, and sugar. A more recent success has been wine, of which exports are now worth more than $600 million per year. Australia now has some of the world's leading wine brands.

Australia's political parties have traditionally pitched conservative forces against those of organized labour—though as elsewhere political parties of right and left have been moving to the centre ground. The conservative party is the Liberal Party, which draws its support from the urban middle class. The Labor Party has relied more on urban workers. The third major force is the National Party, which draws its support from the rural areas. Two minority parties are the Australian Democrats and the Greens, neither of which has ever had seats in the lower House of Representatives, though they do have seats in the Senate.

Labor's longest period in government stretched from 1983 to 1996, initially headed by former trade union leader Bob Hawke. During this period, Labor continued the process of opening up the economy, floating the Australian dollar, dismantling tariffs, and privatizing utilities. Faced with an economic downturn, Labor became increasingly unpopular, but it was not until the 1996 election that it was replaced by a Liberal-National coalition led by John Howard.

Howard continued economic reforms. To gain approval for a new goods and service tax, he called a general election in 1998 and achieved a narrow victory. This election was also notable for the poor showing of the racist One Nation party which had been demanding a halt to Asian immigration.

A continuing saga is Australia's constitutional status. The head of state is still the British monarch. In a 1999 referendum, 55% of Australians rejected the proposal to become a republic, primarily because they disliked the form of republic on offer, which involved an indirectly-elected president, or because they regarded the whole constitutional process as a waste of time and money. For now at least, Queen Elizabeth continues to reign.

Austria

Decades of consensus have been shaken by a resurgence of the far right

Land area: *84,000 sq. km.*
Population: *8 million—urban 65%*
Capital city: *Vienna, 2.1 million*
People: *Austrian*
Language: *German*
Religion: *Roman Catholic 85%, Protestant 6%, other 9%*
Government: *Republic*
Life expectancy: *77 years*
GNP per capita: *$PPP 22,740*
Currency: *Schilling*
Major exports: *Metal goods, textiles, paper products, chemicals, electronics*

Austria is one of Western Europe's most mountainous countries. The western two-thirds of the country fall within the Alps, in ranges that run from east to west divided by broad river valleys. Another smaller and less dramatic highland region extends from the north of the country into the Czech Republic. Lowland Austria is largely in the east, including the Vienna basin through which flows the Danube on its way to Slovakia.

In ethnic terms, Austria is fairly homogenous, though there is some representation of neighbouring nationalities. The end of the cold war also saw a further surge of immigration from Eastern Europe, following the war in former Yugoslavia. As a result, between 1985 and 1997 the proportion of foreign-born rose from 4% to 9%—though these flows have eased now as border controls have been tightened. Immigration did at least temporarily rejuvenate the population. Otherwise, with a fertility rate of only 1.4 children per woman of childbearing age, the population is ageing fast.

Austrians enjoy one of Europe's more generous systems of welfare. Parents are entitled to two years of maternity leave, for example. But welfare benefits have been cut recently and will probably be cut further. Retirement benefits already absorb 9% of GDP, a proportion that, on present trends, could double over the next 35 years.

Most Austrians are now employed in service industries, from banking to transport. And following the opening up of Eastern Europe, many foreign companies use Vienna as a base. One of the more significant service sectors is tourism. Millions of other Europeans are drawn to Austria's rich cultural heritage and to the scenic and winter sports attractions of the Alps. Tourist density is high: the ratio of tourists to the national population is two or three times greater than in other popular European destinations such as France or Spain.

Austria is also an important centre for manufacturing, which employs around one-quarter of the workforce.

More traditional industries such as textiles and footwear have stagnated, but others have been expanding, including electronics, chemicals, and metals. Much of the output consists of medium-technology intermediate goods for other European countries, particularly Germany.

Agriculture employs steadily fewer people—now around only 5% of the workforce, but Austria is still largely self-sufficient in food. Large herds of livestock, particularly in the mountainous west of the country, also allow for the export of some dairy products. And, with around two-fifths of the country forested, there are also exports of timber.

Austria has enjoyed steadier economic progress than many other European countries. Much of this is due to its distinctive system of sozialpartnerschaft (social partnership). This involves regular discussions between employers, trade unions, academics, and agricultural representatives. Most major economic policies derive from this process of consultation which has contributed to stable labour relations, low inflation, and extensive welfare benefits—though it has also reduced the status of the parliament.

Austria has a system of social partnership

Until recently, consensus was also the major characteristic of Austrian politics. For most of the period since the Second World War, Austria has effectively been run by two parties generally in a coalition. From 1970 onwards, the dominant partner has been the centre-left Social Democratic Party, which draws its support from labour and trade unions. In 1997, Viktor Klima took over as party leader and became chancellor—head of the government. The second party was the centre-right People's Party, led by Wolfgang Schüssel, which is linked to the Roman Catholic Church and draws its support more from the middle class and business.

From the mid-1990s, however, the cosy arrangements between the two parties (which included Proporz—sharing out government jobs between their party card-holders) was challenged from the far right by the Freedom Party and its aggressive former leader Jörg Haider who stands on a populist, nationalist, anti-EU, anti-immigrant platform. Haider has in the past praised Hitler, though subsequently he has recanted.

The 1999 elections gave the two major parties a shock. Although Klima and the Social Democratic Party still had the largest share of the vote with 33%, the Freedom Party came second with 29%—narrowly ahead of the People's Party. This resulted in 2000 in the emergence of a People's Party-Freedom Party coalition headed by Schüssel, though without Haider in the cabinet. Freedom's Susanne Riess-Passer became vice-chancellor.

International opinion was outraged, particularly in the rest of EU, where other political leaders fear a return of the far right. Although the EU itself could not take action, many governments decided to freeze bilateral relations to show their disapproval. Haider's subsequent resignation from the party did not seem to placate them. In government, Freedom has toned down its rhetoric, while opinion polls suggest that support for the party has fallen.

Azerbaijan

Oil and gas-rich Azerbaijan could have a prosperous future if it made peace with its neighbours

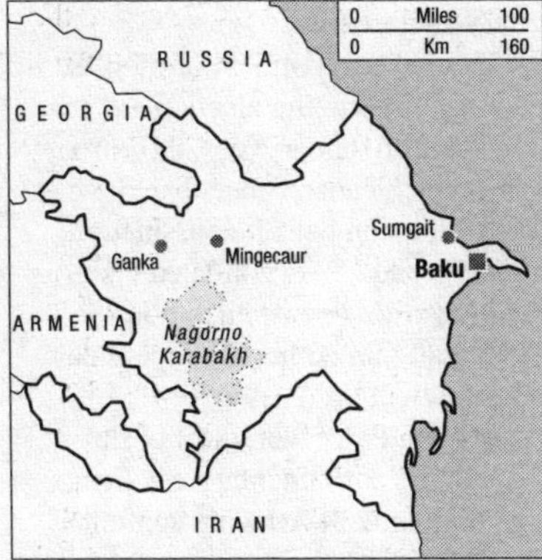

Land area: *87,000 sq. km.*
Population: *8 million—urban 57%*
Capital city: *Baku, 1.8 million*
People: *Azeri: 90%, Dagestani 3%, Russian 3%, Armenian 2%, other 2%*
Language: *Azeri 89%, Russian 3%, Armenian 2%, other 6%*
Religion: *Muslim 93%, Russian Orthodox 3%, Armenian Orthodox 2%, other 2%*
Government: *Republic*
Life expectancy: *70 years*
GNP per capita: *$PPP 1,820*
Currency: *Manat*
Major exports: *Oil, textiles, food*

Around half of Azerbaijan comprises the central lowland area through which flow the two main rivers, the Aras and the Kura which join before draining into the Caspian Sea. These plains are contained by spurs of two mountain ranges, the Greater Caucasus to the north and the Lesser Caucasus to the south-west. In addition, there is a small isolated section of its territory to the south-west, Nakhichevan, sandwiched between Armenia and Iran. Azerbaijan has a varied, and often strikingly beautiful, terrain.

Azerbaijan is ethnically fairly homogenous. Around 90% are Azeris who are Shiah Muslims. But there have always been minority groups. The most prominent are the 100,000 or so Armenians, who are Christians, and who live in the Nagorno-Karabakh region in the south, which since 1994 has been occupied by neighbouring Armenia. There are also many ethnic Azeris elsewhere—indeed more live in Iran than in Azerbaijan itself.

In the past, Azerbaijan's population has had good levels of education and health but government services have been undermined by the current conflict. Between 1990 and 1996, life expectancy fell by two years. One-quarter of the population are unemployed and two-thirds live below the poverty line. The fighting has also made around 1 million people homeless.

One-third of the workforce are employed in agriculture, largely in the fertile lowlands. Most of the former state and collective farms have now been privatized. In addition to growing grains, the country is also a major producer of grapes and other fruits as well as vegetables and particularly cotton.

But the land and water have been heavily polluted by toxic chemicals used in cotton production, and poor drainage has led to salination and a threat from the Caspian Sea which is rising by 25 centimetres per year. Agriculture has also been hit by the fighting: some of the best land for grapes has been lost to the Armenian occupation.

The mainstay of the country's economy remains oil, three-quarters of which is extracted offshore in the Caspian Sea. This area has been an oil producer since the 1850s and by the early 1900s it supplied half the world's oil. Baku still has the ornate grand houses built by the first oil millionaires.

Azerbaijan's significance declined with the discovery of larger deposits elsewhere. Nevertheless, the international oil companies have still congregated here looking for new deposits and were rewarded in mid-1999 with a major new gas find.

In addition to extracting oil and gas, Azerbaijan has also been a major producer of equipment for the oil industry—though much of the plant is now inefficient and obsolete. The city of Sumgait was also one of the main supplier of chemicals to the Soviet Union; now much of the plant there is rusting in what is probably one of the most polluted places on earth.

One of the most polluted places on earth

Efforts have been made to switch to lighter industries, and the country has some textile factories that use local cotton. But production generally has been held back by the slow pace of economic reform and is weakened by extensive corruption.

Given its ethnic fault lines, Azerbaijan's political development was always likely to be painful. Even when it was a Soviet republic, there had been a long-running dispute with Armenia over Nagorno-Karabakh and the difficulties in handling this crisis cost several leaders their jobs. Independence was declared in 1991 and there were initially some successes in consolidating control over the disputed enclave. But in 1993 the Armenians managed to seize this and neighbouring regions—around 20% of Azerbaijan.

The ensuing political turmoil led in October 1993 to the election as president of Heidar Aliev, a former communist leader. Since then, he has survived a number of assassination attempts and he consolidated his position with a new constitution in 1995 that granted him sweeping new powers. In 1996 Aliev's New Azerbaijan Party won most of the seats in the parliamentary elections.

Fighting with Armenia continued until 1994 when a ceasefire was brokered by the Organization for Security and Cooperation in Europe—though Armenia has not withdrawn, and there have been subsequent outbreaks of fighting.

Meanwhile Aliev set about nurturing a personality cult and to no one's surprise was re-elected president in October 1998. The cult continues to flourish. He now has two museums devoted to his life works. There is also a Heidar Mosque, called the Museum of Heidar and Religion, and few public buildings are complete without their Heidar portraits.

Despite the attention lavished upon him, 76-year old Aliev's health is failing. And there are worries about the succession. Aliev has lined up his son Iliam to follow in his footsteps. But Iliam lacks his father's political skills or determination, and seems unlikely to take over.

Bahamas

One of the richest countries in the Caribbean

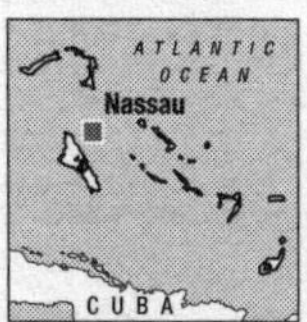

The Bahamas comprises more than 700 islands in the Caribbean, many with sandy beaches and clear water, although only around 30 are inhabited. The majority of people live on New Providence Island, particularly in the capital, Nassau.

Bahamans generally have good standards of education and health and, compared with many other Caribbean countries, incomes are high. However, not everyone has gained from the tourist boom which still leaves many young people unemployed. The islands also attract illegal immigrants, particularly from Haiti, to work in hotels and restaurants.

Tourism accounts for around 40% of GDP and employs a similar proportion of the workforce. Each year there are more than 1.5 million stopover visitors to the country's resorts, and about the same number of cruise passengers—the majority of visitors are from the USA. These numbers are set to rise following more investment in resort hotels. The largest employer is the South African company Sun International.

There are no rivers, and the soil is poor, so opportunities for agriculture are limited. But there is a small fishing industry that catches lobsters for local consumption and export.

The Bahamas also has a significant offshore financial sector that contributes about 7% of GDP and provides some of the highest-paid employment. The industry acquired a dubious reputation in the 1980s through association with drug trafficking and money laundering. Things have improved since US drug enforcement officials established a semi-permanent presence, and the government tightened financial regulations.

Of late, the economy has been growing. In 1999 the Hong Kong-based company Hutchison Whampoa opened a new trans-shipment port.

The Bahamas is a parliamentary democracy whose head of state is the British monarch. In the decades after independence in 1973 the government was largely in the hands of Sir Lynden Pindling, leader of the Progressive Liberal Party (PLP). By the end of the 1980s, however, there was an economic downturn and allegations of corruption. The elections in 1992 resulted in a victory for the Free National Movement (FNM), and Hubert Ingraham became prime minister. With Pindling and other members of the PLP still being investigated for corruption, and a fast-growing economy, the FNM and Ingraham were re-elected in 1997.

Land area:14,000 sq. km.
Population: *294,000—urban 87%*
Capital city: *Nassau, 191,000*
People: *Black 85%, white 15%*
Language: *English, Creole*
Religion: *Baptist 32%, Anglican 20%, Roman Catholic 19%, Methodist 6%, Church of God 6%, other 17%*
Government: *Constitutional monarchy*
Life expectancy: *74 years*
GNP per capita: *$PPP 10,460*
Currency: *Bahamas dollar*
Major exports: *Lobsters, rum*

Bahrain

Bahrain has an absolute monarchy, and a poor record on human rights, but now has a more conciliatory emir

The state of Bahrain consists of around 30 islands in the Persian Gulf. Bahrain island itself, which has more than 85% of the territory, is mostly arid. Wells and springs in the north are used to irrigate fruit and vegetables, but the water table is sinking, so future agricultural prospects are poor.

The native population of Bahrain is largely Arab and divided between the majority Shiah and minority Sunni sects. Bahrainis enjoy high standards of health and education, but, unlike the citizens of most other Gulf oil states, not all are well off, and in 1999 15% were unemployed—with a higher rate among the Sunnis. Even so, Bahrainis employ immigrants, primarily from the Indian sub-continent, to do most of the less popular work.

Bahrain's economy is based on oil, but its reserves are small and may not last beyond 2009. It processes this in its own refineries, along with oil from Saudi Arabia. Since it has less oil than other Gulf countries, Bahrain has had to develop a more diverse economy. Thus, it uses gas reserves to fuel one of the world's largest aluminium smelters and it also has a range of industries that include ship repairing, as well as light engineering and manufacturing.

Land area: *1,000 sq. km.*
Population: *641,000—urban 91%*
Capital city: *Manama, 206,000*
People: *Bahraini 63%, Asian 13%, other Arab 10%, Iranian 8%, other 6%*
Language: *Arabic, English, Farsi, Urdu*
Religion: *Muslim, Shiah 75%, Sunni 25%*
Government: *Absolute monarchy*
Life expectancy: *73 years*
GNP per capita: *$PPP 13,700*
Currency: *Bahraini dinar*
Major exports: *Oil products, aluminium, chemicals*

Bahrain is also a financial, trading, and distribution hub for the other Gulf countries; it is linked by a 25 kilometre causeway to Saudi Arabia. Two-thirds of the workforce are employed in these and other services.

Bahrain is an absolute monarchy. The hereditary emir, from the al-Khalifa family, rules in co-operation with the dominant Sunni business élite. There is no parliament, human rights guarantees have been suspended, and trade unions are banned.

The two Islamic groups often clash violently. The majority Sunni accuse the Shiah of being in league with Iran which once had designs on Bahrain. The Shiah have protested at the lack of democracy and many of their leaders have been imprisoned. An exiled Bahraini Freedom Movement is based in London.

In March 1999, Sheikh Hamad al-Khalifa succeeded to the title of emir. He has been trying to be more conciliatory and has released hundreds of prisoners. He has even spoken of citizens' rights. But he has retained his hard-line uncle, Sheikh Khalifa, as prime minister so for the time being an opening up to greater democracy does not seem to be on the agenda.

Bangladesh

Bangladesh's democracy is being undermined by bitter political feuding

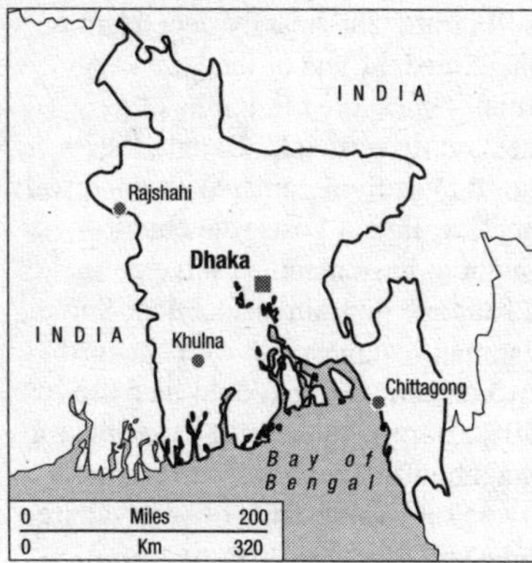

Land area: *144,000 sq. km.*
Population: *126 million—urban 20%*
Capital city: *Dhaka, 10 million*
People: *Bengali, some tribal*
Language: *Bangla*
Religion: *Muslim*
Government: *Republic*
Life expectancy: *57 years*
GNP per capita: *$PPP 1,100*
Currency: *Taka*
Major exports: *Garments, jute products*

Bangladesh consists of a vast alluvial plain. The waters of the Ganges and the Brahmaputra flow in via India to deposit billions of tons of silt each year across this delta before emerging sluggishly into the Bay of Bengal. The only higher areas are the Chittagong Hill Tracts on the eastern border with Burma.

The annual flooding is a welcome event. Even in a normal rainy season, 20% of the landscape is flooded. This recharges the underground aquifers, deposits the silt that makes for fertile and productive soil, and allows for the spawning and migration of 300 or more species of fish. But flooding can also be more destructive. In 1998 floods covered more than two-thirds of the country, killing 1,300 people and causing damage of around $900 million.

The other major natural hazard is cyclones. The funnel-shaped coastline regularly sucks in some of the world's most violent storms. In 1991, winds of up to 240 kilometres per hour combined with a tidal surge 25 feet high to kill around 140,000.

Survival in these climatic extremes has made Bangladesh's people remarkably resilient. As a group, they are also relatively homogenous, with a rich language and culture shared with the state of West Bengal in neighbouring India. Bangladesh means 'land of the Bengalis'. Most people are Muslim, though in practice they tend to have a fairly flexible attitude towards religion. The largest distinctive ethnic groups are the tribal peoples who live in the Chittagong Hill Tracts.

Bar some city-states, Bangladesh has the world's highest population density—818 per square kilometre. However, a massive, largely aid-financed, family planning programme slowed annual population growth from around 2.8% in the early 1970s to 1.8% by 1996 and it is expected to average 1.5% over the next twenty years The government's goal is for population growth to stop altogether by the year 2045, though by this time the population may well have doubled to around 250 million.

Bangladesh remains very poor and standards of health are low. A country where two-thirds of children are malnourished, and where three-quarters of the population do not use sanitary latrines, is unlikely to be healthy, and Bangladesh is not. Millions of children have their lives extinguished all too soon— infant mortality is high at 81 deaths per thousand live births. Only around 50% of the population has access to basic health care.

Bangladesh also has low standards of education. In 1997, the adult literacy rate was below 40%. The government has increased investment in education and many more children are now enrolling in school. But most schools are in decrepit buildings, with overcrowded classrooms, and there are shortages of books and equipment. Not surprisingly, attendance is poor—averaging no more than 60%. Around half of the children do not finish primary school.

Some of this is compensated for by non-formal schools run by non-governmental agencies (NGOs). Bangladesh has some of the world's largest and most enterprising NGOs, such as the Bangladesh Rural Advancement Committee (BRAC). They may offer little more than bamboo huts with mud floors, and teachers who themselves have only a basic education, but they have proved very effective at catching children who have missed out on primary school. Other major NGOs include Proshika, and the NGO-like Grameen Bank, which operates in more than half the country's villages with a system of micro-credit that is being emulated all over the world.

Bangladesh has some of the world's largest NGOs

Most people live in the rural areas and make their living from agriculture. In many respects they have been successful. Over the past twenty-five years, rice production has more than doubled. But harvests are still erratic and heavily dependent on the climate. Plots of land are very small—measured in tenths of a hectare. In principle, Bangladesh need not import foodgrains. With good soils and low labour costs, the country ought to have a comparative advantage in grain production. Some estimates suggest that over the next two decades output could increase by 50%. But yields are still lower than in neighbouring countries, and farmers living on a knife-edge of survival are reluctant to invest. Boosting food production will depend less on supply and more on demand. Since 1995, the price of grain has been stable and reasonably low. However, at current prices half the population still cannot afford to feed themselves properly.

Those unable to find work in the rural areas are heading for the cities, or even overseas. There are probably around 2 million Bangladeshis working in other Asian countries, especially in the Gulf. In terms of industry, Bangladesh's greatest progress has been in light manufacturing, particularly the garment sector, which employs around 1.5 million people, 85% of them women. Bangladesh has enjoyed preferential access to Western markets. This advantage will disappear, but with low labour costs Bangladesh should still be able to compete.

Even so, about one-third of the

work force is unemployed or underemployed and about half the population live below the poverty line. At independence in 1971, the US Secretary of State famously dismissed the new country as an 'international basket-case'. Bangladeshis have defied this gloomy prognostication. Nevertheless, theirs remains one of the poorest developing countries. Economic growth has been no more than 4% or 5% per year, and the country remains heavily dependent on foreign aid.

Bangladesh achieved independence in 1971 after a bloody war of secession from Pakistan. Elections in what was then East Pakistan had produced a victory for the Awami League (AL) led by Sheikh Mujibur Rahman. He demanded greater autonomy and when this was refused the Awami League organized strikes and demonstrations. The Pakistani army responded by attacking Dhaka and a full-scale civil war erupted in which the East Bengalis were supported by India. By the time the war ended, more than 1 million people had died.

A bloody war of secession

After independence, 'Sheikh Mujib' and the Awami League took power, but he became increasingly autocratic and replaced the parliament with a presidential system. The military grew dissatisfied and in 1975 a group of officers assassinated Sheikh Mujib.

Following this, the *de facto* leader of the government was the army chief, General Zia ur-Rahman who took over the presidency in 1977 at the head of his new Bangladesh National Party. In 1981, he in turn was assassinated by rebel army officers led by General Hossain Mohammad Ershad, who took the presidency in 1983. Ershad's rule became increasingly unpopular and, following widespread demonstrations, he was eventually deposed in 1990. Ershad was subsequently convicted of corruption and murder and served seven years in prison.

A general election in 1991 led to a surprising but fair victory for the BNP, which was now led by Zia's widow, Begum Khaleda Zia. She defeated the Awami League, now led by Sheikh Mujib's daughter Sheikh Hasina Wajed. In the same year, a referendum altered the constitution to return executive power to the prime minister.

Though the BNP had achived power in a free and fair election the Awami League embarked on a bitter campaign of destabilization, using 'hartals' which are general strikes enforced by intimidation. The Awami League then boycotted the 1996 election demanding that further voting take place under a neutral administration. Eventually they got their way and the AL won the subsequent election.

Since then, the feuding has continued except that it is Khaleda Zia and the BNP who are organizing the hartals—30 days worth in 1999. All these strikes cost the country up to $100m per day in lost production and exports—to the despair of businesses and aid donors. They also threaten to undermine democracy. Bangladeshi people are becoming increasingly disillusioned with politicians. As yet, there is no indication of military intervention, but history is not encouraging.

Barbados

A Caribbean success story with a growing economy and a stable system of governance

Land area: *430 sq. km.*
Population: *266,000—urban 48%*
Capital city: *Bridgetown, 108,000*
People: *Black 80%, white 4%, other 16%*
Language: *English*
Religion: *Protestant 70%*
Government: *Constitutional monarchy*
Life expectancy: *76 years*
GNP per capita: *$PPP 12,260*
Currency: *Barbados dollar*
Major exports: *Sugar, rum, other foods and beverages*

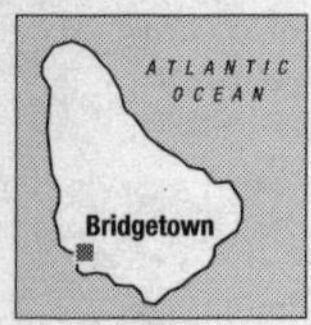

Barbados is the furthest east of the Caribbean islands and, except for low, central mountains, is largely flat. It has few natural resources apart from attractive scenery, a good climate, white beaches, and coral reefs.

With close to 100% literacy and good health standards, levels of human development here rival those in many industrial countries. Education is free and compulsory until the age of sixteen. Nevertheless, unemployment remains high and many Barbadians emigrate to work abroad; their remittances are still an important source of income.

The country's original wealth was based on sugar cultivation, and sugar cane still covers more than 80% of arable land, providing much of the export income. But agriculture has long since given way to tourism as the main economic activity. Tourism went through a dip at the beginning of the 1990s but has since revived strongly.

Barbados has also made efforts to diversify into other services and manufacturing. It has, for example, built up a financial services industry as well as attracting some of the 'back-office' data processing work for US companies. Like other Caribbean countries, Barbados has also become a transhipment point for drugs, though the government has taken a strong line against this and permits US officials to carry out hot-pursuit searches in Barbadian waters.

Barbados was a British colony. Though it had complete internal autonomy in 1961 it subsequently reverted to being a self-governing colony after the West Indies Federation dissolved in 1962. In 1966, Barbados achieved full independence and since then has enjoyed a stable parliamentary system. Two main parties have alternated in office. Between 1986 and 1994 the government was in the hands of the Democratic Labour Party.

The early 1990s, however, were difficult years. The sugar harvest was poor, unemployment was high, and increasing levels of violence were discouraging tourists. In 1994, following a lost vote of confidence and a general election, power passed to the Barbados Labour Party led by Owen Arthur, who increased his majority in the 1999 elections.

At present, the head of state is the British monarch in what has been considered one of the most British of the Caribbean islands. This could soon change. In 1998 a constitutional commission recommended switching to a republic with a ceremonial, elected president.

Belarus

Belarus has changed little since the Soviet era and even cherishes ambitions to reunite with Russia

Land area: 208,000 sq. km.
Population: 10 million— urban 73%
Capital city: Minsk, 1.7 million
People: Belarusian 78%, Russian 13%, Polish 4%, Ukrainian 3%, other 2%
Language: Belarusian, Russian
Religion: Eastern Orthodox 80%, other 20%
Government: Republic
Life expectancy: 68 years
GNP per capita: $PPP 4,850
Currency: Belarusian rubel
Major exports: Vehicles, oil, minerals

Belarus is largely flat—the highest point in this whole landlocked country is only around 350 metres above sea level. One-third of the territory is forested, including the primeval Belovezhskaya Forest on the western border with Poland. There are also extensive peat bogs and marshes, the largest of which are the Pripet Marshes on the southern border with Ukraine.

Most of the population are ethnic Belarusians, but during the Soviet era, Belarus was a significant economic centre, and attracted Russian immigrants, who by 1989 made up 13% of the population. Some have returned, but most remain, and there are also sizeable minorities of Poles and Ukrainians.

The Belarusians had achieved good standards of health and education but since 1990 infant mortality has been rising and life expectancy has been falling. Between 1990 and 1996 men's life expectancy fell from 66 to 63 years. Belarusians are also still suffering the effects of radiation from the 1986 Chernobyl disaster; though the explosion was just across the border in Ukraine, most of the fallout was in Belarus.

Belarus industrialized rapidly from the 1950s onwards, becoming an important centre for oil refining and petrochemical production. In addition, the Soviet Union used Belarus to manufacture military equipment and to supply trucks, tractors, and motor cycles. Unfortunately this involved importing oil, gas, and other raw materials from Russia and elsewhere, so when they had to pay market prices industries shrank rapidly.

By 1996, things had started to stabilize and by 1999 industry accounted for more than 40% of GDP. Nevertheless, the country has been accumulating an energy debt with Russia, and the Russian gas company Gazprom is becoming impatient with receiving much of its payment in bartered goods.

Although the government professes to be following 'market socialism', in practice Belarus still has most of the elements of a command economy and during the first decade of independence only around 10% of state assets were privatized. Foreign investors have not been rushing to Belarus, but Ford at least has established a small factory making cars and trucks to take advantage of Belarus's customs union with Russia.

Agriculture, too, is still mostly a state activity. Small farms have proliferated since independence but most output still comes from state and collective farms. The Soviet Union used Belarus as a source of livestock, but in recent years the government has been switching more to grain production to make the country self-sufficient in food.

Prior to 1991, Belarus had never been an independent state. It did have separate membership of the UN, but this, like the membership for Ukraine, was a legal fiction invented by Stalin to give the Soviet Union another UN vote. Most of the impetus for Belarus's independence came from the Belarusian Popular Front (BFP) whose nominee, Stanislau Shushkevich, was appointed head of state. But it did not take long for the communists to reassert their authority. In 1994, a commission headed by a former state farm manager, Alexander Lukashenka, ousted Shushkevich on charges of corruption.

Belarus had never been an independent state

Lukashenka was able to lever the exposure this gave him into a victory in the 1994 presidential election, and since then he has proved an effective populist, and an astute political operator. In 1996 he successfully conducted a referendum on a new constitution that extended his term of office and created a new bicameral assembly which the president can dissolve if it 'systematically or seriously violates the constitution'. Most of his support comes from unreformed communists.

Opposition has been heavily repressed: in 1996, protests against his regime were crushed and the BFP leader Zyanon Paznyk sought political asylum in the USA. Opposition radio stations and newspapers were also closed down.

One of Lukashenka's main aims is to unite Belarus with Russia, preferably with him as leader. In December 1999, this appeared to move forward with the signing of yet another union treaty with Russia. But genuine union seems some way off. Some communists in Russia are attracted by the kudos that this expansion would bring them, but other Russians have balked at the economic implications of fully absorbing its backward neighbour, especially with its eccentric leader. Lukashenka's prospects of leading a united country shrank even further in 2000 when Vladimir Putin was elected president of Russia.

So far, both the autocratic president and his Russophile inclinations seem to have the support of the majority of the population. Early in 1999, a congress of opposition parties, who had created a 'shadow' parliament called for the overthrow of Lukashenka, but neither this nor widespread international condemnation of his human rights record seem to be having much impact.

Belgium

Belgium has conflicts between its language communities and has been shaken by political scandals

__Land area:__ 31,000 sq. km.
__Population:__ 10 million—urban 97%
__Capital city:__ Brussels, 900,000
__People:__ Fleming 55%, Walloon 33%, mixed or other 12%
__Language:__ Flemish 56%, French 32%, German 1%, legally bilingual 11%
__Religion:__ Roman Catholic 75%, Protestant or other 25%
__Government:__ Constitutional monarchy
__Life expectancy:__ 77 years
__GNP per capita:__ $PPP 23,480
__Currency:__ Belgian franc
__Major exports:__ Iron and steel, transportation equipment, oil products, diamonds

Belgium has three main geographical regions running from north-west to south-east. From the sand-dunes and dykes that fringe the North Sea coast the coastal plain extends inland for up to 50 kilometres—with land that is often marshy and intercut with shipping canals. Then the land rises to the rolling hills of the fertile central plateau, and finally to the dense forests of the Ardennes highlands in the south-east.

In addition to Belgium's political boundaries there is also an invisible cultural frontier running across the country from west to east, passing about 20 kilometres south of the capital, Brussels. To the north is Flanders, home to just over half the population who are Flemish, and speak a dialect of Dutch. To the south is Wallonia, home to the one-third of the population who are Walloons and speak French. There is also a third group, though much smaller, of German speakers on the eastern border.

Superimposed on these divisions is the 0.9 million population of Brussels, which, though within Flanders, is a largely French-speaking enclave. It is also home to many of Belgium's immigrants. Belgium has one of Europe's larger immigrant communities—around 9% of the total population. The inflows continue though the proportion of non-nationals has remained fairly stable because it has become easier to obtain Belgian nationality. Around 60% of immigrants are EU citizens attracted by the status of Brussels as unofficial capital of Europe. Brussels is home to the European Commission and to other international organizations such as NATO that generate around 10% of employment. Of the other immigrants, the largest groups are Moroccan and Turkish. The presence of all these people makes Belgium one of Europe's most densely populated, and most urbanized, countries.

Belgium was one of the first

European countries to industrialize, taking advantage of its formerly extensive coal deposits to process imported raw materials for export. These older industries were in Wallonia, but most of the coal mines and many of the old factories are now shut.

Belgium is still a major steel producer, now using imported coal, but its newer, lighter manufacturing industries have been established in Flanders nearer the important ports.

Antwerp is also the world's largest diamond centre—half the world's diamonds pass through the city. This means that Flanders, which used to be a more backward agricultural area, now has a per capita GDP 40% higher than Wallonia—a shift in industrial power that has fuelled resentment between the two communities. The Flemish complain that their taxes are heavily subsidizing the Walloons.

Resentment between Flemings and Walloons

Belgium has run into economic problems in recent years. Though it has many new service industries, unemployment has been high, around 11%, and despite immigration the population is ageing rapidly. Another issue is debt, since governments have frequently attempted to spend their way out of inter-community problems.

Belgium's political landscape is now dominated by the language issue. To deal with this, Belgium has effectively become a federal state, and very heavily governed: in addition to the bicameral federal government there are now separate assemblies not just for Flanders, Wallonia, and Brussels-Capital, but also individual assemblies for the French, Dutch, and German-speaking communities. These various assemblies have complex overlapping memberships. In total there are around 60 ministers or junior ministers.

The language split is also matched among the political parties. In the two main regions, the three largest—the Christian Socialists, the Socialists, and the Liberals—each have autonomous parties. In addition there are two right-wing nationalist parties: for Flanders, the Vlaams Blok; for Wallonia, the National Front.

Belgians' faith in their political system was rocked in the late 1990s by a series of scandals. These included the failure of the justice system to deal with an extensive paedophile ring, allegations of bribery against senior government officials, brutal police treatment of immigrants, and a number of food scares.

In the past, the two main unifying factors have been Catholicism and the monarchy: King Albert II acceded to the throne in 1993 and has helped to serve as a mediator. So far, only around one-fifth of the population vote for parties that want to break up the country, but different groups of Belgians are increasingly leading separate lives.

The series of setbacks the country suffered led in the 1999 elections to a change in government, ending the 40-year dominance of Christian parties. The right-leaning liberals, became the biggest party nationally, while the greens and the Vlaams Blok also made strong gains. Guy Verhofstadt, leader of the Flemish liberals, formed a coalition government promising to break out of the cycle of crises.

Belize

Belize has resisted aggression from Guatemala, but has become steadily more Hispanic

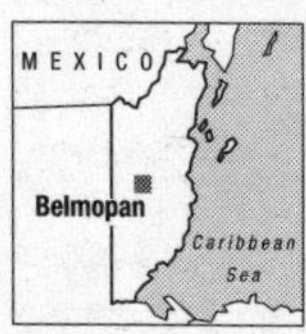

The northern half of Belize consists largely of lowland swamps, while the main feature in the southern half is the Maya mountain range which rises to 1,112 metres. More than 40% of the territory is covered by rainforests. Just off the coastline there are many small islands, or cays, and one of the world's largest barrier reefs.

Belize's ethnic composition has steadily been changing. As a result of flows of migrants and refugees from El Salvador and Guatemala in the 1980s, probably more than half the population is now Spanish-speaking. The English-speaking creoles now form a smaller proportion, partly because many have emigrated to the USA. In addition, there are smaller numbers of Garifuna in the south.

Around one-quarter of the labour force work in agriculture, mostly on small farms growing maize and beans as well as cash crops. The main sources of export income are sugar cane in the north, citrus concentrates in the Stann Creek Valley, and bananas in the south. Forestry is likely to become more important; although there are replanting programmes, concessions granted recently to a number of Asian logging companies raise the prospect of deforestation.

Manufacturing tends to be on a small scale for local consumption, though many foreign garment producers have been attracted to export-processing zones. Tourism is also an increasing source of income; more than 130,000 visitors come each year, many for scuba diving or to visit Mayan archaeological sites.

Since independence in 1981, Belize has had a stable parliamentary system based on two main parties. The head of state is the British monarch, represented by a governor-general. The 1998 elections were won by the People's United Party (PUP) led by Said Musa. The PUP had left-wing origins but has moved to the centre and tends to be supported by the mestizos. The other main party is the conservative United Democratic Party, which has more business links and draws its support from the creoles. Belize had a long-running border dispute with Guatemala but this has been resolved, so relations with neighbours are much improved. An increasingly serious problem, however, is the use of Belize's islands and jungles as transhipment routes for cocaine from South America, which is leading to rising levels of violence and crime.

Land area: *23,000 sq. km.*
Population: *236,000—urban 47%*
Capital city: *Belmopan, 7,000*
People: *Mestizo 44%, Creole 30%, Maya 11%, Garifuna 7%, other 8%*
Language: *English, Spanish, Mayan, Garifuna*
Religion: *Roman Catholic 62%, Protestant 30%, other 8%*
Government: *Constitutional monarchy*
Life expectancy: *75 years*
GNP per capita: *$PPP 3,940*
Currency: *Belize dollar*
Major exports: *Sugar, citrus concentrates, bananas, garments*

Benin

Business has revived, but most is informal so the government gets little tax revenue

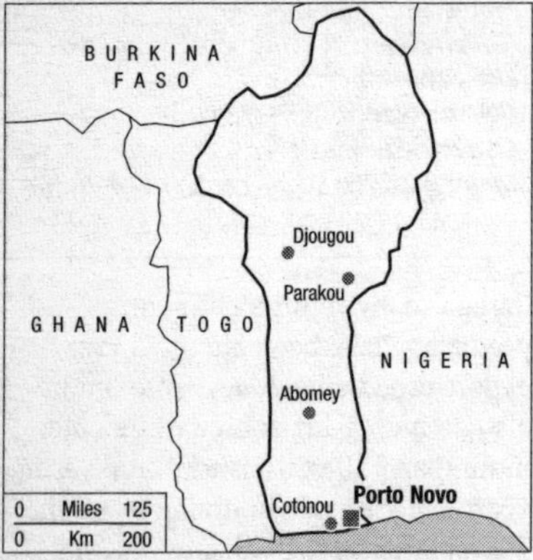

Land area: *113,000 sq. km.*
Population: *6 million—urban 41%*
Capital city: *Porto Novo, 180,000*
People: *Fon, Adja, Yoruba, Barib, and many others*
Language: *French, Fon, Yoruba, and others*
Religion: *Indigenous beliefs 70%, Muslim 15%, Christian 15%*
Government: *Republic*
Life expectancy: *53 years*
GNP per capita: *$PPP 1,250*
Currency: *CFA franc*
Major exports: *Cotton, oil*

Benin has a series of geographical regions that extend northwards from its narrow coastline. Just behind the sandy coast are tidal marshes and lagoons; then there is a flat fertile plateau, the barre. A further series of plateaux lead to the Atakora Mountains in the north-west and to plains that slope down to the Niger River in the north-east.

Benin's people are divided among many ethnic groups, the largest of which are the Fon and the Adja, who make up over half the population. These have an animist religious tradition but there are also significant Muslim influences that come from countries to the north, and Christian influences in the south that are a legacy of the French colonial years, so religious beliefs tend to be a mixture of different ideas.

Benin is one of Africa's poorest countries. Around one-third of the population live below the poverty line. Though there is generally enough food to go round, up to one-fifth of children under 5 suffer from malnutrition, and health standards are poor. Malaria remains a serious problem, along with many cases of gastro-enteritis linked with contaminated water supplies. Only one-third of adults are literate.

Around 60% of the population make their living from agriculture. Farmers grow yams, cassava, millet, sorghum, beans, maize, and rice. Productivity is low, but in a year of reasonable rainfall Benin is self-sufficient in food. Many people also work on cotton and palm-oil plantations. Benin is the world's eleventh largest cotton producer and sales of cotton fibre and seeds make up more than 90% of export earnings. Most industry is linked with processing primary products for export.

Benin is also a bustling centre for trade, which makes up more than half of GDP. Its geographical location makes it a key outlet for the landlocked countries to the north. But most of the trade activity is focused on Nigeria, its giant neighbour to the east. Benin is largely an entrepôt state since less than 20% of imports are consumed locally; the rest are re-exported.

Most of this business flows through the informal sector, particularly the Yoruba traders who deal with their counterparts in Nigeria.

A frenzy of cross-border trade

The fairs and markets along the border with Nigeria are always packed. The Beninois sell rice, cigarettes, and spirits, while they buy cars, plastic products, and electrical equipment. But their most important purchase is petrol: every day around 300,000 litres cross the border illegally; the smuggled price is around half the official price.

Benin's commercial capital, Cotonou, is also a major transit point. Its streets are packed with cars and with motorcycle taxis, the zemidjans. In the 1990s, vehicle ownership more than tripled, and the old bridge that crosses the lagoon and links the country with Togo in the west and Nigeria in the east creaks under the daily weight of traffic.

Much of this frenzy of activity is a response to desperation. Many of those now in the informal sector previously worked in larger enterprises or in government services. But the economic crises and government cutbacks in the 1980s and 1990s resulted in heavy job losses. Even government officials need second or third sources of income: many of the zemidjans are owned by civil servants or teachers, who lease them out.

The government largely turns a blind eye to what the prime minister refers to as 'osmosis' in the border region since it provides an important source of funds to so many people. But it does mean that relatively little income is taxed so government finances are weak.

During the early years after independence from France in 1960 political life was punctuated by a series of military coups. In 1972, Major Mathieu Kérékou seized power and from 1974 tried to set the country on a Marxist-Leninist course and changed its name from Dahomey to Benin.

But in 1989 in the wake of an economic collapse Kérékou abandoned socialism and in 1990 organized a national conference which led to a new constitution for a multi-party democracy. Nevertheless, he lost the 1991 presidential election to Nicéphore Soglo, a former World Bank official.

Soglo struggled to build a free-market economy and was forced to introduce many austerity measures. These did not make him popular, and he narrowly lost the 1996 presidential election to Kérékou. Appropriately, Kérékou campaigned under the symbol of the chameleon.

Benin seems to have taken enthusiastically to democracy. The country has more than 40 political parties. In the March 1999 elections the largest party, with 27% of the vote, was the centrist, Parti de la renaissance du Bénin. There is also a vibrant press, with twelve independent daily newspapers and a similar number of radio stations.

As yet, however, a flourishing democracy has yet to produce a flourishing economy.

Bhutan

This mountain kingdom has suffered from decades of ethnic violence

Land area: *47,000 sq. km.*
Population: *759,000—urban 7%*
Capital city: *Thimpu, 17,000*
People: *Bhote 50%, ethnic Nepalese 35%, indigenous or migrant tribes 15%*
Language: *Dzongkha, Tibeta, and Nepalese dialects*
Religion: *Buddhism 75%, Hinduism 25%*
Government: *Absolute monarchy*
Life expectancy: *61 years*
GNP per capita: *$PPP 1,467*
Currency: *Chetrum*
Major exports: *Electricity*

Bhutan has three main geographical zones. The north falls within the high Himalayas which reach altitudes of 7,300 metres. To the south are the 'inner' Himalayas which include a number of broad, fertile and well cultivated valleys. To the far south these descend to the narrow, subtropical Duars Plain that runs along the border with India.

The main ethnic group are the Bhote, who live mostly in the north and centre. Of the other indigenous groups, the largest are the Sharchops, who live in the east. In addition, there are ethnic Nepalese, who are concentrated in the south as well as refugees from Tibet.

Concerned at this largely illegal influx, the king from the late 1980s declared a 'national culture principle' to enforce a national language and dress. This prompted an exodus of refugees; in 1998 an estimated 100,000 had fled to Nepal, and more than 15,000 to India.

Bhutan's people are generally poor, though few are hungry or homeless. Prior to 1961, Bhutan had scarcely any health centres or schools, or even proper roads. Since then it has made considerable progress. Even so, health standards are poor: the infant and maternal mortality rates are among the highest in South Asia. Only one-fifth of girls enrol in primary school.

More than 90% of people work in agriculture, growing subsistence crops such as rice, maize, and potatoes. The best land is in the fertile valleys and, as a result of land reform in the early 1970s, it is fairly equally distributed though plots are small. Three-quarters of the territory is covered with forests, and timber is an important export.

Industry is still underdeveloped and mostly concentrated along the Indian border. One of the largest projects has been the Chukha hydroelectric scheme. By 1999, power exports to India accounted for one-quarter of government revenue. Tourism is also a useful source of income, though only 5,000 visitors per year are permitted to enter this exclusive and expensive destination.

Bhutan is an absolute monarchy, ruled since 1972 by King Jigme Singye Wangchuk—with the advice of a National Assembly, two-thirds of whose members are elected. In principle the king is required to win a regular vote of confidence from the Assembly, failing which he has to abdicate. He says he is willing to move eventually towards a constitutional democracy but seems to be in no great hurry.

Bolivia

Bolivia has liberalized its economy, but the poorest people have yet to see much benefit

Land area: 1,099,000 sq. km.
Population: 8 million—urban 63%
Capital city: La Paz, 1 million
People: Quechua 30%, Aymara 25%, mestizo 30%, European 15%
Language: Spanish, Quechua, Aymara
Religion: Roman Catholic
Government: Republic
Life expectancy: 61 years
GNP per capita: $PPP 2,820
Currency: Boliviano
Major exports: Soya, zinc, gold, tin, natural gas

Bolivia is one of only two landlocked states in Latin America—having lost its access to the sea in 1883 after a war with Chile. It can be divided into three main regions. First, in the south-west and covering about one-tenth of the country there is the bleak, arid expanse of the Altiplano, a plateau some 3,600 metres above sea level. Second, enclosing this plain, are two branches of the Andes with the highest peak at 6,542 metres. Third, to the east and north, and covering around two-thirds of the country, are the lowlands of the Oriente, which includes grasslands and tropical rainforests.

The Bolivians who occupy this often harsh terrain are mostly of Indian origin. The largest groups are the Quechua and Aymara, who live mostly in the highland regions. The women have often retained their traditional dress with colourful petticoats, and in some regions distinctive bowler hats. The mestizo and white population are more likely to be found in the capital, La Paz, and in the richer valleys and lowlands.

This is one of the poorest countries in South America. The rural areas in particular suffer from lack of safe water and sanitation and poor health services. High levels of infant mortality have depressed population growth. Around two-thirds of Bolivians live below the poverty line. In the face of increasing poverty, many Bolivians, 200,000 or more, have now migrated to work in sweatshops in Argentina, where they earn around $50 per month.

Agriculture employs around half the population but much of this in the highlands is still primitive cultivation of cereals and potatoes. The more productive land is in the eastern lowlands and is often devoted to commercial farming—including cotton, sugar, and particularly soya which is now the leading official export earner.

Much of Bolivia's wealth, and its potential, lies in its minerals—including tin, silver, zinc, and gold—usually extracted with cheap Indian labour working in harsh conditions. This has left Bolivia severely exposed to international commodity markets. One of the worst episodes in recent years was the 1985 crash in the price of tin, which hit Bolivia particularly hard since it is a high-cost producer. Zinc and gold have shown more promise. Other important resources are oil and gas of which there are extensive reserves in the tropical lowlands; 1998 saw the completion of a gas pipeline to Brazil.

Bolivia's largest unofficial export is coca paste. This is derived from coca leaves grown by 35,000 or so peasant farmers in the lowlands. Around 9,000 'laboratories' transform it into coca paste. Bolivians have traditionally chewed the leaf to numb themselves to cold and hunger, but since the 1980s the market for cocaine has transformed this into a lucrative cash crop. Bolivia supplies around 30% of the world's coca paste, with exports worth around $200 million (3% of GDP). With US aid, the government has made some efforts to eradicate coca cultivation. In 1998, for example, at least 7,000 hectares of coca plants were uprooted, though this still left 50,000 hectares under cultivation.

Source of one-third of the world's coca paste

Economic management has often been chaotic. By the mid-1980s, with crashing tin prices, rising international debt, and a world record inflation rate of 20,000%, Bolivia was close to collapse. The subsequent recovery started in 1985 with the shock therapy of the 'New Economic Plan', which dramatically reoriented the economy along free-market lines. Foreign firms were allowed to acquire 50% shares in the main state companies in telecoms, electricity, transport, and oil in exchange for pledges of investment.

One distinctive aspect of this 'capitalization' process was that the income did not go into government coffers. Instead the large minority holdings in the capitalized firms went into a trust fund on behalf of the Bolivian people. In 1997, this was used to pay everyone over the age of 65 a 'solidarity bond' worth $248. These and other innovations enabled Bolivia to enjoy investment-led growth which averaged 4% annually in the period 1990-96.

These radical reforms have been maintained under a series of governments, including that of Hugo Banzer Suarez, a previous military dictator who won the 1997 presidential election. Banzer's party is the populist Nationalist Democratic Alliance, but he runs the country at the head of a four-party coalition.

His administration is now much more popular with international investors and lenders, but Bolivians are less sure. Despite fifteen years of radical reforms only a few people have made progress and many others have lost out. In 1999 economic growth was only 1% and in April, 2000 popular discontent flared into violent protests. For peasant communities this typically takes the form of blocking the roads, but there were also attacks on government buildings.

The government declared a state of emergency and made concessions, but rural unrest is likely to increase unless the Banzer government manages to reduce poverty.

Bosnia and Herzegovina

Bosnia and Herzegovina is held together by aid and diplomatic pressure

Land area: *51,000 sq. km.*
Population: *3 million*
Capital city: *Sarajevo, 520,000*
People: *Serb 40%, Muslim 38%, Croat 22%*
Language: *Serbo-Croatian*
Religion: *Muslim 40%, Orthodox 31%, Catholic 15%, Protestant 4%, other 10%*
Government: *Republic*
Life expectancy: *67 years*
GNP per capita: *PPP$ 1,720*
Currency: *Marka*

The state of Bosnia and Herzegovina, commonly referred to as Bosnia, is a loose federation of two entities created in 1995 following the peace agreement reached in Dayton, Ohio. One is the Serb Republic (RS) with 49% of the territory and approximately 45% of the population. The remainder is itself a federation: the Federation of Bosnia and Herzegovina which had been created in 1994 as a result of the Washington Agreement, and which consists of land controlled by the Muslim and Croat communities—commonly referred to as 'the Federation'.

The region of Bosnia occupies the north and centre of the country while Herzegovina makes up the south and south-west. The political partition gives most of the lower-lying and better agricultural land in the north to the Serb Republic, and the more mountainous remainder, including the Dinaric Alps, to the Federation. The Federation has most of the country's industry and its per capita GDP is around twice that of the Serb Republic.

Bosnia's ethnic strife reflects a long history of occupation and struggles in the Balkans. By the 20th century, this had left the territory with three main communities who appear physically identical but have strong cultural and religious differences: the Croats, who are generally Roman Catholics; the Serbs, who are generally Orthodox; and the Muslims who are a legacy of the long occupation by the Ottoman Empire. The communist government of Marshall Tito managed to keep these groups together, establishing Bosnia and Herzegovina as a republic within Yugoslavia, and in the 1970s also gave the Muslims a distinct ethnic status. The distribution of these groups was complex: some areas had majorities of one group but others were ethnically mixed.

When Yugoslavia started to disintegrate the situation in Bosnia was very difficult. At this point, the Serbs wanted to remain part of Yugoslavia, the Croats wanted to unite with Croatia, while the Muslims preferred a multi-ethnic independence. They maintain these ambitions to this day. However, they did all make a choice of sorts in March 1992 when a referendum, which the Serbs boycotted, opted for secession and Bosnia duly declared its independence.

After independence, the violent conflicts that had accompanied all these events erupted into full-scale civil war as each group sought to seize territory while driving out the members of the other communities in a bitter and savage process of 'ethnic cleansing'. The war was to kill a quarter of a million people, drive 1 million people out of the country as refugees, and displace another million or so internally. Some refugees subsequently returned, but by no means all, and between 1991 and 1997 the population fell from 4.4 million to 3.2 million—2.2 million in the Federation, 1 million in the Serb Republic.

A savage process of ethnic cleansing

In 1994, the USA managed to broker a ceasefire between the Croats and the Muslims which created the Federation. And in 1995 an agreement reached in Dayton, Ohio, brought the war to an end. The agreement established a central government with a collective three-member presidency and a two-chamber parliament that would deal with foreign affairs and monetary policy. But most of the major functions, including economic policy, taxation, defence, and the police forces, would devolve to the two 'entities'. The Dayton agreement also provided for the appointment of a High Representative, a Spaniard Carlos Westendorp, to monitor the agreement and co-ordinate the work of international agencies—and where necessary impose decisions. In addition there is a 30,000-strong NATO 'stabilization force'. Though formally there is a central government, in many respects the three communities continue to function separately.

The peace agreement also served as the launching pad for a $5 billion, four-year reconstruction programme. Construction did kick-start the economy, particularly in the Federation, and industries such as electricity generation, mining, and wood processing revived. Agriculture, which even during the communist era was largely small-scale and private, has also been returning more to normal.

The economy grew by 8% in 1999, though that only brings production back to around 40% of the pre-war level. Unemployment was around 30%. There has been little progress with privatization and not much sign of the economic restructuring needed to drive future growth.

Many of these difficulties arise from the enduring ethnic animosity. The political divisions remain unresolved. Bosnians continue to vote along ethnic lines, though there are signs that people are moving around the country more freely and Muslims have been returning to former homes in eastern Bosnia. In the Serb Republic there has been a power struggle between hard-line nationalists and the moderates who want to implement Dayton.

In 1999, Westendorp was succeeded as high commissioner by Wolfgang Petritsch, but he too has struggled with fractious politicians.

Botswana

Botswana's diamonds have financed public services but have yet to lift its people out of poverty

Land area: *582,000 sq. km.*
Population: *2 million—urban 31%*
Capital city: *Gaborone, 192,000*
People: *Batswana and minorities*
Language: *English, Setswana*
Religion: *Indigenous beliefs 50%, Christian 50%*
Government: *Republic*
Life expectancy: *47 years*
GNP per capita: *$PPP 8,310*
Currency: *Pula*
Major exports: *Diamonds, copper, nickel*

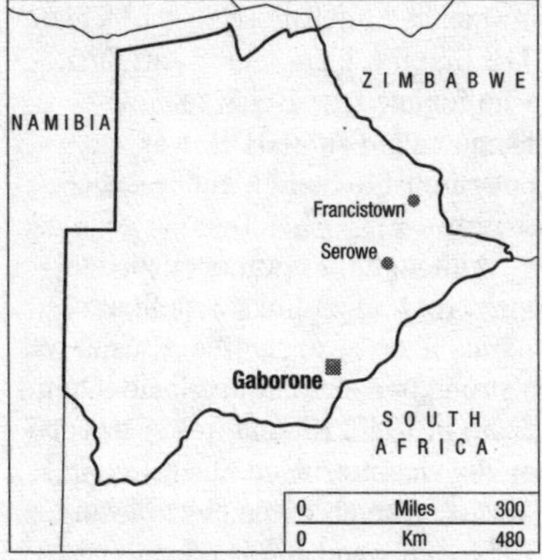

Apart from hills in the south-east, Botswana is largely a flat plateau at around 1,000 metres above sea level. In the north-west is the extensive Okavango Swamp and in the south the Kalahari Desert. Most people live in the east, where the climate is cooler and the soil is more fertile.

Compared with other countries of Sub-Saharan Africa, Botswana has seen little ethnic conflict. Most people are Batswana: a group of eight ethnic clans. The constitution defines these as the 'majority tribe' and they have official representation in an advisory parliamentary chamber, the House of Chiefs. However, there are also small numbers of Bushmen, who frequently face discrimination.

Botswana's income from diamond mining has enabled it to invest in social services. Education is universal and free, and the primary and curative health services are extensive. Infrastructure has also improved. An increasing proportion of the population are now urbanized—as people are attracted in particular to the capital Gaborone which has expanded ten-fold in the past thirty years.

But the economy has yet to diversify and to distribute economic opportunities more widely. Unemployment has been estimated at around 40% and one-third of the population live in poverty.

One of the most alarming recent developments has been the spread of HIV/AIDS. At least one-quarter of young adults are thought to be infected. This has had a dramatic impact on average life expectancy: in the early 1990s this was around 65 years but by 1998 it had slumped to 47. This has also served to slow the population growth rate which had been around 3.3% per year but is now around 2.2%.

Many people still rely on agriculture—through subsistence farming and particularly raising livestock. But even when rainfall is good, they only grow enough food to meet around one-third of national needs. And in 1997 an outbreak of lung disease required the compulsory slaughter of 330,000 cattle—depriving many people of their primary source of income. Agriculture by 1997 had fallen to around 4% of GDP.

Nowadays, Botswana's economy is dominated by the diamond industry, which accounts for around 40% of GDP. Diamonds were discovered under the sands of the Kalahari Desert shortly after independence and large-scale extraction was started in 1971 by the Debswana Mining Company—a joint enterprise between the government and the South African company De Beers. Botswana is now one of the world's largest producers of diamonds and new diamond 'pipes' are still being discovered.

There are also significant deposits of copper-nickel and other minerals, including coal, soda-ash, and gold, but the enterprises that are mining these reserves have proved less successful.

Mining employs few people directly—less than 4% of the workforce. But it does support a large public sector which employs around half of all those working in the formal sector. The government is anxious to build up manufacturing industry and is offering substantial tax concessions for new investment. This makes it an appealing place in which to produce cars. The Motor Company of Botswana is under contract to Hyundai and Volvo to assemble cars for export virtually duty-free into South Africa.

Making Volvos for South Africa

Mining has also enabled the government to build up large savings in anticipation of its diamond reserves eventually being exhausted. Botswana had foreign reserves of around $5 billion in 1998 and was in the fairly unique position for an African country of lending currency to the IMF.

Botswana has long been one of Sub-Saharan Africa's more democratic countries. Since independence in 1966, it has had a 40-member National Assembly which elects an executive president, in addition to its 15-member advisory House of Chiefs. The first president, Seretse Khama, who founded the Botswana Democratic Party (BDP) was determined to build a multiracial society.

Although the country needed to maintain trading links with South Africa in order to survive, Khama was a strong opponent of apartheid. On his death in 1980, Khama was succeeded by his vice-president, Quett Ketumile Masire, who also won elections in 1984, 1989, and 1994. When he retired in 1998, he in turn was replaced by his vice-president Festus Mogae. Significantly, Mogae's vice-president is Ian Khama, son of the first president.

The BDP has now been in power for more than three decades, but its grip seems to be slipping. High levels of unemployment and allegations of corruption have allowed the opposition to make inroads. Until recently, opposition came from the left-wing Botswana National Front (BNF), led by Kenneth Koma, but in 1998 eleven of the BNF's assembly members broke away to form the Botswana Congress Party, led by Michael Dingake. With the opposition split, the BDP achieved yet another convincing victory in the 1999 National Assembly election, taking 54% of the votes and 33 of the 40 seats.

Brazil

Destined by size to be the leading country of South America, Brazil has yet to realize its potential

Land area: *8,512,000 sq. km.*
Population: *166 million—urban 80%*
Capital city: *Brasilia, 1.8 million*
People: *White 55%, mixed white and black 38%, black 6%, other 1%*
Language: *Portuguese*
Religion: *Roman Catholic 70%, other 30%*
Government: *Federal Republic*
Life expectancy: *69 years*
GNP per capita: *$PPP 6,160*
Currency: *Real*
Major exports: *Manufactures, soya, iron, coffee*

Brazil's huge landmass occupies almost half the continent of South America. Geographically, the country's two main features are the Brazilian Highlands and the Amazon Basin. The Brazilian Highlands cover most of the south and east of the country and consist of a vast plateau with an average elevation of 1,000 metres interspersed, particularly in the east, with rugged mountain ranges, some of which rise above 2,800 metres. Much of this area is forested or opens up to extensive prairies.

The Amazon Basin to the north and west covers more than 40% of the country. This is the world's largest river drainage system and most of it is covered with tropical rainforest. While there are still unexplored areas, many parts of the rainforest have now been penetrated by settlers, ranchers, or mining companies, a process of deforestation that has alarming environmental implications globally—in terms of climate change and loss of biological diversity. This area contains around one-fifth of world plant species. Most of Brazil has a humid subtropical climate, but the land to the north-east, known as the sertão, suffers from frequent droughts.

Brazil has long been a racial melting pot. There is little overt discrimination, but people of European origin hold the most powerful positions, followed by those of mixed race (who call themselves 'brown') and blacks, with the small and declining Indian population the most marginalized of all. This mixture of races has generated a vibrant and diverse culture. So although Brazil is unified by the Portuguese language and by Roman Catholicism it also has strong African influences.

This social stratification contributes to severe inequalities. The cities in the south, like Rio de Janeiro or São Paulo, are similar in many respects to those in Europe, though also have desperate shanty towns, called favelas. The north-east is almost another country—deep in the Third World. Brazil has one of the world's most unequal distributions of income. In 1995, the richest fifth of the population got 63% of the income while the poorest fifth got only 2.5%. Around one-quarter of Brazilians live on less than $1 per day.

These contrasts are evident in education. Though Brazil has a small proportion of highly educated professionals, most people drop out of school very early. Health services too are skewed. One estimate suggests that 40% of health expenditure is used for sophisticated curative treatments that benefit only 3% of the population.

The richest 20% of Brazilians get 63% of the income

In many respects, Brazil is an advanced industrial economy. Around one-quarter of the labour force works in industry. With such a large population, Brazil was for decades able to direct most of its manufacturing output at its domestic market, not just basic industries, such as food and clothing, but also more sophisticated products from cars to petrochemicals to aircraft—all of which benefited from protection from foreign competition.

By the late 1980s, however, the limitations of this strategy were becoming clear—Brazilian personal computers, for example, were much more expensive than foreign equivalents. From 1990 therefore, the government opened up the markets. This helped stimulate greater efficiency in some areas—though others such as garments or shoes have shrunk in the face of Asian competition.

Brazil's industry has benefited from its wealth of mineral resources. It has around one-third of the world's reserves of iron ore, as well as large deposits of bauxite, coal, zinc, gold, and tin. It also has extensive offshore oil reserves that have enabled the state oil company, Petrobrás, to supply more than half the country's needs. Most electricity, however, comes from hydroelectric plants—one of the largest in the world being the Itaipú dam shared with Paraguay on the Paraná River.

With such a huge landmass, Brazil might also be expected to be a major agricultural producer. Brazil is largely self-sufficient in basic foods. It also has a large livestock herd, and is an exporter of cash crops like soya and coffee. But output is less than might be expected. This is partly because much of the land area, particularly in the Amazon Basin, is unsuitable for farming. But even the better farming land is often used very inefficiently. Indeed, much of the land held by the largest landowners is scarcely used at all. Some 58,000 large landowners hold half the country's farmland, while 3 million small farmers make do on 2%, and millions more have no land. Many governments have promised land reform. Few have delivered, but the current Cardoso government claimed that between 1994 and 1998 280,000 families received land.

Brazil's vast territory also complicates the task of government. For much of the country's history it has been under centralized authoritarian rule, including a military government from 1964 to 1985. In 1988 the country adopted a new constitution that provided for a directly elected executive president in addition to elections for the two houses of Congress. The 1988 election was won by the conservative Fernando Collor de Mellor. He resigned in 1992, having been impeached for corruption, and Vice-President Itamar Franco took over.

Brazil has often been plagued by inflation—usually at least in two digits and sometimes four or five. This pattern appeared finally to have been broken early in 1994 when Franco's finance minister, Fernando Enrique Cardoso, introduced a new currency, the 'real', which was pegged to the US dollar. The 'real plan' was so successful at halting inflation that Cardoso was easily elected president at the end of 1994. Having secured a constitutional change to permit a second term he won again in 1998.

Any Brazilian president's task is complicated by the dispersed and fragmented nature of the political system. Brazil is a federal democracy and each of the 26 states has its own legislature and administration. States and their municipalities control over two-fifths of total tax revenues and have considerable freedom. Thus, Cardoso's former boss Itamar Franco subsequently became governor of of Minas Geraís and caused a major problem when he announced a unilateral moratorium on paying the state's debts.

Brazilian states have considerable freedom

Federalism has the merit of permitting decentralization, but it also produces confusing overlaps. Universities and hospitals, for example, may be controlled either by the federal or state governments. There are also huge disparities between the states: in 1996 the average per capita income in the state of São Paulo was more than ten times that of the north-eastern state of Piaui or of Amazonas. Governments have tried to narrow these gaps by building infrastructure and offering tax breaks. As a result, many new electronics factories have sprung up in Manaus in the middle of the rainforest.

The federal structure also complicates political manoeuvres in the capital, Brasilia. The president does in theory have considerable power of patronage. And Cardoso in 1998 could also rely on majority support in Congress since his Brazilian Social Democratic Party had made an alliance with the Party of the Liberal Front. Other centre-right parties also gave their support. But party allegiances are notoriously weak and temporary—over the period 1994-98, almost half the 513 members of the lower house switched allegiance. Most have greater loyalty to their local power base and are focused on extracting federal largesse for their state or municipality. Party organization is also blurred by powerful cross-party interest groups such as the ruralistas, who lobby for large landowners.

Still, Cardoso can rely on the weakness of the opposition. The main opposition comes from the left-wing Workers' Party. Its charismatic leader, Luis Inácio 'Lula' da Silva, achieved 33% of the vote in the 1998 presidential election but his party got only 12% of the seats in Congress. The Workers' Party has a strong anti-corruption platform and is making progress at the local level, but seems unlikely to gain power unless it moves further to the centre.

Brunei

A high-income sultanate floating on oil, but subjected to autocratic rule

Land area: *6,000 sq. km.*
Population: *314,000—urban 71%*
Capital city: *Bandar Seri Begawan, 47,000*
People: *Malay 64%, Chinese 20%, other 16%*
Language: *Malay, English, Chinese*
Religion: *Muslim 63%, Buddhism 14%, Christian 8%, indigenous and other 15%*
Government: *Constitutional sultanate*
Life expectancy: *76 years*
GNP per capita: *$PPP 29,773*
Currency: *Bruneian dollar*
Major exports: *Oil, gas*

Brunei occupies a small section of the north coast of Borneo, surrounded by the Malaysian state of Sarawak. A narrow coastal plain rises to low hills in its eastern section and to mountains in the west. Unusually for this part of Asia, forests still cover around 85% of the territory—thanks to its other main natural resource: oil.

Since 1929, oil and gas have been the main sources of wealth. Oil not only gives Brunei's citizens a high per capita income; it also funds extensive free, or highly subsidized, health and education services. The major health concerns are those of affluence: a high-fat diet and a sedentary lifestyle.

Most Brunei citizens are of Malay extraction, and tend to seek work either in the public sector, or in large prestigious companies such as Brunei Shell Petroleum or Royal Brunei Airlines. Most of the entrepreneurial energy comes from the less privileged Chinese minority, who are considered non-citizens, and also from temporary foreign residents—who make up around 40% of the labour force.

Brunei's oil and gas reserves are expected to last 40 years, and, given the country's extensive foreign investments, should provide an income long beyond that. Even so, oil and gas represent a shrinking proportion of GDP—down from 80% in the early 1980s to 36% in 1995, as a result of falling oil prices and an extension of government services. Moreover, there are doubts about the value of the Brunei Investment Agency's holdings. As a result the Brunei Economic Council concluded early in 2000 that on the basis of current income and expenditure the economy was unsustainable.

In theory, Brunei is a constitutional sultanate; in practice it is an absolute monarchy. When the country became independent in 1985, Sultan Hassanal Bokiah (whose family have ruled the country for 600 years) dissolved the existing Legislative Assembly and has since ruled by decree in a biennially renewed 'state of emergency'. Political parties are proscribed and no public criticism is permitted. The sultan occupies numerous government posts, including prime minister, head of the police force, and leader of the Islamic faith.

Fundamental change seems remote, but there have been some attempts to economize. In 2000, the sultan sued his profligate younger brother, Prince Jefri, who owns dozens of houses and thousands of cars, accusing him of embezzling billions of dollars of Brunei's investment funds.

Bulgaria

Bulgaria now seems to be making faster economic progress and is negotiating to join the EU

Land area: *111,000 sq. km.*
Population: *8 million—urban 69%*
Capital city: *Sofia, 1.1 million*
People: *Bulgarian 85%, Turk 9%, other 6%*
Language: *Bulgarian, Turkish*
Religion: *Bulgarian Orthodox 85%, Muslim 13%*
Government: *Republic*
Life expectancy: *71 years*
GNP per capita: *$PPP 4,010*
Currency: *Lev*
Major exports: *Base metals, chemicals, textiles, machinery, agricultural products*

Bulgaria has three main natural regions, each of which extends across the country from west to east. The most northerly, starting from the banks of the Danube, which marks the border with Romania, is a plain with low hills that takes up around one-third of the country. To the south of this plain is the second main region, the Balkan Mountains. Further south still, separated from these mountains by the narrow Thracian Plain, is the third region, the Rhodope Mountains, which form the border with Greece.

Bulgaria has a fairly homogenous population and has so far avoided serious ethnic conflict. The largest minority are around 800,000 ethnic Turks, who live largely in the north-east or in the east of the Rhodope Mountains. The Turks tend to be worse off than most Bulgarians, and in the communist era suffered legal discrimination. They have their own political party but are not very assertive. Many have, however, been emigrating to Turkey. Even worse off are the Roma, or gypsies, who are economically marginalized and frequently the victims of heavy-handed policing.

Like many other countries of Eastern Europe, Bulgaria now has a shrinking population—a result of a falling birth rate, a higher death rate, and emigration. From 1990 to 1996 the total population fell from 8.7 million to 8.3 million. In the mid-1990s there were around 30,000 emigrants per year, particularly to Turkey.

Public services have deteriorated since the collapse of communism. Spending on education has fallen and more children are dropping out of school. There has also been a disturbing rise in infant mortality and an increase in infectious diseases such as tuberculosis.

During the communist era, Bulgaria's economy was heavily industrialized, but production fell steeply during the transition. In the period 1989-93 output more than halved. The industries that held up better were basic metallurgy and chemicals, which along with textiles have been the major exports. By 1997, industry accounted for around 30% of GDP.

Part of the problem has been an erratic process of privatization that has seen the emergence of 'red capital'—large private conglomerates that feed off corrupt and inefficient state enterprises. By 1996, around 60% of GDP was produced by the private sector. Foreign enterprises have so far chosen to stay away—dissuaded by economic and political turmoil and a weak judicial system.

One-quarter of the population still make their living from agriculture, growing basic grains. Although most output is now in private hands, few people yet have title deeds to their land. Nevertheless, the late 1990s saw some good harvests and an expansion of cultivation of crops such as grapes for the production of wine—with most exports going to the UK.

A leading wine exporter to the UK

Bulgaria's development has been hampered by political conflicts—and by the persistence in power of many former communists. The latter have regrouped as the Bulgarian Socialist Party (BSP), which has support among older people in the rural areas and among those with strong nationalist sentiments.

Opposing them, the other main grouping is the Union of Democratic Forces (UDF), a coalition of centre-right organizations that has greater support in the cities and among the younger and more educated. But neither group has followed a clear political direction and both are prone to shifts and splits based more on personalities than policies. The other important parties include the party for ethnic Turks (the Movement for Rights and Freedom) and the Bulgarian Business Bloc, which despite its name has proved as likely to ally itself with the BSP as the UDF.

The BSP won the first post-communist election in 1990. But this government did not last and was followed by a number of short-lived administrations led either by the BSP or the UDF. In 1994, the BSP won an absolute majority but did not achieve much. Privatization and other structural reforms slowed, the currency collapsed, the country suffered a banking crisis, and the economy crashed. Large-scale corruption, including extensive smuggling rackets, continued.

This once again opened the way for the UDF, whose candidate, Petar Stoyanov, won the 1996 election for the largely ceremonial role of president. Then in April 1997, an alliance led by the UDF won the parliamentary elections on a law-and-order platform, choosing Ivan Kostov as prime minister.

Kostov has had some success. He has brought more coherence to his own party and faced up to the power of the conglomerates. He has also imposed greater financial discipline, bringing inflation down to single figures in 1999—from over 1,000% in 1997. The pace of privatization has also picked up and the World Bank has now declared that Bulgaria is a good place in which to invest.

In 2000, Bulgaria started negotiations to join the EU—though it has has a long way to go before acceptance.

Burkina Faso

Burkina Faso has few natural resources, a fragile environment, and a rapidly growing population

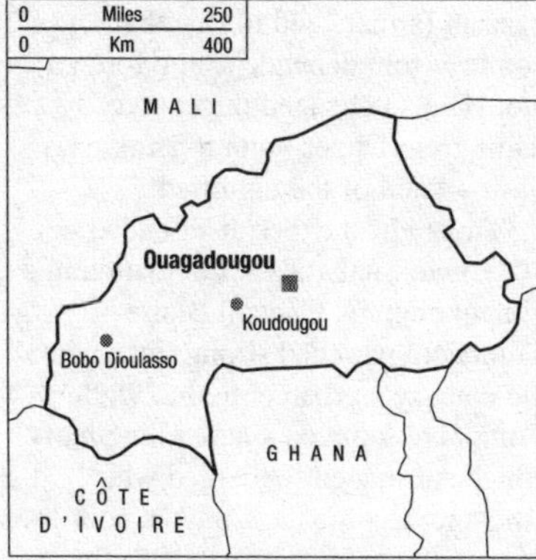

Land area: *274,000 sq. km.*
Population: *11 million—urban 17%*
Capital city: *Ougadougou, 690,000*
People: *Mossi 52%, Peulh 11%, Bobo 7%, other 30%*
Language: *French and local languages*
Religion: *Muslim 50%, indigenous beliefs 40%, Christian 10%*
Government: *Republic*
Life expectancy: *44 years*
GNP per capita: *$PPP 1,020*
Currency: *CFA franc*
Major exports: *Cotton, livestock, gold*

Burkina Faso extends over a broad plateau in the Sahel—the fringe of the Sahara Desert. Most of the territory is savannah grassland scattered with small bushes and trees. The climate is generally arid with a short rainy season and a long dry season. But the rains are unpredictable and the land is vulnerable to drought. The country does have major rivers, including the Red, White, and Black Voltas, though these frequently dry up.

Burkina Faso has numerous ethnic groups, of whom the largest, the Mossi, make up more than half the population. Most people live in the rural areas in the east and centre of the country. Half live below the poverty line and one-quarter are in extreme poverty. Between 30% and 50% of pre-school children are chronically malnourished and the population is largely uneducated: only around one-third of children enrol in primary school—one of the lowest proportions in the world. Health standards are undermined by endemic diseases like malaria and bilharzia, as well as by sleeping sickness transmitted by the tsetse fly, which makes land alongside the rivers virtually uninhabitable.

Most people make their living from agriculture—which provides around 80% of jobs, 40% of GDP, and 50% of export income. Farmers grow subsistence food crops such as millet and sorghum. Food production has increased in recent years—though this was due more to bringing additional land under cultivation than to increases in productivity. Between 1984 and 1994, the area planted with cereals increased by more than 70%. The other main crop is cotton. In the early 1990s Burkina Faso was one of the region's leading producers, but production has been lower in recent years as a result of erratic rainfall and severe insect infestations. Other cash crops include shea nuts, sesame seeds, and sugar cane. Even so, only around 13% of the land is under cultivation: much of the rest of the territory, particularly in the north, is given over to livestock, largely for export to neighbouring countries such as Ghana and Côte d'Ivoire.

Burkina Faso also has mineral potential. At present, most extraction is of gold. But the government has attracted a number of foreign mining companies which are looking at the possibilities for zinc, manganese, limestone, phosphates, and diamonds.

The population continues to grow rapidly, by 2.8% annually, and is putting increasing pressure on the environment. Many of the traditional systems for managing the fragile ecology are breaking down. Much of the thin topsoil has been lost and in the past fifteen years or so, a combination of drought, over-grazing, brush fires, and unregulated felling has removed nearly 60% of the trees. Over a similar period the water table has fallen by around 20 metres. Many parts of the country have already gone beyond what is considered to be a critical limit of 50 inhabitants per square kilometre.

Tsetse fly makes land uninhabitable

Bringing the country's population and resources into balance will be an increasingly difficult task. Though economic growth and population growth have roughly kept pace, already millions of people migrate seasonally to neighbouring countries in search of work, and these numbers are likely to increase.

As one of the world's poorest countries, Burkina Faso has been a major recipient of foreign aid. Its high levels of poverty, and its participation in an IMF-backed structural adjustment programme have also qualified it for various debt cancellation schemes.

Since independence from France in 1960, governments in Burkina Faso have rarely been free of military influence. One of the most distinctive periods was between 1983 and 1987, when a group of army officers led by Thomas Sankara seized power and embarked on a left-wing agenda determined to redistribute resources to peasant farmers and to free the country from dependence on foreign aid. He also changed the country's name from Upper Volta to Burkina Faso—'land of the dignified'.

This radical experiment ended in 1987 with Sankara's assassination in a violent coup by Captain Blaise Compaoré who had strong links with the country's urban élite. In 1989, Compaoré founded a new ruling party which subsequently merged with others to become the Congrès pour le démocratie et le progrès (CDP). In 1991, under pressure from donors, he introduced a new constitution permitting the operation of opposition parties.

Nevertheless, this is still essentially a one-party state. Burkina Faso is one of the few West African countries that has not ratified the UN International Covenant on Civil and Political Rights. Human rights activists have protested over the 1998 murder of journalist Norbert Zongo, over which the government took little action.

The opposition remains weak and divided; it boycotted the presidential elections in 1991 and again in 1998 allowing Compaoré to be re-elected with a large majority. When in May 2000 opposition groups tried to organize a mass rally with other civil organizations the government responded by banning the rally and blocking the streets.

Burma (Myanmar)

Burma has suffered years of repression in the grip of a military regime that renamed it Myanmar

__Land area:__ 677,000 sq. km.
__Population:__ 44 million—urban 27%
__Capital city:__ Rangoon (Yangon), 3.3 million
__People:__ Burman 68%, Shan 9%, Karen 7%, Rakhine 4%, Chinese 3%, Mon 2%, Indian 2%, other 5%
__Language:__ Burmese and minority languages
__Religion:__ Buddhist 89%, Christian 4% Muslim 4%, other 3%
__Government:__ Military dictatorship
__Life expectancy:__ 60 years
__GNP per capita:__ $PPP 1,199
__Currency:__ Kyat
__Major exports:__ Food, timber, prawns

Burma consists largely of the central fertile valley of the Irrawaddy River, encircled by a horseshoe-shaped mountain system running north to south. The highest mountains are to the north, while to the west are two lower ranges, the Chin Hills and the Arakan range. To the east is the extensive Shan Plateau which consists of mountains that intersect with broken ranges of hills and river valleys.

Three-quarters of the population, mostly Burmans, live in the central valley and the coastal strips. Although sparsely settled, Burma has a complex ethnic mix, with 21 major groups and over 100 languages. The largest group are the Shan, who live on the Shan plateau. The Karen live in the delta and in the coastal areas to the south, and the Rakhine live in the south-west. These ethnic groups have engaged in long struggles with the military government. Around 90,000 live in refugee camps in Thailand.

Education standards are low, and over the period 1989-95 almost one-third of children under 3 years were thought to be malnourished. Intravenous drug use is growing and increasing numbers are now HIV-positive. Over one-third of public spending is used to finance the army.

Most people make their living from agriculture, which accounts for around half of GDP. But they are short of fertilizer and other inputs so productivity is low. Another source of rural income is forestry. Burma has around 80% of the world's teak reserves, but over-logging, often through government contracts with Thai companies, is rapidly stripping the forests. The most profitable crop is opium poppies, which are abundant in the eastern mountains and in Shan and Kachin states, enabling Burma to supply around 60% of the world's heroin.

Burma has made slow progress in industrial development since many foreign companies worry about dealing with the military regime. A number of Hong Kong and Korean companies have been attracted by labour costs that can be one-tenth of those in neighbouring Thailand and have established a garments industry, most of whose output goes to the USA. But faced with consumer boycotts many larger companies such as Levi Strauss and Reebok have pulled out. Similarly Texaco has withdrawn from oil and gas production, leaving exploration in the hands of the independent British company Premier Oil.

Premier Oil is one of the few companies prepared to work in Burma

The present regime dates to a coup in 1988. Millions of people had taken to the streets to protest against military rule. The response was brutal. Soldiers sprayed bullets indiscriminately into the crowds and during this incident and the subsequent repression 10,000 people may have died. At this point, a new group of senior military officers seized power. They called themselves the State Law and Order Restoration Council (SLORC), and renamed the country Myanmar. In 1989, they placed under house arrest the leading opposition politician Aung San Suu Kyi, daughter of Aung San, a hero of Burma's independence struggle.

In 1990 SLORC, presuming wrongly that their grip on power would intimidate people into voting for military-backed parties, held multi-party elections for representatives to design a new constitution. In the event, 80% of the seats were won by Aung San Suu Kyi's party, the National League for Democracy. SLORC refused to accept the results. The assembly never met.

This marked the onset of one of the world's most repressive regimes. The UN Human Rights Commission has accused the government of torture, summary executions, and forced displacement and oppression of religious and ethnic minorities. SLORC also overturned the previous regime's socialist model—opening the country up to foreign companies, particularly for timber extraction and the export of natural gas. To build the country's infrastructure it has frequently resorted to forced labour, displaying what an ILO report called: 'a total disregard for the human dignity, safety and health of the people'.

Much of the assault has been born by different ethnic groups which have stubbornly resisted the regime. However, the army, largely staffed by Burmans, has steadily subdued them and all the guerrilla groups except the Karen National Union have signed ceasefires.

The most potent focus of non-violent opposition remains Aung San Suu Kyi, who in 1991 won the Nobel Peace Prize. She was released from house arrest in 1995 but her movements are very restricted, and she is unable to speak in public.

In late 1997, SLORC reformed as the State Peace and Development Council—with most of the same people but a less forbidding acronym. Faced with growing boycotts and denied international aid, the economy is under increasing strain with collapsing trade and rising inflation. Without a change in government, the prospects for Burma are bleak.

Burundi

Burundi has been plagued by ethnic violence, though has avoided genocide on the scale of neighbouring Rwanda

Land area: *28,000 sq. km.*
Population: *7 million—urban 8%*
Capital city: *Bujumbura, 140,000*
People: *Hutu, 85%, Tutsi 14%, other 1%*
Language: *Kirundi, French, Swahili*
Religion: *Christian 67%, indigenous beliefs 32%, other 1%*
Government: *Republic*
Life expectancy: *42 years*
GNP per capita: *$PPP 620*
Currency: *Burundi franc*
Major exports: *Coffee, tea, cotton*

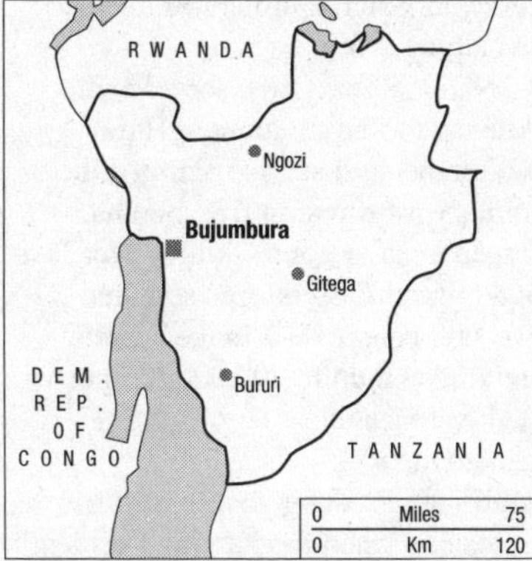

The west of Burundi lies along the Great Rift Valley, with Lake Tanganyika forming the southern two-thirds of the border. To the east the land rises first to high mountains and then descends across a hilly plateau to the border with Tanzania. Much of this area was originally forested, but most of the land has now been cleared for cultivation. This has resulted in extensive soil erosion.

Burundi's population remains sharply divided between two main ethnic groups. The majority are the Hutu, who are agriculturalists. For centuries, they have been dominated by the minority Tutsi, most of whom raise cattle.

In recent decades, there have been a series of Hutu challenges to Tutsi domination, following which the security forces have taken revenge on the Hutu. Waves of killings occurred in 1965, 1969, 1972, 1988, and 1991. In 1993 it was Hutu militias, however, who killed more than 100,000 Tutsi. And from 1994 onwards, a number of Hutu armed opposition groups, have fought the Tutsi-dominated armed forces. Half a million people, mainly Hutu, have fled into Tanzania and the Democratic Republic of the Congo—and similar numbers, mainly Tutsi, have been displaced within Burundi.

The continuing civil war has largely brought development to a halt. Only around half the population is literate and the proportion is probably falling. Schools have frequently been a target of the militias and many teachers and pupils have been killed. Government and opposition forces also force children as young as 12 years old to serve as porters. Health standards too are falling. At least 40% of children are malnourished and health services have deteriorated as medical staff have been caught up in the fighting.

More than 90% of people live in the rural areas, mostly growing subsistence crops such as cassava, sweet potatoes, bananas, beans, and maize. Rapid population growth in recent decades has intensified pressure on the land. Even so, the soil is relatively fertile and until the mid-1990s the country was mostly self-sufficient in food. Since then, however, Burundi has become reliant on international food aid. The main cash crops are coffee, tea, and cotton, which are also grown on peasant small holdings.

Until independence in 1962, Belgium administered Burundi and neighbouring Rwanda as one country. In fact, they have always been fairly distinct territories, naturally divided by rivers, and with people speaking different languages.

Burundi's independence movement was led by the Union pour le progrès national (Uprona). This party had been formed by Tutsis related to their king and also had the support of many Hutu. But traditional conflicts soon resurfaced.

Burundi achieved independence as a monarchy but in 1966 the king was deposed by a Tutsi police commander who declared himself president and the country a republic. The decades that followed saw regular purges, massacres and reprisals, the worst of which in 1972 resulted in the death of at least 100,000 Hutu. Another coup by another Tutsi in 1974 brought Colonel Jean-Baptiste Bagaza to power. He continued to exert Tutsi dominance but his authoritarian rule brought him into increasing conflict with the Catholic Church and others, and he was eventually overthrown in another coup in 1987 by Major Pierre Buyoya. He was a more conciliatory figure and, following another cycle of ethnic violence, he deliberately included Hutu leaders into the government.

Regular purges, massacres and reprisals

In 1993 Burundi had its first free elections. These were won by a new party, the Front pour la démocratie au Burundi (Frodebu). Although ethnically mixed, it had a large Hutu following. A Hutu president, Melchior Ndadaye, took office with a Tutsi prime minister. Uprona had the remaining seats.

National unity was short lived. Attempts to promote more Hutu within the civil service alarmed the military, who within five months staged another coup—killing Ndadaye and other ministers. An estimated 100,000 people died in the ensuing fighting and up to 700,000 refugees fled to Tanzania.

Attempts to re-establish a legitimate Frodebu government were weakened when the interim president was killed in a plane crash, and in 1996 in yet another coup Buyoya returned. Burundi's Hutu have organized themselves in a number of militant movements in Congo and Tanzania, from where they carry out raids—these include the National Council for the Defence of Democracy, Palipehutu, and Frolina.

Early in 2000, Nelson Mandela took over as mediator from the late Julius Nyerere with a plea to Burundi's politicians to 'join the modern world' . He criticized the government for herding people into camps. Unsurprisingly, he soon ran into opposition. In February 2000, Tutsi parties warned Mandela against conclusions that 'tend to imply that the basis of the Burundi conflict is the political, economic and military domination of the minority Tutsi group over the majority Hutu one'.

Cambodia

Decades of war and political upheaval have torn Cambodia apart. It has yet to regain a stable government

Land area: 181,000 sq. km.
Population: 11 million—urban 21%
Capital city: Phnom Penh, 900,000
People: Khmer 90%, Vietnamese 5%, Chinese 1%, other 4%
Language: Khmer, French
Religion: Theravada Buddhism
Government: Constitutional monarchy
Life expectancy: 53 years
GNP per capita: $PPP 1,240
Currency: Riel
Major exports: Logs, timber, rubber, manufactured goods

Three-quarters of Cambodia consists of a large central plain, through which passes the Mekong River on its way from Laos in the north-east to Vietnam in the south. The plain also includes a large lake, the Tonle Sap, which drains into the Mekong—though during the rainy season, while the Mekong is flooding it also sends water back into the lake. Cambodia has a number of mountainous regions—including the Dangrek Mountains on the northern border with Thailand, as well as ranges to the east and south-west.

Cambodians are mostly Khmers, but there are also significant Vietnamese and Chinese minorities. The vast majority live and work in the rural areas. Their standards of literacy and health are poor; less than one-fifth of the population have access to safe drinking water. The health system is weak, offering care only to about half the population.

Three-quarters of the labour force work in agriculture and fishing. But years of conflict have reduced their acreage of rice, which is lower than it was in the 1960s. This is partly because farmers have to avoid the hazard from landmines which still lie in one-third of potential agricultural land. Yields are low. Since farmers largely rely on seasonal rains, they can only get one crop per year.

Forests cover around half the territory, and rubber, logs, and timber are also important exports. In 1997 timber accounted for 43% of foreign trade. But logging companies are cutting down large numbers of teak trees, often illegally, and deforesting vast areas. According to the World Bank, Cambodia's forests could be commercially exhausted by 2003.

So far Cambodia has had little industrial development. Since the mid-1980s the country has been opening up to private enterprise, though many of the largest companies are still state owned. Some foreign companies have invested in light manufacturing, including garments, but their production has been disrupted by the fighting, which has also impeded exploitation of the country's mineral deposits. Economic growth has fluctuated along with the scale of warfare. In 1996, growth was 7% but by 1998 it was down to 1%. Around 40% of GDP comes from foreign aid.

Cambodia's recent political history has been both tragic and complex. One constant figure has been Norodom Sihanouk. Between 1941 and 1970, he ruled either as king or, for a five-year period, as prime minister, attempting to steer a neutral course between right and left. In 1970, he was deposed by more conservative forces in a US-backed coup, though this republic only lasted until 1975 when it fell to the communist Khmer Rouge.

The constant figure of Sihanouk

Headed by Pol Pot, the Khmer Rouge unleashed a regime of extraordinary ruthlessness and brutality. They abolished money, cleared people out of Phnom Penh, and forced a return to peasant agriculture. Their regime is thought to have killed 2 million people. Sihanouk returned, only to find himself under house arrest.

But the Khmer Rouge made the mistake of antagonizing neighbouring Vietnam. In 1979, the Vietnamese responded by invading Cambodia and installing a new regime, forcing the Khmer Rouge back underground. In 1989, the Vietnamese finally withdrew and in 1991 a UN-brokered peace process led to an agreement between the various warring factions and to elections in 1993. The outcome was evenly balanced between a royalist party, Funcipec, led by Sihanouk's son Prince Ranariddh, and the Cambodian People's Party, led by a political strongman, Hun Sen, a former Khmer Rouge defector who had been prime minister in the Vietnamese-installed regime. In the same year, a new constitution established a constitutional monarchy with Sihanouk once again as king.

Hun Sen worked with Prince Ranariddh as joint prime minister until 1997 when he ousted him in a violent coup. Ranariddh fled, but returned for new elections in 1998. These were marked by intimidation and violence, but observers held the result to be fair. Again, the Cambodian People's Party came out ahead, but without the two-thirds majority required to rule outright. Funcipec came second, and they and the 'self-named' party of Sam Rainsy, a former finance minister, denounced the elections as fraudulent. Nevertheless, Ranariddh subsequently agreed to join Hun Sen's coalition government in an uneasy alliance. The year 1998 also saw the death of Pol Pot—unrepentant to the last.

But it looks as though some of his Khmer Rouge followers may go on trial if the government and the UN can agree on a mechanism. By April 2000, talks had lasted for nearly two years. Hun Sen wants a majority of Cambodian judges and prosecutors, while the UN doubts that the Cambodian legal system could administer justice.

In practice Hun Sen is probably more interested in political peace than in justice. In any case a number of the more prominent Khmer Rouge leaders who were implicated in the genocide have been offered immunity or are unlikely ever to be prosecuted.

Cameroon

Potentially one of Africa's richer countries, Cameroon has squandered its oil wealth

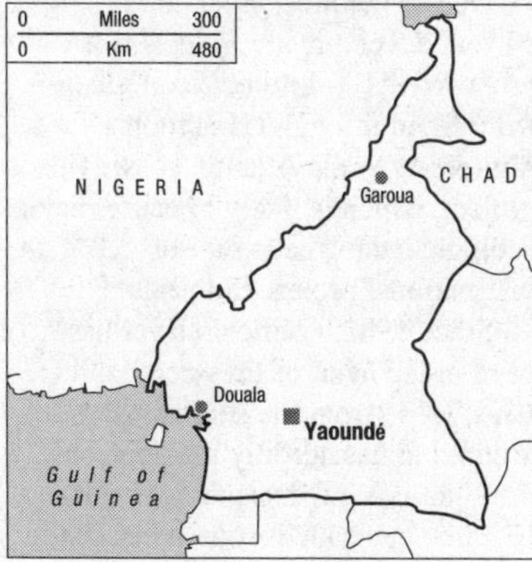

Land area: *475,000 sq. km.*
Population: *14 million—urban 55%*
Capital city: *Yaoundé, 1.1 million*
People: *Fang 20%, Bamiléké 20%, Duala 15%, Kirdi 11%, Fulani 10%, and numerous other groups*
Language: *24 African language groups, English, French*
Religion: *Indigenous beliefs 51%, Christian 33%, Muslim 16%*
Government: *Republic*
Life expectancy: *55 years*
GNP per capita: *$PPP 1,810*
Currency: *CFA franc*
Major exports: *Oil, timber, cocoa, cotton*

Cameroon can be divided into four main regions. First, there is a coastal belt with mangrove forests and swamps that stretch up to 60 kilometres inland. These give way to the east to rocky plateaux. Much of the far north is a broad savannah plain with occasional hills leading to the shores of Lake Chad. The highest part of the country is along the border with Nigeria, a region that includes Mount Cameroon, the highest point in West Africa.

Cameroon has a diverse population, fractured along lines of ethnicity and language. There are thought to be around 200 ethnic groups. In the west the largest include the Bamiléké, who are one of the main commercial influences in the larger cities. In the north there are the Fulani and the Kirdi. And in the south there are the politically more powerful Fang and Beti. These differences open up a number of potential divisions: between the Islamic north and the Christian south, for example, and between pastoralists and farmers. But the most significant political differences arise from the colonial experience. The east of Cameroon was colonized by the French and the west by the British. Today the country is around two-thirds Francophone, and one-third Anglophone—with the latter tending to be marginalized.

Although they had been doing well by the standards of Sub-Saharan Africa, most Cameroonians have seen a fall in living standards since the mid-1980s. The proportion of children going to school has dropped by around one-fifth and the literacy rate is falling. Their health too has been hit by reductions in public expenditure. Only around half the population have access to clean water and sanitation.

More than 60% of Cameroonians still rely directly or indirectly on agriculture. The land is fertile and the country is usually self-sufficient in basic food crops like cassava, corn, millet, and plantains. The most important cash crops are cocoa, coffee, bananas, and cotton, which are mostly grown on small holdings, though they are marketed through state corporations. In the south, there are also plantations growing palm oil and rubber. The country's extensive grasslands also offer grazing for livestock, which provide meat both for local consumption and export.

Cameroon's dense forests in the centre and south, as well as in the coastal belt, have also been an important source of income. Around one-third of the forest area has been exploited, chiefly for the export of mahogany, teak, and ebony. This activity is largely in the hands of multinational companies, but there have been increasing concerns about the over-exploitation of the forests as well as the effects on the country's oldest inhabitants, the pygmies—hunter-gatherers who live in the southern forests.

Rainforests threatened by logging and a proposed oil pipeline

Economic prospects brightened with the discovery of offshore oil in 1976. Production started in 1978 and peaked in 1985. Since then, some of the better fields have matured and companies are having to exploit more marginal deposits. There has been little new investment and current known reserves suggest that output may not be sustained at current levels beyond 2005. Oil flows provided a sudden injection of wealth into the economy, but much of this was dissipated in unwise public expenditure, and through corruption. When the oil price crashed in the mid-1980s, Cameroon crashed with it, suffering one of Sub-Saharan Africa's steepest economic declines. Over the same period, Cameroon also suffered from the overvaluation of the CFA franc. The 50% devaluation in 1994 caused a surge in inflation, though the economy subsequently recovered and growth resumed after 1996.

One of the most contentious current development projects is a proposed 1,100-kilometre oil pipeline from Chad through Cameroon's rainforests to the Atlantic coast. This project, which is likely to cause major ecological damage is the subject of an international protest campaign.

Since 1982, political power has been in the hand of President Paul Biya. He is from the southern Beti group, but has adroitly manipulated the country's various ethnic divides. Initially, he headed a one-party state, but a wave of social agitation in 1990 forced Biya to permit multi-party politics. In a 1992 election alleged to have been rigged, Biya was elected president at the head of his own party the Rassemblement démocratique du peuple Camerounais (RDPC)—narrowly defeating John Fru Ndi of the main Anglophone opposition party, the Social Democratic Front (SDF).

Biya won again in 1997, but this time all three opposition parties boycotted the election after the government refused to appoint an independent electoral commission. The SDF, whose power base is among the Bamiléké, wants to see constitutional reform, and its more radical elements demand secession for the English-speaking provinces. Thus far, Biya has successfully resisted these pressures, but increasing levels of poverty throughout the country could weaken his position.

Canada

Canada is perennially on the brink of splitting between English and French speakers

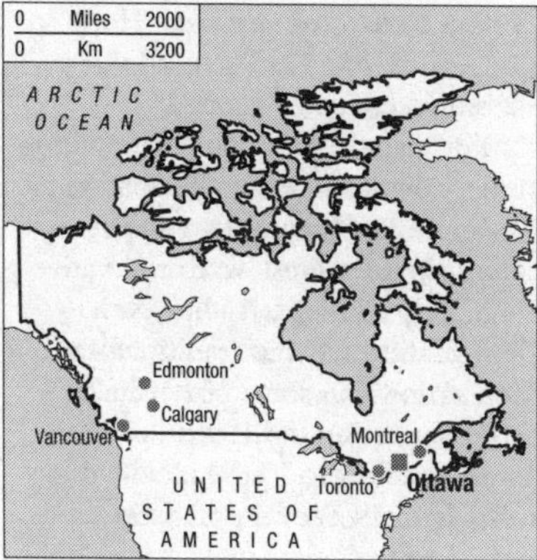

Land area: *9,976,000 sq. km.*
Population: *31 million—urban 77%*
Capital city: *Ottawa, 1.0 million*
People: *British origin 40%, French origin 27%, other European 20%, Amerindian 2%, other 11%*
Language: *English, French*
Religion: *Roman Catholic 45%, Protestant 40%, other 15%*
Government: *Constitutional monarchy*
Life expectancy: *79 years*
GNP per capita: *$PPP 24,050*
Currency: *Canadian dollar*
Major exports: *Newsprint, pulp, timber, oil, machinery, vehicles, gas*

Canada is, after Russia, the world's second largest country, though much is barren and sparsely populated. The more remote areas include the icy wastes of the Arctic archipelago in the north, the splendour of the Rocky Mountains in the west, and the stormy Newfoundland coast in the east. The largest region, around Hudson Bay, is the flat, rocky Canadian Shield which is studded with thousands of lakes. To the west are the lowlands of the interior plains. And to the south-east the Great Lakes-St Lawrence region that borders on the USA. Around 90% of Canadians live in a belt of land along the southern border that amounts to only 10% of the territory.

Canada's original population, the 'first nations', now make up less than 2% of the population, and are among the poorest people. Many are now claiming land and other rights from provincial governments. In 1997, the Supreme Court ruled that the government has 'a moral, if not legal, duty' to negotiate to settle their claims—which could prove an expensive business.

Everyone else is of immigrant descent, and Canada remains a country of immigration. In 1996, 17% of the population were foreign-born. Immigration is strictly limited to around 200,000 per year, but the pattern of arrivals altered dramatically from the 1960s, following changes that removed the privileges of European immigrants. Now more than half of immigrants come from Asia, many of them of Chinese origin who settled on the Pacific coast. Despite this influx, Canada remains relatively free of racial tension.

Three-quarters of Canadians are employed in service industries, with the most dynamic growth in larger cities like Toronto and Vancouver. Manufacturing, particularly in high-technology goods, has also been expanding and, in 1998, accounted for 19% of GDP.

Mining now employs only around 1% of the workforce but still makes a vital contribution to the economy.

Canada is the world's largest exporter of nickel, zinc, uranium, and potash and is an important source of many other metals, including platinum, copper, and titanium. It also has considerable oil and gas deposits, and is the world's tenth largest oil exporter.

The Canadian prairies produce vast quantities of wheat, oats, barley, and many other crops, as well as livestock. But agriculture employs only 3% of the workforce. Canada's forests also enable it to be the world's leading exporter of wood pulp and newsprint. And its rich fishing grounds on both Pacific and Atlantic coasts also make it the world's largest exporter of fish.

Around 80% of exports go to the USA—trade which has been boosted by the 1994 establishment with the USA and Mexico of the North American Free Trade Agreement (NAFTA). There had been fears of a flood of imports but Canada seems to have retained a strong trade balance with the USA. A greater problem is that NAFTA encourages movement of professional labour and is sending skilled Canadians to the USA.

The wealth of natural resources and a dynamic immigrant population have made Canada one of the world's richest countries. It also has strong health and education services. In 2000, it once again took first place in the United Nations Development Programme's Human Development Index. Nevertheless there have been some economic problems in recent years, notably an increase in unemployment, which early in 2000 was 7%.

Number one in human development

Canada's head of state is the British monarch—a constitutional anomaly that seems unlikely to change since Canada has a strong federal system with semi-autonomous provincial governments—each of which would have a right of veto. In 1999, a former refugee from Hong Kong, Adrienne Clarkson, was appointed governor-general.

For many years, Canadian politics at the federal level was the domain of the centre-left Liberal Party or the centre-right Progressive Conservative Party. The smaller left-wing New Democratic Party has traditionally been stronger in some provincial parliaments. But the 1990s saw dramatic changes. These included the collapse in 1993 of the Conservative Party, and the emergence of the right-wing Reform Party, along with a strong federal representation for the Bloc Québécois which argues for independence for the French-speaking province of Quebec.

The 1997 federal election saw the Liberal Party led by Prime Minister Jean Chrétien returned to power, though with a reduced majority, and the Reform Party confirmed as the main opposition.

The most contentious issue remains the potential secession of Quebec. A number of English-speaking provinces are vigorously opposed to secession. Even the citizens of Quebec are as yet unconvinced: in a 1995 provincial referendum, they narrowly rejected a proposal for independence. By early 2000, however, the Bloc Québécois was already touting the idea of yet another referendum, though opinion polls suggested only 45% of Québécois were in favour.

Cape Verde

One of Africa's smallest countries—heavily dependent on emigrants' remittances

Land area: *4,000 sq. km.*
Population: *412,000—urban 58%*
Capital city: *Praia, 61,000*
People: *Creole 71%, African 28%, other 1%*
Language: *Portuguese, Crioulo*
Religion: *Roman Catholicism and indigenous beliefs*
Government: *Republic*
Life expectancy: *68 years*
GNP per capita: *$PPP 2,950*
Currency: *Cape Verde escudo*
Major exports: *Footwear, garments, fish*

Cape Verde is an archipelago of ten islands off the coast of West Africa. Much of the territory is mountainous with little arable land. Combined with frequent droughts, this has made agriculture difficult, and has resulted in serious environmental degradation.

Two-thirds of Cape Verdeans are creole, of mixed Portuguese and African descent, and half live on the island of Santiago. Because of the harshness of the terrain and the resultant poverty, they have had a strong tradition of emigration. Today there are probably twice as many Cape Verdeans living abroad as there are at home.

Aid-financed public investment in education and health services in the decades following independence in 1975 helped to give Cape Verde one of Sub-Saharan Africa's higher levels of human development. However this made the country very dependent on donors who have been providing around one-third of the budget. The country has also benefited from emigrants' remittances which annually are equivalent to 70% of GDP.

Agriculture still employs more than half the workforce. But this does not offer much prospect of future employment and the government has been liberalizing the economy in an attempt to attract foreign investment for light industry and to develop tourist facilities. This may help, but seems unlikely to be sufficient to absorb the large numbers of unemployed. Cape Verde will probably rely on emigration and aid for some time.

Cape Verde, which was in union with Guinea-Bissau until 1980, was one of the first African one-party states to democratize. Multi-party elections in 1991 saw a defeat for the socialist Partido Africano da Independência de Cabo Verde (PAICV) and victory for the more market-oriented Movimento para a Democracia (MPD)—a victory repeated in 1995 with Carlos Veiga as prime minister.

Antonio Mascarenhas Monteiro, also of the MPD, was elected president in 1991 and re-elected unopposed in 1996. The PAICV remains as a left-wing opposition, led after 1997 by former prime minister Pedro Pires.

Since 1997, there have been further constitutional reforms and plans to increase the powers of the president. The MPD's enthusiasm for liberalization, which has included a series of privatizations, has continued to attract donor support.

Central African Republic

After years of instability and violence, international interventions have brokered an uneasy peace

Land area: *623,000 sq. km.*
Population: *3 million—urban 40%*
Capital city: *Bangui , 542,000*
People: *Baya 34%, Banda 27%, Sara 10%, Mandjia 21%, Mboum 4%, M'baka 4%*
Language: *French, Sangho, Arabic, Hunsa, Swahili*
Religion: *Indigenous beliefs 24%, Protestant 25%, Roman Catholic 25%,* **Muslim** *15%, other 11%*
Government: *Republic*
Life expectancy: *45 years*
GNP per capita: *$PPP 1,290*
Currency: *CFA franc*
Major exports: *Diamonds, timber, cotton*

The Central African Republic is a landlocked country that sits on a plateau around 700 metres above sea level. The north of the country is savannah with some extensive grasslands. The south has more luxuriant vegetation, particularly along the river valleys and in the dense tropical rainforests.

The country is sparsely populated but ethnically complex. The main division is between savannah dwellers such as the Sara and Mandjia, and the more dominant, 'riverines' those such as the M'baka who live in the south along the Ubangi River and who had greater contact with the French colonists. There are many languages, though the national lingua franca is Sangho, and the official language in the education system is French. Years of unrest and ethnic strife have taken their toll on human development. The education system is weak and only around 40% of the population are literate. Health standards too are low: in the rural areas where more of the people live few have access to safe water or sanitation, and around one-third of all children are malnourished.

Two-thirds of the population make their living through subsistence agriculture, growing such crops as cassava, peanuts, corn, and millet. They also grow cash crops, including coffee and cotton, but the poor state of communications means that many households effectively live outside the cash economy. The most important transport artery is the Ubangi River along the southern border with the Democratic Republic of the Congo.

One-fifth of the country is covered by tropical rainforests and there are more than 50 species of commercially viable trees. Transport difficulties have so far hampered the development of forestry but logging is increasing, making timber one of the most important exports. The government has attempted to conserve the rainforest by reducing the proportion of wood exported as timber and encouraging the production of veneers and plywood.

The Central African Republic also has a number of mineral resources, including iron ore, uranium and gold, but these have not been exploited because of low prices and high transport costs.

More important are alluvial diamonds. Found in the west of the country, these are often mined by individuals and co-operatives and offer a significant source of rural employment. Diamonds are also the leading export earner, though at least half the output is smuggled out of the country. Official export and cutting operations are in the hands of a joint venture between the state and South Korean and Belgian companies.

The Central African Republic achieved independence in 1960, but from 1965 the country's development was overshadowed by the bizarre, tyrannical rule of Jean-Bedel Bokassa, who, in 1977 in an extravagant ceremony had himself crowned Emperor Bokassa I. France sustained him in power but in 1979 finally lost patience and sent in troops to remove him. However the chosen successor was himself removed (again with French support) in a military coup in 1981 by General André Kolingba.

Emperor Bokassa I, one of Africa's most notorious dictators

Kolingba offered a degree of stability and put more emphasis on economic development. He also attempted to legitimize his rule by creating a single political party, the Rassemblement démocratique centrafricain (RDC). But in the face of popular and international pressure in 1992, he had to legalize other parties.

In 1993 Kolingba lost the ensuing presidential election to Ange-Félix Patassé, who had been one of Bokassa's prime ministers. His party, the Mouvement pour la libération du peuple centrafricain, gets most of its support from the north-west of the country, where Patassé himself comes from. Kolingba's RDC has its support in the south.

Patassé's government soon proved inept and corrupt and in 1996 the army staged a mutiny, demanding back pay for themselves and other government workers. The French army, who maintained a garrison in the country, came to his rescue.

In 1997, following diplomatic interventions from Gabon and Mali, the government, rebels, and political parties reached a more lasting settlement. UN-monitored legislative elections for the 109-seat National Assembly held in December 1998 were generally considered to be free and fair. Opposition parties won 55 seats while the ruling party and its allies won 54. But the post-election defection of an opposition legislator gave the ruling coalition a one-seat majority in the assembly.

In September 1999, Patassé beat Kolingba fairly convincingly in a UN-monitored presidential election. The UN peacekeeping mission left in February 2000, raising security fears. In May 2000, in an effort to consolidate the peace, UN Secretary-General Kofi Annan paid a visit. At the request of opposition parties, Annan asked the president to introduce some kind of power sharing—though he seems unlikely to contemplate this at present.

Chad

Chad has had decades of civil war, but now seems more stable, and its future could be transformed by oil

Land area: *1,284,000 sq. km.*
Population: *7 million—urban 23%*
Capital city: *Ndjamena, 610,000*
People: *Numerous Muslim and non-Muslim groups*
Language: *French, Arabic, many others*
Religion: *Muslim 50%, Christian 25%, indigenous beliefs 25%*
Government: *Republic*
Life expectancy: *47 years*
GNP per capita: *$PPP 970*
Currency: *CFA franc*
Major exports: *Cotton, livestock, textiles*

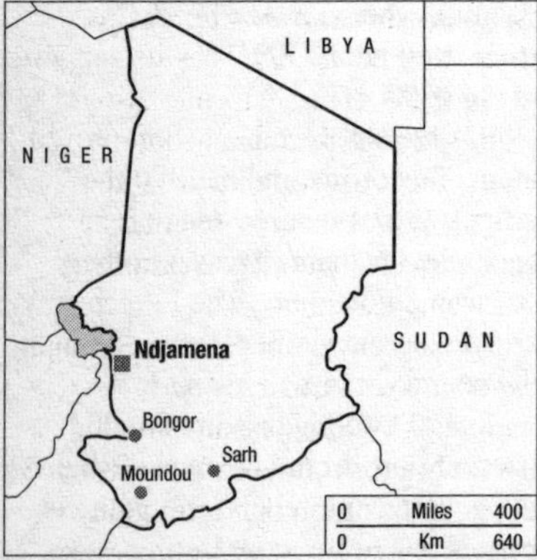

Chad's territory forms a basin centred on Lake Chad on the western border. The terrain rises steadily, eventually reaching mountains in the north and east between which, in the north-east, lies a sandstone plateau. The climate varies from hot and dry in the north to tropical in the south, where the country's small amount of arable land is to be found.

Chad is ethnically very diverse, with more than 200 distinct groups. Conventionally, these are divided into the Islamic north, where most people raise cattle and the common language is Arabic, and the Christian or animist south, where people are farmers and the common language of the élite is French. The dividing line is taken to be the Shari River. Though the two parts have roughly the same population, the south represents less than one-tenth of the territory. This north-south divide is something of a simplification, since each part has numerous internal divisions, but generally the north has been more traditional, and the south, which was more effectively colonized by the French, is economically more modern. Throughout the country, poverty is severe and widespread. Infant mortality is high, life expectancy is low, and the literacy rate is around 50%. The country is dependent on foreign aid and is heavily in debt.

Chad's economy has seen little progress since independence, hampered by poor infrastructure and endemic political conflict. Around 40% of GDP is generated by agriculture, which employs 60% of the workforce. Sedentary agriculture is almost entirely in the south, on the lake shore, and along the river valleys. In a good year, production of rice, sorghum, millet, wheat, and other foodstuffs is sufficient for local consumption, but output has frequently been constrained by drought and civil conflict. Cash crops include sugar and peanuts, but the most important, and the major export earner, is cotton—which directly or indirectly is thought to employ about 1 million people. In the centre and north of the country people rely for income on their livestock—around 5 million cattle and 6 million sheep and goats.

Chad has little industry. Most is linked to the processing of agricultural products—ginning cotton and producing meat and hides. But things could change radically if oil production gets underway. Following oil discoveries in 1994, Elf, Exxon, and Shell proposed to develop oilfields in Doba in the south and build a 1,100-kilometre pipeline to the port of Kribi in neighbouring Cameroon.

There are two major complications. First, the pipeline will pass through some of Chad's scarce agricultural land, displacing thousands of people, and then in Cameroon it will pass through an ecologically fragile rainforest region. Secondly, Doba has been a focus of intense rebel activity—some of which is organized around opposition to the pipeline. All this has given the World Bank, which is to provide most of the finance, pause for thought. Even if the project goes ahead, oil production is unlikely before 2002.

A controversial World Bank-financed pipeline

Chad's conflicts became evident soon after independence in 1960, and have usually involved direct or indirect participation by neighbouring countries. The first, one-party regime, supported by the French, came to be seen as a southern dictatorship. This prompted the emergence in the north of a guerrilla movement, the Front de libération du Tchad (Frolinat).

Following a military coup in 1975, the new regime, although again composed mostly of southerners, tried to make peace with Frolinat. This failed, not least because the rebellion was being funded by Libya. In 1982, however, Hissène Habré, a northern leader, seized power, backed by the USA Sudan, and Egypt, but opposed by Libya. This provoked a rebellion in the south and warfare that was to claim 40,000 victims.

In 1990, Habré's former army head, Idriss Déby, launched the Mouvement patriotique du salut (MPS). With Libyan support, this rapidly ousted Habré and installed Déby as president.

So far Déby seems to have brought a measure of democracy and stability—by Chad's standards. In 1996, a national referendum approved a new constitution that introduced multi-party politics. Elections were held in 1996, and multi-party elections for the National Assembly were held in 1997. Although the opposition claimed that there were irregularities, President Déby won with 67% of the vote, and the MPS obtained a majority of the seats in the National Assembly. Déby has concentrated on co-opting as many opposition groups as possible, and has achieved a measure of peace. Even so, the conflict continues with violent abuses of human rights by both security forces and rebels.

Early in 2000, former-President Habré was arrested in Senegal and charged with murder and torture. This was the first case of African victims asking another country to prosecute a former African dictator. In July 2000, however, the charges were dismissed following intervention by President Wade of Senegal.

Channel Islands

Dependencies of the British crown—constitutionally odd and financially rich

Land area: *300 sq. km.*
Population: *149,000—urban 29%*
Main towns: *St Helier, St. Peter Port*
People: *British and Norman French*
Language: *English, French*
Religion: *Christian*
Government: *Dependencies of the British crown*
Life expectancy: *78 years*
GNP per capita: *$25,000*
Currency: *Jersey pound, Guernsey pound*
Major exports: *Vegetables, fruit, flowers*

The Channel Islands consist of four main islands and numerous other islets. They are governed as two separate 'bailiwicks' based on the two largest islands: Jersey, with 58% of the population; and Guernsey, with 42%, which also covers the two smaller islands of Alderney and Sark.

Natives of the islands generally speak either English or French, though there are vestiges of a Norman-French dialect. There are also large numbers of settlers: in Jersey only half the resident population were born on the island; most of the rest come from elsewhere in the British Isles, often as tax exiles, and there are also many immigrant workers from Portugal.

The islands have traditionally exported horticultural produce to the UK—fruit, flowers, tomatoes, and potatoes. But agriculture now accounts for only 5% of GDP. Tourism is more significant, accounting for 24% of GDP in Jersey and 14% in Guernsey. Around 80% of visitors come from the UK, attracted by the mild climate and pleasant scenery, though most come only for short breaks.

More recently, the islands' economies have become dominated by financial services—55% of GDP in Jersey, and 60% in Guernsey. With little or no corporation tax, they became very attractive to British companies in 1979 after the abolition of exchange controls. By 1998, the two had between them around $400 billion in bank deposits. The business is fairly clean, though a 1998 British government report concluded that 'the extent of disreputable business is hard to judge' and the scale of tax evasion and fraud 'unusually hazardous' to assess. The report also discovered a strangely high level of entrepreneurial activity on Sark, whose 575 inhabitants between them held 15,000 company directorships.

These opportunities are created by the islands' unusual constitutional position, with respect to both the UK and the EU. They are neither sovereign states nor part of the UK, but remnants of the duchy of Normandy, a legacy of William the Conqueror, and come under the jurisdiction of the British monarch rather than of the state. They have autonomy in domestic policy, including fiscal policy, and Jersey issues its own coins and notes. The monarch appoints a lieutenant-governor to each of the bailiwicks. Each also has an appointed bailiff who is president of the local Assembly of the States, which has both elected and appointed members.

Chile

Chile has its first socialist president since Allende, and appears to have set aside the Pinochet years

Land area: *757,000 sq. km.*
Population: *15 million—urban 84%*
Capital city: *Santiago, 4.9 million*
People: *European and mestizo 95%, Indian 3%, other 2%*
Language: *Spanish*
Religion: *Roman Catholic 89%, Protestant 1%*
Government: *Republic*
Life expectancy: *75 years*
GNP per capita: *$PPP 12,890*
Currency: *Peso*
Major exports: *Copper, fruit, cellulose, fishmeal*

Chile is remarkably narrow: 4,329 kilometres long and on average no more than 180 kilometres wide. From north to south run the rolling hills of the coastal highlands in parallel with the massive ranges of the Andes to the east. Between them lies a central valley that is most evident in the middle third of the country. Chile's length also offers striking climatic variations, from the heat of the Atacama Desert in the north, through a temperate centre, then a cool, wet south extending through the lakes and fjords and on to the stormy Straits of Magellan.

Most of Chile's people live in the central valley and around the middle of the country. One-third live in the capital, Santiago. Chileans are almost entirely of mestizo or of European descent. The small Mapuche Indian population is concentrated in an area 700 kilometres south of Santiago.

Chile has at times viewed itself as more European than South American. And it can claim higher standards of education and health than its neighbours as well as a more broadly-based economy. Even so, its wealth is very dependent on natural resources. One of the economic mainstays is mining in the northern deserts. Chile has one-quarter of global copper reserves and is the world's largest producer. Since copper makes up two-fifths of export earnings, Chile is vulnerable to swings in the prices. The country is also rich in other minerals, including gold, molybdenum, silver, and iron; and it can count on substantial reserves of oil and gas.

Chile's climatic diversity also permits a diverse agricultural output. Agriculture and fisheries employ around 15% of the workforce. Chile's climate in the central zone is ideal for growing apples, pears, and grapes during what is winter in the northern hemisphere. The 5,000 or so growers and the largely multinational packing plants are doing well, though the wages and working conditions of the largely female labour force are poor. Also less fortunate are the 200,000 wheat-growing campesino farmers who in a very liberal trade regime are suffering from cheaper imports. Land ownership is becoming ever more concentrated into larger farms.

Chilean manufacturing has been diverse. In the past, it was designed for import substitution. But Chile's open economy, which in 1998 had a uniform external tariff of 11%, means that it tends to operate in areas where it has the greatest competitive advantage. Even leading manufactured exports are usually closely linked to agriculture, including cellulose and fishmeal, as well as very popular wines.

Chile's economic and political history was transformed in 1973. Previously, the country had enjoyed a long sequence of democratic governments, but this pattern was shattered by a CIA-supported military coup which ousted socialist President Salvador Allende and ushered in the era of General Augusto Pinochet. For the next seventeen years, Chile became a byword for torture, repression, and the abuse of human rights: within three years about 130,000 people had been arrested. Ultimately 3,197 people were to die for political reasons, including 1,102 who 'disappeared'.

Pinochet made Chile a byword for torture and repression

Pinochet's political ferocity had been combined with radical economic liberalism—and subsequent governments followed the same economic path. But the 'Chilean model' is actually a mixture of policies. It does espouse open markets, low trade tariffs, deregulation, and privatization, including a privatized pension scheme. But it also has significant elements of regulation—including controls on capital flows and some indexing of wages and prices.

Democracy was restored only in 1990, and a government was formed by the Concertación alliance—a thirteen-party coalition that included parties from moderate conservative to the far left. The Concertación won again in 1993 led by Christian Democrat Eduardo Frei. For most of the 1990s the right-wing opposition had been hampered by its association with Pinochet. But Pinochet's detention in the UK in 1998 muddied the waters. Frei's government felt obliged to ask for the former dictator's return (which took place in 2000).

It was thought that the Pinochet case would affect the 2000 presidential election. In the event, voters were more interested in bread and butter issues of employment and income. But this election also showed that the right was no longer tainted by its association with Pinochet. Their candidate was Joaquín Lavin, a right-wing populist who came close to defeating the Concertación candidate Ricardo Lagos.

Lagos won in the second round, thanks to the support of left-wing parties. Although he is the first socialist president since Allende, he is likely to follow a social-democratic path. The new government has also said that Pinochet could be tried in Chile but that it is determined to leave the issue to the justice system. There are indications that the courts might deprive him of some immunity from prosecution but he is unlikely ever to face trial.

China

China is reforming into an economic superpower, but the Communist Party retains its political grip

Land area: *9,561,000 sq. km.*
Population: *1,239 million—urban 30%*
Capital city: *Beijing, 12.2 million*
People: Han Chinese 92%, Zhuang, Uygur, Hui, Yi, Tibetan, Miao, Manchu, Mongol, Buyi, Korean, and other nationalities 8%
Language: *Mandarin, Yue (Cantonese), Wu (Shanghaiese), Minbei (Fuzhou), Minnan (Hokkien-Taiwanese), Xiang, Gan, Hakka dialects, minority languages*
Religion: *Taoism, Buddhism, Muslim, Christian*
Government: *Communist state*
Life expectancy: *70 years*
GNP per capita: *$PPP 3,220*
Currency: *Renminbi (yuan)*
Major exports: *Electrical machinery, clothing, footwear, coal*

China's vast landmass incorporates immense topographical and climatic diversity. But it can be divided into three broad areas. First, there is the north-western region, which is predominantly mountainous, including the Tien Shan ranges that average around 4,000 metres—though this area also includes the Tarim and Dzungarian basins and the Takla Makan Desert. A second main region lies to the south-west and includes the Tibetan Plateau and other highlands. The remainder of the country, extending east to the coast, has some mountains but is mostly low-lying and includes extensive river systems flowing west to east: the Huang Ho (Yellow River) to the north and the Yangtze to the south.

This huge territory also has considerable climatic variation—colder and dryer to the north and on the mountains and steppes in the interior, and warmer and wetter to the south and east.

Most people live in the eastern part of the country and are ethnically fairly homogenous—more than 90% are Han Chinese. Nevertheless the Han differ regionally, particularly in language. The standardized common language is based on the Mandarin dialect and is used in government as well as in schools and universities, but there are also a number of Han dialects that share most of the same characters though are mutually incomprehensible.

In addition to the Han there are around 75 million Chinese who belong to any of 55 or more different ethnic groups who are settled across more than half the territory. These include the Zhuang, the Hui (Muslims), the Miao, the Mongols, and the Tibetans. Where they are concentrated in specific areas, they theoretically have some autonomy, though this is fairly limited.

One of China's central preoccupations has been population

growth. Population control efforts intensified after 1979 with the introduction of the 'one-child family' policy—with fines for parents who had two or more children. Although subsequently relaxed somewhat, this has had a dramatic effect. By 1999, total fertility was down to 1.5 children per woman of childbearing age, which is well below replacement level. This has slowed the growth of the population, which is expected to reach 1.6 billion by 2050. But it has also increased the average age: by 2030 on current trends, one in five people will be over 60. An unusually high proportion will be men. When Chinese parents faced the one-child policy they wanted that child to be a son—and many used abortion or even infanticide to ensure this. By 1995, for every 100 girls under five there were 118 boys.

China will have more men than women

China remains a poor country and in 1995 one-fifth of the population lived below the poverty line. Life in the countryside is often harsh. Rural families only earn around half as much as those in the cities, and services remain poor. Few rural people have access to safe sanitation and one-third of the rural population does not have an adequate supply of drinking water. Their health services are also inferior to those in the cities.

The situation in the rural areas began to improve after 1978, when the first round of market reforms dismantled the collective farms and passed responsibility to households. They could now choose what to grow and, after producing their quota for the government, they could sell the rest in private markets. In response, farm output increased by 50%. But in recent years agriculture has stagnated. Farmers do not have title to their land, so they are reluctant to make improvements.

China is still able to feed itself—indeed in the late 1990s there were often food surpluses. But the long-term prospects are more worrying. The country already has a relatively small proportion of agricultural land—only around 16% is cultivable—and this continues to shrink as a result of environmental degradation and industrial and housing development.

Another reason for the stagnation in agriculture has been the much greater emphasis on industry. Until the late 1970s, industry was dominated by state-owned heavy industrial enterprises. Since then, there has been a dramatic shift towards the private sector and light industry. Between 30% and 50% of national output is now in the private sector, and China now manufactures one-third of the world's suitcases, and one-quarter of its toys. In 1997 there were still around 100,000 state-owned enterprises employing more than 100 million people, but they accounted for only 25% of output and around half are making a loss.

Agriculture stagnates while cities expand

In order to stem migration from the countryside, the government from 1978 promoted township and village enterprises (TVEs). This boosted rural incomes and employment, and around one-quarter of the rural labour force is now non-agricultural. By 1997, TVEs and other kinds of collective enterprise accounted for 40% of industrial production.

China can also rely on a wide variety of mineral deposits. It has enough iron ore to feed its steel industry. It also has extensive coal reserves, particularly in the north. In addition, a number of provinces have small onshore oil deposits, and there are off-shore possibilities. Hydroelectric power is also important and has benefited from extensive investment, most recently in the controversial $28-billion 'Three Gorges' dam on the Yangtze, a project that has already displaced more than 1 million people.

The Three Gorges dam will displace 1 million people

In recent years, many foreign businesses have also arrived, tempted by the world's most populous market. Most have invested in coastal areas—one-quarter in Guangdong alone. China acquired another major block of foreign investment when it took control over the former British colony of Hong Kong, which remains a global financial and business centre.

China's transformation is the legacy of the late Deng Xiaoping. Deng emerged as the leading figure after the death of Chairman Mao Zedong in 1976. In economic policy, Deng was fairly pragmatic. He described his approach as 'crossing the river by feeling for the stones'. Politically, he was more orthodox. Though Deng opened the labour camps and reduced government interference in people's private lives he was less tolerant of political dissent. This became chillingly clear on 4 June 1989 when troops opened fire on pro-democracy demonstrators in Beijing's Tiananmen Square, killing hundreds of people.

When Deng died in 1997 he was replaced by his chosen successor Jiang Zemin. But Jiang has less authority than Deng enjoyed and China's leadership is now more collective.

China's constitution of 1982, as amended in 1988, declares the country to be a socialist dictatorship led by the working class. In practice, it continues to be run by the Communist Party. The party and the government are more or less the same thing, run by the same people. Jiang is general-secretary of the Chinese Communist Party as well as state president and chairman of the Central Military Committee. Second in the hierarchy is Li Peng, who chairs the National People's Congress—a 3,000-member rubber-stamp parliament. Third is Premier Zhu Rongjii. But the real decision-making body is the party's seven-member Politburo Standing Committee.

The army has also been a major political and economic force, but its influence has receded and one of Jiang's most radical moves has been to force the army to give up all its lucrative commercial interests.

In the short term, Jiang seems to be trying to make the current political system work better, attacking corruption and making the government more responsive to the people. In the long term, however, his authority and that of the Communist Party is likely to be eroded as the market economy makes steady inroads. The next generation of Chinese will probably be more interested in business than in politics.

Colombia

Colombia is as violent as ever, though the deaths nowadays are linked to drugs as well as politics

Land area: *1,139,000 sq. km.*
Population: *41 million—urban 74%*
Capital city: *Bogotá, 4.9 million*
People: *Mestizo 58%, white 20%, mulatto 14%, black 4%, mixed black-Indian 3%, Indian 1%*
Language: *Spanish*
Religion: *Roman Catholic*
Government: *Republic*
Life expectancy: *70 years*
GNP per capita: *$PPP 7,500*
Currency: *Peso*
Major exports: *Oil, coffee, chemicals, coal*

The western half of Colombia is dominated by three Andean mountain chains. To the west, they descend to the Pacific and Caribbean coasts. To the east, their foothills lead from plains on to savannah and to rainforests that cover around two-thirds of the country.

Colombia's diverse ethnic make-up changes from one region to another. The highest proportions of blacks and mulattos—mixtures of black and white—are to be found in the coastal regions. The whites and mestizos—mixtures of white and Indian—who make up most of the population, live in the valleys and basins between the mountain ranges. The Indian population are mostly to be found in the isolated lowlands. Though now only 1% of the population they are still very diverse, with more than 180 languages and dialects. Colombia is a very polarized society with wide disparities in income—the richest 10% of the population, predominantly white, get 47% of national income.

Around one-third of the workforce are employed in agriculture. They grow a range of food crops such as maize and rice, as well as cash crops for export, of which the most important is coffee; Colombia is the world's leading producer of the mild arabica variety. Colombia also exports large quantities of cut flowers as well as bananas and sugar.

Colombia has rich mineral resources. The most important is oil, which accounts for around one-quarter of exports. The newer and more promising reserves, including gas, lie to the east of the Andes in remoter areas of the tropical lowlands. In addition, Colombia has Latin America's largest coal reserves and is a significant producer of gold, emeralds, and nickel. The country also has a diverse manufacturing sector—in areas such as food processing, chemicals, textiles, and clothing, most of which is controlled by large conglomerates.

The great unknown element in Colombia's economy is the drugs trade—whose worth is estimated at anything up to $4 billion per year. Colombia processes its own heroin poppies and coca leaf, as well as coca paste imported from Peru and Bolivia. The government is reported to spend more than $1 billion per year combating drugs, but the traffic continues unabated, and it supplies around 80% of the cocaine that reaches the USA.

Blessed with resources legal and illegal, Colombia has enjoyed steady economic growth. Its economic management has also been fairly steady by Latin American standards, avoiding the cycles of boom and bust as well as the debt crises. Even so, in 1999 the economy was deep in recession, shrinking by 5% and unemployment reached 20%. The government has had to keep public spending high to pay for the war against the guerrillas. The government budget more than doubled in the 1990s. The government has promised the IMF that it will cut the deficit but is doing so very slowly.

Colombia is also distinctive in South America for having had a series of democratically elected non-military governments. Even so, the political system has long been steeped in violence. Between 1948 and 1957 this was essentially warfare between the Liberal and Conservative parties—a period known as 'la violencia' that cost 300,000 lives. Then the 1960s saw the rise of left-wing guerrilla movements, including the Revolutionary Armed Forces of Colombia (FARC), the National Liberation Army (ELN), and M-19.

In recent years there have been a series of ceasefires and amnesties. Eventually, M-19 laid down its arms and entered politics, ultimately unsuccessfully. But political resolution is more difficult nowadays since the guerrillas are less concerned about revolutionary ideals and more preoccupied with making money through drugs, kidnapping, and extortion. Add to these the private armies of drug dealers and right-wing militias and Colombia is always on the brink of anarchy and civil war. This takes a terrible human toll. Colombia has the world's highest incidence of violent death—80 per 100,000 population. Over the past ten years, around 35,000 people are thought to have died.

Colombia is on the brink of civil war

When Andres Pastrana of the Conservative Party was elected president in 1998, he promised to make peace with the rebels and reform the army but has had little success. Part of his strategy was to withdraw the armed forces from a 'demilitarised zone' of mountainous jungle—leaving around 100,000 civilians effectively under the rule of some 15,000 FARC troops. He also hoped to engage in talks with the smaller ELN.

But the situation appears little better, and a particularly brutal murder of a farmer with a 'collar bomb' in May 2000 caused the president to postpone the next round of peace talks. Added to the violence from the army, the guerrillas, and the right-wing death squads, Pastrana has had to deal with an economic slump. He hopes that some of this can be tackled with more aid from the USA—in return for efforts to combat drug smuggling. An alternative scenario is all-out civil war.

Comoros

Already one of the world's smallest countries, Comoros faces demands for secession

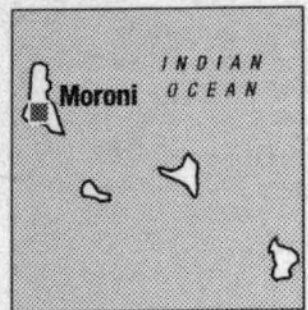

Comoros consists of three volcanic islands in the Indian Ocean. The largest is Grande Comore (also called Ngazidja), which includes Mount Karthala, an active volcano. To the south-east is the island of Anjouan, and between them is the smallest island, Mohéli. The terrain includes steep hills and some fertile valleys, but much of the land has been over-exploited and the soil has been eroded.

Comorans are descended from immigrants from Africa, Asia, and beyond, so the population is very diverse. The majority speak Comoran, which is a Bantu language, though the official languages are French and Arabic. Comorans are as poor as the poorest people in other African countries, and their country's limited resources offer a narrow range of opportunities.

Most people still make their living from agriculture. They do grow food but not enough, so much has to be imported. They also grow cash crops, notably vanilla, cloves, and ylang-ylang (a perfume essence) but the country remains reliant on foreign aid. Population density and a general shortage of land are forcing more people into the towns—where they find little by way of industry or trade. Most economic activity is dominated by the government.

Land area: *2,000 sq. km.*
Population: *531,00—urban 32%*
Capital city: *Moroni, 16,000*
People: *Antalote, Cafre, Makoa, Oimatsaha, Sakalava*
Language: *Arabic, French, Comoran*
Religion: *Sunni Muslim 86%, Roman Catholic 14%*
Government: *Republic*
Life expectancy: *59 years*
GNP per capita: *$PPP 1,480*
Currency: *Comoran franc*
Major exports: *Cloves, vanilla, ylang-ylang*

The islands were a French colony grouped with the nearby island of Mayotte. Following a referendum in 1974, the three islands voted for independence while Mayotte chose to remain with France. Even so, France has remained a significant influence—and French and other foreign mercenaries have regularly provided the personnel for a series of coups.

In 1997, eyeing the subsidies and aid showered on Mayotte, the islands of Anjouan and Mohéli seceded from the federation, demanding to be returned to French control. France declined the offer but the Comoran army were still unable to regain control of Anjouan. In April 1999 the country suffered its eighteenth coup since independence as the army took over 'to preserve national unity'.

In January 2000, Anjouans held a referendum on independence and voted to secede, but the Organization of African Unity said that the referendum had been held in a climate of terror and intimidation and refused to recognize the result.

The coup leader, Colonel Azali Ansumani, then ruled that there would be no elections until the separatist crisis was resolved.

Congo

The smaller and more urban of the two Congos is potentially oil-rich, but continues to be racked by civil war

Land area: *342,000 sq. km.*
Population: *3 million—urban 61%*
Capital city: *Brazzaville, 1.0 million*
People: *Kongo 48%, Sangho 20%, M'Bochi 12%, Teke 17%, other 3%*
Language: *French, Lingala, and Monokutuba*
Religion: *Christian 50%, animist 48%, other 2%*
Government: *Republic*
Life expectancy: *49 years*
GNP per capita: *$PPP 1,430*
Currency: *CFA franc*
Major exports: *Oil, timber*

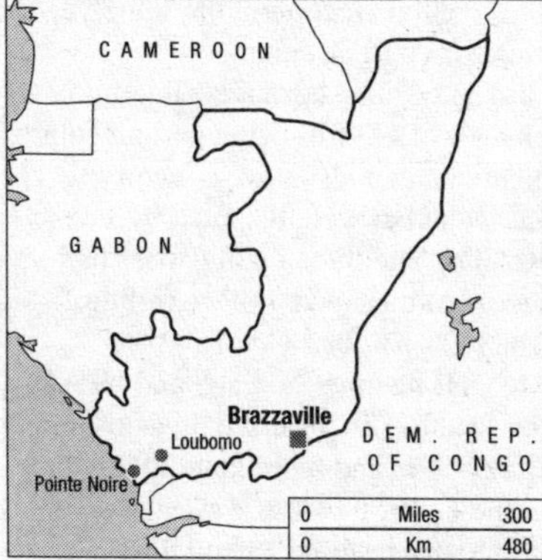

The country's official name is the Republic of the Congo. Its territory consists largely of two river basins separated by mountains and plateaux. The smaller of the two is the Niari basin in the south and south-west. To the north-east of this the land rises to the Batéké and Bembe plateaux, and then descends to the basin of the Congo River, which also serves as the border with the Democratic Republic of the Congo to the east. More than half the land area is covered by dense tropical forests.

Ethnically, Congo is diverse, though around half the population belong to the Kongo ethnic group, who are concentrated in the capital, Brazzaville, and in the south. The Sangho live in the remote forests of the north, the M'Bochi are in the centre-north, while the Teke are in the Batéké plateau. Congo is the most urbanized country in Sub-Saharan Africa and prior to its civil war from 1997 the concentration of people in Brazzaville helped to ensure relatively good educational standards. But the war has undermined the education system and has also taken a toll on health—not only killing more than 10,000 people and destroying clinics but also enabling HIV/AIDS to spread more rapidly: up to 10% of the population could now be infected.

Since the late 1970s, the Congo's main source of income has been oil. Oil makes up most of export earnings and around 40% of GDP. Reserves are large and more are being discovered, mostly offshore serviced by the port of Pointe Noire, with Elf and Agip as the leading producers. Though this income has given the country a relatively high per capita GNP, the wealth has not percolated through to the rest of the economy. There is little other industry and most people in Brazzaville who do not work for the government are employed in the informal sector. The country's infrastructure is also weak—even Pointe Noire and Brazzaville are not connected by an all-weather road, though there are a number of railways.

People outside the cities generally survive through farming. Though the country has good soil and ample rainfall, agriculture is underdeveloped. Most farmers grow crops like cassava, plantains, and groundnuts for their own consumption. But because road links are so poor they find it difficult to market their crops, so most of the food consumed in Brazzaville is actually imported, usually across the Zaire River from Kinshasa.

The country's vast forest resources have also been underexploited. For loggers too the main handicap is a lack of transport. The only forests that have been felled are near the coast. Environmentalists are now, however, worried about the arrival of a number of Asian logging companies looking for new opportunities.

Fighting between Cobras, Ninjas, and Zulus

Congo's current political rivalries have their roots in the 1960s and 1970s when this was the Marxist People's Republic of the Congo run by the Parti congolais du travais (PCT). In 1979, Colonel Denis Sassou-Nguesso, a northerner from the M'Bochi ethnic group—from which the PCT drew most of its support—took over the leadership and was elected president in 1984, and again in 1989. But by the early 1990s, popular pressure forced the PCT to legalize other political parties, and in 1991 a national conference approved a new multi-party constitution and changed the country's name to the Republic of the Congo.

The PCT lost the democratic parliamentary elections in 1992 when the two leading parties were the Union panafricaine pour la démocratie sociale (UPADS), led by Pascal Lissouba whose support came from the centre-south, and the Mouvement congolais pour la démocratie et le developpement intégral (MCDDI), led by Bernard Kolélas with strong support in Brazzaville. The presidential election in the same year was won by Lissouba.

The country began its slide into chaos in 1993 following parliamentary elections that also gave a victory to Lissouba but were disputed by Kolélas. The three main parties had recruited their own private militias. The PCT had the 'Cobras', the MCDDI had the 'Ninjas', and UPADS the 'Zulus'. Each seized areas of Brazzaville and more than 2,000 died in the ensuing battles. Order was eventually restored when UPADS and the MCDDI agreed to share power while Sassou-Nguesso retired to his northern power base.

When Sassou-Nguesso returned to Brazzaville with his Cobras for the next election in 1997, Lissouba tried to arrest him and disband his militia. He failed and following a six-month civil war, in which much of Brazzaville was destroyed, Sassou-Nguesso regained power and Lissouba fled. Fighting resumed in 1999 when the Ninjas teamed up with the Cobras to attack government troops, again causing thousands of people to flee Brazzaville.

Early in 2000, in an agreement brokered by President Bongo of Gabon, the protagonists pledged to lay down their arms and 'initiate dialogue'. In May 2000, former-President Kolélas was sentenced to death in his absence.

Congo, Democratic Republic

Formerly Zaire, the Democratic Republic of the Congo has become a regional battlefield

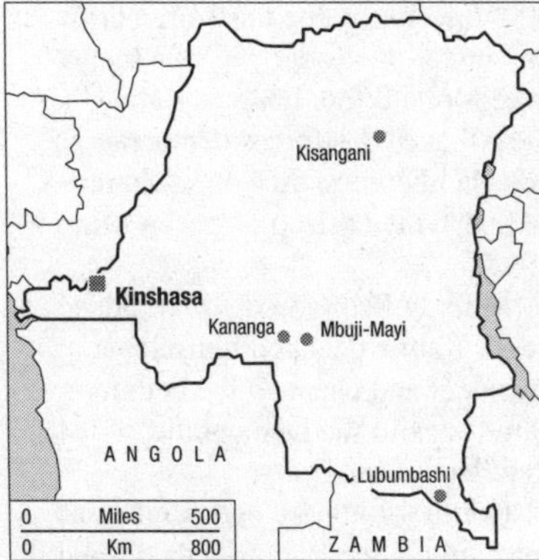

Land area: *2,345,000 sq. km.*
Population: *48 million—urban 30%*
Capital city: *Kinshasa, 5 million*
People: *Mongo, Luba, Kongo, Mangbetu-Azande and many others*
Language: *French, Lingala, Kingwana, Kikongo, Tshiluba*
Religion: *Roman Catholic 50%, Protestant 20%, Kimbanguist 10%, Muslim 10%*
Government: *Republic*
Life expectancy: *51 years*
GNP per capita: *$PPP 750*
Currency: *Congolese franc*
Major exports: *Diamonds, cobalt, coffee, copper, oil*

The dominant feature of this vast country, accounting for around 60% of its territory, is the Congo River basin centred on the north-west. This includes some of the world's most dense tropical rainforests. From this depression the land rises to the south and west to plateaux, and then to mountains along the country's borders.

With more than 200 ethnic groups, the population is very diverse. The majority, including the Mongo, Luba, Lunda, and Kongo are Bantu speakers. But in the north there are major Sudanese groups such as the Mangbetu-Azande. There are also pygmy people in the forests. Relations between these groups have often been tense and violent—divisions that politicians have exploited.

Standards of human development have been falling steadily—a result of government neglect, withdrawal of international aid, and civil war. Incomes have declined steeply: GDP per capita dropped by two-thirds between 1975 and 1999. Most education is provided by Catholic missionaries but fewer children are now attending school and the literacy rate is thought to be falling. Because children are less likely to be immunized, infant mortality is rising, and at least one-third of children are malnourished. AIDS is a growing threat—in some regions one-fifth of the population is HIV-positive.

Two-thirds of the workforce are employed in agriculture. Most are subsistence farmers who use fairly primitive techniques, growing plantains, cassava, sugar cane, and maize. Despite ample fertile land, huge quantities of food need to be imported—a result primarily of government indifference to agriculture, and poor transport facilities, as well as the disruption of warfare. There are also some cash crops such as coffee, palm oil, and cotton, but output has declined steeply in recent years. The country's vast forest potential could also be exploited on a sustainable basis.

In the past much of the country's income has come from its lucrative mineral deposits. Traditionally the major earner has been copper in the Katanga region in the south-east. This, along with the cobalt industry, is the responsibility of the state-owned company, Gécamines. But production has fallen steadily as a consequence of low investment and warfare; copper and cobalt now account for only one-fifth of exports.

In 1997 more than half of export earnings came from diamonds, most of which come from Kasaï in the south. This is the world's third largest diamond producer, though of industrial rather than gem quality. Diamond production, which is mostly in the hands of the private sector, has been less affected by the recent wars.

The country also has some manufacturing industry, often centred on the processing of minerals. Most foreign investors have stayed away, though Société de Belgique and Unilever have extensive interests.

For most of the period since independence in 1960 the country was under the control of one man, Mobutu Sese Seko. Mobuto came to power in a US-backed military coup in 1965 and established his own political party—which from 1970 became the only party. In 1991 he changed the country's name from the Democratic Republic of the Congo to Zaire.

From Congo to Zaire

Mobuto was subsequently elected unopposed for three consecutive terms of seven years—a period during which he ruthlessly repressed all opposition and looted the economy.

Mobutu's grip weakened in 1996 following a rebellion in Kivu province in the east. This was originally centred on a rebellion by an ethnic group he had persecuted, the Banyamulenge, who are the local section of the Tutsi who had by then seized power in neighbouring Rwanda. With Rwandan help they overcame the Zaïran army and under the leadership of a long-time Mobutu foe, Laurent Kabila, as the Alliance des forces démocratique pour la libération du Congo-Zaire (AFDL), they seized power in May 1997.

Mobutu fled (and died later that year). Kabila declared himself president and changed the country's name back to the Democratic Republic of the Congo.

Hopes for a more democratic and peaceful era were soon dashed. First it became clear that Kabila was going to be just as heavy-handed—favouring his own group, jailing his opponents, and alienating investors and donors. Most extraordinary of all he sufficiently antagonized his former Tutsi allies that in 1998, with backing from Rwanda and Uganda, they launched another rebellion, but this time against him. Zimbabwe, Angola, and Namibia soon sprang to his defence, leading to a complex and dangerous regional conflict.

A peace agreement was agreed in July 1999, though the fighting continued. Early in 2000 there was another ceasefire following a UN-brokered plan for disengagement of all foreign troops. With so many different armed groups engaged in such a profitable war it seems unlikely, however, that this will be seen as much more than an opportunity to regroup for the next offensive.

Costa Rica

Long an island of peace in a troubled region, Costa Rica is struggling to maintain its social achievements

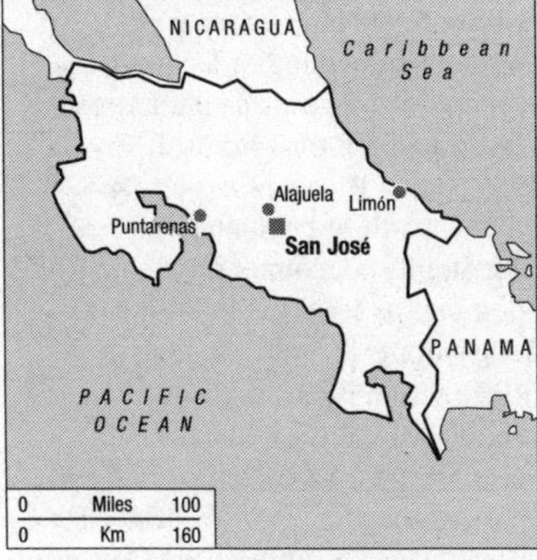

Land area: *51,000 sq. km.*
Population: *4 million—urban 51%*
Capital city: *San José, 968,000*
People: *White or mestizo 96%, black 2%, other 2%*
Language: *Spanish, English*
Religion: *Roman Catholic*
Government: *Republic*
Life expectancy: *76 years*
GNP per capita: *$PPP 6,620*
Currency: *Colón*
Major exports: *Electronics, coffee, bananas, meat*

Mountain ranges form a rugged backbone extending down the centre of Costa Rica. On the Pacific side they descend to coastal lowlands and sandy beaches. On the Caribbean side they come down more gradually to heavily-forested lowland areas with a rich variety of plant and animal life. Most of the population, however, live in the highlands, in the Meseta Central where the climate is milder and soil more fertile. Unfortunately, this is also a geologically active zone subject to earthquakes and potentially dangerous volcanoes.

Most people are of European or part-European descent. Few Amerindians remain and the largest minority group consists of black descendants of workers brought from Jamaica at the end of the 19th century to build the railroads and work on plantations. This English-speaking group make up around 30% of the population of the province of Limón on the Caribbean coast.

Christopher Columbus, who christened Costa Rica (rich coast), had visions of gold and treasure. But the country's wealth has been based on more mundane products—particularly coffee and bananas. Costa Rican coffee takes advantage of the volcanic soils in the central highlands. It is produced largely by small farmers—the average grower has 5 hectares earning around $1,000 per year. Quality is good, cultivation is intensive, and yields are among the highest in the world. Coffee, however, has since 1989 been overtaken in export value by bananas—20% of export value—produced on both the Caribbean and Pacific coasts. Prices have been lower in recent years, but Costa Rica stands to benefit from a greater opening of European markets to Central American bananas.

Though still relying significantly on these crops, Costa Rica has nevertheless achieved a very diverse economy. Indeed this is now primarily an industrial country. The basis was laid in the 1950s and 1960s with investment in import-substitution industries. Costa Rica now has a substantial manufacturing sector in areas like food processing, chemicals, textiles and metals—though they often rely on imports for inputs.

Costa Rica's development has also been relatively equitable and it has created one of the most extensive welfare states in Latin America. Much of this can be traced back to the constitution adopted in 1949, which, among other things, gave the state a strong role in social welfare, established labour rights, and introduced free secondary education. Remarkably, it also abolished the army, to avoid coups and save money—though the country does have a 7,500-strong police force.

Home to Intel and Microsoft, Costa Rica is becoming a 'chip republic'

Costa Rica's extensive welfare state and stable democracy gave it an enviable reputation as the 'Switzerland of Central America'. It avoided the 1980s warfare in neighbouring states; indeed Costa Rica was the driving force of the Central American Peace Agreement of 1987, for which then President Oscar Arias Sánchez was later awarded the Nobel Peace Prize.

The fabric started to unravel to some extent in the 1970s and 1980s. Import substitution did not ultimately produce very efficient industries. As public investment increased and revenues fell, the government was deeply embroiled in the debt crisis that swept through Latin America in the early 1980s. Like other countries, Costa Rica found itself in the hands of the IMF.

Unlike neighbouring countries who are chasing investment for low-value assembly factories, Costa Rica is more interested in capitalizing on its high standards of education by attracting high-tech investors. It has the advantage of a sound democracy, a well-educated workforce, and a good legal system.

The arrival in 1998 of a $500 million Intel chip factory was therefore something of a coup—as was establishing this as the Latin American base for Microsoft. By 1999, Costa Rica was exporting $2 billion-worth of computer chips per year and its economy as a whole was booming. In 1999 Costa Rica had a trade surplus for the first time in fifteen years. Even so, this new course may be risky if the country again becomes over-dependent on one product. Despite growth, social infrastructure is crumbling and inequality is rising.

Costa Rica is also now a prime tourist destination. More than 1 million people come each year to visit the rain forests, volcanoes, and beaches. Tourism is now the biggest foreign exchange earner.

Over much of this period, Costa Rica has been ruled by the centre-left National Liberation Party (PLN), and occasionally by the more conservative Social Christian Unity Party (PUSC). But there is less of an ideological division than before. The 1998 parliamentary and presidential elections were won by the PUSC, with Miguel Ángel Rodríguez elected president. In May 2000, a survey by Latinobarometro, a Chilean polling company, confirmed that Costa Ricans were among the Latin Americans most satisfied with the way their democracy was working.

Côte d'Ivoire

Land area: *322,000 sq. km.*
Population: *14 million—urban 45%*
Capital city: *Yamoussoukro, 120,000*
People: *Baoulé 23%, Bété 18%, Senoufou 15%, Malinke 11%, and more than 60 others. Many immigrants.*
Language: *French, Dioula and many local languages*
Religion: *Animist 60%, Muslim 25%, Christian 15%*
Government: *Republic*
Life expectancy: *47 years*
GNP per capita: *$PPP 1,730*
Currency: *CFA franc*
Major exports: *Cocoa, palm oil, wood,*

Côte d'Ivoire has ambitions to be one of Africa's leading industrial nations

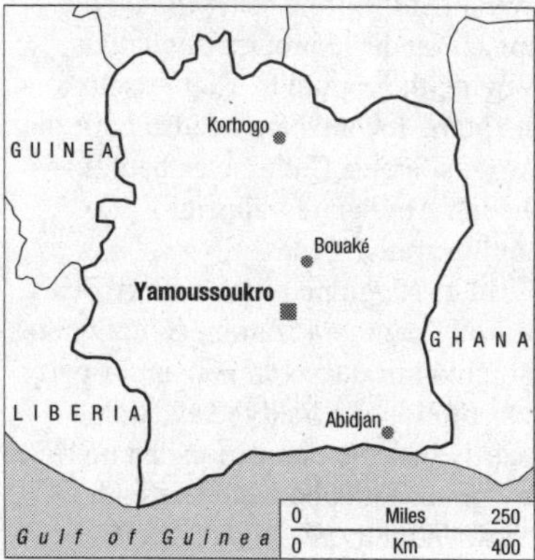

Côte d'Ivoire has a narrow coastal strip of land, which includes in the east a series of deep lagoons. Behind this are two forest areas. The one to the west still has dense rainforest, while the one to the east has now largely been cleared to grow plantation crops. Beyond these to the north the land is mostly savannah, used for grazing cattle.

The population is very diverse with 60 ethnic groups that can be classified roughly according to language and area of the country. The majority group, mostly living in the towns and villages of the south-east, includes the Baoulé. Those in the forests of the south-west include the Bété. In the north-west are the Malinke, and in the north-east a number of Voltaic groups including the Senoufou.

For the first twenty years following independence in 1960, Côte d'Ivoire had rapid economic growth based on exports of cocoa and coffee. These crops are mostly grown by peasant farmers, who, in the early years, benefited from stable, guaranteed prices. Côte d'Ivoire became the world's largest cocoa exporter and the fifth largest coffee exporter. Other important agricultural exports are tropical hardwood and palm oil.

The benefits spread to the rest of the country and in the 1970s the then capital, Abidjan, became one of Africa's most cosmopolitan cities. The country's wealth also attracted millions of immigrants who even now make up almost 30% of the population. Most come from Burkina Faso, Guinea, and Mali to work on plantations and in domestic service, but there are also substantial Lebanese, Syrian, and French communities.

Export crops helped to develop Côte d'Ivoire but they also increased its vulnerability to international commodity prices. Dramatic price falls in the late 1970s, exacerbated in 1994 by the devaluation of the CFA franc, led to a severe economic crisis and the country was soon plunged deeply into debt, which in 1996 stood at $20 billion. Annual debt servicing was eating up almost half of export earnings. The crisis provoked high levels of unemployment and many people migrated to the cities. Around one-third of the population now live in poverty. It was not until 1994, with better commodity prices, that growth resumed, but even now the recovery is fragile.

The government has pronounced its determination to diversify and industrialize the economy. Taking their cue from the South-East Asian 'tigers', the Ivorians would prefer to emulate the strong and stable African elephant. The first task is to modernize agriculture, aiming for food self-sufficiency—particularly for yams, maize, rice, and plantains and all the other foods popular at the distinctive 'maquis': informal outdoor restaurants.

Côte d'Ivoire wants to emulate the African elephant

At the same time, under pressure from the IMF, the marketing of most major crops has been privatized. The government also wants to exploit the Côte d'Ivoire's energy and mineral resources—including recently-discovered deposits of oil and gas that could make the country self-sufficient, and even an exporter. In terms of manufacturing, the greatest opportunity probably lies in more intensive local processing of primary commodities like cocoa—at present only around one-fifth is transformed into higher value products like chocolate.

Much of Côte d'Ivoire's political stability rested on the 23-year autocratic reign of the country's first president, Félix Houphouët-Boigny. For many years, his Parti démocratique de la Côte d'Ivoire was the only legal political party. With a liberal, business-oriented administration he helped to attract investment. But he also promoted some grandiose projects including moving the capital to Yamoussoukro, his home town where he also built the world's largest Catholic cathedral—though Abidjan remains the administrative centre.

In 1990, going along with Africa's wave of democratization, Houphouët-Boigny introduced an new multi-party constitution but held the election so swiftly that the opposition had no time to organize and he won a seventh presidential term.

Houphouët-Boigny died in office in 1993. He was replaced by Henri Konan-Bédié, who was confirmed as president by an election in 1995. This election had been boycotted by the main opposition parties, who came together in 1997 as the Front populaire ivorienne. Konan-Bédié consolidated his grip and forced his presidential rival, Alassane Ouattara, to flee into exile.

But Konan-Bédié over-estimated the support of the army, which had been protesting at poor pay, and in December 1999 they overthrew him in Côte d'Ivoire's first coup, led by General Robert Guéi. Guéi has promised a swift return to democracy.

Ouattara returned to Côte d'Ivoire in early 2000. He could be the next president, but will probably have to defeat Guéi in any election. The next steps will be a constitutional referendum in July 2000 and perhaps a presidential election in October.

Croatia

Croatia's fierce nationalism sparked the Balkan wars. A new government could sustain a lasting peace

Croatia's eccentric shape encloses a variety of landscapes and climates. The north-west includes a part of the Dinaric Alps. To the south the dramatic, broken coastline of Istria and Dalmatia consists of mountains that drop steeply into the sea, creating numerous inlets and bays as well as more than 1,100 islands.

When it was a republic within Yugoslavia, this territory had a clear majority of Croatians, as well as around 12% ethnic Serbs. The differences between these two Slav peoples are cultural rather than physical: the Croats are Roman Catholic and Western in outlook; most Serbs are Eastern-oriented Orthodox Christians. As a result of the wars of the 1990s, more than half of the Serbs fled and by early 2000 few had returned. In addition there are around 800,000 Croatians in Bosnia.

Land area: *57,000 sq. km.*
Population: *5 million—urban 57%*
Capital city: *Zagreb, 900,000*
People: *Croat 78%, Serb 12%, Muslim 1%, other 9% (1991)*
Language: *Serbo-Croatian*
Religion: *Catholic 77%, Orthodox 11%, other 12%*
Government: *Republic*
Life expectancy: *73 years*
GNP per capita: *$PPP 4,895*
Currency: *Kuna*
Major exports: *Transport equipment, chemicals, textiles*

Croatia was, after Slovenia, the second richest of the republics of former Yugoslavia and had an economy similar to that of Western European countries. But the war precipitated a steep economic decline: between 1989 and 1993 GDP fell by more than 40%. After 1994, growth resumed, fuelled first by efforts at reconstruction and later by a revival of tourism.

The break-up of Yugoslavia cost Croatia many of its markets and forced it to re-orient more towards the west. It has, for example, re-established some industries such as textiles under contract to foreign companies, and others, including vehicles and furniture, have also shown strong growth. But official unemployment in 2000 was still some way above 20%.

The government did little to restructure enterprises before privatization—merely transferring ownership. It sold some shares in state-owned enterprises to their managements. And from mid-1998 it distributed vouchers to almost a quarter of a million people who generally exercised them through investment funds. In addition, the government has restored some assets to the descendants of former owners. All these transfers have tended to create a new élite, particularly among those who have been able to exploit their connections.

Most agricultural land was already privately owned, though many farms are small and not very profitable. The best land and most of the larger holdings are to be found in Slavonia in the north-east, which is where most of the capital-intensive production of cereals and other cash crops takes place. Before the war, Croatia was a food exporter, but production by the end of 1999 still languished far below pre-war levels.

Croatia's spectacular Adriatic coastline had long been a major package-tourist attraction—notably the ancient city of Dubrovnik, which took a severe battering from the Yugoslav army in 1991. Tourism revived after 1995 and in 1997 there were around 30 million visitors. But Croatia's tourist infrastructure needs to be rebuilt and modernized.

Historic Dubrovnik took a battering during the war

Croatia's transition from communism was dominated for the first decade by a former general, Franjo Tudjman, who, in 1990, created a new party, the Croatian Democratic Union (HDZ). In the first free elections in May 1990 the HDZ won a majority of parliamentary seats and Tudjman became president. Tudjman's hard-line nationalism alarmed Serbs in Krajina and Slavonia who feared breaking with Serbia, and rejected the idea of independence and in mid-1990 they established 'Serbian Autonomous Regions' which Tudjman refused to recognize. When Croatia did declare independence in July 1991, this provoked a full-scale civil war as the Serb paramilitaries united with the Yugoslav army to seize more than one-quarter of Croatia. The UN negotiated a ceasefire in January 1992, but in August 1995 the Croatian forces regained control over the whole country, causing the Serbs to flee. In December 1995 Tudjman joined in the signing of the Dayton peace accords which laid the foundations for the return of the Serb refugees, though even by early 2000 few of these people had come back.

Croatia is a parliamentary democracy, but in the early years the HDZ had a majority in both houses and Tudjman had a fairly free hand. He was elected president in 1992 and re-elected in 1998, and used his status as a war hero to build a centralized and authoritarian state that refused to welcome back Serb refugees and always threatened to seize parts of neighbouring Bosnia.

To many people's relief, Tudjman died in December 1999 and the parliamentary elections in January 2000 resulted in a surprising turnaround. The main centre-left opposition alliance of Social Democrats (SDP) and Social Liberals (HSLS) won almost half the seats. The SDP's leader, Ivica Racan, became prime minister and a presidential election in February 2000 was won by Mate Granic. The new government, which has ambitions to join the EU, has promised to make a break with the past—toning down the nationalism and liberalizing the economy.

Cuba

Cuba now has elements of a market economy, but political change is unlikely in Castro's lifetime

__Land area:__ 111,000 sq. km.
__Population:__ 11 million—urban 77%
__Capital city:__ Havana, 2.2 million
__People:__ Mulatto 51%, white 37%, black 11%, other 1%
__Language:__ Spanish
__Religion:__ Roman Catholic
__Government:__ Communist
__Life expectancy:__ 76 years
__GNP per capita:__ $PPP 3,100
__Currency:__ Peso
__Major exports:__ Sugar, nickel, tobacco, seafood

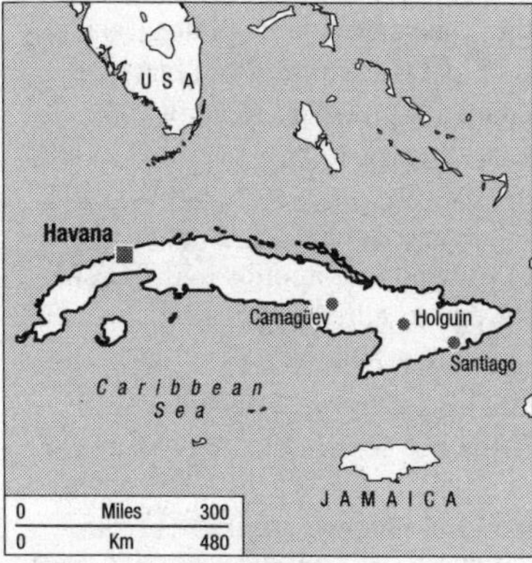

Around one-quarter of Cuba's territory is mountainous, with three main systems, of which the most extensive is the Sierra Maestra in the south-east. Most of the island, however, consists of plains and gently rolling hills. For a relatively small island, the environment is biologically rich—particularly in its mangrove forests and wetlands.

Cuba's population is racially mixed: most people are mulatto. There is little overt discrimination, but those with darker skins tend to have the worst jobs. In 1998, only one member of the Communist Party's politburo was black.

Though they are far from rich, Cubans enjoy some of the world's best levels of social development. Health and education services are free, though they have deteriorated somewhat as underpaid staff seek more lucrative employment—a tour guide can earn twenty times as much as a teacher.

Agriculture accounts for only around 7% of GDP and directly employs only 20% of the workforce, but it remains critically important to the economy since it provides around 60% of export earnings. The main crop is still sugar, which the Soviet Union used to buy at a favourable price. Nowadays, Russia is the main buyer but the price has dropped by two-thirds. Moreover, Cuba's sugar harvest is less than half what it was prior to 1990—a result in part of low prices, the high cost of inputs, and low investment. Other crops, such as tobacco, fruit, and vegetables, have done better. But Cuba only grows around one-quarter of its staple food, rice, and has to import the rest.

Cuba's land reform created state farms, but also left around 20% of the land with small-holders and co-operatives who proved more productive—growing about 40% of the food. Since 1993, most state farms have been dissolved and transformed into 'Unidades Básicas de Producción Cooperativa' (UBPCs). This involves the government leasing land rent-free to former workers who are responsible for running financially independent co-operatives. This seems to have raised production, though even by 2000 few of the UBPCs were profitable. Farmers can sell surplus production in 'agropecuarias'—farmers' markets.

Manufacturing has suffered from the loss of the Soviet market and the continuing US boycott. To generate more industrial jobs, the government has now created free-trade zones and has been concentrating official investment in areas such as biotechnology and pharmaceuticals, where it sees export potential. Mining is also an important source of foreign exchange. Cuba has large reserves of nickel and cobalt, which are mined in conjunction with the Canadian corporation Sherrit International.

The most vigorous part of the economy has been tourism. Between 1990 and 1997 annual arrivals quadrupled to 1.2 million, with Canadians, Italians, and Spanish in the lead—chiefly heading for beach resorts on the northern coast. Tourism brings in around $2 billion annually but three-quarters of this goes straight out again to pay for related imports and as profits to the many foreign companies who run the hotels. There is also considerable unofficial income from informal ancillary enterprises, including prostitution.

Tourism to Cuba encourages unofficial enterprise

Since 1993, Cubans have been able to hold dollars which they might get from relatives in the USA or from contact with tourists. They can spend these in 'dollar shops', which are virtually the only source of non-essential consumer goods. 'Peso shops' distribute food rations, though Cubans can also buy more expensive produce from farmers' markets.

Despite economic liberalization, political change seems some way off. Cuba remains a 'socialist workers' state' in which the only legal party is the Cuban Communist Party, headed by Fidel Castro, who has been the country's president since the revolution in 1959. The only opposition comes from human rights organizations and small groups linked to Cuban communities in the USA. Several hundred political prisoners are in jail. Despite the lack of democracy and the economic privations, Castro remains a remarkably popular leader.

Many of Cuba's difficulties are the result of hostility from the USA, which, under pressure from a powerful exile lobby in Miami classifies Cuba as an enemy state and imposes rigid economic sanctions. Relations with the USA are alternately warm and cool.

One of the severest freezes has been the 1996 US Helms-Burton Act which threatens to impose sanctions in the US on foreign companies that do business with Cuba. Nevertheless, there have also been some thaws which have enabled agreements on the flows of emigrants between the two countries and in 1998 the restoration of some direct flights.

Things turned difficult again in 2000 with the emotive case of Elián González, a 6-year-old shipwrecked refugee boy whom the Miami Cubans wanted to keep in the USA. In the event, however, the US government agreed that the boy should go back with his father.

Cyprus

An island bitterly divided between Greek and Turkish communities

Land area: *9,000 sq. km.*
Population: *753,000—urban 54%*
Capital city: *Nicosia, 257,000*
People: *Greek 78%, Turkish 18%, other 4%*
Language: *Greek, Turkish*
Religion: *Greek Orthodox 78%, Muslim 18%, other 4%*
Government: *Republic*
Life expectancy: *78 years*
GNP per capita: *$PPP 13,500*
Currency: *Cyprus pound*
Major exports: *Citrus fruit, potatoes, grapes*

The island of Cyprus has two main mountain ranges. The Kyrenian Mountains extend along the northern coast, while the Troodos Mountains are in the south and centre. Between these is the most fertile part of the country, the Mesaorian plain, which includes the capital, Nicosia.

Cyprus is more sharply divided than ever between Greek and Turkish Cypriots. Greeks are still in a large majority, virtually all of them living in the south and centre. The Turks are confined to the north. They have been joined by many immigrants from Turkey who with their children may now outnumber Turkish Cypriots.

The Greek part of the island has shifted decisively away from agriculture and now depends heavily on service industries. The most important is tourism. More than 2.2 million tourists arrived in 1998, the majority from the UK—accounting for around 20% of GDP. The other main service activity is business and finance. By 1997 there were more than 30,000 registered companies, with most of the newer arrivals coming from Russia. The economy in the north lags far behind: the main activity is agriculture, growing the traditional export crops of citrus fruit and potatoes.

At times, Greek and Turkish Cypriots have coexisted peacefully, and the constitution adopted at independence in 1960 involved explicit power-sharing. But by 1964 there were violent confrontations and the UN sent in a peacekeeping force, which is still there, 1,200 strong. Matters came to a head after a military coup in 1974. Turkey sent in 30,000 troops to protect Turkish Cypriots and established control over the northern one-third of the island. In a precursor to ethnic cleansing, people moved from one part of the island to the other.

In 1983, the Turkish Cypriot leader Rauf Denktash proclaimed the north to be the Turkish Republic of Northern Cyprus, a claim recognized only by Turkey. The rest of the world recognizes the Republic of Cyprus, even if it controls only 57% of the territory. In 2000 Cyprus had a rather unstable five-party coalition government headed by the Democratic Rally party, which favours a federal solution.

A likely turning point will be the negotiations for both Cyprus and Turkey to join the EU. It is unlikely that both could be accepted without a political settlement. Joint sovereignty seems inevitable, but some way off.

Czech Republic

A formerly communist country that had a 'velvet revolution' and a fairly painless transition to a market economy

Land area: *79,000 sq. km.*
Population: *10 million—urban 66%*
Capital city: *Prague, 1.2 million*
People: *Czech 94%, Slovak 3%, other 3%*
Language: *Czech, Slovak*
Religion: *Atheist 40%, Roman Catholic 39%, Protestant 5%, other 16%*
Government: *Republic*
Life expectancy: *74 years*
GNP per capita: *$PPP 10,510*
Currency: *Czech crown*
Major exports: *Machinery, manufactures*

The Czech Republic has two main geographical areas. The largest, to the west; is Bohemia, a broad elevated plateau of plains and low hills centred on Prague and ringed by mountains. Beyond the mountains to the east lies the second main area, the Moravia Valley centred on Brno, whose eastern boundary is formed by the Carpathian Mountains that separate the country from Slovakia.

Ethnically the population is fairly homogenous: more than 90% are Czech. But throughout the country there are also small numbers of Slovaks, who moved here when the country was part of Czechoslovakia, and also many Romany, or gypsies, whose different lifestyle exposes them to both economic and racial discrimination. Until the 1980s, the Czech Republic had a relatively high proportion of children and a low proportion of elderly people, but recent falls in the birth rate are causing the population to age rapidly.

Levels of human development here are fairly high for a formerly communist country. But secondary education was weak since the main demand was for unskilled labour: in 1991, only one-third of the population had completed secondary school.

Health standards too were reasonable, though lifestyles were not particularly healthy: high fat consumption and heavy smoking substantially reduced life spans, particularly for men.

Though production fell during the 1990s, the Czech Republic remains a highly industrialized country. In the past it has concentrated on heavy industry such as engineering and steel, but more recently some manufacturers have been exporting intermediate goods, particularly to Germany. Lighter industries such as food processing have also been expanding.

Privatization of state-owned assets took place quite rapidly. By 1996 more than 75% of GDP was in private hands, mostly through vouchers which small investors rapidly sold to institutions. This transfer of ownership did little to transform the management of enterprises. But some companies acquired an injection of expertise from foreign companies: the reputation of Skoda cars, for example, was transformed when it was taken over by Volkswagen—and by 1997 the company provided 8% of exports.

The agricultural sector accounts for only about 5% of employment and is now entirely in private hands, either commercial farms or co-operatives. Output has fallen while productivity has risen—between 1990 and 1996, the agricultural labour force halved.

Meanwhile, many more people are working in services particularly in retailing and catering and in all those dealing with tourism which by 1996 brought in 6% of foreign exchange. Most new jobs have been created in the region around Prague, heightening the disparities with poorer regions such as northern Bohemia and northern Moravia.

From a velvet revolution to a velvet divorce

From 1918 to 1938, and from 1945 to 1992, what is now the Czech Republic was united with Slovakia. As Czechoslovakia, their joint transition from communism in 1989 was so smooth it was termed the 'velvet revolution'. Within the Czech lands, the democracy movement was called the Civic Forum, one of whose leaders was the writer Václav Havel. Civic Forum won most of the Czech seats in the election of 1990 while a corresponding movement in Slovakia won the seats there. The new parliament elected Havel as president.

Civic Forum soon reformed into a number of parties, of whom the most important subsequently have been the right-wing Civic Democratic Party (ODS), and the centre-left Czech Social Democratic Party (CSSD).

The union with Slovakia did not last. The disagreements were partly ideological, since the leading Czech party at that point was the right-wing ODS led by prime minister Václav Klaus, while the leading Slovak party was the centre-left Movement for a Democratic Slovakia. The Slovaks thought reform was taking place too quickly for their less developed economy. Eventually, the politicians decided to disband the federation—despite the absence of popular support for the split.

On 1 January 1993, they became two countries and in February Havel was elected president of the new Czech Republic—a symbolic, though significant role—while Klaus remained prime minister.

The reforms proceeded apace but Klaus lost popularity as the economy slowed and his government became embroiled in corruption scandals. As a result, the 1996 elections reduced the ODS to a minority government which soon collapsed amid scandals around party funding, along with general economic chaos.

In the ensuing election in 1998 voters' allegiances swung left. The CSSD became the largest party, the ODS came second, and the unreconstructed Communist Party came third. The new prime minister was Milos Zeman but, without an overall majority, he was obliged to enter into a somewhat surprising parliamentary pact, though not a full coalition, with the ODS. The Czech Republic is still making steady if slower progress and should be one of the first ex-communist countries to join the EU.

Denmark

A bridge from continental Europe to Scandinavia that has had a vacillating relationship with the EU

Land area: *43,000 sq. km.*
Population: *5 million—urban 86%*
Capital city: *Copenhagen, 0.5 million*
People: *Danish, Inuit, Faroese*
Language: *Danish, Faroese*
Religion: *Evangelical Lutheran 91%, other Christian, 2%, other 7%*
Government: *Constitutional monarchy*
Life expectancy: *76 years*
GNP per capita: *$PPP 23,830*
Currency: *Krone*
Major exports: *Meat products, furniture, pharmaceuticals*

Denmark is one of Europe's more physically fragmented countries. The largest part, with around 70% of the territory of Denmark itself, is the Jutland peninsula. To the east of this lie the two largest of Denmark's 400 or so islands: Funen and Zealand; the capital, Copenhagen is located on the east of Zealand. In addition, Denmark has two distant dependent states—Greenland and the Faroe Islands. Most of Denmark itself is low-lying and fertile, broken only occasionally by hills, particularly in the centre and east of Jutland.

Denmark's population is ethnically fairly homogenous, though flows of immigrant workers from the 1970s, and asylum-seekers during the 1980s and 1990s, added variety. Around 5% of the population are foreign-born, with the largest numbers coming from former Yugoslavia and Turkey.

The standard of living is high and the government gives a high priority to education, on which it spends 8% of GDP, one of the highest proportions in Europe. Danes also enjoy free medical care and extensive welfare benefits. Although public provision is not as generous as in other Nordic countries, social welfare spending is equivalent to more than one-quarter of GDP. A 1999 opinion poll found that 70% of people liked paying high taxes. This is just as well since income tax rates touch 60% and there is a flat VAT rate of 25%.

Even so, it is doubtful that the Danish welfare state will survive in its current form, given the ageing population. The arrival of immigrants rejuvenated the population somewhat but a falling birth rate is still leading to a rising proportion of older people. In the next thirty years the ratio of working people to those over sixty years old will fall from 3 to 2.1.

Agriculture itself accounts for only around 5% of GDP, but is still vital to the economy, since it feeds into industry and exports. Two-thirds of Denmark is used for crops or pasture. Most activity is concerned with livestock—either growing animal feed or raising cattle and pigs. Farms are small and family owned but technologically very sophisticated. Since they produce around three times Denmark's own requirements, they export most of their output. Denmark also has a major fishing fleet, though over-fishing and controls by the EU have been constraining output.

Agriculture provides important raw materials for Danish industry—some of the cereal crop finishes up, for example, in cans of Carlsberg beer, one of the world's most venerable brands. Other distinctive Danish exports include stylish furniture, the hi-fi equipment of Bang & Olufsen, and the ubiquitous plastic Lego bricks—which have also been used in the construction of Legoland, one of Europe's largest theme parks.

Denmark is the home of Carlsberg and Lego

Apart from its soil, Denmark has limited natural resources. It does not have much coal or many minerals, but oil and gas fields in the North Sea supply the bulk of local needs. With a lot of flat and exposed land, Denmark can also generate a significant amount of wind power.

Denmark is a constitutional monarchy, with Europe's oldest royal family, currently headed by Queen Margarethe II. Most governments have been coalitions or minority administrations. For decades after the Second World War, the main party was the Social Democratic Party, which had promoted the welfare state. This pattern was broken decisively in the 1982 election when the reins of government passed to Poul Schluter of the Conservative Party at the head of a centre-right coalition. As a result, Denmark became the first of the Nordic countries to rein in public spending and deregulate its economy. Schluter eventually resigned in 1993, implicated in a scandal around immigration policy.

Though there was no election, he was replaced as prime minister by a Social Democrat, Poul Nyrup Rasmussen, at the head of a coalition that included the Radical Liberals, the Centre Democrats, and the Christian People's Party. The Social Democrats had by this time moved closer to the centre and continued with many of the neo-liberal economic policies. They were also returned at the head of coalitions in the 1994 and 1998 elections. In fact, all nine parties in the Danish parliament crowd into the political centre and the government works by consensus.

One of the most contentious issues is immigration. At the end of 1999 protests against immigration policy led to street violence. Such views have also contributed to the rise of the right-wing populist Danish People's Party (DPP) led by Pia Kjaersgaard who has been compared with Jörg Haider in Austria. However, there seems little prospect of any of the mainstream parties allying themselves with the DPP.

The Danes joined what is now the EU in 1973, but have not been strong federalists. They gave their fellow members a shock in 1992 when they voted against the Maastricht treaty which set the stage for monetary union. After various amendments, they endorsed it the following year. Since then, attitudes towards Europe seem to have become more positive and Denmark may even join the European Monetary Union.

Djibouti

A city-state still suffering from the aftermath of its own civil war as well as the conflicts around it

Land area: 23,000 sq. km.
Population: 600,000—urban 83%
Capital city: Djibouti, 270,000
People: Somali 60%, Afar 35%, other 5%
Language: French, Arabic, Somali, Afar
Religion: Muslim 94%, Christian 6%
Government: Republic
Life expectancy: 50 years
GNP per capita: $PPP 1,266
Currency: Djibouti franc
Major exports: Hides and skins, coffee

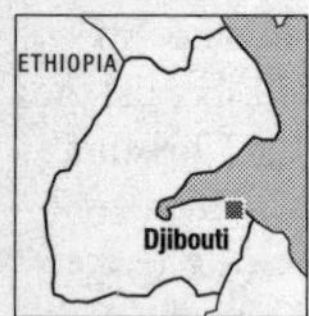

Though there are mountains in the north of this small country, most of Djibouti consists of a bare arid plateau—one of the world's hottest places. Most activity centres on the capital, also called Djibouti, and particularly its port, which is crucial to its now landlocked neighbour, Ethiopia.

The country's brief period since independence in 1977 has been soured by conflict between its two main ethnic groups. More than half the population are Somalis of the Issa and other clans, while around one-third are the Afar, who are of Ethiopian origin. However, the precise ethnic division is uncertain, partly because of the flows of refugees, but also because the ethnic population balance is a sensitive issue. Three-quarters of the population live in the capital; most of the remainder are pastoral nomads.

Djibouti is a poor country with low standards of health and education. It is also remarkable for its consumption of a mild intoxicant: qat. Every day, Djiboutians together chew their way through a remarkable 11 tons of the drug—which is imported from Ethiopia—devoting a high proportion of household expenditure to the habit. Djibouti's population growth rate, well over 4%, is also one of the world's highest.

Most of Djibouti's economy depends on its location as a transit point for neighbouring countries: trade and services make up around 70% of GDP. But this makes Djibouti vulnerable to developments around it. During the 1999 war between Ethiopia and Eritrea, throughput doubled—putting the elderly infrastructure under strain.

Road and rail links with Addis Ababa are now in a very poor state—and in need of investment. Most food has to be imported and there is little industry.

Since independence in 1977, Djibouti has been ruled by the Rassemblement populaire pour le progrès (RPP), which from 1981 to 1992 was also the only legal party. But the government could not contain the Somali-Afar rivalry and in 1990 there was an armed rebellion by the Afar front pour la restauration de l'unité et la démocratie (FRUD). A peace accord was signed in 1994 with a minority faction of FRUD; but there are still regular clashes with Afar guerrillas.

Most decision-making is centralized around the president. Until April 1999, Djibouti had had only one president, Hassan Gouled Aptidon, who was then replaced by his close confidant, Ismael Omar Geulleh.

Dominican Republic

The expansion of manufacturing industry and tourism has yet to benefit most of the poor

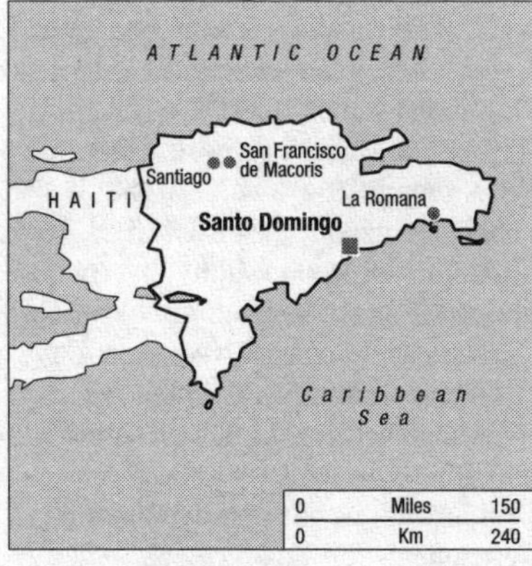

Land area: *49,000 sq. km.*
Population: *8 million—urban 64%*
Capital city: *Santo Domingo, 2.2 million*
People: *Mulatto 73%, white 16%, black 11%,*
Language: *Spanish*
Religion: *Roman Catholic*
Government: *Republic*
Life expectancy: *71 years*
GNP per capita: *$PPP 4,700*
Currency: *Dominican peso*
Major exports: *Manufactured goods, ferronickel, sugar, gold, coffee*

The Dominican Republic occupies the eastern two-thirds of Hispaniola, an island that it shares with Haiti. Much of the territory is mountainous—the highest peaks in the central highlands rise above 3,000 metres. The best land for agriculture and the most densely populated area, apart from the capital, is the Cibao Valley, which stretches across the north of the country.

Most people are of mixed race, or mulatto—the result of intermarriage between the predominantly Spanish colonists and the slaves brought to work in mines and sugar plantations. Wealth generally correlates with colour of skin—the blacks being the poorest. But the population as a whole has been getting poorer. Despite industrial development, the proportion of people living in poverty rose between 1985 and 1998 from 47% to 57%. Services are inadequate: around half the rural population lack clean drinking water. Education standards are low: half the children do not finish primary school.

Poor as the Dominican Republic is, neighbouring Haiti is even poorer, and up to 800,000 Haitians, many coming to work on the sugar harvest, are thought to live in the Dominican Republic. Most have no legal status and live in squalid conditions.

Sugar is still important—and one of the largest sources of export earnings, taking advantage of preferential access to the US market. But shrinking demand and under-investment have reduced production. Other minor export crops, such as cocoa and coffee, have also suffered setbacks due to disease and drought. Exports of tobacco and cigars have done better. Food production too has been slowing. Again this has been the result of low investment—discouraged both by high interest rates and government subsidies for imported food—particularly in election years. By 1997, only 20% of the population worked in agriculture.

Mining is another source of revenue, though it employs few people. The Canadian-owned Bonau nickel mine has been a major source of export earnings but has been hit by falling world prices.

A more dynamic part of the economy has been manufacturing—which by 1997 employed 21% of the workforce. Apart from more traditional industries like food processing, the fastest growth has been in the free-trade zones. More than 400 companies, the majority US-owned, have established factories in 40 or more zones scattered around the country. Around two-thirds of these factories make garments, while others produce footwear, leather goods, and electronics. The zones do provide employment for a predominantly female workforce, but working conditions are poor and wages are desperately low.

Another rapidly growing source of income and foreign exchange is tourism. In 1997 the Dominican Republic welcomed more than 2.5 million visitors, more than half from Europe. Few of these venture out onto the streets, preferring the self-contained beach resorts. But even here they are vulnerable to the country's poor infrastructure—particularly to pollution from inadequate sanitation.

Free trade zones provide low-paid work

The Dominican Republic is still struggling to build a stable democracy. For thirty years after his first election victory in 1966, the government of the Dominican Republic was dominated by Joaquín Balaguer and his conservative Social Christian Reform Party, whose administrations were generally corrupt and repressive and sustained by fraudulent elections. These years were marked by instability and violence. There were, however, a couple of interludes of rule by the centre-left Dominican Revolutionary Party (PRD).

In 1996, when he was 88 years-old and virtually blind, Balaguer's seventh and last term ended prematurely following allegations of electoral fraud. The ensuing election was won by Leonel Fernández Reyna of the Dominican Liberation Party (DLP), formerly a Marxist split-off from the PRD, though now a party of the centre. Fernández promised to eliminate corruption, fight poverty, and modernize the economy.

The past few years have seen stronger economic growth but the poor have yet to gain much from this and 1997 saw frequent street demonstrations and a general strike. Fernández's job was further complicated by the 1998 congressional elections which resulted in a decisive majority for the opposing PRD.

Fernández could not stand again in the May 2000 presidential elections. This was won by the PRD candidate Hipolito Mejia, who was up against the DLP candidate and, inevitably, the veteran Balaguer. Mejia won just under half the vote, but in an encouraging development the other candidates conceded without requiring a second round of voting. Mejia ran a populist campaign promising to increase social spending and to review some of Fernández's more unpopular privatization measures—though reprivatization is unlikely.

The Dominican Republic seems on an upward trend with an established democracy and a more enlightened generation of politicians.

East Timor

Land area: *15,850 sq. km.*
Population: *800,000—urban 8%*
Capital city: *Dili, 60,000*
People: *Maubere, Chinese, Indonesian*
Language: *Tetum, Bahasa Indonesian*
Religion: *Roman Catholicism and traditional religions*
Government: *UN administration*
Life expectancy: *45 years*
GNP per capita: *n.a.*
Currency: *US dollar (transition period)*
Major exports: *Coffee, oil, gas*

East Timor has broken free of Indonesia and now has a UN administration

East Timor comprises the eastern half of the Pacific island of Timor and the north-western enclave of Oecussi Ambeno. The territory consists largely of forested mountains that descend to coastal plains and mangrove swamps. Most people are Maubere, a mixture of Melanesian and Malay. Although their traditional beliefs are animist, the Catholic Church has also been important—particularly as a focus of resistance against Indonesia.

The Timorese have always had a very basic lifestyle. During the conflict with Indonesia, thousands were herded into cramped and unsanitary settlement camps. This added to existing problems, including TB, pneumonia, and parasitic infections. By the mid-1990s around two-thirds of children were malnourished, and infant mortality was among the highest in the world.

Most Timorese have made their living from agriculture, growing food crops such as sweet potatoes or corn, along with cash crops—especially coffee, which had been the leading export. Farmers on the coastal plains also grow rice and plantation crops such as rubber, tobacco, and coconuts. In addition the forests yield many kinds of timber, including sandalwood. During the occupation, however, much of the best land was seized by the Indonesian military.

The island of Timor had been divided between the Dutch colonists in the west and the Portuguese in the east. The Portuguese hung on much longer and East Timor declared its independence only in November 1975. Indonesia promptly invaded. Within three months, 60,000 people had died. But the struggle continued—led by the Revolutionary Front of Independent East Timor (Fretilin). Its leader, Xanana Gusmao, was captured in 1992. In 1996 the exiled political leader Jose Ramos-Horta and the Catholic Bishop Carlos Belo, were awarded the Nobel Peace Prize.

It took a near-revolution in Indonesia for East Timor to be freed. Despite widespread killings and intimidation by army-backed militias, which drove 200,000 people into West Timor, 80% of people voted in favour of independence in a referendum in August 1999. This led to an interim UN administration with an international military presence to ward off Indonesian militia gangs. Towns like Dili had been virtually destroyed and the World Bank estimates that reconstruction will cost $300 million. Gusmao, who has now returned, is the most plausible president, though says he does not want the job.

Ecuador

Ecuador has defaulted on international bond debts, and suffered a 'quasi-coup'

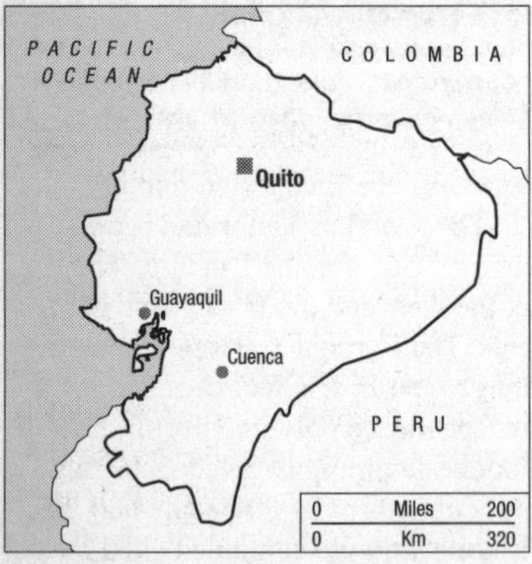

Land area: *284,000 sq. km.*
Population: *12 million—urban 61%*
Capital city: *Quito, 1.4 million*
People: *Mestizo 55%, Amerindian 25%, Spanish 10%, black 10%*
Language: *Spanish, Amerindian languages*
Religion: *Roman Catholic*
Government: *Republic*
Life expectancy: *70 years*
GNP per capita: *$PPP 4,630*
Currency: *Sucre*
Major exports: *Bananas, coffee, oil*

Ecuador has three main geographical areas. To the west, containing around one-quarter of national territory, are generally low-lying coastal plains. These rise abruptly to two Andean mountain chains that run down the centre of the country from north to south and are separated by high valleys. Beyond the Andes lies the 'Oriente'—the Ecuadorian part of the Amazon basin with its tropical rainforests. In addition, Ecuador has sovereignty over the Galapagos Islands 1,000 kilometres to the west in the Pacific Ocean. As its name indicates, Ecuador sits astride the Equator, and outside its mountain regions has a year-round humid climate.

Most Ecuadorians are mestizo—mixtures of Amerindians and white immigrants who came chiefly from Spain and other European countries, though there are also descendants of other immigrants including the Lebanese who arrived in the 1900s. The various Amerindian groups are largely Quechua-speaking and can be found throughout the country but particularly in the highlands. They have not in the past exerted much influence but have become more assertive in recent years. There are also two main black groups—one in Esmeraldas on the north-east coast and the other in the Chota Valley in the northern highlands.

Standards of health and education are poor for most people, particularly in the highlands. Per capita expenditure on health is lower than in most other countries in the region, and although the constitution mandates that 30% of the national budget be devoted to education the quality is low and underpaid teachers frequently go on strike.

Ecuador's distinct geographical areas have tended to impede national integration. People in the mountains, particularly those in the capital, Quito, have generally been more traditional and conservative compared with the more commercially oriented communities on the Pacific coast centred on the port city of Guayaquil which has been pressing for greater autonomy.

This divide is evident too in agriculture, which is the country's major employer. In the mountains, production is chiefly for national consumption—typically corn, potatoes, and beans as well as livestock. But productivity is low and landholdings are small—tempting some farmers to colonize the sparsely populated Oriente, where they face resistance from indigenous groups. On the coast, much of the land is devoted to large plantations of export crops, especially bananas, of which Ecuador is the world's largest exporter. Fishing is also an important source of both food and export revenue—particularly the cultivation of freshwater prawns.

Ecuador is the world's leading exporter of bananas

Industry and manufacturing in Ecuador have generally operated behind high tariff walls, producing goods for local consumption. But participation in the Andean Community and the WTO has required liberalization and stimulated exports particularly of paper and wood—for which the country has abundant raw material.

The largest export industry continues to be oil. This has been extracted in the Oriente since the 1970s. One of the main constraints is pipeline capacity, and because local refining is limited much fuel still has to be imported.

Governance in Ecuador has been fragile. Since the end of military rule and the subsequent democratic elections in 1979, successive governments have switched between centre-right, centre-left and populist—though none has managed to hold the country together sufficiently to follow a coherent development strategy.

One of the stranger fates was that of Abdalá Bucaram of the Partido Roldista Ecuatoriana, who was elected president in 1996 and dismissed by the Congress in 1997 on the constitutionally dubious grounds of 'mental incapacity'.

He was temporarily replaced by the leader of the Congress, Fabián Alarcón. And then the 1998 presidential election was won by ex-mayor of Quito, Jamil Mahuad of the centre-right Democrácia Popular party. He had an encouraging start in that he ended the long-running border dispute with Peru. But the catastrophic economic situation in 1999, with the government deep in debt and with unemployment at 20%, forced Ecuador to become the first government in recent history to default on some of its sovereign debt.

Mahuad's downfall came in January 2000 when he proposed to replace the sucre with the US dollar. Trade unions protested and Indian groups marched on Quito. At this point, the army stepped in and removed Mahuad in favour of his vice-president, Gustavo Noboa.

Noboa nevertheless proceeded with the 'dollarization' plan and attempted to start widespread economic reforms in order to qualify for IMF support. But even if IMF aid is forthcoming Ecuadorians face an even tougher future. Prices rose by one-quarter in the first few months of 2000. The same trade unions and peasant organizations that brought down the previous president will probably take to the streets again.

Egypt

Egypt is the largest Arab country and is struggling with Islamic militancy

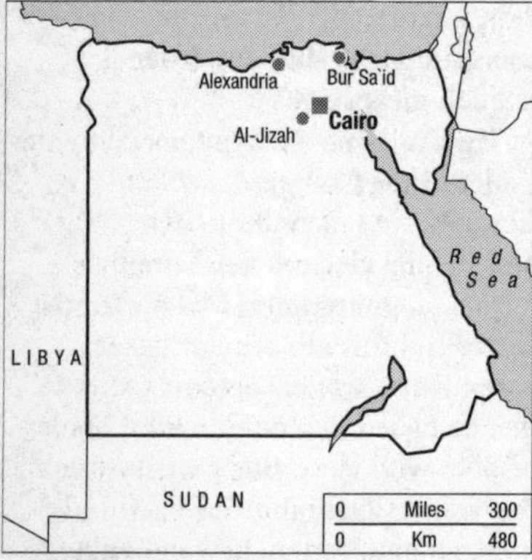

Land area: *1,001,000 sq. km.*
Population: *61 million—urban 45%*
Capital city: *Cairo, 6.8 million*
People: *Eastern Hamitic (Egyptians, Bedouins, and Berbers) 99%, others 1%*
Language: *Arabic, English, French*
Religion: *Muslim 94%, Coptic Christian and other 6%*
Government: *Republic*
Life expectancy: *68 years*
GNP per capita: *$PPP 3,130*
Currency: *Egyptian pound*
Major exports: *Petroleum products, cotton products*

Egypt's vast territory consists of two main desert areas separated by the fertile Nile Valley. The western desert occupies around two-thirds of the country, a rocky sandy plateau with occasional inhabited oases. The eastern desert, with around one-quarter of the territory, is even less hospitable and more sparsely populated. The country's lifeline, the Nile, provides most of the water, and its valley and delta are home to more than 95% of the population.

Ethnically most Egyptians are the result of generations of intermarriage between Arabs and other groups. Most people are Sunni Muslims, but an important minority are members of the Coptic Orthodox Church, whose religion predates the Arab conquest, and who have a strong influence in both commerce and government. The Copts have also at times been the target of Islamic militancy; early in 2000, for example, twenty were killed in a village shoot-out.

Despite recent bursts of economic growth, Egypt remains poor. One-third of the population live below the poverty line and one-third of children are malnourished. Around half the workforce is unemployed or under-employed. Some 2 million Egyptians also work abroad, chiefly in the Gulf countries, sending home around $3 billion each year in remittances.

One-third of the workforce are still engaged in agriculture, mostly in small plots in the Nile Valley. With intensive applications of fertilizer, and manual irrigation systems, these farms are quite productive—though many are affected by waterlogging and salination. One of the main crops is Egypt's high-quality, long-staple cotton, which is an important source of export income. The main food crop is wheat, but production is insufficient for a fast-growing population, and Egypt is one of the world's largest food importers.

To increase production the government has plans to increase its usable land area with a $29 billion land reclamation programme in Sinai and the western desert.

Egypt's most important industrial enterprise is oil production. Though by Middle Eastern standards the reserves are modest, the oil and petroleum products from Egyptian refineries are still the main export earners, and recently the government has made further investment in gas. These industries, along with others like cotton spinning, are in the hands of state enterprises which employ around one-third of the workforce. The government started a privatization programme in 1996, but has made slow progress.

Within the service sector, one of the most important sources of income is the Suez Canal. Around 15,000 vessels pass through each year. Another vital service industry is tourism. Some 4 million people arrive each year, chiefly visiting its historical sights and spending some $4 billion. A 1997 Islamic terrorist attack at Luxor that killed 58 tourists was a serious setback, but the industry seems to have recovered.

15,000 vessels per year through the Suez Canal

Since it became a republic in 1952, Egypt has never had a pluralist democracy. The early years were dominated by Gamel Abdel Nasser, who pursued Arab socialism and nationalized many industries, including the Suez Canal. He was replaced on his death in 1970 by Anwar el-Sadat. In 1978, Sadat established the current ruling party, the National Democratic Party (NDP). Sadat was assassinated in 1981 by Islamic terrorists and was replaced by the current president, Hosni Mubarak. Egypt has an elected assembly, the Majlis al-Shaab, in which the NDP has a large majority, but the president has extensive powers.

Much recent history has been dominated by the relationship with Israel. Both Sadat and Mubarak have been peace-brokers between other Arab states and Israel and have been rewarded with more than $2 billion annually in US aid.

There is little effective opposition to Mubarak or the NDP, which achieved 95% of the vote in the 1995 election, amid widespread fraud and intimidation. The president is elected by a two-thirds majority of the parliament, and his appointment is then endorsed in a referendum. There are 15 weak opposition parties. The government carefully vets each application to form a new party and has turned down every request for the past 20 years.

The most direct political opposition has come from the Muslim Brotherhood. Religion-based parties are illegal so it has to operate underground. There are also a number of Islamic terrorist groups. Until the Luxor attack, the most active was the Gamaat Islamiya (Muslim Groups) but widespread condemnation and a security crackdown have effectively brought its activities to a halt.

Despite this success the government has taken an even tighter grip. In March 2000 it extended its emergency law for a further three years. The government has even been restricting conventional non-governmental organizations. Added to all this is the question of who will succeed President Mubarak who has now been in charge of Egypt for eighteen years.

El Salvador

El Salvador has moved from a debilitating civil war to an often violent peace

Land area: *21,000 sq. km.*
Population: *6 million—urban 46%*
Capital city: *San Salvador, 10 million*
People: *Mestizo 94%, Amerindian 5%, white 1%*
Language: *Spanish*
Religion: *Roman Catholic, Protestant*
Government: *Republic*
Life expectancy: *69 years*
GNP per capita: *$PPP 2,850*
Currency: *Colón*
Major exports: *Coffee, manufactures*

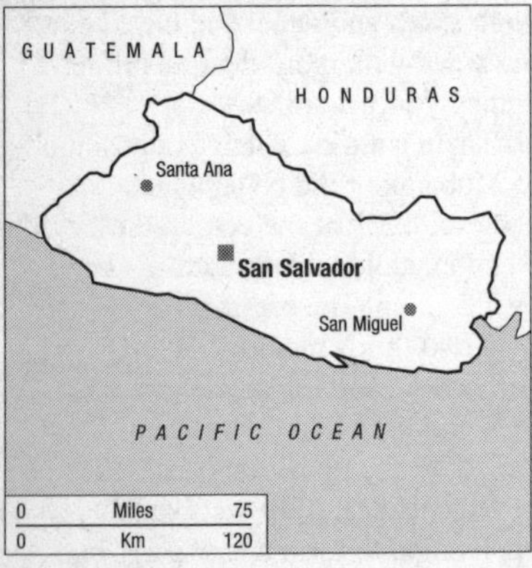

El Salvador is the smallest and most densely populated country in the continental Americas. It has two highland areas: to the north, a rugged mountain range along the border with Honduras, and to the south a range of twenty major volcanoes separated by a series of basins that make up the central plain. The major lowland areas are the valley of the Lempa River that runs from north to south, and a narrow plain along the Pacific coast.

The volcanoes have dominated El Salvador not just physically but also economically. The rich and porous volcanic soils that cover one-quarter of the land area are ideal for coffee cultivation, and the struggle for control over this and other fertile land has shaped the country's history. Land clearing for cultivation has removed most of the forest cover.

Little of El Salvador's Amerindian culture remains. In the 1930s the army launched a vicious military campaign La Matanza, the 'killing', which not only cost 30,000 lives but also laid waste to the indigenous culture.

Agriculture employs 40% of the labour force and meets 70% of domestic food needs. But the best land is still controlled by a few wealthy people: about 1% of landowners control more than 40% of the arable land. Coffee is one of the main export earners, grown on the slopes of the mountains. Sugar and cotton are cultivated in the lowlands on the coastal plain. The main food crops are corn, beans, and rice, but much of the food has to be imported.

One of the most pressing issues now is environmental degradation. With most of its forest cover removed, El Salvador suffers from extensive soil erosion. This made it vulnerable to Hurricane Mitch which caused massive mudslides in October 1998.

El Salvador's economy is now dominated by services and manufacturing. With its dense population, this has become the most industrialized country in Central America. Lacking oil, it had to rely heavily on hydroelectricity, and some geothermal power. Manufacturing was originally designed for import substitution, but in recent years the emphasis has been on manufacturing for export in 'maquila' factories engaged in offshore assembly. Most of this involves the production of garments which have now overtaken coffee as the leading export earner. Garment factories employ 52,000 people, the majority of them women. However these factories and other exporters are facing stiffer competition from Mexico and other countries in Latin America. This has led to pressure for devaluation or even for 'dollarization'—abandoning the national currency in favour of the US dollar.

Nowadays the largest source of foreign exchange is actually the million or more Salvadorans now living in the USA who send home around $1.3 billion annually in remittances.

El Salvador's long history of injustice and bitterness finally erupted into armed revolt in the 1970s. A series of guerrilla groups united in 1980 as the Farabundo Martí Liberation Front (FMNL), and when Archbishop Oscar Romero was assassinated in 1980, his death provoked an armed insurrection that launched the country into a full-scale civil war.

In 1982, the right-wing ARENA party took over the government and was sustained by massive US aid which at the height of the war amounted to around $1 million per day. Death squads roamed the country killing trade unionists or anyone promoting peaceful reform. The war lasted until 1992 and cost 80,000 lives. About 1 million people were displaced—many ending up in the USA.

In April 1990, UN-supervised negotiations began and a ceasefire was finally achieved in January 1992. The FMLN agreed to end the armed struggle, while the government agreed to dismantle the death squads, reduce the size of the armed forces, and distribute some land.

The presidential elections in 1994 were of dubious validity since around one-third of the electorate were unregistered. This, combined with poor organization by the FMLN, which had become a political party, resulted in an ARENA victory with Calderón Sol elected president. Subsequently, there was some land reform but little real change to show for all those years of fighting. Around half the population live below the poverty line.

An amnesty law that effectively grants impunity to many of those responsible for atrocities, including those who murdered Archbishop Romero, also hampers reconciliation.

Aside from the human and economic costs of the war, El Salvador has another pernicious legacy. Violence from ex-combatants on both sides results in around 6,000 murders a year—one of the highest rates in the world.

6,000 murders per year

The 1997 legislative elections saw something of a revival for the parties of the left, with the FSLN only one seat behind ARENA. Even so, the others found it difficult to sustain a united progressive alliance. In 1999, ARENA's Francisco Guillermo Flores Pérez was elected president, though on a very low turnout by a disillusioned electorate.

Equatorial Guinea

Land area: *28,000 sq. km.*
Population: *432,000—urban 45%*
Capital city: *Malabo, 45,000*
People: *Fang, Bubi*
Language: *Spanish, French, pidgin English, Fang, Bubi*
Religion: *Roman Catholic*
Government: *Republic*
Life expectancy: *50 years*
GNP per capita: *$PPP 4,400*
Currency: *CFA franc*
Major exports: *Oil, timber*

Equatorial Guinea has discovered oil but has yet to find democracy

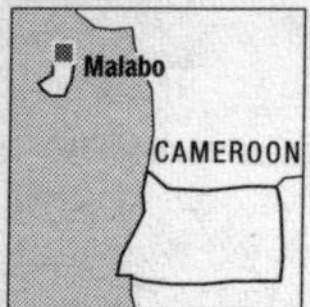

The mainland of Equatorial Guinea, called Río Muni, consists of a coastal plain and then forested hills and plateaux that extend east to the border with Gabon. The country also includes several islands, the largest of which is Bioko, several hundred kilometres to the north in the Gulf of Guinea and has the capital, Malabo.

The majority ethnic group are the Fang, though these are divided into many subgroups. Those on Bioko, 15% of the population, are mostly Bubi—many of whom are politically and economically marginalized. This was Spain's only colony in Sub-Saharan Africa, and Spanish is the official language. Health standards are poor, but literacy is higher than in neighbouring countries.

During the Spanish period, the country had thriving cocoa plantations, but most of these withered away during the early years of independence. Around 85% of the labour force still work in agriculture. Most farmers grow subsistence crops like cassava and sweet potatoes, along with some cocoa and coffee. The main agricultural export, however, is timber.

Equatorial Guinea's prospects were transformed in 1991 by the discovery of oil off the coast of Bioko. By 1998, the various fields were producing more than 100,000 barrels per day. This gave a jolt to the economy: between 1994 and 1998 economic growth was 24% annually, though much of the benefit has gone to Western oil companies.

Democracy has never had much of a foothold. At independence the country was in the hands of Francisco Macías Nguema, a corrupt and oppressive dictator who dragged Equatorial Guinea into a social and economic abyss. In 1979, after a bloody coup supported by Spain and Morocco, he was overthrown by his nephew, Teodoro Obiang Nguema Mbasogo, who merely delivered a different brand of dictatorship.

In 1991, under pressure from aid donors, Obiang opened the country up to multi-party democracy, but his Partido Democrático de Guinea Ecuatorial (PDGE) remains the dominant force. In 1996, he was re-elected president, achieving 98% of the vote in an election marked by fraud and intimidation.The only real opposition comes from an underground Bubi opposition group which has attacked government installations. At the trial of some of those arrested for this, Amnesty International reports that many defendants appeared with broken bones and parts of their ears cut off.

Eritrea

Independent Eritrea was soon at war with former ally Ethiopia

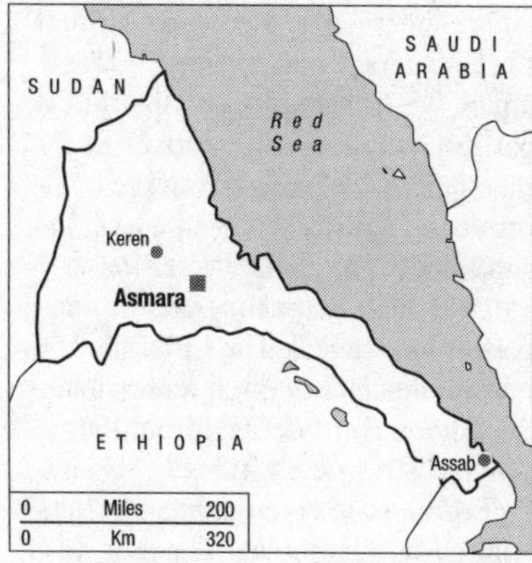

Land area: *125,000 sq. km.*
Population: *4 million—urban 18%*
Capital city: *Asmara, 400,000*
People: *Ethnic Tigrinya 50%, Tigre and Kunama 40%, Afar 4%, Saho 3%, other 3%*
Language: *Afar, Amharic, Arabic, Tigre and Kunama, Tigrinya*
Religion: *Muslim, Coptic Christian, Roman Catholic, Protestant*
Government: *Republic*
Life expectancy: *51 years*
GNP per capita: *$PPP 950*
Currency: *Nafka*
Major exports: *Livestock, textiles, food*

Eritrea can be divided into three main areas. The eastern part of the country is a long, arid coastal plain inhabited by nomadic herders or fishing communities. The savannah and shrub-covered western lowlands descend to the border with Sudan. The main part of Eritrea is the central highlands which are part of the Ethiopian Plateau. This is the most densely populated part of the country and has the more fertile land, though many of the hills have suffered severe soil erosion.

Eritrea has a number of ethnic groups of which the largest are the Tigrayans, who speak Tigrinya. They form most of the population of the highlands and are also to be found in the adjacent Ethiopian region of Tigray. Another major group are the similarly named Tigre, who speak Tigre, and are to be found in the north of the plateau, as well as in parts of the lowlands. Though their languages have the same root and script, they are mutually unintelligible. Hundreds of thousands of Eritrean refugees who fled during the wars still live in Sudan and Ethiopia, though many were expelled from Ethiopia in 1999 during a border war.

Decades of war have kept Eritreans desperately poor. In 1998, more than 40% of children were reported to be malnourished, only 22% had access to safe water, and 13% to safe sanitation. Education levels are also low. During the Ethiopian period, schools were forced to teach in Amharic, though most schooling was confined to urban areas. In 1999, only one-third of children were enrolled in primary school, and literacy is probably not much above 20%.

More than two-thirds of the population depend on agriculture or fishing. Farmers grow subsistence cereal crops and raise a small number of animals, but output is low. They have little irrigation and have to rely on erratic rainfall. And in the densely populated highlands their land has become increasingly eroded. Given Eritrea's long coastline, the fishing industry has considerable potential both for local consumption and export.

Before its incorporation into Ethiopia in the early 1950s, Eritrea had started to develop a number of industries. But Ethiopian priorities steadily undermined Eritrean enterprises and subsequent conflicts destroyed many of the rest. Even so, there are still light industries processing food and producing textiles and garments, mostly in state-run enterprises.

When it achieved independence from Ethiopia in 1993, Eritrea gained the entire coastline, so in principle Eritrea's ports should be a useful source of income—though this does depend on an abiding peace with Ethiopia. Another important source of income is remittances from Eritreans abroad—around $200 million in 1997.

On achieving independence, Eritrea got Ethiopia's coastline

Formerly an Italian colony, Eritrea was federated into Ethiopia in 1952, and in 1962 was formally, and illegally, annexed by Ethiopia. By then an independence struggle had already started but it was weakened by a long conflict between two groups. The Eritrean Liberation Front (ELF), which emerged in 1958, was organized along ethnic and regional lines. But in 1973 a splinter group appeared with a more socialist orientation—what is now the Eritrean People's Liberation Front (EPLF). The two groups fought each other as well as the Ethiopians.

By 1991, the EPLF was dominant and had seized control of the territory. Meanwhile the Ethiopian government in Addis Ababa had been overthrown by Tigrayan TPLF guerrillas, another Marxist-inspired group which had good relations with the EPLF. In 1993, this led to an amicable parting, and independence for Eritrea.

Early in 1994, the EPLF disbanded and re-emerged as the People's Front for Democracy and Justice (PFDJ), which was to incorporate all political parties, including some former ELF members, with Isaias Afwerki as president. Eritrea achieved a new and supposedly pluralist constitution in 1997, though in practice opposition parties are banned. The PFDJ tends to impose this less through repression than moral force derived from long years of struggle.

Eritrea soon entered into conflicts with all its neighbours. The first was with Sudan: each country accusing the other of harbouring its dissidents. Then there were arguments with Yemen and Djibouti.

The most damaging and surprising, conflict, however, was with Ethiopia. In May 1998, a border skirmish erupted into a full-scale war that by mid-1999 had cost around 50,000 lives and displaced hundreds of thousands of people from Ethiopia to Eritrea. Ostensibly, the war was being fought over a few barren hectares of loosely defined border which Eritrea claims that Ethiopia had been encroaching on, and taxing its people. A Framework Agreement, brokered by the Organization of African Unity, was reached in July 1999. But this achieved very little and by May 2000 the war was in once agin in full swing as Ethiopia launched a major offensive displacing around one-third of a million people within Eritrea.

Estonia

Estonia is one of the more successful ex-Soviet republics and has turned decisively towards Europe

Land area: *45,000 sq. km.*
Population: *1 million—urban 74%*
Capital city: *Tallinn, 400,000*
People: *Estonian 64%, Russian 29%, Ukrainian 3%, Byelorussian 2%, other 3%*
Language: *Estonian, Russian, Ukrainian*
Religion: *Evangelical Lutheran, Russian Orthodox, Estonian Orthodox*
Government: *Republic*
Life expectancy: *69 years*
GNP per capita: *$PPP 5,240*
Currency: *Kroon*
Major exports: *Mechanical equipment, food, textiles, wood products*

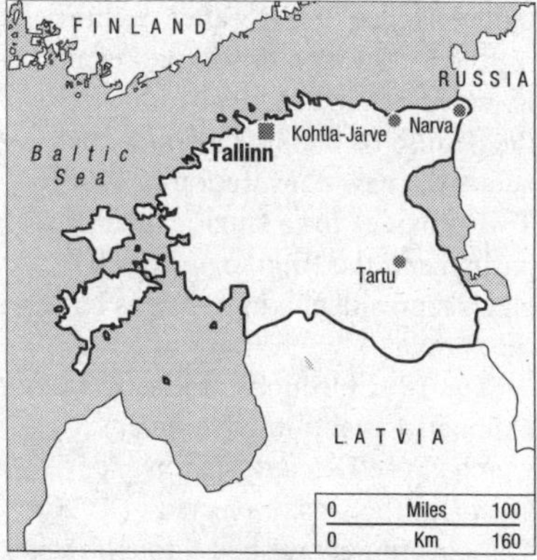

Estonia's mainland consists largely of a plain that includes many lakes. Around 40% of the territory is covered with forests. In addition, it has more than one thousand islands and islets in the Baltic Sea.

Estonians were disturbed when many Russians moved into the country following the Soviet invasion in 1940. Once Estonians recovered their independence in 1991 they were therefore determined to re-exert their national identity and demanded that anyone who wished to become a citizen, or to work in public administration, should speak Estonian—not an easy language to learn. For the Russians, who made up one-third of the population, this was a significant obstacle. Some have been emigrating but most have stayed.

At the start of 1999, there were around half a million people who were not of Estonian ethnic origin. Of these, around 30% had Estonian citizenship, 19% were Russian citizens, while 3% were citizens of other countries. However that still left around one-quarter of a million people in limbo—described as alien, of non-determined citizenship, without documents, or stateless. At least half of these cannot meet the language requirement.

Russia has frequently complained about discrimination against Russians, and Estonia's relations with its giant neighbour remain tense. Estonia has, however, been strengthening ties with Finland: Estonian is related to Finnish, which helps to sustain cultural and commercial ties.

Of the former Soviet republics, Estonia made one of the most rapid transformations towards a market economy. The government started the privatization programme with land and housing by distributing vouchers to all households, and later extended the scheme to large companies. By 1997, more than two-thirds of the economy was run by the private sector.

After independence, Estonia's economy contracted suddenly as ties with Russia were cut. But from around 1995 the economy revived, thanks in part to foreign investors impressed with Estonia's enthusiastic liberalization, open trading regime, and low wage rates. This meant that basic industries such as textiles and timber products, along with chemicals, plastics, and metals revived fairly quickly, finding new markets in Europe.

Finland has been one of the main investors. The electronics company Elcoteq, for example, attracted by wages one-sixth of those in Finland, assembles mobile phones and other items for Nokia and other Scandinavian companies, and is now Estonia's largest exporter.

Estonia has some of its own energy supplies, based on extracting oil from shale, but this is an expensive and polluting process, and the country still relies on Russia for additional, and now much more expensive, supplies of oil.

Agriculture, which is largely based on livestock, has not performed so well. Between 1989 and 1997, its share of GDP fell from 20% to 7%.

Estonia is a favourite destination for Finns seeking cheap liquor

The government rapidly dismantled the former collective farms to create more than 6,000 private farms. But having lost their subsidies these have struggled to match EU standards. The only brighter spots have been forestry and fishing.

Estonia's market economy has also opened up the potential for a larger and more vigorous service sector that had been stifled during the Soviet years. Tourism has certainly benefited. Estonia abolished visa requirements for visitors from Nordic countries and now welcomes more than 1 million tourists a year—the majority from Finland arriving by ferry and often to take advantage of low prices for liquor.

Estonia, which had first gained independence in 1918 after centuries of rule by Sweden or Russia, regained its independence in 1991 following the demise of the Soviet Union and adopted a new constitution in 1992. This provides for a single-chamber parliament, the Riigikogu, which elects a president whose role is largely ceremonial.

The 1992 elections produced a nationalist coalition government which chose Lennart Mari as president (he was re-elected in 1996). The government pushed through rapid reforms, but its popularity was undermined by economic contraction along with some political scandals. The 1995 elections produced a swing to the left—though this did not seem to reduce the drive for economic reform of the government led by Mart Siimann.

The 1999 elections were contested by more than 30 parties, and though the populist, left-leaning Centre Party won the most seats, the government was formed by a centre-right coalition with Mart Laar as prime minister. A notable positive feature of this election was that ethnic Russians seem to have voted for Estonian parties, rather than Russian nationalist parties.

In 1998, Estonia became the first former Soviet republic to start negotiations for EU membership. Also on the agenda is membership of NATO.

Ethiopia

Ethiopia has been racked by war and political violence and a series of famines

Land area: *1,097,000 sq. km.*
Population: *61 million—urban 17%*
Capital city: *Addis Ababa, 2.1 million*
People: *Oromo 40%, Amhara and Tigrean 32%, Sidamo 9%, others 19%*
Language: *Amharic, Tigrinya, Orominga, Guaraginga, Somali, Arabic, English*
Religion: *Muslim 45%, Ethiopian Orthodox 35%, animist 12%, others 8%*
Government: *Republic*
Life expectancy: *43*
GNP per capita: *$PPP 500*
Currency: *Birr*
Major exports: *Coffee, hide and skins, qat*

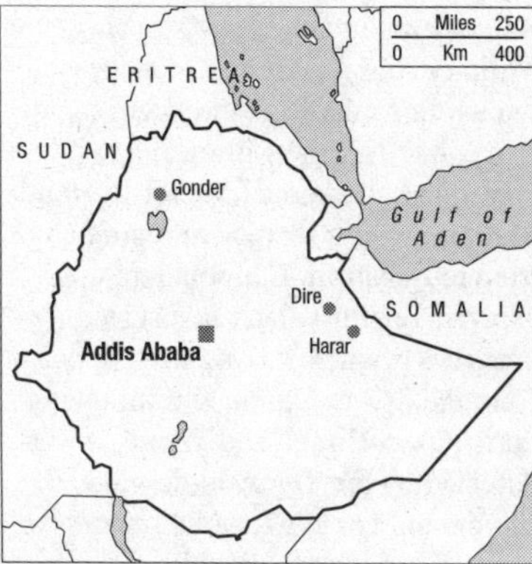

More than half of Ethiopia consists of two high tablelands—the western and eastern highlands which are split, south-west to north-east, by the East African Rift Valley. To the east, much of the territory consists of the lower arid plains of the Danakil depression and the Ogaden.

Ethiopia's population is very diverse, the result of many centuries of linguistic and racial mixing. Officially, there are 64 recognized ethnic groups, but there are probably 200 or more languages. Following a new constitution in 1995, the country became a federal republic and now has nine regions or 'nationalities', though each of these actually contains a mixture of ethnic groups. The largest group are the Oromo, who are to be found in the centre and south, followed by the Amhara and the Tigrayans, who occupy the north and the north-west. Many are Christians, belonging to the previously dominant Ethiopian Orthodox Union Church, but nowadays more are Muslims.

Ethiopia remains one of the world's poorest countries. Half the population are malnourished, infant mortality is high, and life expectancy short. Fewer than 20% of Ethiopians have access to modern health care services and their health status is among the worst in the world. AIDS is a major threat: around 1.7 million Ethiopians were infected with HIV in 1996. Education standards are also very low: only one-quarter of people are literate. The population continues to grow by around 3% per year and by the year 2025 it could exceed 145 million.

Some 85% of the population live in the rural areas, and survive mostly through farming—growing a range of subsistence cereal crops, including teff, which is a cereal grass. But agricultural output has been extremely variable. The high population density in the highlands and ensuing deforestation have led to extensive soil erosion. And since almost all agriculture is rain-fed it is very vulnerable to the often unreliable climate. Per capita food production has declined sharply. In a good year Ethiopia is just about self-sufficient, but when the rains fail it has to rely on emergency shipments of food aid. Ethiopia's strategies to improve food security include, on the one hand, stronger early warning systems, and on the other, efforts to increase output through greater use of fertilizers.

But some of the problems are political. In the past farmers had greater freedom to migrate temporarily to help harvest cash crops and supplement their incomes. Now they need permission to travel. In 2000, Ethiopia was again in the grip of a famine that was affecting an estimated five million people.

The main cash crop is coffee, which is grown mainly in the south by small-holders and usually provides around two-thirds of export earnings. Another important agricultural export is qat, a bush whose leaves can be chewed and which provides a mild stimulant popular in neighbouring Somalia and Djibouti.

Cultivating qat for its neighbours

Ethiopia has little industry. Most is controlled by the state and is concentrated in food processing. However, some industries, particularly textiles and garments, are being privatized, and there is probably potential for more private-sector activity in the processing of hides and skins, which are also major exports.

In the past three decades, Ethiopia has been through a series of political traumas and civil wars. Following a famine in 1972-4, which cost an estimated 200,000 lives, political unrest led to the overthrow of the monarchy of Haile Selassie and in 1975 to the establishment of a socialist republic. Although the original rebellion included a wide range of civilian groups, they failed to cohere into viable political parties, leaving the way clear for the establishment of a seventeen-year military regime, the Provisional Military Administrative Council, known in Amharic as the 'Derg'.

From 1977, the Derg was controlled by Colonel Mengistu Haile Mariam, whose repressive regime tried to transform Ethiopia into a Marxist-Leninist state. It survived until 1991, when, having lost support from the Soviet Union, and following uprisings in Eritrea and Tigray, it was defeated by the Tigrayan-dominated Ethiopian People's Revolutionary Democratic Front (EPRDF).

This led in 1993 to independence for Eritrea—leaving Ethiopia landlocked. It also meant that in Ethiopia the Tigrayan minority had displaced the previously dominant Amharic groups. Meles Zenawi, Ethiopia's prime minister, is regarded as one of Africa's 'new leaders'. However, his strategy of 'ethnic federalism', while understandable, is also seen as a policy of divide and rule. Most political power is concentrated in the Tigrayan-dominated EPRDF.

To the surprise of many people, the former allies Ethiopia and Eritrea declared war in 1998 over a border dispute. The war appeared all the more senseless since both countries were suffering from famine. A ceasefire was agreed in mid-1999, but the war flared up again. In mid-2000, Ethiopia effectively emerged victorious and new talks started.

Fiji

Another coup and a racist constitution will isolate Fiji

Land area: *18,000 sq. km.*
Population: *827,000—urban 41%*
Capital city: *Suva, 200,000*
People: *Fijian 51%, Indian 44%, other 5%*
Language: *English, Fijian, Hindi*
Religion: *Christian 52%, Hindu 38%, Muslim 8%*
Government: *Republic*
Life expectancy: *73 years*
GNP per capita: *$PPP 3,580*
Currency: *Fiji dollar*
Major exports: *Sugar, garments, gold*

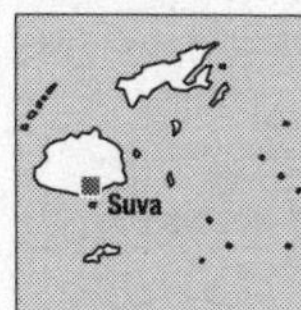

Fiji comprises hundreds of islands and islets in the South Pacific. The two largest islands, Vitu Levu and Vanua Levu, account for more than 80% of the territory.

The population is finely balanced between Fijians, who are of mixed Melanesian and Polynesian origin, and Indians, who are descendants of 19th century immigrant sugar workers. Indians were narrowly in the majority until 1987, when many fled after the first coup; now the balance again favours Fijians.

Sugar remains the backbone of Fijian agriculture, but drought and worries about land tenure have affected production. Sugar processing used to dominate industrial production as well, but manufacturing industry has become more diverse and by 1998 garments were bringing in as much export income. Earnings from the Vatukoula gold mine are also important. In addition, Fiji depends heavily on tourism: in 1998 more than 360,000 tourists arrived, with expenditure close to 10% of GDP.

Politics in Fiji has long been afflicted by conflicts between ethnic Fijians and those of Indian origin. One of the most important issues is the ownership of land which has largely been monopolized by indigenous Fijians who lease it to Indians—who produce virtually all the sugar. Many of these leases are now becoming due, and a proposal to offer new leases sparked the latest round of conflict.

From independence in 1970, indigenous Fijians had controlled the government through the Alliance Party. The 1987 election, however, was won by two parties that were largely supported by Indians. The Fijians responded with a military coup and a constitutional change to bar Indians from power. This led to international isolation that only ended in 1994 when a new constitution gave the Indians a fairer deal. Eventually, in 1999, with the Fijian vote split among five parties, the Indian-dominated Fiji Labour Party won a majority in parliament and Mahendra Chaudhry became the first Indian prime minister.

But his promise of 30-year land leases to Indians incensed the Fijians. In May 2000 businessman George Speight, along with a section of the army, held the prime minister hostage in the parliament building. After ten days the army chief, Frank Bainimarama, took control of Fiji. Finally in July Speight signed a peace deal in exchange for the army firing the prime minister and abandoning the multiracial constitution. For Fiji the outlook is grim. Years of isolation and economic crisis could lie ahead.

Finland

The least-rich Scandinavian country, Finland is also the world's most wired country

Land area: *338,000 sq. km.*
Population: *5 million—urban 64%*
Capital city: *Helsinki, 532,000*
People: *Finn 93%, Swede 6%, Lapp 1%*
Language: *Finnish, Swedish*
Religion: *Evangelical Lutheran 89%, Greek Orthodox 1%, none 9%, other 1%*
Government: *Republic*
Life expectancy: *77 years*
GNP per capita: *$PPP 20,270*
Currency: *Markka*
Major exports: *Metals and machinery, forestry products*

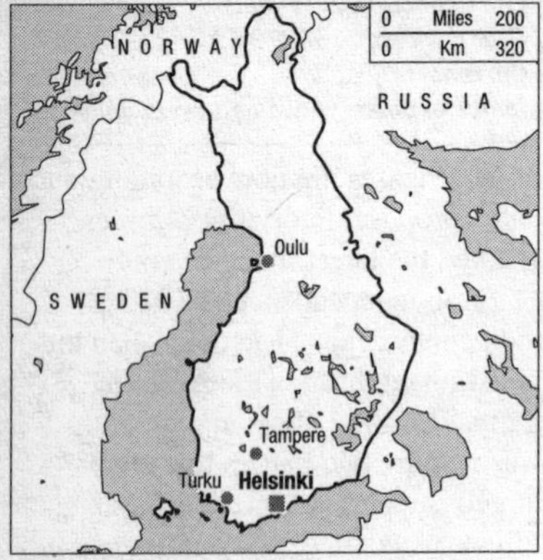

Most of Finland is fairly low-lying and the country as a whole is heavily forested. One of its most striking features is the complex of thousands of shallow lakes in the south. Here the climate is fairly temperate but even some of the ports on the Baltic Sea are icebound during the long winter. Most of the higher ground is in the northern one-third of the country, and since this lies within the Arctic Circle the climate is severe.

Finland's population, which is concentrated in the south, is ethnically fairly homogenous. Nevertheless, there are also significant numbers of Swedes, mainly in the southern coastal areas and on the Åland Islands, which lie between the two countries. Swedish is also an official language. Another minority, though now very small in number, are the Sami, or Lapps, who herd their reindeer in the far north. The break-up of the Soviet Union also caused some immigration of ethnic Finns from Russia and Estonia, but the proportion of foreign-born is less than 2% and immigration has often been exceeded by emigration, particularly during recent periods of high unemployment. By European standards, Finland is also fairly rural—more than one-third of people live in the countryside.

Agriculture is not a major source of income. The fierce climate and poor soils mean that less than one-tenth of the land is suitable for farming. Even so, the country is largely self-sufficient in basic foods.

The most important rural activity is forestry. Finland's vast forests of pine, spruce, and birch support a number of major industries. The extensive pulp and paper sector, which is dominated by four main companies, is responsible for around one-quarter of world paper exports. In addition, Finland is an important producer of building materials and furniture, and has used its forestry experience to specialize in the production of forestry machinery.

Finland's other industries have also been expanding fast. Remarkably, most of this development has come from one company, Nokia, which makes one-quarter of the world's mobile phones as well as other telecommunications equipment. Finland was among the first countries to deregulate its telecommunications industry and is now the world's most connected country: two-thirds of the population had a mobile phone in 1999 and Finland now has the highest per capita number of internet connections.

Finland had made steady economic progress for decades but was rocked by a deep recession in the early 1990s and by the collapse of trade with the Soviet Union, which had taken around one-fifth of exports. In three years the country's economy shrank by 13%. Unemployment, which was only around 3% in 1990, had jumped to 18% by 1994, and social security payments contributed to a serious budget deficit.

The government made determined efforts to tackle the problems. It made deep cuts in public expenditure and this, combined with contributions from the forestry and electronics industry, helped Finland to emerge from the worst of the crisis. Over the past five years economic growth has averaged 4% per year, more rapid than in most European countries. Unemployment has also been cut and by 1999 was down to 11%. However this development has been increasingly concentrated in the south of the country in the region bounded by Helsinki, Turku and Tampere, to which many people have been migrating.

Nokia produces one-quarter of the world's mobile phones

For most of the 20th century, the government of Finland was in the hands of coalitions or minority administrations, typically led either by the Social Democratic Party or the rural-based Centre Party.

Since 1995, however, the mosaic has taken on a new pattern. In that election the Social Democrats, led by Paavo Lipponen, had the largest share of the vote for the parliament, though that only amounted to 25%, and encouraged the formation of a 'rainbow', five-party coalition that included all shades of the political spectrum from the Conservative Party to the ex-communists of the Left-Wing Alliance.

The rainbow coalition reformed after the 1999 election still with Lipponen as prime minister, though the Democratic Party lost seats to the conservatives, now called the National Coalition Party.

In February 2000, the Finns elected as president former foreign minister Tarja Halonen, a social democrat and the first woman to hold the office. She is also further to the left than most of her predecessors. However the president now has relatively few powers.

Finland is likely to pursue greater integration into Europe. It joined the EU in 1995 and was one of the first eleven countries to adopt the common currency, the Euro. Finnish enthusiasm for Europe is due as much to security as to economic concerns. Finland had a mutual security treaty with the Soviet Union but since 1990 it has tried to follow a neutral course. This means that Finland is reluctant to join NATO but Finns hope that membership of the EU will afford them similar protection.

France

One of Europe's most centralized states, with a distinctive and influential culture

Land area: 552,000 sq. km.
Population: 59 million—urban 75%
Capital city: Paris, 9.3 million
People: French, including ethnic minorities from former colonies
Language: French
Religion: Roman Catholic 90%, Protestant 2%, other 8%
Government: Republic
Life expectancy: 78 years
GNP per capita: $PPP 22,320
Currency: Franc
Major exports: Machinery, cars, food and agricultural products, chemicals

France has the largest territory in Western Europe. Around two-thirds is lowlands, chiefly to the north and west, including the Paris basin and the Loire Valley. But there are also dramatic mountain ranges. To the south-west the Pyrenees mark the border with Spain. To the south, occupying one-sixth of the territory is the Massif Central, consisting mostly of plateaux at between 600 and 900 metres. And to the south-east, forming a barrier with Italy and Switzerland, are the towering French Alps, beyond which to the south is the Mediterranean coastline—the Côte d'Azure.

The French population has been formed by successive waves of immigration, but France has been determined to sustain a national identity. Thus for more than 250 years, the Académie Française has protected and promoted the French language. The French government has also made strenuous efforts to resist the encroachment of American culture. National identity and a centralized style of management are reinforced by its education system. Most of the country's leadership has been processed through the 'grandes écoles', so they tend to share the same values.

Nevertheless, France does have strong regional identities, and even regional languages such as Breton and Catalan. And the French population continues to be stimulated by immigration. Had there been no immigration this century, France's population would be around 10 million smaller. Around 6% of the population have foreign nationalities, the majority coming from Algeria and Morocco. But millions more immigrants have become French citizens. There may also be up to half a million undocumented immigrants.

Most French workers are now employed in services and often work for the government. The French state continues to play an important part in the economy—spending more than half of GDP and employing more than one in four workers.

Agriculture employs far fewer—only 6% of the labour force—chiefly on smaller farms. Even so, output has increased and France is the EU's leading food producer. The country is largely self-sufficient in food and is a leading exporter of wheat, beef, and other foodstuffs—as well as the world's leading exporter of high quality wine.

France is also the world's fourth-largest industrial power and has many globally important companies. Danone, for example, is the world's largest dairy products firm, and two major car companies, Peugeot-Citroën and Renault, account for one-eighth of France's exports. Another distinctive manufactured export has been the high-speed train, the TGV. Many of these companies are also run by ex-bureaucrats from the grandes écoles. With no oil, France has invested heavily in nuclear electricity which it also exports.

Exporting high-speed trains

Like many other European countries, France has been afflicted by high unemployment—around 10% overall, but often above 25% for young people. Many employers blame this on over-regulation of the labour market and a high minimum wage. In order to reduce unemployment and share work more widely, the government from 2000 introduced an official 35-hour week.

Government in France frequently requires 'cohabitation' between a president of one party and a prime minister of an opposing one. The current constitution, which dates from 1958, strengthened the position of the president, who is directly elected for a seven-year term. However, many people think this is too long and there are proposals to reduce the term to five years. The president appoints the prime minister and chairs the weekly Council of Ministers.

When François Mitterand from the Parti socialiste (PS) won the presidential election in 1981, he could also count on support from his party in the National Assembly and used it to push through many radical measures, including nationalization of important industries. But this did not last. The centre-right party, the Rassemblement pour la république (RPR), subsequently made gains in the National Assembly and obliged Mitterand to appoint a prime minister from its ranks.

By 1997 the situation was reversed. The RPR had won the 1993 elections to the National Assembly and in 1995, with Mitterand ill, their candidate, Jacques Chirac, won the presidential election, defeating Lionel Jospin of the PS. Chirac, hoping to increase the RPR majority, called a snap National Assembly election in 1997. This was a miscalculation. The PS won, obliging Chirac to appoint Jospin as prime minister at the head of a coalition that included the communists and the greens.

Jospin proved an adroit politician and his first two years in office were reasonably successful. Unlike most other leaders of centre-left parties in Europe he is still an avowed socialist, though less radical than before—and has put a number of state-owned enterprises up for sale. Meanwhile the parties of the right are in some disarray.

French Guiana

One of the richest, but most impenetrable, countries of South America

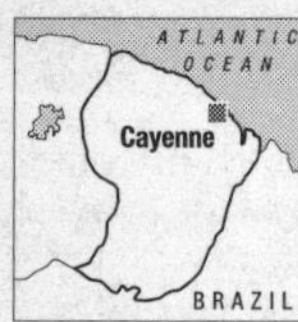

French Guiana's hot and humid territory is largely flat. There are low mountains in the south along the border with Brazil, but most of the country is a vast plateau covered with dense tropical rainforest. The majority of people live along the swampy coastal plain or in the capital, Cayenne.

France used the territory as a penal colony until 1953—most notoriously Devil's Island. Even after they had served their sentences, it was difficult for prisoners to leave. However, most of those who stayed succumbed to tropical diseases.

Today, most people are creole or black, but there is also a significant French population. The others include the original Amerindians in the jungles of the south, the Marons, who are descendants of prisoners who escaped to the interior, and immigrants from other French territories. There are even some people from the Hmong ethnic group from Laos.

The country benefits from generous aid from France, particularly since the establishment in 1968 at Kourou, 60 kilometres west of the capital, of the rocket-launching base now used by the French and European space agencies, as well as by a commercial company. There are around a dozen launches each year.

Land area: *90,000 sq. km.*
Population: *163,000*
Capital city: *Cayenne, 55,000*
People: *Black or mulatto 66%, white 12%, other 22%*
Language: *French*
Religion: *Roman Catholic*
Government: *Overseas territory of France*
Life expectancy: *77 years*
GNP per capita: *$PPP 6,000*
Currency: *French franc*
Major exports: *Shellfish, gold, timber*

This and other government services employ not just French people but also many local workers. As a result, the average per capita income is one of the highest in South America, though this is distributed somewhat unequally between rocket scientists and Amerindian hunter-gatherers.

The other main economic activities are agriculture, fishing, and forestry. Most farms are small, growing subsistence crops, but there are also a few large commercial fruit plantations that export their produce to France. In addition, fishing for shrimp provides an important source of export income. Because of the European tastes of many inhabitants, the country remains highly dependent on imports from France of food and other goods.

As an overseas territory of France, the country elects two representatives to the French National Assembly and one to the Senate. Locally, there are also consultative general and regional councils

In the 1994 elections to the General Council, the Socialist Party of Guiana took the most seats. Local people are in favour of greater autonomy but also want more aid; few want independence from France, which for many people could result in a catastrophic drop in income.

French Polynesia

Tahiti and the other islands have become increasingly reliant on tourism

Land area: *4,000 sq. km.*
Population: *228,000*
Capital city: *Papeete*
People: *Polynesian 78%, Chinese 12%, French 10%*
Language: *French, Tahitian*
Religion: *Protestant 54%, Roman Catholic 30%, other 16%*
Government: *Overseas territory of France*
Life expectancy: *72 years*
GNP per capita: *$PPP 8,000*
Currency: *CFP franc*
Major exports: *Pearls, coconut products*

French Polynesia consists of around 130 islands in five groups in the Pacific, of which the largest and most populous are Tahiti and nearby Moorea. These two islands are volcanic and mountainous, though many others are little more than coral atolls with scant vegetation.

The majority of people are Polynesian, but there is also an influential French minority. Since the islands are a French overseas territory, EU citizens are free to travel and work there, and many have done so. But there have been concerns that they may be taking the better jobs and altering the social balance.

The islanders' relatively high standard of living reflects substantial French investment, particularly during the period of nuclear testing that ended in 1996. Early in 2000, a new campaign was launched to investigate the long-term medical effects of nuclear testing.

In recent years the economy has shifted decisively towards tourism, which is the main source of foreign exchange. Many people also work in government. As a result, more than two-thirds of the population are now employed in services. But many people still work in various forms of agriculture and in fisheries, notably oyster farming and the production of cultured pearls, which are the main source of export revenue. The islands continue to enjoy aid from France, which insulates them from many of the economic disturbances elsewhere, though unemployment is increasing.

As citizens of a French overseas territory, the islanders elect members to the French parliament, but they also have their own territorial assembly which chooses the president of the territorial government of French Polynesia. Since 1991, this has been Gaston Flosse of the Rassemblement pour la république, though early in 2000 a French court convicted him for corruption.

The islands already have considerable autonomy, but they have been pressing for greater authority to act independently on regional issues, and there is a strong pro-independence party led by Oscar Temaru. Flosse has also argued for some restrictions on the arrival of immigrants from 'metropolitan France'. In 1999, the French government responded to these concerns, promising that French Polynesia could become an 'overseas country' within the French republic, though early in 2000 it seemed that implementation of this might be delayed.

Gabon

Oil-rich Gabon is one of Africa's most prosperous countries, but the oil is running out

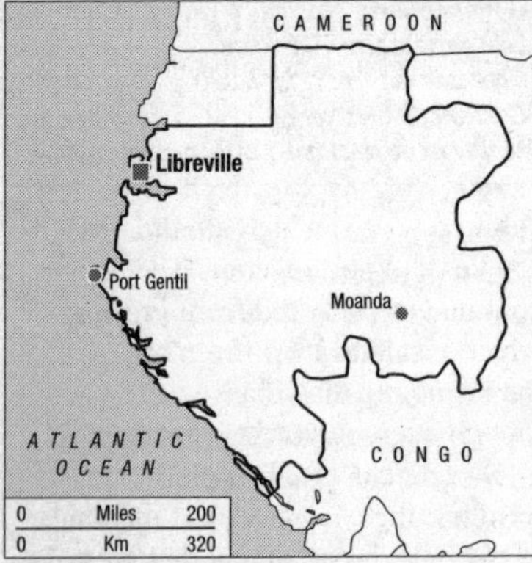

Land area: *268,000 sq. km.*
Population: *1.2 million—urban 52%*
Capital city: *Libreville, 362,000*
People: *Four major Bantu groupings: Fang, Eshira, Bapounou, Bateke. Many immigrants*
Language: *French, Fang, Myene, Bateke, Bapounou/Eschira, Bandjabi*
Religion: *Christian, animist, Muslim*
Government: *Republic*
Life expectancy: *52 years*
GNP per capita: *$PPP 6,660*
Currency: *CFA Franc*
Major exports: *Oil, timber, manganese, uranium*

Gabon consists almost entirely of the basin of the Ogooué River and its tributaries, broken by mountains in the centre and the north, with a narrow strip of coastal lowlands. Three-quarters of the country is covered in dense tropical forest—a rainforest second in area only to the Amazon Basin. This has more than 250 species of trees and provides living space for more than four-fifths of the world's chimpanzees and gorillas.

Gabon's rapid development as an oil producer has made it one of the most urbanized countries in Sub-Saharan Africa—more than half the population are now thought to live in urban areas. This has also left its forest resources relatively unscathed by development. Though there has been some deforestation, particularly along the coast and the river banks, Gabon still has thousands of plant species and thriving wildlife.

The population is very diverse, with more than 40 ethnic groups. But there is also a strong French influence and most of the population is Roman Catholic. The urban population is largely to be found in the coastal strip—in Libreville, the capital, or in Port Gentil, the centre of oil production. The skyline of Libreville was transformed by the oil boom which gave it some very distinctive 1970s architecture. It has also made this one of the world's most expensive cities for visitors.

The interior, on the other hand, is sparsely settled, largely along river banks. Communications generally are poor. Even Port Gentil has no road link with the rest of the country; it must be reached by boat or by air.

Oil has given Gabon Africa's second-highest per capita GNP but the wealth is unequally distributed. In the rural areas basic services for health and education are in a poor state. And even in the urban areas 20% of the population live below the poverty line.

Agriculture is largely for subsistence, but only 0.6% of the total land area has been cultivated and more than half the country's food has to be imported. Most of this, from vegetables to cheese, comes from France, at considerable cost.

The most important rural product is timber, which, before the discovery of oil, was the country's leading source of wealth. Timber is still a major export and is thought to employ around half the labour force. Gabon is the world's leading producer of okoume, a softwood used for making plywood. Other cash crops include rubber, coffee, and cocoa.

Since the late 1960s, Gabon's development has been fuelled by oil, most of which is offshore. Oil accounts for around 60% of the country's total income. Some fifteen international companies are involved in exploration or production in a large number of oilfields. The most important are the Gamba field, which is operated by Shell, and the giant Rabi Kounga field and its satellites, which are operated by Shell and Elf.

Future prospects are uncertain. Apart from the danger of low world prices, Gabon has the disadvantage of being a high-cost producer with a price per barrel that can be twenty times higher than that in Saudi Arabia. More worrying still, reserves could be exhausted within the next few decades.

President Bongo has ruled for thirty years

Another major mineral export is manganese. Here the prospects are better. Gabon is the world's third largest producer and its open-cast mines in the Moanda region in the south-east have around 30% of global reserves. Mining is in the hands of the Comilog company, which is largely foreign owned, though there is some state and Gabonese participation. The other important mineral is uranium, but the reserves are now almost exhausted.

Gabon embarked on an economic structural adjustment programme in 1995, liberalizing the economy and privatizing a number of state enterprises. But life without oil will be difficult; apart from the possibilities of eco-tourism there do not seem to be many new options on the horizon.

For most of the period since independence in 1960, Gabon has been ruled by President Omar Bongo. He came to power in 1967, and in 1968 established the Parti démocratique gabonaise (PDG) as the only legitimate political party. Subsequent oil wealth allowed Bongo and his supporters to entrench their position and distribute patronage. Protests were met with violent repression. The regime maintained close relations with France and even today Gabon has a contingent of French soldiers.

A fall in the oil price in the late 1980s, combined with general extravagance and corruption, produced a financial crisis. The resulting austerity measures led to violent protests and in 1991 eventually forced Bongo to amend the constitution and introduce a multi-party system. He nevertheless won the 1993 presidential election.

Later, a number of new opposition parties emerged, the most prominent was the 'National Rally of Woodcutters' which came second in the 1996 legislative elections. But this soon split into a number of factions—helping Bongo to be re-elected as president in 1998.

Gambia

A holiday destination with a repressive government

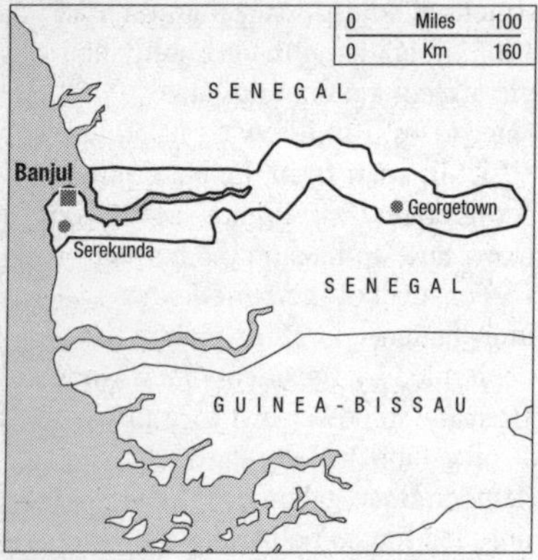

Land area: *11,000 sq. km.*
Population: *1.2 million Urban 30%*
Capital city: *Banjul, 40,000*
People: *Mandinga 42%, Fula 18%, Wolof 16%, Jola 10%, Serahuli 9%, other 5%*
Language: *English, Mandinka, Wolof*
Religion: *Muslim 90%, Christian 9%, other 1%*
Government: *Republic*
Life expectancy: *47 years*
GNP per capita: *$PPP 1,430*
Currency: *Dalasi*
Major exports: *Groundnuts*

This long, thin country extends within Senegal for around 300 kilometres inland from the coast, along both banks of the lower Gambia River. The river is fringed with swamps beyond which are flats that give way to low hills and a sandy plateau. The better land is up-river and most people have settled between the river flats and the uplands.

The Gambia has a large number of ethnic groups, but the majority are the Malinke (also called the Mandingo), who are largely to be found higher up the river. Only one-third of the population is urban, but the capital, Banjul, is more than usually crowded since it effectively occupies an island at the mouth of a river and has few opportunities for expansion. There are also a large number of middle-class refugees from Sierra Leone.

The Gambia is one of the world's poorest countries, and it has been getting poorer. According to official estimates, more than half the population is poor and more than one-third are extremely poor. Three-quarters of the population make their living from agriculture. They use the lower land that benefits from annual flooding to grow rice, which is the staple food. But yields are low and most of the country's rice now has to be imported. Other subsistence crops include millet, sorghum, maize, and vegetables.

Most farmers get their cash income by growing groundnuts, which are ideally suited to the sandy soil on the higher ground. Groundnuts occupy around half the country's cultivable area and most of the crop is sold through Senegal. The government has made some attempts to diversify by promoting the cultivation of flowers and fruit for air-freighting to Europe, but so far has had little success.

In fact, more than 90% of the country's exports are 're-exports'—manufactured goods that have been imported into the port of Banjul but are *en route* to neighbouring countries such as Senegal, Mali, Guinea, and Guinea-Bissau.

The other major export earner is tourism. The Gambia's coastline may be short but it has a number of sandy beaches that have attracted package tourism from Europe, particularly from the United Kingdom which provides more than half the visitors. Tourism creates hotel jobs for local workers but the benefits do not extend very far beyond the resorts. A military coup in 1994 deterred visitors for a couple of years, but they have now returned and there has been more investment in new hotels and holiday cottages.

Politically and geographically, the Gambia seems an anomalous country that one might expect to be part of Senegal. Its status derives from its history as a colony of the British, whose main preoccupation was to deprive the French of an important navigable waterway. The Gambia's relations with Senegal have sometimes been fraught.

For many years following independence in 1965, the Gambia was held up as a model, albeit imperfect, of African democracy. The first prime minister was the leader of the People's Progressive Party (PPP), Sir Dawda Jawara, who was the first president in 1970 when the country became a republic. Jawara survived a Libyan-backed coup attempt by Muslim dissidents in 1981 with the help of troops from Senegal. This intervention also led in 1982 to the formation of a federation 'Senegambia' that seemed destined to unite the two countries. Jawara resisted this, however, and the federation was disbanded in 1987.

The Gambia gets aid despite its poor human rights record

In 1992 Jawara was re-elected as president but in 1994 was overthrown by a military coup led by Lieutenant Yahyah Jammeh. The coup, following which all political parties were banned, was widely condemned internationally. The Gambia found itself isolated and had most of its international aid withdrawn.

International pressure did eventually result in a democratic opening. In 1996, Jammeh formed a new party, the Alliance for Patriotic Reorientation and Construction. Just before the election, however, he took the precaution of banning the three largest opposition parties—and anyone who had held ministerial office for the previous thirty years. This left the United Democratic Party as the main opposition. Jammeh won the presidential election with more than half the vote.

Though formally subscribing to democratic principles, the government has shown scant regard for democratic freedoms. It continues to ban the three largest political parties and to harass the United Democratic Party, whose leaders it arrests and detains. There have also been regular raids on radio stations and newspapers.

Throughout his regime, Jammeh has been subject to real or supposed plots. In 1998 three lieutenants were executed for plotting against him. And early in 2000 Jammeh claimed to have uncovered another plot hatched by his palace guards, several of whom died while 'resisting arrest'.

Despite the country's poor record for human rights, international aid has started to flow again. The IMF returned in 1997 and links with other bilateral donors, including the USA, the UK, and Germany have largely been restored.

Georgia

Georgia is racked by secessionist struggles that undermine economic and social development

Land area: *70,000 sq. km.*
Population: *5 million—urban 60%*
Capital city: *Tbilisi, 1.3 million*
People: *Georgian 70%, Armenian 8%, Russian 6%, Azeri 6%, Ossetian 3%, Abkhazi 2%, other 5%*
Language: *Georgian 71%, Armenian 7%, Azeri 6%, Russian 9%, other 7%*
Religion: *Georgian Orthodox 65%, Russian Orthodox 10%, Muslim 11%, Armenian Apostolic 8%, other 6%*
Government: *Republic*
Life expectancy: *73 years*
GNP per capita: *$PPP 1,960*
Currency: *Lari*
Major exports: *Food, tobacco, machinery*

Georgia is dominated by the Caucasus mountains. Its northern border is formed by the Greater Caucasus and the southern border by the Lesser Caucasus; more than one-third of the mountains are forested. Between these are the major rivers and their valleys—the Kura which flows east into Azerbaijan and the Rion and others flowing west into the Black Sea. The latter have deposited masses of silt to form the Kolkhidskaya lowlands which make up most of the coastal land. Formerly a sub-tropical swamp, this has been drained to create valuable agricultural land.

Most people live in the lower parts of the country. While ethnic Georgians—who call themselves Kartveli—make up around 70% of the population, they are divided into many regionally based subgroups. Georgians have a distinctive language, alphabet, and culture. Most are Christian, though an important subgroup in the south-west, are Muslim. Two of the non-Georgian ethnic groups have been trying to secede: the South Ossetians on the northern border with Russia; and the Abkhazis, who live in the north-west.

Levels of human development have been high, with good standards of education and health: some Georgians are reputedly very long-lived. But war and economic crisis have devastated health and education systems and standards are falling. Two-thirds of the population now live below the poverty line—per capita income is half that in Russia.

Agriculture has been the most important employer. The country's geographical diversity permits a wide variety of crops, including tea, citrus fruits, grapes, and tobacco. Most of the land has yet to be privatized and instead is leased out by local authorities. Food production is low.

The Soviet Union had promoted heavy industry, but much of this is now uncompetitive. By the end of 1996 output was less than one-fifth of the 1989 level. Georgia has some oil and gas of its own but chiefly relies on imports from neighbouring former-Soviet republics who have been trying to charge higher prices. Georgia does have some important mineral resources, including manganese, iron ore, and gold, but high energy costs and falling demand have affected production.

Georgia has attractive scenery and beach resorts so could have a tourist industry, but political instability and poor infrastructure keep people away.

Many important businesses are still run by the state, but the government has sold majority stakes in some others to foreign companies. The Borjomi mineral water plant, for example, is run by French and Dutch investors. More surprisingly, part of the customs administration is run by a British company.

British-run customs service

Economic development has been held back by Georgia's painful struggles to build a coherent democratic state. The first president, following independence in 1991, was Zviad Gamsakhurdia, who was driven from office in 1992 following accusations of corruption and of human rights violations—sparking a civil war that ended only with his death at the end of 1993.

He was replaced by Eduard Shevardnadze, who had been Soviet foreign minister. Shevardnadze was invited back, and eventually in 1995 he was elected president. His new party, the Union of Georgian Citizens, also took the most seats in parliament. The party was returned to power in the 1999 parliamentary elections, and Shevardnadze, now 72, was re-elected president in April 2000 with 80% of the vote. Somewhat surprisingly, since Shevardnadze was in little danger of losing, the election was marred by ballot stuffing and other irregularities.

Shevardnadze has had a torrid time, battling organized crime and corruption, and surviving several assassination attempts. So far, he has concentrated more on playing one corrupt group off against the other than on tackling them head on, but he could now be in a position to institute more thorough reforms.

Shevardnadze has also had to deal with a number of secessionist struggles. In 1990, South Ossetia hoped to unite with Alania (North Ossetia) in the Russian Federation. Fighting here ended with a cease-fire in 1992 and the result will probably be greater autonomy.

The second secessionist struggle, in Abkhazia, has proved more intractable. The Abkhazis declared independence in 1992, and subsequently expelled more than 250,000 Georgians. Various ceasefires have been negotiated, with the involvement of 1,500 Russian peace keeping troops. But fighting has persisted between the Abkhazis and the Georgian guerrillas who have been supporting the refugees. This is not just economically disruptive, it also threatens Georgia's potential Black Sea outlet for oil pipelines from the Caspian.

Georgia is popular with Western countries and gets considerable sums of aid, particularly from the USA which is keen to see a resilient Georgia as a barrier to the extension of Russian influence.

Germany

Politically powerful in Europe, Germany also has a large and successful economy, though it is becoming less competitive

Land area: *357,000 sq. km.*
Population: *82 million—urban 87%*
Capital city: *Berlin , 3.4 million*
People: *German 92%, Turkish 2%, other 6%*
Language: *German*
Religion: *Protestant 38%, Roman Catholic 34%, Muslim 2%, unaffiliated or other 26%*
Government: *Republic*
Life expectancy: *77 years*
GNP per capita: *$PPP 20,810*
Currency: *Deutsche mark*
Major exports: *Machinery, cars, chemicals, manufactured goods*

Germany has three main geographical regions. From the North Sea and Baltic coasts southwards, covering roughly one-third of the country, are the lowlands of the North German Plain. This leads to a belt of central uplands running west to east, cut through by major rivers, including the Rhine and the Weser. Further south still are the South German Highlands culminating in the Alps at the borders with Austria and Switzerland.

The 1990 reunification of Germany created by far Europe's largest national population. Today there are 16 million in what was East Germany and 66 million in what was West Germany. Germany also has the largest number of immigrants in Europe—around 9% of the population are foreign nationals, the largest proportion from Turkey. Many of these are former 'guest workers', who arrived in the 1970s and have chosen to settle. Others are refugees and asylum seekers who came at the end of the 1980s, including more than 2 million people of German ancestry.

From the 1950s, West Germany developed into Europe's most dynamic industrial nation. East Germany lagged far behind and the merger of the two economies has proved difficult and expensive. Since 1991, around 5% of GDP has been taken up annually by the costs of reunification, which include extending social benefits to the East, raising wages, and repairing extensive environmental damage. Even so, wide gaps remain. In early 2000, unemployment in the West was 8% but in the East was 17%.

Nevertheless, this remains a powerful industrial economy—the world's third largest after the USA and Japan. Its strength has been highly efficient manufacturing industry, which accounts for around one-quarter of GDP and four-fifths of exports of goods and services. The most important sectors are machinery, cars, and chemicals. Built around this is a large service sector. Agriculture employs few people but the country is still 75% self-sufficient in food.

The economy has been organized in a more coherent way than in other countries—built around the idea of the 'social market'. Rather than relying on the short-term vagaries of stock markets, investment has been based on long-term partnerships between banks and companies. There are also extensive cross-holdings of equities. Another feature has been co-operation between companies and the powerful trade unions. Though membership has been falling, one-third of workers still belong to trade unions and wages are settled annually in national rounds led by IG Metall, the union of 3.4 million engineering workers. In addition, workers are entitled to participate in management through works councils and have half the seats on the supervisory boards of the largest companies.

Germany also has one of the most generous welfare systems with high unemployment benefits and pensions. This comes at a cost, since total deductions shared between employers and workers now amount to more than 40% of pay. Employers argue that having to meet these costs is making the country increasingly uncompetitive. Hourly wage costs are one-third higher than in the USA or the UK. Another notable feature of the German economy and society is a concern for the environment. The country has intensive systems of recycling—around 700,000 jobs are linked with environmental protection.

Germany is one of the world's most dedicated recyclers

Germany is a federal state with fifteen states, or Länder (ten from the West, five from the East), plus the federal capital Berlin. Each Land has its own parliament and government responsible for such issues as policing and education. The state governments are also represented in the federal parliament's upper house, the Bundesrat. But most power rests in the 656-member lower house, the Bundestag. In 1994, the parliament elected Roman Herzog to the largely ceremonial function of president.

After 1949, most West German governments were coalitions and the tradition continues in the new Germany. The 1998 election was won by the Social Democratic Party (SPD), governing in alliance with the Green Party. This ended the sixteen-year rule of Helmut Kohl, leader of the centre-right Christian Democratic Union (CDU) and architect of German reunification. In a startling development in 2000, Kohl faced prosecution for party finance irregularities. In April 2000 the CDU leadership was taken by Angela Merke, who comes from the east, and is thus untainted by the activities of the party in the west.

The leader of the SPD was Oskar Lafontaine but the more popular Gerhard Schröder was chosen to be Chancellor (head of government). Lafontaine became finance minister but resigned after several clashes with Schröder. The post of foreign minister went to a leading green politician, Joschka Fischer.

The SPD (formerly Marxist) is further to the left than the CDU, and more protective of the welfare system, but in many respects their policies are similar—in particular their support for European integration.

Ghana

Heralded as one of Africa's economic successes, but now in trouble

Land area: *239,000 sq. km.*
Population: *18 million—urban 37%*
Capital city: *Accra, 1 million*
People: *Akan 44%, Moshi-Dagomba 16%, Ewe 13%, Ga 8%, other 9%*
Language: *English, Twi and other African languages*
Religion: *Indigenous beliefs 38%, Muslim 30%, Christian 24%, other 8%*
Government: *Republic*
Life expectancy: *60 years*
GNP per capita: *$PPP 1,610*
Currency: *Cedi*
Major exports: *Gold, cocoa, timber*

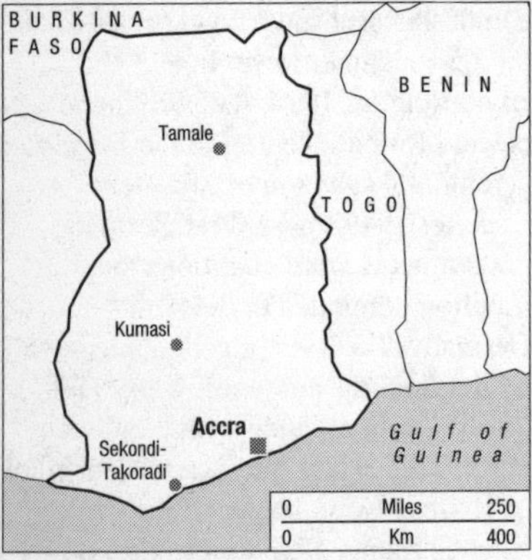

Apart from scattered hills and plateaux along the eastern and western borders, Ghana consists mostly of lowlands. These include a coastal plain that extends up to 80 kilometres inland and incorporates many lagoons and marshes. Almost two-thirds of thc country, however, consists of the basin of the Volta River, which now includes Lake Volta, which was formed by the Akosombo dam—the largest artificial lake in the world. There is a sharp climatic division between the dry north and the wetter and lusher south.

Ghana's population comprises dozens of ethnic groups of whom the largest are the Akan. By the standards of Sub-Saharan Africa, Ghana is relatively well off. Even so, around one-third of the population live below the poverty line—and poverty is generally more severe in the north. Less than half of Ghanaians have access to health services. Education services too came under pressure following budget cuts during the economic collapse of the 1970s and 1980s, and many parents cannot afford the fees introduced during the 1990s. The population has been growing rapidly—at around 3% per year, though this rate is expected to drop.

The majority of people still make their living from agriculture, which accounts for around 40% of GDP. The main food crops are maize, yams, and cassava, while the main cash crop, and for many years consistently the leading export earner, is cocoa. Cocoa is produced by more than 1.5 million peasant farmers and although production collapsed in the mid-1980s it has now bounced back—partly because the government has raised producer prices and farmers have been replacing their trees.

Even so, overall agricultural productivity has been falling, a consequence of low investment and the removal of subsidies on inputs such as fertilizers, which many farmers can no longer afford. Some are now reverting to subsistence production. Another important agricultural export is timber, though there are concerns about deforestation.

Ghana,whose colonial name was the 'Gold Coast', once again has gold as its leading export. Production rose by 40% in 1998. The main producer is the Ashanti Goldfields Corporation. Other important mining activities involve manganese and diamonds. Ghana also has a diverse collection of manufacturing industries, a legacy of earlier efforts at self-sufficiency.

In 1983, Ghana started to follow the market-led structural adjustment recipes of the IMF and the World Bank, selling off public enterprises and reducing protection for local manufacturers. Donors rewarded Ghana with considerable flows of aid. This stimulated entrepreneurial activity, particularly in financial services and trade, and imports flooded in, making Accra a much more stylish city. Tourists too started to arrive to visit Ghana's ecological reserves as well as its historical sites related to slavery. GDP growth over the 1990s averaged more than 4%. But development did not reach far into the rural areas, and the loans steadily piled up. By 1999, Ghana's total debt was equivalent to four years of export earnings and the economy was in steep decline.

Ghana has important historical slavery sites

Most of this activity has been presided over by Jerry Rawlings. He first entered the political scene in 1979 as 28-year-old Flight-Lieutenant Rawlings, leading a military coup that resulted in the murder of a number of senior figures. He briefly handed power over to a civilian administration but, dissatisfied with their performance, he returned in a second coup in 1981. His Provisional National Defence Council (PNDC) government opted for party-less government to be run by technocrats. Initially this had a strong socialist orientation but, following a crippling drought and economic recession, Rawlings turned sharply to the right into the embrace of the IMF and from 1983 embarked on the sustained programme of structural adjustment that donors have at times held up as a model of success.

Donors were less happy with Rawlings's dictatorial, if popular, rule. In 1992 he responded with a new constitution that allowed multi-party elections and he refashioned the PNDC as a political party—the National Democratic Congress (NDC). Rawlings won the 1992 presidential election, overcoming the candidate of the main opposition party, the business-oriented New Patriotic Party (NPP). The NPP alleged that this election had been rigged, so boycotted the legislative elections leaving the field to the NDC. In 1996 the NDC again proved victorious, though the NPP did gain one-third of the seats. Rawlings was re-elected president with 57% of the vote.

Ghana's constitution prevents Rawlings seeking a third term in 2000. His unofficial successor is vice-president John Atta Mills, but he may struggle to hold the NDC together. Another possibility is Rawlings's wife, Nana Konadu Agyeman. If the election goes to plan, Ghana would be the first African state in which an ex-military leader who was subsequently elected president departed peacefully and left the choice of his successor to the electorate.

Greece

The poorest member of the European Union, Greece is now mending fences with its old adversary, Turkey

Land area: *132,000 sq. km.*
Population: *11 million—urban 60%*
Capital city: *Athens, 3 million*
People: *Greek*
Language: *Greek*
Religion: *Greek Orthodox*
Government: *Republic*
Life expectancy: *78 years*
GNP per capita: *$PPP 13,010*
Currency: *Drachma*
Major exports: *Manufactures, food*

Most of Greece is mountainous. The mainland is dominated by the rugged Pindus Mountains, which extent from the northern border to the hand-shaped peninsula of the Peloponnese. The main lowland areas are the plains in the north-east along the Aegean coast. Greece's coastline is highly indented so the country is penetrated from all directions by the sea. Around one-fifth of the territory consists of 2,000 or more islands, the largest of which is Crete, to the south.

Officially, the population is almost entirely ethnic Greek, though it can also be considered a mixture of the many different groups that have arrived from neighbouring countries, including Turkey, Macedonia, Albania, and Bulgaria. Greeks may not be rich but have been relatively long-lived—thanks to a healthy diet.

Greece continues to be a country of emigration and immigration. Emigration was still continuing to richer countries of the EU in the 1990s, notably to Germany. In 1996, Greeks overseas sent home $3 billion in remittances. But many people are also arriving. The break-up of the Soviet Union encouraged more than 60,000 ethnic Greeks to move to Greece. There are also around 600,000 undocumented immigrants, mostly from Albania.

Greece is the poorest country in the EU, which it joined in 1981—though it has benefited considerably from EU subsidies. One-fifth of the population still work in agriculture, but only one-quarter of the land is cultivable, and since the soil is poor and there is not much rain, yields are often low. The coastal plains are used for the cultivation of major cereal crops and sugar beet as well as cash crops such as cotton and tobacco. Greece is also a major producer of olives, tomatoes, grapes, and other fruits.

Though Greece is bounded everywhere by the sea, its fishing industry is in poor shape, the result partly of an ageing fleet and over-fishing.

By European standards, industry is underdeveloped. The country has few minerals, apart from lignite, and its manufacturing tends to be small-scale.

Even so, wages have risen in recent decades and some of the simpler industries such as garments and textiles have migrated to poorer neighbouring countries.

Many of the larger industrial activities are controlled by the state, either owned directly or through state-owned banks—though this is as much a legacy of military centralization as of socialist government. So far the government has been slow to deal with the inefficient state-owned enterprises, such as Olympic Airways, since it has been reluctant to take on the public-sector unions.

Historically, one of the most successful industries has been shipping. Greece owns around one-sixth of the global fleet, typically bulk carriers, though most of these sail under other flags using foreign, and cheaper, crews.

Another important source of foreign exchange has been tourism—an industry that employs 9% of the labour force. With many historical sites, and spectacular scenery and beaches on its many islands, Greece often attracts more tourists than its total population. While these are welcome for the income they bring—$4 billion per year—the sheer numbers have been causing environmental damage.

Greece attracts more tourists than its population

The Greek economy has been struggling to keep up with the rest of the EU. But its democracy too has had some ground to make up. In 1967, after years of political instability and friction between the king, the government and the army, a coup installed a military junta. This ruled until 1974, when it backed a failed coup in Cyprus that resulted in a Turkish invasion, following which democracy was restored. In addition to elections there was also a referendum which confirmed that Greece would be a republic—the junta had declared this unilaterally in 1973.

Since 1974, Greece has been ruled by one of two parties: the conservative New Democracy Party (NDP), or the Panhellenic Socialist Movement (Pasok). The period 1989-90 saw a series of hung parliaments until the NDP, led by Constantine Mitsotakis, briefly took the reins and tried to balance the books. But the sacrifices proved unpalatable and early elections in 1993 were won by Pasok, led by Andreas Papandreou.

When the latter fell ill he was replaced in 1996 as prime minister by Costas Simitis. Pasok has steadily drifted towards the centre and Greece has achieved sufficient financial discipline to qualify for the European Monetary Union. Meanwhile the NDP, now led by Constantine Karamanlis, is in disarray.

Pasok won a third consecutive term in April 2000 although by a very narrow margin which gave the party only 158 of the 300 parliamentary seats.

Greece has often had difficult relationships with neighbouring countries, particularly Turkey with which it has had a long-running dispute over Cyprus and whose accession to the EU it had long opposed. But in 1999 there was an unexpected thaw in relations when both countries suffered serious earthquakes and each came to the other's aid.

Guadeloupe

An overseas department of France that occasionally agitates for independence

Land area: *2,000 sq. km.*
Population: *431,000*
Capital city: *Basse-Terre*
People: *Black or mixed race 90%, other 10%*
Language: *French*
Religion: *Roman Catholic*
Government: *Department of France*
Life expectancy: *77 years*
GNP per capita: *$PPP $9,200*
Currency: *French franc*
Major exports: *Sugar, bananas*

Guadeloupe comprises two volcanic islands in the Caribbean, Basse-Terre and Grande-Terre, that together form a butterfly shape, along with several smaller islands. The western wing, Basse-Terre is mountainous, with dense rainforests as well as mangrove swamps. It also has a smoking volcano, La Soufrière, though this has not erupted for thirty years, along with some spectacular waterfalls. Much of the island has now been designated a national park. Grande-Terre has lower hills and plains and is more suitable for agriculture.

The population is mostly black or of mixed race and speaks French, though many also use a creole dialect. The majority of the workforce are employed in the service sector, particularly in tourism. Most tourists come from the USA, many on brief visits from cruise ships, to enjoy the French colonial atmosphere of the largest town, Basse Terre, also known as Pointe-à-Pitre, or to head for the beaches, the rainforests, or the outer islands.

Agriculture is less significant nowadays and much of the country's food has to be imported from France. Historically, sugar was the major crop but efforts have been made to diversify into bananas and other fruits as well as aubergines and flowers. There is also some light industry, including rum manufacture.

Guadeloupe enjoys substantial subsidies from France—which help to offset high levels of unemployment. Since Guadeloupians are French citizens many young people take the opportunity to emigrate to France.

As an overseas department, Guadeloupe sends representatives to the French parliament—two senators, and four representatives in the National Assembly. But it also has its own elected general council and regional council.

During the 1960s and 1970s, there was some agitation for independence. The pro-independence movement organized strikes and demonstrations, but never managed to gain control of the local assemblies, and the French government continued to insist that Guadeloupe would remain part of France. Since then enthusiasm for independence seems to have waned.

The local assemblies have usually been dominated by centre and right-wing parties, though the left gained power during the 1980s. In the 1998 elections for the Regional Council the majority of seats went to the centre-right Rassemblement pour la république.

Guam

As a US military outpost, Guam has been hard hit by recent defence cuts

Land area: *1,000 sq. km.*
Population: *151,968—urban 38%*
Capital city: *Hagåtña/Agaña*
People: *Chamorro 47%, Filipino 25%, white 10%, Japanese and other Asian 18%*
Language: *English, Chamorro, Filipino*
Religion: *Roman Catholic*
Government: *Unincorporated territory of the USA*
Life expectancy: *77 years*
GNP per capita: *$PPP $19,000*
Currency: *US dollar*
Major exports: *Transhipments of oil products, construction materials, fish*

Guam is one of the Mariana Islands in the Pacific between Hawaii and the Philippines. The northern half of the island is a limestone coral plateau, much of which has been levelled to form airfields. The southern half has a range of volcanic hills. Around one-third of the territory is owned by the US military—and the country has suffered from much indiscriminate dumping of waste, either on the land or in the ocean.

The oldest inhabitants are the Chamorro people, who still make up around half the population. They have their own distinctive language and culture. But years of colonization, by Spain and then by the USA, have taken their cultural toll. Guam has, for example, the world's highest per capita consumption of Spam.

Many other people have arrived. In addition to more than 20,000 US military and other federal employees and their dependants, the bases have drawn immigrants from elsewhere in the Pacific, particularly the Philippines. In a few decades it seems likely that Filipinos could outnumber Chamorros. More recently, Guam has also been attracting illegal immigrants, some from China seeking political asylum.

Guam's military bases, mostly those of the navy, with around $10 billion-worth of infrastructure, are one of the mainstays of the economy. But military cutbacks are likely to see many defence-related jobs disappear. One of the first to close was a ship-repair operation. In 1999, the USA was still investing $100 million in upgrading some facilities, but the longer-term prospects are limited. The return of military land to the Guamanians is also raising many contentious political issues.

The second main source of income is tourism. More than 1 million visitors arrive each year, mostly from Asia and the Pacific. But efforts to extend visa-waiver systems in order to promote tourism, particularly from the Philippines, have been opposed by the US Immigration and Naturalization Service, which worries that Guam could offer a back door into the USA.

Guamanians are US citizens and send a delegate to the US House of Representatives with limited voting rights. In 1998, Democrat Robert Underwood was re-elected as the delegate. The 1998 elections for the local governor also re-elected a Democrat, Carl Gutierrez, though the legislative elections that year produced a Republican majority.

Guatemala

Guatemala endured thirty-six years of civil war. But the issues that led to the war remain unresolved

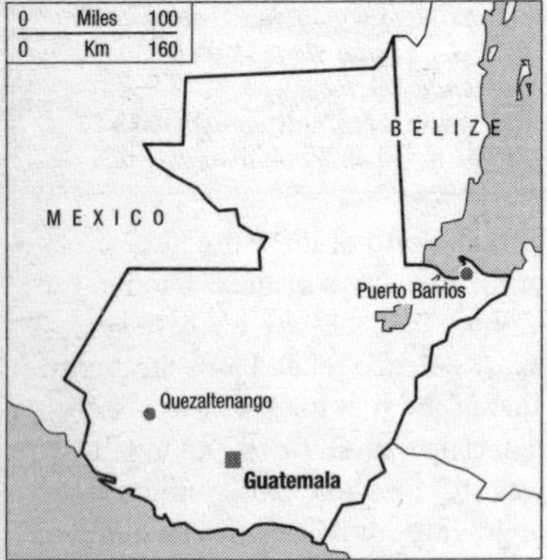

Land area: *109,000 sq. km.*
Population: *11 million—urban 40%*
Capital city: *Guatemala City, 1.2 million*
People: *Ladino 56%, Amerindian 44%*
Language: *Spanish. Amerindian*
Religion: *Roman Catholic, Protestant*
Government: *Republic*
Life expectancy: *64 years*
GNP per capita: *$PPP 4,070*
Currency: *Quetzal*
Major exports: *Coffee, sugar, bananas, cardamom*

Guatemala is one of the most picturesque countries in Central America. The northern, sparsely inhabited part juts out between Mexico and Belize. But around 60% of the population live either on the narrow Pacific coastal plain or in the mountainous areas of the south and west that are studded with spectacular lakes and volcanoes.

Guatemala's population distribution still reflects the legacy of the Spanish conquest. The invaders seized the most fertile soil on the plains and lower slopes, driving the Indian population up to the steeper, less valuable land—where their descendants more or less remain.

Today 60% of the population would consider themselves 'ladinos'—though the term is more social and cultural than racial: apart from Spanish descendants it also includes Amerindians who have adopted Spanish language and culture.

The other 40% of the population consist of 23 Mayan indigenous groups, whose women are particularly noticeable because of their unique and colourful form of dress. Most are Roman Catholics but Protestant evangelical groups have been making increasing inroads.

Around 60% of the population make their living from agriculture. But this covers vast disparities. Guatemala has probably the most unequal land distribution in Latin America. The most recent data refer to 1979, when 3% of farms had 65% of the land, and 88% of farms had only 16%, and since then the situation has probably deteriorated. The larger holdings mostly grow export crops such as sugar and bananas on the coastal plantations, while on the lower mountain slopes they grow coffee and cardamom. The poorest subsistence farmers concentrate on corn, rice, and beans, but as many as 650,000 have to make the annual pilgrimage to work on the plantations.

Manufacturing industry accounts for only 13% of employment, mostly concentrated around Guatemala City. Some efforts have been made to expand simple assembly work for export to the USA, with Korean-owned plants making T-shirts and underwear. But competition from Mexico has been stiff and many factories have closed.

Agriculture also accounts for around half of export earnings, led by coffee, sugar, and bananas. But poor prices in the 1990s encouraged diversification into such crops as mange-tout, fruit, and flowers. The production of staple crops, like corn and beans, has also fallen as a result of, among other things, cheap imports and the high cost of inputs.

The unequal distribution of resources and overt discrimination have kept the Mayan population poor.

Discrimination against Mayan Indians

Compared with the Ladinos, the Mayans' life expectancy is seventeen years less and their literacy rates are only half. The governing élite have made few efforts to redistribute income: only 3,000 of the nation's estimated 100,000 professionals pay income tax. In 1997, tax revenues were only 9% of GDP .

This inequality has been sustained by a long history of repression. For 39 years after a US-inspired coup in 1954, the country was dominated by the army and its right-wing supporters. Many of those on the left joined guerrilla groups that in 1982 came together as the Unidad Revolucionária Nacional Guatemalteca (URNG). From the early 1980s in particular, the government tried to eliminate this opposition with an onslaught on the countryside that wiped out 400 villages. Over the whole period this 'dirty war' is thought to have cost up to 100,000 lives and a further 40,000 'disappearances'.

Formal democracy was restored only in 1985, and in 1990 the government started negotiations with the URNG. International support for the process included awarding the 1992 Nobel Peace Prize to a leading Mayan woman activist, Rigoberta Menchú.

The peace agreement was signed in December 1996. This included constitutional amendments to rein in the military, to outlaw discrimination, and to allow use of Mayan languages in schools. But most of the programmes established in the accords are behind schedule, under-funded, and beset by political bickering.

At the time of the peace agreement, the presidency was in the hands of the right-wing Partido de Avanzada Nacional, headed by Alvaro Arzú. He made little headway in curbing the human rights abuses and in April 1998 a Roman Catholic bishop, Juan Geradi, was murdered after issuing a critical report on the army. Low world prices for bananas, coffee, and sugar, combined with the disastrous effects of Hurricane Mitch in 1998 and general economic mismanagement further disillusioned the voters.

In the December 1999 election, Arzú lost to Alfonso Portillo, the candidate of the opposition, and equally right-wing, party, the Frente Republicano Guatemalteco. The party that represented former guerrillas came a poor third. Portillo has promised to find the killer of Bishop Geradi, but for now there seems little prospect of that, or of Guatemala achieving a peaceful, stable society.

Guinea

Despite rich agricultural and mineral potential, this West African state has yet to make much economic progress

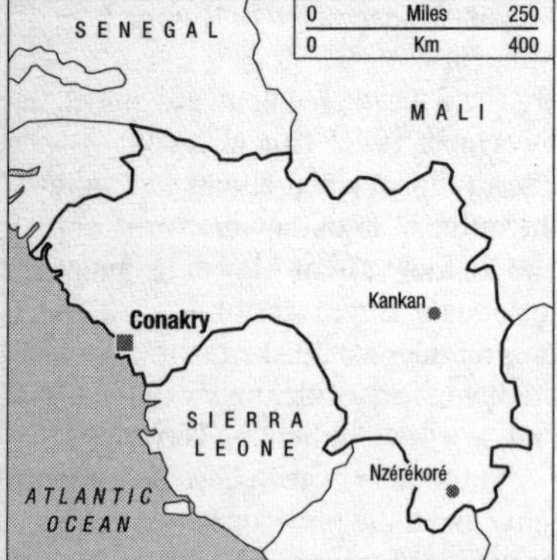

Land area: *246,000 sq. km.*
Population: *7 million—urban 31%*
Capital city: *Conakry, 1.1 million*
People: *Peuhl 40%, Malinke 30%, Soussou 20%, others 10%*
Language: *French, Sousou and others*
Religion: *Muslim 85%, Christian 8%, indigenous beliefs 7%*
Government: *Republic*
Life expectancy: *47 years*
GNP per capita: *$PPP 1,760*
Currency: *Guinean franc*
Major exports: *Bauxite, alumina, gold, coffee*

Moving in from the coast, Guinea has four main geographical regions. The coastal plain reaches around 50 kilometres inland, leading to the Fouta-Djallon Highlands which rise to more than 1,500 metres. Then there are the savannah plains of Upper Guinea which slope towards the Sahel in the north-east, and finally the forested highlands of the far south-east. Guinea is also the 'reservoir' of West Africa. The region's major rivers, the Senegal, the Gambia, and the Niger all have their origins in Guinea.

Ethnic divisions correspond to the four regions. The largest group are the Peuhl (also called the Fulani), who are mostly to be found in the Fouta-Djallon Highlands. Then there are the Malinke in Upper Guinea, the Soussou who occupy the coastal plain, and a number of smaller groups, many of whom can be found in the forested highlands. The local population was also swollen in the late 1990s by more than 700,000 refugees from fighting in neighbouring Liberia and Sierra Leone. In the 1980s, up to 2 million Guineans also fled the repressive regime in their own country and do not seem to have returned in significant numbers.

Their lack of enthusiasm reflects the country's persistently low achievements in human development. Around 40% of the population live below the poverty line. Life expectancy is short, health services are poor, and the literacy rate is still less than 40%. Ironically, for a country that has the sources of many major rivers, 45% of the population do not have access to drinking water.

Most people depend for survival on agriculture—the main food crops being rice, cassava, maize, plantains, and vegetables. Despite having much fertile agricultural land, only around 20% of the available land is cultivated. Most production is for subsistence, leaving a wide food gap that must be met with imports of rice.

With the help of international donors, the government has been struggling to increase food production and to diversify into cash crops such as coffee, cotton, and fruits. This has required extensive investment in infrastructure, particularly in road building.

Nevertheless, Guinea's fortunes still depend critically on bauxite. Guinea has 30% of global reserves—which are to be found both in the coastal region and in Upper Guinea. Guinea is the world's second largest producer. In the past, bauxite has been responsible for 90% of the country's exports and 70% of government revenue. These proportions have been falling in recent years as a result of falling world prices and inefficient production at the major smelter that converts part of the output to alumina (aluminium oxide). Much of the industry has been controlled by state-owned enterprises—though there has been greater foreign investment in the past few years, with the participation of companies from Russia, Ukraine, Iran, and Australia.

The world's second largest bauxite producer

Guinea also has significant exports of gold and diamonds. But mining has mostly been in the hands of smaller enterprises and the trade is largely clandestine. Only around 15% of diamond production is recorded. In addition, Guinea has extensive reserves of other minerals, particularly iron ore (6% of world reserves) that remain largely unexploited. And it has enormous hydroelectric potential.

Guinea's economic weaknesses and its over-centralized and corrupt bureaucracy are a legacy of the 26-year dictatorship of Sékou Touré. He led the country to independence in 1958 and his Marxist-tinged and ultimately repressive and isolated regime only ended with his death in 1984. At this point the army took over, led by Colonel Lansana Conté who embarked on limited economic reforms putting more emphasis on the free market.

Political reform had to wait until 1991 and a new 'fundamental law' that offered the potential for greater democracy. In 1993, Conté, as leader of his newly constituted Parti de l'unité et du progrès (PUP), won the presidential election, and in 1995 the PUP won the majority of seats in the National Assembly. The PUP's power base is mostly in the coastal areas but it is extending its influence in other regions—while opposition parties, grouped as the Co-ordinated Democratic Opposition, are more regionally confined.

In 1996, Conté withstood a coup attempt by officers protesting against poor working conditions and wages. The coup's failure helped sustain the regime. But probably more significant was the appointment as prime minister of a technocrat, Sydia Touré. This reassured international donors, and particularly the IMF, that the country was serious about structural reform.

In 1998, Conté beat four other candidates to win a second presidential term. Though he was never in much danger of losing, after the election Conté cracked down and started arresting opposition leaders—saying that security needed to be tightened because of the chaos in neighbouring Sierra Leone where Guinean soldiers are part of the peacekeeping force.

Guinea-Bissau

Guinea-Bissau in West Africa is probably the world's most indebted country, and has recently suffered a civil war

Land area: *36,000 sq. km.*
Population: *1.1 million—urban 22 %*
Capital city: *Bissau, 200,000*
People: *Balanta 30%, Fulani 20%, Manjaca 14%, Mandinga 13%, Papel 7%, other 16%*
Language: *Portuguese, Criolo, African languages*
Religion: *Indigenous beliefs 65%, Muslim 30%, Christian 5%*
Government: *Republic*
Life expectancy: *44 years*
GNP per capita: *$PPP 750*
Currency: *CFA Franc*
Major exports: *Cashew nuts*

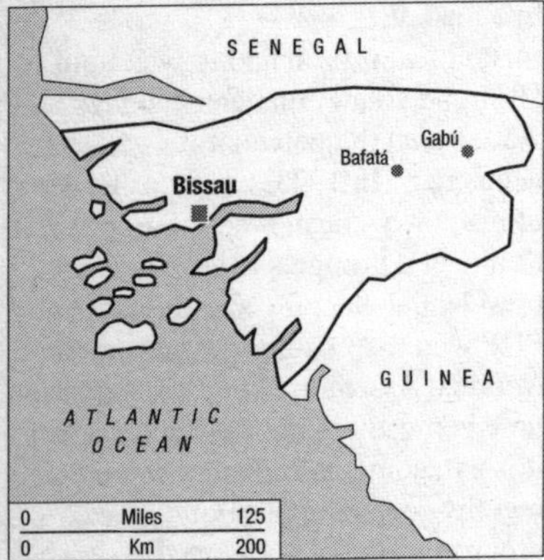

Guinea-Bissau is low-lying and monotonously flat. Much of the territory comprises coastal swamps, and daily tidal flows through the mangrove forests stretch up to 100 kilometres inland. Beyond the swamps and plains are dense forests leading in the north to broad savannah.

The country has a large number of ethnic groups, though around half the population are either Balanta or Fulani. Most follow traditional animist religions, but Islam has been making strong progress, particularly among the economic and political leadership.

Standards of human development are low and 87% of the population live below the poverty line. Life expectancy at 45 years is one of the lowest in the world. Only one-quarter of people have access to health services or to safe water and sanitation. The poor environment is also fertile territory for AIDS—around 10% of the population are thought to be HIV-positive.

Education standards are also very low. Years of economic crisis and structural adjustment have taken their toll on the school system, closing off many opportunities, particularly for women whose literacy rate is only around 14%.

Most economic life centres on agriculture, which represents more than 50% of GDP, more than 80% of employment, and more than 90% of exports. The staple food crop is rice, which is grown on one-third of arable land, along with millet, sorghum, cassava, and other root crops. But the country still has to import around 40% of its rice. In the interior, the Fulani and other groups raise cattle.

The main cash crop is cashew nuts, which provide most export income. Cashew nut trees can survive even on very poor land and require little or no cultivation. Production has been rising but Guinea-Bissau has earned less than it could from this. It has few facilities for processing, so most of the nuts are exported to India and then make their way to Europe where they are eaten as a cocktail snack. There are other cash crops such as groundnuts, and mangoes are another with export potential.

Fishing could also make a greater contribution. Fishing employs only 10% of the workforce but provides additional revenues as a result of licences sold to European fleets.

Confusing patterns of land holding

One of the obstacles to better agricultural performance is land tenure or, more precisely, deciding who owns what. Most food is produced by the 90,000 small villages, the tabancas. But there are also 1,200 larger farms, the poteiros, that are operated under state concessions. Unfortunately, many of these two types of holding overlap and it has proved difficult to resolve ownership.

Until around the mid-1980s, Guinea-Bissau's government attempted to develop along state-socialist lines. But recent decades have seen a decisive shift towards a market economy. This made the country more acceptable to international donors and since 1987 Guinea-Bissau has been engaged in World Bank-financed structural adjustment programmes that have involved large-scale privatization.

The country has also received many other forms of multilateral and bilateral aid, particularly from Portugal, the ex-colonial power. But not all aid has been well used and a combination of corruption and economic crisis led Guinea-Bissau deeply into debt—which by the end of 1996 was equivalent to more than three times the country's GDP.

In an effort to stabilize the economy, the government in 1996 took the unusual step of abandoning its currency, the peso, and entering the currency zone of the former French West African countries. Now Guinea-Bissau uses the CFA franc. This move promised more financial discipline but also required some unpopular tax changes that heightened political instability.

Guinea-Bissau became independent in 1974, at which point it was federated with Cape Verde. Between 1974 and 1999 the country was ruled by one party—the Partido Africano da Independência de Guiné e Cabo Verde (PAIGC). In 1980, the party leadership was seized by General João Bernardo Vieira in a bloodless coup. He broke the union with Cape Verde and from 1985 he steered the PAIGC away from state socialism and from the early 1990s opened the political system to other parties.

Faced with a divided opposition he won subsequent presidential elections in 1991 and the PAIGC won the 1994 parliamentary election.

By 1998, a combination of corruption, economic mismanagement, and public dissatisfaction with the political process was provoking widespread civil unrest. This exploded into civil war in mid-1998 with an army mutiny led by Brigadier Ansumane Mane. A peace accord was signed in November 1998 but did not hold, and in May 1999 Vieira was finally overthrown. Presidential and legislative elections were held in November 1999. These were won by the Partido para a Renovaçao Social (PRS), whose presidential candidate, Kumba Yala, convincingly defeated his PAIGC opponent.

Guyana

Guyana in South America remains split between its Indian and black communities

Guyana has a narrow coastal plain that soon leads into the dense tropical rainforests that cover more than 80% of the territory—though there are mountains in the west along the borders with Venezuela and Brazil.

The country's ethnic mix reflects its colonial history. Most of today's Guyanese, concentrated along the coast, are descendants of slaves from Africa and subsequent indentured labourers from India who came to work on coastal sugar cane plantations. The surviving Amerindian population are generally now found only in scattered communities along river banks in the forests.

Guyana, with a relatively sparse population, still has good potential for agricultural development. And in recent years output has increased. Sugar remains the main crop and, following investment in the 1990s, the industry has been reinvigorated. Rice too has seen record crops in response to demands from new export markets. As yet, the country's forests have been relatively under-exploited but the arrival of several South-East Asian logging companies should change that—and raise fears of deforestation.

Guyana also has important mineral deposits. The opening of the Omai gold mine in 1993, jointly owned by two Canadian companies, led to a rapid increase in production. Bauxite from two government-owned enterprises used to be a leading export but high production costs have reduced their competitiveness.

Politics in Guyana has usually divided sharply along racial lines. The two main parties are the People's Progressive Party (PPP), which represents the Indo-Guyanese, and the People's National Congress (PNC), which represents the Afro-Guyanese. Elections have typically been bitterly contested affairs marked by violence and accusations of fraud; 1997 was no different. The majority of seats in the single-chamber parliament went to a coalition formed by the PPP and CIVIC, a small party formed by professionals. The PPP leader Janet Jagan, widow of its former leader Cheddi Jagan who died in 1997, became president (elected by the National Assembly). CIVIC leader, Samuel Hinds became prime minister.

Though an investigation found no evidence of fraud, PNC leader Desmond Hoyte refused to recognize the government, provoking yet more riots. In 1999, Mrs Jagan resigned due to ill health, to be replaced by Bharrat Jagdeo.

Land area: *215,000 sq. km.*
Population: *857,000—urban 36%*
Capital city: *Georgetown, 151,000*
People: *East Indian 49%, black 32%, mixed 12%, Amerindian 6%*
Language: *English, Amerindian languages*
Religion: *Christian 57%, Hindu 33%, Muslim 9%, other 1%*
Government: *Republic*
Life expectancy: *64 years*
GNP per capita: *$PPP 2,680*
Currency: *Guyanese dollar*
Major exports: *Sugar, gold, bauxite, rice, shrimp, molasses*

Haiti

The poorest country in the Americas—decades of violence have pushed Haitians even deeper into poverty

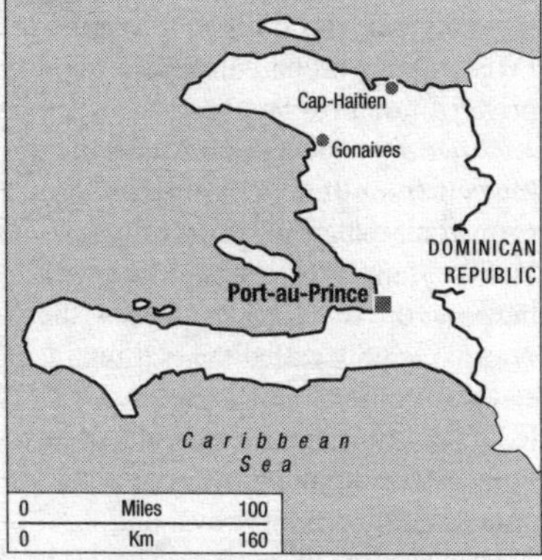

Land area: *28,000 sq. km.*
Population: *8 million—urban 34%*
Capital city: *Port-au-Prince, 1.4 million*
People: *Black 95%, mulatto plus white 5%*
Language: *French, creole*
Religion: *Roman Catholic 80% Protestant 16%, other 4% (also voodoo)*
Government: *Republic*
Life expectancy: *54 years*
GNP per capita: *$PPP 1,250*
Currency: *Gourde*
Major exports: *Coffee*

Haiti occupies the western one-third of the island of Hispaniola, the rest of which is the Dominican Republic. The territory consists of mountain ranges interspersed with fertile lowlands. Around half takes the form of two peninsulas to the north and south of the Golfe de la Gonâve, within which there are a number of offshore islands.

Decades of plunder by the dictatorial Duvalier family, followed by years of violent political turmoil, have reduced an already poor population to destitution and even starvation. Average income is now less than one-quarter of that in the Dominican Republic. Around one-third of children are malnourished, 60% of the population lack access to safe water, and more than half are illiterate. There is scarcely any tax revenue and social services are weak or non-existent.

Unsurprisingly, many Haitians are driven to migrate—either across the border to work on the sugar plantations of the Dominican Republic, where up to 800,000 Haitians are now thought to live, or to the USA; around 300,000 live in New York. In 1998, their remittances were around $1 billion—one of the country's main sources of income.

Two-thirds of the population struggle to make a living from agriculture. Much of this is subsistence farming on tiny plots growing maize, sorghum, millet, and beans. The better, irrigated land is also used to grow rice and beans for sale in the urban areas. The main cash crop is coffee, whose production has revived somewhat after years of upheaval and trade embargoes. Sugar used to be an important export earner but falling prices and foreign competition have discouraged production.

Agriculture in Haiti has also suffered from environmental degradation. Over-exploitation of the soil has been compounded by erosion resulting from deforestation. Most people rely on wood for fuel and have steadily stripped the hillsides of trees—only around 2% of the land is now forested.

In the early 1980s, there was some

prospect of industrial development in two free-trade zones near Port-au-Prince, but the fighting and the trade embargo drove most companies away. That leaves the majority out of work. Unemployment in 1999 was around 60% and many people were relying for survival on feeding programmes and other support from international aid agencies.

The country's current troubles are the persistent legacy of the years of dictatorship. From 1957 to his death in 1971, 'Papa Doc' Duvalier ruled through fear and repression, supported by a vicious armed gang, the Tontons Macoutes—whilst draining the country of its meagre resources. His son Jean Claude, 'Baby Doc', continued in the same fashion until national and international pressure ousted him in 1986. Several years of upheaval ensued until 1990, when a fiery Catholic priest, Jean-Bertrand Aristide, heading a grass-roots movement called Lavalas ('avalanche'), became president in February 1991 following an internationally supervised election. However, his radical policies favouring the poor so upset the army and the business community that he was ousted that September in a military coup by General Raul Cédras.

The arrival of Aristide

The coup in turn outraged the international community. First the Organization of American States and later the UN applied sanctions on trade and travel in an attempt to force Aristide's return. Ultimately, it took the threat of a US invasion to make Cédras withdraw—and 20,000 US troops did arrive to supervise the restoration of democracy and Aristide's return.

Constitutionally, Aristide was not eligible to stand in the 1991 elections. In his place the Lavalas candidate, duly elected, was René Préval who had previously been prime minister. His appointee as prime minister was Rosny Smarth, who, under pressure from donors, was obliged to impose IMF-style spending cuts and privatization programmes.

Aristide made a point of distancing himself from these measures and formed a breakaway party called Fanmi ('family') Lavalas. Struggles between the two Lavalas parties (the original is now called the National Lavalas Political Organization, OPL) led to disputes over Senate elections. Smarth, feeling his position was being undermined by both Préval and Aristide, resigned in 1996. This and several postponed elections left the country without a functioning government, obliging several donors to cut back their aid programmes.

Elections were eventually held in April 2000 giving Aristide's Lavalas 16 of the 17 seats in the Senate and a majority in the lower house, as well as most of the mayoral positions contested. The election was marred by irregularities but not sufficiently to have the results disallowed. Aristide looks set to return as president. The opposition warns of an electoral dictatorship.

Through all the political bickering, the people of Haiti have to struggle on. Haiti is still riddled with corruption and violence. The army was disbanded in 1994. The UN-trained civil police force is as likely to collaborate with the drug runners as with the system of justice.

Honduras

In 1998 Honduras was devastated by Hurricane Mitch. Reconstruction continues

Land area: *112,000 sq. km.*
Population: *6 million—urban 48%*
Capital city: *Tegucigalpa, 800,000*
People: *Mestizo 90%, Amerindian 7%, black 2%, white 1%*
Language: *Spanish, Amerindian dialects*
Religion: *Roman Catholic 97%, Protestant 3%*
Government: *Republic*
Life expectancy: *69 years*
GNP per capita: *$PPP 2,140*
Currency: *Lempira*
Major exports: *Coffee, bananas*

Honduras occupies the centre of the Central American isthmus. Most of the land is mountainous—around three-quarters has slopes of 20 degrees or more. Lowland areas are confined to the narrow coastal strips and to the river valleys.

The majority of Hondurans are of mixed Indian-European extraction. There are some Indians who live mostly along the Guatemalan border and on the Caribbean coast there are groups of Garifuna, who are descendants of the Carib Indians and black Africans.

More than half of Hondurans live below the poverty line and the income distribution is very skewed: the top 10% of the population get 42% of the income, while the bottom 10% get only 1%. The rural population in particular has poor standards of education and health and there are increasing problems of TB and malaria. City dwellers fare little better. They are concentrated in the capital, Tegucigalpa, and in the northern commercial capital, San Pedro Sula. The latter, for reasons as yet unclear, has also become an epicentre for the AIDS epidemic in Latin America. In 1997, WHO estimated at least 43,000 people to be HIV-positive.

Poor enough already, in October 1998 Hondurans were on the receiving end of Hurricane Mitch. The ensuing floods and mudslides killed more than 5,000 people and drove more than a quarter of a million people from their homes, causing damage worth around $5 billion.

Agriculture employs around one-third of the workforce though only 14% of the total land area is suitable for arable farming. Half the population are in the rural areas struggling to make a living, cultivating corn and beans on the steep slopes. Agriculture is also responsible for more than half of export earnings. Nowadays the leading export crop is coffee, which is produced by around 40,000 independent producers.

The other main export crops are grown in the lowland areas which have the best and most fertile land. The Caribbean coast in particular has one of the world's best climates for bananas.

Since the beginning of this century, the Honduran banana industry has been dominated by two corporations which are subsidiaries of US multinationals: Standard Fruit (selling under the Dole brand name) and United Fruit (Chiquita). These companies have had a powerful influence on commercial and political life. They employ around 15% of the workforce. Hurricane Mitch destroyed about 70% of the banana plantations but by the end of 2000 around 90% of these will probably have been replaced. Honduras should benefit from the World Trade Organization's controversial ruling that the EU should liberalize its banana market.

Recent developments in shrimp farming have also offered new export markets along with lobsters, most of which come from 5,000 Miskito Indian divers who risk their lives for the catch.

Perilous diving for lobsters

Land distribution remains a critical issue. Pressure from peasant farmers in the 1960s and 1970s resulted in some land reform. In 1992, however, an Agrarian Modernization Law removed most of the grounds for automatic confiscation—hoping instead to redistribute through the market.

In the urban areas, one of the most important new sources of employment has been the 'maquila' factories which assemble goods for export. Around 80,000 people work in a number of zones around San Pedro Sula, chiefly in garment manufacture using imported US cloth. The maquila output has been growing strongly and sales of around $2 billion have made this the leading source of foreign exchange.

Honduras has many of the same contrasts between rich and poor as its neighbours, but somehow it managed to escape the civil wars that devastated other countries in Central America. Nevertheless, it was still deeply involved and heavily militarized, since the country offered military bases both for the 'contra' fighters from Nicaragua and also for the US forces—for which it was rewarded generously with military aid.

The military have also had a major influence on politics, though this has diminished in recent years and there are fewer abuses of human rights. A more worrying security threat comes from the drug cartels who use Honduras as a transit point.

Politics in Honduras has long been a two-party struggle between liberals and conservatives—strongly influenced by US commercial and political interests. The centre-right Liberal Party, headed by Carlos Flores Facussé, won the 1997 presidential elections. Facussé vowed to reform the Honduran economy and to take a firm line with the military—and in 1999 he did indeed dismiss a number of army officers. But the reforms have not been very extensive, and many officers have yet to be prosecuted for human rights violations committed in the 1980s.

The government has been criticized for the slow pace of post-hurricane reconstruction, and Honduras has also been accused by an NGO, Transparency International, of being, after Paraguay, the second most corrupt country in Latin America.

Hungary

Hungary will probably be one of the first former-communist countries to join the European Union

Land area: *93,000 sq. km.*
Population: *10 million—urban 66%*
Capital city: *Budapest, 1.9 million*
People: *Hungarian 90%, Romany 4%, German 3%, Serb 2%, other 1%*
Language: *Hungarian*
Religion: *Roman Catholic 68%, Protestant 25%, Atheist and other 7%*
Government: *Republic*
Life expectancy: *71 years*
GNP per capita: *$PPP 7,200*
Currency: *Forint*
Major exports: *Machinery, manufactured goods*

Hungary is divided into roughly two halves by the Danube, which cuts through the country from north to south. The area to the west is called Transdanubia. The land is predominantly flat but has two higher areas: the uplands of Transdanubia in the south-west and the loftier Northern Mountains along the border with Slovakia. Hungary's plains also come in two main parts. In the north-west of Transdanubia is the Little Hungarian Plain. To the east of the Danube is the Great Hungarian Plain, which accounts for more than half the country.

Most of Hungary's people are related to Finns and Estonians and are ethnically distinct from their Slavic neighbours. The most significant minority population are half a million or so Romanies, or gypsies, who are among the country's poorest people.

Most Hungarians suffered a steep drop in living standards after 1990 and by 1994 around one-quarter of the population were living in poverty. Education standards are high, but health is worse than might be expected: middle-aged men tend to have particularly poor health, due to bad diet, smoking, and high alcohol consumption; by 1998 their life expectancy was less than it had been in 1970.

Around one-quarter of ethnic Hungarians live outside Hungary. As a result of the historical redrawing of boundaries there are around 2 million in Romania, half a million in Slovakia, and many others in Serbia and Ukraine. This has frequently been a source of friction: Hungary has protested to Slovakia in particular about discrimination against Hungarians, though Hungary tends to have better relations with Romania.

Industry employs around one-quarter of the workforce and their output of machinery, other equipment, and chemicals accounts for most exports. Production slumped when markets in Eastern Europe collapsed, but thanks to extensive foreign investment these have now been replaced by sales to Germany and Austria. Hungary produces around 1 million of Audi's engines, for example, and around 70% of all Hungary's exports go to the EU.

Even in the communist era, Hungary had been creating elements of a market economy. Many of its state enterprises already operated autonomously and the government carried out a fairly effective privatization programme: by 1998 the private sector was responsible for more than 80% of GDP.

With fertile soils and a helpful climate, Hungary can grow a wide range of crops. And though agriculture accounts for a rapidly falling proportion of its GDP and employs less than one-tenth of its workforce, the country is generally self-sufficient in food. The government has converted collective farms to co-operatives but there are still many state farms.

Foreign investment is concentrated in Budapest

Workers leaving agriculture and industry have mostly been absorbed into a mushrooming service sector which generates around two-thirds of GDP. One-third of economic activity is now thought to be in the informal sector. Unemployment is a persistent problem: in 1999 the average was 10%, but much higher in northern regions.

Over the last decade the political scene has seen regular swings between left and right. By 1989, the Communist Party had itself become a leading advocate of reform. Renamed the Hungarian Socialist Party (HSP), it had brought together the more liberal intellectuals, social democrats, and trade unions. Even so, it lost the 1990 election to the right-wing Hungarian Democratic Forum, which formed a coalition with two other conservative parties.

In the 1994 election, the socialists came out ahead. Led by Prime Minister Gyula Horn, they entered into an alliance with a smaller liberal party. But faced with an economic crisis they were forced to make cuts in welfare spending. And although foreign investment was creating new wealth the benefits were spread unevenly—concentrated around Budapest, leaving much of the east of the country behind. Corruption was also an issue, both within the government and the wider economy—along with rising levels of crime.

In the 1998 elections, the voters rejected the socialists. But this time they chose a different alternative—Fidesz. This party started life in 1988 as a liberal student organization but now had a populist conservative stance. The prime minister is Viktor Orban, leading a coalition that includes the right-wing Smallholders Party, which appeals to older rural voters.

In 1998, Hungary started negotiations to join the EU and with a well developed and liberal economic system will probably be one of the first countries to qualify. However, Hungarians seem to be wary of encroachment on sovereignty. Oban, for example, was disturbed at the EU countries' reaction to the rise of the Freedom Party in neighbouring Austria. In 1999 Hungary joined NATO—just before that alliance started bombing another neighbour, Yugoslavia.

Iceland

A rich country, but over-dependent on fish

Land area: *103,000 sq. km.*
Population: *274,000—urban 92%*
Capital city: *Reykjavik, 107,000*
People: *Icelandic*
Language: *Icelandic*
Religion: *Evangelical Lutheran*
Government: *Republic*
Life expectancy: *79 years*
GNP per capita: *$PPP 22,830*
Currency: *Krona*
Major exports: *Fish, aluminium*

Despite its proximity to the Arctic Circle, the climate in most of Iceland is relatively mild. The landscape varies from Mount Hvannadals at 2,119 metres, which is on the edge of a vast glacier, through grassy lowlands to a complex coastline indented with fjords. Iceland is one of the most geologically active places on earth, and has regular minor earthquakes, numerous active volcanoes, and bubbling hot springs.

The country's isolated position has sustained a very homogenous population, but they are far from insular. In addition to Icelandic, most speak English, and education standards are high: Iceland publishes more books per person than any other country and its people are enthusiastic users of the internet. They are also among the richest people in the world and have a good system of welfare.

Much of the wealth has been based on fish. The fishing industry still employs around 10% of the workforce and accounts for three-quarters of exports. The main catches are of cod and capelin, though over-fishing has required the introduction of quotas. In 1975 Iceland imposed a 200-mile fishing zone—provoking the 'Cod War' with the UK—and since it also takes 15% of its catch from distant waters it frequently has disputes with other fishing nations.

Iceland's geological activity is also a major resource, providing geothermal energy that heats most urban homes. The fractured landscape also has numerous steeply falling rivers that have huge hydroelectric potential. This is already being exploited by US and Swiss-owned companies for smelting aluminium and, with a cable to Scotland, Iceland could export electricity.

Iceland has one of the world's oldest parliaments, the Althing. Since independence from Denmark in 1944, the system of proportional representation has never given one party an absolute majority and politics has usually been consensual. In 1980 Vigdís Finnbogadóttir became the world's first elected woman president—though this is a largely ceremonial role; she was replaced in 1996 by Ragnar Grimsson.

The 1999 Althing elections gave the most seats to the conservative Independence Party, and returned David Oddsson as prime minister in coalition with the agrarian-based Progressive Party. The new government has continued with economic liberalization. Ever-protective of its fishing industry, Iceland is unlikely to join the EU, but still has strong trading links with many European countries.

India

The world's largest democracy has a rich and diverse culture, but its bureaucracy and rigid social structure continue to hamper its development

Land area: *3,288,000 sq. km.*
Population: *980 million—urban 28%*
Capital city: *New Delhi, 10 million*
People: *Indo-Aryan 72%, Dravidian 25%, Mongoloid and other 3%*
Language: *Hindi 30%, plus 14 other official languages and English*
Religion: *Hindu 80%, Muslim 14%, Christian 2%, Sikh 2%, other 2%*
Government: *Federal republic*
Life expectancy: *63 years*
GNP per capita: *$PPP 1,700*
Currency: *Rupee*
Major exports: *Garments, gems and jewellery, cotton textiles, cereals*

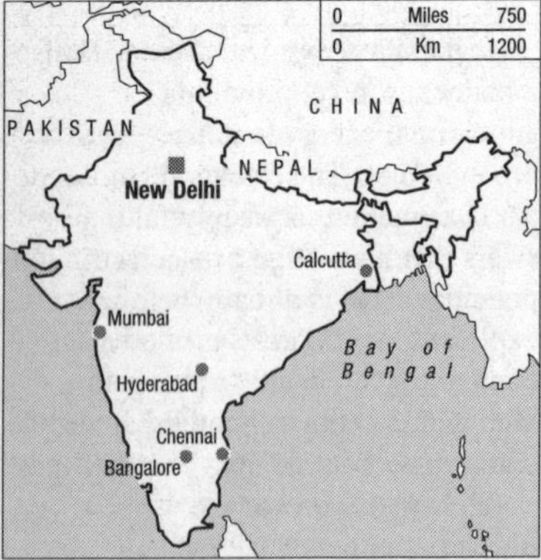

India's vast territory can be divided into three main regions from north to south. The far north and north-east of India cover part of the Himalayas including Kanchenjunga, the world's third-highest mountain. To the south, these mountains descend to the second region, a broad northern plain formed by the deposits of a number of major river systems, the most important of which is the Ganges, which emerges from the southern slopes of the Himalayas, flowing slowly south-east across the plain before spreading out into a broad delta in the Bay of Bengal.

To the west, the plain becomes a desert that extends into Pakistan. To the east, beyond the Ganges delta, India's territory circles round that of Bangladesh. The third main region, to the south of the plain beyond the Narmada River, is the Deccan plateau, a triangular region of low hills and extensive valleys, bounded along the coasts by two mountain systems: the eastern and western Ghats.

India has one of the world's most diverse populations, which can be subdivided in many different ways. The broadest distinction is in terms of religion. India's constitution declares it to be a secular state, but religious intolerance, known here as 'communalism', is never far below the surface. Hindus now account for around 80% of the population and Muslims 14%, and there has always been tension between the two. The other main source of friction has been with the Sikh community concentrated in the northern state of Punjab. More recently Christians too have come under attack.

Beyond religious divisions, India is also a source of vast cultural and linguistic diversity. The national language, Hindi, is widely spoken in the north but elsewhere it is displaced by dozens of other languages, from Malayalam to Tamil to Bengali, many of which use different scripts.

Another way of dividing India is

by caste—a hereditary social system that has Brahmins at the top and the 'untouchables', who perform the most menial social tasks, at the bottom. The latter, who are now referred to as 'scheduled castes', have specific allocations or 'reservations' of government jobs and parliamentary seats. Similar positive discrimination is exercised in favour of 'scheduled tribes'—another, smaller disadvantaged group of tribal communities.

In terms of average income, India is still very poor. But the population is so large that the top 10% of the population would on its own constitute one of the world's largest industrial nations. India also has an extraordinary pool of engineers and other highly educated people, though seeing limited opportunities at home many choose to emigrate.

Most people are not so lucky. Half the population are illiterate and 70% lack access to basic sanitation facilities. Around half the population live below the poverty line, but there are striking regional contrasts. Thus, one of the wealthier states, Punjab, has a per capita income twice that of West Bengal. And the state of Kerala, which is notable for its many enlightened social policies, has a literacy rate of 90%.

India has striking regional contrasts

In India it is also important to consider gender distinctions. In most states women fare worse than men. Two-thirds of women are illiterate, and women's health and nutrition are frequently neglected—more than 80% of pregnant women suffer from anaemia.

Three-quarters of India's people are still to be found in the rural areas and rely on agriculture for survival. Land is scarce. By the mid-1980s, the average farm size was down to 1.7 hectares and today one-third of rural households have no land at all. Despite the shortage of land, India's food production has, thanks to the 'Green Revolution', largely kept pace with population growth. India's self-sufficiency in food only means, however, that it grows enough to meet effective market demand. Millions still go hungry because they cannot afford to buy the food. More than 60 million Indian children are malnourished.

While this remains primarily an agricultural country, its size also establishes India as one of the world's major industrial powers. For the first forty years after independence, industrial policy was based on building up heavy industry—often with Soviet aid—combined with private production of consumer goods which were protected from foreign competition by high tariffs. At the same time, entrepreneurs had to fight their ways through thickets of regulations and licences and negotiate with often corrupt officials.

All this began to change from 1991 when the finance minister, Manmohan Singh, took the first steps, by cutting tariffs, liberalizing imports, and encouraging foreign investment. Liberalization has a long way to go. The state still employs around 70% of formal-sector workers who are deeply resistant to change. But India is now much more open to the outside world. And economic growth, which between 1960 and 1990 had averaged only 4% per year (known as the 'Hindu rate of growth'), in the late 1990s was averaging around 6%.

All industries, including textiles, steel and petrochemicals, have been affected by liberalization, but some of the most visible changes have been in areas such as cars and other consumer goods. There has also been a boom in consumer electronics and computers. The latter can take advantage of India's large pool of computer programmers, especially in Bangalore, India's 'cybercity', most of whose work is now exported. Many of these people are also being tempted to work overseas.

India has become a nursery for software talent

These developments have been transforming the face of India's cities. TV programming, long confined to the dull output of the state, has now been opened up to a multitude of satellite channels. Life in the rural areas is slower to change. Villagers may have satellite TV but little prospect of buying the wares on offer.

India can rightly be proud of having maintained a democratic government for almost the entire period since independence. This is based on a federal constitution. Each of the states has its own chief minister and Regional Assembly. In the past, with a centrally planned economy, and little finance of their own, the states have had relatively little power. Nevertheless, Kerala and West Bengal have had communist governments that have been able to pursue more distinctive policies of income redistribution.

India's federal government for most of the first fifty years was the domain of the Congress Party, which was led for most of that period by the Nehru dynasty, first by the leader of the independence struggle, Jawaharlal Nehru, later by his daughter Indira Gandhi (assassinated in 1984 by Sikh extremists), and then by her son Rajiv (assassinated in 1991 by a Tamil extremist).

Congress's almost uninterrupted rule ended with the election in 1996 that gave the majority of seats to the right-wing Hindu nationalist Bharatiya Janata Party (BJP). The BJP briefly led a coalition government until replaced by a diverse United Front coalition that included communists and regional parties. In 1997, the United Front government collapsed when the Congress Party withdrew its tacit support. The ensuing election in 1998 again resulted in a BJP-led coalition with Atal Behari Vajpayee back as Prime Minister.

The BJP has also toned down some of the shriller Hindu rhetoric, but on the other hand it has further chilled the traditionally frosty relations with the old enemy, Pakistan. In May 1998, India carried out five nuclear tests—provoking similar tests in Pakistan. And in June 1999 the two came perilously close to all-out war following a Pakistani incursion in the disputed territory of Kashmir. This eventually resulted in a Pakistani withdrawal.

This victory helped Vajpayee in the election in October 1999, which the BJP fought as the leader of a 24-party National Democratic Alliance. This alliance gained a comfortable majority, and one that did not leave Vajpayee so vulnerable to threats from smaller regionally based parties.

Indonesia

Decades of enforced stability have given way to massive uncertainty—and possible disintegration

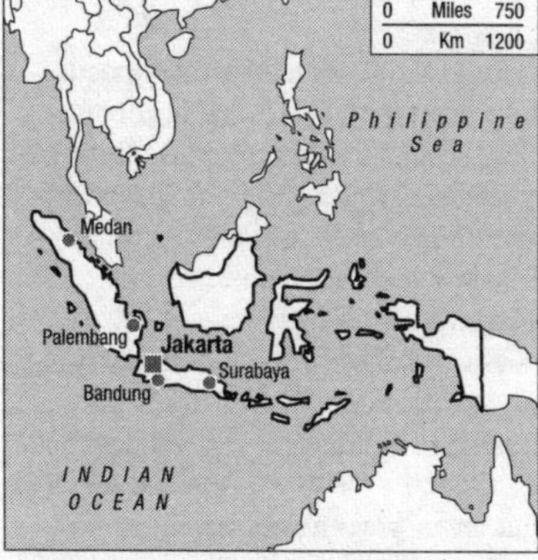

Land area: *1,905,000 sq. km.*
Population: *204 million—urban 28%*
Capital city: *Jakarta, 8.2 million*
People: *Javanese 45%, Sundanese 14%, Madurese 8%, coastal Malays 7%, other 26%*
Language: *Bahasa Indonesia, English, Dutch, local dialects*
Religion: *Muslim 88%, Protestant 5%, Roman Catholic 3%, Hindu 2%, Buddhist 1%, other 1%*
Government: *Republic*
Life expectancy: *65 years*
GNP per capita: *$PPP 2,790*
Currency: *Rupiah*
Major exports: *Oil, gas, plywood, garments, rubber*

Indonesia is one of the world's largest and geographically most dispersed countries, consisting of more than 17,000 islands. Of the southern chain of islands, the largest are, from west to east: Sumatra, Java, Bali, Lombok, Sumbawa, and Flores.

To the north of this chain is the island of Borneo, the southern part of which is the Indonesian state of Kalimantan. To the east of Borneo is the island of Sulawesi, and furthest east is New Guinea, the western half of which is the Indonesian state of West Papua. Most of these islands have volcanic mountains covered in dense tropical rainforests that descend to often swampy coastal plains.

Indonesia's people are as diverse as its topography. By some counts, there are more than 300 ethnic groups with almost as many languages. Many of these groups are related and most are of Malay origin. The largest are the Javanese, who live on the centre and east of Java—the western portion of which is occupied by the Sundanese.

Other large groups are the Madurese and the coastal Malays. The many smaller groups include tribal peoples, such as the Dayak, who inhabit the interior of Kalimantan, and people of Melanesian descent in West Papua. In addition, Indonesia also has 8 million people of Chinese origin who live mostly in the cities and allegedly control more than half the economy.

Despite the large land area, Indonesia's population is fairly concentrated. Half the islands are uninhabited and around two-thirds of the population live on Java, Madura, and Bali. The majority of people profess to be Muslim, though religion has not so far been a dominant force in political life. The official language is Bahasa Indonesia, which is based on Malay. Only around 10% of people use this as their first language; most have it as their second.

Faced with a fast-growing population, the government in the

1970s and 1980s instituted a programme of family planning so by early 1997, the annual growth rate was only 1.6%. A more controversial demographic initiative has been the 'transmigration' programme which has moved people from densely settled areas like Java—which has around 60% of the population—to other islands. In 1997 more than 80,000 families were resettled. At the same time, there has also been extensive labour migration—particularly to Malaysia, where over 1 million Indonesians work on plantations.

More than half the population still make their living from agriculture. Only about one-tenth of the country is suitable for agriculture, but the rich volcanic soil on the major islands is very fertile. Farmers here, most of whom are small-holders, primarily grow rice in the lower areas, and fruit, vegetables, tobacco, or coffee on the higher slopes. By the mid-1980s, with heavy use of 'green revolution' techniques, they had made the country self-sufficient in rice, though imports have now resumed. The land on the outer islands is less fertile and is primarily used for tree crops such as oil-palm, rubber, and coconuts, as well as cocoa and coffee.

Another important source of rural income is forestry. Forests cover around 60% of the land area and the timber industry has grown rapidly, mostly based on hardwoods such as teak and ebony. The government has become increasingly concerned about deforestation and has banned the export of logs, though Indonesia is still the world's largest exporter of plywood. Another source of deforestation has been forest fires—a result of slash-and-burn cultivation as well as companies clearing land for plantations. These fires are usually doused by the monsoon rains, but in drought years they can spread out of control, sending a vast pall of smog across neighbouring countries.

Choking forest fires

Indonesia's rich mineral deposits have been a major source of income. State companies exploit these through production-sharing agreements with foreign investors. Among the major minerals are tin, bauxite, copper, nickel, gold, and silver.

But the most important mineral is oil. Proven reserves in 1996 were around 10 billion barrels. Oil accounts for around 12% of exports and one-quarter of government revenue and is controlled by the state company Pertamina which has production-sharing agreements with transnational oil companies. Nevertheless, oil output has been fairly low and without more investment Indonesia could become a net importer.

Indonesia has also developed a highly diversified manufacturing sector. This includes iron and steel, aluminium smelting, oil refining, cement, and, more recently, pulp and paper production. Manufacturing for export has concentrated more on labour-intensive items such as garments and footwear. Indonesia has also had ambitions to move into higher technology areas such as cars, aircraft, and telecommunications.

Indonesia's political system has generally been authoritarian with a strong military influence. Between 1950 and 1967, following independence from the Dutch, the country was controlled by President Sukarno. During the mid-1960s his army chief, Mohamed Suharto, successfully suppressed an allegedly communist coup—and followed up with a slaughter of suspected communists and others that cost up to 1 million lives. In 1967, Sukarno was removed from office, and in 1968 Suharto was elected president. Backed by his political group, Golkar, Suharto was subsequently re-elected unopposed for six further terms.

Suharto reinvigorated the economy, initiating what he called the 'New Order', and drawing in large amounts of foreign capital. Economic growth averaged 6% annually between 1970 and 1996. But much of the wealth was seized by Suharto, his family, and associates. One of Suharto's most notorious acts of nepotism was to hand over the development of a national car to one of his sons.

Suharto's notorious nepotism

Meanwhile Suharto, with the help of the army, brutally suppressed most opposition. The constitution accorded the army a dual function—security and 'socio-political' activities. It exercised these through reserved seats in the Consultative Assembly, through state-owned enterprises, and through general violence and terror.

Suharto's reign ended in 1998 as a result of economic collapse. In Indonesia, as elsewhere in Asia, companies had over-borrowed, banks became insolvent, and thousands of companies crashed. This left millions of poor people even worse off than before. Faced with rises in food prices they rioted—targeting Chinese businesses as scapegoats. Others took to boats, desperately seeking work in Malaysia and Singapore.

In May 1998, Suharto resigned, handing over power to his vice-president, B.J. Habibie. Habibie never seemed likely to retain the office, but he did make one crucial decision: to offer the people of East Timor a referendum on independence. Despite widespread intimidation by army-inspired militias, in August 1999 80% of East Timorese voted to break away.

In Indonesia the president is elected indirectly by the People's Consultative Assembly, which is a complex mixture of directly elected representatives, regional appointees, and reserved army seats. In June 1999, elections for the assembly gave most seats to the Democratic Party of Struggle (PDI-P), which is led by Megawati Sukarnoputri—Sukarno's daughter. Golkar came second, followed by the moderately Islamicist National Awakening Party (PKB), and the more strongly Islamic United Development Party (PPP). When the assembly met in October 1999 it made a surprising presidential choice: Abdurrahman Wahid of the PKB—an elderly and partially blind Muslim scholar. Megawati Sukarnoputri was appointed vice-president.

Wahid will need to demonstrate his considerable political skill. On the one hand he faces other fractious provinces, notably Aceh and West Papua, where there have been violent demonstrations in favour of independence. In a number of islands there are also rising Muslim-Christian religious tensions. Wahid has had some success in dealing with the military, but his handling of the economy has been less sure.

Iran

Islamic Iran is struggling to modernize its political system but economic progress has proved even more difficult

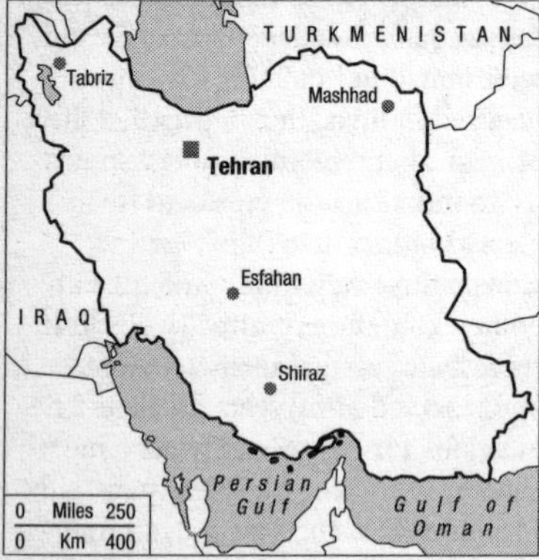

Land area: *1,648,000 sq. km.*
Population: *62 million—urban 61%*
Capital city: *Tehran, 6.8 million*
People: *Persian 51%, Azeri 24%, Gilaki and Mazandarani 8%, Kurd 7%, Arab 3%, Lur 2%, Baloch 2%, other 3%*
Language: *Persian and dialects 58%, Turkic and dialects 26%, Kurdish 9%,*
Religion: *Shiah Muslim 89%, Sunni Muslim 10%, other 1%*
Government: *Islamic republic*
Life expectancy: *69 years*
GNP per capita: *$PPP 5,817*
Currency: *Rial*
Major exports: *Oil and gas, carpets, fruit*

Much of Iran consists of a high central plateau ringed by mountains, the highest of which are in the volcanic Elburz range in the north. Iran is not very fertile—more than half the territory is barren wasteland, most of which is salt desert and uninhabited. Only around 10% is suitable for arable farming, much of this in the fertile northern plateau. Another 20% can be used for grazing.

Ethnically, Iran is quite diverse. Just over half the people are ethnic Persians, who are to be found throughout the country. But one-quarter are Azeris, who live in the north-west. The least assimilated minority are the Kurds, who make up 7% of the population and have a largely nomadic existence in the mountains of the west. This diversity is also reflected in language. Persian (Farsi) is the official language but one-quarter of people use Turkic languages. Iran is also home to several million refugees, chiefly from Afghanistan and Iraq. On the other hand, more than half a million Iranians live abroad.

Religion plays a central part in Iranian life. Most people are Shiah Muslims, but around one-tenth, including the Kurds, belong to the Sunni sect. In theory there is religious freedom, but in practice those who are not Shiah Muslims are second-class citizens. Islam also places restrictions on women, particularly on their dress. But by the standards of other Islamic countries, Iran is relatively liberal—women have good access to education and can enter most professions.

Despite Iran's hostile terrain, agriculture accounts for about one-fifth of both GDP and of the workforce. The main crops are wheat, barley, and potatoes. But productivity is low: development has been hampered by poor management and political uncertainties—land reform is considered un-Islamic. Around one-third of agriculture is based on livestock, chiefly sheep and goats.

At the heart of Iran's industrial

economy is oil. Iran has around 9% of global reserves. In 1997, oil accounted for 14% of GDP and provided 80% of export earnings. Reserves are in the south-west, and also offshore in the Persian Gulf. Iran also has massive reserves of natural gas, the second largest in the world—after Russia—but these remain under-exploited.

Iranian industry was nationalized after the 1979 revolution. Most is inefficient and runs far below capacity. Foreign investors have been discouraged by official coolness to foreigners, and also by a US ban on trade and foreign investment imposed since 1995. The most promising manufacturing area is petro-chemicals though steel and cement also offer prospects for diversification from oil.

Most Iranians struggle to survive. Unemployment was officially 14% in 1999 but was probably far higher. Many professional people are on such low salaries that they need to take on two or three extra jobs. Corruption is widespread.

Political life in Iran was transformed by the 1979 revolution that swept aside the Pahlavi dynasty of the Shah and by 1981 had established a strict Islamic Republic which was to be run by 'religious jurists'. At the head of these was the formerly exiled Ayatollah Khomeini, supported by another cleric, Hashemi Rafsanjani, who in 1980 became the speaker of the Majlis, the 207-member parliament.

An Islamic republic run by religious jurists

The early years of the revolution were chaotic and turbulent and included an eight-year war with Iraq, 1980-8, and a persistent enmity with the 'Great Satan', the USA. Khomeini's death in 1989 left no obvious successor. Instead, political and religious functions were re-allocated. The role of rahbar, or religious leader, was taken by Sayed Ali Khamenei, while most of the political functions were to be vested in the president. Rafsanjani was elected president.

This set up a tension between the conservative religious leadership and the more reformist presidency that persists to this day. Rafsanjani set about opening up the economy, with limited success. He was succeeded in 1997 by an even more progressive cleric, Muhammad Khatami. The struggle between the reformers and conservatives took a violent turn with anti-clerical student protests in mid-1999.

The parliamentary elections in February 2000 altered the picture again, giving a resounding majority to the reformers—the Islamic Iran Participation Front led by Muhammad Reza Khatami, who is the brother of the president.

The problem for the reformers is that the parliament has only limited powers. The Conservatives remain entrenched in the judiciary and elsewhere and could thwart future progress.

This became all too clear in April 2000 when the judiciary shut down 16 newspapers and journals which religious leader Khamenei had accused of 'disparaging Islam and the religious elements of the Islamic Revolution'. A number of journalists were arrested. Khatami did not respond. Later in the year there were signs of rising student unrest.

Iraq

Saddam Hussein continues to defy the rest of the world—and there seems little prospect of political change

Land area: *438,000 sq. km.*
Population: *21 million—urban 75%*
Capital city: *Baghdad, 5.3 million*
People: *Arab 75%-80%, Kurdish 15%-20%*
Language: *Arabic, Kurdish*
Religion: *Muslim*
Government: *Republic*
Life expectancy: *38 years*
GNP per capita: *$PPP 3,197*
Currency: *Iraqi dinar*
Major exports: *Oil*

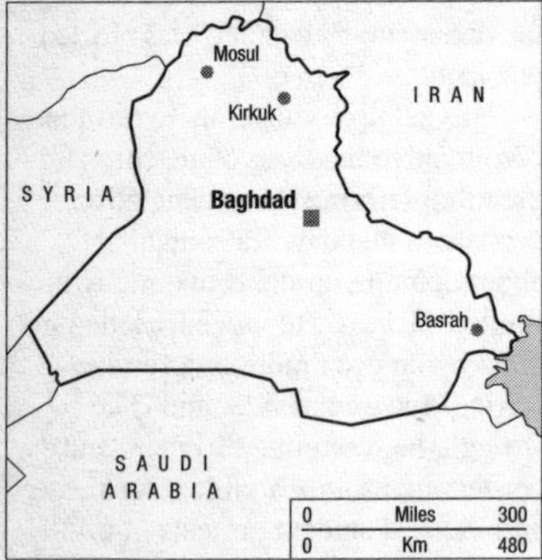

The heart of Iraq, forming around one-third of the territory, is the alluvial and often marshy basin of the Tigris and Euphrates. These rivers flow the length of the country before uniting as the Shatt al-Arab River, which flows into the Persian Gulf. To the north of this basin are uplands, and in the north-east is the mountainous region of Kurdistan. The rest of the country, to the west and south, around two-fifths of the territory, is largely desert.

There are three main population groups. The largest, accounting for around half the population, are Arab Shiah Muslims, who live mostly in the centre and south. Next are the Arab Sunni Muslims who are around one-third of the population and are concentrated in the east around Baghdad. Then there are the Kurds, also Sunni Muslims, who make up one-fifth of the population and live in the north and north-east.

These three groups have frequently fought each other. Politically the most powerful are the Arab Sunnis, who include the president Saddam Hussein. Following the Gulf War in 1990, both the Kurds and the Shiah rebelled against the government—but were brutally crushed. To protect the Kurds, the US and British governments in 1991 established a 'no-fly zone' above the 36th parallel. In 1992, to protect the Shiah they established a similar zone below the 32nd parallel. As a result, the Iraqi air force is not free to fly over more than half the country.

The lives of most Iraqis have been devastated by UN trade sanctions imposed since 1990 in an attempt to force the government to abandon its chemical and biological weapons. Studies by UNICEF concluded that by the end of 1998 around half a million children under five had died. This was a result of the poor health of mothers, the general collapse of health services, and the lack of power for the country's water system.

Iraq's economy has long depended on the export of oil. In 1996, the country had 10% of world reserves. And prior to 1990 oil accounted for 60% of GDP and 95% of export earnings. But when sanctions were imposed most of those earnings were cut off. Since 1996, the UN has permitted Iraq to export fixed values of oil—now $4.5 billion-worth every six months—with the revenues being used largely for humanitarian relief under UN supervision. But Iraq has been hard-pressed to export even these quotas, partly because of the low oil price, but also because war and sanctions have crippled much of the oil infrastructure.

Many factories have also been forced to close because they have been unable to get spare parts.

Government officials have two or three jobs

Government employees still have jobs but with salaries of around $2 per month many officials and other professions have had to make ends meet by selling their possessions or by fishing, or even turning to crime or prostitution.

Iraq's farmers should have been less affected. The rich alluvial soil with ample supplies of water ought to make the country very productive. In 1992, 14% of the labour force were engaged in farming. In practice, many peasant farmers, who often lease government land, have reverted to subsistence production. This is partly because of political uncertainties and shifts of policy, but also because the arrival of food aid has kept prices down.

In 1979, Saddam Hussein came to power in a coup. He immediately consolidated his position by summarily executing his rivals. In theory the country is run by the Revolutionary Command Council and the Ba'ath Socialist Party. In practice all power is centralized in the council's chairman, Saddam Hussein, who has dealt ruthlessly with any opposition. Hussein is politically cunning but he has also made disastrous mistakes—notably the war with Iran over the period 1980-88, which ended in a stalemate, and the 1990 invasion of Kuwait that provoked intervention by a US-led coalition and a defeat in the Gulf War.

Since the Gulf War there have been a number of attempts to topple Saddam Hussain. Efforts to monitor his weapons production by a UN inspection force UNSCOM were eventually aborted in 1998. Although inspections had forced Saddam to abandon his nuclear weapons programme, he called a halt when the UN started searching for biological weapons. The USA and the UK responded with bombing raids—15,000 in 1999—and continue to enforce the no-fly zones.

Meanwhile, there seems little prospect of effective internal opposition. The Shiah groups have been efficiently repressed. The Kurds are undermined by rivalry between their two main groups, the Kurdish Democratic Party and the Patriotic Union of Kurdistan. They are as likely to fight each other as to take on Saddam Hussain. And the internal security services are brutally effective at discouraging other opposition. Even if Saddam Hussain were to go, the most likely successor appears to be his equally ferocious son Udai.

Because economic sanctions have done little damage to Saddam or his entourage, while hurting millions of innocent Iraqis, there have been increasing calls for the UN to take a different approach.

Ireland

Ireland has prospered as a member of the EU and has become a centre for high-tech manufacturing

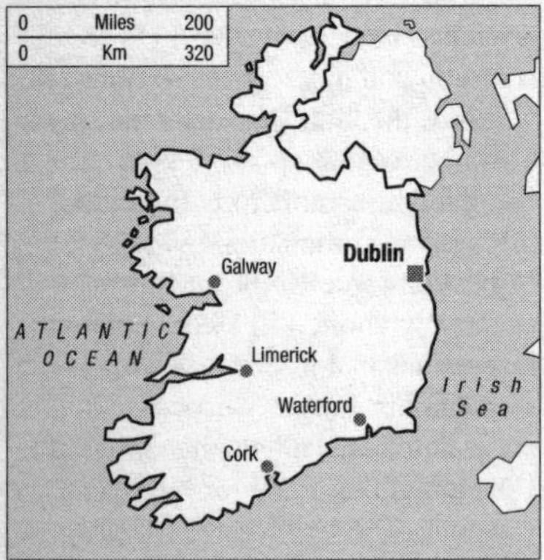

Land area: *70,000 sq. km.*
Population: *3.6 million—urban 58%*
Capital city: *Dublin, 1.2 million*
People: *Irish*
Language: *Gaelic, English*
Religion: *Roman Catholic*
Government: *Republic*
Life expectancy: *76 years*
GNP per capita: *$PPP 18,340*
Currency: *Irish pound (punt)*
Major exports: *Machinery, chemicals, food*

The Republic of Ireland occupies 80% of the island of Ireland. The remainder, Northern Ireland, is a part of the UK. The interior is mostly lowlands interspersed with numerous lakes and bogs. Ringing the lowlands, around most of the coast, are a series of low mountain ranges—the highest peak is only 1,040 metres above sea level.

Ireland's people are largely of Celtic descent and Roman Catholic, though there are also small numbers of Anglo-Irish Protestants, a legacy of the period of English rule. Irish, or Gaelic, is the first official language but only a tiny minority use it; English is spoken almost universally.

Until recently, Ireland was a country of emigration, chiefly to the UK and the USA. More than 1 million Irish-born people live abroad—around 40 million Americans claim Irish ancestry. But recent years of rapid development have encouraged some of the diaspora to return—and attracted many other nationalities. In mid-1999 around 1,000 people a week were arriving to work. More than half of these were returning Irish but 19% were from the UK.

Agriculture remains an important part of the economy, particularly the rearing of livestock and along with the export-oriented food processing industry it still employs around one-fifth of the workforce. Ireland's agriculture benefited greatly from the EU's Common Agricultural Policy (CAP). In 1996, for example, more than 40% of farm income came from EU subsidies. But reform of the CAP and changes demanded by the World Trade Organization will hit Irish agriculture hard.

Fortunately, there are plenty of alternatives. In the past decade manufacturing and service industries have been booming. Most of this is due to foreign investment. Ireland now has affiliates of more than 1,000 foreign companies employing more than 90,000 workers. They account for around 30% of the economy and 40% of exports, and include major computer companies such as IBM, Intel, Fujitsu, and Dell. Tourism is also a major earner—from more than 3 million visitors each year.

The Irish government can take credit for this transformation. It has offered generous grants and tax concessions while restraining wage claims through a series of 'social contracts' with the trade unions. It has also invested heavily in higher education.

Attracted by financial incentives and an inexpensive, well-educated, English-speaking population within the European Union, foreign companies have understandably flocked. This stimulated rapid economic growth—turning Ireland into an 'emerald tiger'. In 1999, Ireland was the EU's fastest growing economy for the sixth year running. Unemployment, which was 16% in 1993, was down to 5% in 2000. But the wealth has not been evenly spread: property prices in Dublin have been rocketing while the west of the country trails far behind.

Ireland has also been going through rapid social and political changes. Under the influence of the Roman Catholic Church, Ireland has been very conservative in such matters as abortion, homosexuality, and divorce. But the Church's influence has waned and divorce finally became legal in 1997.

The Catholic Church's influence has waned

At the same time, the political landscape is being transformed by the prospect of a settlement of the long-running conflict in Northern Ireland. The island was partitioned by the1921 Anglo-Irish Treaty and the south became independent in 1922. Since then, Irish politics has been shaped by attitudes towards the north. The largest party, the nationalist Fianna Fail, was formed in opposition to the treaty, insisting on Irish jurisdiction over the whole island—the name means militia of Fál, a stone monument. The second largest is the centre-right Fine Gael ('Irish nation'), which represented landowners and the business community who accepted the terms of the treaty. Irish politics did not therefore split along right-left lines, but according to attitudes to partition. There is also a Labour Party, but it has always been much smaller.

In recent years, electoral outcomes have usually required coalitions of one of the major parties with one of the smaller ones. After the 1997 election for the parliament, the Dáil, a Fine Gael-Labour coalition gave way to one between Fianna Fail and the Progressive Democratic Party, which was a 1985 right-wing breakaway from Fianna Fail. Bertie Ahern became Taoiseach—prime minister. There was also an election for the largely ceremonial post of president which resulted in the liberal, Mary Robinson (now the UN Commissioner for Human Rights), being succeeded by the more conservative Mary McAleese.

In 1998 Ahern signed the 'Good Friday' Northern Ireland peace agreement with the UK. This required Ireland to remove from its constitution a claim on Northern Ireland—subsequently confirmed with 94% approval in a referendum.

Assuming the agreement holds, this could also stimulate a realignment in Irish politics since on most economic and political issues the two main parties have now converged.

Israel

After half a century of war and hostility, the peaceful creation of a Palestinian state still remains in doubt

Land area: *21,000 sq. km.*
Population: *6 million—urban 91%*
Capital city: *Jerusalem, 613,000*
People: *Jewish 80%, others, mostly Arab, 20%*
Language: *Hebrew, Arabic, English*
Religion: *Judaism 80%, Islam 15%, Christian 2%, other 3%*
Government: *Republic*
Life expectancy: *78 years*
GNP per capita: *$PPP 17,310*
Currency: *Shekel*
Major exports: *Industrial goods, cut diamonds*

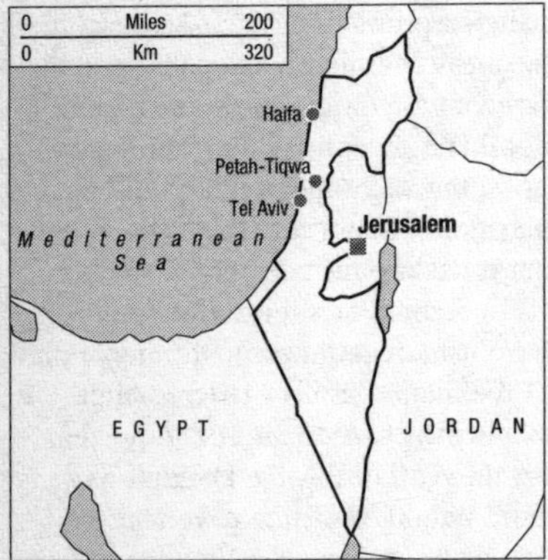

Israel can be considered to have four main geographical regions. To the north is a hilly region that includes the hills of Galilee and extends down through the Israeli-occupied West Bank. Along the Mediterranean coast there is a narrow plain that is home to most of the country's commerce and population. The border in the north-east is formed by the valley of the river Jordan which flows south into the Dead Sea—the lowest point on earth—and the same fissure continues south to the Gulf of Aqaba. Most of the south is the Negev Desert.

The state of Israel was established in what was formerly Palestine in 1948 as a Jewish homeland and has since attracted immigrants from almost every country. By the end of the 20th century the population was 80% Jewish, of whom more than half were native-born and the remainder immigrants. Immigration accelerated after 1989 with the arrival of more than 800,000 Jews from the former Soviet Union—swelling the total population by more than one-quarter. In addition, around one-fifth are descendants of the original Arab population—who are typically the poorest people.

The Jewish population is usually divided into two groups. First are those of European and North American origin—the Ashkenazim—who tend to be richer. Second are those from North Africa and the Middle East— the Sephardim or Misrahi—who form most of the working class. But there are many other distinctions within these groups, principally between secular and religious Jews.

Israelis have generally good standards of health and are also highly educated. About 22% of immigrants in the 1990s were professionals. Israel has the highest proportion of scientists and engineers per capita in the world.

Over its lifetime, Israel has shifted from a simple agricultural society to an export-driven high-tech industrial economy—particularly during the 1990s, with the influx of new professionals and the establishment of communications technology and software enterprises concentrated around Tel Aviv.

Israel also has high-tech agriculture which has to make sophisticated use of limited water resources. As well as being self-sufficient in food, Israel is a major exporter of citrus and other fruits. Most farming, reflecting the country's socialist origins, is still organized by kibbutzim (collectives) or moshavim (co-operatives). Although fairly efficient, their survival still depends on cheap supplies of water and subsidies and many are now heavily in debt.

Israel has high-tech farms that work with little water

Israel's Zionist and socialist origins have also influenced its politics, which have largely been dominated by the Labour Party—though now more liberal and renamed 'One Nation'. Labour was for decades the majority ruling party, but was dislodged in 1977 by the conservative Likud Party. Since the mid-1980s, neither has been able to muster a majority and each has had to govern in coalition with a plethora of smaller religious parties.

Throughout its existence, Israel's governments have been embroiled in conflicts with their Arab neighbours, most notably in the six-day war of 1967 as a result of which Israel seized the Gaza Strip from Egypt, the West Bank from Jordan, and the Golan Heights from Syria. The status of these territories has been disputed ever since. Generally, Likud and the orthodox religious parties have wanted to keep them—and encouraged Jewish settlements there—while Labour has been more equivocal.

In the event, it now seems inevitable that most of these lands will be returned and that the West Bank and Gaza will constitute an independent Palestine. The most decisive steps were taken in 1993 when, following secret negotiations in Oslo, Labour Prime Yitzhak Rabin signed in Washington a peace agreement with Palestine Liberation Organization chairman Yasser Arafat that allowed for Palestinian self-rule. Rabin was assassinated in 1995 by an Israeli right-wing nationalist and was replaced by Shimon Peres, who continued negotiations.

The peace process faltered after 1996 when Likud returned to power. In that year, following a change in legislation, Likud's Binyamin Netanyahu became the first prime minister to be directly elected, and in the corresponding parliamentary election Likud and other right-wing groups formed a coalition government.

Peace negotiations came back on track, however, following the 1999 election for prime minister, which was won by One Israel's Ehud Barak. In the parliamentary elections, however, the vote was very fragmented, so Barak had to assemble an unlikely-looking coalition. This included a number of hardline religious parties which subsequently left the coalition, leaving Mr Barak with a fragile minority government.

Meanwhile talks with the PLO stutter onwards. In principle these could produce a result in 2000, though agreement seems unlikely. The key sticking point will be the status of Jerusalem.

Italy

Despite deep regional disparities and unstable governments, Italy has had rapid economic growth

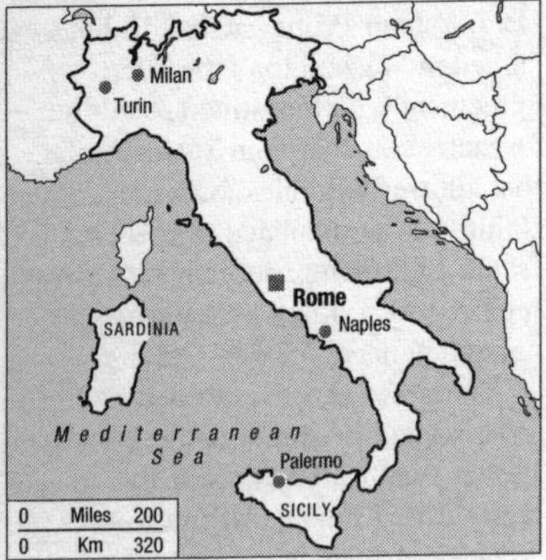

Land area: *301,000 sq. km.*
Population: *58 million—urban 67%*
Capital city: *Rome, 2.7 million*
People: *Italians*
Language: *Italian and some regional*
Religion: *Roman Catholic*
Government: *Republic*
Life expectancy: *78 years*
GNP per capita: *$PPP 20,200*
Currency: *Lira*
Major exports: *Machinery, textiles, clothing, cars*

Italy is dominated by mountains. The Alps loom over the north of the country and merge with the Apennine Mountains, which run down the centre. Mountains also make up much of the Italian islands of Sicily and Sardinia. Overall, more than one-third of Italy's territory is covered by ranges higher than 700 metres.

The difficult terrain is one reason why the country has been regionally divided. Italy was united as one country only in 1871, at which point only 3% of the population spoke Italian. Since then there has been a steady process of integration, but strong regional identities persist.

For much of the 20th century, Italy's population grew rapidly, and with limited prospects of work at home, millions of Italians emigrated: even as late as 1968-70 net emigration was over 250,000. Now the position is reversed. The fertility rate, at 1.2 children per woman, is among the lowest in the world.

Italy has become a country of net immigration: currently it has about 1.2 million immigrants, most of whom have come from outside the EU, chiefly from Morocco, former Yugoslavia, Tunisia, and Albania.

Thin soils and steep terrain have always made agriculture difficult, and as a result Italy has been a net importer of food. It is also poorly endowed with other natural resources: it has no coal and has to import three-quarters of its energy needs.

In economic terms, the country's great strength has been in manufacturing. It does have some large multinational companies, notably Fiat (cars) and Olivetti (telecommunications), but manufacturing is dominated by networks of thousands of small firms, chiefly in clothing, furniture, kitchen equipment, and 'white goods' such as refrigerators and cookers. These often cluster together regionally: wool textiles in Prato, for example, shoes in Verona, spectacles in Belluno. Until recently, there was also a large state sector, but since 1992 there has been a steady process of privatization.

These small and medium-sized

enterprises have been the engine for economic growth. There have certainly been periods of recession, particularly after the 1974 oil shock, which hit Italy hard, but overall the country has made striking progress even if growth has slowed over the past few years.

Economic activity remains concentrated in the north. Here manufacturing accounts for 30% of value-added compared with 13% in the south. Indeed, the GDP of the south is only 70% of the Italian average. There are also striking differences in employment—virtually full employment in the north but 25% or more unemployment in the south. In the 1950s and 1960s, this led to mass south-north migration. But this appears to have halted, partly because the cost of living in the north is much higher. The impact of unemployment is also cushioned by the extended family which remains stronger in Italy than in most other industrial countries. Around two-thirds of unmarried men under thirty still live with their mothers. And when they marry they do not move very far away.

Many Italian men still live with their mothers

Tourism also makes an important economic contribution, with 30 million visitors per year.

Italy's economic progress has not been matched by its system of governance. The post-war period has seen a sequence of weak and transient administrations: between 1947 and mid-2000 it had no fewer than 58 governments. This weakness was to some extent deliberate. In an effort to avoid repeating the experience of the fascist governments of the 1930s and 1940s, the constitution adopted in 1948 resulted in reduced powers for the prime ministers—who were often beholden to party leaders who were not themselves in government. Governance was also undermined by widespread corruption and the power of the Mafia. Between 1947 and 1992, all coalition governments were dominated by the Christian Democrats.

After 1993, the political scene shifted dramatically when Italians voted overwhelmingly to move from a system of proportional representation to one in which most seats in both houses of parliament would be determined by straight majorities. This produced a different set of alignments. The 1996 election was won by the 'Olive Tree' coalition: chiefly centrist and left parties. Romano Prodi took over as prime minister. Even so, Italy's parliament still has around 40 parties.

Prodi's government fell in 1998 following a dispute between the coalition partners, and Massimo D'Alema, a former communist, took over at the head of yet another coalition. D'Alema also headed the next government in 1999, but he departed in April 2000. He was replaced by Giuliano Amato who put together yet another frail coalition. Meanwhile, waiting in the wings is Silvio Berlusconi of the right-wing Forza Italia, which could take power if there were an early election.

There have been efforts to remove the final vestiges of proportional representation. But a series of referenda have failed to achieve this since too few people have voted.

Jamaica

Culturally vigorous and a tourist attraction—but prone to political violence

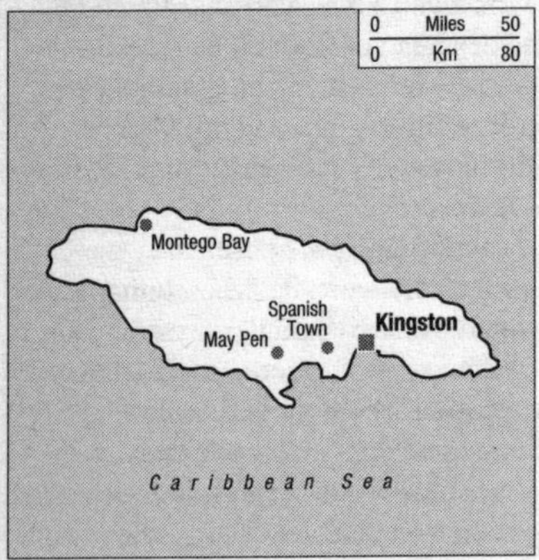

Land area: *11,000 sq. km.*
Population: *2.6 million—urban 55%*
Capital city: *Kingston, 631,000*
People: *Black 90%, mixed 7%, East Indian 1%, other 2%*
Language: *English, Creole*
Religion: *Christian 65%, other 35%*
Government: *Parliamentary, with the British monarchy*
Life expectancy: *75 years*
GNP per capita: *$PPP 3,210*
Currency: *Jamaican dollar*
Major exports: *Alumina, bauxite, sugar*

Jamaica's mountainous, and often thickly wooded, territory rises to 2,200 metres at the peak of the Blue Mountain in the east—a landscape criss-crossed by rivers and attractive waterfalls. In the centre of the island, and accounting for around half the country is a limestone plateau that includes extensive systems of underground caves. The most densely cultivated parts of the country, however, are the coastal lowlands of the south and west.

Jamaica's people are predominantly descendants of slaves brought to work on the sugar plantations, along with smaller communities of Asian and European origin. While officially speaking English and mostly professing Christianity, Jamaicans have developed their own characteristic culture, notably their distinctive dialect, the Rastafarian religion, and reggae music.

On the whole, Jamaicans are well educated and have a good health service. But limited economic opportunities have driven successive generations of young Jamaicans to emigrate—in the 1960s and 1970s to the UK, but more recently to the USA and Canada.

Around one-quarter of the population still make their living from the land. Apart from food crops such as plantains, yams, and corn, Jamaica also has major agricultural exports, notably sugar on plantations in the coastal plain and bananas grown on small farms. But agriculture in general has been stagnating—hit by droughts, floods, and hurricanes. One of the more consistent crops has been ganja, or marijuana, which provides solace to about half the male population.

Jamaica's most dependable export earner has been bauxite—of which it is the world's third-largest producer. Most deposits are in the centre of the island and because they are not very deep extraction is relatively cheap Some is exported as raw ore, but most is now first converted to alumina (aluminium oxide). With around half of export earnings from this source, Jamaica is vulnerable to world prices, particularly because it is a relatively high-cost producer.

Jamaica has also been trying to develop exports of manufactured goods. The most significant success in the 1980s was the growth of a garment industry which, at its peak in the mid-1990s, employed 35,000 people. By 1998, however, the industry had shrunk by around one-third—hit by, among other things, the arrival of the North American Free Trade Agreement (NAFTA) through which the USA gives preference to imports from Mexico.

The other main source of foreign exchange and employment is tourism. Jamaica attracts more than 1.8 million visitors each year, most of whom come from the USA and head for the beautiful beaches of the north and west. Directly and indirectly, tourism probably employs around a quarter of a million Jamaicans. The industry grew rapidly in the 1980s and early 1990s, but seemed to stall in the late 1990s, perhaps due to the relatively high rate of exchange—as well as the country's reputation for street violence.

Tourism employs 250,000 Jamaicans

Another source of export income is drugs. Some of this is marijuana, but the greatest profits come from transshipping Colombian cocaine.

Politics in Jamaica has frequently been a dangerous business, involving armed confrontations between the two main parties. The violence has its roots in the mid-1970s. Between 1972 and 1982, the prime minister was former union organizer Michael Manley who led the People's National Party (PNP). Manley tried to pursue socialist policies and gain greater control over the foreign-dominated bauxite industry, and became a leading international figure. Opposing him was the pro-business, anti-communist, Edward Seaga, who led the Jamaican Labour Party (JLP). But their left-right confrontations spread far beyond the parliament to become a kind of tribal warfare with pitched battles between gangs in the streets of Kingston.

Manley could not deliver the economic prosperity he had promised and Seaga won convincing victories in the 1980 and 1983 elections, pursuing more market-friendly policies and opening the country up to foreign investment. But with low prices for bauxite and the effects of the 1988 Hurricane Gilbert, economic development was slow and Seaga's popularity waned.

In 1989, the PNP and Manley returned to power, though now more or less continuing the same liberalization policies as the JLP. Following Manley's retirement in 1992, Percival Patterson took over as prime minister and won subsequent elections over Seaga in 1993 and 1997. A small third party, the National Democratic Movement, was created in 1995 to challenge the two main parties but has had little impact.

Politics may be less ideologically charged nowadays, but the gangs live on, thriving on income from drugs and extortion. Kingston is a dangerous city, with a murder rate twenty times that of London. In 1998, there were 953 murders. And citizens frustrated by high prices, poverty, and unemployment frequently protest by erecting roadblocks.

Japan

Japan had an enviable record for growth and prosperity, but its economic and political frailties have been exposed

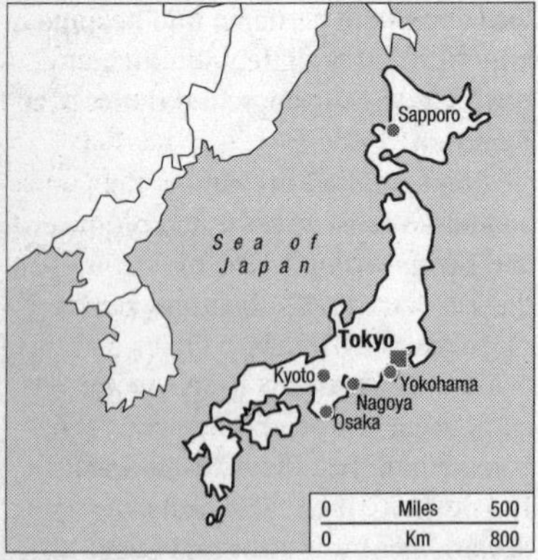

Land area: *378,000 sq. km.*
Population: *126 million—urban 79%*
Capital city: *Tokyo, 7.9 million*
People: *Japanese 99%, other 1%*
Language: *Japanese*
Religion: *Shinto and Buddhist*
Government: *Constitutional monarchy*
Life expectancy: *80 years*
GNP per capita: *$PPP 23,180*
Currency: *Yen*
Major exports: *Cars, semiconductors, office machinery, chemicals*

Though the Japanese archipelago has more than 1,000 islands, most of the territory comprises four main islands. From north to south these are: Hokkaido, Honshu, Shikoku, and Kyushu, of which the largest, with more than half Japan's land area, is Honshu. These islands have mountain chains running north to south divided by steep valleys and interspersed with numerous small plains. The mountains include a number of extinct and active volcanoes, of which the highest, at 3,700 metres, is the distinctively symmetrical and snow-capped Mount Fuji on Honshu.

This is one of the world's most unstable geological zones and Japan experiences more than 1,000 tremors per year. The most recent severe earthquake hit the city of Kobe in 1995, killing more than 5,000 people. Japan's climate runs from the sub-arctic to the sub-tropical but most of the country enjoys fairly mild temperatures with plentiful rain that supports lush vegetation.

Japan has one of the world's most homogenous populations. This is partly due to isolationism, since for centuries Japan effectively cut itself off from the rest of the world. There is one small indigenous ethnic group, around 24,000 Ainu people on Hokkaido, but the largest group of non-Japanese are the 630,000 Koreans, many of whom are descendants of people brought to Japan during the Second World War to work as forced labourers. During the post-war boom years, however, Japan was the only developed country not to rely extensively on foreign workers to meet labour shortages. Although immigrants arrived from elsewhere in Asia, they often did so illegally.

The only group actively welcomed, were the 'nikkeijin', the descendants of a previous generation of Japanese emigrants. From the early 1900s, many Japanese had emigrated to the Americas, and in the 1990s thousands of their descendants came back—around 230,000 from Brazil.

Japan's rapid economic development has been accompanied by striking social changes. With a healthy diet and a good health service average life expectancy, at 80 years, is among the highest in the world. Education standards are high—though learning by rote tends to stifle creativity. Japanese houses are well equipped but cramped, typically with less than half the floor area found in other rich countries. Many workers commute long distances.

Japan's population is ageing rapidly. There are now only 1.5 children born per woman of childbearing age—well below replacement rate. By 2007, one-fifth of the population will be over sixty-five. With a steady breakdown of the extended family, this has serious implications for the country's pensions system.

Social security has already come under pressure as economic crisis has forced large companies to abandon their former commitment to loyal employees, the 'salarymen', whom they had offered jobs for life. As a result of corporate downsizing and the recession, unemployment in 2000 was at least 5%, alarmingly high by Japanese standards, and homelessness is rising fast in the major cities.

Salarymen no longer have jobs for life

Japan's development surged after the Second World War—boosted by demand from the Korean War and by high levels of savings that could be channelled into heavy industries such as steel and chemicals, and later into the provision of consumer goods and services. This process was based on 'keiretsus'—tightly knit groups of manufacturers, suppliers, and distributors that work closely with the banks. The Ministry of Trade and Industry (MITI) also had a pivotal influence. This, combined with protectionism, helped to trigger two major economic booms: 1965-70 and 1986-91.

Manufacturing still accounts for around one-quarter of GDP, and cars and semiconductors are the leading exports. But rising labour costs, an appreciating currency, and the need to operate closer to overseas markets have long obliged Japanese companies to invest in other countries. By the mid-1990s around 10% of manufactured output was located overseas.

Japan's manufacturing success has been all the more striking since it has few mineral resources and has to import more than 80% of its energy needs. This has meant exploiting nuclear energy—Japan has more than 50 nuclear power plants.

Agriculture employs relatively few people—less than 5% of the labour force. But unlike many other rich countries, they work predominantly on small family farms, chiefly growing rice. This is the legacy of an extensive post-war land reform imposed by the USA. Since then, farmers have remained a politically powerful lobby and have benefited from protection and high subsidies. In recent years the government has deregulated the system somewhat, but Japan still has highly protected food markets.

Japan's economic expansion began to falter after 1991 when the escalating property prices and booming stock market could not be sustained. This exposed the weaknesses of the keiretsu system. Many banks had continued to lend to unsound companies. This left an overhang of bad loans and rendered many banks insolvent. By 1998, the economy had slipped into recession and in 1999 grew by only 0.6%. Meanwhile, companies have been reluctant to restructure to reduce massive over-capacity and the government has been slow to force banks into liquidation.

Japan finds it difficult to take tough decisions because its political system is neither as robust nor transparent as might be expected in one of the world's richest and technologically most advanced countries. For most of the period since 1955 Japan has been ruled by the conservative Liberal Democratic Party (LDP). The LDP has always had close links with both the business community and the farmers—each of whom allied themselves with different LDP factions. The main opposition party has been the centre-left party now called the Social Democratic Party (SDP).

A weak and scandal-hit government

The LDP continued in office despite a series of scandals that included the prosecution of one prime minister for taking bribes in 1976 from the Lockheed corporation. The most dramatic example, however, was in 1989, when almost all the LDP factions were found to have received bribes from Recruit, a large Japanese conglomerate.

Throughout this period, it had seemed that the Japanese electorate would continue to forgive a party that had delivered such a long period of prosperity. But the LDP's rule came to an end in 1993. A series of defections caused it to lose a no-confidence motion in the Diet—the lower house of parliament. It was replaced by a coalition that included the SDP and others. But this too collapsed in 1994 and the LDP returned, though this time in a coalition that included the SDP.

By the 1996 election the LDP had more or less recovered its former position. Led by Ryutaro Hashimoto, it almost achieved an overall majority in the Diet and was able to rule alone, with less formal support from its former coalition partners. Later, receiving defections from other parties, it achieved a simple majority.

In recent years, most opposition parties have been in a state of upheaval—changing names and policies with bewildering rapidity. In 1998, the leading opposition party was Minshuto, followed by New Komeito.

By 1998, the LDP government was again becoming less popular, as a result of the worsening economic climate and it did badly in elections to the upper house. This led to the resignation of Hashimoto, who was replaced as prime minister by Keizo Obuchi.

In April 2000, however, Obuchi suffered a stroke, and he died in May. He was replaced as prime minister by Yoshiro Mori who said he would continue with the same policies. The Japanese voters were less confident about this. In the July 2000 election the LDP lost its majority in the Diet, though it is still the largest party. Mori has not proved a very adept prime minister and his government could be threatened by a series of bribery allegations. He will probably do well to survive in office beyond the end of 2000.

Jordan

Jordan's King Abdullah has started to establish a more stable democracy

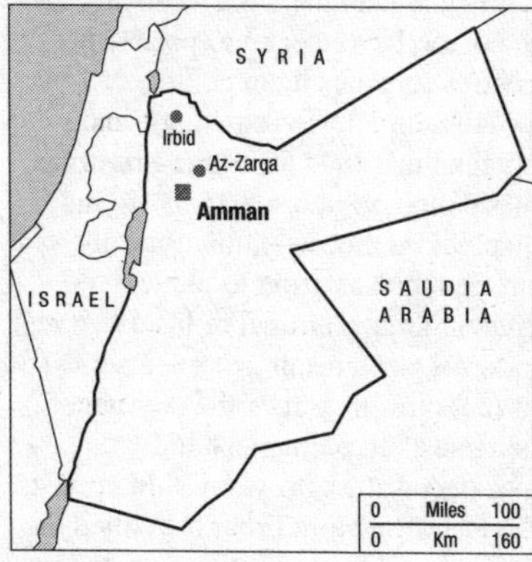

Land area: *89,000 sq. km.*
Population: *5 million—urban 73%*
Capital city: *Amman, 900,000*
People: *Arab*
Language: *Arabic*
Religion: *Sunni Muslim*
Government: *Constitutional monarchy*
Life expectancy: *70 years*
GNP per capita: *$PPP 3,230*
Currency: *Dinar*
Major exports: *Phosphates, potash*

Jordan has three main zones. First, there is the Jordan Valley region, which lies to the east of the Jordan river and finishes in the south at the Red Sea, which is the world's lowest body of water. Secondly, further to the east and running parallel with the valley, are the eastern uplands, whose elevation is mostly 600 to 900 metres. Thirdly, beyond the uplands, and occupying around 80% of the country to the east and north is the desert.

Most people live in the upland areas and almost everyone is Arab. But there are numerous social divisions based on politics and history. One group consists of the 'East Bankers'—descendants of the people who lived on the East Bank of the Jordan prior to 1948. The second, and probably the largest, is made up of descendants of the Palestinian refugees who crossed the river from the West Bank following the formation of the state of Israel in 1948—who were followed by another surge in 1967 when Jordan lost control of the West Bank to Israel. A third group are the 180,000 or more immigrant workers—the majority from Egypt, with some from India and elsewhere in Asia.

The population is young and growing fast—at around 3% per year. This has put severe pressure on health and education services. One-quarter of families live in poverty. Most richer people send their children to the private schools that educate 15% of the school population.

With relatively little by way of industry or natural resources, Jordan has relied heavily on the service industries that account for around two-thirds of GDP. Many of these, including transport and communications, derive from Jordan's close links with neighbouring countries.

Agriculture is divided between fairly primitive rain-fed cereal production in the uplands and the higher-tech irrigated farms of the Jordan valley that are largely given over to fruit and vegetables, some of which are exported—and rely significantly on immigrant labour. Water is a perennial problem. There have been suggestions for a canal to link the Red Sea with the Dead Sea, along with desalination plants that would provide drinking water for Jordan and Israel.

Industry is limited. The most significant enterprises are the state-owned mining operations that extract potash and phosphates. Jordan is the world's second largest exporter of raw phosphates.

One of the most reliable sources of foreign exchange, however, is migrant remittances. Though Jordan is home to many immigrants, it sends even more of its own people overseas. Around 900,000 Jordanians, most of whom work in the Gulf states, send home more than $1 billion in remittances each year.

Jordan receives $1 billion in migrant remittances

Though it has no oil of its own, Jordan benefited from business generated in the Gulf states during the late 1970s. After 1982, a recession set in and by 1989 Jordan had been forced to embark on an IMF structural adjustment programme. The Gulf War in 1990 offered some respite: Kuwait and other Gulf countries expelled around 300,000 Palestinians, who came back to Jordan with most of their assets which they invested in construction and other businesses—setting off a mini-boom. Since then, however, the economy has slowed.

In principle, Jordan is a constitutional monarchy with executive power vested in its 80-member parliament and its prime minister. In practice, the parliament has always been directed by the king. For most of the second half of the 20th century, this was King Hussein, who reigned in an often autocratic fashion—bolstered by his links with tribal leaders and with the army. In the middle of one of the world's most unstable regions he sustained an intricate balancing act. On the one hand, he cultivated close ties with Israel and kept the USA as an ally. On the other, he managed to placate his vociferous Palestinian citizens.

Hussein allowed a democratic opening in 1989—instituting reforms that permitted new elections. To his displeasure, however, this gave a strong representation to radical Islamic groups critical of his overtures to Israel. As a result he took a series of measures to reduce the number of Islamicists in parliament and introduced strict press laws. In protest, the Islamic Action Front boycotted the 1997 election.

Hussein died early in February 1999. He was succeeded by his son Abdullah who knows relatively little of Jordanian politics, and does not speak Arabic very well. Even so, King Abdullah has made some decisive early moves. He has, for example, clamped down on the radical Palestinian group, Hamas, producing a surprisingly muted response from Jordan's main Islamic organization, the Muslim Brotherhood. Abdullah has also been conciliatory. He has modified the press law, and promised further electoral reform, encouraging Islamic politicians to end their parliamentary boycott. Frequently accompanied by his Palestinian wife, Queen Rania, he has also been trying to get Palestinians and East Bankers to put old divisions behind them. At the same time he has been trying to persuade Israel to take a more positive line in negotiations with the PLO.

Kazakhstan

Kazakhstan has yet to capitalize on its rich mineral resources, or the opportunity for democracy

Land area: *2,717,000 sq. km.*
Population: *16 million—urban 60%*
Capital city: *Astana, 300,000*
People: *Kazakh 46%, Russian 35%, Ukrainian 5%, German 3%, Uzbek 2%, Tatar 2%, other 7%*
Language: *Kazakh, Russian*
Religion: *Muslim, Russian Orthodox*
Government: *Republic*
Life expectancy: *61 years*
GNP per capita: *$PPP 3,400*
Currency: *Tenge*
Major exports: *Oil, gas, metals*

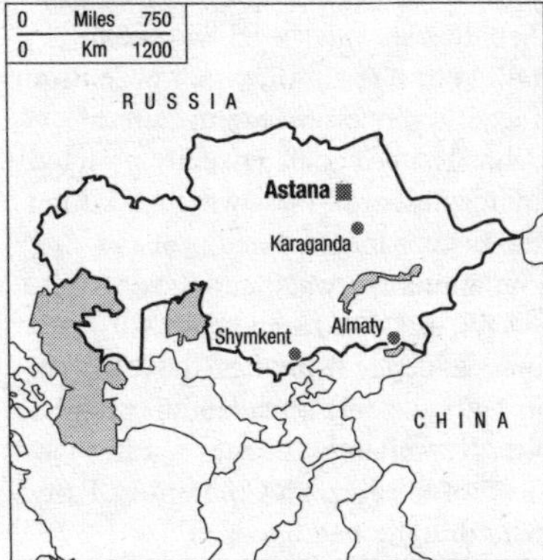

Kazakhstan is a landlocked country in central Asia that consists of a vast plain stretching from the Caspian Sea in the west to the mountainous border with Kyrgyzstan and China to the east. Most of the territory consists of grassy steppes or desert.

Kazakhs form less than half the population in a country with more than 100 ethnic groups. Russian settlers moved in from the 18th century and continued to do so during the Soviet era, along with ethnic Germans who were exiled here by Stalin in the 1930s. Most Kazakhs live in the east, while Russians are in the majority in the north.

Since independence, there have been efforts at 'Kazakhization', particularly the promotion of the Kazakh language. When Kazakhstan was effectively a Russian colony, Kazakhs had to learn Russian; now about half can scarcely speak their own language.

Demography, too, is starting to swing back in the Kazakhs' favour. This is partly due to emigration. Many emigrants were Russians: between 1989 and 2000, 1.6 million left. Others were ethnic Germans, heading for Germany: their numbers fell from 1 million to about 170,000. Since the Kazakhs' birth rate is higher than that of Russians they should soon be in a majority again—the average age of Kazakhs is 20, while that of Russians is 46.

Nevertheless the fall in population is worrying. Villages in some parts of the country are now virtually empty. The German government has been helping—trying to persuade the remainder of ethnic Germans to stay by sending around $50 million each year in supplies along with capital to invest in small businesses. But in an era of general instability the exodus continues.

Kazakhstan's people had reasonable standards of human development in the past. But health services have been deteriorating, and there have been sharp rises in infectious diseases such as tuberculosis, as well as lifestyle diseases, particularly alcoholism. People have also been getting poorer: between 1989 and 1996, real wages dropped by two-thirds. In 1996, more than one-third of the population was living below the poverty line.

One-quarter of the workforce are employed in agriculture, though this now generates a shrinking proportion of GDP. The soil is good but the climate is unpredictable and it swings between hostile extremes—fiercely hot summers and bitterly cold winters.

Agriculture has not developed much since the Soviet era. Privatization has been slow. Most farmers lease their land from the state and are often so short of credit, inputs, and equipment that they cannot complete their harvests.

Kazakhstan's other major source of employment—though more for Russians and Ukrainians—is heavy industry which centres on the production of oil and gas. Oil was first found here in 1899. Kazakhstan still has substantial oil deposits along the Caspian Sea coast, and there have been major new finds coast—1.6% of world reserves. There are also fields in the north-west. Despite the difficulties of exporting from this landlocked country, these deposits have proved very attractive to companies from all over the world who are keen to engage in joint ventures. The country also has substantial deposits of metal ores—including chromium, lead, copper, zinc, and tungsten, but production of these has been restricted in recent years by falling world demand.

Oil companies have flocked to Kazakhstan

Kazakhstan's oily industrial past has bequeathed severe environmental problems. It was also a Soviet nuclear test site—between 1949 and 1989, 470 tests were carried out in the north, which now has to deal with a legacy of cancer and birth defects. In the south, the main environmental problem is the drying up of the Aral Sea, whose water level has been falling as a result of withdrawals from feeder rivers elsewhere in Central Asia. The sea is also heavily polluted by fertilizer run-off—which is killing the fishing industry and is also contaminating water supplies.

When Kazakhstan achieved independence from the Soviet Union in 1991 the sole presidential candidate was Nursultan Nazarbaev—a former head of the Kazakh Communist Party, who initially had opposed independence. Like other leaders in Central Asia, he continued to rule in much the same autocratic fashion. And when it was time for re-election in 1999 he took no chances—suddenly bringing the election forward while the economy was in better shape, and banning his most serious rival. Standing against a communist candidate, he was duly re-elected with 82% of the vote.

Nevertheless Nazarbaev does have genuine popular support—he is credited with creating peace and stability, if at the cost of harassing the opposition and controlling the press. Voters had more of a choice in October 1999 in the election for a new lower house of parliament, the Majlis. Most of the seats went to the Otan (fatherland) Party, which has promised to engage in more rapid economic reform—though the parliament has relatively little power.

Kenya

Kenyans have had to cope with an increasingly inept and corrupt administration

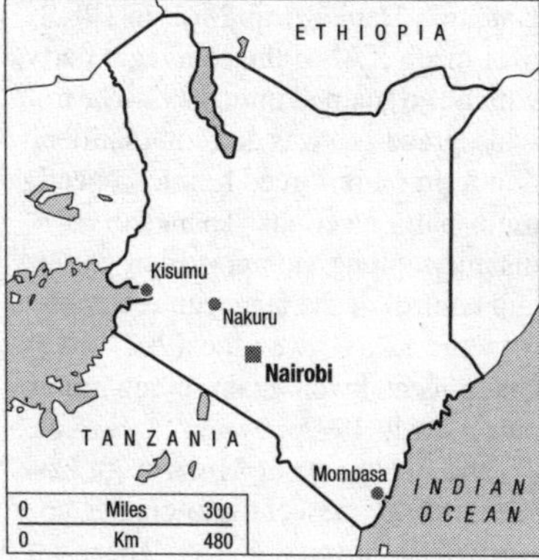

Land area: *580,000 sq. km.*
Population: *29 million—urban 28%*
Capital city: *Nairobi, 1.3 million*
People: *Kikuyu 22%, Luhya 14%, Luo 13%, Kalenjin 12%, Kamba 11%, Kisii 6%, Meru 6%, other 16%*
Language: *English, Swahili, and many other languages*
Religion: *Protestant 38%, Roman Catholic 28%, indigenous beliefs 26%, other 8%*
Government: *Republic*
Life expectancy: *52 years*
GNP per capita: *$PPP 1,130*
Currency: *Kenyan shilling*
Major exports: *Tea, coffee, horticultural products*

Most of the eastern half of Kenya consists of a broad plateau with scattered hills that slope down to a narrow coastal strip. This is an area of uncertain rainfall, merging into the arid and semi-arid lands of the north and north-east. The western half has several mountain systems split in two by the snaking line of the Rift Valley, while to the south-west the mountains descend to a basin around the shores of Lake Victoria.

Most of the population is concentrated in the western half of the country, particularly on the fertile central highlands and on the land to the west. The land in the north-east is occupied mostly by nomadic herding communities. Kenya has many different ethnic communities, but they can be divided into three main groups. The largest, with about two-thirds of the population, are the Bantu group which includes the Kikuyu and the Luhya. A second group, the Nilotic, making up around a quarter of the population, includes the Luo and Kalenjin and the Masai nomads. A third, smaller, group are the Cushitic. Others are of European, Asian, and Arab descent.

Kenya has had very rapid population growth, averaging 3.5% per year over the period 1970-95. The growth rate has fallen slightly since then as a result of more intensive family planning as well as the death toll from AIDS—12% of the adult population is HIV-positive. Even so, the population density is already high in the areas that have better land, putting pressure on the environment and driving people into the cities, particularly to the slums of Nairobi.

Kenya also suffers from wide income disparities. At independence, much of the best land was taken and kept by the Kikuyu élite. And subsequent liberal free-market development led to rapid economic growth but also heightened inequality. The richest fifth of the population get half of national income. Half the population live below the poverty line.

Agriculture accounts for around one-quarter of GNP and for around one-fifth of formal employment. Kenya's small farmers grow food crops such as cassava and maize for subsistence, and also produce around half the two largest export items, tea and coffee—the rest being grown on large estates. Over recent decades Kenyan farmers have also found important new markets for fruit, vegetables, and even for cut flowers, which are air-freighted to Europe.

Manufacturing accounts for around 10% of GDP, with the emphasis on food processing and small-scale consumer goods. But industry has been hit by a lethal combination of liberalization and corruption. Kenya's textiles industry, for example, has been undermined by duty-free imports brought in by people who enjoy close connections to the ruling élite. Kenya also has a vast informal sector which employs around two-thirds of the workforce.

Kenya has a vast informal sector

In 1999, economic growth fell yet again, to 1.3%—which the National Bank attributed to poor infrastructure, the high cost of credit, and inefficient public services. In addition a severe drought not only hit agricultural production, but also reduced output of the hydroelectric power on which Kenya depends. Most parts of the country face frequent power cuts.

Tourism has been a further source of foreign exchange, and accounts for around one-fifth of GDP. Visitors head for the game reserves or the beaches, though nowadays more are choosing neighbouring countries.

For much of the period following independence in 1963, Kenya has effectively been a one-party state—run by the Kenya African National Union (KANU). The first president was a Kikuyu, Jomo Kenyatta, who on his death in 1978 was succeeded by a Kalenjin, Daniel Arap Moi. In 1982, Moi made KANU the sole legal party, which it remained until 1992 when widespread protests and international donor pressure forced him to concede multi-party elections. Thanks to disunity among the opposition groups, and control of the state-run media, Moi and KANU won the 1992 elections and won again, though more narrowly, in 1997.

The final years of Moi's reign have seen a steady descent into greater corruption, poverty, and violence. Politics in Kenya has always had a strong ethnic element. KANU was originally a Kikuyu-dominated party, but Moi has steadily transformed it into one that primarily serves the needs of his own group, the Kalenjin. KANU still has the broadest-based support but Kikuyu, Luo, and Luhya voters now tend to opt for one of the two main opposition parties.

Meanwhile, the economy is unravelling, the infrastructure is collapsing, and aid donors have lost patience with the administration's corruption and incompetence. In 1997, the IMF refused to lend any more and other donors followed suit.

In an attempt to placate them, Moi brought a former opponent, Richard Leakey, into the government to clean up the civil service. Unfortunately, most of the corruption problems remain within the government itself, and the IMF has yet to relent.

Korea, North

The prospect of a collapsed state persuades neighbouring countries to prop up North Korea

Land area: *121,000 sq. km.*
Population: *23 million—urban 61%*
Capital city: *Pyongyang, 2.3 million*
People: *Korean*
Language: *Korean*
Religion: *Confucianism*
Government: *Communist*
Life expectancy: *63 years*
GNP per capita: *$PPP 1,000 (est.)*
Currency: *North Korean won*
Major exports: *Minerals, agricultural products*

Officially, this is the Democratic People's Republic of Korea. Around four-fifths of the territory comprises mountains or high plateaux—the highest of which are to be found in the north-east. The main lowland areas, home to most of the population, and where most agriculture takes place, are to be found in the south-west.

The population is ethnically among the most homogenous in the world, a factor that has helped sustain national solidarity in the face of extreme hardship. There are also several million ethnic Koreans living across the border in China—including around a quarter of a million refugees.

One of the successes of the communist regime is education. Children have good access to pre-school activities, partly to allow their mothers to work, but also to expose them early to the ideals of the state. Health standards were also good until undermined by the famines of the 1990s. In 1999, two-thirds of children were thought to be malnourished. Estimates of the death toll from famine since 1995 range from 1 million to 3.5 million.

Agriculture still employs one-third of the workforce, primarily growing rice, corn, and potatoes. Officially, this is produced almost entirely by co-operatives and collectives—though in recent years much has also been traded through markets. Until the mid-1990s, agriculture was relatively successful, but from 1995 a series of climatic setbacks, including floods, droughts, and tidal waves, combined with mismanagement, crippled production and triggered a sequence of famines. The daily food ration is 100 to 300 grams of rice, but since 1997 the government has been unable to deliver even this.

North Korea had a flourishing industrial sector because the partition of Korea in 1948 left it with most of the minerals and heavy industry. Though it has no oil, the country has plenty of brown coal and considerable hydroelectric potential. Industry, which is largely on the east coast, is dominated by iron and steel, machinery, textiles, and chemicals. But much of the equipment is now antiquated and since 1990 production has been halved. There is little light industry, though some South Korean firms have invested: Daewoo has a factory making Pierre Cardin shirts for export.

The Democratic People's Republic of Korea is a communist state which has been underpinned by a bizarre personality cult. The state was formed in 1948 from the territory of Korea above the 38th parallel which had been occupied by the Soviet Union. With Soviet help, the communist leader Kim Il Sung rapidly took control. In 1950, he also attempted to seize South Korea, provoking the 1950-3 Korean War. Although he failed, Kim nevertheless entrenched his position and with the support of China, the Soviet Union, and a highly disciplined party, he managed to rebuild the country.

By the mid-1950s, however, he had drifted away from the Soviet sphere and developed his own philosophy 'Juche', an obscure mixture of communism and self-reliance, woven into a personality cult around Kim himself. The country was never as self-reliant as it proclaimed. When the Soviet Union collapsed and China started to liberalize its economy and build stronger ties with the West, North Korea lost its two main props.

A bizarre personality cult

North Korea frightens its neighbours. It has the world's fifth-largest army—1.2 million strong—which soaks up around one-third of GDP. Even more alarming, it has the potential to develop nuclear weapons and the early 1990s it threatened to withdraw from the Nuclear Non-Proliferation Treaty. The tension subsided in 1994 when North Korea and the USA signed the General Framework Agreement, through which North Korea would cap its nuclear weapons programme in exchange for US aid for the construction of new light-water reactors. Since then, however, there have been fears the North Korea has been backtracking.

When Kim Il Sung died suddenly in 1994 he left a confusing power vacuum. For four years, the country had no head of state. The situation became clearer in 1998 when the late Kim Il-Sung was posthumously elevated to 'president for eternity' while his son Kim Jong-Il became Chairman of the National Defence Committee and head of state. Even so, the real location of power remains unclear—distributed between the state, the party, and the army.

With persistent famines and a bankrupt government, North Korea seems permanently on the brink of implosion. South Korea does not want the economic burden of having North Korea fall into its lap and has been sending fertilizer and food aid. It has also established a fund of $450 million to help the north. China, nervous of a capitalist Korea on its doorstep, has been allowing hundreds of thousands of starving North Koreans to enter in search of food.

Reunification seems inevitable—only a matter of time and conditions. Kim Jong-Il was remarkably forthcoming during the ground-breaking visit of the South Korean prime minister in June 2000, helping to defuse some tensions.

Korea, South

South Korea's economic crisis exposed its over-reliance on huge and cosseted conglomerates

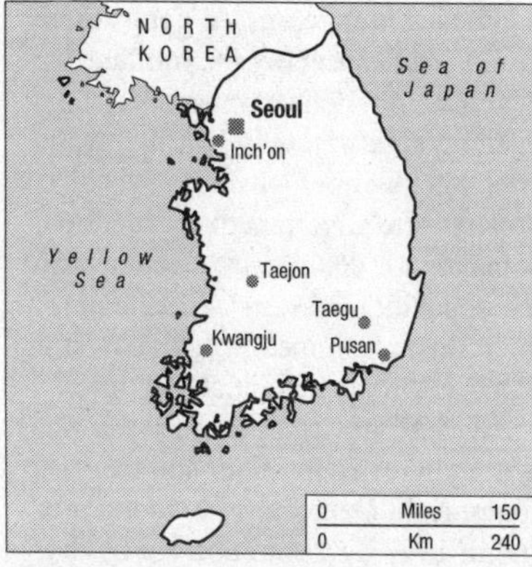

Land area: *99,000 sq. km.*
Population: *46 million—urban 84%*
Capital city: *Seoul, 11 million*
People: *Korean*
Language: *Korean*
Religion: *Christianity, Buddhism*
Government: *Republic*
Life expectancy: *72 years*
GNP per capita: *$PPP 12,270*
Currency: *Won*
Major exports: *Electronic goods, textiles, cars, ships*

The country's official name is the Republic of Korea. Almost three-quarters of its territory is mountainous—the largest range being the T'aebaek, which occupies most of the eastern half of the country. Most of the population are to be found in the lowlands of the north-west and south-west and in the Naktong River basin in the south-east.

Almost everyone is ethnically Korean—and speaks the Korean language. Traditionally most Koreans have followed Confucian and Buddhist principles, but Christianity has had an increasing impact, particularly the evangelical protestant sects. One of these, though less significant now, is the controversial Unification Church of Reverend Sun Myung Moon, which has been exported around the world. South Korea is one of the world's most densely populated countries.

Until the early 1980s, South Korea sent emigrant workers to other countries, but the flow has now been reversed and South Korea has attracted more than 200,000 foreign workers, legal and illegal, to do the more menial work. Most come from South-East Asia and China and many are of Korean ethnic origin.

Koreans have good standards of health and are well educated. But the curriculum puts much emphasis on rote learning that does not encourage creativity—something of a handicap for future development.

Today few Koreans work as farmers. Between 1980 and 1997, the proportion of the labour force working in agriculture fell from 37% to 6%. The people remaining are mostly small-holders with rice as their main crop. Food prices are heavily subsidized.

Nowadays around one-third of the workforce are employed in manufacturing industry. The partition of Korea left the South worse off—since the North had most of the mineral resources and the heavy industry. Manufacturing in the South initially concentrated therefore on light industry for local consumption and then for export. But from the

1970s South Korea turned its attention to heavy industry, particularly steel and cars—largely in the Seoul-Inchon region—and later to advanced electronic products. The result was a phenomenal rate of growth, from the 1990s until 1997 it averaged around 9% per year. This led to steady rises in income, and in labour costs. Between 1970 and 1997, average monthly earnings went from $70 to $1,394. As a result, much of the simpler labour-intensive assembly work in footwear and toys has now moved overseas.

Service industries, on the other hand, are less sophisticated than those of other countries of similar wealth—whether in retail, finance, or entertainment. Seoul seems, for example, less cosmopolitan than other leading Asian cities.

At the heart of South Korea's rapid economic expansion were the 'chaebol'— vast diversified family-owned conglomerates. In 1999, five of these—Hyundai, Samsung, Daewoo, LG, and the SK group—still accounted for one-third of sales and almost half of exports. They benefited from decades of state favours and easy credit but recklessly overstretched and were deep in debt by 1997 when the Asian financial crisis struck. The currency lost half its value, and in the year from June 1997 the stock market fell by 65%.

South Korea's chaebol are deep in debt

Since then, the economy has bounced back. In 1999, growth was 9%. But in 2000 the Daewoo group still owed $87 billion. And unemployment in late 1999 was 6%—three times higher than before the crisis. The economic crisis has also widened the gap between rich and poor—in a country that had prided itself that its development had been egalitarian.

For most of its period of rapid growth, South Korea was in the grip of authoritarian military-backed regimes, which repressed opposition groups and especially the militant labour unions. The democratic opening appeared only in 1987, when, after weeks of demonstrations and protests, the government acceded to demands for democratic elections. But the opposition was divided, allowing the military nominee Roh-Tae-Woo to win the 1988 presidential election.

In 1992, however, the election was won by Kim Young-Sam and the centre-right Democratic Liberal Party, and in 1997 by a coalition led by the left-of-centre, and formerly exiled, Kim Dae-Jung. The military are still in the background, but their influence has waned—in 1996 Roh-Tae-Woo was imprisoned for corruption.

Kim Dae-Jung's job was complicated by the parliamentary election in April 2000 when his Millennium Democratic Party came second. Kim has to struggle with structural reform, widespread corruption, and an insolvent banking system. At the same time he faces stiff resistance from the chaebol and from the labour unions which oppose layoffs.

A permanent anxiety is North Korea: the South is worried about the cost of taking over the North so is anxious to stave off its collapse. Relations improved following Kim's historic official visit to the North in June 2000.

Kuwait

After the Gulf War, Kuwait wanted to become less reliant on foreigners, but failed

Land area: *18,000 sq. km.*
Population: *2 million—urban 97%*
Capital city: *Kuwait City, 192,000*
People: *Kuwaiti 45%, other Arab 35%, South Asian and other 20%*
Language: *Arabic, English*
Religion: *Muslim 85% (Sunni 45%, Shiah 40%), Christian, Hindu, Parsi, and other 15%*
Government: *Hereditary emirate*
Life expectancy: *76 years*
GNP per capita: *$PPP 25,314*
Currency: *Kuwaiti dinar*
Major exports: *Oil, oil products*

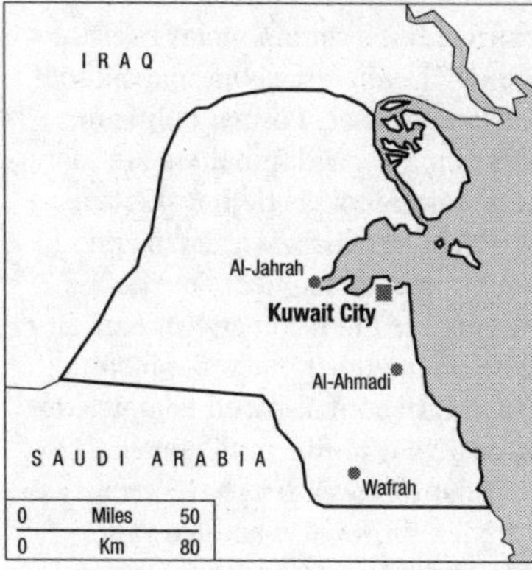

Kuwait is a small state at the north of the Persian Gulf between Iraq and Saudi Arabia. It has some oases and a few small fertile areas, but the country consists largely of a sloping plain that is almost entirely desert.

A couple of generations ago, Kuwaitis were nomadic tribesmen. But since 1946 oil has made Kuwait very wealthy. Kuwaitis are among the richest people in the world—and are also entitled to free education, health care, and electricity, and are spared the inconvenience of income tax.

They can also pay other people to do much of the work. In 1997 Kuwaitis made up only 16% of the labour force—the rest being immigrant workers. The largest numbers nowadays are from Egypt, Palestine, and Lebanon, but there are also many from South Asia. Kuwaiti citizens make up only one-third of the total population. Almost all employed Kuwaitis choose to work for the government or for public corporations.

Kuwait is still floating, if less buoyantly than before, on a sea of oil which accounts for 45% of GDP and around 95% of export earnings. Kuwait has about 10% of world reserves, mostly in the Burgan field south of Kuwait City. At present rates of extraction, this should last for 100 years or more.

Since the 1970s, the oil industry has been nationalized. The government owns local refineries and also markets around 40% of its own oil. Kuwait Petroleum International operates more than 5,000 petrol stations using the 'Q8' brand name in 10 European countries. It also now has more than 100 stations in Thailand. In addition, Kuwait has large reserves of gas.

In addition, the country has some manufacturing industry—also linked to oil. In the past this has typically involved such low-value products as ammonia, urea, and fertilizers. But there have been efforts to move to more profitable products such as polypropylene One of the largest petrochemicals companies, Equate, is a joint venture between Kuwait's

Petrochemical Industries Company and Union Carbide.

Much of the oil infrastructure has been restored since the 1990 Gulf War, but Kuwait's economy will never be the same. To pay for the war the government had to sell off around half its $100-billion overseas investments. To make matters worse, the price of oil was low for much of the 1990s.

With scarcely any arable land or water for irrigation, Kuwait's agriculture is very limited. Some farms grow vegetables and fruits but almost all the country's food has to be imported. There is also a fishing industry whose catches are dedicated to the local market.

With a generous welfare system, Kuwait is now living far beyond its means and government finances have gone deeply into the red—the 1998-9 budget showed a $5-billion deficit. The government has been suggesting the possibility of charging for health, or education, or even for local telephone calls. But there is stiff opposition from conservatives who argue that the government should reduce the deficit by attacking corruption and reducing defence expenditure, which is around one-fifth of the budget. For the time being Kuwait will continue to sell off its investments.

Kuwait is living far beyond its means

Kuwait is a hereditary emirate and the ruling al-Sabah family holds all the key government posts. Since 1977, the emir has been Sheikh Jaber al-Sabah, though after the Gulf War he started to leave most decisions to his cousin Sheikh Saad. There is also a degree of palace intrigue since the deputy prime minister, Sheikh Sabah, is from a rival branch of the family.

Kuwait does have a parliament whose 50 members are elected for four-year terms. The last elections were in 1999. However this has little power, and the electorate is also very restricted—to certain males over the age of 21, who are about one-sixth of Kuwaiti citizens. Formal political parties are banned, but there are more informal groupings both inside and outside the parliament. On the one hand, there are the liberals who are concentrated in the centre of Kuwait City; on the other, there are more conservative tribal-based Islamic groupings who live in the outer areas.

Relations with Iraq have been complex. In 1961, when Kuwait achieved full independence, Iraq refused to recognize the state and claimed the territory as part of Iraq. Nevertheless, when Iraq fought Iran Kuwait supported Iraq. This did not stop Saddam Hussain invading Kuwait in August 1990. Though he rapidly overran the country his forces were expelled by a US-led coalition in Operation Desert Storm.

After the war, the USA tried to pressure the emir to establish a democracy, reduce dependence on immigrant workers, and liberalize the economy. Little of this has happened. In 1998, a bill that proposed votes for women was rapidly defeated. And though many migrant workers fled, particularly the Palestinians who had been accused of siding with the Iraqis, they have now been replaced. The government wants to 'Kuwaitize' private-sector companies, but few Kuwaitis have the qualifications or the inclination for this work.

Kyrgyzstan

Kyrgyzstan is one of the faster-reforming ex-Soviet republics in Central Asia

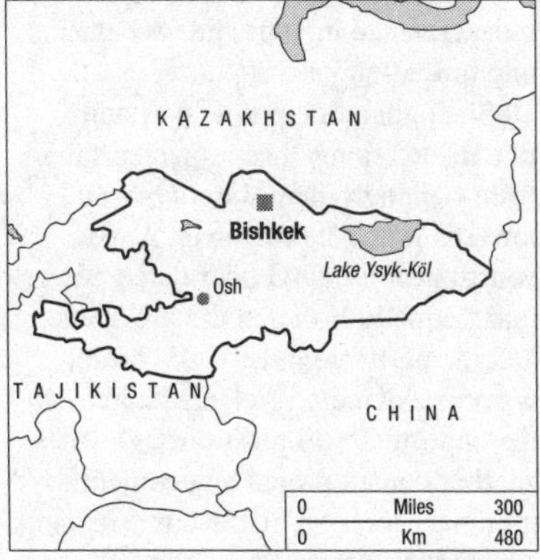

Land area: *199,000 sq. km.*
Population: *5 million—urban 40%*
Capital city: *Bishkek, 631,000*
People: *Kirghyz 53%, Russian 18%, Uzbek 13%, Ukrainian 3%, German 2%, other 11%*
Language: *Kyrgyz, Russian*
Religion: *Muslim 75%, Russian Orthodox 20%, other 5%*
Government: *Republic*
Life expectancy: *68 years*
GNP per capita: *$PPP 2,200*
Currency: *Som*
Major exports: *Food, metals, electricity*

Kyrgyzstan is a landlocked country with spectacular scenery. It is almost entirely mountainous, lying at the junction of several ranges that run mostly east to west and whose peaks are permanently covered in snow and ice. More than half the territory is above 2,500 metres. Some of the main lowland basins are in the south-west and there is one in the north where the capital Bishkek is to be found. The main river, flowing east to west, and a major source of irrigation, is the Naryn. The country also has many lakes, the largest of which, Ysyk-Köl in the north-east, is 1,500 metres above sea level.

The Kyrgyz people make up more than half the population—a proportion that is rising as a result of the exodus of Russians and ethnic Germans: between 1990 and 1995 half a million departed, more than 12% of the population. The majority of Kyrgyz live in the rural areas. The second largest minority are the Uzbeks, who are concentrated in the south, around the city of Osh. Ethnic relations have at times been tense. In 1990, for example, the Kyrgyz had been moving into territory previously occupied by the Uzbek. Clashes between the two communities left 230 dead.

While standards of health have generally been good, health services are deteriorating and there have been outbreaks of contagious diseases. Poverty increased rapidly after 1990. Since then there has been some improvement—but around half the population are still considered poor.

Agriculture is the largest source of income, employing one-third of the workforce. Livestock production has long been a mainstay of the economy—producing wool, hides, and meat. And many people still work as nomadic herders, setting up camp in their traditional round felt tents, called 'gers'. Only about 7% of the land is arable, but it benefits from extensive irrigation from rivers rushing down from mountain peaks. Crops include cotton, wheat, and vegetables. Most of the previous collective farms are now joint-stock companies and relatively efficient—the country is now self-sufficient in grains.

During the Soviet period, Kyrgyzstan underwent a rapid process of industrialization, chiefly based on the exploitation of mineral deposits. The country has extensive coal reserves, as well as non-ferrous metal deposits, including gold, uranium, mercury, and tin. Much of the heavy industrial manufacturing has been fairly inefficient. But the mining sector, along with perhaps the expansion of hydroelectric power, will be one of the keys to future development. Gold production, for example, has recently been stepped up following the start of mining at Kumtor, near Bishkek. Although a state-owned company still controls gold mining, it has also been working in tandem with foreign enterprises.

This has been one of the fastest reforming countries of the ex-Soviet republics in Central Asia. By mid-1997, for example, around 60% of eligible enterprises had been privatized. This, combined with tight macroeconomic policies ensured considerable support from international donors and financial institutions. But the economic and social cost was high and the economy has been slow to respond—hampered by the exodus of skilled Russian workers. Growth only really resumed after 1995 and dipped again in 1998. The economic outlook remains problematic—the country's relative isolation has been deterring foreign investment in anything other than mining.

Kyrgyzstan has lost many skilled Russians

The country's economic reforms have been driven largely by President Askar Akaev, who has been in office since 1990. The riots in that year had fatally weakened the Communist Party and opened the way for reformists to elect Akaev, a former physicist, as president. He subsequently banned the Communist Party and, following independence in 1991, he was elected unopposed.

Since then, the political system, like the economy, has remained fairly open—though increasingly biased towards presidential power. A new constitution in 1993 distributed power fairly equally between the president and the parliament. In 1995, Akaev was convincingly re-elected and took the opportunity to push through yet another constitutional amendment to tilt power more in his favour. The new constitution offers Akaev the opportunity to stand for president twice more, since he had been elected under the old constitution.

The parliament has three main groups: the communists, who are now legal again but are hostile to reform, Akaev's Union of Democratic Forces (SDS), and a social democratic grouping that tries to resist the increasing presidential powers.

By the democratic standards of Central Asia, which are not high, Kyrgyzstan does fairly well and has a free press. But Akaev has at times overridden parliamentary opposition and there were alarming developments before the February 2000 elections: three of the main parties were excluded—probably to undermine the opposition prior to the presidential election. In the event, the communists were again the largest party with 27% of the vote. The SDS came second with 18%.

Laos

An isolated communist state that is slowly opening up to the rest of the world

Land area: *237,000 sq. km.*
Population: *5 million—urban 22%*
Capital city: *Vientiane, 400,000*
People: *Lao-Loum 68%, Lao-Theung 22%, Lao -Soung including Hmong and Yao 9%, Vietnamese/Chinese 1%*
Language: *Lao, French, English, and various ethnic languages*
Religion: *Buddhist 60%, animist and other 40%*
Life expectancy: *53 years*
GNP per capita: *$PPP 1,300*
Currency: *Kip*
Major exports: *Wood products, coffee, electricity*

Laos is a landlocked and almost entirely mountainous country—nine-tenths of the territory is 180 metres or more above sea level. The highest mountains are to the north, while another range lies to the east along the border with Vietnam. The only extensive lowland areas are to the south in the floodplains of the Mekong River—where around half the population live. Only around 5% of the territory is suitable for agriculture and most of the rest is covered with forests—broadleaf in the north, but tropical hardwoods in the south.

Laos is sparsely populated but it has, according to the government, around 68 'nationalities' divided into three main groups. The largest, and politically the most dominant, are the Lao-Loum, who live in the cities and in the lowlands of the Mekong delta. The Lao-Theung, also called the Mon-Khmer, live in the uplands throughout Laos and can also be found in neighbouring countries. Finally, there are the highland Lao-Soung, who include the Hmong (Meo) and the Yao (Mien).

Levels of human development are low. In 1995, 22% of the population were estimated to be living below the poverty line, consuming less than 2,100 calories per day. With the loss of aid from the former Soviet Union, Laos has had to turn instead to international institutions including the UN agencies, the IMF, and the World Bank. By 1998, foreign aid accounted for 15% of GDP.

More than 80% of Laotians depend for survival on agriculture, which accounts for more than half of GDP. But farming is not very efficient. Upland farmers rely on slash-and-burn techniques and even in the more fertile lowlands rice yields are low—vulnerable to droughts and floods and hampered by lack of credit and inputs, as well as by crumbling infrastructure that has suffered from decades of war and low investment.

More recently, Laos has been trying to produce more cash crops for export—including cotton, groundnuts, sugar cane and tobacco. But the most notable export success has been coffee. This was originally introduced by the French colonialists and is now being revived by small farmers, who grow good-quality robusta coffee for export to Europe.

Nevertheless, the country's leading export earners remain timber and wood products. Laos has valuable forest resources, including teak, rosewood, and ebony. A less official crop is opium. Laos is thought to be the world's third largest producer of opium and heroin. The country also serves as a transit route for heroin from Burma.

Laos has no heavy industry but does have some small-scale manufacturing around Vientiane.

Laos exports hydro-electricity

Some of the more successful products include handicrafts, garments, foodstuffs, and wood products. Another export prospect is hydro-electric power. Laos's rugged terrain is cut through with fast-flowing rivers, some of which are dammed to produce power for export to Thailand. But projects for dams funded by World Bank loans have fallen foul of international environmental protests—and the power demand from Thailand has slumped.

Political life in Laos is controlled by the Lao People's Revolutionary Party (LPRP). Laos has been a communist country since 1975 and the most recent constitution in 1991 confirmed that power would remain exclusively in the hands of the governing party. But whether Laotian communism amounts to socialism is more questionable. Politics is based less on class and more on regional, family, and ethnic loyalties. From the outset, it looked as though socialism would remain a long-term goal, and it seems more distant than ever.

Since the mid-1980s the government has pursued a more liberal economic path. In 1986 it abandoned collectivization of farms and introduced the 'New Economic Mechanism', which also removed many restrictions on private enterprise. Since 1988, the government has also been selling stakes in many state-owned enterprises—though only a few have been sold outright. Because Laos is economically dependent on Thailand it was hard hit by the Asian financial crisis in 1997—which cut demand for timber and electricity—and inflation hit 100%.

Politically, the situation is less fluid and the party hardliners retain their grip. Non-communist political parties are proscribed and the government clamps down on all forms of dissent. In the National Assembly elections in 1997, only four non-party members won seats; the other 98 were taken by members of the LPRP. There seems little prospect of any political liberalization in the near future.

The only visible opposition comes from insurgent Hmong tribesmen, known as the 'Chao Fa'. They are the remnants of a guerrilla army that the CIA financed during the Vietnam War. As a result of increasing discontent with the government, they seem to be getting more popular support and they stepped up their activities during 1999. In March 2000 they were blamed for an explosion in a restaurant in Vientiane.

Latvia

Latvia is turning to the West, but EU membership is a long way off and relations with Russia are often tense

Land area: *65,000 sq. km.*
Population: *2 million—urban 74%*
Capital city: *Riga, 804,000*
People: *Lett 56%, Russian 30%, Belarusian 4%, Ukrainian 3%, Polish 3%, other 4%*
Language: *Lettish, Lithuanian, Russian*
Religion: *Lutheran, Roman Catholic, Russian Orthodox*
Government: *Republic*
Life expectancy: *68 years*
GNP per capita: *$PPP 3,940*
Currency: *Lat*
Major exports: *Timber, wood products, textiles, metals*

Latvia consists of gently rolling plains interspersed with low hills. Around one-quarter of the land is forested and there are numerous lakes, marshes, and peat bogs. The long coastline includes major ports as well as holiday resorts and extensive beaches.

Latvia's people, the Letts, have come close to being a minority in their own country. Before Latvia was annexed by the Soviet Union in 1940 the Letts were 77% of the population, but a combination of deportation of Latvians and immigration from other Soviet republics, particularly Russia, dramatically altered the ethnic balance. In 1997, the Letts made up only 54% of the population. After Latvia regained independence in 1991 the government was determined to reassert Latvian control and in 1994 introduced a rigorous Citizenship Law. Although, under pressure from Russia, this was relaxed somewhat in 1998 it still requires people taking Latvian citizenship to pass stiff tests in language and history. And unless you are a citizen you cannot vote, buy land, or enter a number of professions. Russians who arrived after 1940 are regarded as 'occupiers' and do not get automatic citizenship. Of the 700,000 ethnic Russians, around 60% are potentially stateless.

Latvia has been one of the more successful ex-Soviet republics, but it still has high levels of poverty. In 1997, the government estimated that 60% of the population lived below the 'crisis subsistence minimum', though this proportion was down somewhat on the previous year. At the same time inequality is rising.

Industry in Latvia had been geared to producing industrial and consumer goods, including processed food, for the Soviet Union. But after independence, when the country was opened up to foreign competition, many industries went into steep decline. Some of the largest are still in state hands. Privatization, which started with a voucher distribution in 1993, proceeded fairly slowly.

Although the smaller enterprises changed hands quickly, many of the larger ones were not privatized until 1999. Even so, by 1997 the private sector accounted for around two-thirds of GDP.

Agriculture had been collectivized during the Soviet era but by 1997 almost all the land had been returned to its original owners. The main activities are dairy farming and livestock raising, along with cereal production. Output fell during the transition period and farmers have been hit by weak demand from the food processing industry. Probably the most important rural activity is timber production. Forests cover around 45% of the land area and timber and wood products make up around one-third of exports.

The most striking economic development in recent years has been the rise of the service sector, which now accounts for around two-thirds of GDP. Much of this is connected with trade since Latvia, with three important ports, is a major transit route for goods in and out of Russia. Latvia is also dependent on Russia for oil, though is trying to construct a pipeline to Finland through Estonia.

Latvia is a major transit route to Russia

Much of Latvia's economic growth has been driven by foreign investment. Latvia has become one of the most popular investment choices in Eastern Europe.

Since independence in 1991, politics has been a shifting and unstable affair, producing a series of weak governments. At the outset the country was governed by the Latvian Popular Front. But the steep economic decline of the early years eroded support and after the first free parliamentary elections in 1993, the party with the most seats in the Saeima, the unicameral parliament, was the centre-right Latvia's Way Party which governed in coalition with the Farmers' Union. In the same year Guntis Ulmanis of the Farmers' Union was elected to the largely ceremonial post of president (and re-elected in 1996).

That coalition fell apart in 1995. The ensuing election did not produce a much clearer answer but eventually resulted in a multi-party 'rainbow' coalition led by businessman Andris Skele. This survived until 1997 when the centre-right parts of the coalition withdrew their support, backing instead a new coalition led by Gunter Krasts of the nationalist For Fatherland and Freedom (FFF) party. He, however, also had difficulty in keeping a coalition together. In 1998, Vilis Kristopans of Latvia's Way put together a centre-right minority administration.

In 1999 in an interesting twist, the parliament, after a long deadlock in its selection for the post of president, chose an outsider, a 61-year old returned emigré, Canadian psychology professor Vaira Vike-Freiberga. Soon after her election, Kristopans resigned and Andris Skele was back as prime minister. In 2000 Latvia started negotiations for EU membership.

By May 2000, however, this government too had collapsed and Skele was replaced as prime minister by Andris Berzins, heading a similar coalition. Since 1991 Latvia has had nine governments.

Lebanon

Reconstruction has stalled, but could revive if there is a settlement in Palestine

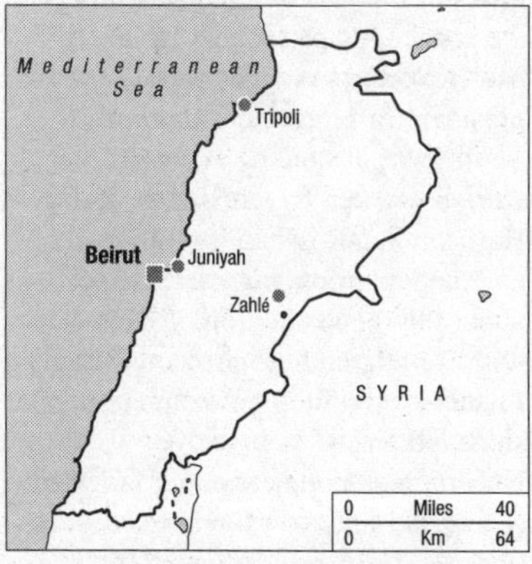

Land area: *10,000 sq. km.*
Population: *4 million—urban 89%*
Capital city: *Beirut, 1.5 million*
People: *Arab 95%, Armenian 4%, other 1%*
Language: *Arabic, French*
Religion: *Islam 70%, Christian 30%*
Government: *Republic*
Life expectancy: *64 years*
GNP per capita: *$PPP 6,150*
Currency: *Lebanese pound*
Major exports: *Paper products, foodstuffs, textiles*

Along its Mediterranean coast Lebanon has a narrow, flat coastal plain. Inland it has two parallel mountain ranges running north-east to south-west: the Lebanon Mountains, which ascend abruptly from the plain; and the Anti-Lebanon Mountains along the border with Syria. Between these two ranges is the fertile Bekaa Valley.

Almost all Lebanese are ethnically Arab, but they are sharply divided into 'confessional' groups—Muslim and Christian sects. At independence in 1943, political leaders established an unwritten National Pact that shared political power according to the proportions of each sect in the 1932 census. At that point, the most numerous were the Maronite Christians, followed by Sunni Muslims, Shiah Muslims, Greek Orthodox Christians, Druze (Muslims), and Greek Catholics. Overall, Christians were in a narrow majority and for many years were politically dominant. Since then, however, waves of immigration, notably of Palestinians, have altered the balance. Of today's 4 million population, around 70% are Muslim, including around 200,000 Palestinian refugees living in camps. In addition, there are around 300,000 Syrian migrant workers.

Prior to the civil war of 1975-90, Lebanon was one of the most developed Arab states—a major centre for trade, finance, and tourism. Much of that was wrecked in the war which virtually levelled the city of Beirut. Today, the Lebanese population remains highly educated with good standards of health, but many people are unemployed and around one-quarter of the population live in poverty.

The economy is recovering slowly. Unsurprisingly, one of the most vibrant sectors has been construction. From 1992, funds raised from government bonds have flooded in for the rebuilding of Beirut, often from Lebanese expatriates.

But as before, the main sources of employment are services of various kinds, many connected with trade, which account for around 60% of

GDP. The financial sector is also being redeveloped and tourists have been coming back—more than half a million in 1998. Manufacturing too has been important. Many new enterprises have sprung up—one-third of companies were launched after 1990. Most of these are small, engaged, for example, in food production, furniture-making, and in textiles and clothing.

Agriculture has been less significant. Farmers grow fruit and vegetables on the coastal plain, and wheat and barley in the Bekaa Valley, but there has been relatively little investment and many farmers in the Bekaa are turning again to cannabis, which was a major source of income for various militias during the war.

Lebanese farmers are turning to cannabis

Lebanon's most recent troubles date back to the late 1960s when the Palestine Liberation Organization (PLO) started using Lebanon as a base. The Muslims, many of whom supported the PLO, had long resented Christian political domination and from 1975 their disagreements erupted into a full scale civil war. In 1978, as part of its campaign against the PLO, Israel invaded and seized a 'security zone' on Lebanon's southern border.

The war stopped in 1990—after 150,000 deaths and $25 billion-worth of damage. The end came when Syrian forces effectively took control, helping the government to disarm the militias.

Political loyalties in Lebanon align not behind parties but more along personal or religious lines. The largest group now are the Shiah, who include the militant Hizbullah. The Sunni are a less coherent group and during the war had weaker militias.

In the deal that ended the war, Lebanon's National Pact was amended to increase the powers of the prime minister (always a Sunni Muslim) and the speaker of parliament (a Shiah Muslim), and to reduce those of the president (a Maronite Christian).

In 1992, following elections that were boycotted by Christians, Rafiq Hariri, a Saudi-Lebanese billionaire emerged as prime minister. He set about the reconstruction of Beirut, with some grandiose projects—largely financed by selling government bonds since aid was slow to arrive. Unfortunately, the economy failed to revive and Lebanon found itself deep in debt. Hariri was criticized for spending the money on buildings rather than on social welfare.

In 1998 in order to reduce corruption Syria supported the election as president of a Christian former army commander, Emile Lahou. Hariri feared that this would produce a stronger Christian influence so resigned, and was replaced by Salim al-Hoss.

The Barak administration in Israel had pledged to withdraw from southern Lebanon during 2000. In the event, however, the departure was more abrupt: the Israelis, and their local proxy militia, the South Lebanon Army, were suddenly driven out in May 2000 by the Hizbullah forces. This is unlikely to see the end of hostilities since Hizbullah could well start striking at targets within Israel. The UN also has forces in southern Lebanon but probably insufficient to maintain control.

Lesotho

Lesotho's democracy is fragile—and dependent on support from South Africa

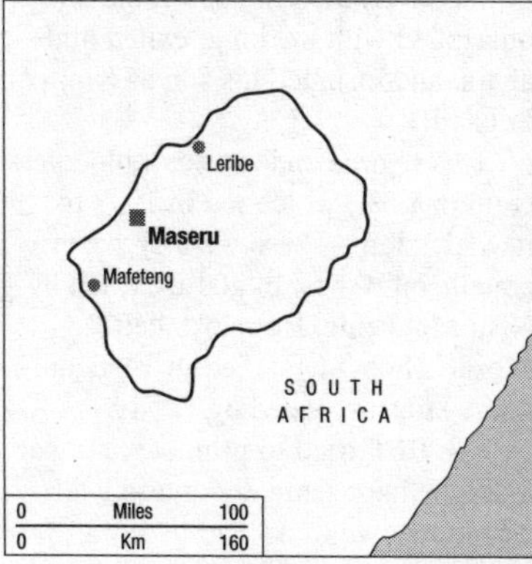

The landlocked kingdom of Lesotho is embedded in South Africa. Most of the territory is mountainous with its highest points in the east and north-east. The lowest and most densely populated areas, which have the best land, are in the north-west, particularly in the valley of the Caledon River.

The kingdom was formed in the 19th century when the Basotho ethnic group took refuge in the mountains to avoid being killed by the more aggressive Zulus and Boers. Today, almost all the people are still Basotho, though this includes a number of subgroups.

Lesotho is a poor country but has relatively high levels of human development. More than 80% of the population are literate, and more than 70% of children are enrolled in secondary schools. Health standards too are quite good, partly as a result of the non-tropical climate.

Land area: *30,000 sq. km.*
Population: *2 million—urban 26%*
Capital city: *Maseru, 150,000*
People: *Basotho*
Language: *Sesotho, English, Zulu, Xhosa*
Religion: *Christian 80%, indigenous beliefs 20%*
Government: *Constitutional monarchy*
Life expectancy: *56 years*
GNP per capita: *$PPP 2,320*
Currency: *Loti*
Major exports: *Garments, footwear*

Many of Lesotho's people live temporarily or permanently in South Africa, working on farms and mines. However their numbers have been dropping. Between 1989 and 2000 the number of Basotho mineworkers in South Africa halved to 64,000. And while their remittances in 1990 contributed around 67% of the country's GDP, by 1996 the proportion was down to 33%.

However, this still means that around 10% of the labour force is in South Africa. This has had a major social impact. Family structures are very disrupted, and most of the agricultural work in Lesotho is done by women. A large migrant population also exposes Lesotho to AIDS, and a significant proportion of the population is HIV-positive.

For most people, however, the main source of income is still farming. Only around one-tenth of the land is suitable for agriculture, and even this has become less productive as a result of over-exploitation and soil erosion. The main crops are maize, wheat, and sorghum, but even in good years around one-quarter of food needs to be imported. Many people also raise cattle which they buy with migrant remittances. They also raise sheep and goats which generate some export income from wool and mohair.

In recent years, Lesotho has seen a surge in manufacturing industry. East Asian investors have established a series of joint ventures with the Lesotho National Development Corporation to manufacture clothing and footwear for export to South Africa and elsewhere. Other companies are now making handicrafts.

Making garments and shoes for South Africa

Another new, if more temporary, source of employment has been the $4 billion Lesotho Highlands Water Development Project. Started in 1986, with the first phase of dam construction due to finish in 2003, this aims to provide electricity for Lesotho and water for South Africa.

Lesotho's political relationship with South Africa has always been close. During the colonial era, South Africa had wanted to incorporate what was then Basutoland. The Basotho successfully resisted and in 1966 Lesotho was born as a constitutional monarchy. Elections the previous year had narrowly been won by the Basotho National Party (BNP), led by Chief Leabua Jonathan who became prime minister. Chief Jonathan was soon in conflict with King Moshoeshoe II, who had tried to extend his authority.

But Jonathan was no democrat. In 1970, when it looked as though the opposition Basotho Congress Party (BCP) had won the election, Chief Jonathan suspended the constitution, dispatched the king temporarily into exile, arrested opposition politicians, and continued to rule by force.

In 1974 the BCP, following a failed uprising, formed the Lesotho National Liberation Army. But Jonathan was not overthrown until 1986, when the military took over and re-established King Moshoeshoe as the titular head of the government. In 1990, the army quarrelled with the king, exiled him again, and installed his son as King Letsie III.

This regime ended after a bloodless coup in 1991, which led in 1993 to new elections. These were convincingly won by the BCP, led by Ntsu Mokhehle. He reinstalled Moshoeshoe—who died in 1996 and was again succeeded by Letsie.

The BCP tried to promote national dialogue but eventually quarrelled within its own ranks and in 1997 Mokhehle himself quit to form the Lesotho Congress for Democracy (LCD). The LCD won only 61% of the vote in the 1998 election but gained 78 of the 79 seats.

In September 1998, an electoral commission refused to overturn this unbalanced result, provoking street riots and a revolt by junior officers. The government asked South Africa, Botswana, and Zimbabwe for help—under the rules of the Southern African Development Community, a threatened member can call on support from the others. In the event, almost all the troops and helicopters that arrived in Maseru were South African. This 'invasion' provoked further riots and looting that caused 70 deaths before a fragile peace was restored.

The next elections, which are unlikely to take place before 2001, will probably involve an element of proportional representation.

Liberia

Slowly emerging from a long civil war, Liberia remains highly armed and violent

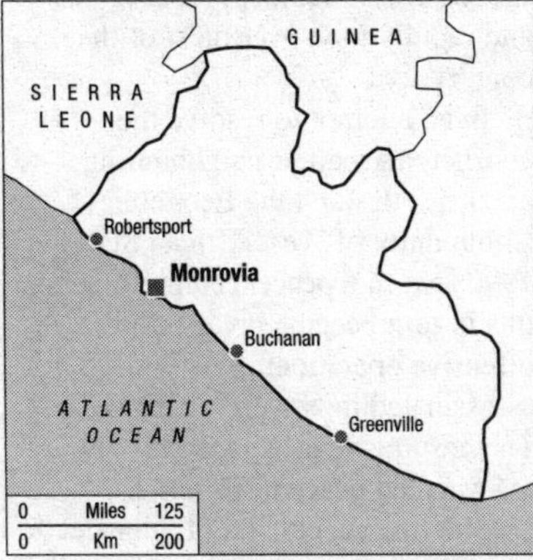

Land area: *98,000 sq. km.*
Population: *3 million—urban 50%*
Capital city: *Monrovia, 1.3 million*
People: *African 95%, Americo-Liberian 5%*
Language: *English and about 20 other languages*
Religion: *Traditional 70%, Muslim 20%, Christian 10%*
Government: *Republic*
Life expectancy: *47 years*
GNP per capita: *$PPP 490*
Currency: *Liberian dollar*
Major exports: *Iron ore, timber, diamonds*

The most developed part of Liberia is the narrow coastal strip that extends around 50 kilometres inland. Behind this rises a belt of low hills and plateaux, and beyond this is the densely forested mountainous interior.

Liberia's fifteen or more ethnic groups were left relatively undisturbed by the colonial powers until freed American slaves arrived in the mid-19th century and established the Republic of Liberia. Nowadays, the Americo-Liberians make up only around 5% of the population but until the early 1980s they dominated political life. The 1989-97 civil war was partly a struggle between this élite group and the rest of the population, as well as between other ethnic groups.

The war is thought to have killed around 200,000 people, displaced around 700,000 within Liberia, and sent 750,000 refugees into neighbouring countries. By early 2000, most of the internally displaced had returned home—as had many refugees. Even before the war, this was one of Africa's most urbanized countries, but the fighting and the flows of refugees will probably have raised the proportion now to 60% or more.

In the past agriculture has provided work to more than half the workforce—the staple foods being rice and cassava. But the fighting drove many subsistence farmers from the land, and the population remains heavily dependent on food imports. Prices are high because the president has given many lucrative import concessions as monopolies to businessmen who supported him during the war.

Many small farmers were also responsible for the country's major cash crop, rubber. One-third of this was produced by small-holders and the rest on large plantations now owned by the Japanese Bridgestone Company. The rubber industry now needs to be rebuilt—with investment not just in plantations but also in roads and in employee housing, much of which was destroyed in the war.

Logging was also an important

source of income. About 50% of Liberia is covered with trees and there are an estimated 3.8 million hectares of productive forests. Before the war there were 36 logging companies but by 1997 these had been reduced to five—and there were no functioning sawmills or plants for processing plywood or veneer. Now the government, or at least the president, is liberally handing out timber concessions to his allies.

Logging licences granted to political allies

Liberia is well-endowed with minerals, including iron ore, gold, and diamonds. Indeed much of the fighting involved struggles for control over these resources. Iron ore was the most significant in terms of export income. Production had already fallen in the mid-1980s as a result of a global slump in the demand for steel. But the war brought the industry to a rapid halt. Between 1988 and 1992, production fell from 12.9 to 1.7 million tons and virtually to zero subsequently. Again, heavy investment will be needed to replace the damaged or looted equipment—and production is unlikely to resume for some years.

Gold and diamond production, which are smaller-scale operations, will revive more quickly. But since much of the output is smuggled out of the country these make a limited contribution to tax revenue or the national economy.

The seeds for Liberia's civil war were sown in 1980 when a military coup led by Master-Sergeant Samuel Doe ended 150 years of domination by the Americo-Liberians. His regime promoted the interests of his own ethnic group, the Kahn, and rapidly degenerated into ruthless repression. He won a rigged election in 1985 but this was soon followed by another attempted coup by the Gio group. Full-scale civil war erupted in 1989 when Charles Taylor (an Americo-Liberian) invaded with rebel forces and rapidly took over most of the country.

In an attempt to resolve the conflict, a group of neighbouring countries through the Economic Community of West African States in 1990 sent in a peacekeeping force, but this in turn became involved in offensive operations. Doe was assassinated in November that year. The ensuing years of anarchy saw many failed peace deals and a bewildering succession of alliances and splits between warring factions.

Finally in 1995, the thirteenth peace deal was signed, leading to elections in 1997. Taylor's lavish presidential campaign was financed from logging and mining operations. But he and his National Patriotic Front of Liberia won a convincing 75% of the vote in what seems to have been a reasonably fair election, largely because people thought he was the only person who could bring the fighting to an end.

Taylor rules in lavish style, with a heavy hand, and with the benefit of armed guards, as well as an 'Anti-Terrorist Unit' commanded by his son. Most opposition politicians have fled or have 'disappeared'. Aid donors are still suspicious of Taylor and have not resumed large flows of aid. Most aid is channelled through local non-governmental organizations. Foreign companies too have been reluctant to invest.

Libya

Sanctions over Lockerbie have ended, but democracy is still not on the agenda

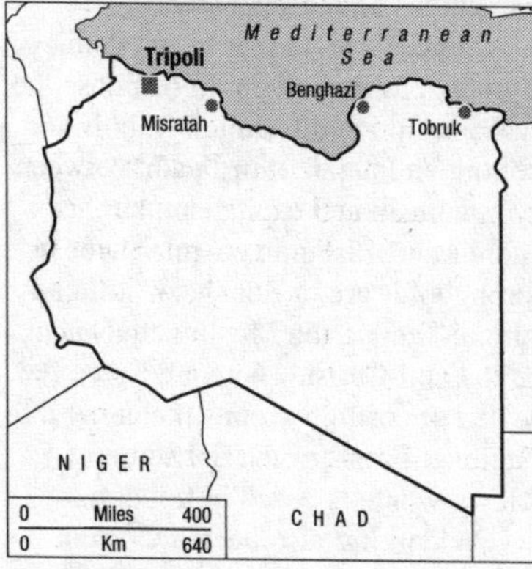

Land area: *1,760,000 sq. km.*
Population: *5 million—urban 86%*
Capital city: *Tripoli, 1.7 million*
People: *Berber and Arab*
Language: *Arabic, Italian, English*
Religion: *Muslim*
Government: *Military dictatorship*
Life expectancy: *70 years*
GNP per capita: *$PPP 6,697*
Currency: *Libyan dinar*
Major exports: *Oil, petroleum products, natural gas*

Most of Libya is a vast barren plain of rocks and sand. The majority of the population live in Tripolitania, in the north-west of the country, a region that includes the capital and a number of coastal oases. The other main inhabited area is Cyrenaica in the north-east.

Many of Libya's people descend from Bedouin Arab tribes—and the tribe is still often the basic social unit. The original Berber population has also largely been absorbed into Arab culture. Nowadays, however, most people live in the cities and the population is very young—60% are under 20 years old.

Libya's oil wealth has not been widely distributed. Most Libyans work in one way or another for the government at salaries less than $70 per month. And standards of living have fallen steadily since the early 1990s as a result of falling oil prices and international sanctions. Nevertheless, Libyans do benefit from subsidized housing and largely free medical care and education. Notably, for an Arab country, women are at least as well educated as men. There have been periods of deliberate cultural isolation. But this seems to be breaking down. Schools have started teaching English after a ten-year ban.

In addition to the native population, there are also more than 1 million immigrant workers, chiefly from Egypt, who at times have been arbitrarily expelled.

Since 1959, when oil was first discovered, Libya has become one of the world's largest producers. Oil makes up more than 90% of exports and provides 80% of government income. At current rates of extraction the oil should last fifty years or more. Most oil production is controlled by the National Oil Company but there are many exploration and co-production contracts with European oil companies. Libya also has huge reserves of natural gas that have yet to be exploited.

Most other industrial operations are run by the state. They do now produce many consumer goods, though companies from Italy and Korea are manufacturing some items like refrigerators and video recorders.

Less than 2% of the land is suitable for farming so agriculture is limited and around 80% of cereals must be imported. The main problem is water. Along the coast, groundwater has been over-extracted for drinking and irrigation and there is a danger of sea water seeping in to replace it. The government's solution is the $30-billion 'great man-made river' scheme which will pump groundwater from aquifers in the south-east to the north. This now delivers water, at great expense, to Tripoli and Benghazi, but its irrigation potential seems limited since much is lost in evaporation.

For the past thirty years, Libyan politics has centred around Muammar Qaddafi. Following a military coup in 1969 Libya's monarchy was overthrown and a group of military officers led by then 29-year-old Captain Qaddafi seized control and redirected Libya along a path of Arab socialism.

In 1977 he changed the country's name to the Socialist People's Libyan Arab Jamahiraya ('state of the masses'). In theory this is popular government, with everyone participating in Basic People's Congresses and choosing representatives to a General People's Congress which selects members of the government. The underlying philosophy is spelled out in Qaddafi's 'Green Book', which is a mixture of Islam and socialism.

Libya is a 'socialist state of the masses'

In reality, all power resides with the idiosyncratic Colonel Qaddafi, whose picture is ubiquitous. He is assisted by 'revolutionary committees' who control most institutions, including the media. Citizens also find their activities scrutinized by 'purification committees'. Human rights abuses range from arbitrary arrest and torture to extra-judicial executions and disappearances.

Qaddafi's main fear is an Islamic uprising, as in Algeria. In response, he has appropriated Islamic symbols and set out an Islamic 'third path' between communism and capitalism, but his more radical Islamic enemies, whose strongholds are in Benghazi, still call him al-Tagout, the Muslim equivalent of the anti-Christ. There are also a few exiled opposition groups including the National Front for the Salvation of Libya, which is based in London.

Qaddafi has also been a thorn in the side of Western governments, particularly the USA, using Libya's oil wealth to bankroll a range of guerrilla groups from the PLO to the IRA. A series of terrorist incidents allegedly culminated in the bombing in 1988 of a Pan Am jet over Lockerbie in Scotland, killing 270 people.

Qaddafi denied Libyan involvement, but the US and British governments indicted two suspects. Qaddafi's initial refusal to allow their extradition resulted in 1992 in UN-backed economic sanctions that were only suspended in 1999 when the suspects were sent to the Netherlands for a trial under Scottish law which started in May 2000.

For the time being, Qaddafi seems secure. In 2000 he was still only 56 and could be around for some time. In any case, his three sons all have public roles so there is the potential for a dynasty.

Lithuania

The slowest reformer of the Baltic states, but negotiating for EU membership

Land area: *65,000 sq. km.*
Population: *3.7 million—urban 72%*
Capital city: *Vilnius, 579,000*
People: *Lithuanian 81%, Russian 9%, Polish 7%, Belarusian 2%, other 1%*
Language: *Lithuanian, Polish, Russian*
Religion: *Roman Catholic*
Government: *Republic*
Life expectancy: *69 years*
GNP per capita: *$PPP 4,310*
Currency: *Litas*
Major exports: *Mineral products, textiles, machinery*

Lithuania's terrain is mostly flat—a plain dotted with low hills and around 3,000 small lakes. The highest points are in the Baltic Highlands in the east and south-east. A feature of the sandy coastline is the narrow 100-kilometre sand spit that creates a distinctive lagoon.

Compared with the other Baltic states—Estonia and Latvia—Lithuania's population has a higher proportion of its own national group: more than 80% of people are ethnic Lithuanian. As a result, when it regained independence in 1991 Lithuania was less nervous than the other Baltic states about offering automatic citizenship to all, an offer that most people took up. Lithuanians also differ in that, like the Poles to the south, they maintain a strong Roman Catholic tradition.

The population has shrunk since 1991, initially as a result of emigration to Russia, Poland, and elsewhere, but more recently because of falling birth rates and rising death rates. Mortality rates, particularly from heart disease and cancers linked to poor diets rose steeply until 1995 though since then have levelled off.

The transition also caused an increase in poverty: beggars and street children are becoming part of a new underclass. In early 2000 official unemployment was only 10% but the real figure is certainly much higher. And in any case most workers have to do a second job in order to survive.

Lithuania had industrialized rapidly in the Soviet era, but after 1991 the country lost its major markets and its sources of cheap energy. By 1997, the private sector accounted for 70% of GDP but there has not been much interest from foreign investors.

By 1995, industrial output had halved. Having reoriented more towards the West, some industries, particularly textiles, chemicals, and wood products, have since recovered. But with only small amounts of domestic oil and gas, the country remains very dependent on energy imports. Two Chernobyl-style reactors at Ignalia provide over 80% of electricity—making this probably the most nuclear-dependent country in the world. Under EU pressure Lithuania has promised to close them by 2005—which means it will have to buy more gas from Russia. However the EU has also pledged around $150 million in aid to help with the shutdown.

Independence boosted the service sector, which by 1998 accounted for more than half of GDP. Much of this is concerned with transport and communications with Russia. A significant proportion of exports are actually re-exports to Russia of imported cars and consumer goods. Moreover, Russians have to cross Lithuania to reach their 'orphaned' province of Kaliningrad.

Lithuania embraces an orphaned Russian province

Agriculture continues to make an important if declining contribution—chiefly livestock and cereals. By 1998 it accounted for 10% of GDP. One of the first steps after independence was to break up the collective farms and co-operatives and return land to the descendants of former owners. By mid-1996 over 1 million hectares had been handed back. Since most of this was in fairly small plots, efficiency and output fell. One-quarter of the country is covered by forests which supply raw materials for wood and paper industries.

Lithuania's independence struggle had been led in the late 1980s by Sajudis—the Lithuanian Movement for Restructuring. But at a time of economic crisis, Sajudis rapidly lost popularity. In 1992 in the first free election to the unicameral parliament, the Seimas, the voters reverted to the former communist party which had reinvented itself as the Democratic Labour Party (DLP). In 1993, the DLP candidate Algirdas Brazauskas was elected president.

The DLP government made some progress but was rocked by a banking crisis, and following the 1996 election Sajudis, now renamed the Homeland Union Party (HU), formed a coalition with the Christian Democratic party with Gediminas Vagnorius as prime minister.

The 1997 presidential election was surprisingly won by an independent candidate, a returning US emigré, Valdas Adamkus, at that point still a US national. The president has considerable powers—including the appointment of ministers. By mid-1999 Adamkus, however, was at loggerheads with Vagnorius.

In 1999 there were two changes of prime minister: first Rolandas Paksas took over, and then Andrius Kubilius. These changes reflected various divisions in, and defections from, the HU-led government which has become increasingly unpopular in the face of a severe economic crisis.

Meanwhile Paksas is waiting in the wings. He defected from HU to become leader of the Lithuanian Liberal Union which in the event of an election would probably form a coalition with the Centre Union, the party which had sponsored Adamkus as president.

Late in 1999 Lithuania was invited to join negotiations for EU membership. These will be complicated by Lithuania's porous borders with Russia and Belarus, which would make it difficult to keep out immigrants. In any case the EU is unconvinced that Lithuania has a functioning market economy.

Luxembourg

Land area: *3,000 sq. km.*
Population: *404,000—urban 89%*
Capital city: *Luxembourg-Ville, 75,000*
People: *Luxembourgish and immigrants*
Language: *Luxembourgian, French, German, English*
Religion: *Roman Catholic*
Government: *Constitutional monarchy*
Life expectancy: *76 years*
GNP per capita: *$PPP 37,420*
Currency: *Luxembourg franc*
Major exports: *Steel, chemicals, rubber products*

Luxembourg is the world's richest country—but with a lot of help from foreigners

The northern one-third of Luxembourg is mountainous, with dense forests. The more fertile part of the country is in the southern two-thirds—the rolling plains of the 'Bon Pays'.

Luxembourg's people have their own dialect and a strong national identity, but most also speak French and German. They have the world's highest per capita income—and usually Europe's lowest rate of unemployment.

But the birth rate is also low, so immigrants are needed to fill the labour gaps. Foreign-born residents make up one-third of the population, and more than half the labour force. Portugal is the main provider. In addition there are some 60,000 'frontaliers'—cross-border workers who commute daily from France, Belgium, and Germany.

Most immigrants used to come to work in Luxembourg's heavy industry, particularly the Arbed steel company which took advantage of iron-ore deposits along the southern border. Steel is still an important industry, and the main export, and there are also other major manufacturing industries, including a Goodyear tyre plant and a DuPont chemical plant. Today, however, the core of Luxembourg's economy is formed by financial and business services, which contribute around one-third of government revenue. Luxembourg is one of Europe's leading financial centres. Its low tax rates attract funds from Germany, and it controls more than 90% of Europe's offshore investment funds—though the arrival of the Euro could undermine some of this business.

Luxembourg is a constitutional monarchy—a Grand Duchy. Grand Duke Jean has ruled since 1964, but since 1998 his son Henri has exercised sovereign, if largely ceremonial, powers.

All governments since 1919 have been coalitions, usually led by the centre-right Christian Socialist Party (CSV). The CSV were the major party after the 1984 election and governed in coalition with the Socialist Party (LSAP), with Jacques Santer as prime minister. They were re-elected in 1989 and 1994.

In 1995, Santer left for an ill-fated presidency of the European Commission. He was replaced in Luxembourg by Jean-Claude Juncker. In the 1999 elections, however, the LSAP were pushed into third place by the right-wing Democratic Party which became the junior party in the coalition.

Macedonia

Macedonia avoided the worst of the Balkan wars, but still has ethnic tensions

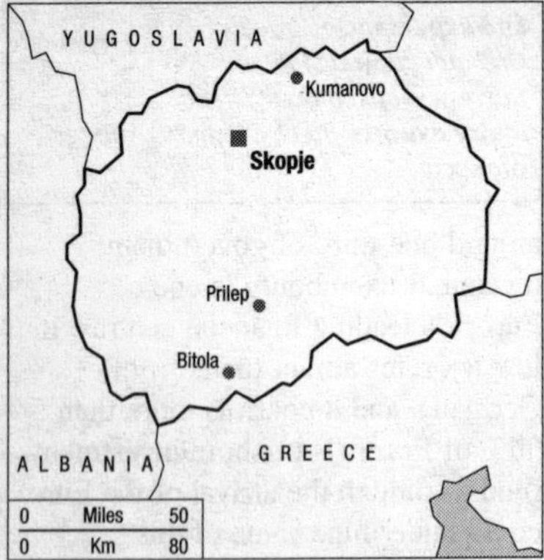

***Land area:** 26,000 sq. km.*
***Population:** 2 million—urban 61%*
***Capital city:** Skopje*
***People:** Macedonian 66%, Albanian 23%, Turkish 4%, Serb 2%, Gypsies 3%, other 2%*
***Language:** Macedonian 70%, Albanian 21%, Turkish 3%, Serbo-Croatian 3%, other 3%*
***Religion:** Eastern Orthodox 67%, Muslim 30%, other 3%*
***Government:** Republic*
***Life expectancy:** 73 years*
***GNP per capita:** $PPP 3,660*
***Currency:** Macedonian denar*
***Major exports:** Food, tobacco, machinery*

This landlocked country is largely mountainous. In the past it was also heavily forested, and though forests remain, particularly in the west, the cleared land revealed thin soil, much of which has now been eroded. The best land is to be found in the valley of the Vardar River, which runs through the centre of the country from north to south. Tectonic fault lines run in the same direction and the country remains vulnerable to earthquakes.

Macedonia's ethnic composition is a source of political tension. The 1994 census showed 66% of the population as ethnic Macedonian who belong to the Eastern Orthodox Church. There are also small minorities of Turks, Romanians, and Serbs.

But the most significant minority were ethnic Albanians, who made up 23% of the population. The Albanians, who are Sunni Muslims, live largely in the north-west. They claim they were under-counted and that in fact they represent around one-third of the population. Albanians are in many respects treated as second-class citizens. They also object to the 1991 constitution which defines the country as 'the nation-state of the Macedonian people'. These tensions were exacerbated in 1999 by the flood of more than 200,000 ethnic Albanians from Kosovo. The Albanian population want to see Albanian-language schools and a university.

Macedonia was the poorest of the constituent republics of former Yugoslavia. It had developed heavy industries such as steel, chemicals, and metal-based manufacturing, and was mining its deposits of lead, zinc, copper, chromium, and coal. It also had light industries such as textiles. But the break-up of Yugoslavia and subsequent trade embargoes sent industry into a steep decline. By 1995, output had dropped by more than one-third. Some of these industries have since recovered but even by late 1999 were operating far below capacity.

Agriculture also suffered in the early years but has recovered more strongly. Even as part of Yugoslavia,

Macedonian agriculture depended largely on small private farms which produced most of the food as well as important cash crops such as tobacco. The country could be self-sufficient in food, and even export vegetables and fruit, but at present has to import much of its requirements. Efforts to privatize the 30% of the arable land that is state-owned have been slowed by claims by former owners.

Officially the unemployment rate in 1999 was above 40%, but since many people actually work in the black economy the true rate was probably nearer 25%.

Macedonia's emergence as an independent republic in 1991 was a tortuous process. Neighbouring Greece immediately objected to the new country's name on the grounds that this and the constitution implied sovereignty over the adjacent Greek province of the same name. Greece also objected to a sixteen-pointed star on the flag which had historical resonance in Greece too. Greece's objections, reluctantly backed by fellow members of the EU, blocked international recognition.

The flag problem was resolved by dropping the star, and the name problem by referring to the 'Former Yugoslav Republic of Macedonia'. Officially that is still the name, though few people use it. Greece's economic blockade ended in 1995.

Objections to Macedonia's name have subsided

Macedonia joined the UN in 1993 and almost immediately requested a UN peacekeeping force to prevent annexation by Serbia. The 1,000-strong UN Preventive Deployment force, known as Unpredep, achieved this objective though its role was overtaken by the Kosovo war in 1999.

The 1992 parliamentary election was won by the ex-communist Social Democratic Alliance of Macedonia (SDSM), which entered into a coalition with the moderate Albanian Party for Democratic Prosperity. The SDSM increased its representation in the 1994 parliamentary elections which were boycotted by the leading opposition party the Internal Macedonian Revolutionary Organization (VMRO). But the government was beset by scandal over pyramid schemes and in 1997 by riots in the Albanian-dominated city of Gostivar, where the mayor wanted to fly the Albanian flag.

In the general election in 1998, the VMRO led by Ljubcho Georgievski did stand, gained the largest number of seats, and formed a centre-right coalition government. Its main partner was the new pro-business Democratic Alternative (DA) Party, run by Vasil Turpurkovski—an ex-leader of Yugoslavia's communist youth movement. The more difficult partner is the Democratic Party of Albanians (DPA), a radical separatist group that for the time being has been moderating its demands. The coalition has frequently come under strain. However these differences appeared to be resolved in December 1999 when Turpurkovski accepted the post of deputy prime minister.

In 1999, the election for the largely ceremonial post of president was won by Boris Trajkovski of the SDSM, a Methodist pastor who has promised to keep the peace between Macedonia's rival ethnic groups.

Madagascar

Madagascar's drive for foreign investment is doing little for the rural poor

Land area: *587,000 sq. km.*
Population: *15 million—urban 28%*
Capital city: *Antananarivo, 1.7 million*
People: *Merina, Betsileo, Betsimisaraka and others*
Language: *French, Malagasy*
Religion: *Indigenous beliefs 52%, Christian 41%, Muslim 7%*
Government: *Republic*
Life expectancy: *45 years*
GNP per capita: *$PPP 900*
Currency: *Malagasy franc*
Major exports: *Coffee, vanilla, cloves*

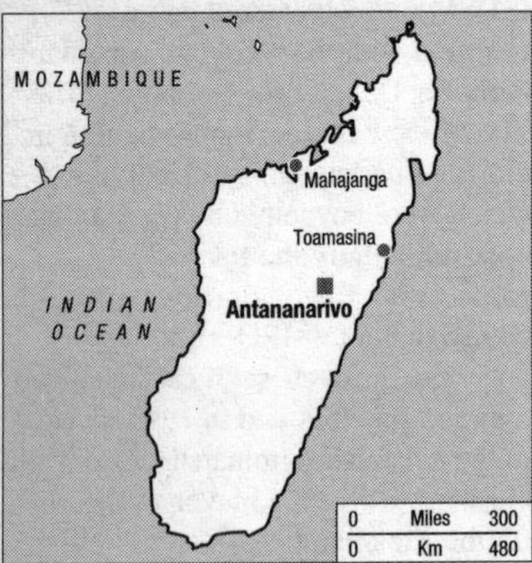

Madagascar is dominated by a central, mountainous plateau that covers around two-thirds of the island—the highest peak is 2,800 metres. To the east, the mountains drop steeply to a narrow coastal strip. To the west the slope is more gentle to broad fertile valleys. Most of the original forest cover on the mountains has been lost and Madagascar now suffers from severe erosion as millions of tons of soil are washed each year into the sea. Deforestation has also stripped the natural habitats of many rare plant and animal species. Madagascar is frequently battered by cyclones—and in early 2000 was hit by three in fairly rapid succession that caused widespread damage.

Most Malagasy are descendants of immigrants who arrived more than 2,000 years ago from South-East Asia. Today, these consist of around twenty ethnic groups, of whom the largest are the Merina (around one-quarter of the population) and the Betsileo. Some groups such as the Betsimisaraka are of mixed African, Malayo-Indonesian, and Arab ancestry. All speak dialects of Malagasy, though the education system also works in French.

Levels of human development in Madagascar have fallen steadily. Around three-quarters of the population live in poverty. Literacy also seems to be dropping—from over 68% in 1985 to 47% by 1997. Life expectancy, however, is a little higher than in other countries of Sub-Saharan Africa, and the island's relative isolation offers some protection from the rapid spread of HIV/AIDS. Nevertheless, more than 40% of children are malnourished and only one-quarter of the population have access to safe water.

Madagascar's poverty is concentrated in the rural areas where most people struggle to survive by agriculture. Much of this is at a subsistence level, primarily growing rice, along with cassava, sweet potatoes, maize, and other crops. But farms are generally small, yields are low, and food has to be imported. The main cash crops are coffee, vanilla, sugar, and cloves, but here too output has been stagnant. Some of the problems result from under-investment and there is relatively little irrigation. Prices for cash crops have been liberalized in recent years, so farmers' rewards are linked more to world prices, which for vanilla and cloves have been low. Livestock is also an important source of income—indeed it often takes up land that might better be used for growing crops. But agriculture will take some time to recover from the ravages of the cyclones in 2000.

Fishing, especially for prawns, should be an important source of income but the local industry is relatively under-developed, so much of the income actually comes from licences sold to European and Japanese fleets that fish in Madagascan waters.

Madagascar has some basic industries. The major ones process agricultural produce, notably the textiles industry which is based on locally-grown cotton. Others include plastics, pharmaceuticals, and footwear. Discouraged by the poor state of infrastructure, foreign investors have not been very prominent, though some have established plants in an export-processing zone.

A cyclone in 2000 caused extensive damage

Madagascar's main political figure in recent decades has been Didier Ratsiraka. He first came to power at the head of a military government in 1975 and held a referendum which approved a new constitution that allowed for only one political organization. This was to be a 'national front' that embraced all the political parties, though it was actually controlled by Ratsiraka's party which was subsequently renamed the Association pour la renaissance de Madagascar (Arema).

Ratsiraka embarked on a socialist transformation that involved nationalizing banks and other major companies, but he soon ran into economic problems and by 1980 was seeking the support of the IMF. The ensuing austerity measures contributed to growing political unrest. By 1990, he had agreed to allow other political groups to operate. This led to the formation of a new opposition front, the Forces vives (FV), led by Albert Zafy. In 1991, after Ratsiraka had ordered troops to fire on strikers, he was faced with further widespread protests and after another referendum introduced a fresh constitution that led to elections in 1993.

Zafy and the FV won the elections. But his chaotic presidency was fraught with problems, including internal disputes over co-operation with the IMF. In August 1996, Zafy was impeached for corruption and abuse of power. The interim administration that followed duly finalized an IMF agreement.

Such was the disenchantment with Zafy that in the presidential elections at the end of 1996 the electorate voted Ratsiraka back into office. By this time he had abandoned socialism and was promising a 'humanist and ecological republic'. His party, Arema, also did well in the 1998 legislative elections.

Economic growth had shown signs of revival but the cyclones in early 2000 caused extensive damage to infrastructure.

Malawi

Malawians now have a democracy, but they remain desperately poor and are vulnerable to HIV/AIDS

Land area: *118,000 sq. km.*
Population: *11 million—urban 15%*
Capital city: *Lilongwe, 233,000*
People: *Chewa, Nyanja, Tumbuko and others*
Language: *English, Chichewa, and others*
Religion: *Protestant 55%, Roman Catholic 20%, Muslim 20%, other 5%*
Government: *Republic*
Life expectancy: *39 years*
GNP per capita: *$PPP 730*
Currency: *Kwacha*
Major exports: *Tobacco, tea, sugar, coffee*

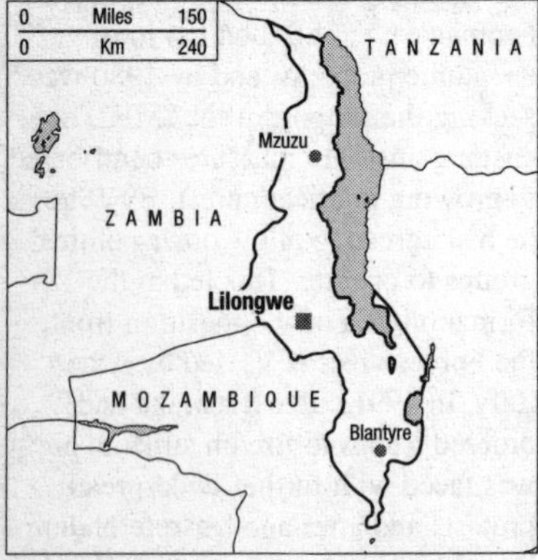

Malawi's dominant geographical feature is the East African Rift Valley, which cuts through the country from north to south. This includes Lake Malawi, through which runs most of the eastern border, and the Shire River valley, which drains the lake southwards into Mozambique. To the west of the Rift Valley in the centre of the country, there is an extensive plateau area. There are also high plateaux in the north and intensively cultivated highlands in the south.

The main ethnic groups are the Chewa, who make up the majority of people in the centre of the country and whose language is the most widely spoken. The Nyanja are found mostly in the south, and the Tumbuko in the north.

By African standards, Malawi is densely populated and with few people using contraception the population growth rate prior to the AIDS epidemic was 3.5% per year.

Malawi is a poor country. Around two-fifths of people live below the poverty line. Its education levels are higher than in some African countries and it even has its own version of an élite English public school, the Kamuzu Academy. But most children are less fortunate and drop-out rates at ordinary government schools are high. Half the children are malnourished and one-fifth do not live beyond their fifth birthday.

Mortality rates will climb even more steeply as a result of AIDS. By the end of 1997, 8% of the population were HIV-positive and it is believed that one-quarter of the urban workforce will die from the disease by 2010. This will plunge the survivors even deeper into poverty, since those who will die are the main breadwinners and the country will also face the heavy cost of caring for AIDS patients.

With 85% of people living in the rural areas, this is one of the world's least urbanized countries. Farmers have cultivated virtually all the arable land—in the mid-1980s more than half of rural households had less than 1 hectare each. Most concentrate on subsistence crops like maize, sorghum, or millet, and the country is largely self-sufficient, though at low levels of consumption.

Cash crops have also been important, particularly tobacco, which has provided more than two-thirds of export income, along with tea, sugar, and cotton. Previously the policy was to concentrate cash crops on large commercial estates (which still occupy around 20% of arable land) but the government is now encouraging small-holders by offering better prices. Even so, prospects for both food and cash crops are limited since many farmers cannot afford the inputs, and much of their land has been over-exploited. Another important source of food is Lake Malawi, whose fish provide more than two-thirds of animal protein consumption—though catches have fallen in recent years.

Malawi relies heavily on exports of tobacco

Malawi does have some mineral deposits but has never had a substantial mining industry. In recent years British and French companies have been exploring for tin and other metals.

For the first three decades following independence in 1962, political life in Malawi was overshadowed by the diminutive but dictatorial figure of Dr Hastings Banda at the head of his Malawi Congress Party (MCP). He was first prime minister and then president, and finally in 1970 declared himself 'president for life'. Banda's rule became increasingly ruthless. He had an extensive network of spies and secret police to monitor internal discontent and to enable him to jail and torture opponents. His collaboration with the apartheid regime in South Africa proved very fruitful—helping to finance the building of a new capital, Lilongwe, as well as a presidential palace.

Banda's regime started to fall apart in the early 1990s following strikes and riots—and the suspension of international aid. Eventually he was forced to concede a 1993 referendum which approved a return to multi-party democracy. In the ensuing presidential election in 1994, Banda was defeated by a former cabinet minister, Bakili Muluzi, at the head of the United Democratic Front (UDF). The legislative election in the same year also give the UDF the most seats, ahead of the MCP, but without a majority it initially entered into a coalition with the third party, the Alliance for Democracy (Aford).

After his election Muluzi released a number of political prisoners. He also had Banda arrested on a murder charge, though he was acquitted, and died (101 years old) in 1997. In the 1999 elections, Muluzi scraped through to a second five-year term ahead of Gwanda Chakuamba, the MCP candidate.

The UDF government has offered Malawians greater political freedom, but not greater prosperity. Violent clashes followed Muluzi's swearing-in for his second term, and opposition supporters attacked mosques and businesses linked to the UDF. Early in 2000, the opposition took the case to the courts arguing that the election commission had acted illegally in declaring Muluzi the winner but they did not have any success.

Malaysia

Malaysia's social stability is jeopardized by an autocratic government

Land area: *330,000 sq. km.*
Population: *22 million—urban 56%*
Capital city: *Kuala Lumpur, 1.1 million*
People: *Malay and other indigenous 59%, Chinese 32%, Indian 9%*
Language: *Malay, English, Chinese, Tamil and tribal dialects*
Religion: *Muslim, Buddhist, Hindu, Confucian, Christian, tribal religions*
Government: *Constitutional monarchy*
Life expectancy: *72 years*
GNP per capita: *$PPP 6,990*
Currency: *Ringgit*
Major exports: *Manufactured goods, rubber, palm oil*

Malaysia has an unusual geographical composition. Its territory is evenly divided between a portion on the Asian mainland and a similar area on the north-west of the island of Borneo. On the mainland, peninsular Malaysia, which has around 80% of the population, is largely mountainous in the north, with coastal lowlands to the west and south. Eastern Malaysia, 600 kilometres away across the South China Sea, is more sparsely populated, with a swampy coastal plain rising to high mountains that form the border with Indonesia.

Malaysia also has a distinctive racial composition. The majority are classified as ethnic Malays, most of whom are Muslims. But around one-third of the population are of Chinese origin, who live chiefly in the urban areas. There are also a number of South Asians, as well as small tribal groups who are found particularly in Eastern Malaysia. Standards of education and health have improved rapidly though there remain wide disparities between urban and rural areas and between richer and poorer states. The population grew rapidly in the 1980s, particularly among rural Malays, but the growth rate has slowed in recent years, it is projected to be 1.5% annually for 1997-2015.

Since the early 1970s, Malaysia has transformed itself into an export-oriented industrial country. More than one-quarter of the population now work in manufacturing industry, which is largely concentrated in states on the west of the peninsula—on the island of Penang and in the coastal area to the west of Kuala Lumpur. Much of this has been driven by multinationals in the electronics industry who have used Malaysia simply as an assembly base.

The government has, however, been making efforts to have more manufacturing take place in Malaysia and use higher levels of technology. The most ambitious project is a 'multimedia super-corridor', including a cybercity which is currently being carved out of land that previously was either jungle or palm-oil plantations.

Malaysia's industrial success has, however, affected agriculture. Attracted by better paid jobs in the cities, many people have been leaving the land. As a result production has fallen and Malaysia is now a net importer of rice. Production of rubber, long a major export, has also been declining—though partly because plantations have switched to the more lucrative palm oil for which output continues to expand.

Malaysia has also become reliant on immigrant labour. In 1997, there were an estimated 2 million migrant workers in Malaysia, half of them illegal, making up around one-quarter of the workforce. During the Asian financial crisis, there were pressures for them to return—though there is little sign that Malaysians want to do those jobs again.

Malaysia's distinctive ethnic mix has also had a profound impact on its political processes. The country is a federal constitutional monarchy, and formally it is an Islamic state. Each of the thirteen states has a state assembly and an executive council that deals with state issues. Nine of the states have hereditary rulers who take turns to serve a five-year term as king. Since independence in 1957, political power at the federal level has been in the hands of the main Malay political party, the United Malays' National Organization (UMNO), which has ruled in a National Front coalition with parties representing other racial groups.

Rulers take turns as king of Malaysia

The political system in Malaysia turned decisively in a new direction following riots in 1969 when Malays protested against the pervasive economic power of the Chinese minority. From 1971, the government embarked on a 'new economic policy' that would deliberately favour Malays and indigenous ethnic minorities, referred to as 'bumiputra' (sons of the soil). This included preferential access to government jobs, to higher education, and to a share of equity in national and foreign investment. Because the economy was growing rapidly, the bumiputra were able to progress without having to make the Chinese worse off so the process was relatively smooth.

Since becoming prime minister in 1981, UMNO leader Dr Mahathir Mohammed has built a dominant position. He has also established himself as a spokesman for developing countries in Asia, notably accusing foreign currency speculators of provoking Asia's financial crisis. In 1997, Malaysia became one of the first countries to introduce new controls on financial capital.

But his position was weakened in 1998 when he had his obvious successor, Anwar Ibrahim, jailed on charges of corruption and sexual misconduct. This provoked widespread criticism which was reflected to some extent in the December 1999 elections. The National Front coalition again won a convincing majority in the federal parliament. But it gained a smaller share of the popular vote, and in the northern states in particular voters started to turn to Islamic parties. The substantial Chinese minority still supports Mahathir; the Malays are no longer so sure.

Maldives

One of the most prosperous, if least democratic, countries in South Asia

Land area: *300 sq. km.*
Population: *262,000—urban 27%*
Capital city: *Male, 62,000*
People: *Sinhalese, Dravidian, Arab, African*
Language: *Maldivian Divehi, English*
Religion: *Muslim*
Government: *Republic*
Life expectancy: *67 years*
GNP per capita: *$PPP 3,690*
Currency: *Rufiyaa*
Major exports: *Marine products*

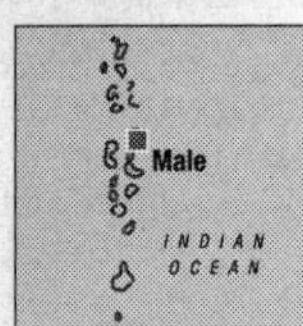

The Maldives consists of 1,190 coral islands grouped in atolls, spread out over a wide area. Only around 200 are inhabited, and since few rise more than 1 metre above sea level, global warming could swamp most of the country. Some defences are already in place. The government has built what is known locally as the 'Great Wall of Male': a two-metre high concrete barrier around much of the capital. There are also plans for a new and higher artificial island.

Culturally, the Maldives is a blend of influences from India, Sri Lanka, Arabic countries, and elsewhere. All Maldivians speak the national language, Divehi, and are Muslims. By South Asian standards, they also have high levels of human development: adult literacy is over 90%; and between 1970 and 1997 life expectancy increased from 50 to 67 years.

The country's major source of income is tourism, which brings in around 400,000 visitors per year mostly at the top end of the market—providing 40% of government revenue and 70% of foreign exchange.

Fishing is also an important source of income and employment. The main catch is tuna, which is processed locally and exported frozen or canned. Most other industry tends to be on a small scale.

The Maldives has a distinctive constitution. It has no political parties. Citizens elect members to the 50-seat parliament, the Majlis, which chooses a president whose appointment then has to be confirmed in a national referendum. Though the constitution was modified in 1998 to ensure that the Majlis could choose from more than one candidate, this made little difference.

Since 1978, they have chosen Moumoon Abdul Gayoom, who in the 1998 referendum got more than 90% of the vote. The authorities do not allow members of the Majlis to criticize the government.

President Gayoom has survived a sequence of coup attempts: in 1980, 1983, and most notably in 1988 when some Maldivians engaged Tamil mercenaries from Sri Lanka—an attack that was repelled with Indian support.

Gayoom, who is now one of the world's longest serving leaders, has made some gestures towards a more inclusive style of government, bringing a former opponent, Iliyas Ibrahim, into his cabinet. Some of the younger generation want to go further, with a parliamentary system based on political parties, but there seems little hope of that in the near future.

Mali

Mali has become one of West Africa's more democratic countries

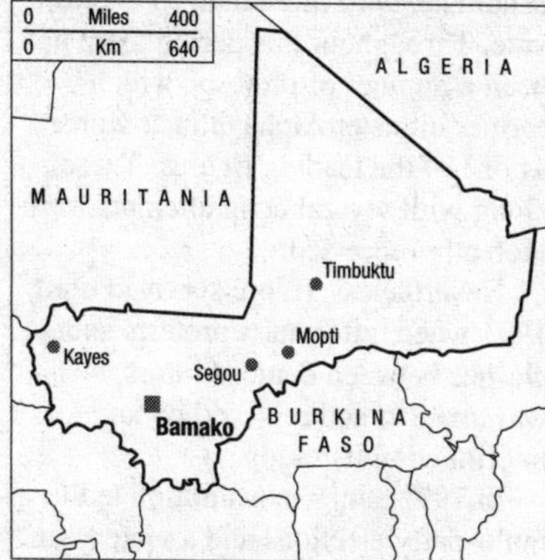

Land area: *1,240,000 sq. km.*
Population: *11 million—urban 29%*
Capital city: *Bamako, 1 million*
People: *Mandé 50%, Peuhl 17%, Voltaic 12%, Songhai 6%, Tuareg and Moor 10%, other 5%*
Language: *French, Bambara, other African languages*
Religion: *Muslim 90%, indigenous beliefs 9%, Christian 1%*
Government: *Republic*
Life expectancy: *53 years*
GNP per capita: *$PPP 720*
Currency: *CFA Franc*
Major exports: *Cotton, gold, livestock*

Mali is almost entirely flat with only occasional broken rocky hills. The northern one-third of the country falls within the Sahara Desert. The centre is the semi-arid Sahel belt, which gives way further south and south-west to grasslands and to the valley of the Niger—a broad river that periodically floods the land, depositing rich alluvial soil.

Mali has a diverse collection of ethnic groups and clans which tend to be concentrated in specific areas. The main distinction is between the Berbers and the black groups. Berbers include the Tuareg and the Moors, who are nomadic herders and occupy the Sahelian zone. Of the black Mandé group, the largest are the Bambara who are farmers along the Niger River. The Peuhl are another nomadic herding group in the Sahel. Most Malians are Muslims, though religious affiliations are also divided along ethnic lines. Islam is not as strong a political force as in other countries but there are a number of fundamentalist groups. Mali's ethnic diversity has frequently led to conflict, particularly between the nomadic and sedentary groups.

The Tuareg in particular have felt marginalized and in 1991 they rebelled, demanding autonomy from the central government. The army responded forcefully, driving more than 80,000 Tuareg into neighbouring countries. Hostilities largely ended in 1996, and most Tuareg refugees have since returned, but there are still occasional conflicts.

There are also around three million Malians working as emigrants, primarily in neighbouring countries such as Côte d'Ivoire but there are also many in France.

Malians are among the world's poorest people, particularly those living outside the towns. More than half the children are malnourished, less than 10% of the population have access to safe sanitation, and only 30% are literate. Mali also has one of the highest rates of maternal mortality: 1,200 women die from pregnancy-related causes for every 100,000 live births.

Most people depend for survival on subsistence agriculture and livestock. They grow food crops in the south on irrigated land around the Niger and its tributaries, their main crops being millet, rice, wheat, and corn. This is also where they grow the principal cash crops: peanuts and particularly cotton which is the source of export income. Most cotton is grown by small farmers and co-operatives; quality is high and output has been increasing. Although there are some plans to process cotton locally, most is exported raw.

Livestock production accounts for around one-fifth of GNP. This used to be the preserve of nomadic herding communities, but nowadays most of the cattle are on small farms. Fishing in the Niger river is also an important source of income and around one-fifth of the catch is exported to Côte d'Ivoire.

Mali has little industry beyond processing agricultural output. Most consumer goods are imported, or smuggled in, from neighbouring countries. But one increasingly important activity is gold mining. Output in 1998 was around 20 tons, mostly through Canadian and South African companies working with the government. The country's reserves are equivalent to at least 500 tons and since production costs are low Mali is likely to rely more on gold exports in future.

Mali has around 500 tons of gold

For 23 years, Mali was under the autocratic rule of Moussa Traoré, who became president in 1969 following a military coup. In 1979 the country returned to single-party civilian rule. This made little difference since Traoré was elected president at the head of a military-backed party and re-elected in 1985—as the only candidate, with more than 99% of the vote. Throughout this period there had been a number of protests, with a former minister Alpha Oumar Konaré as one of the leading figures. These along with several coup attempts were violently repressed.

Nevertheless Traoré survived until 1991 when, after mass protests and clashes between demonstrators, he was arrested and replaced by an interim administration.

In 1992, a new constitution led to multi-party elections and a victory in the National Assembly for a coalition led by Konaré and the Alliance pour la démocratie au Mali (Adema). Konaré was elected president.

Konaré is an archaeologist and veteran pro-democracy campaigner. He has taken human rights and clean government more seriously than many other African leaders and has been rewarded with support from donors.

Opposition parties have tended to split along factional lines, though since 1997 they have come together as a loose alliance, the Collectif des partis politiques de l'opposition (COPPO). They have accused Konaré of trying to recreate a one-party state and have boycotted elections.

Konaré was re-elected president in 1997, in a low turnout. Since then he has attempted to increase popular participation—holding national one-day forums in which anyone can stand up and complain to the president in front of national television.

Malta

Land area: *316 sq. km.*
Population: *378,000—urban 90%*
Capital city: *Valletta, 16,000*
People: *Maltese*
Language: *Maltese, English*
Religion: *Roman Catholic*
Government: *Republic*
Life expectancy: *77 years*
GNP per capita: *$PPP 13,610*
Currency: *Maltese lira*
Major exports: *Clothing, electronics*

Malta's EU aspirations have been confounded by fractious politics

Malta comprises a small group of islands in the Mediterranean, of which the largest are Malta, Gozo and Comino. The land is largely low-lying and dry, without permanent rivers or lakes, so most water comes from desalination plants across the country.

Malta is a bridge between Europe and North Africa, and its language has both Latin and Arabic components. In the past, young Maltese often chose to emigrate, creating a Maltese diaspora around the world, notably in Australia. Nowadays people tend to stay, and the population continues to grow, if only slowly. The Maltese enjoy an extensive welfare state with free education and health care.

Not many work in agriculture, which is restricted by thin soil and the lack of water, so although farmers do have crops of cereals, fruits, and vegetables, most food has to be imported.

One-fifth of the workforce are in manufacturing industry, either in small-scale factories making goods for local consumption or in the export factories established as a result of foreign investment—typically in clothing and light engineering, and a large SGS-Thomson electronics factory. Until 1979, Malta had a major British naval base and still has a ship-repair industry. The other mainstay of the economy is tourism, which accounts for 30% of GDP. Malta attracted more than 1.6 million visitors in 1999—40% from the UK.

Maltese politics is frequently a confrontational and animated business, and as a result electoral turnouts above 90% are common. For much of the 1970s and 1980s, the country was governed by the then socialist Maltese Labour Party led by Dom Mintoff, who built up the Maltese welfare state. Even today, 40% of the workforce are employed in the public sector.

Since 1987, however, with a brief 1996-8 Labour interruption, the country has been in the hands of the centre-right Nationalist Party, led by Eddie Fenech Adami, who has been trying to privatize and to cut down the public sector.

Ideologically, the two parties have moved closer together. The most divisive issue is membership of the EU. The Nationalist Party is strongly pro, and applied in 1990. The Labour Party, now led by Alfred Sant, withdrew the application when in charge in 1996, arguing for neutrality and better links with North Africa. Restored to power in 1998, Adami renewed the application and in 1999 the EU said that Malta could start negotiations in 2000.

Martinique

A French dependency with hopes for independence

Land area: *1,000 sq. km.*
Population: *397,000—urban 79%*
Capital city: *Fort-de-France, 100,000*
People: *African and African-white-Indian mixture 90%*
Language: *French, creole*
Religion: *Roman Catholic*
Government: *Overseas department of France*
Life expectancy: *79 years*
GNP per capita: *$PPP $10,000*
Currency: *French franc*
Major exports: *Petroleum products, bananas, rum*

Martinique is a mountainous island in the eastern Caribbean with an active volcano, Mont Pelée, though it does have some flatter parts in the southwest. Abundant rainfall for most of the year sustains lush vegetation: more than one-third of the island is covered with tropical rainforests. There are also many sandy beaches.

The people of Martinique are a rich racial mixture of black, white, and Indian. Thanks to steady flows of French aid, their standard of living is fairly high. The capital, Fort-de-France, is a smart cosmopolitan city, combining French and West Indian cultures, though its attractions have also encouraged many younger people to emigrate onwards to metropolitan France. The descendants of the white settlers, the Béké, still own plantations but most political and economic power nowadays is in the hands of the creole élite.

Historically, Martinique was a major sugar producer and there are still sugar plantations, which supply the raw material for the rum distilleries, but farmers have been diversifying more into tropical fruits including pineapples, avocados, and bananas. Agriculture only contributes around 5% of GDP and most food has to be imported.

Today, the main industry is tourism. More than three-quarters of the workforce are employed in services, working in hotels and restaurants, as well as in government.

There is also a refinery which produces oil products for local consumption and for other French dependencies in the Caribbean.

As an overseas department of France, Martinique sends two representatives to the French Senate and four to the French National Assembly. For local consultation, it also has a general council and a regional council.

Of thc French dependencies, Martinique has had the most persistent agitation for independence. Some local political groups just want greater autonomy, and to attract more investment, but others have independence in their sights and some local representatives have been elected on pro-independence platforms: after the 1998 legislative elections the largest party was the Mouvement indépendantiste martiniquais.

Given the high levels of unemployment, however, and the dependence of many people on welfare payments and other transfers from France, a vote for independence seems unlikely.

Mauritania

Nomadic communities have settled in the towns, but many traditional practices remain—including slavery

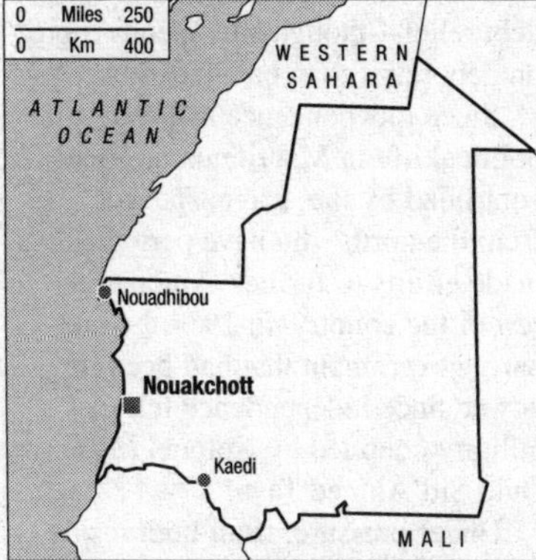

Land area: *1,026,000 sq. km.*
Population: *3 million—urban 55%*
Capital city: *Nouakchott, 1.0 million*
People: *Mixed Maur/black 40%, Maur 30%, black 30%*
Language: *Hasaniya Arabic, Pular, Soninke, Wolof*
Religion: *Muslim*
Government: *Republic*
Life expectancy: *53 years*
GNP per capita: *$PPP 1,660*
Currency: *Ouguiya*
Major exports: *Fish, iron ore*

Mauritania is essentially the western section of the Sahara Desert. It does have a strip of arable land alongside the southern border that is formed by the Sénégal river, and the territory to the north of this consists of dry grasslands with occasional bushes, but more than half the country is covered with sand dunes.

The population represents an overlap between ethnic groups from the north and south. Those from the north are lighter coloured and of mixed Arab and Berber descent. Those from the south are black, from a number of groups, including the Fulani, Soninke, and Wolof. But there has also been extensive intermarriage, so most of the population is a mixture of the two groups.

Mauritanian society has traditionally been very hierarchical—with noble families at the top and then a series of different castes extending down to servants and slaves. Slavery was abolished during the French colonial period, and the prohibition was reiterated with new laws in 1980. However, the Mauritanian Human Rights Association reports that slavery and serfdom continue—even if owners can no longer call on the law to pursue runaway slaves. The slaves may belong to any ethnic group, but particularly the blacks.

Living standards are very low. Around 40% of children are malnourished and infant mortality is high—especially for those outside the towns and cities who have few facilities for health care. About half the population live in poverty.

In the past, most Mauritanians lived in nomadic herding communities, and livestock still contributes around one-sixth of GNP—cattle in the south and goats and sheep further north. But the numbers of nomadic herders have been falling. To some extent this is a response to desertification—a result in part of over-grazing. A series of droughts also wiped out herds, driving destitute families to the cities. Moreover, the urban life in general is attractive to younger generations.

Mauritania's little available agricultural land is used mostly to grow millet and sorghum. Some rice is produced on irrigated land—usually by agricultural labourers working for richer landlords. Nevertheless, most cereals have to be imported. Many rural communities also maintain herds of cattle, camels and goats.

The Atlantic coastline opens up opportunities for fishing. This is one of the richest fishing areas in the world and catches increased considerably during the 1980s, but over-fishing by local and foreign boats, the 'supertrawlers', eventually depleted the stock and output declined. The government has taken measures to combat over-fishing—including tighter surveillance and new agreements for sharing production with fleets from the EU.

Mauritania's fishing grounds are depleted by foreign supertrawlers

With limited agricultural potential, Mauritania's economic survival has rested on the exploitation of mineral resources which have generated around half of export revenue. The most important is iron ore. The Zouérat mine near the border with Western Sahara has rich deposits of iron ore that have been extracted since the early 1960s. Most of the output goes to the EU which has also been supporting measures to increase production. A number of foreign companies are also prospecting for other minerals, particularly gold and diamonds.

Mauritania's poverty and vulnerability to shocks, whether from the climate or international commodity markets, have frequently obliged it to turn to the IMF which had demanded programmes of structural adjustment. Popular protests against these austerity measures have usually been dealt with fairly harshly. Mauritania is, however, a major aid recipient and has also qualified for debt relief—though still spends more on debt relief than on education.

Since independence in 1960, political life in Mauritania has been controlled by the Arabic speakers from the north who have periodically made efforts to further 'Arabize' the rest of the country. In 1984 the one-party government that had been in power since independence fell to a military coup led by Colonel Maaouya Ould Sid'Ahmed Taya.

Under pressure, from both inside and outside the country, Taya brought in a new constitution, approved by a referendum in 1991, that legalized political parties, including his own Parti républicain démocratique et sociale (PRDS).

Taya won the first presidential election in 1992. The main opposition party, the Union des forces démocratiques (UDF), charged that this was fraudulent and boycotted the 1997 election, which Taya duly won with 90% of the vote. The PRDS also achieved a majority in the Legislative Assembly, again thanks to a boycott.

The president's power base is in his home region of Atar but he also gets strong support from the army. Opposition is difficult to organize because the political process is based on rivalries between different clans and ethnic groups, which tend to generate a large number of competing parties.

Mauritius

A human development success story with a booming economy

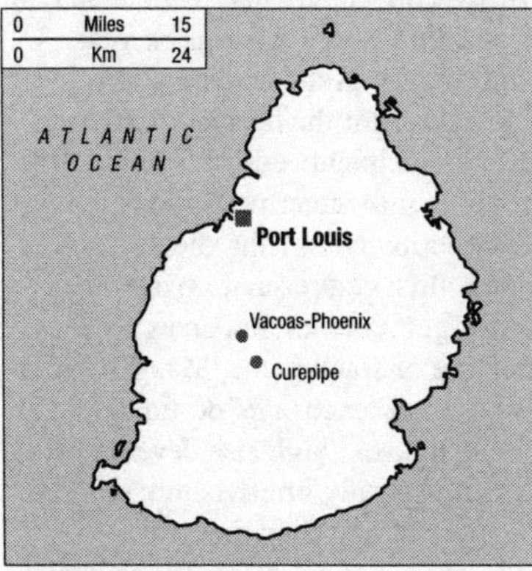

Land area: *2,000 sq. km.*
Population: *1.1 million—urban 41%*
Capital city: *Port Louis, 137,000*
People: *Indo-Mauritian 68%, creole 27%, other 5%*
Language: *English, creole, French, Hindi, Urdu*
Religion: *Hindu 52%, Christian 28%, Muslim 17%, other 3%*
Government: *Republic*
Life expectancy: *71 years*
GNP per capita: *$PPP 9,400*
Currency: *Mauritian rupee*
Major exports: *Textiles, garments, sugar*

Mauritius, an island in the Indian ocean surrounded by coral reefs, is the site of an ancient volcano. The rainiest and most mountainous part of the island is in the south, falling to a plateau in the centre and then to a drier broad plain in the north.

The Mauritian population contains distinct and diverse groups. Two-thirds are of Indian origin—descendants of about half a million Indians who after 1850 were brought to work as indentured labourers in the sugar plantations—of these around one-quarter are Muslim and the rest Hindu. Then there are the creoles, descendants of slaves—the previous sugar workers. There are also smaller numbers of whites, the European colonizers, as well as Chinese and other Asian immigrants who came later as traders.

While there has been relatively little tension, the communities do remain fairly distinct. This is probably the only country where the end of Ramadan, All Saints' Day, and the Chinese New Year are all official holidays.

Each community uses its own languages but three have become dominant: English is the official administrative language; French is the language of the major newspapers; creole the unofficial language used in the streets.

Communal divisions used also to correspond to a division of labour—with the Indians as farmers, creoles as artisans, Chinese as traders, and whites as large landowners. Today, these distinctions have been blurred. This is partly the result of education which is free up to university level. But it also reflects a rapid modernization of the economy which has offered new opportunities to all. Indeed, Mauritius is one of Africa's rare success stories—its economy is now as large as that of Zambia which has nine times as many people.

Up to a few decades ago the major source of wealth was sugar—capitalizing on preferential access to the European market. Sugar still covers around 90% of all arable land and in 1997 was responsible for around 6% of GNP, but sugar now employs only around 7% of the workforce and future prospects are poor as a result of trade liberalization that will reduce preferential access. With little land on which to grow rice, most food has to be imported.

Fortunately, Mauritius has invested much of the earnings from sugar into creating a new manufacturing sector based in export-processing zones. Since the early 1980s, the country has attracted 500 companies, employing 17% of the workforce—two-thirds of them women. Around 80% of production is of garments—again taking advantage of preferential access to markets in Europe and North America. Companies were also attracted by Mauritius's stable, healthy, and well-educated society, good infrastructure and cheap labour. Most investment has come from Hong Kong and from France and other European countries.

Nevertheless, there are clouds on the horizon. The removal of trade barriers as a result of globalization will erode the Mauritian advantage. And there has been a steady rise in local wages which makes low-tech manufacturing here less competitive: direct labour costs are now around 50% higher than in southern Africa, and one-third higher than in South-East Asia. Employment in garments has already started to fall. This will demand a move to higher value products. With this in mind the government has now built an 'informatics park', which, among other things, can provide bilingual office services for international companies.

A new informatics park'

The third main pillar of the economy is tourism, which accounts for around 5% of GDP and, directly and indirectly, employs more than 10% of the population. More than half a million visitors arrive each year, with France as the leading source. Most head for the beaches, but there is also an incipient eco-tourism industry. A number of sugar plantations are considering converting themselves into tourist centres and laying out trails, golf courses and areas for the hunting of small game. Mauritius sees itself as an 'exclusive' destination and wants to avoid high-rise development. It will probably limit visitors to three-quarters of a million per year.

Surprisingly perhaps, for a country with a booming private sector, politics in Mauritius has been dominated by political parties that are avowedly socialist. So far, all heads of government in Mauritius have been Hindu. In 1991 the country, which until then had the British monarch as head of state, introduced a new constitution and became a republic, electing the then governor-general, Cassan Uteem, as president.

The 1995 election for the National Assembly was won by the Labour Party, led Navin Rangoolam, who became prime minister. The main opposition party is the Mouvement militant mauricien, led by Paul Berenger which was initially in a coalition with the Labour Party but withdrew in 1997. Policies tend, however, to be broadly similar. The government largely leaves the private sector to its own devices and concentrates on providing good social services.

Mayotte

Mayotte is a part of France and anxious to remain so

Land area: *375 sq. km.*
Population: *126,000—urban 41%*
Capital city: *Dzaoudzi, 6,000*
People: *Mahorais*
Language: *Shimaore, French*
Religion: *Muslim*
Government: *Territory of France*
Life expectancy: *60 years*
GNP per capita: *$PPP 600*
Currency: *French franc*
Major exports: *Ylang-ylang, vanilla, copra*

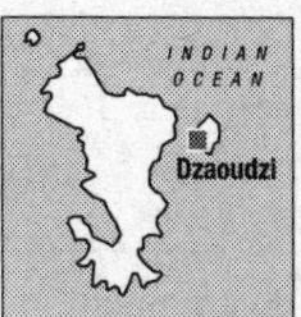

Mayotte is a volcanic island in the Indian Ocean between Madagascar and Mozambique. Its capital, and port, Dzaoudzi, is not on the main island, but on a rock linked by a causeway to the nearby islet of Pamandzi.

The people, the Mahorais, are of Malagasy origin and the vast majority are Muslim. In addition there are minorities of Indians, Creoles and Madagascans. There are also some 'M'Zoungous'—the local name for people who have come from metropolitan France. The official language is French though most people use Shimaore which is based on Swahili.

Here, French law and Muslim law work in tandem—the latter allowing polygamy, for example. Many young children also attend Koranic school before going to a French primary school later in the day. The population is very young: 60% are under 20 years and continues to grow rapidly, a result both of natural increase and immigration from neighbouring Comoros.

Most people are farmers, and grow some food crops as well as cash crops such as vanilla, cloves, and trees for the perfume extract ylang-ylang. Their island has few natural resources, but their link with France entitles them to free education and health services, a guaranteed monthly minimum wage of $400, and French citizenship.

Mayotte was the fourth island of the Comoros when they were a French overseas territory. The split occurred in 1975 when the Comoros as a whole unilaterally declared its independence—despite protests from Mayotte.

In 1976, France held a referendum in Mayotte which produced a 99% vote in favour of retaining the link with France. France reluctantly gave them the temporary designation of 'special collectivity'—a compromise between an overseas territory and a full department of France. Though they have their own general council, the Mahorais also elect members to the French National Assembly and to the Senate.

The Comoros continue to claim the territory and in 1991 the UN General Assembly confirmed that they should have sovereignty. France would be happy to let go what is becoming an expensive colonial memento but says it will only relinquish control if the local people want this.

There seems little prospect that the Mahorais will sever the link in the near future, given the general state of chaos and poverty in the Comoros. Indeed they have been pressing to become a fully-fledged department, though that is an unlikely outcome.

Mexico

Mexico's political landscape changed dramatically after its presidential election in 2000

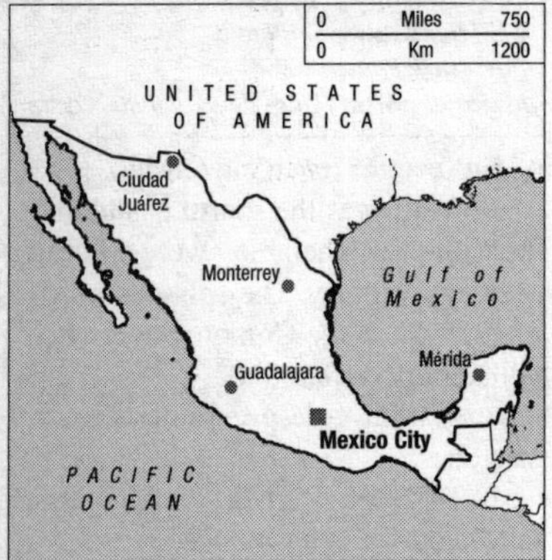

Land area: *1,958,000 sq. km.*
Population: *96 million—urban 74%*
Capital city: *Mexico City, 16 million*
People: *Mestizo 60%, Amerindian 30%, other 10%*
Language: *Spanish and some Indian*
Religion: *Roman Catholic*
Government: *Republic*
Life expectancy: *72 years*
GNP per capita: *$PPP 8,190*
Currency: *Peso*
Major exports: *Cars, oil*

Some have suggested that Mexico's most important geographical feature is the 2,000-mile border it shares with the USA. But Mexico has a striking diversity all of its own—from the snow-capped mountains of the Sierra Madre, to the deserts of Sonora, to the tropical rainforests of Yucatán. Most of the population is to be found, however, in the central region in the high plateau and the surrounding mountains.

Today's Mexicans are largely mestizo, a mixture of Indian and European ancestry. But about one-third are of purer Indian origin, concentrated in the poorer areas of the south. In the first half of this century, Mexico's population expanded rapidly, but annual growth has now slowed to around 1.6%. Population expansion and rural-urban migration also contributed to an explosive growth of cities, particularly of Mexico City, which with a population of 16 million is the third largest city in the world. It also has the dubious distinction of having some of the most polluted air, with levels of sulphur dioxide and lead more than twice the acceptable limits.

Apart from migrating to cities, Mexicans have also been moving to the USA. By 1994, 5 million Mexicans were living in the USA, equivalent to 6% of Mexico's population, and sending $3 billion in remittances. Every working day about 2,000 Mexicans apply for US visas.

A major stimulus for emigration has been the poor state of Mexican agriculture. Only about one-fifth of the country is suitable for arable farming, and even then the soil is often thin and levels of technology are low. Around two-thirds of this land is devoted to maize and beans. Some three million farmers work on the 'ejidos', small collective farms.

From the mid-1980s, in an attempt to improve efficiency, the government liberalized agriculture—reducing subsidies and changing the land-tenure system, allowing the ejidos to be sold and consolidated. But this has brought few benefits to small farmers who find it difficult to get bank loans, or buyers for their crops now that there are no price guarantees.

Mexican maize farmers also find it very hard to compete with imports from the USA. As a result, since 1990, more than half a million subsistence farmers abandoned their farms. The brightest agricultural development has been in the north, where irrigation has permitted a flourishing export trade in fruit and vegetables to the USA.

Aside from the land, one of Mexico's greatest natural assets is oil. Mexico is the world's fourth-largest producer, exporting 1.3 million barrels per day. Another valuable asset is silver: Mexico has the world's largest silver production.

Most industrial employment is in manufacturing. After the economic liberalization of the mid-1980s, many small companies collapsed in the face of international competition. But others gained from international trade, particularly the 'maquiladoras', the 3,300 or more duty-free assembly plants strung along the border with the USA which by 1999 were employing more than 1.1 million people. In January 1994 Mexico joined the North American Free-Trade Agreement (NAFTA). The opening up of the economy has exposed it more to the vagaries of the global market. The most dramatic episode was in 1995, when the peso came under speculative attack, and had to be rescued with a $20 billion loan package from the USA.

3,300 assembly plants on the US border

Though the export-linked 'dollar economy' often seems to be doing well, the vast majority of Mexicans working in the 'peso economy' have a much tougher time. Liberalization is thought to have increased inequality. The richest 10% of the population get 40% of national income while the poorest 40% get only 13%. One-third of the population live below the national poverty line.

Presiding over Mexico's development for 71 years was the Institutional Revolutionary Party (PRI), which was in power continuously between 1929 and 2000. This one-party electoral dictatorship at times lapsed into brutal episodes of repression. But the monolith started to crumble in 1990s. This was partly because in a liberalized economy the state had fewer opportunities for lavish patronage, but also because of more vigorous opposition, most dramatically from the Zapatista National Liberation Army which in 1994 led an uprising in the poor southern state of Chiapas. More disruption comes from the growing drug mafias that control routes from South America into the USA.

Despite having democratized its method for selecting candidates, the PRI was finally defeated in the July 2000 presidential election. The victor, by a surprisingly large margin, was Vicente Fox of the right-wing National Action Party. Fox is a businessman, a former head of Coca-Cola in Mexico, and will take over on December 1.

Fox has vowed to tackle Mexico's entrenched corruption through a 'transparency commission'. He also aims to get the taxation system working properly. However, his party lacks a majority in Congress so it will have to work either with the PRI or with the smaller, left-wing Party of the Democratic Revolution.

Micronesia

Heavily dependent on US aid, Micronesia will need other sources of income

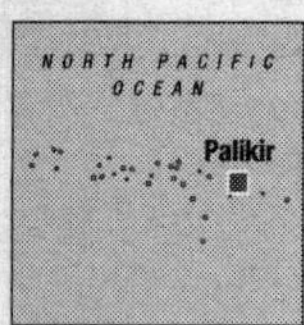

The Federated States of Micronesia are Yap, Chuuk, Pohnpei, and Kosrae, and consist of more than 600 islands and coral atolls in the Pacific.

The people of the federation, though few in number, include a great variety of cultures and languages. Chuuk is the largest state, with around half the population, followed by Pohnpei.

Most productive activity centres on subsistence farming and fishing. The main crops include breadfruit, taro, and coconuts, and there is a small export income from copra, black pepper, and handicrafts. The most important fishing catch is tuna though much of the catch goes to foreign fleets.

The islanders' primary source of cash income, however, is the government, which relies on transfers of US aid through a 'Compact of Free Association'. Over the period 1986-99 the country received $1.3 billion in US grants—$10,000 per person. The government is the main employer, providing 40% of total employment in 1997 and its expenditure in 1996 accounted for over 40% of GDP.

This assistance is due to end in 2001 and the government has been struggling to adjust by reducing its employees' working hours as well as through large-scale layoffs. It does appear to have made progress and aid donors seem encouraged by the reduction in public-sector spending and in the budget deficit.

Land area: *1,000 sq. km.*
Population: *113,000—urban 28%*
Capital city: *Palikir*
People: *Micronesian and Polynesian groups*
Language: *English, Chukese, Pohnpeian, Yapese, Kosraean*
Religion: *Roman Catholic 50%, Protestant 47%, other 3%*
Government: *Republic in free association with the USA*
Life expectancy: *67 years*
GNP per capita: *$PPP $1,760*
Currency: *US dollar*
Major exports: *Copra, fish, pepper*

Tourism offers some potential, but so far has been confined to niche markets such as eco-tourism, visits to some ancient ruins, and shipwreck diving. However there are concerns about the impact that greater numbers of visitors would have on the fragile environment.

There has also been some investment in industry, notably in garment production, but expansion is hampered by poor infrastructure and the distance from markets.

Until 1986, the states were part of a UN Trust Territory. Then they became an independent federation, self-governing but in free association with the USA. Each of the four states has its own elected governor and legislative assembly. There are no political parties. In addition, there is an elected federal congress, which chooses the president. In March 1999, it selected Leo Falcam. However, in many respects Micronesia functions more as four separate states than one country.

Moldova

Moldova has effectively been split in two by a long fight for secession

Land area: *34,000 sq. km.*
Population: *4 million—urban 54%*
Capital city: *Chisinau, 667,000*
People: *Moldavian/Romanian 65%, Ukrainian 14%, Russian 13%, Gagauz 4%, other 8%*
Language: *Moldovan, Russian, Gagauz*
Religion: *Eastern Orthodox*
Government: *Republic*
Life expectancy: *68 years*
GNP per capita: *$PPP 1,500*
Currency: *Moldovan leu*
Major exports: *Food products, beverages, tobacco*

Most of Moldova lies between two rivers that flow into the Black Sea: the Prut, which forms the western border with Romania; and the Dniester which flows roughly in parallel with the eastern border with Ukraine. The land is largely a hilly plain, though also cut through with many steep ravines. The soil—the rich, black 'chernozem'—is very fertile, and two-thirds of the country is forested.

Moldova's difficulties in building a new nation since 1991 reflect its fairly recent assembly as one territory. In 1940, the Soviet Union united the land from the Prut to the Dniester, Bessarabiya, which had been part of Romania, with the strip of land from the Dniester to the eastern border, Transdniestria. The two were merged as the Moldavian Soviet Socialist Republic.

After the Second World War, the Soviet Union made strong efforts to weaken the republic's Romanian past. This included changing the name of the language from Romanian to Moldovan, and switching from the Roman to the Cyrillic alphabet, as well as encouraging immigration from Russia and Ukraine. As a result, ethnic Moldovans make up only around two-thirds of the population; and in Transdniestria they are only around 40%.

The break-up of the Soviet Union provoked a crisis of national identity that persists to this day. During the late 1980s, two separatist movements had appeared. When the Moldavian Republic declared its independence in 1991, as 'Moldova', both groups feared that independence would lead to unification with Romania and both declared themselves independent. The smaller group were the Gagauz in the south-east—135,000 Christians of Turkish origin—who subsequently laid down their arms in exchange for a measure of autonomy.

The larger, and more debilitating, rebellion came from the Russians in Transdniestria, and in 1992 this escalated into a civil war, in which Russia backed the separatist while Romania backed Moldova. A peace treaty was signed in 1992 and has been enforced with Russian troops.

This has left the country effectively partitioned in two. Transdniestria, which has 11% of the territory, and 17% of the people, is ruled by its own government in Tiraspol headed by Igor Smirnov, an unreconstructed communist whose heavy-handed and repressive rule is attempting to sustain the Soviet economic model. This is particularly damaging for Moldova since Transdniestria has around 38% of the total industrial production capacity—including about 80% of energy, 90% of steel and plastics, and 40% of food-canning plants.

Transdniestria has its own government

Meanwhile the rest of Moldova is struggling with market reforms. From 1990 the economy went into a deep recession though it started to revive after 1997. The government privatized many industries by distributing vouchers and also made some cash sales. By 1998, the private sector controlled around 45% of the economy.

With limited immediate prospects for industrial development, Moldova remains highly dependent on agriculture which accounts for around one-third of GDP and employment, and is the main source of export income. The most important crops are cereals, sugar beet, tobacco, grapes, and other fruit. Although the land is fertile it has suffered from over-intensive cultivation and the heavy use of fertilizers, and production is vulnerable to the weather: harvests are regularly hit by droughts and floods. More than half the land is still in the hand of co-ops and collectives, many of which run at a loss. More than half the national food output comes from household plots.

In 1994, Moldovans voted for a new constitution to maintain the country's current borders but grant extensive autonomy to Gagauz and Transdniestria.

The head of state is the president, who appoints the council of ministers and nominates the prime minister—though these must be approved by the single-chamber assembly, the Parlamentul. The 1996 presidential election was won by Petru Lucinschi, a leading official from the Soviet era. And the 1998 parliamentary elections made the Party of Moldavian Communists the largest party, with 30% of the vote.

Since then the political situation has been fairly unstable. In 1999 the government of Ion Sturza, for example was dismissed, partly as a result of manoeuvring by Lucinschi who wants to increase the powers of the presidency in advance of the 2000 presidential elections.

Moldova's future as a state, however, now seems reasonably secure. The prospect of unification with Romania has receded, particularly since the current Romanian administration seems less keen. Even the leaders of Transdniestria accept that they will not achieve independence, but are aiming for a confederation of equal states. In 1997 they signed a memorandum with the Moldovan government calling for a peaceful settlement of the conflict. One hopeful sign is that Transdniestria has now allowed its footballers to play in the Moldovan national team.

Mongolia

Long a Soviet satellite state, Mongolia is struggling to create a market economy

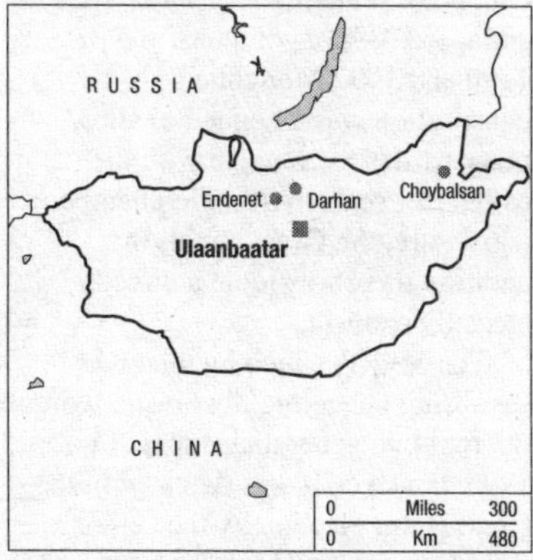

Land area: *1,567,000 sq. km.*
Population: *3 million—urban 60%*
Capital city: *Ulaanbaatar, 573,000*
People: *Mongol 90%, Kazakh 4%, Chinese 2%, Russian 2%, other 2%*
Language: *Khalkha Mongol 90%, Turkic, Russian, Chinese*
Religion: *Tibetan Buddhist*
Government: *Republic*
Life expectancy: *62 years*
GNP per capita: *$PPP 1,520*
Currency: *Togrog*
Major exports: *Fuels, minerals, metals, garments*

Mongolia's territory, which is around the size of Western Europe, consists largely of a vast plateau between 900 and 1,500 metres above sea level. It has a harsh semi-arid climate, with bitterly cold winters, but has extensive pasture land. The greatest mountain ranges are to the north and west, while the land to the east and south stretches out into rolling steppes and the Gobi Desert.

Most Mongolians now live in cities—one-quarter in the capital, Ulaanbaatar. In ethnic terms the country is fairly homogenous, the largest minority being Kazakhs in the south. In the 1930s, a Stalinist government purged much of the country's Tibetan Buddhist heritage, though with a democratic government and freedom of religion Buddhism is now staging a revival.

In 1991, following seven decades of socialism and the sudden withdrawal of Soviet aid, the government embarked on a course of 'shock therapy', shutting some industries, privatizing others, and making severe cuts in social services. For most people, this meant a serious drop in income. Between 1990 and 1993, real wages in industry dropped by one-fifth and in agriculture by nearly one-third. More than one-third of the population are still classified as poor or very poor.

Education services are also deteriorating and the government has reduced the number of dormitory places that are essential for herder children. One of the most disturbing developments has been the emergence of 4,000 street children in Ulaanbaatar. Because winter temperatures can drop to 30 degrees below zero the children have to live in the sewers.

Around 45% of the workforce work in agriculture. Nomadic Mongol tribes, with their circular felt tents, or 'gers', and their huge herds of sheep, goats, horses, and yaks, offer a distinctive picture of Mongolian life. Their herds had been collectivized during the communist period and then privatized again—29 million animals—after 1990. The land remains in state ownership. Privatization revived production but it has also increased inequality and larger herds are harming the pastures—two-thirds of which are now degraded to some extent. To make matters worse, the winter in early 2000 was disastrously cold, even by Mongolian standards, killing around 2 million animals.

Larger herds degrade the pasture

Mongolia also has considerable mineral wealth—with rich deposits of coal, iron ore, copper, molybdenum, fluorspar, and tungsten. Fuels, minerals, and metals are responsible for more than two-thirds of exports. Revenues have fallen with the decline in world prices, but mineral extraction is one of the country's main priorities. Efforts have also been made to increase manufacturing production, and the next largest export sector is garments and textiles, including cashmere from goat hair.

Mongolia's main trade disadvantage is its isolation. Getting goods out to a seaport overland involves a three-day railway journey through Russia or China. Nevertheless, there have been efforts to promote trade and in 1997 Mongolia briefly became the only country with no taxes on trade.

Mongolia's economy shrank rapidly following the withdrawal of Soviet aid, which had been equivalent to 30% of GDP. It also lost supplies of cheap oil. Since then, the economy has recovered somewhat. By 1998 growth was positive again and inflation was down to 6%.

Mongolia became the world's second communist state in 1924. From then on it was ruled by the Mongolian People's Revolutionary Party (MPRP) and for 70 years was bankrolled by the Soviet Union as a buffer state against China. When communism collapsed in the Soviet Union it duly collapsed in Mongolia too, and in 1990 and 1992 Mongolia's constitution was amended to allow other parties to compete with the MPRP for seats in a single-chamber legislature, the Great Hural. In addition there was to be a directly elected president.

The MPRP, which by then was espousing economic liberalism, won the first two general elections. In 1996, however, it was defeated in the Great Hural election by the centre-right Democratic Union, consisting of the Mongolian National Democratic Party and the Mongolian Social Democratic Party. But matters were complicated later that year when an MPRP candidate, Natsagiin Bagabandi was elected president.

In 1998 this conflict produced a political crisis when the MPRP started to boycott the Great Hural and the president rejected a series of candidates for prime minister. Things seemed to settle down subsequently with a new government and Janlaviin Narantsatsralt as prime minister. But rising levels of poverty made the government increasingly unpopular. In the July 2000 parliamentary elections the MPRP was returned to power with a substantial majority. The prime minister is 42-year old Namburiin Enkhbayar. He is a modernizer who has dubbed himself the 'Tony Blair of the steppes', though he still has to deal with his communist old guard.

Morocco

Morocco now has a more liberal monarch but continues its illegal occupation of Western Sahara

Land area: *447,000 sq. km.*
Population: *28 million—urban 54%*
Capital city: *Rabat, 1.7 million*
People: *Arab-Berber 99%, other 1%*
Language: *Arabic, Amazigh, French, Spanish*
Religion: *Muslim*
Government: *Constitutional monarchy*
Life expectancy: *67 years*
GNP per capita: *$PPP 3,120*
Currency: *Dirham*
Major exports: *Phosphate rock, phosphoric acid, textiles*

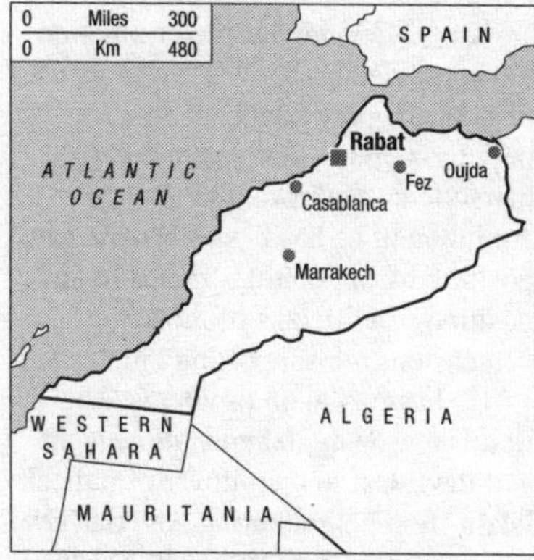

Morocco is the most mountainous country of North Africa. The two main chains are the Er Rif, along the Mediterranean coast, and the Atlas Mountains which dominate the country from north-east to south-west. Most people live in the lowlands that lie between these two chains and the Atlantic coast. Morocco also controls the desert area of Western Sahara to the south.

Morocco's people are largely Arabized Berbers, but around one-third are less-assimilated Berbers, most of whom live in the mountains and whose language, Amazigh, was given official recognition in 1994. Morocco has striking rural-urban disparities. Only half the rural population have access to health services and only one-fifth have safe water and sanitation. Even in urban areas there are high levels of poverty, and unemployment is around 20%. As a result, many Moroccans have chosen to emigrate illegally, making the perilous 15-kilometre sea-crossing to Spain. Around 1.7 million Moroccans now live overseas, chiefly in France and Spain; their annual remittances are around $2 billion—the second largest source of foreign exchange.

Agriculture employs about two-fifths of the labour force. Most of the land is in the hands of smaller farmers growing cereals, potatoes, and other staples. Since they lack irrigation they have to rely on fairly erratic rainfall. The tenth of the arable land that is irrigated is mostly in larger farms which grow citrus fruits, grapes, and other export crops. Meanwhile, especially during drought years, much of the country's cereal needs have to be imported.

One of the Morocco's main priorities is to improve the irrigation network taking water from the areas of good rainfall to those regularly hit by drought. A new canal was opened in 1999 to take water from Guerdane in the east to the south of the country to irrigate citrus crops.

Many of the smaller farmers in the mountains also raise cattle, sheep, and goats. Morocco's fishing industry is a major supplier of sardines to the EU, though catches have fallen due to over-fishing by both Spanish and Moroccans.

Morocco's main industrial enterprises are state-owned and linked to phosphates. With Western Sahara, Morocco has most of the world's reserves, and is the third largest producer. The other major export industry is textiles, which expanded rapidly in the 1980s. Many smaller enterprises also produce high-quality leather goods, rugs, and carpets.

Of the service industries, one of the most important is tourism. Around 2 million visitors arrive each year and provide employment to 6% of the labour force. Earnings have been falling, however, and many of Morocco's tourist facilities are in need of a facelift. Some of this investment is already underway. The French Accor Group, for example, which owns a number of hotel chains, plans to treble its number of hotel rooms in Morocco by 2006.

Morocco is a constitutional monarchy ruled by King Mohammad VI, who in 1999 succeeded to the throne following the death of his father, King Hassan II. In Morocco, the monarch acts like an executive president and Hassan was an autocratic ruler whose determination to retain tight control resulted in thousands of arbitrary arrests and disappearances.

The king is known as M6

King Mohammad seems different. One of his first actions was to free 8,000 political prisoners and he has welcomed back a number of high-profile exiles, notably Abraham Serfaty, who had been jailed for seventeen years and then exiled. King Mohammad has also established a commission to investigate more than 4,000 cases of political repression. Most dramatically of all, he sacked the notorious interior minister, Driss Basri, who had been Hassan's chief enforcer.

King Mohammad's determination to extend democracy and improve the lives of the poor has made him hugely popular—young people copy his hairstyle and refer to him as 'M6'. And though he has been bolstering his position by appointing friends to key positions, politicians of most persuasions are supporting him.

He has two main problems. The first is a growing Islamist movement and the threat of a spillover of radical Islam from neighbouring Algeria. The more radical elements are still banned and the security forces have had regular clashes with Islamic students who strongly oppose some of the reforms to improve women's rights.

The second major concern is Western Sahara. Morocco seized the former Spanish colony when Spain withdrew in 1975 and despite armed resistance from the Polisario guerrilla movement, and international protests, has stayed there ever since. Following a ceasefire in 1991 the UN started a long series of negotiations that have promised the local people, the Saharawis, a referendum to choose between independence and union with Morocco.

Meanwhile Morocco has been flooding the territory with settlers in order to swing the vote. King Mohammad has been taking a more conciliatory approach, but seems unlikely to allow a fair referendum.

Mozambique

Devastating floods set back Mozambique's efforts to capitalize on a period of peace and stability

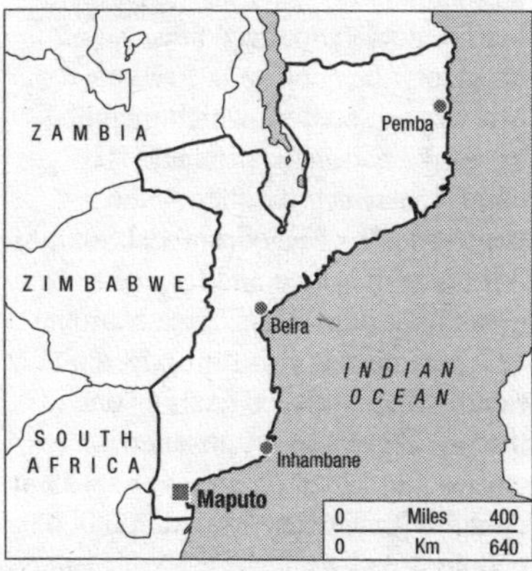

Land area: *802,000 sq. km.*
Population: *17 million—urban 38%*
Capital city: *Maputo, 1.4 million*
People: *Makua-Lomwe, Tsonga, Yao, Sena-Nyanja.*
Language: *Portuguese, indigenous dialects*
Religion: *Indigenous beliefs 50%, Christian 30%, Muslim 20%*
Government: *Republic*
Life expectancy: *45 years*
GNP per capita: *$PPP 850*
Currency: *Metical*
Major exports: *Prawns, cotton, cashew nuts*

Mozambique can be divided by the Zambezi River into two main geographical regions. The southern part of the country is mostly flat and low-lying, apart from highlands on the eastern border. North of the river the land rises to plateaux and to mountains along the border with Malawi.

The Zambezi also divides the country's many different ethnic groups. Most of the population is concentrated in the better land north of the river, particularly in the north-east. Groups here include the Makua, who are farmers, and the Muslim Yao. South of the river, where people live more along the coast, are groups such as the Tsonga. None of their languages is widely spoken around the country so the official language is Portuguese.

Mozambique's civil war, which ended in 1992, devastated much of the country's social infrastructure, destroying schools, hospitals, and clinics—in what was already one of the world's poorest countries. Since then, the government has managed to rebuild most of the schools. School attendance has been rising and by 1997 around 60% of children were enrolled in primary schools. Even so, adult literacy had still only reached 40%. The health system also still needs considerable investment.

Most people are very poor. Although the capital, Maputo, is now a lot smarter, around 70% of the population languish below the poverty line. Poverty is severe in the rural areas and particularly in the north. Those who have had few employment opportunities at home have traditionally migrated to neighbouring South Africa which currently has around 1 million immigrant Mozambicans.

Around 80% of the workforce make their living from agriculture. Given good weather, Mozambique should be self-sufficient in basic foodstuffs such as maize and cassava. By 1996 it had even managed to export some maize—though imports of wheat and rice will continue. The main cash crops are cotton and especially cashew nuts. Production of both food and cash crops has increased, but farmers are still hampered by the hazard of landmines scattered in the civil war.

Since much of the land in Mozambique is under-exploited, the government has invited Boer farmers to resettle from South Africa. All land nevertheless remains state-owned; farmers, even local ones, can only lease it.

Mozambique's most important exports are prawns along with some shellfish. The fishing industry was less affected than others by the war. Even so, the local fleet is relatively small and the government gains extra income by selling licences to boats from Europe, South Africa, and Japan.

Mozambique's industrial sector was badly damaged by the fighting. Since the mid-1990s, however, and following one of Africa's most extensive programmes of privatization, industrial output has revived. A large new aluminium smelter is almost finished. More foreign investors are coming, and over the period 1997-9 the economy grew annually by around 10%. Much of this activity, however, has been in the southern half of the country, which also tends to be economically more integrated with neighbouring countries, thus sharpening the north-south divide.

Development is widening the north-south divide

Mozambique remains heavily dependent on aid which accounts for 40% of GNP—around $60 per person per year. Overall development efforts were set back by widespread flooding early in 2000 which destroyed roads and other infrastructure. However, this did at least encourage the country's creditors to suspend debt repayments.

Since independence in 1975 the government has been in the hands of the Frente de Libertação de Moçambique (Frelimo). Frelimo's Marxist orientation, which included extensive nationalization and state control, alarmed the then white governments of Rhodesia and South Africa, who armed and funded a guerrilla group, Resistência National de Moçambique (Renamo). Renamo rapidly distinguished itself as one of the world's most vicious guerrilla armies and Mozambique sank into a civil war that killed around 900,000 people.

The war ended with a stalemate and a peace accord in 1992, followed by very effective UN-organized programmes which demobilized the soldiers and repatriated more than 1 million refugees. In the elections in 1994, Frelimo, by then headed by Joaquím Chissano, won a surprisingly narrow victory over Renamo—which, to its credit and everyone's relief, accepted the result.

By the mid-1980s Frelimo had renounced Marxism and continued economic liberalization. Poverty is still widespread, but Chissano and Frelimo remain fairly popular, especially in Maputo and the south.

In 1999, Chissano won another narrow victory over the Renamo leader, Afonso Dhlakama, in the presidential election and Frelimo gained a small majority in the legislative assembly.

Namibia

Namibia is one of the world's most unequal societies, and now faces an AIDS crisis

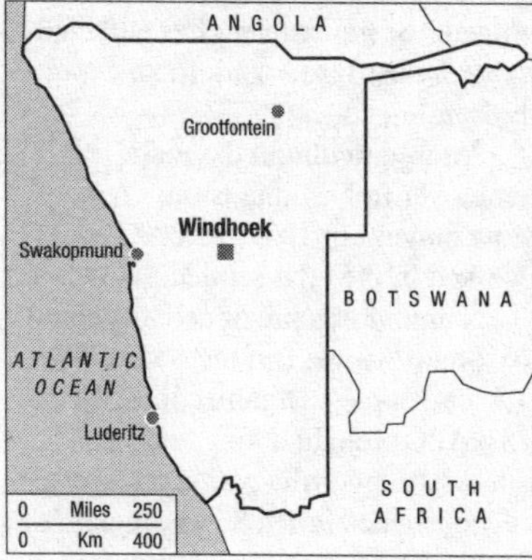

Land area: *824,000 sq. km.*
Population: *2 million—urban 39%*
Capital city: *Windhoek, 190,000*
People: *Ovambo 50%, Herero 7%, Damara 7%, white 7%, mixed 7%, Nama 5%, other 17%*
Language: *English, Afrikaans, German, Oshivambo, Herero, Nama*
Religion: *Christian 80%, indigenous religions 20%*
Government: *Republic*
Life expectancy: *52 years*
GNP per capita: *$PPP 4,950*
Currency: *Namibian dollar*
Major exports: *Diamonds, uranium, gold,*

Namibia has three main geographical regions. Its long, distinctive Atlantic coastline consists of the dunes and rocks of the Namib desert. This rises to a broad plateau that includes mountains rising to 2,500 metres. To the east, the plateau descends to the sands of the Kalahari desert. The climate is hot and dry and the rainfall is erratic—the only year-round rivers flow along the northern and southern borders.

Namibia is sparsely populated. Around half the population live in the far north. The other area of concentration is in and around the capital, Windhoek. Namibia has a number of different ethnic groups. The largest are the Ovambo, who are also politically dominant. Linguistically, Namibia is very diverse. Only a small minority speak English, which is the official language; most others use languages of the Ovambo or their own ethnic group, though many also understand Afrikaans or German.

Of the minority groups, the most discontented have been the 100,000 or so Lozi who live in the Caprivi strip, an odd sliver of land in the far north-east, originally carved out to give the German colonists a corridor to the Zambezi. This cuts across the land of the Lozi people, who are spread across Angola, Botswana, and Zambia and have been fighting for independence. In August 1999 a Lozi uprising was brutally repressed by Namibian security forces.

Another fundamental division is between the whites and the rest. Namibia's per capita income is fairly high but it has one of the world's most unequal distributions of income—the richest 1% of households, mostly whites, consume as much as the poorest 50%. Efforts to overcome this imbalance have included heavy investment in education, which now takes up more than 25% of the budget. Health too is a major problem; most facilities are concentrated in the urban areas. Though Namibians suffer from diseases like malaria and tuberculosis, the leading cause of death is now

HIV/AIDS—around 10% of the population are infected. UNAIDS has estimated that over the next five years life expectancy could fall to 41 years.

Agriculture represents only a small proportion of GDP, but up to two-thirds of the population rely on farming for at least part of their livelihood. The staple crop is millet, which is grown by subsistence farmers in the north—though output is vulnerable to erratic rainfall and Namibia normally has to import almost half its food.

Commercial farming, which is mostly the prerogative of white settlers in the centre and south, is devoted primarily to livestock—raising cattle and sheep for export to South Africa and the EU. One of the most contentious political issues is land reform, since whites own around half the land area. So far, there has been little reform because the constitution requires the government to provide full compensation for any land taken—and the government is also nervous of provoking a white exodus.

Whites own around half the farm land in Namibia

A larger component of Namibia's GDP comes from mining, and particularly from diamonds. Namibia has high-quality diamonds that are extracted by the Namdeb Diamond Corporation, a joint venture between the government and the South African De Beers company. In 1997, they extracted diamonds worth half a billion dollars. An increasingly high proportion of these are now coming from offshore fields. The other important minerals are uranium and gold, though mining of these has been curtailed by low world prices. In future there could also be an expansion of copper and zinc extraction.

Other industrial activity is more limited. Manufacturing has been concentrated in food processing, though the government has attracted other industries to work in an export-processing zone.

After agriculture, the main employer in Namibia is the government. In 1997, 76,000 people worked in the civil service.

Namibia was previously occupied by South Africa. But the South-West Africa People's Organization (SWAPO) fought a long and successful guerrilla war and since independence in 1988 it has held political power.

SWAPO won the first election for the national assembly in 1989 and its leader Sam Nujoma was also elected president. The main opposition came from the Democratic Turnhalle Alliance—which had formed the government during the South African occupation and which is particularly weak in the north.

SWAPO consolidated its position in the 1994 National Assembly and presidential elections. But Nujoma's rule has grown increasingly autocratic—handing out most of its favours to the Ovambo people, while clamping down on the Lozi. He also changed the constitution to let him run for president a third time in 1999. Nujoma won that election convincingly, though against a new and more credible opposition party, the Congress of Democrats, whose leader Ben Ulenga is a former SWAPO dissident.

Nepal

A poor and remote mountain kingdom that has suffered years of political turmoil

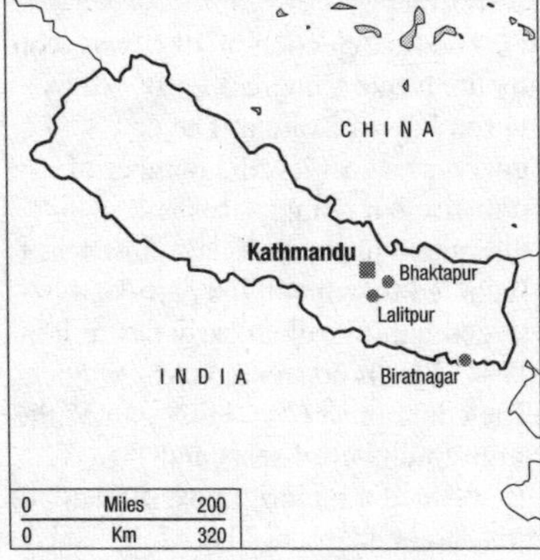

Land area: *141,000 sq. km.*
Population: *23 million—urban 11%*
Capital city: *Kathmandu, 535,000*
People: *Newars, Indians, Tibetans, and 70 other ethnic groups*
Language: *Nepali and 30 tribal languages*
Religion: *Hindu 90%, Buddhist 5%, Muslim 3%*
Government: *Constitutional monarchy*
Life expectancy: *54 years*
GNP per capita: *$PPP 1,090*
Currency: *Nepalese rupee*
Major exports: *Carpets, garments*

Nepal's territory can be divided roughly into three bands descending from north to south. The northernmost band includes the Great Himalayas dominated by Mount Everest at 8,848 metres. The central band has the lower Mahabharat range and a number of major river systems and valleys, including the densely-settled Kathmandu Valley. The band along the southern border with India has forested lower slopes which descend to the fertile Terai plain.

Nepal's people comprise more than 70 ethnic groups that can be considered in two sets. The first and smaller, the Tibeto-Nepalese, are the result of immigration from Tibet. They are found in the bleak high mountain areas as well as in the middle band, and are usually Buddhist. The larger set, of Indo-Aryan ancestry, have immigrated from India and elsewhere, and are largely Hindu and rigidly stratified into higher and lower castes.

The Nepalese have in recent years become even poorer. Despite economic growth the proportion of people living in poverty has increased from 36% to 45% as a result of rising inequality: economic growth has bypassed the poor.

Standards of education and health are very low. Only 27% of the population are literate. Four-fifths have no access to safe sanitation, and around two-thirds of children are malnourished. The situation is particularly severe for women. While in most countries women's biological advantage enables them to live longer than men, in Nepal women's lifespan is somewhat shorter. This is the outcome of many kinds of discrimination, especially in health care, which results in high rates of maternal mortality—more than 500 mothers die in childbirth per 100,000 live births.

Survival in Nepal depends primarily on agriculture, which generates about 40% of the country's GDP and involves more than 80% of the workforce—primarily cultivating rice, maize, and wheat, as well as raising livestock. But productivity is low and output is erratic. Cultivation is particularly arduous in the terraced farms of the hilly regions. Land holdings are small, irrigation is difficult, and the situation is being aggravated by soil erosion and deforestation. The position is somewhat better in the land of the Terai plain, which accounts for about half the cultivable land and where there are better prospects for irrigation. But land ownership here is highly concentrated so the benefits are unevenly spread.

Most of Nepal's industry is on a small scale for local consumption. One of the main export industries is carpet weaving, but carpet sales in Europe have been affected by accusations of the exploitation of child labour. Some Indian garment manufacturers have also established factories to take advantage of Nepal's quotas. The service sector has been growing too but this is primarily the result of government development expenditure, two-thirds of which is financed by foreign aid.

Another important source of income is tourism. In 1996 there were 390,000 arrivals providing 18% of the country's foreign exchange. But it is difficult to travel around Nepal, and the vast majority of tourists get little further than Kathmandu. The government has been trying to encourage more arrivals and longer stays, but it is doubtful that the infrastructure could cope with many more people.

Few tourists get much further than Kathmandu

Until 1990, Nepal was an absolute monarchy and political parties were banned. Inspired by democratic changes elsewhere, many political groupings organized a series of protests that culminated in a mass march on the royal palace. Eventually, King Birendra gave way and in November 1990 he introduced a new constitution based on multi-party democracy.

The first election in 1991 was won by the Nepal Congress Party, led by Girija Prasad Koirala. The new government achieved a number of reforms, but rising prices and discontent about Koirala's closeness to India led to splits in the party and forced him to call an early election in 1994. This produced no clear winner. The communist CPN-ULN gained the largest number of seats and established a minority government but this soon collapsed. There followed a rapid sequence of different coalition or minority administrations.

Since 1996 the political situation has been further destabilized by a Maoist insurgency originating in the poorest rural areas of western Nepal, and demanding land reform and a republican state. This conflict has cost hundreds of lives and led to abuses of human rights on both sides. Amnesty International has charged Nepal's government with jailing political activists without trial and killing suspects in police custody.

In May 1999, there was a parliamentary election. This produced a victory for the Congress Party—thanks to splits in parties to the right and left of it. For a year or so the prime minister was Krishna Prasad Bhattarai, but he was ousted early in 2000 by the now 76 year-old Koirala, who returned as Nepal's tenth prime minister in ten years.

Netherlands

One of Europe's most tolerant, and most prosperous, societies

Land area: *37,000 sq. km.*
Population: *16 million—urban 89%*
Capital city: *Amsterdam, 1.1 million; jointly with The Hague, 0.7 million*
People: *Dutch 95%, other 5%*
Language: *Dutch*
Religion: *Roman Catholic 34%, Protestant 25%, Muslim 3%, other 2%, unaffiliated 36%*
Government: *Constitutional monarchy*
Life expectancy: *78 years*
GNP per capita: *$PPP 21,620*
Currency: *Guilder*
Major exports: *Manufactured goods, chemicals, food, and agricultural products*

True to its name, most of the Netherlands is 'low lands': more than one-quarter of the country lies below sea level, protected from flooding by coastal dunes and by specially constructed dykes. For centuries, the Dutch have been reclaiming land from the sea and keeping it drained, using pumps that initially were powered by windmills. But even the higher and drier parts of the country seldom rise much above 60 metres.

This is one of Europe's most densely populated countries—456 per square kilometre, most of them are concentrated in the west and centre. This makes land expensive and its use is controlled and regulated more closely than in most other countries.

The Dutch enjoy one of the world's most advanced systems of social welfare. They also have very liberal social attitudes: in 1994, this was the first country to permit euthanasia, and since 1998 registered homosexual partnerships have had almost the same rights and obligations as married couples. The Dutch have also gone a long way towards decriminalizing the use of soft drugs—with marijuana readily available in thousands of 'coffee houses'.

Like other European countries, the Netherlands is facing a falling birth rate; its fertility rate is only 1.5 children per woman of childbearing age. This has been offset to some extent by immigration. The foreign born make up 4% of the population; initially they came from former colonies such as Indonesia or Suriname, though nowadays the largest groups are from Turkey and Morocco.

Reclaiming land from the sea helped make the Netherlands one of Europe's leading agricultural nations, and it maintains that position today, even though only around 2% of the labour force work on the land. Thanks to very productive small farms, it has steadily increased agricultural output. The country is largely self-sufficient in food and also exports dairy products, meat, flowers, and bulbs.

Because it had few raw materials,

the Netherlands did not develop as much heavy industry as other advanced economies. Instead it based its economy more on processing imported materials and on international trade. Thus Rotterdam is the world's largest port, and a transhipment point for imported oil that is heading for other European countries. Amsterdam's Schipol airport is Europe's second largest hub for air freight. The Netherlands' external orientation has given rise to important multinational companies such as Unilever, Royal Dutch/Shell, Philips, and Heineken. Even so, two-thirds of the workforce are employed in service industries.

One of the most important economic developments in the 20th century was the discovery in 1959 of huge deposits of natural gas in the north of the country. This rapidly turned the Netherlands into a major gas exporter. Unfortunately, this also distorted other aspects of development, driving up the exchange rate and wages, and making industry less competitive—a phenomenon subsequently dubbed the 'Dutch disease'. The disease now seems to have been cured. Following decades of wage moderation, the Netherlands has enjoyed rapid growth, low inflation and low unemployment.

Acquired and cured the 'Dutch disease'

This success is the result of a unique social model that allows many different groups to participate in setting social and economic policy. Thus there is a Social Economic Council, with representation from employers and trade unions that considers such issues as collective agreements and welfare provision and has helped keep wage claims within manageable limits. However, the pact has sometimes come under strain—especially when union members see their income falling behind inflation. Nor has there been much improvement in inequality: 5% of households still have half the private wealth.

Dutch politics is similarly consensual. The head of state is Queen Beatrix, but her role is largely ceremonial since almost all power rests in the parliament. In the past, political parties have been divided by ideology or by religion—Catholic or Protestant. But these distinctions have steadily been eroded. The religion-based parties which, in one form or another, had run the country since 1917 merged in 1977 to form Christian Democratic Appeal and continued to dominate politics until 1994, when, as a result partly of a plan to cut pensions, they lost the general election.

The party with the most seats was the centre-left Labour Party, whose leader, Wim Kok, became prime minister. Labour governed in partnership with the centre-right Liberals, and the smaller libertarian party, D-66. This coalition, which retained power in the 1998 election, is ideologically so diverse that it has been termed the 'purple' partnership. The opposition is the Christian Democratic Party, which is opposed to euthanasia and expresses concern for the decline of 'family values'. But with the country so prosperous, and apparently so cohesive, much of the vigour has been drained from Dutch political debate.

Netherlands Antilles

A dispersed Dutch federation in the Caribbean

Land area: *800 sq. km.*
Population: *213,000—urban 70%*
Capital city: *Willemstad, 140,000*
People: *Mixed black 85%, Carib Amerindian, white, and East Asian, 15%*
Language: *Dutch, Papiamento, English*
Religion: *Roman Catholic, Protestant, Jewish, Seventh-Day Adventist*
Government: *Dependency of the Netherlands*
Life expectancy: *75 years*
GNP per capita: *$PPP $11,500*
Currency: *Netherlands Antilles guilder*
Major exports: *Petroleum products*

The Netherlands Antilles comprises five Caribbean islands. The northern group has the three smaller and greener islands of Sint Eustatius, Saba, and Sint Maarten (the southern part of St Martin). The southern group, off the coast of Venezuela, is formed by the two larger and drier islands of Curaçao and Bonaire.

The people are racially mixed—of combined African, European, and Amerindian ancestry. Those in the northern islands have a stronger black component; those in the south have a stronger Latin component. Though the official language is Dutch, on the northern islands the usual spoken language is English, while in the south it is the creole language Papiamento. Around three-quarters of the total population live in Curaçao. Standards of human development are quite high, boosted by aid from the Netherlands, but there have been persistently high levels of unemployment.

The islands have few natural resources and rely mostly on oil refining, tourism, and financial services. The proximity of Curaçao to Venezuela, and its location on important shipping lanes, made the island a major centre for oil storage and transhipment, cargo handling, and ship repair. The collapse in oil prices of the 1980s created serious problems, though with investment from Petróleos de Venezuela the oil-related business has recovered. While this business has brought many economic benefits it has also caused some environmental damage.

The expansion of tourism helped to offer alternative employment, particularly on Sint Maarten, though it has been hit by a series of hurricanes. Bonaire is another tourist centre, with some spectacular scuba diving.

The islands are also an important stopping-off point for money. This is an offshore financial centre, with more than 40 registered banks which, the USA complains, are used for laundering drug money. Agriculture is very limited, though farmers grow oranges to make the liqueur Curaçao.

The islands are a federation. They have a Dutch-appointed governor, as well as an autonomous government for internal affairs. The legislature, the Staten, has representative from each island. In addition, each island has its own general council.

Most political organization is based on individual islands, and at times it has seemed that the federation might break up. Aruba left in 1986. In the last referendum in 1993, however, the islands voted to stay together.

New Caledonia

A nation divided over the question of independence from France

Land area: 19,000 sq. km.
Population: 206,000—urban 62%
Capital city: Nouméa , 65,000
People: Melanesian 43%, European 37%, Wallisian 8%, Polynesian 4%, Indonesian 4%, Vietnamese 2%, other 2%
Language: French and Melanesian languages
Religion: Roman Catholic 60%, Protestant 30%, other 10%
Government: Overseas territory of France
Life expectancy: 73 years
GNP per capita: $PPP $11,400
Currency: CCP franc
Major exports: Ferronickel, nickel ore

Most of this Pacific country is formed by Grande Terre, a long island dominated by a mountain range that runs its entire length and descends steeply to hills and a narrow coastal plain. The country also includes many other islands, notably the Loyalty Islands and the Isle of Pines.

The original Melanesian inhabitants, known as the Kanaks, are now in a minority. France established New Caledonia as a country of settlement with immigrants from France, the 'Caldoches', and indentured workers from elsewhere in the Pacific and Asia.

New Caledonia's main resources are its mineral deposits. The country is the world's fourth-largest producer of nickel and has around one-third of world reserves. This, combined with French aid of around $900 million per year, given New Caledonians a relatively high standard of living, but low prices for nickel have reduced the income, increasing the need to develop other resources such as fishing and tourism to combat rising levels of unemployment.

New Caledonia is an overseas territory of France and sends deputies to the French parliament, as well as electing members to local assemblies. Since the 1970s, there has been a running, and often violent, conflict between the Kanaks, who favour independence, and the Caldoches, who favour continuing as French territory. The main pro-independence political group is a coalition, the Front de libération nationale kanak socialiste, led by Rock Wamytan, while the anti-independence party is the Rassemblement pour la Calédonie dans la république, led by Jacques Lafleur.

Although a referendum on independence was planned for 1998, this was ultimately considered too divisive, and instead the two sides reached the Nouméa Accords through which France would allow considerable autonomy between 2000 and 2014, at which date there would finally be a referendum on independence.

The outcome remains uncertain. The Kanaks have a higher birth rate than the Caldoches, and if migration from France declines they could be in the majority by 2014. On the other hand, the next generation of Kanaks will have benefited from fifteen or more years of French aid, so may have grown to depend on it. Years of dispute lie ahead.

New Zealand

New Zealand now has one of the world's least regulated economies

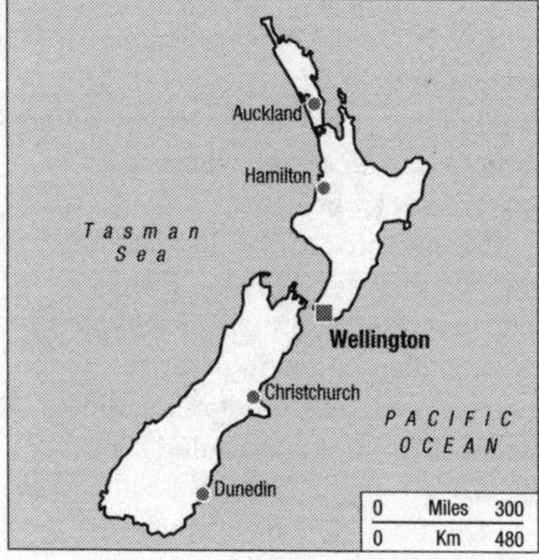

Land area: *271,000 sq. km.*
Population: *3.7 million—urban 87%.*
Capital city: *Wellington, 350,000*
People: *New Zealand European 75%, Maori 10%, other European 5%, Pacific Islander 4%, Asian and others 6%*
Language: *English, Maori*
Religion: *Protestant 52%, Roman Catholic 15% , others 33%*
Government: *Constitutional monarchy*
Life expectancy: *76 years*
GNP per capita: *$PPP 15,840*
Currency: *New Zealand dollar*
Major exports: *Wool, meat, dairy products, chemicals, forestry products*

New Zealand consists of two main islands. The larger, South Island, is also the more mountainous, dominated by the snow-capped Southern Alps which run down its western half. In North Island the mountains are on the eastern side and are somewhat lower. Parts of New Zealand are of volcanic origin and there are a number of hot springs and geysers.

Three-quarters of the population live in the North Island. Most are of European, and particularly British, extraction—the product of more than a century of immigration that gave preference to 'traditional source countries', a policy that ended officially only in 1986. New Zealand has also been a country of net emigration, primarily to Australia. Worried about this brain drain, the government from 1991 made greater efforts to attract skilled immigrants and investors. This increased immigration, primarily from Asia, a shift that has created a political reaction.

The earlier arrivals came around the 14th century. These are the Maori who are now a minority, almost all of whom live on the North Island. Maori is Maori for 'normal people', a name they used to distinguish themselves from the whites, the 'Pakeha'. The Maori name for New Zealand is Aotearoa, 'land of the long white cloud'. For a hundred years, the Maori community remained bitter that the 1840 Treaty of Waitangi that had guaranteed their land rights had not been honoured. They got some recognition in 1994 and 1995 in the form of compensation treaties with the government—and a formal apology from the British Queen Elizabeth II.

The third largest group of New Zealanders come from various Polynesian islands, many of whom arrived from the 1960s onwards to meet the demand for unskilled labour.

Agriculture still employs around 10% of the population. New Zealand's soil is not particularly fertile, but the temperate climate and its grassy hills and meadows sheltered by the mountains make it ideal for pastoral farming. The vast sheep herd enables New Zealand to be one of the world's leading producers of lamb, mutton, and wool. It also exports beef and dairy products. The main arable crop is barley for animal feed. Other crops include kiwifruit and apples for export, along with the grapes that have enabled New Zealand to become a leading wine producer.

Manufacturing industry is dominated by the processing of meat and dairy products for export, but New Zealand is now also a major producer of pulp and paper.

New Zealand has the service industries common to most industrial countries. But its tourist industry is increasingly important. More than 1.5 million visitors come each year to the see the country's attractive scenery.

New Zealand is a constitutional monarchy, headed by the British queen. Because the population are of overwhelmingly British origin there seems to be little of the pressure for change to a republic that has been evident in Australia.

New Zealanders keep the British queen

Until the mid-1980s, New Zealand had an extensive and highly regulated welfare state. This changed dramatically from 1984 following an electoral victory by the Labour Party. The new Labour government, led by Prime Minister David Lange, embarked on a radical programme of economic liberalization, removing agricultural subsidies and import controls, and in its next term from 1987 it privatized many public enterprises.

By the end of the second term, splits in the Labour Party between the new right and old left had contributed to the party's downfall. In the 1990 elections the right-wing National Party returned to power and with Jim Bolger as prime minister, continued and extended Labour's liberalization programme, while reducing trade union power and cutting many welfare benefits. In 1993, the National Party government was narrowly re-elected.

Meanwhile an ex-National Party cabinet minister, Winston Fletcher, had launched a new nationalist party, New Zealand First, in order to campaign against foreign investment and immigration, particularly from Asia.

The 1996 election was the first to be fought under a new system of proportional representation and resulted in a coalition government that paired the National Party with New Zealand First. This soon started to unravel. First, Mr Bolger was ousted as National Party leader in a neat coup that opened the way for Jenny Shipley to become New Zealand's first woman prime minister. Then New Zealand First exited from the coalition, leaving Shipley in charge of a minority government.

The election in 1999 brought Labour, led by Helen Clark, back to power in a coalition with the centre-left Alliance Party. After years of neo-liberal economic policies, Labour plans to shift slightly to the left, increasing the top rates of income tax and probably giving more help to poor families, especially the Maoris. The Alliance Party, however, will probably want to pull the government further to the left.

Nicaragua

Nicaraguans of left and right now seem more prepared to work together

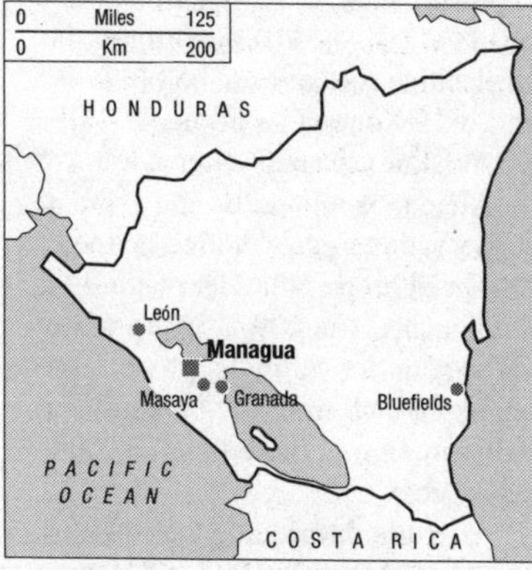

Land area: *130,000 sq. km.*
Population: *5 million—urban 64%*
Capital city: *Managua, 900,000*
People: *Mestizo 69%, white 17%, black 9%, Amerindian 5%*
Language: *Spanish, English, Amerindian*
Religion: *Roman Catholic*
Government: *Republic*
Life expectancy: *68 years*
GNP per capita: *$PPP 1,790*
Currency: *Córdoba*
Major exports: *Coffee, seafood, meat, sugar*

Nicaragua is the largest country in Central America—and the least densely populated. The emptiest area consists of tropical forests in the east that stretch down to the marshy area called the Miskito coast, named after the Miskito Indians who inhabited it when British buccaneers arrived in the 17th century. Even today, this region, which is also home to most of Nicaragua's black English-speaking population, remains relatively isolated from the rest of the country.

The majority of the population, mestizo and white, are to be found in the plains on the Pacific coast or in the central volcanic highlands, though in the north even these are sparsely populated. Basic education standards are high, thanks to a literacy drive by the Sandinistas in the 1980s, but have slipped in recent years. They also started mass health campaigns—the latter reducing the infant mortality rate which fell over the period 1979-89 from 121 to 41 per thousand live births. Since then, however, public health services have deteriorated.

For such a large and poor country, Nicaragua has a relatively large urban population—almost a million of them are in Managua, a city still eerily dotted with vacant lots, following a 1972 earthquake.

Around one-third of the workforce make their living from agriculture. Many grow basic food crops while in the uplands coffee is the main crop. Good prices and a bumper coffee harvest in 1999-2000 have improved the agricultural outlook.

Nicaragua also has some light industry but nowadays more than half the workforce are engaged in services. Even so, around 12% of the population were unemployed in 1999 and a further 20% underemployed; the situation is particularly bad on the Atlantic coast.

Even the richer émigrés returning from Miami after the end of the civil war, the 'Nicas Ricas', did little to boost the economy, using their wealth more to increase imports than to invest in local activities.

Nicaragua found itself the focus of world attention after the 1979 overthrow of corrupt dictator Anastasio Somoza and the arrival of the government of the Frente Sandinista de Liberación National (FSLN). The 'Sandinistas' had strong socialist principles, and distributed land and property to the peasants. Between 1979 and 1989, the proportion of land held by large landowners fell from 41% to 7%.

But the Sandinistas faced resolute opposition from the Reagan administration in the USA, which accused it of fostering communism. For most of the 1980s, the USA imposed a trade embargo and funded the 40,000 'contra' rebels operating from bases in Honduras.

The debilitating civil war that ensued, combined with poor economic management, brought the country to its knees. By 1992, real GDP per capita was down to one-third of its level fifteen years earlier.

Sandinistas rejected at the polls

Many people were surprised in 1990 when Nicaraguans voted the Sandinistas out. But as well as protesting against poverty, they were also disillusioned with a party that seemed to have become less democratic. They opted instead for a right-wing coalition led by Violeta Chamorro. She set the country out on a new course, reducing public expenditure, and by 1994 had privatized 340 state enterprises.

She also adopted a conciliatory line with the FSLN, accepting their land reforms and retaining a Sandinista general as head of the armed forces. The Chamorro government did reduce hyperinflation, but growth was slow to materialize.

The 1997 election was a violent affair which again saw a victory for the right wing, this time a coalition of parties led by Arnoldo Alemán of the Partido Liberal Constitutionalista (PLC) which won both the presidential election—by 51% to the FSLN's 38%—and a majority in the Legislative Assembly. The FSLN is still led by one of its original personalities, Daniel Ortega.

Alemán is a populist and conservative figure, though he too has also been prepared to deal with the Sandinistas. The 1997 Property Law agreement, for example, protects those who benefited from the Sandinista redistribution of more than 100,000 properties.

After the devastation caused by Hurricane Mitch in 1998, aid donors stepped up their assistance and in 1999 pledged an additional $1.3 billion. Donors had been encouraged by signs of further collaboration between old antagonists.

But lately they think reconciliation may have gone too far. Early in 2000 the government made a number of constitutional changes which entrenched the position of the PLC and the FSLN. Many of the most important institutions, such as the Supreme Court, will now have their members nominated by the two main parties.

There have also been sweeping changes to the electoral law. These inhibit the formation of small new parties. In response, the existing minor parties are trying to come together to offer a third force. European donors in particular have raised objections, but have been told this is not their concern.

Niger

Niger's underground wealth has been of little benefit to most of its people

Land area: *1,267,000 sq. km.*
Population: *10 million—urban 23%*
Capital city: *Niamey, 420,000*
People: *Hausa 56%, Djerma 22%, Fulani 9%, Tuareg 8%, Beri Beri 4%. other 1%*
Language: *French, Hausa, Djerma*
Religion: *Muslim 80%, indigenous beliefs and Christian 20%*
Government: *Republic*
Life expectancy: *49 years*
GNP per capita: *$PPP 830*
Currency: *CFA Franc*
Major exports: *Uranium, livestock, cotton*

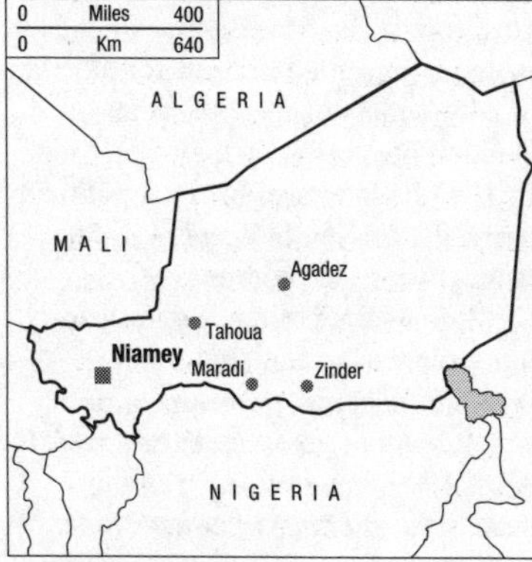

Niger has three main geographical zones. The zone to the north, approximately half the country, falls within the Sahara Desert. This arid territory includes the Air Mountains with sandy desert on either side. The central zone falls within the Sahel, with thin soil, scrubland, and sparse vegetation. The most fertile zone is the south, which benefits from annual rains, as well as, in the far south-west, flooding from the Niger River which flows south into Nigeria.

Most people live in the fertile south where sedentary farming groups include the Hausa and Djerma. The nomadic herding communities, including the Fulani, who raise cattle, and the Tuareg, who also have extensive herds of goats and camels, are likely to be found in the Sahel area, and sometimes in the desert to the north. But creeping desertification and over-use of the land by a growing population is steadily undermining the nomadic lifestyle—and many nomads are settling as farmers or moving to the cities. The population growth rate over the period 1970-95 averaged 3.2% annually, and at the current rate the population will double by 2015.

Levels of human development are desperately low. Niger is one of the few countries that even in peacetime has seen no improvement in social indicators over the past decade. In 2000, Niger came last but one in UNDP's human development index, a consequence not just of low income but also of dismal standards of health and education. One-fifth of children die before their fifth birthday. Less than one-third of children enrol in primary school.

Most people make their living from agriculture which accounts for around 40% of GNP and employs 90% of the labour force. Their food crops include millet, sorghum, rice, and cassava, and their cash crops include cotton and groundnuts. Since most of this cultivation is rain-fed it remains very vulnerable to the often erratic climate. In a good year the country is more or less self-sufficient in food. Even then, during the dry season many Nigeriens migrate temporarily to neighbouring countries in search of work. The main agricultural export is livestock, much of which walks across the border to Nigeria to escape taxation.

Niger's main export and an important source of government revenue has been uranium ore. Niger has extensive deposits of high-grade uranium ore in the desert to the east of the Air Mountains. Niger is the world's second largest producer, sending a lot of its output to nuclear-power reactors in France. The mines are run by two independent companies though the government has shareholdings in both.

Niger's uranium fuels French reactors

In the 1970s uranium provided a much-needed boost to national income, but since the late 1980s the uranium price has collapsed and revenues have fallen drastically.

This also led the country deep into debt—equivalent in 1995 to over 90% of GNP, most of it owed to bilateral and multilateral agencies. Aid temporarily ceased following a coup in 1996, but most donors have now returned. The bulk of the aid comes from France and from the EU.

Niger's democratic performance since independence in 1960 has not been impressive. Brief periods of multi-party governance have been interspersed with bouts of military rule. There have also been armed rebellions by the Tuareg, who, with the support of Libya, have at times pressed for independence, though they signed a ceasefire in 1995.

The last coup-but-one was in 1996, when Colonel Ibrahim Baré Maïnassara seized power claiming impatience with seemingly endless bickering between the politicians. He arrested both the president and the prime minister and banned political activity. Later that year he did, however, introduce a new constitution that put power much more firmly in the hands of the president. Unsurprisingly, Maïnassara, by then a general, presented himself for election and took most of the vote in an election boycotted by the opposition. In 1997 he launched his own political party, the Rassemblement pour la démocratie et le progrès.

Maïnassara's rule became steadily more repressive and any group protesting against government policy was subject to harassment or arrest. In April 1999, however, he was shot dead by soldiers in what the prime minister called an 'unfortunate accident', but is assumed to have been a palace coup.

At any rate, the military seized power until fresh elections were held in November 1999 when Mamadou Tandja, a retired army colonel, won the presidential election and his party, the Mouvement national pour la societé de développement, won 38 of the 83 seats in the National Assembly. Those who assassinated Maïnassara were subsequently pardoned, and Tandja has resisted calls for a further investigation.

International donors, notably France, seem convinced that democracy has been re-established and have resumed aid. Tandja will need all the help he can get. The government's coffers are empty and health workers, teachers, and other public servants have engaged in a series of strikes to protest at non-payment of salaries.

Nigeria

The new democratic government will struggle to reverse Nigeria's economic and social decline

__Land area:__ 924,000 sq. km.
__Population:__ 121 million—urban 42%
__Capital city:__ Abuja, 300,000
__People:__ Hausa, Fulani, Yoruba, Igbo, Kanuri, Ibibio, Tiv, Ijaw
__Language:__ English, Hausa, Yoruba, Igbo, Fulani
__Religion:__ Muslim 50%, Christian 40%, indigenous beliefs 10%
__Government:__ Republic
__Life expectancy:__ 50 years
__GNP per capita:__ $PPP 820
__Currency:__ Naira
__Major exports:__ Oil, cocoa, rubber, cotton

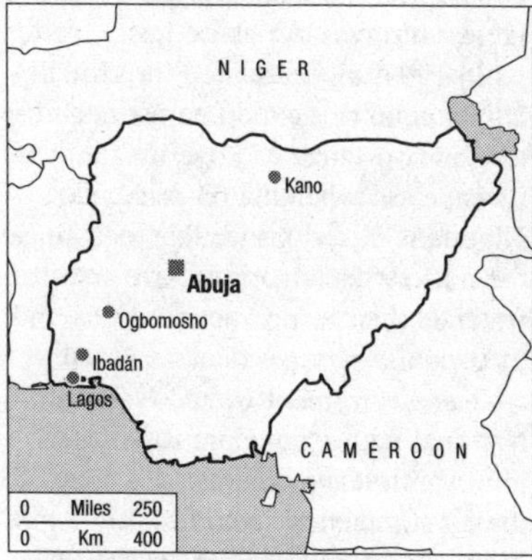

Nigeria can be divided into four main regions. The humid coastal belt includes extensive swamplands and lagoons that can extend 15 kilometres inland, and further still in the area around the Niger River delta. Further inland the swamps give way first to hilly tropical rainforests and then the land rises to several plateaux—the Jos plateau in the centre and the Biu plateau in the north-east. Further north, these descend to savannah grasslands and eventually to semi-desert areas. The principle feature of the east-central border area with Cameroon is the Adamawa plateau, which includes the highest point in the country, Mount Dimlang.

Nigeria has Africa's largest population, though the actual size is a matter of some dispute. The government has claimed that the 1998 total was 109 million, though other estimates have it up to 20% higher. As with much else, this is a highly political issue since it has a critical bearing on the distribution of funds between the federal government and the states. The population is likely to grow at an average of 2.2% per year over the next decade or so—and could reach 240 million by 2025.

Nigeria is a federation of 36 states with more than 400 ethnic groups, though more than half belong to the three main groups: the Hausa-Fulani, who are Muslims and live in the north; the Yoruba, who are followers of both Christian and Islamic faiths and live in the south-west; and the Igbo, many of whom are Christians and live in the south-east. Though they largely live together peacefully, there are at times outbreaks of violence. In 1999, for example, there were clashes between Yoruba and Hausa and hundreds of people died in various outbreaks of ethnic violence. Even more alarming were the deaths in early 2000 of hundreds of Christians and Muslims in disputes over the latter's determination to impose Shariah law in northern states in which Muslims are in the majority.

Despite its potential wealth,

Nigeria has been slipping backwards. In 1997 half of all Nigerians lived on less than 30 cents per day. The education system is in poor shape and the literacy rate is stuck at around 60%. Those who can afford private education make progress but most children are packed into crowded and dilapidated classrooms. The public health system too is increasingly over-burdened. Maternal mortality is three times the average for developing countries. HIV/AIDS is also taking a heavy toll: in 1999 an estimated 5% of adults were HIV-positive.

Nigerian children packed into crowded classrooms

Despite rapid urbanization, most Nigerians still earn their living from agriculture, which makes up around 40% of GDP. The vast majority are subsistence farmers who have small plots and use primitive tools. In the south they tend to grow root crops like yams and cassava, while in the north the main crops are sorghum, millet, and maize. With little investment, and over-exploitation of the land, output has lagged way behind population growth.

As a result Nigeria, which used to export food in large quantities, is now a major importer. Small farmers also grow some cash crops, but of these only cocoa now provides any significant export income—and output has halved in the last thirty years.

Agriculture, as with much else in Nigeria, has been pushed into the background by the oil industry. Oil was discovered in 1956 and output grew rapidly in the 1960s and 1970s, helped by the high quality and low sulphur content and also by the location—most of the fields are onshore in the Niger delta and convenient for export. One-third goes to the USA. In 2000, proven reserves were around 25 billion barrels—sufficient for another thirty years. Nigeria also has some of the world's largest reserves of natural gas.

In 1997, oil accounted for virtually all the country's export earnings and around two-thirds of government revenue. So when the oil price falls Nigeria is in serious trouble, and since the mid-1980s Nigerians have watched their infrastructure decay and their public services decline.

The government-owned Nigerian National Petroleum Company has joint venture agreements with most of the oil companies, including Elf, Agip, Mobil, and Chevron. But around half the oil output comes from one company, Royal Dutch/Shell, which has been coming under increasingly heavy local criticism. People in the Niger delta have seen little benefit from oil production that has often caused environmental damage.

The Ogoni people in particular have been demanding greater control over the oil, and in 1995 Ken Saro-Wiwa and eight other Ogoni were executed. Shell was accused of collusion with the government and although it denies this, the company has now accepted greater responsibility for community development in the area. In 1999, when it announced an $8 billion oil investment plan, it also said it would spend around $40 million per year in the 1,500 communities where it

Shell accused of collusion in human rights abuses

works, though that has stopped neither the hostage taking, nor the inter-ethnic violence.

Most of the $280 billion received in oil wealth since the early 1970s has been squandered, either in wasteful development projects, or in graft or theft. Corruption started at the top. Military leaders simply stole hundreds of millions. But scarcely any service is available without the payment of what is known as 'chop'. One of the most ironic effects of corruption is that Nigeria has suffered from chronic shortages of petrol. Local refineries have been deliberately run down so that government officials can get their chop from the sale of lucrative licences to import petrol, much of which finishes up on the black market.

Oil wealth squandered

From the early 1970s, the government used some of the oil money to invest in nationalized heavy industry—particularly petro-chemicals, steel, and fertilizers—though such industries have been poorly managed and Nigeria still depends to a large extent on imports. Most productive industrial activity is based on small-scale manufacturing, and a high proportion of the urban populations struggle to survive in the informal sector.

Nigeria's political history since independence in 1960 has been fraught with ethnic conflicts and demands for greater independence for the states, which wanted to seize greater shares of the oil revenue. In 1967 the military governor of the Eastern Region attempted to secede, provoking a bloody civil war that lasted two and a half years and killed 1 million people. Most of the years since then have involved a series of coups with brief interludes of civilian rule.

The most recent military regime, that of General Sani Abacha starting from 1993 was, by general consent, the most brutal and rapacious. Abacha had come to power following the annulment of a presidential election that gave victory to a Yoruba, Chief Abiola. Abacha subsequently imprisoned Abiola and launched ferocious attacks on opposition figures and hanged Saro-Wiwa—an act that drew widespread international condemnation. Abacha had planned to restore 'civilian' rule, with himself as president. But to widespread relief he died in 1998—as did Abiola in prison (of a heart attack).

This led to a presidential election and victory for Olesegun Obasanjo, who took office in 1999. Although a former military ruler, he can at least claim credit for having relinquished power voluntarily in 1979. Now he faces the task of rooting out corruption, fending off the army, and trying to hold the country together in a period of lower oil prices. With a $30 billion debt, the equivalent in 1999 of $250 per person, he will seek and need international aid—which seems likely to arrive less from sympathy and more from donor self-interest. The early indications were positive as he released political prisoners and arrested former military leaders for crimes they committed during Abacha's regime. But it is not yet clear whether he can respond effectively to inter-ethnic violence or build a strong and coherent administration.

Norway

Norway is one of the world's richest countries, but is trying to wean itself from over-reliance on oil

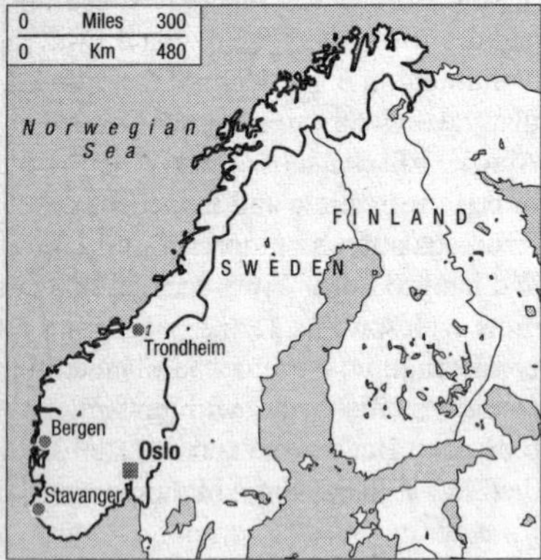

Land area: *324,000 sq. km.*
Population: *4 million—urban 74%*
Capital city: *Oslo, 490,000*
People: *Norwegian, Sami*
Language: *Norwegian (Bokmål, Nynorsk)*
Religion: *Evangelical Lutheran*
Government: *Constitutional monarchy*
Life expectancy: *78 years*
GNP per capita: *$PPP 24,290*
Currency: *Norwegian krone*
Major exports: *Oil and gas, metals and machinery*

Norway is a mountainous country with a distinctively complex coastline. Much of the landscape consists of rolling plateaux, called 'vidder', interspersed with high peaks. To the west the mountains descend steeply to the coast which, during the Ice Age, was deeply cut by glaciers creating long, narrow inlets, the 'fjords', beyond which lie hundreds of islands, Though one-third of the country is above the Arctic Circle, the warm waters of the gulf stream usually keep the fjords above freezing point.

Norway is ethnically fairly homogenous. Almost everyone speaks the same language, though this exists in two mutually intelligible forms. The older of the two, Bokmål, is more widely used—in the national newspapers and in most schools—and is the product of previous centuries of Danish occupation of Norway. 'New Norwegian', Nynorsk, is both newer and older—the result of efforts to revive earlier dialects of Norse.

The oldest minority are the country's original inhabitants, the Sami, who herd their reindeer in the far north. But from the 1980s Norway started to receive significant flows of asylum seekers, first from Asia and Africa and later from former Yugoslavia. By 1997, 4% of the population were foreign-born, and in 1999 there was rising racial tension. In 2000, Norway also occupied second place in the UNDP human development index—a reflection of the country's wealth and its comprehensive system of welfare.

Norway's economic prospects were transformed in 1969 by the discovery of the Ekofisk oilfield in the North Sea. This and numerous other fields discovered subsequently have made Norway the world's fourth largest oil producer. Oil production will probably peak in the early years of the 21st century but this is likely to be offset by continuing discoveries of gas.

Despite falling prices, oil and gas have fuelled economic growth, providing more than half of export income and making a huge contribution to the national coffers. Unlike many other countries, Norway has been setting much of this windfall aside into a national savings account, which by 1999 had reached $16 billion. One disadvantage of the oil bonanza, however, is that it has stifled investment in other activities. Manufacturing, for example, accounts for only 12% of GDP. Meanwhile, some older industries have been stagnating.

Norway's dramatic, serrated coastline has ensured a close relationship with the sea, and the country has established a strong shipping industry that in 1999 still gave it around 10% of the world's commercial fleet—including a quarter of all cruise vessels—but this business too seems becalmed.

Agriculture has long been in decline, though the government has subsidized it heavily to sustain rural communities. Fishing too, for herring, cod, and mackerel, has also been suffering, though in this case more a result of over-fishing. Even so, Norway's unemployment rate in 2000 was only around 3%.

Norway is a constitutional monarchy, currently ruled by King Harald, who acceded to the throne in 1991. For most of the 20th century Norway was governed by the social-democratic Labour Party. One of the leading figures in the 1980s and 1990s was Gro Harlem Brundtland, who was a Labour prime minister in the periods 1986-9 and 1990-9. Brundtland applied for Norwegian membership of the EU and achieved significant concessions. But the electorate did not share her enthusiasm and in a referendum in 1994 declined to join—52% voted against. Brundtland resigned in 1996. She had already been a major international figure, having chaired the World Commission on Environment and Development, and in 1998 became head of the World Health Organization.

Norwegians reject EU membership

Brundtland was replaced as Labour leader by Thorbjorn Jagland. Although Labour received 35% of the vote in the 1997 election, this was less than what Jagland had declared he needed to govern and he gave way to a minority centrist government led by Lutheran priest Kjell Magne Bondevik of the Christian People's Party in coalition with the rural Centre Party and the free-market Liberals. Bondevik took the unusual step in late 1998 of disappearing from view as a result of 'a depressive reaction to overwork'—an act which, if anything, seemed to enhance his popular standing.

A less liberal development, however, has been the rise of the right-wing populist and anti-immigration Progress Party, which in local elections in 1999 became the third largest party.

In February 2000 Labour replaced Jagland as their candidate for prime minister by the more media-friendly Jens Stoltenberg. This contributed to a sudden surge in popularity for Labour which overtook the ruling coalition in the opinion polls.

The EU continues to be a divisive issue, both within and between parties. Norway is a member of NATO and also of the European Economic Area, which obliges it to obey many EU rules without having any say in writing them, so may still reconsider its membership.

Oman

Oman is less well endowed with oil than its neighbours, and is keen to diversify

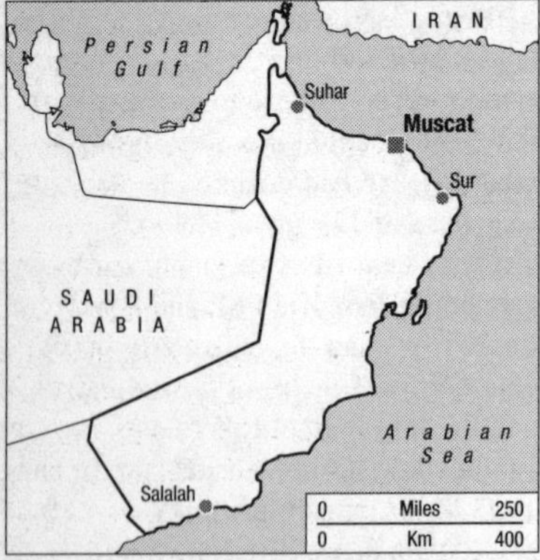

Land area: *212,000 sq. km.*
Population: *2 million—urban 79%*
Capital city: *Muscat, 600,000*
People: *Arab, Baluchi, South Asian*
Language: *Arabic, English, Baluchi, Urdu, Indian dialects*
Religion: *Ibadhi Muslim 75%, Sunni Muslim, Shiah Muslim, Hindu, or other 25%*
Government: *Sultanate*
Life expectancy: *73 years*
GNP per capita: *$PPP 9,960*
Currency: *Omani rial*
Major exports: *Oil, animal products, textiles*

Oman has three main geographical areas. The Al-Batinah plain extends for about 270 kilometres along the northern coast but only about 10 kilometres inland. From here, the land rises to the Al-Hajar mountain range, whose highest peak is around 3,000 metres. Beyond the mountains to the south, the rest of the country, around three-quarters of the land area, is largely desert until it reaches the mountains of Dhofar in the far south-west.

Oman's people are culturally diverse. Most Omani citizens are Arab and Muslim, though around three-quarters belong to the Ibadhi sect, an early breakaway from the Shiah. The rest are Sunni or Shiah. But this is not a strict Islamic state.

One-third of the population are immigrants, who make up more than 40% of the workforce. Most come from the Indian subcontinent, though there are also expatriate Europeans. Immigrants do all the lowliest jobs—more than two-thirds earn less than the minimum wage.

From around 1970, thanks to oil income, Oman's people made swift improvements in human development—some of the most rapid progress ever recorded. Between 1970 and 1997 life expectancy increased from 40 to 71 years, and over the same period, infant mortality fell from 126 per thousand live births to 15. Education too expanded rapidly, though it has not produced an optimum balance of skills.

Most Omani graduates expect managerial or professional jobs, preferably with the government, and are less willing to acquire vocational skills. But with the population of Omanis growing at around 3% per year there are not enough of these jobs to go around.

Oil has fuelled much of Oman's progress, but it is a dwindling asset. It must be extracted from over 100 small and complex fields in the interior of the country and in Dhofar. As a result, production costs are higher than in neighbouring countries. In 1998, reserves were around 5 billion barrels, but they are being extracted at a rate of 300 million barrels per year. There are other reserves but these would probably be too expensive to extract. Most production is in the hands of one company, Petroleum Development Oman.

The other main source of income is agriculture. Though accounting for only 2% of GDP, it employs around half of working Omanis. On the northern Batinah plain, their main crop is dates, while, on a smaller scale, farmers on the southern coastal plain grow coconuts and bananas. There is also some subsistence agriculture in the mountains as well as livestock rearing in the interior. But Omani agriculture is running short of water. Most has to be pumped from underground and the advent of diesel pumps has encouraged over-extraction. Coastal areas also suffer from intrusion of saline water.

Farmers are running out of water

Oman's first attempts to diversify involved creating new industrial estates for manufacturing. These factories are now working, producing textiles and other goods for export. But they remain over-reliant on foreign workers.

Better prospects seem likely to emerge from recent discoveries of natural gas which have encouraged three major industrial projects. The most important is a large liquefaction plant to enable gas exports—primarily to South Korea and Japan. The other possible uses are more problematic. Plans to develop an ammonia-urea fertilizer plant have been set back by low world prices for fertilizers. And plans to use the gas to fuel aluminium smelting still seem to be at an early stage.

As well as diversification Oman is also pursuing 'Omanization' of private industry, setting quotas for different industries and establishing fines and other penalties for enterprises that fall short. But with so few trained or willing recruits most companies will be hard pressed to meet their targets.

Presiding over these developments is an absolute monarch. Since the 18th century Oman has been controlled by the Al bu Said tribe, and since 1970 the sultan has been Qaboos bin Said. In his early years he was faced with a communist insurrection in Dhofar. He finally crushed this in 1975 with the help of the USA, which still has a military presence. Since then opposition has been much more limited and the sultan has managed to satisfy the various tribes, regions, and interest groups.

He has also been edging towards democracy. In 1997 the sultan promulgated a new 'Basic Law' (based on Islamic law) that serves as a constitution and establishes some limited democratic rights. In addition, he has set up two consultative bodies. The first is the Majlis al-Shura which in 1997 had 82 elected members. The second is the State Council whose members are appointed from tribal leaders and former government officials.

The Basic Law also establishes that the sultan's successor must come from the Al-Turki branch of his family. It says too that if the family cannot agree on a suitable successor within three days of the sultan's death, they will have to accept his choice—which will be left in a letter.

Pakistan

Asia's great underachiever. Semi-feudal landlords, excessive military spending, and corruption continue to stifle human development

Land area: 796,000 sq. km.
Population: 132 million—urban 35%
Capital city: Islamabad, 204,000
People: Punjabi, Sindhi, Pathan, Baluch Muhajir
Language: Urdu, Punjabi, Sindhi, Siraiki, Pashtu and others
Religion: Muslim
Government: Republic
Life expectancy: 64 years
GNP per capita: $PPP 1,560
Currency: Pakistani rupee
Major exports: Cotton yarn, garments, cotton textiles

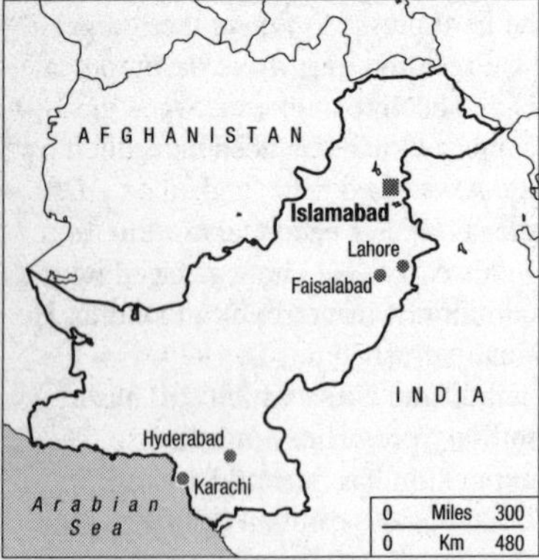

Pakistan has four main geographical regions. First, in the far north is the Hindu Kush and Pakistan's section of the Himalayas, including K2, the world's second-highest mountain. Second, in the west and south-west, are a number of other mountain ranges and the Baluchistan plateau. Third, to the east are the desert areas which join with the Thar Desert across the border in India. Fourth, in the centre of the country, is the rich agricultural plain of the Indus River, which traverses the entire length of Pakistan, emerging from the foothills of the Himalayas and flowing down to the Arabian Sea.

Pakistan is also divided politically into four provinces: Baluchistan in the west; North-West Frontier Province, on the border with Afghanistan; Sindh in the south; and Punjab in the heartland of the Indus Valley. The population of Pakistan has been formed by waves of migration from many different directions and is a mixture of many influences with relatively few ethnic divisions. The Punjabis account for around two-thirds of the population, and the Sindhi for 13%. The other main groups are the Baluchs and the Pathans in North-West Frontier. Added to these are the Muhajir ('refugees'), descendants of the 8 million Muslims who fled from India in 1947 at the time of partition—most of whom are in the urban areas of Sindh and particularly Karachi.

Faced with limited opportunities at home, millions of Pakistanis have headed overseas, chiefly to the Gulf states. They send home remittances worth around $1 billion per year.

Almost all Pakistanis are Muslims. Pakistan was created out of the partition of British India specifically to provide a state for the Muslim community. Even so, it was not initially envisaged as an Islamic state. Only in recent years has Islam come to be a dominant political force, having frequently been exploited by authoritarian governments seeking to unify the population behind their regimes. There have been frequent clashes between Sunni and Shiah Muslims.

Economically, Pakistan appears at times to have been more successful than India. Thus, one-quarter of the population live below the poverty line, compared with close to half in India. But Pakistan has failed to translate economic growth into real improvements in human well-being. Education levels are low. Half of Pakistani children fail to complete primary education, and two-thirds of the adult population are illiterate. There are similar problems in health. Half the population lack access to basic health facilities or to safe water and three-quarters do not have safe sanitation. All this reflects low spending on public services.

Particularly disturbing is the slow advance of women. Thus while boys on average have 2.9 years of schooling, girls have only 0.7 years, and the literacy rate for women is only half that of men. Women also have fewer opportunities for employment outside the home—particularly in the socially more conservative provinces of Baluchistan and North-West Frontier.

Pakistani women have been making very slow progress

Women's generally low status is also reflected in poor standards of reproductive health, a consequence of official neglect, religious intransigence and considerable violence against women. Contraceptive use is low, so the birth rate is high and thousands of women die each year in childbirth. This also contributes to Pakistan's high population growth rate. According to UN projections, by 2050 Pakistan will be the world's third most populous nation—after China and India.

Agriculture still employs around half the population and makes up one-quarter of GDP. But over half the land is controlled by rural élites in farms of 50 acres or more where it is often used poorly—growing the most profitable crops like cotton but using inefficient farming methods that have made the land waterlogged or saline. Since 1959, there have been half-hearted efforts at land reform, but little has happened since the main landowners are also usually politicians. Pakistan used to be self-sufficient in wheat and rice but production has not kept pace with population growth and each year millions of tons of wheat now have to be imported.

Industry has been fairly slow to develop. Pakistan is one of the world's major cotton producers but still exports most of its output as yarn rather than cloth. Immediately after independence, manufacturing was aimed at import-substitution.

More recently there have been efforts to open up the economy—removing some bureaucratic restrictions and lowering tariffs. But manufacturing industry is still unimpressive—dominated by low-tech enterprises. Industrialists claim they cannot invest because they, unlike the politically powerful landowners, have to pay so much tax.

Pakistan has been equally slow to develop its mineral deposits. The country does have some oil and gas. But oil production is only sufficient for about 20% of the country's needs, while reserves are falling. And exploitation of gas in remote areas of Baluchistan is hindered by opposition from belligerent tribesmen. Pakistan also has large deposits of rock salt, limestone, and a number of other minerals but these have been little exploited.

Democracy in Pakistan has at best been fragile. For more than half its history since independence in 1947 the country has been under military rule. From 1978, the military ruler was General Zia ul-Haq, who, in order to boost his popularity, had been steering Pakistan towards becoming an Islamic state.

Following Zia's death in 1988, Pakistan then had a series of short-lived administrations that terminated with their dismissal by the president. Thus the 1988 election resulted in victory for Benazir Bhutto and the Pakistan People's Party (PPP) the party founded by her father—a former prime minister whom Zia had executed. Her administration was regarded as incompetent and corrupt and she was dismissed in 1990.

A series of governments have been dismissed for corruption

The ensuing election resulted in a victory for a coalition headed by Nawaz Sharif, a Punjabi businessman whose party was the Pakistan Muslim League. He too soon fell foul of the president for much the same reasons. He was dismissed in 1993. Bhutto then returned only to be dismissed again in 1996. The 1997 election saw Sharif back at the helm though this time as leader only of a faction of his party the PML(N). One of the more radical measures he proposed in 1998 was to make Islamic sharia law the 'supreme law of Pakistan'.

Throughout this period of political upheaval, Pakistan was embroiled in serious disputes with its neighbours, particularly India. In 1998, Pakistan responded to Indian nuclear tests with six tests of its own, provoking the wrath of the USA and other donors who promptly imposed economic sanctions and withdrew aid. The most dangerous issue is Kashmir, a territory whose sovereignty Pakistan disputes with India. For many years, this has involved just sporadic gunfire, but it took an alarming turn in June 1999 when Pakistan encouraged rebel fighters to cross into Indian-held territory, though they were later forced to retreat.

There has also been violence closer to home—in Karachi and centred on the Muhajir. When their political party, the Muhajir Quami Movement (MQM), came to power in Karachi in the early 1990s it took ferocious revenge on other groups. Bhutto sent in paramilitaries and Sharif subsequently made peace with the MQM, but the violence continues.

Sharif's downfall came in October 1999 when he was deposed by the army chief, General Pervez Musharraf. Most Pakistanis seemed to regard this with some relief. One of Musharraf first steps was to try Sharif, who in April 2000 was sentenced to life imprisonment for terrorism and hijacking. In May 2000 the Supreme Court accepted that Mussharaf's takeover had been in the national interest, confirming his government's legitimacy, but said he should hold an election by the end of 2002.

Palestine

Palestine's political independence might soon be settled, but economic independence is remote

Land area: *6,000 sq. km.*
Population: *2.0 million— urban n.a.*
Capital city: *East Jerusalem, 320,000*
People: *Palestinian Arab and other 83%, Jewish 17%*
Language: *Arabic, Hebrew, English*
Religion: *Muslim 75%, Jewish 17%, Christian and other 8%*
Government: *Republic*
Life expectancy: *75 years*
GNP per capita: *$PPP 2,000*
Currency: *Israeli Shekel, Jordanian dinar*
Major exports: *Industrial goods, food*

Palestine comprises two territories linked by land corridors through Israel. The larger of the two is the West Bank, most of which consists of hills of up to 900 metres that descend eastwards from the border with Israel down to the Jordan river and the Dead Sea. The land in the north-west is relatively well watered, but rainfall is much sparser in the south. The remainder of Palestine is the Gaza Strip, which makes up only 6% of the territory—a flat and sandy region on the Mediterranean coast between Israel and Egypt.

The people are predominantly Arab, but the territory is dotted with Israeli settlements. In 1997, the population was 1.7 million in the West Bank and 1.0 million in the more densely settled Gaza Strip. Of these, the UN classifies 1.3 million as refugees who live in nineteen camps in the West Bank and eight in Gaza. Thanks to international aid, standards of education and health are relatively high, though services have been disrupted by decades of violence and unrest. The population is young—47% are under 15 years.

Long years of conflict and poverty have also caused many Palestinians to seek work and refuge overseas. In 1997, in addition to 2.7 million Palestinians at home, there were a further 4.2 million abroad, chiefly in Jordan (2.2 million), Israel (1.0 million), Lebanon (0.4 million), Syria (0.3 million,) as well as in other Arab countries, in Europe, and in the Americas.

Until fairly recently, both the West Bank and Gaza were predominantly agricultural, and agriculture still accounts for around 14% of GDP. Most of this is on small family farms, chiefly growing olives, citrus fruits, and vegetables in sufficient quantities for export, as well as raising livestock. But much of Palestine's cereal requirements have to be imported.

Industry remains largely undeveloped, accounting for 16% of GDP in 1996. This consists mostly of small enterprises engaged in food processing, textiles, clothing, leather, and metal working. But political uncertainty has hampered investment so productivity is low.

Israel's invasion of 1967 effectively incorporated what is now Palestine into Israel—and made it dependent on Israel for most of its markets; 90% of exports still go there. Just as important Israel became a major source of work: by 1992 one-third of the workforce were commuting to Israel. But in 1993 Israel started to close off the West Bank both for imports and for incoming workers so by 1997 the proportion of the labour force working in Israel was down to 21%. This had a devastating effect on the economy—a loss of $10 million per day—and unemployment and underemployment together reached around 30%.

Israel crippled the West Bank's economy

Were it not for international aid Palestine would be even worse off. Following the peace agreement in 1993, in addition to ongoing aid from the UN and from non-governmental organizations, bilateral aid donors committed $2.9 billion of which more than half had been disbursed by mid-1997.

Until the Israeli invasion of 1967, Jordan controlled the West Bank. Jordan continued to claim it until 1987, when it relinquished the claim in favour of the Palestine Liberation Organization (PLO).

The PLO had been formed in 1964 and was recognized by the Arab League as the representative of the Palestinians. From the outset, the PLO had been engaged in armed conflict and in 1987 it embarked on a more general uprising called the 'intifada'. Subsequently, however, it shifted towards political activity and negotiations took a dramatic turn in 1993 when secret talks in Oslo produced a peace agreement. This involved mutual recognition between Israel and the PLO, as well as a staged Israeli withdrawal.

As a result, by 1996 much of Palestine was being administered by a Palestinian National Authority run by the PLO. Elections in that year gave 87% of the vote to PLO chairman Yasir Arafat as 'rais' (Israelis translate this as chairman, and Palestinians as president) and also gave a majority to Arafat's Fatah faction of the PLO in the Legislative Council.

In practice, power has been highly centralized round Arafat, though his popularity has been falling as his largely aid-financed administration has been accused of corruption.

The prospects for a final peace settlement dimmed during the Israeli administration of Binyamin Netanyahu. The process seemed to get back on track following the victory by Ehud Barak in the 1999 Israeli elections, after which talks resumed.

But they did not move very fast. By May 2000 there should have been a 'framework agreement' on borders, settlements, water, the rights of refugees, and the status of East Jerusalem. But the deadline came and went. Israel has also been reluctant to release the 1,600 political prisoners.

Mounting frustration in the West Bank and Gaza resulted in a fresh outbreak of violence in May—underlining the fragility of Arafat's control over Fatah. Negotiations with Israel started again in July at Camp David in the USA but made little progress.

Panama

Panama now controls the canal. But the US withdrawal raises doubts about security

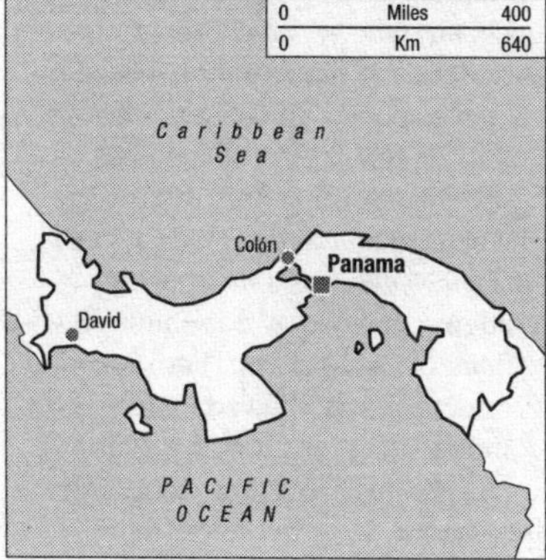

Land area: *76,000 sq. km.*
Population: *3 million—urban 57%*
Capital city: *Panama City, 800,000*
People: *Mestizo 70%, West Indian 14%, white 10%, Amerindian 6%*
Language: *Spanish, English*
Religion: *Roman Catholic 85%, Protestant 15%*
Government: *Republic*
Life expectancy: *74 years*
GNP per capita: *$PPP 6,940*
Currency: *Balboa (US dollar)*
Major exports: *Bananas, seafood*

Panama does have mountain ranges, including an extinct volcano, and a temperate zone above 2,000 feet. But 85% of the country is lower and flat, and one-third is forested. Its most significant geographical feature, however, is that at its narrowest it is only 80 kilometres wide—an ideal location for a canal to help link the eastern and western coasts of the USA.

The USA has long been the dominant influence here. In 1903, it leased from Colombia the strip of land on either side of a canal that had been started and abandoned by a French company. When the Colombian senate refused to ratify the agreement the USA organized a rebellion that resulted in the secession of Panama from Colombia. A treaty with the new country gave the USA rights to the land in perpetuity and the canal was completed in 1914.

Panama's location as a communications crossroads has given it a very diverse population, most of whom would be considered mestizo. The largest single group are the black descendants of the West Indians who were brought in to build first a railway and then the canal itself. But there are also significant Amerindian communities, including the Guaymí who live in the west of the country.

Most Panamanians occupy the land on either side of the canal—although population pressure is forcing people to push further into the rainforest to clear more land for cultivation. Around one-third are engaged in agriculture, growing subsistence crops or producing for export—chiefly bananas and sugar—or fishing for shrimps.

In the past most other employment has been derived from canal services. The canal remains vitally important. It charges ships up to $110,000 per transit and has annual revenues of around $600 million. But Panama has also diversified into other industries. At the Caribbean end of the canal, Colón has the largest free trade zone in the western hemisphere, home to more than 800 companies and employing 13,600 people, chiefly in electronics, textiles and clothing, and turns over $5 billion per year. On the other side of the country, Panama City also became a major financial centre with more than 100 offshore banks.

Compared with their neighbours, Panamanians are relatively well off, with good standards of health and education, though there are often striking contrasts between those linked with the canal and the modern sector and those working in the rest of the economy.

Panama's turbulent political history has been shaped by its relationship with the USA. The US bases in the Canal Zone, were home to the 'Southern Command'. But years of pressure and occasional riots provoked a nationalist backlash and Panamanians demanded sovereignty over the canal. In 1978, the military government of General Omar Torrijos, which had introduced popular measures such as agricultural reform, also negotiated a new treaty with US President Jimmy Carter, who agreed a handover to take place at the end of 1999.

This did not signal an immediate end to US involvement in Panamanian political life. The most dramatic intervention in recent years was in 1989 when the USA invaded to overthrow the government of General Manuel Noriega—later tried and jailed for 40 years in Miami for corruption and drug smuggling. Several hundred people were killed.

The USA invades to overthrow Noriega

The 1994 presidential election was won by Ernesto Pérez Balladares of the populist Partido Revolucionario Democrático. But he was not to supervise the handover of the canal. Although his party won a heavy majority in the 1999 legislative elections, he was defeated in the presidential election by Mireya Moscosa of the conservative-populist Arnulfista party (named after her late husband, who was three times elected president and three times deposed by military coups). She became the country's first woman president.

The handover of the canal went ahead as planned. But the Stars and Stripes was lowered in a rather grudging manner, as no senior US official chose to attend. Former-President Carter showed up to complete the process he had started.

As well as providing more direct income for the government the handover of the canal has also created a property bonanza. The School of the Americas, for instance, where Latin American military officers were once trained in dubious practices, is to reopen as a five-star Spanish-owned 'Hotel of the Americas' catering to eco-tourists. But the poorer sections of the population have seen little of this and many are doubtful about the benefits of US withdrawal if it just lines the pockets of the rich.

Panamanians are well qualified to run the canal; by April 2000, after 100 days of Panamanian administration, 3,700 vessels had passed through, paying $143 million in tolls. The doubts are more about security. After the 1989 invasion the Panamanian army was disbanded leaving only a national police force. Colombian guerrillas and drug smugglers have long used the far south of Panama as a staging area. Now there are fears that they could attack the canal itself.

Papua New Guinea

More than 800 groups live in the rainforests—above some of the world's richest deposits of minerals

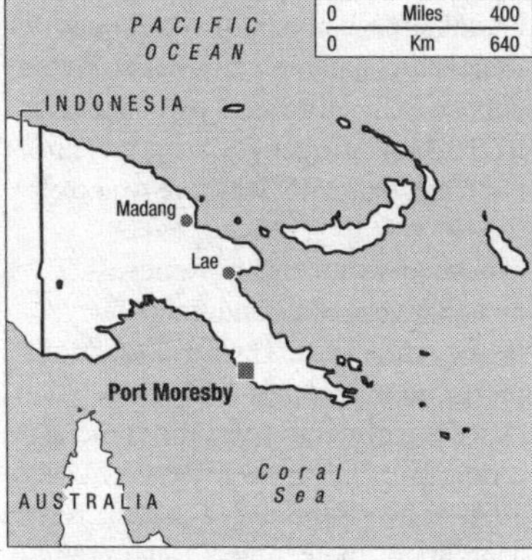

Land area: *463,000 sq. km.*
Population: *4.7 million—urban 17%*
Capital city: *Port Moresby, 260,000*
People: *Melanesian, Polynesian*
Language: *Pidgin English, English, and more than 700 indigenous languages*
Religion: *Christian 66%, indigenous beliefs 34%*
Government: *Constitutional monarchy*
Life expectancy: *58 years*
GNP per capita: *$PPP 2,400*
Currency: *Kina*
Major exports: *Gold, copper ore, oil, logs, palm oil, coffee, cocoa*

Papua New Guinea consists of the eastern half of the island of New Guinea, along with around 600 other islands. The mainland, with around 85% of the territory, includes extensive swampy plains to the north and south and a rugged chain of central highlands. But there are a number of other substantial islands, mostly of volcanic origin, including New Britain, New Ireland, and Bougainville. More than 80% of the country is covered with dense tropical rainforest.

Communications are difficult and much internal travel is only feasible by air, which makes it hard to help isolated communities at times of natural disaster, as when a tidal wave swept into the north-west coast of the mainland in July 1998, killing up to 10,000 people.

Papua New Guinea has one of the world's most complex societies, with 800 or more ethnic groups or languages. The lingua franca is Tok Pisin—Pidgin English. For most Papua New Guineans, the primary allegiance is to their tribe or clan linked by a common language, called in Pidgin a wontok ('one talk').

Papua New Guineans have a rich culture, but low levels of human development. Around one-third of children under 5 years old are underweight, and less than one-third of households have access to safe water or sanitation. Nevertheless, almost everyone benefits from basic health services, whether provided by the government, the churches, or non-governmental organizations. And since people have access to commonly held land few are likely to starve unless there is a severe drought.

The country is also making some progress in education: primary school enrolment is now around 80% and the literacy rate is above 70%, though secondary education is weak.

More than 80% of the population depend on agriculture. They grow mainly subsistence food crops such as sweet potatoes, bananas, sugar cane, and maize. But small-holders also grow cash crops for export including coffee, cocoa, and copra. In addition, there are large estates producing rubber, palm oil, and tea. Forestry is another source of export income. But commercial agricultural development generally has been slow—hampered by difficult communications.

Modernization is drawing more people to the towns, and particularly to the capital, Port Moresby, where 40% of people live in shanty towns with no sanitation or basic services. Here and in other urban areas there has been considerable civil unrest, along with high levels of crime—both of which have served to slow social and economic development.

Port Moresby has very high levels of crime

Papua New Guinea's greatest cash wealth lies underground in extensive mineral deposits that generate more than 60% of exports. The earliest to be exploited was gold in the 19th century, then copper, notably on the island of Bougainville. The main copper mine now, however, is the Ok Tedi mine near the western border, owned by an Australian company BHP. Since 1989 a series of major gold mines have opened up. More recently, there have also been discoveries of oil and gas. Gas could be particularly important, with an undersea pipeline to Australia.

Distributing the country's mineral wealth has long been a vexed issue—complicated by communal land ownership. There is also severe environmental damage. In 1999, BHP admitted that the pollution from the Ok Tedi mine was so severe that the only solution would be to close down—an alarming economic prospect for Papua New Guinea.

Papua New Guinea's political structure matches the complexity of its society. This is a constitutional monarchy, headed by the British monarch. But since independence from Australia in 1975 its single-chamber parliamentary system has yet to develop a stable party basis. Voters choose MPs largely on personality or tribe. Party allegiances are weak and, once elected, MPs feel free to 'cross the floor'.

All governments have been unstable coalitions and none has yet lasted a full term. The 1997 election produced a four-party coalition which chose as prime minister the somewhat erratic Bill Skate. He resigned in July 1999 to be replaced by Sir Mekere Morauta of the People's Democratic Movement. Morauta faces a deep economic crisis and has been doing the rounds of aid donors—Australia is still the main supporter.

A perennial problem for all governments has been the threat of secession by Bougainville. Local people felt they were getting little benefit from the Panguna copper mine. An armed insurrection in 1989 closed the mine permanently and the next ten years of fighting cost around 15,000 lives.

Following mediation, from Australia and particularly from New Zealand, the fighting ended in January 1999 with the Lincoln Agreement. In March 2000 under the Loloate Understanding, a Bougainville Interim Provincial government was established to offer autonomy. Later there could be a referendum on independence.

Paraguay

Paraguay produces more electricity per person than any other country, but remains very poor

Land area: *407,000 sq. km.*
Population: *5 million—urban 55%*
Capital city: *Asunción , 0.6 million*
People: *Mestizo 95%*
Language: *Guaraní, Spanish*
Religion: *Roman Catholic 90%, Protestant*
Government: *Republic*
Life expectancy: *70 years*
GNP per capita: *$PPP 3,650*
Currency: *Guarani*
Major exports: *Electricity, soya, timber, cotton*

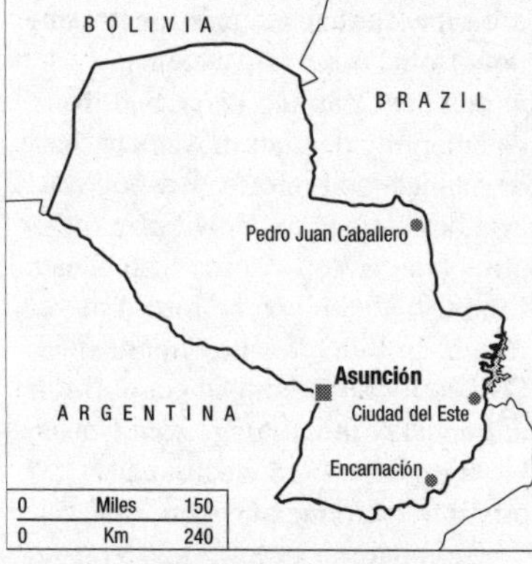

The Paraguay River, which flows through the country from north to south, divides Paraguay into two very different geographical zones. To the west, making up three-fifths of the country is the flat, featureless scrubland of the Gran Chaco, which extends into Bolivia, Argentina, and Brazil. To the east, the remaining two-fifths, where most of the population live, is more fertile and humid and is an extension of the Brazilian Highlands. Much of the eastern and southern border is formed by another major river, the Paraná.

The majority of Paraguayans are mestizo, a mixture of European and Guaraní Indian. But the Guaraní influence remains strong. For about one-third of the population Guaraní is the first language, and most people understand it as well as Spanish. More recent immigrants have been Brazilian farmers who have settled on land in the east. There are also small numbers of Indians—in seventeen ethnic groups who live both in the Chaco and the east.

Paraguayans are among the poorest people in South America. Two thirds of them live in poverty, only one-fifth have access to sanitation and only half have electricity. Around one-fifth are infected with the debilitating, insect-transmitted Chagas' disease.

Agriculture remains an important source of income, accounting for one-quarter of GDP and employing 40% of the workforce. But land is very unevenly distributed, with the top 1% of landowners controlling more than three-quarters of the land. The main export crop used to be cotton, which is grown primarily by 200,000 or so peasant farmers on small plots of land, but of late they have been trying to diversify into other crops like wheat, rice, and sunflowers. Nowadays, the major export crop is soya, which is typically grown on the more efficient farms. Both cotton and soya, however, remain vulnerable to the vagaries of the weather and international prices.

Livestock is also important, with cattle raising in the Chaco and in the south. Again, ownership is highly concentrated—1% of producers own around three-fifths of the total herd.

Paraguay has little manufacturing industry. Most is in the hands of small firms producing for local consumption. Foreign investors have shown little interest—deterred by the poor state of infrastructure and the low levels of education and skill.

But one important and expanding industry is electricity production. Paraguay's rivers have enormous hydroelectric potential. The world's largest single source of hydro-electricity is the Itaipú dam on the Paraná River. This $20 million project, most of whose funding came from Brazil, began production in 1985. Since Paraguay's share of the output is more than twenty times its total consumption, it sells most of the electricity to Brazil where the dam provides one-quarter of that country's electricity.

A second, more controversial joint enterprise is with Argentina further down the Paraná at Yaciretá. This started production early in 1998 but has been the subject of international protests against environmental damage and the displacement of 50,000 local people—as well as general corruption and heavy handedness.

Protests over construction of a new dam

Paraguay's political system has yet to develop any coherent shape following the end of the dictatorship of General Alfredo Stroessner. He seized power in 1954, along with the leadership of Paraguay's dominant Colorado Party, and his dictatorship continued until he was ousted in a coup in 1989 by General Andrés Rodríguez. Rodríguez subsequently won the 1989 election as the Colorado candidate and opened up the economy to some extent but had little interest in social reform. He imposed as the Colorado candidate for the 1993 presidential election a leading businessman Juan Carlos Wasnoy.

Wasnoy tried to liberalize the economy further but faced resistance both from conservative elements within the Colorado Party, and from an emerging peasant movement that demanded land reform. Wasnoy was also determined to depoliticize the army but crossed swords with General Lino Oviedo, whom he forced to resign. In 1996, Wasnoy imprisoned Oviedo for an attempted coup. But he did not stay in jail long. Raul Cubas Grau won the 1998 election and promptly pardoned Oviedo.

Grau was opposed in this by his vice-president, Luis Maria Argaña, who threatened to impeach him. Matters came to a head in March 1999 when Argaña was murdered and Grau resigned to avoid impeachment. Oviedo fled to Argentina. One of Argaña's supporters, senate president Luis Gonzalez Macchi, was sworn in as president, refusing to submit to an election and vowing to run a coalition administration until 2003.

His government has been unpopular and seems unlikely to last that long. After Argentina threatened to deport him, Oviedo suddenly disappeared and now claims to be living in secret in Paraguay. In May 2000 it looked as though he might also return to power when a group of army officers attempted a coup on his behalf. In the event, the army high command chose not to support the rebels.

Peru

President Fujimori has liberalized the economy and defeated guerrillas, but at a severe cost to democracy

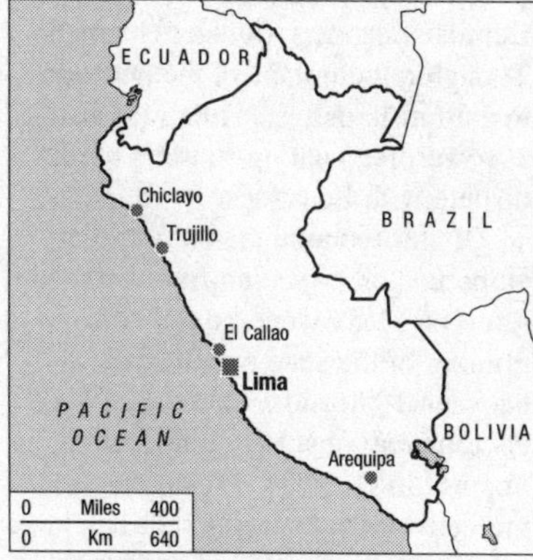

Land area: *1,285,000 sq. km.*
Population: *25 million—urban 72%*
Capital city: *Lima, 6.5 million*
People: *Indian 45%, mestizo 37%, white 15%, other 3%*
Language: *Spanish, Quechua, Aymara*
Religion: *Roman Catholic*
Government: *Republic*
Life expectancy: *68 years*
GNP per capita: *$PPP $4,420*
Currency: *Nuevo Sol*
Major exports: *Copper, fish products, gold*

Peru's striking terrain falls into three well-defined zones. The Pacific coastal region is a long strip of desert, broken only by 60 or so rivers crossing to the sea. Further inland, rise the dramatic Andean mountains, whose plateaux and valleys nurtured the Inca civilization. Then to the west, the mountains descend more gently through densely forested foothills to the vast, sparsely populated tropical rainforest of the Amazon Basin.

The Quechua and Aymara Indian descendants of the Incas still make up close to half the population. Millions of them are to be found in peasant farming communities in the highlands. But many others, driven by violence or poverty, have now made their way to the towns and cities, particularly to those on the coast.

The warmer tropical land to the east, though it makes up more than 60% of the country has only around 5% of the population, mostly native Indians living in scattered settlements.

Peru remains very poor. In 1997, 37% of the population were classified as poor, and 16% as extremely poor. In recent years, the government has increased spending on basic social services but investment still lags far behind what is required. There is also a wide gap between the urban and rural areas. Child malnutrition and under-five mortality are twice as high in rural areas as in the towns and cities. But even in the sprawling capital Lima half the population struggle to make a living in the informal sector.

Agriculture employs around one-third of the workforce. The most productive areas are around the rivers in the coastal areas where farmers grow cotton, sugar, and food for the cities. Agriculture in the highlands, the altiplano, remains fairly primitive. Peasant farmers grow maize and potatoes and raise alpacas and llamas. However, the most lucrative crop in the highlands is still coca—worth perhaps $1 billion per year though production has been falling.

On the coast one of Peru's most important activities is fishing. Peru is one of the world's largest fishing nations, catching around 10 million tons per year, mostly sardines and anchovies that are processed locally into fishmeal for export.

Peru's most important official foreign exchange earner, however, is still mining. Copper, gold, zinc, and lead provide more than 40% of export earnings. Privatization of many of the mines since 1994 has encouraged new foreign owners to step up investment. Peru also has reserves of oil, both in the jungle regions and offshore, as well as large natural gas fields.

Tourism to the spectacular Inca sites has also provided important income, and has revived now that guerilla warfare has subsided.

In the 1970s Peru had a series of military or autocratic governments. But even the restoration of democracy in the 1980s did little to improve the lot of the poor. On one side a populist government had by the late 1980s contributed to rampant inflation—7,650% by 1990. On the other side, two guerrilla movements had emerged: the Cuban-inspired Movimiento Revolucionario Tupac Amaru (MRTA); and the Maoist Sendero Luminoso. The ensuing struggles killed 28,000 people and forced more than 700,000 to flee.

Warfare with Sendero Luminoso

It was in this chaotic environment that Peruvians in 1990 elected as president Alberto Fujimori, a former university rector and descendant of Japanese immigrants. Fujimori was to prove an effective antidote to many of these problems—though at a democratic cost. In 1992, in an army-backed 'autocoup' he closed the Congress and suspended the judiciary. Though in 1995 with a new constitution he later won a free election, he still had to rely on close relations with the army since he lacked a party power base of his own.

On the military front, his successes included the 1992 arrest of Sendero Luminoso leader, Abimael Guzmán. Though not eliminated, the guerrilla threat has largely subsided. He also in 1998 resolved a long-running border dispute with Ecuador.

On the economic front, Fujimori embarked on sweeping free-market reforms. Many were painful. His pruning of the state bureaucracy between 1990 and 1993 cost 200,000 government jobs. His cutting of import tariffs exposed formerly protected manufacturing industry to foreign competition closing around 2,000 companies.

Privatization also opened up the economy to foreign owners of everything from mines to Aeroperú, the national airline. This has cut inflation and stimulated economic growth but most of the poorest people have yet to see the benefits.

Constitutionally, Fujimori was not strictly eligible for a further term in office. But on the grounds that his earlier term had been served under a previous constitution he ran again in 2000. Despite widespread manipulation of the media and the electoral processes, he narrowly failed to win in the first round against Alejandro Toledo—an economist of Amerindian descent. Toledo withdrew from the second round, accusing Fujimori of fraud. Fujimori duly claimed victory, to widespread international condemnation.

Philippines

The Philippines has lagged behind the 'tigers' of South-east Asia—always on the brink of economic take-off

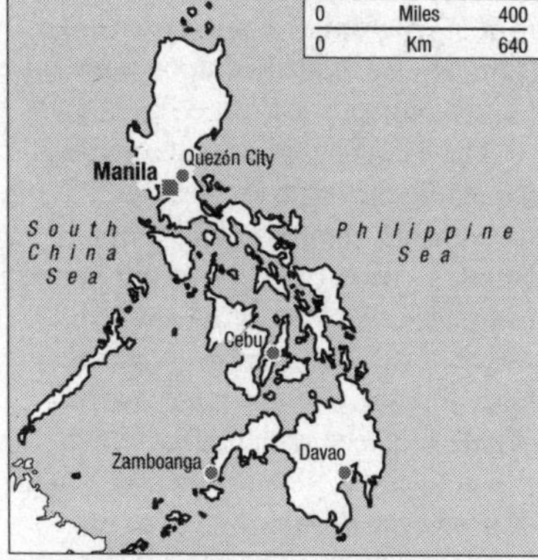

Land area: *300,000 sq. km.*
Population: *75 million—urban 57%*
Capital city: *Manila, 12 million*
People: *Christian Malay 92%, Muslim Malay 4%, Chinese 2%, other 2%*
Language: *Pilipino, English*
Religion: *Roman Catholic 83%, Protestant 9%, Muslim 5%, Buddhist and other 3%*
Government: *Republic*
Life expectancy: *68 years*
GNP per capita: *$PPP 3,540*
Currency: *Peso*
Major exports: *Electronics, machinery and transport, garments*

The Philippines is an archipelago of more than 7,000 islands, though many are tiny and less than half are named. The two largest are Luzon in the north and Mindanao in the south. In between lie the group of islands known collectively as the Visayas. Most of the islands are mountainous, with the ranges running from north to south, and they include twenty active volcanoes. The Philippines is environmentally rich and diverse but since the 1970s much of the forest land has been cleared and tropical forests now cover only around one-fifth of the territory.

Filipinos are ethnically relatively homogenous, though there are a number of small indigenous groups. The main distinction is between Christians, who make up the majority of the population, and Muslims, most of whom are to be found on Mindanao. The country had two major periods of colonization, first by Spain and later by the USA, and it bears strong traces of both. Though the main language is Pilipino, many people also speak English, which is the principal language for higher education. There are also smaller ethnic groups on different islands.

Many Filipinos are well educated, and the literacy rate is high, but health and nutrition standards are less impressive. Over the period 1990-7, around 30% of children were malnourished. Services are very unequally distributed: half the doctors work in the National Capital Region.

In 1997 around one-third of people were living below the poverty line—of whom most were in the rural areas. Emigration is one solution to poverty, and there are thought to be around 4 million Filipinos abroad. One-third of Filipino children live in households where at least one parent has gone overseas. Their remittances which probably amount to $6 billion per year not only sustain families, they also prop up the economy.

The largest source of employment at home remains agriculture, which employs more than 40% of the population. But the Philippines is a very unequal society, especially in landholding. In 1988 2% of landowners had 36% of the land. The main food crop is rice, most of which is grown in Luzon. The second largest crop is coconuts, with half the production in Mindanao. Sugar used to be a major cash crop, particularly on the island of Negros, but, following a collapse in the world price, output has declined steeply. Fishing is another source of livelihood, though over-fishing by commercial fleets has been hitting the catches of inshore subsistence fishing communities.

The Philippines was slower than many other South-East Asian countries to modernize its industries. Like land, industry is often in the hands of powerful families. But its educated, and often English-speaking, population is proving increasingly attractive to foreign investors despite constitutional restrictions on foreign ownership of certain enterprises.

Assets controlled by rich families

Many companies have now established factories in export processing zones, particularly for assembly of electronic products, which in 1998 made up two-thirds of exports. The Philippines also has some mineral potential: though it has little oil, it does have deposits of copper, nickel, gold, and silver.

One factor that has slowed development in the Philippines has been a weak political system based more on personality than ideology or principle. This was particularly evident during the period of authoritarian rule by Ferdinand Marcos from 1965 to 1984. Although the economy grew during this period, he and his high-profile wife, Imelda, siphoned off much of the wealth. Marcos was eventually ousted by a 'people-power' revolution. and Corazon Aquino, wife of a murdered opposition leader, was elected president in 1987. She was succeeded in 1992 by former army leader Fidel Ramos, who embarked upon a period of economic reform.

The Marcos regime had also seen the emergence of two guerrilla movements: the communist New People's Army (NPA); and the Moro National Liberation Front (MNLF), which was fighting for independence for Mindanao. Ramos made some degree of peace with both. Though still active, the NPA is down to a rump of 6,000 and does not seem to have much of a future. The MNLF signed an agreement in 1996 through which Mindanao became an autonomous region that would receive considerable development funds.

Two other major political forces are the Catholic Church, which had helped oppose Marcos, and a plethora of non-governmental organizations that emerged during the Marcos period as an alternative form of political organization.

In 1998, Ramos was succeeded as president by a former movie actor, Joseph Estrada. He made a good start, having surrounded himself with able technocrats, but his economic reforms have stalled, and by early 2000 there were accusations that his government was reverting to the cronyism and corruption of the Marcos years.

In May 2000 he was also facing a return to hostilities, and hostage-taking, by the MNLF.

Poland

Economic shock therapy seems to have worked in Poland, which is now aiming for EU membership

Land area: *313,000 sq. km.*
Population: *39 million—urban 65%*
Capital city: *Warsaw, 1.6 million*
People: *Polish*
Language: *Polish*
Religion: *Roman Catholic*
Government: *Republic*
Life expectancy: *73 years*
GNP per capita: *$PPP 6,740*
Currency: *Zloty*
Major exports: *Manufactures, machinery, mineral fuels*

Poland has swamps and sand dunes along its northern coast. But the main part of the country comprises the central plains and lowlands; 'Poland' derives from a Slavic word for 'plain'. The mountainous one-third of the country includes the Carpathians along the southern border with Slovakia.

Poland's population has become ethnically more homogenous—largely as a result of the deaths and expulsions of Jews and other minorities during the Second World War. At the same time, many ethnic Poles have also emigrated, a trend which continued in the early 1990s as many people moved to Germany and elsewhere in search of work. In 1999, around one-third of ethnic Poles were thought to live abroad. An important unifying factor has been the Catholic Church, which played an important part in the struggle against communism—and also provided the current Pope, Karol Wojtyla, John Paul II. However, the Church's political influence has diminished and it now restricts itself more to social teaching.

Poles have not just become wealthier, they have also become healthier. Since the early 1990s, life expectancy has been increasing, and infant mortality falling. This was helped by better food and by cleaner air: between 1980 and 1996 sulphur dioxide output, for example, fell by more than 40%. Not all have benefited, however, and inequality has been rising.

Poland is considered a successful example of economic 'shock therapy'. From 1989, the government rapidly liberalized prices, imposed wage controls, and reduced subsidies to state-owned enterprises while encouraging private businesses. This helped to control inflation but ushered in a deep recession with high unemployment. From around 1992, however, the economy started to recover and by the mid-1990s Poland embarked on rapid economic growth. Overall, between 1989 and 1999 the Polish economy grew by more than 25%. Manufacturing led the way, fuelled by foreign investors who had been encouraged by a liberal economic environment, good skills, and low wages. Some of the older industries have faded but there has been strong growth in lighter industry, notably food and drink and some heavier manufacturing such as automobiles. Between 1989 and 1996, the private sector's share of GDP rose from 18% to 52%. This has still not been enough to reduce unemployment which was 12% in 1999.

Poland has, on the other hand, been slow to privatize. Sales started in 1995 but have not made much progress. In 1999, state-owned firms still accounted for one-third of industrial sales and employed more than 40% of industrial workers—while producing only 5% of the profits. These firms, particularly coal and steel, are in urgent need of restructuring; many are making heavy losses. In 1999, the government estimated they had 170,000 excess workers.

Agriculture did not need privatizing since Polish farmers had managed to resist collectivization during the communist period. They also kept their farms small—of the 2 million farms, more than half are of less than five hectares and they are very labour intensive. The government is anxious to increase productivity, with the prospect of competing within the EU, but has not had much success.

Poland has 2 million small farms

Poland's political transformation out of communism was famously the work of the Solidarity trade union based in the shipyard in Gdansk. This momentum also swept Solidarity into political power and its leader, Lech Walesa, was elected president in 1990. Solidarity pushed through dramatic economic reforms but subsequently fragmented into numerous centre-right groups.

In 1993, after a series of short-lived Solidarity governments, parliamentary elections resulted in a victory for the former communists of the Left Democratic Alliance (SLD) and in 1995 its founder, Aleksander Kwasniewski, was elected president. Even so, the SLD continued Solidarity's economic reforms. In May 1997, a national referendum narrowly approved a new constitution that reduced the powers of the presidency. This was in the face of opposition from Solidarity and from the Catholic Church, which opposed the failure to outlaw abortion.

Nevertheless Solidarity had been regrouping, and under the leadership of Marian Krzaklewski came back together as a 37-party coalition Solidarity Electoral Action (AWS). As a result, after the 1997 parliamentary election, AWS was able to form a government in coalition with another group, Freedom Union (UW) with Jerzy Buzek as prime minister. Krzaklewski will be Solidarity's presidential candidate in the November 2000 elections. But Kwasniewski is very popular and is more likely to win.

In 1999, Poland joined NATO. It is also in negotiations to join the EU—which could be tricky on both sides. The EU is worried about an exodus of Polish migrant workers. The Poles are concerned about the cost of accession and the risks to agriculture. Only around half the population are thought to be in favour of EU entry.

Portugal

Political stability and EU membership have stimulated development

Land area: *92,000 sq. km.*
Population: *10 million—urban 37%*
Capital city: *Lisbon, 600,000*
People: *Portuguese*
Language: *Portuguese*
Religion: *Roman Catholic*
Government: *Republic*
Life expectancy: *75 years*
GNP per capita: *$PPP 14,380*
Currency: *Escudo*
Major exports: *Textiles, garments, cars, footwear, wood products*

Portugal's major river, the Tagus, flows across the country from east to west, reaching the Atlantic ocean at the capital, Lisbon. To the north of the Tagus, the land is mountainous and the climate cooler and wetter. The southern part of the country, the Alentejo ('beyond the Tagus') consists of rolling and generally arid lowlands. Portugal also includes the Madeira Islands and the Azores.

Portugal is one of the least industrialized countries in Western Europe and two-thirds of the population still live in rural areas, with greater concentrations in the north.

By the standards of most European countries, the population is fairly homogenous, with only small numbers of immigrants from its former African colonies. Indeed until the 1980s Portugal was one of Europe's leading sources of emigrants who were drawn away by higher wages in France and Germany. Some 4.6 million Portuguese still live overseas and even in 1995 their remittances amounted to 4% of GDP.

Though unemployment is low, wages are low too—20% of those in Germany. And by European standards health and education levels are poor. But joining the EU has transformed the country's prospects. Between 1986 when it joined and 1999, Portugal's per capita income grew from 54% to 74% of the EU average. As a result, emigration has slowed. Indeed around 20,000 people per year are now returning.

Portugal's slow development is linked to the relatively poor state of agriculture, which employs one-fifth of the workforce. Most farms, particularly in the north, are small and relatively unproductive. Thin soil and unreliable rainfall, combined with low levels of investment, lead to yields less than one-third of the EU average. More than half the country's food has to be imported.

Nevertheless, Portugal does have agriculturally based exports, notably tomato paste, port, and other wines. Forestry also generates important exports: more than one-third of the country is forested, much of this with cork-oak trees. Portugal has one-third of the world's cork trees. The country's long coastline also supports a significant fishing industry, largely catching cod for local consumption and sardines for export, though over-fishing has caused catches to fall steeply in recent years.

Manufacturing in Portugal is still fairly low-tech—much of it concentrated in textiles, clothing, and footwear—but the government has gone out of its way to attract higher tech investment. One of the most striking examples was the record $1-billion subsidy for the joint Ford-Volkswagen Auto Europa car factory just outside Lisbon which by 1998 was responsible for more than one-tenth of merchandise exports. Portugal also has some mineral resources, particularly in the Alentejo which has the Neves Corvo copper mine as well as centres of marble production.

Portugal offers $1 billion for a car plant

Within the service sector, one of the most important industries is tourism. Portugal attracts more than 10 million tourists each year, mostly from Europe's chillier countries, heading for Madeira and the southern Algarve coastline. Tourism employs around 6% of the workforce and makes a major contribution to the balance of payments.

The years after 1976, which marked the end of the 36-year dictatorship of Antonio Salazar, and the introduction of a democratic constitution, were a period of rapid political change. In the first fifteen years of democracy, there were twelve changes of government. In the mid-1980s, however, the situation settled down. In 1985 the largely ceremonial post of president was taken by Mario Soares, formerly prime minister and leader of the centre-left Socialist Party. And in 1987 the Social Democratic Party achieved a parliamentary majority and Anibal Cabaço Silva became prime minister. This pairing, which was to last until 1995, ushered in a period of relative stability—due in part to Portugal's 1986 entry into the EU which triggered an economic boom that lasted until 1992.

Discontent with the Social Democrats led to their defeat in the 1995 parliamentary elections, following which the Socialist Party took over again, this time with the urbane Antonio Guterres as prime minister. In 1996 Cabaço Silva ran for president but was defeated by the socialist candidate Jorge Sampaio.

The socialist administration, which moved towards the centre, benefited from several years of rapid economic growth. It suffered a major setback late in 1998 when a plan for greater regionalization was decisively rejected in a referendum.

Nevertheless, with the economy doing well, unemployment below 5%, and inflation under control, Guterres remained popular. As a result, in the 1999 parliamentary elections the socialists substantially increased their representation, coming close to an outright majority, which should help Guterrez's plans to reform the health, taxation, and legal systems. Guterrez has become a widely admired figure on the European stage, having led the Portuguese presidency of the EU in 2000. He also successfully steered Portugal into the Euro zone.

Puerto Rico

Puerto Rico has decided not to become a US state, yet. Now it wants greater economic independence

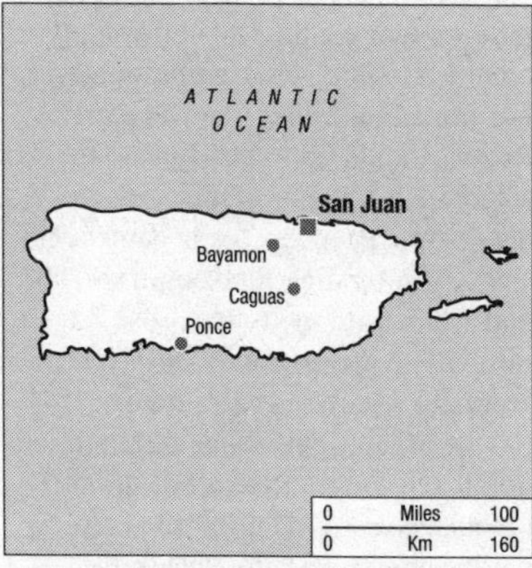

Land area: *9,000 sq. km.*
Population: *4 million—urban 71%*
Capital city: *San Juan, 438,000*
People: *White 80%, black 20%*
Language: *Spanish, English*
Religion: *Roman Catholic 85%, other 15%*
Government: *Commonwealth (US)*
Life expectancy: *75 years*
GNP per capita: *$PPP $8,600*
Currency: *US dollar*
Major exports: *Chemicals, manufactures, food*

Puerto Rico is largely mountainous. The Central Cordillera range extends east-west along most of the length of the island, descending steeply to the narrow southern coastal plain, and more gently to the broader plains of the northern coast. There is also a north-south distinction in climate: humid and tropical in the north; drier in the south.

The population is racially fairly homogenous, and there is little overt discrimination though, as elsewhere in Latin America, the people in positions of power tend to be those with lighter skin colour. Puerto Ricans are US citizens, but their standard of living is far lower than that in the USA. The per capita income is around half that of the poorest US state, Mississippi, the unemployment rate is around twice as high as in the USA, and half the population lives below the US poverty line. Not surprisingly, many people driven by poverty and unemployment have headed for the USA, which now has around 3 million people of Puerto Rican descent, most of whom are in New York.

Almost everyone speaks Spanish, which is the main language of instruction in schools. English is also an official language, but far fewer speak it fluently and many people want to resist any further imposition.

Puerto Rico's main economic activity is manufacturing, which accounts for more than 40% of GDP. Many US firms have been attracted to Puerto Rico by low wages. Although Puerto Rico is subject to US minimum wage legislation, wages tend to be one-quarter less than in the USA. In the past there have also been significant tax concessions, though the latter are now being phased out.

Initially this drew in firms engaged in labour-intensive industries like garments manufacture. But in recent decades companies have invested in higher levels of technology—more than half of current manufacturing is in chemicals, and another fifth is in metal products and machinery. Most of this output is for export, primarily to the USA.

Though some garment production

remains, and employs around 30,000 people, many labour-intensive industries subsequently migrated in search of even cheaper labour elsewhere. This kind of change accelerated after the signing of the North American Free-Trade Agreement (NAFTA) which gave Mexico a new advantage in low-wage work.

Little is left of Puerto Rican agriculture, which now contributes less than 1% of GDP and continues to shrink.

Another increasingly important source of employment and income is tourism. San Juan, the capital, is a favourite port of call for cruise liners. Around 1 million cruise visitors come each year as well as 3 million other tourists, primarily from the USA.

The USA acquired Puerto Rico in 1899 at the end of the Spanish American War. Since then, its status has remained unresolved. The US Supreme Court has asserted that Puerto Rico is an 'unincorporated territory of the United States'—a possession of, but not a part of, the USA. A new constitution in 1952 established a system for local government, making Puerto Rico a 'Commonwealth'.

Puerto Rico has an odd constitutional status

So although Puerto Ricans are US citizens, they cannot vote in presidential elections, and do not pay federal income tax. They elect their own governor and Congress which have autonomy in many areas such as tax, education, and criminal justice. The US government deals with defence, monetary issues, and trade and also extends some, but not all, federal social programmes to the island, amounting to around $10 billion annually.

In recent years, there have been a number of attempts to change the relationship, since Puerto Rico's position is anomalous in international law; unless it is a US state or an independent country it is effectively a colony. On this view, 'commonwealth' is a transitional status and Puerto Ricans should periodically vote to select their ultimate status—to become independent, or become a US state. Non-binding plebiscites in 1993 and 1998, with more than 70% turnouts, voted narrowly in favour of retaining commonwealth status.

Given the significance of this issue, politics in Puerto Rico tends to be organized around it. The two main parties are the Partido Nuevo Progresista (PNP), which is pro-statehood, and the Partido Popular Democrático (PDP), which is pro-commonwealth. Since 1968 power has tended to alternate between these two. The third party, though it rarely gets more than 5% of the vote, is the Partido Independendista Puertorriqueño, which is pro-independence.

The argument for statehood is chiefly financial. As part of the USA, the island would get full representation in Washington; people would pay federal income tax but they would also qualify for more federal funds. The argument against is chiefly cultural—Puerto Rico would lose its distinctive identity.

Since 1992, the governor has been the PNP's Pedro Rosselló and the PNP has retained a healthy majority in congress. Even so, this has not been sufficient to carry the statehood vote.

Qatar

With a huge new gas field, Qatar could become the world's richest nation

Land area: *11,000 sq. km.*
Population: *742,000—urban 92%*
Capital city: *Doha, 0.2 million*
People: *Arab 40%, Pakistani 18%, Indian 18%, Iranian 10%, other 14%*
Language: *Arabic, English*
Religion: *Muslim*
Government: *Absolute monarchy*
Life expectancy: *72 years*
GNP per capita: *$PPP 20,987*
Currency: *Qatari riyal*
Major exports: *Petroleum products, fertilizers, steel*

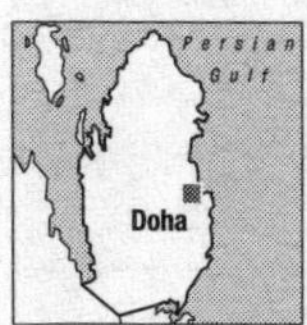

Though it has some wells and sand depressions that provide water for limited agriculture, the peninsula of Qatar is mostly a flat and arid desert.

Native Qataris are in the minority—only around one-third of the population. Though they are entitled to free education, this is not compulsory and around 20% of adults are illiterate. The health service is also free, though some charges are being introduced.

Most of the manual work is done by Qatar's large immigrant workforce, drawn from the Indian subcontinent and Iran.

Oil was discovered in 1939 and has fuelled this small state's rapid development, providing two-thirds of government revenue. The country has also made efforts to diversify. Qatar has had a steel industry since 1978 and many foreign companies have invested in the production of fertilizers and other petro-chemicals.

Even so, the future lies with gas. Qatar's Dukhan field has been exploited since 1980, but most attention is now focused on the North field, which is the world's largest gas field not associated with oil. In order to earn the $25 billion required for investment in gas Qatar has been over-pumping oil at a rate that could exhaust reserves by 2012, and also borrowing abroad. But this investment should pay off over the next few decades, probably doubling the country's income.

Qatar is ruled by the emir, Sheikh Hamad al-Thani, an absolute monarch who took over in 1995 when he ousted his father in a bloodless coup. As crown prince Sheikh Hamad had been working to open up Qatar economically and politically and when he became emir he immediately ended press censorship and established one of the region's most outspoken TV stations.

In March 1999 he also offered Qatari citizens, including women, the opportunity to vote. This was only for a council to advise on municipal affairs, but by the standards of Gulf governments it was a radical move, especially since it even permitted women to stand as candidates.

For the long term, the emir has announced his intention of turning the country into a constitutional monarchy and has appointed a committee to draft a constitution, with parliamentary elections promised in 2000. This is an unsettling precedent for neighbouring Gulf countries, though Qatar has a reputation as a regional maverick.

Réunion

A French dependency in the Indian ocean—and likely to stay that way

Land area: *2,500 sq. km.*
Population: *700,000—urban 68%*
Capital city: *Saint-Denis, 104,000*
People: *African, French, Malagasy, Asian*
Language: *French, creole*
Religion: *Roman Catholic 94%, Hindu, Islam, Buddhist*
Government: *Republic*
Life expectancy: *75 years*
GNP per capita: *$PPP $4,800*
Currency: *French franc*
Major exports: *Sugar, rum, molasses, perfume essence*

Réunion is a volcanic island with rugged mountains surrounded by basins and plateaux that lead down to the tropical coastal lowlands. The island is often exposed to violent cyclones, and there is still a live volcano.

Most people are of African or creole (mixed) descent, though there are also significant French and Asian minorities. Poverty is high among the black and creole communities. The population continues to grow rapidly, and unemployment has been 40% or more. This has at times led to violent protests as people have demanded social security payments equivalent to those in France. Many have also emigrated to France in search of work.

The island was colonized as a potential sugar producer, and sugar still dominates the economy, providing 80% of exports as well as the raw material for rum and molasses. Other crops include vanilla beans and geraniums, which are grown for perfume essences. The government has also been trying to promote Réunion as a tourist destination. But the country remains heavily dependent on aid from France.

Réunion is an overseas department of France and sends five deputies and three senators to the French National Assembly. Locally, it is administered by a French-appointed prefect and has a general council and a regional council.

Political parties on the island include the main French parties, the right-wing Union pour la démocratie française (UDF), the Gaullist Rassemblement pour la république (RPR), and the Parti socialiste.

But two local parties have also held sway. One is the Parti communiste réunionnais (PCR); the other had a more distinctive origin, arising out of a pirate television station Télé-Free-DOM. The authorities tried to suppress the station but found that in the 1992 regional council election the largest number of seats went to candidates whose platform was simply the station's right to broadcast. In new election in 1993 Free-DOM won again and the station-owner's, wife Marguerite Sudre, was elected president of the council.

After four years there was a reshuffle of parties and control was taken by a coalition of Free-DOM, the RPR, and the UDF. The last general council election in March 1994 gave victory to an alliance of communists and socialists. In the past, there has been minority pressure for independence but this has now subsided.

Romania

Romania has avoided ethnic disaster, but has suffered from political confusion and an increase in poverty

Land area: *238,000 sq. km.*
Population: *22 million—urban 57%*
Capital city: *Bucharest, 2.3 million*
People: *Romanian 88%, Hungarian 9%, Gypsy 2%, other 1%*
Language: *Romanian, Hungarian*
Religion: *Romanian Orthodox 70%, Roman Catholic 6%, Protestant 6%, unaffiliated 18%*
Government: *Republic*
Life expectancy: *70 years*
GNP per capita: *$PPP 3,970*
Currency: *Leu*
Major exports: *Textiles, footwear, basic metals*

Western Romania is dominated by the Carpathian Mountains, which take up around one-third of the land area and run from the northern border with Ukraine down the centre of the country before veering west and exiting south-west into Yugoslavia. East of the mountains are broad plains that extend to the south before reaching the coast of the Black Sea.

Most people are ethnically Romanian but there are significant minorities that have given rise to ethnic tensions. The largest minority are the 2 million Hungarians who are concentrated in the north-west of the country and have been pressing for greater language rights, including a Hungarian-language university. Such requests are resisted, however, by a number of Romanian nationalist groups. The other important minority are the Romany, or gypsies. The official figure is around 400,000 but there are probably nearer 2 million. They tend to live apart from other Romanians and have been subject to widespread discrimination and abuse. Many have fled to other countries, notably Germany. Prior to 1989, the country also had large numbers of ethnic Germans but most of these have now left for Germany.

Romania is one of the poorest countries in Eastern Europe and has yet to regain ground lost in the transition. By 1999, per capita income was still 20% lower than the 1989 figure. In 1997, around one-quarter of the population were below the poverty line. Health standards are desperately low: the rates for infant and maternal mortality are among the highest in Europe.

Moreover, population is falling. Communist Romania had been determined to boost the population and had prohibited abortion and contraception. As a result, many unwanted children finished up in grim orphanages that became symbols of the failures of communism. Now, as a result of economic uncertainty and family planning, the birth rate is very low. Combined with a rising death rate and emigration, this has led to a steady fall in population.

Only one-third of the workforce are employed in agriculture. By the end of 1998, three-quarters of agricultural land was in private hands. Privatizing the rest is hampered by disputes over land title. This uncertainty, combined with low levels of technology and investment, has reduced yields and output.

The communist governments had given a high priority to heavy industry, particularly engineering and chemical, but most of the equipment is now obsolete. Romania's manufacturing potential now lies in more labour-intensive light industries, such as textiles and footwear. But this has yet to take off and in 1999 industrial output was still only half what it had been in 1989.

Romania's economic reforms have been slow—resisted by the bureaucracy, the trade unions, and by politicians who have milked the state enterprises. Only after 1997 was there any serious effort to restructure production and to close loss-making enterprises. In 2000 the Romanian economy seemed likely to shrink further.

Politicians have milked state enterprises

Romania had one of the most traumatic transitions from communism. From 1965 it had largely been the personal fiefdom of a brutal dictator, Nicolae Ceausescu, who was finally overthrown and executed in 1989. But the government remained in the hands of former communists, and their new party, the National Salvation Front (NSF) won the 1990 parliamentary and presidential elections. A new constitution approved in 1991 was followed by further elections in 1992 which again chose Ion Iliescu as the president—who has a strong executive role and appoints the prime minister. By this time however, the NSF had split and subsequently it merged with several other parties. In 1993 it was renamed the Party of Social Democracy in Romania (PSDR). For much of this period the government was essentially in thrall to the old politicians and bureaucrats as well as to nationalist forces who delayed economic reforms.

This era ended in 1996 with the election of an anti-communist government, led by a centre-right coalition, Democratic Convention (DC). Emil Constantinescu of the DC also defeated Iliescu in the presidential election and appointed Victor Ciorbia as prime minister. The DC governed in conjunction with the third-largest party, the Social Democrat Union (SDU), which consists largely of ex-communists now turned entrepreneurs.

The new government set about modernizing the economy but lost momentum and the coalition started to fracture. The SDU ousted Ciorbia, who was replaced by Radu Vasile. He attempted to get the reforms moving again—and obtain more funds from the IMF, but was faced with widespread strikes and protests. In December 1999 the president sacked him and replaced him with Mugur Isarescu, a non-party technocrat. Meanwhile, the EU said that Romania could start negotiations for entry—though accession seems a distant prospect.

Russia

President Putin may exert greater political and economic control, but at the cost of political freedom

Land area: *17,075,000 sq. km.*
Population: *147 million—urban 77%*
Capital city: *Moscow, 8.6 million*
People: *Russian 82%, Tatar 4%, Ukrainian 3%, Chuvash 1%, Bashkir 1%, Belarusian 1%, Moldavian 1%, other 7%*
Language: *Russian*
Religion: *Russian Orthodox, Muslim*
Government: *Republic*
Life expectancy: *67 years*
GNP per capita: *$PPP 3,950*
Currency: *Rouble*
Major exports: *Fuels, metals, machinery*

Russia, officially the Russian Federation, is by far the world's largest country, spanning two continents—more than 10,000 kilometres across. The territory is huge and diverse but can be considered as a series of regions west to east. First, to the west are the rolling plains and uplands of the European plain, through which flow major rivers including the Don and the Volga. These plains terminate in the east at the Ural mountains, which, running north to south, form a dividing line between Europe and Asia.

Beyond the Urals lies the vastness of the West Siberian plain, a mostly featureless and often marshy landscape that stretches east to the Yenisey River. This leads on to the Central Siberian Plateau and then to Russia's Far East, which ends in a number of mountain ranges before reaching the Pacific coast. Russia's climate is often harsh, with bitterly cold winters and short summers, especially in the north and east.

The majority of people, more than four-fifths, are ethnic Russians, but the country also has 70 or more other nationalities, of which the largest are Tartars, Ukrainians, and Chuvash. The ethnic spectrum corresponds to some extent to the country's complex administrative structure. Russia has 89 different administrative units, including 21 'minority' republics, such as Tatarstan, Chechnya, and Karelia. However, these account for only around 20% of the total population, and even they have majority Russian populations.

Russia's people have endured a series of shocks since the demise of communism. Living standards have fallen steeply. In 1999, around two-thirds of Russians lived near or below subsistence level and more than one-quarter lived below the official poverty line of just under $40 a month.

One of the most serious effects has been a decline in health standards. Between 1989 and 1995, Russia's death rate rose steeply and life expectancy for men dropped from 65 years to 59, though for women the drop was less steep—74 to 72. This has been ascribed to a combination of stresses and uncertainties that have contributed to heart problems, strokes, and alcoholism. The decline in the health system will also have played a part. Russia still has enough doctors, but they often work in poorly equipped hospitals.

A sudden fall in life expectancy

The education system too has come under strain. School attendance is compulsory and free, but standards have been slipping. Teachers' salaries are frequently in arrears and many teachers have been abandoning their profession for business activities.

In the first half of the 20th century Russia, as the core of the Soviet Union, had made striking economic progress—particularly in heavy industry. But by the 1980s its centrally planned economy was unable to produce the goods evident in the rest of the world. After the collapse of the old Soviet Union in 1989, Russia from 1992 undertook radical reforms—privatizing industries, liberalizing prices, and reducing tariffs.

The first phase of privatization involved selling off small enterprises, such as shops or small restaurants, primarily to their workers. More difficult was the disposal of large-scale enterprises. Initially this was done in 1992 by giving every Russian citizen a voucher to buy shares. This dispersed ownership very widely but left management unchanged.

After 1995, the government started selling enterprises for cash, often at low prices, to large industrial groups, typically those with good political contacts. As a result, the old communist élite, the 'nomenklatura', got most of the assets. Few companies have been restructured—and even fewer have gone bankrupt. Industrialists have used their political contacts to get cheap credit and have siphoned off many of the assets.

Russian manufacturing was antiquated and once exposed to international competition went into steep decline. Between 1990 and 1997, output halved. And most industrial enterprises continue to lose money—paying wages late, if at all, and very few taxes. Probably the majority of trading is based on barter. Plenty of luxury goods are available for the few who can afford them, but most are imported or manufactured locally by foreign companies.

One of the largest industrial sectors, and the one with the greatest potential, remains energy. Russia has vast reserves of coal, oil, and natural gas—with about one-tenth of global oil reserves and 30% of natural gas. Privatization created major oil companies of which Yuksi is the world's third largest. But this industry too is sorely in need of investment, particularly for pipelines. Russia also has large deposits of many other minerals, including diamonds, nickel, and platinum.

Vast mineral reserves

The most promising industries in Russia are now controlled by a series of 'financial-industrial groups', based on banks that have strong political connections. The largest in 1999 was Oneksimbank, whose interests ranged across telecoms, oil, automobiles, and the media, including *Izvestia*.

The establishment of this new oligarchy has been accompanied by a proliferation of organized crime. Commerce is now dominated by the 'mafia' which exacts protection money from the largest company to the smallest street kiosk or café. The forces of law and order tend to be in league with the racketeers.

Agriculture, which still employs around 15% of the workforce, has also suffered a sharp decline. Between 1990 and 1996, grain production fell by 40%—though with better weather it subsequently revived. Here privatization has been much slower. In 1996, only 9% of the cultivable area was in private hands. Most of the rest is cultivated by partnerships or by companies created by reorganizing former state or collective farms. Even today, land cannot be treated as a normal commodity. This has reduced the potential for investment, and both the cultivated land area and the yields have been falling.

The new era in Russia can be traced from 1985 when Mikhael Gorbachev started to open up the Soviet Union. This unleashed tensions between conservative and reformist forces that culminated in August 1991 in a failed coup by hard-line conservatives which triggered the break-up of the Soviet Union.

Until the end of 1999, political life in Russia was dominated by Boris Yeltsin who had been elected president of the Russian Federation in 1991. Yeltsin was determined to push forward economic reform but met stiff opposition from communists. He was, however, able to strengthen his position in 1993 after winning an overwhelming victory in a referendum that gave the president strong executive powers and allowed him to take many actions without endorsement by the state parliament, whose lower house is the Duma. The upper house is the Federation Council, which is made up of regional governors and heads of regional assemblies.

But Yeltsin's grip was constantly shaken by a number of rebellions both within government and in the regions. The most serious was in the southern republic of Chechnya where Yeltsin unleashed a fierce civil war. This lasted first from 1994 to 1996 and was re-ignited in 1999. By the end of 1999 around 80,000 people had died.

Brutal war in Chechnya

Despite serious health problems, Yeltsin was re-elected in 1996. He had long struggles with the Duma, which remained dominated by communists, and he appointed and sacked a sequence of prime ministers. His final appointee in 1999, was a former KGB colonel, Vladimir Putin. In December 1999 Putin and other liberals won a striking victory in the Duma elections. Even more remarkable was Yeltsin's sudden resignation on January 1, 2000—following which he handing over presidential power to Putin.

Portraying himself as a strong war leader, Putin easily won the March 2000 presidential election. His ruthlessness may stand him in good stead for imposing control in Russia's chaotic political and economic environment. But Putin's KGB past, for which he is unrepentant, and his disdain for press freedoms and human rights, have worrying implications for Russian democracy.

Rwanda

Rwanda has emerged from the period of genocide and has the beginnings of a democratic government

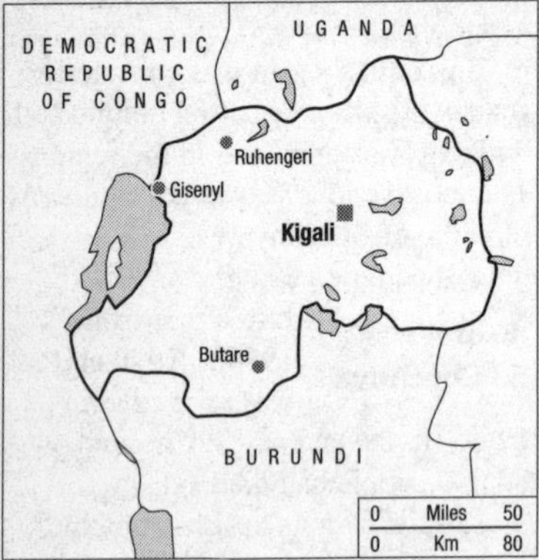

Land area: *26,000 sq. km.*
Population: *8 million—urban 6%*
Capital city: *Kigali, 240,000*
People: *Hutu 80%, Tutsi 19%, Twa 1%*
Language: *Kinyarwanda, French, English, Kiswahili*
Religion: *Roman Catholic 65%, Protestant 9%, Muslim 1%, indigenous beliefs and other 25%*
Government: *Republic*
Life expectancy: *44 years*
GNP per capita: *$PPP 690*
Currency: *Rwandan franc*
Major exports: *Coffee, tea, hides*

From Lake Kivu on the western border, Rwanda's territory rises to a steep mountain range, with the volcanic Virunga Mountains in the north. To the east of these is the broad hilly plateau that covers most of the country before descending to the marshy land along the border with Tanzania.

The people of Rwanda are sharply divided between two main groups: the Hutu and the Tutsi, though the demarcation is more political and economic than cultural, since they speak the same language and follow the same religions.

Traditionally, the minority Tutsi, who were primarily cattle herders, had formed the ruling élite; the majority Hutu worked for the Tutsi while raising their own crops. Conflict between them culminated in genocide in 1994. Up to 1 million people, primarily Tutsi, were killed. Many more fled as refugees.

Since then, a traumatized population has been struggling to rebuild. Most refugees have returned, though often more segregated than before, reducing the prospect of reconciliation. Rwanda already had 70% of its population living below the poverty line. Now those people are even poorer. Between 1992 and 1996, per capita income fell by 20% and the child mortality rate rose by one-third.

The vast majority of Rwandans live in the rural areas and depend on subsistence agriculture. Population density is high and most households survive on less than 1 hectare. For decades, their intensive cultivation of steep slopes has been eroding the land.

The violence of 1994 resulted in part from competition for scarce land. Farmers primarily grow staple crops like plantains, sweet potatoes, cassava, and maize, but output is far less nowadays because of the massive population movements—which have also resulted in complex, competing land claims. The fighting also reduced livestock numbers, though by 1999 the herds had largely recovered.

Rwandan farmers also grow cash crops, notably high-quality coffee in the north-west. And there is also a good export market for locally grown tea. Most industrial activity is devoted to processing coffee, tea, and other crops, along with production in a few textiles factories and others making simple consumer goods.

Some of today's antagonisms can be traced to the 1950s and the lead-up to independence from Belgian colonial rule. The Hutu knew democracy could lead to their majority rule and had become more assertive. In 1959, following a number of violent incidents the Tutsi king fled into exile along with hundreds of thousands of refugees. In 1962, Rwanda achieved independence—with a Hutu government led by the first president, Grégoire Kayibanda. The ethnic strife continued. The exiled Tutsi made several coup attempts and thousands of people died in reprisals.

Early indications of conflict

Kayibanda's government ended in 1973 after he had been accused of favouring people from his own region and he was overthrown in a coup by the Hutu army chief, General Juvénal Habyarimana. More violence followed, with massacres of both Hutu and of Tutsi, more of whom fled to Uganda and Burundi. In a one-party state, Habyarimana was subsequently elected at the head of the Mouvement révolutionaire national pour le développement (MRND)—and re-elected in 1989.

Violence surged again in 1990 when the exiled Tutsi united as the Rwandan Patriotic Front (RPF) and launched another series of offensives. Meanwhile, under donor pressure the Hutu government had allowed other political parties to organize, and in 1991 Habyarimana agreed to the formation of a transitional government with the participation of opposition parties. In 1993, this government made a peace agreement with the RPF at Arusha in Tanzania, though many in the MRND opposed this and started training Hutu militias, the 'Interahamwe'.

In 1994, President Habyarimana died in a plane crash. MRND dissidents took over and together with the Rwandan army they launched a genocidal massacre, mostly of the Tutsi. In response, the RPF intensified its campaign and by July 1994 had taken over the country. This ended the genocide, but by then up to 1 million people had died.

The RPF have remained in power. They have included Hutu leaders in government but are reluctant to hold a full-scale election. In 1996, trials began of those accused of the genocide—a number of whom have since been executed. At the same time the Interahamwe, now based in the Democratic Republic of the Congo, have continued their attacks, particularly in the north-west, on what they call the 'Tutsi dictatorship'.

Until April 2000, the president was, Pasteur Bizimunguy, an ethnic Hutu, but he resigned and the electoral college replaced him with Paul Kagame, an ethnic Tutsi, who in any case had really been running the country, as vice-president.

Rwanda received more than $2 billion in aid between 1994 and 1999, and aid now finances two-thirds of the state budget.

St Lucia

A Caribbean island nation building a diverse economy

Land area: *620 sq. km.*	
Population: *160,000—urban 37%*	
Capital city: *Castries*	
People: *Black 90%, mixed 6%, East Indian 3%, white 1%*	
Language: *English, French creole*	
Religion: *Roman Catholic 90%, other 10%*	
Government: *Constitutional monarchy*	
Life expectancy: *70 years*	
GNP per capita: *$PPP 4,610*	
Currency: *East Caribbean dollar*	
Major exports: *Bananas, clothing, cocoa, vegetables, fruits, coconut oil*	

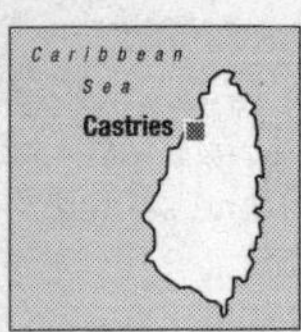

St Lucia is a volcanic island in the Caribbean, and subterranean activity surfaces via a number of hot springs. The mountain range that runs from north to south still has some dense forest cover though most of the land lower down has been cleared for agriculture.

Most St Lucians are black and English-speaking. But there is also a French influence: the majority are Roman Catholic and many also speak a French creole language.

Around 40% of the labour force work in agriculture on small farms that take advantage of generally fertile soil. They raise subsistence crops such as breadfruit and cassava. In addition, many have traditionally grown bananas which are the country's leading export.

But in recent years prices for bananas have been low. As a result, almost half of St Lucia's banana farmers are thought to have quit in the 1990s and their numbers are still falling. The situation will get worse when the island loses its preferential access to the EU.

The other main source of income is tourism. The island has a number of beach resorts that provide all-inclusive holidays. More than a quarter of a million visitors stay each year, and there is a similar number of short visits by cruise-ship passengers. Most tourists come from Europe and the USA. Poorer St Lucians argue that relatively little of the income percolates down to them.

Manufacturing output is more diverse than in other Caribbean islands. As well as processing agricultural goods, local factories produce clothing and assemble electronic items.

St Lucia is a parliamentary democracy with the British monarch as its head of state represented locally by a governor-general. The first elections after independence in 1979 were won by the St Lucia Labour Party (SLP), which established links with Cuba and North Korea. In 1982, power passed to the more conservative United Workers' Party (UWP), which opened up the economy and embarked on a series of IMF structural adjustment programmes.

However, these measures failed to relieve persistently high levels of unemployment—30% or more—and this, combined with allegations of corruption, contributed to the UWP's downfall in the 1997 elections. The SLP won convincingly and Dr Kenny Anthony took over as prime minister, though since its earlier period in office the SLP has shifted towards the centre.

St Vincent & the Grenadines

Rural poverty alongside hedonistic luxury

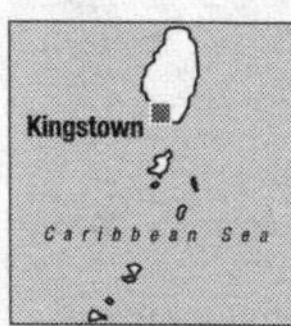

The country comprises one main island, St Vincent, which has around 90% of the territory and population, and the Grenadines, a group of 30 or more smaller islands, or cays, to the south. St Vincent is rugged and mountainous, with an active volcano, Soufrière, which last erupted in 1979.

Much of St Vincent is covered with dense tropical rainforests. The Grenadines have white sandy beaches and coral reefs.

There are still a few of the original Carib Indians, but most of the people on St Vincent, who are concentrated on the coast, are black or mulatto. They depend for survival primarily on agriculture, growing subsistence crops such as sweet potatoes and plantains.

The main cash crop, and the core of the country's economy, is bananas. These are grown both on small farms and large estates. New irrigation projects have boosted production and quality. But the loss of preferential access to the EU will strike a severe economic blow, and add to already high unemployment, which in 1999 was officially 25%.

Efforts to diversify have had limited success, though marijuana could now be the second-largest export. US marines arrived in 1998 to destroy an estimated $1 million-worth of the crop, prompting local farmers to demand compensation from President Clinton.

Land area: *390 sq. km.*
Population: *113,000—urban 51%*
Capital city: *Kingstown, 16,000*
People: *Black 70%, mulatto 20%, other 10%*
Language: *English, French creole*
Religion: *Protestant, Roman Catholic*
Government: *Constitutional monarchy*
Life expectancy: *73 years*
GNP per capita: *$PPP 4,090*
Currency: *East Caribbean dollar*

The Grenadines are famous for secluded luxury tourism on islands like Mustique, and are occasionally home to celebrities, but the islands also attract more than 60,000 other tourists each year, as well as many visitors from cruise liners.

The Grenadines have a drugs trade too, though in this case the drug is cocaine: the Grenadines are said to tranship 10% of Colombia's cocaine traffic to the USA.

A small offshore financial sector provides another source of income—sustained by strict legislation to preserve secrecy and a declared policy not to co-operate in cases of foreign tax evasion.

The country is a constitutional monarchy whose head of state is the British monarch, represented by a governor-general. Government is based on a two-chamber legislature, with a fifteen-member house of assembly and a six-member appointed senate.

Since 1984, the government has been in the hands of Sir James Mitchell and the New Democratic Party. It looked as though he would lose in 1998 to the opposition parties which had merged to form the Unity Labour Party. But in the event he narrowly scraped through again.

Samoa

Samoa is forging closer links with its American neighbour

Land area: 3,000 sq. km.
Population: 176,00—urban 21%
Capital city: Apia, 34,000
People: Samoan
Language: Samoan
Religion: Christian
Government: Constitutional monarchy
Life expectancy: 69 years
GNP per capita: $PPP 3,440
Currency: Tala
Major exports: Copra, cocoa

Samoa, which in 1998 changed its name from Western Samoa, consists of two principal Pacific islands: Upolu and Savai'i—volcanic islands surrounded by coral reefs. Less than one-quarter of the territory is covered by tropical forests. Samoa lies just east of the international date line, so had the dubious distinction of being the last country to enter the 21st century.

Two-thirds of Samoans live on Upolu. Standards of human development are fairly high. The literacy rate is close to 100% for both men and women, and the leading diseases are those associated with a rich lifestyle, including hypertension, diabetes, and coronary heart disease. Although fertility rates are high, population growth has been slowed by emigration.

Two-thirds of the workforce are engaged in agriculture, mostly working on communally owned land. As well as growing subsistence crops, such as breadfruit and taro, they also grow the cash crops that produce the country's major exports—including cocoa and coconuts. Samoa also has substantial forest reserves, though these are being depleted by illegal logging and land clearance. Both agriculture and forestry are often affected by the cyclones that regularly hit the islands. Fishing has also expanded in recent years, primarily for tuna.

Samoa has been strengthening its links with neighbouring American Samoa—though the country's change of name to Samoa caused some friction between the two. Cooperation helps promote tourism; the islands between them welcome more than 70,000 visitors each year. Closer integration should also help boost trade; Samoa sends tuna to be canned in American Samoa, it also exports large quantities of beer to American Samoa.

Since independence from New Zealand in 1962, Samoa has been a constitutional monarchy, based on traditional systems of authority. The head of state is the high chief, who in 2000 was Malietoa Tanumafili II. When he dies his successor will be elected by the legislature, the Fono. The power structure is also influenced by the heads of the extended family, the matai. Until 1990, the matai also made up the majority of people entitled to vote.

Since 1982 the government has been formed by the Human Rights Protection Party, whose co-founder, the long-serving Tofilau Eti Alesana, again became prime minister after the 1996 elections. On his death in 1999, he was succeeded by Tuilaepa Sailele Malielegaoi.

São Tomé and Príncipe

Bankrupted by political rows and falling cocoa earnings

Land area: *1,000 sq. km.*
Population: *142,000—urban 56%*
Capital city: *São Tomé , 50,000*
People: *Mestiço, African*
Language: *Portuguese, creole languages*
Religion: *Roman Catholic, Protestant*
Government: *Republic*
Life expectancy: *64 years*
GNP per capita: *$PPP 1,350*
Currency: *Dobra*
Major exports: *Cocoa*

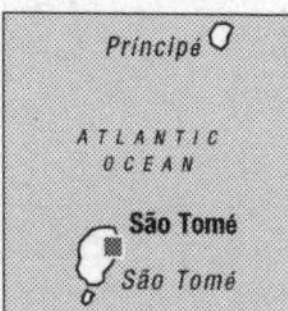

This small country consists of two main volcanic islands, as well as a number of smaller islets, in the Gulf of Guinea off the coast of West Africa. São Tomé has around 85% of the land area and almost all the people.

The islands were largely uninhabited until the Portuguese established plantations here—producing first sugar, then coffee, and now cocoa. Today, most people are of mixed race, though of distinctly defined origins.

The forros, the ruling élite, are of Portuguese-African origin. The angolares are descendants of slaves from Angola. The serviçais, are descendants of former contract labourers from Angola, Cape Verde, and Mozambique. Half the population still live in the rural areas, mostly on plantations.

In 1975, when the country achieved independence, the plantations passed into state hands. Largely as a result of subsequent poor management, production of the main crop, cocoa, dropped by more than half, though this still accounts for almost all the country's export earnings. There is also limited production of coffee. The second largest source of foreign exchange is licences from foreign vessels, mostly from Europe, fishing for tuna.

Poor management, falling world prices and political turmoil, have brought the country to its knees. Poverty has escalated and unemployment in 1998 was over 75%. By the mid-1990s, debt had rocketed to five times the GDP and by 1998 external aid accounted for 70% of GDP. So far, a series of IMF and World Bank-directed structural adjustment programmes have imposed strict austerity measures but brought little benefit.

Since independence, the government has largely been controlled by the Movimento de Libertação de São Tomé e Principe (now the MLSTP-PSD). Initially this was a Marxist party and until a new constitution in 1990 it was the only legal one. Today the political scene has less to do with ideology than with personal power struggles and party infighting. Between 1991 and 1999, there were seven governments.

Much of the internecine conflict has been between the National Assembly and the president, who has wide and loosely-defined powers. Miguel Trovoada was re-elected president in 1996 and Guilherme Pósser da Costa was appointed prime minister in 1999, after a 1998 election in which the MLSTP-PSD obtained an absolute majority. The feuding continues.

Saudi Arabia

Even Saudi Arabia has to tighten its belt when expenditure outpaces income

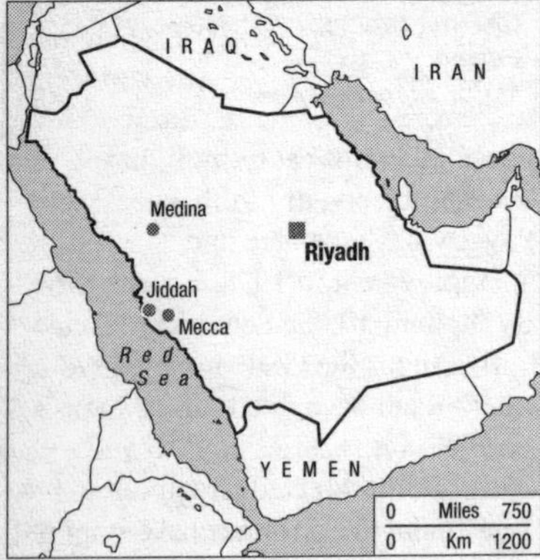

Land area: *2,150,000 sq. km.*
Population: *21 million—urban 85%*
Capital city: *Riyadh, 1.8 million*
People: *Arab 90%, Afro-Asian 10%*
Language: *Arabic*
Religion: *Muslim*
Government: *Monarchy*
Life expectancy: *71 years*
GNP per capita: *$PPP 10,120*
Currency: *Riyal*
Major exports: *Oil*

Along the Red Sea, Saudi Arabia has a narrow coastal plain. From here the land rises sharply to highlands that vary from 1,500 metres in the north to 3,000 metres in the south. Beyond these western highlands is a vast plateau that descends gently to the eastern coast along the Persian Gulf. In the centre of this plateau is the rocky expanse of the Najd, around which circles an arc of desert, which includes in the south the world's largest area of sand, the Rub' al-Khali—the 'empty quarter'. Saudi Arabia has no rivers and must take all its water from underground sources.

The native population is almost entirely Arab, though along the Red Sea coast there is also a black population. This is the original home of Islam. Most people are Sunni Muslim, but there are also up to 2 million Shiah Muslim who live largely in the east and have suffered repression. Many live abroad in exile. The population is growing fast—3.3% per year. Saudi Arabian citizens generally have benefited from the oil wealth. All receive free education and health care, and enjoy a wide range of subsidies. Those not independently wealthy are also entitled to a plot of land.

Though women have traditionally been kept behind closed doors, and are still not allowed to drive, their education levels are rising and many are now entering businesses. They can also take full advantage of the internet—two-thirds of Saudi users are women.

Around one-quarter of the resident population consists of foreigners. This includes immigrant workers from other Arab countries and from South and South-east Asia, who do the more menial jobs as well as Europeans and Americans who do more specialized or technical work. Nevertheless with lower oil prices the boom years now seem to be over. Since the population has been growing faster than the economy Saudi Arabia's per capita income has been falling—it has more than halved in the past 20 years. As a result, Saudi nationals are having to accept more routine jobs, and are now appearing as security guards and taxi drivers.

Most economic activity revolves around oil, which is responsible for more than one-third of GDP, three-quarters of government revenue, and 90% of exports. Saudi Arabia has the world's largest oil reserves—one-quarter of the global total. This is extracted from huge oil-fields—most of which are in the east, though there have also been discoveries elsewhere. At current rates of extraction reserves should last eighty years or more.

The business is almost entirely in the hands of the government through Saudi Aramco. As well as having local refineries, the company also owns extensive refining and marketing operations in other countries.

Saudi Arabia has other important natural resources. Thus it has 4% of global gas reserves and is well endowed with many other minerals, including gold, iron, copper, and phosphates. Having concentrated on oil, it has barely exploited these, but is planning to do so in the future.

The government has been making efforts to diversify and to encourage and build industries that would offer more employment—including petrochemicals, fertilizers and steel. It has also been making greater efforts to attract foreign investment.

Exhausting underground water

Despite its lack of water, and its under-developed agriculture, the country in the 1980s aimed to be self-sufficient in food, even in wheat. This meant extracting huge quantities of water from underground aquifers at rates that would exhaust the resource in around thirty years. Wheat production costs are four times the world price. In recent years, however, the government has been withdrawing subsidies and encouraging farmers to grow vegetables.

Another source of income is tourism. The annual 'haj' pilgrimage to Mecca draws in around 1.6 million foreigners a year, many of whom take advantage of the opportunity to stock up on consumer goods. The government is now more interested in promoting tourism and has set up a tourist board.

Since the 1930s Saudi Arabia has been governed by the Al-Saud family, which in its various branches has 20,000 members, many of whom pursue a profligate lifestyle. The current leader is King Fahd, though since he is in poor health much of the responsibility has already passed to his chosen successor, 71-year-old Prince Abdullah.

Successive kings have usually governed with some degree of consultation and in 1992 Fahd introduced a 'Basic Law' which serves as a kind of constitution. There is also the Majlis al-shura, a consultative council with 90 appointed representatives, chiefly from former officials and tribal leaders.

The Al-Saud rulers have governed with some skill, using their extensive patronage to dampen dissent. The most direct opposition comes from radical Islamic clerics who, along with their supporters, have frequently been jailed. Their chief complaint is Saudi Arabia's liaison with the USA which still maintains military bases. Meanwhile the royal family's lavish expenditure continues. A current pet project of one of Fahd's sons is a replica of Spain's Alhambra palace.

Senegal

Senegal's democracy has finally produced a change in government

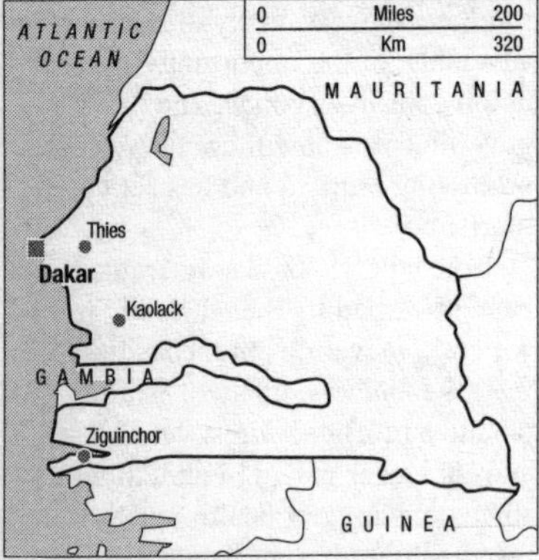

Land area: *197,000 sq. km.*
Population: *9 million—urban 46%*
Capital city: *Dakar, 2 million*
People: *Wolof 36%, Fulani 17%, Serer 17%, Toucouleur 9%, Diola 9%, Mandingo 9%, other 3%*
Language: *French, Wolof, Pulaar, Diola, Mandingo*
Religion: *Muslim 92%, indigenous beliefs 6%, Christian 2%*
Government: *Republic*
Life expectancy: *52 years*
GNP per capita: *$PPP 1,710*
Currency: *CFA franc*
Major exports: *Fish, chemicals, groundnuts, cotton, phosphates*

Senegal's northern border is formed by the Sénégal River whose valley provides a fertile strip of land. This soon gives way in the south and west to the flat, dry savannah of the Sahel, suitable only for raising livestock. The centre of the country consists largely of grasslands that are used more intensively for agriculture. Further south, beyond the 'finger' of the Gambia, a country that Senegal completely encloses, the Casamance region is greener, with more dependable rainfall and some tropical forests.

Senegal has more than a dozen ethnic groups of whom the largest are the Wolof, who are found particularly in the west. They make up only around two-fifths of the population and their language is also spoken by many others—though the official language remains French. Another large group, found in the west, are the Serer. Senegal also has a large number of Fulani (or Peulh). They are found throughout the country, and although traditionally they raise livestock many are now settled farmers. One of the politically most powerful groups is the Islamic Sufi sect, the Mourides.

The most significant dissident group are the Diola people in the Casamance region in the south who feel they have been exploited by northerners. Their armed organization, the Mouvement des forces démocratiques de la Casamance, signed a peace agreement in December 1999, but there have been frequent violations.

Senegal is more developed than its immediate neighbours, and Dakar is one of the region's more cosmopolitan cities, but the Senegalese are still very poor. More than half the population are below the poverty line, only one-third are literate, and average life expectancy is 52 years.

Most people still depend directly or indirectly on agriculture, typically in small farms using basic production methods. The main food crops are sorghum and millet, grown in the north and centre, and rice in the Senegal river valley and in the Casamance region in the south. Even so, Senegal is a net importer of rice.

Most farmers also grow cash crops, of which the most important traditionally has been groundnuts. Groundnuts were also the main export earner but harvests over the last decade have been affected by erratic rainfall, and government income has been reduced by extensive smuggling of the crop into the Gambia where it has fetched a better price. Another important cash crop is cotton. Livestock production too has been affected by drought and the country also has to import meat.

Senegal's Atlantic coastal waters are a rich source of fish, particularly tuna. Most is caught from small boats by fishermen, who make up 15% of the workforce, but there is also industrial fishing. Tuna is canned and exported to the EU. The industry has expanded recently, making fish the largest source of export income, but over-fishing and increasing international competition have been reducing Senegal's tuna sales.

Catching too much tuna

Senegal is one of the more industrialized countries in West Africa though productivity is not very high. Most manufacturing involves processing local raw materials. Thus, in addition to the fish canneries, there are groundnut-crushing mills, and four cotton ginning plants, as well as textiles factories.

There is also a significant chemicals industry, based on the deposits of phosphates in the west of the country. This produces phosphoric acid and fertilizer for export.

Senegal has a reputation for being more democratic than most African countries, though in fact for the first four decades after independence in 1960 it was ruled by the same party, now called the Parti socialiste (PS). The PS tended to win largely because of its power of patronage and a system that deliberately blurred the lines between the state, the government, and the party. And over the years the whole system had become increasingly corrupt.

From 1981 to 2000 the president was Abdou Diouf. He and the PS won elections in 1983 and 1988—though the main opposition party, the Parti démocratique sénégalais (PDS) and its leader Abdoulaye Wade alleged that the elections were fraudulent. In 1991, under pressure from donors, Diouf brought Wade into the government.

Change came at last in February 2000. Wade had been gathering greater support from the younger urban population, and from the Mourides, and won the presidential election with 60% of the vote.

To his credit, Diouf accepted defeat with good grace and stepped aside—one of the few elected African presidents to have done so.

Wade finally arrived in office at the age of 74. He has suggested that he might instigate constitutional changes, reducing the holding of presidential office to a limit of two-five year terms. His more immediate preoccupation has been to get on good terms with France, which is Senegal's main trading partner and its major donor. He has also promised that the dispute in Casamance will be resolved.

Sierra Leone

As a result of incessant warfare Sierra Leone has sunk to last place in UNDP's human development index

Land area: *72,000 sq. km.*
Population: *5 million—urban 35%*
Capital city: *Freetown, 470,000*
People: *Mende 30%, Temne 30%, and many smaller groups*
Language: *Mende, Temne, Krio, English*
Religion: *Muslim 60%, indigenous beliefs 30%, Christian 10%*
Government: *Republic*
Life expectancy: *37 years*
GNP per capita: *$PPP 390*
Currency: *Leone*
Major exports: *Rutile, diamonds, bauxite, cocoa*

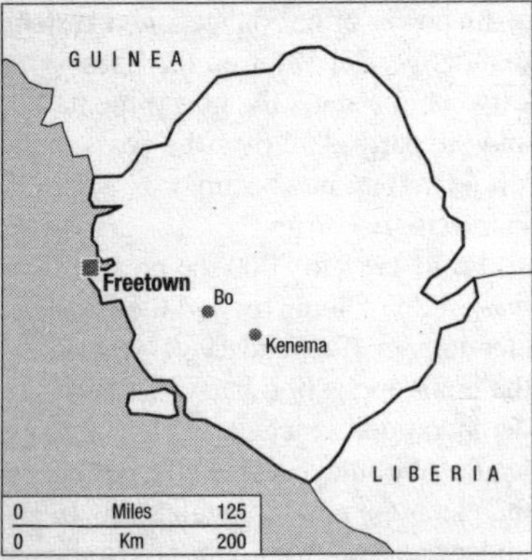

Sierra Leone takes its name ('lion mountain') from the distinctive shape of the mountainous peninsula that is the site of the capital, Freetown, and north of which there is a fine natural harbour. Most of the coastal area however is swampy for about 60 kilometres inland. Beyond this for around 100 kilometres is a broad plain of grasslands and woods, rising to a plateau broken by mountains that covers the eastern half of the country.

Sierra Leone's largest ethnic groups are the Temne and the Mende, each of which incorporates many subgroups. There is also a small population of Krios—descendants of liberated slaves who settled here from the end of the 18th century. Though few in number, they have had a disproportionate influence in the professions and the civil service.

Sierra Leone's people have one of the world's shortest life expectancies—37 years. More than one-quarter of children die before their fifth birthday and around 2% of all births result in the death of the mother. They can count on little medical support as public health services barely function. Education standards are low. Less than one-third of the population is literate.

The level of human development, already low, is sinking further in a country torn apart by violence. In recent years, half a million people fled to neighbouring countries and even more were internally displaced, deserting the rural areas for the relative safety of the cities, where they added to already critical problems of over-crowding, poor sanitation, and poverty.

Prior to the most recent phase of fighting, around two-thirds of people made their living from agriculture, principally growing rice along with cash crops such as food and coffee. Indeed, Sierra Leone was a major rice exporter. But for most of the 1990s its people have had to rely largely on food aid. With the prospect of a reduction in the fighting, some farmers started to return to the land, but it will be some years before full production can be resumed.

Sierra Leone should have been able to invest in much higher standards of human development, given its rich mineral resources. In the south it has extensive deposits of rutile (titanium ore) and bauxite (aluminium ore) that in the past provided the bulk of the country's export earnings. Again, the fighting has dramatically cut production.

Sierra Leone's other main mineral output—diamonds—has also been affected by the fighting, if less so. Because the diamonds are alluvial, larger mining companies can use mechanical systems but individuals can simply dig and pan. Informal mining is easier to sustain in the middle of a war but the resulting diamonds are also more likely to be smuggled out of the country.

Since independence in 1961, Sierra Leone has suffered from economic mismanagement and corruption on a grand scale. For two decades after 1970 this was effectively a one-party state. The government was overthrown partly as a result of the spillover of the fighting in neighbouring Liberia when in 1991 a local rebel group the Revolutionary United Front (RUF), with Liberian help, launched an uprising in the south-east.

Corruption on a grand scale

Then in 1992, a group of army officers, who had been fighting with the rebels staged a coup. This intensified the ferocious civil war that killed around 15,000 people, and drove millions of people from their homes. The RUF were particularly brutal, recruiting thousands of child soldiers and frequently cutting the hands off anyone who got in their way.

It was not until 1996, following a peace accord signed in Abidjan, that Sierra Leoneans had the opportunity to vote in an election. They chose Ahmed Tejan Kabbah, a former UN bureaucrat, as president. For a while it looked as though this might lead to a lasting peace. Hopes were dashed, however, in 1997 when the same army officers staged another coup and invited the RUF led by Foday Sankoh to share power. The Economic Community of West African States, and its peacekeeping force ECOMOG, largely with Nigerian troops, helped to restore Kabbah as president.

But the fighting continued until a UN-sponsored peace deal in July 1999. This kept Kabbah as president but gave the RUF four cabinet posts, and put Sankoh in charge of diamond mining. The agreement was heavily criticized by international human rights groups, who argued that it rewarded Sankoh for his butchery, and they doubted it would work. In the event they were proved right. The RUF did not disarm and in April 2000, when Nigerian peacekeepers handed over to UN troops, the RUF captured hundreds of UN soldiers and started to advance towards Freetown.

This alarmed the international community, and particularly the former colonial power, the UK, which sent troops to supervise the evacuation of foreigners. These troops were not part of the UN force and most were eventually withdrawn when a measure of stability was restored. Sankoh was captured in May 2000 but the RUF fights on.

Singapore

An autocratic city-state that has become a leading manufacturing and financial centre.

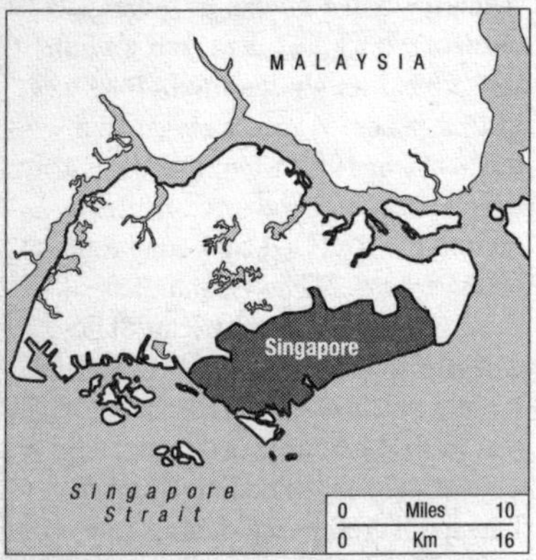

Land area: *643 sq. km.*
Population: *3.5 million—urban 100%*
Capital city: *Singapore 3.5 million*
People: Chinese 75%, Malay 15%, Indian 6%, other 4%
Language: *Chinese, Malay, Tamil, English*
Religion: *Buddhist, Muslim, Christian, Hindu*
Government: *Republic*
Life expectancy: *77 years*
GNP per capita: *$PPP 28,620*
Currency: *Singapore dollar*
Major exports: *Petroleum products, machinery, chemicals*

Singapore lies at the tip of the Malay peninsula, occupying the island of Singapore, along with 60 other adjacent islets. The city covers the southern part of the main island, but it has extended itself further so that there is now little distinction between the city and the countryside. There is a small, highly productive agricultural sector but this is essentially an urban environment.

Singapore has a diverse immigrant-based population. The majority are of Chinese origin, though since they come from a range of provinces they often speak different dialects. The Indian population is also disparate, including Tamils, Malayalis and Sikhs. The Malay population is linguistically more uniform. But most Singaporeans are at least bilingual and also speak English, the language of government and business. Previous racial tensions have declined.

Singapore's rapid development has also created labour shortages—at both the bottom and the top of the market. In 1998 there were 450,000 immigrant workers. This included 100,000 Filipina maids as well as 60,000 foreign professionals. The government has a well-organized system for controlling this workforce, involving special levies on employers.

In terms of purchasing power, Singapore is the world's fifth richest country. Standards of education and health are good. The education system is highly competitive, with a strong emphasis on the literacy and numeracy requirements of a modern economy—though there are worries that regimented instruction is producing workers who are not sufficiently creative.

Most of these workers are employed in manufacturing and services. Singapore has for a century or more been an important regional centre for trade and business, and since the early 1960s the government has relentlessly propelled the economy along a path of export-led growth.

Manufacturing accounts for one

quarter of GDP, around half of which comprised electronics: Singapore is now, for example, the world's leading producer of computer disk drives. Since the early 1970s, Singapore has become the world's third largest oil-refining centre—based on imported crude oil—and is a significant producer of chemicals and pharmaceuticals. It is also a centre for high-quality printing and publishing. Most of this activity is in the hands of 5,000 or so international companies along with a few large local enterprises.

A further one-quarter of GDP comprises finance and business services. Singapore's strong financial services sector combines a protected local banking system, dominated by four domestic banks, with a more open offshore banking sector. All are closely regulated.

Singapore's development has demanded a hectic process of construction. Until the mid-1980s this largely meant razing slums and replacing them with soulless apartment blocks and skyscrapers. More recently there have been attempts to preserve older buildings. High urban density has also created serious environmental problems, particularly from the automobile. In response, the government applies a sophisticated electronically monitored system of road pricing, along with a good network of public transport. One persistent problem is a shortage of water, which has to be piped from Malaysia.

Hectic construction of soulless apartments

This frantic expansion has been directed by a fairly autocratic government. For two years following independence in 1963, Singapore was part of the Malaysian Federation but it broke away in 1965 to become an independent country.

From the outset, Singapore has been governed by the multi-racial People's Action Party (PAP), which for three decades was presided over by Lee Kuan Yew, who became a major figure on the international stage—and a proponent of the idea that Singapore had succeeded because of distinctive 'Asian values'. In 1990, Lee stepped down in favour of the current prime minister Goh Chok Tong.

The PAP has shown little tolerance for opposition. A familiar tactic is to sue political opponents for defamation, often rendering them bankrupt and thus ineligible to stand for parliament. In the 1997 election the PAP won 65% of the vote and only two opposition candidates were elected. The government also maintains wide powers to detain people arbitrarily and to restrict their travel, freedom of speech, and rights to free association.

The government has a similarly fierce attitude towards the media, intimidating local journalists into self-censorship, and keeping a close watch on the foreign media.

The autocratic impulse also extends into the social sphere, with laws, for example, against chewing gum, and fines for not flushing public toilets. But Singapore's wholehearted embrace of the internet and its ambition to wire the country up as an 'intelligent island' could erode its efforts at tight control.

Slovakia

The poorer part of former Czechoslovakia has been slow to reform and has a dubious human rights record

Land area: *49,000 sq. km.*
Population: *5 million—urban 60%*
Capital city: *Bratislava, 441,000*
People: *Slovak 86%, Hungarian 11%, Romany 2%, other 1%*
Language: *Slovak, Hungarian*
Religion: *Roman Catholic 60%, atheist 10%, Protestant 9%, Orthodox 4%, other 17%*
Government: *Republic*
Life expectancy: *73 years*
GNP per capita: *$PPP 7,910*
Currency: *Slovak crown*
Major exports: *Manufactured goods, machinery*

Slovakia is dominated by the Carpathian Mountains. Three ranges run east to west and cover the northern half of the country. The highest point is in the Tatra Mountains—the Gerlachovský Peak at 2,655 metres. Most of the river valleys run north-south, so east-west communications are difficult. The main lowland areas are along the border with Hungary—one in the south-west including the capital Bratislava, and one in the east which includes the second city, Košice.

The majority of people are Slovaks but there are also important minorities. The largest group are ethnic Hungarians along the southern borders who since independence have been subject to increasing discrimination—especially against the use of their languages. There is also a sizeable Romany, or gypsy, population, officially 2% but probably nearer 5%, many of whom are concentrated in the Tatra Mountains and live in constant fear of racist attack. Thousands have fled overseas as refugees, particularly to the UK.

Health standards and life expectancy are lower than in the more developed European countries. Though curative health services are extensive, much less effort has gone into preventive health. As a result, men in particular have high death rates in middle age—probably the result of smoking, poor diet, and exposure to pollution. Education levels have been high, and secondary school enrolment increased in the 1990s.

Industry accounts for one-third of GDP but production has fallen steeply, particularly in armaments. During the Czechoslovakia period, Slovakia also transformed imported raw materials into intermediate products such as steel and chemicals to be sent to more sophisticated manufacturing plants in the Czech lands. This pattern has continued, though at lower levels of production. One serious consequence of industrialization has been pollution:

many factories have been located in valleys that trapped the smoke generated by burning brown coal.

By 1997, more than 80% of industry was ostensibly in the private sector, though often actually owned by state-controlled banks that obliged the firms to maintain high levels of employment. As a result, many have continued to function while technically insolvent.

Employment in agriculture fell steeply in the 1990s and by 1996 employed only 9% of the labour force. Nevertheless, production has been maintained and the country is largely self-sufficient in food. Privatization has been slower than elsewhere: by 1998, one-fifth of output still came from state farms. People who lost their jobs in industry and agriculture moved to services which by 1996 employed more than half the workforce. But at least 10% of people now work in the informal sector.

Slovakia breaks with the Czechs

Slovakia's peaceful transition to a democratic free-market system was part of Czechoslovakia's 'velvet revolution' in 1990. But differences soon emerged between the two parts of the country. Slovakians thought that economic liberalization was going too fast for their less-advanced economy and wanted greater autonomy. Matters came to a head after the elections of 1992. In Slovakia the leading party was the Movement for a Democratic Slovakia (HZDS), led by a hard-line nationalist, Vladimir Meciar. This consisted predominantly of nationalists and former communists. Meciar negotiated with the Czech prime minister the terms for the 'velvet divorce'—which was not subject to a referendum since the split actually had little public support in either part of the country.

On 1 January 1993 Slovakia became an independent republic with Meciar as prime minister and another HZDS politician, Michel Kovác, as president (elected by parliament). Meciar's heavy-handed authoritarian instincts soon came to the fore as he concentrated power in his own hands, stifling opposition and curbing the press. He temporarily lost power in 1994 but was soon back and intensified his repression and intimidation of ethnic minorities. This drew international condemnation and in June 1997 both the EU and NATO refused to consider Slovakia for membership because of a lack of democracy.

But by the elections of 1998 Meciar's grip was slipping and he lost power to a four-party centre-right coalition led by the Slovak Democratic Coalition (which itself is a group of five parties), with Mikulas Dzurinda as prime minister. Dzurinda set the country back on a more liberal path though he has had trouble in holding even his own part of the coalition together.

In May 1999, Slovaks had their first direct election for president and chose the government-backed candidate, Rudolf Schuster. Though Meciar lost the election, and in April 2000 was arrested on corruption charges, he remains a powerful and influential figure.

Slovakia is negotiating to enter the EU. Economically the country is now in better shape to join but its human rights record will prove an obstacle.

Slovenia

The richest country of ex-communist Europe and on course to join the EU

Land area: *20,000 sq. km.*
Population: *2 million—urban 52%*
Capital city: *Ljubljana , 0.3 million*
People: *Slovene 91%, Croat 3%, Serb 2%, Muslim 1%, other 3%*
Language: *Slovenian 91%, Serbo-Croatian 6%, other 3%*
Religion: *Roman Catholic 71%, other 29%*
Government: *Republic*
Life expectancy: *74 years*
GNP per capita: *$PPP 11,800*
Currency: *Tolar*
Major exports: *Manufactured goods, machinery, chemicals*

Slovenia is predominantly mountainous. The highest areas are the Julian and Karavanken Alps on the north-western borders with Austria and Italy. These descend to a sub-alpine region on the edge of which is the Ljubljana basin. Slovenia has a short strip of coastline, which includes attractive beaches as well as the major port of Koper.

Slovenia's people have more in common with Germans, Austrians, and Italians than with the other former Yugoslav republics to the south. Slovenia also acquired around 7,000 refugees from neighbouring republics as a result of the wars of the 1990s. State benefits are relatively generous, and the standard of living is on a par with some of the poorer countries of the EU, though liberalization has caused a rise in inequality.

Like other richer European countries, Slovenia is concerned about the ageing of the population since it offers relatively generous pension benefits.

Slovenia only had about one-tenth of former Yugoslavia's population, but was responsible for around 20% of the output and was effectively subsidizing the poorer republics. The years immediately following independence were difficult as Slovenia lost markets in the other republics, but the economy revived after 1993 as exporters found new buyers in the West. About 70% of trade is now with the EU.

Major manufacturing industries include metal products, furniture, paper, footwear, and textiles as well as chemicals and electronic appliances. Nevertheless, manufacturing industry has steadily been shrinking in significance and by 1997 was down to 28% of GDP.

After 1992, following the Law on Ownership Transformation, many of the previously 'socially owned' enterprises were transferred into private hands. Some went to investment funds or were sold for cash. But many others were transferred 'internally' to workers and management in exchange for ownership certificates, or for cash at heavily discounted rates. So far, Slovenia has not gone out of its way to attract foreign investment, and has discouraged companies who wanted to borrow abroad.

Agriculture has become steadily less important, employing no more than 1% of the workforce, mostly on small farms engaged in dairy farming and livestock rearing. Around half the country is covered in forests, most of which are still owned by the state.

Nowadays, most people work in services. Many are employed in trade and transportation: the high-tech port of Koper is a major outlet for goods from Austria. It also services trade between Eastern Europe and Asia: the port's largest customer is the South Korean car maker Daewoo. The capital, Ljubljana, is also at the crossroads of two of the EU's proposed new highways, from Venice to Kiev, and from Munich to Istanbul. Italy also has a strong interest in better links since its north-eastern city of Trieste is virtually surrounded by Slovenia.

Another important service industry is tourism, though so far most tourists are Austrians making day trips for cheap fuel, and Italians attracted by the casinos.

Relatively painless exit from Yugoslavia

By Balkan standards, Slovenia's independence struggle was relatively painless. Following the declaration of independence in June 1991, the Yugoslav army made a half-hearted attempt to reassert control, but the Slovenians fended them off in a largely bloodless ten-day war. In 1992, voters chose Milan Kucan for the largely ceremonial role of president. He is a former communist president and a skilled diplomat (who was re-elected in 1997). In the first post-independence parliamentary election in 1992 they also opted for familiar figures. The largest single party was the centre-left Liberal Democracy of Slovenia (LDS), led by Janez Drnovsek, a member of the previous communist establishment who had briefly served as president of Yugoslavia. Drnovsek formed a coalition that included the Slovene Christian Democrats.

Slovenia has continued to be ruled by members of the old communist establishment. At the end of 1996 voters once again made the LDS the largest party, though with fewer seats—which hampered coalition building. The government that emerged early in 1997, again headed by Drnovsek, also included the populist, centre-right Slovene People's Party and the smaller Democratic Party of Slovene Pensioners.

In April 2000, the government collapsed when the coalition lost one of its members. At this point a new figure emerged as a stop-gap leader, probably until the next election at the end of 2000. He is Andrej Bajuk, a recent returnee from Argentina—an unlikely choice since he scarcely speaks the language.

Slovenia is negotiating to join the EU. It will probably be one of the first former-communist countries to be accepted. Certainly its standard of living is approaching that of the EU's poorest members. And the EU will welcome a useful transport route for trade. Doubts will probably centre on the slow speed of privatization.

Solomon Islands

Ethnic tension has raised the prospect of civil war

Land area: *29,000 sq. km.*
Population: *415,000—urban 18%*
Capital city: *Honiara, 35,000*
People: *Melanesian 93%, Polynesian 4%, other 3%*
Language: *Solomon Islands Pidgin and other languages*
Religion: *Christian*
Government: *Constitutional monarchy*
Life expectancy: *70 years*
GNP per capita: *$PPP 2,080*
Currency: *Solomon Islands dollar*
Major exports: *Timber, fish, copra, palm*

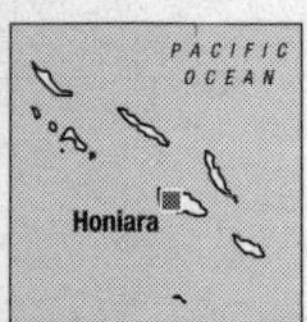

The Solomon Islands consists of several hundred islands stretched over approximately 1,500 kilometres. Many have steep mountain ranges and more than 60% of the country is forest or woodland. The main islands are Guadalcanal, Malaita, New Georgia, Makira, Santa Isabel, and Choiseul.

The population is almost entirely Melanesian, mostly living in scattered rural communities. The islanders have more than 80 indigenous languages, but most also speak Solomon Islands Pidgin and the official language is English.

In 1999, the country was shaken by an outbreak of ethnic violence in Guadalcanal in a struggle over land rights and jobs. Indigenous Guadalcanal islanders, the 'Isatambu Freedom Fighters', fought immigrants from Malaita, who responded through the 'Malaita Eagle Force'. The dispute led to a coup attempt in June 2000.

Most islanders rely on subsistence agriculture. Their principal cash crops are coconuts, palm oil, and cocoa. But the main sources of export income has been timber—which has provided more than 40% of government income. Logging accelerated during the 1990s and by 1997 timber was being felled at more than twice the sustainable rate—threatening a loss of most forest cover by 2010. Given the local vested interests, it has been difficult to reduce the felling and some overseas aid has been withdrawn in protest.

Fishing, primarily for tuna, is also an important source of food and of income. The islanders have one of the world's highest per capita consumptions of fish. The largest private-sector employer is the Solomon Taiyo tuna canning plant.

The country's head of state is the British monarch, represented by a governor-general who must always be a Solomon Islander. In 1999, this was Sir Moses Pitakaka. Politics tends to be organized around people and issues rather than ideas—Prime Minister Francis Billy Hilly, for example, was toppled in 1994 when he tried to enforce a moratorium on log exports.

The 1997 elections were won by a coalition, the Alliance for Change, from which Bartholomew Ulufa'alu emerged as prime minister. His immediate priority was to tackle an economic crisis, but ethnic upheaval made it difficult to take action. Matters came to a head in June 2000 when the Maita Eagle Force seized the capital during an attempted coup. Ulufa'alu was forced to resign, and was replaced by opposition leader, Mannasseh Sogavare.

Somalia

A 'failed state', fought over by rival clans, that somehow seems to function

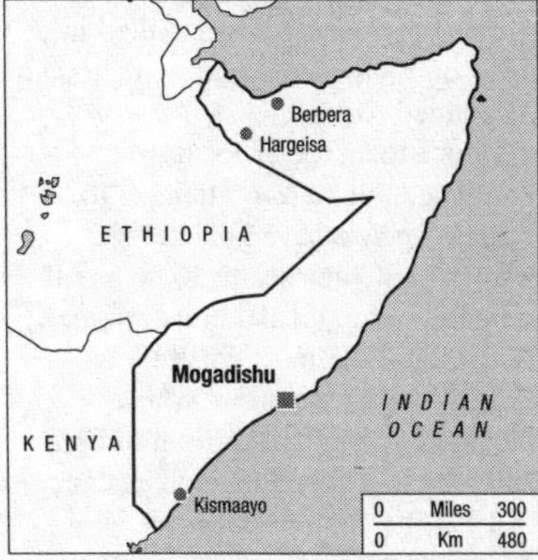

Land area: *638,000 sq. km.*
Population: *9 million—urban 24%*
Capital city: *Mogadishu, 1.0 million*
People: *Somali 85%, Bantu, Arab and others 15%*
Language: *Somali, Arabic, Italian, English*
Religion: *Sunni Muslim*
Government: *None*
Life expectancy: *47 years*
GNP per capita: *$PPP 210*
Currency: *Shilling*
Major exports: *Livestock, bananas (1990)*

Somalia is largely semi-desert. It has rough grasslands suitable for pasture but little arable land. The highest part of the country is in the north, where rugged mountain ranges face the Gulf of Aden. To the south of these lies the Hawd plateau, beyond which there are flat sandy plains with extensive dunes along the Indian Ocean coastline.

Somalis have always been desperately poor and the incessant wars of recent decades have made them even poorer. Health standards are low and deteriorating. One-fifth of children die before their fifth birthday. Only one-third of the population have access to safe water. The education system has virtually collapsed, and less than 10% of children enrol in primary school. There is also the ever-present threat of famine, whether from poor rains or from a collapse in the distribution system caused by the fighting. Dismal conditions in and around the refugee camps have also resulted in frequent outbreaks of cholera, which is now endemic.

UNHCR says that at one point 900,000 people fled to neighbouring countries. Many have since returned but there are still thousands outside the country, chiefly in Ethiopia and Kenya. In addition there are probably similar numbers internally displaced.

Through the civil war people still struggle to make a living. The most important source of income is rearing livestock—goats, sheep, and cattle. Two-thirds of the population are nomadic or semi-nomadic herders. Most of the others are farmers, growing sorghum and maize, chiefly in the river valleys. The most lucrative crop, and an important export, has been bananas. Indeed, some of the clan battles have been fought over control of banana production. Although Somalia, with its long coastline, could be a significant producer of fish most of the catch is taken by foreign vessels. Nevertheless, there are parts of the country that function fairly well commercially, and satellite telephone systems are building new trade networks.

Since independence in 1961, Somalia has been riven by ethnic and clan divisions. Following the assassination of a newly elected president in 1969, the army took over, led by General Mohammad Siad Barre. Siad Barre, initially with Soviet help, declared that his would be a non-tribal socialist government. However, his rule became increasingly authoritarian and his 'non-tribal' credentials were also undermined by choices of members of his own Marehan clan for senior positions.

Throughout the 1980s, the other clans formed a number of armed opposition forces and made an informal alliance against Siad Barre. There were three main groups: the United Somali Congress (USC—Hawiye clan); the Somali Patriotic Movement (SPM—Darod clan) in the centre and south of the country; and the Somali National Movement (SNM—Issaq clan) in the north. By January 1991, they had successfully driven Siad Barre from Somalia but they had less success forming a replacement government.

The USC claimed to establish an interim government but this was immediately rejected by the SPM, which started fighting USC forces in the south, and by the SNM, which in the north proclaimed independence for the 'Somaliland Republic'. Then the USC itself split between factions led by Ali Mahdi Mohammad and General Mohamed Farah Aideed, who fought for control of Mogadishu. Meanwhile, the country was stricken by a famine that killed 300,000 people.

Famine in the midst of war

An uncertain peace was established in 1992 with the arrival of a US-led UN peace-keeping force. This served as cover for the distribution of humanitarian aid but soon became bogged down in its efforts to exert military control and to capture Aideed, and there were frequent encounters between UN and Somali forces. In 1995, the UN's mandate ended and its forces withdrew. Aideed declared himself president but was killed in 1996 and replaced by his son Hussain Mohamed Aideed.

Since then, the chaos has continued. Numerous attempts to broker a peace have failed. The likeliest outcome seems to be based on building up local administrations.

Of these the most coherent is Somaliland in the north, whose president is Mohamed Ibrahim Egal and which declared its independence in 1991. Its capital, Hargeisa, is relatively prosperous with wage rates higher than in some other African countries. The population is around 2 million and most of the government revenue comes from customs duties. Services such as electricity and telecommunications are run by the private sector.

Another region which has been autonomous since the end of 1998, though it has not declared itself as a state, is Puntland, whose administration is based in the north-east. Each administration has been organized so as to strike a balance between the clans.

In early 2000 UN agencies and others struggled to deliver aid, faced with another drought. Meanwhile a number of other governments in the region were attempting a fresh peace initiative, though hopes receded when the war between Ethiopia and Eritrea flared up again since each supports rival factions.

South Africa

Post-Mandela South Africa is trying to heal the old wounds of apartheid

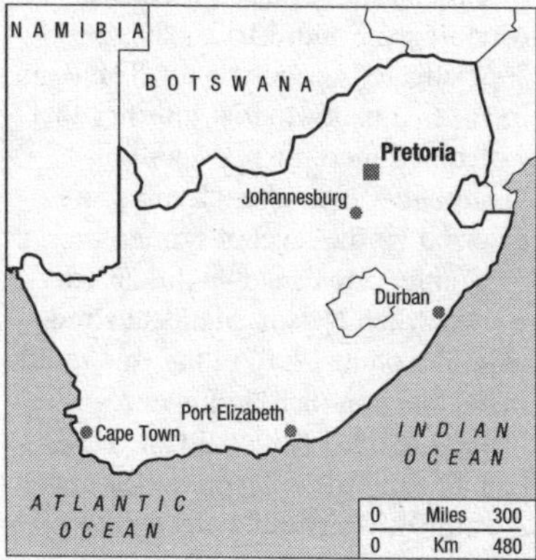

Land area: *1,221,000 sq. km.*
Population: *41 million—urban 50%*
Capital city: *Pretoria, 1.0 million*
People: *Black 75%, white 14%, coloured 8%, Indian 3%*
Language: *Afrikaans, English, Ndebele, Pedi, Sotho, Swazi, Tsonga, Tswana, Venda, Xhosa, Zulu*
Religion: *Christian 68%, traditional and animist 28%, Muslim 2%, Hindu 2%*
Government: *Republic*
Life expectancy: *55 years*
GNP per capita: *$PPP 6,990*
Currency: *Rand*
Major exports: *Gold, diamonds and other minerals and metals*

South Africa has narrow coastal plains in the east, west, and south. These rise to a chain of mountains that curves around the coast. The mountains are at their highest in the east where the Great Escarpment culminates in the Drakensbergs in the north. Within these mountains lies the vast plateau that makes up around two-thirds of the country.

Three-quarters of the population are black. The largest groups are the Zulu and the Xhosa, though official status has been extended to nine African languages. Of the white population, just over half speak Afrikaans, while the rest largely speak English. The 'coloured' population is of mixed African, Asian, and European descent and most speak Afrikaans. The majority of Asians originate from India and are English-speaking. In addition, there are thought to be up to 8 million illegal immigrants from neighbouring countries.

Since the end of apartheid and the first all-race elections in 1994, the government has been struggling to redress the injustices of apartheid—in a country where the per capita income of the richest 20% is sixteen times greater than that of the poorest 20%. The greatest success has been political—to keep this divided society together without major racial violence or a mass exodus of minority groups.

But the government has had less success with social programmes. Ambitious targets for housing, for example, are unlikely to be achieved. The education system is still in a poor state. And while there has been more investment in health, the infant mortality rate for black children is ten times that for white children. Around 60% of black South Africans live in poverty. The government in 2000 was planning to spend about 3% of GDP on welfare, including pensions, housing, and child-care. But the social security system is very inefficient so this target is unlikely to be achieved.

Exacerbating the poverty problem is the spectre of HIV/AIDS. Around

10% of the population are infected and one-third could eventually die. President Mbeki has disturbed many people by his willingness to believe dissident scientists who argue that AIDS is caused not by the HIV virus but by poor health and poverty.

In recent years there has also been an explosion of violent crime. In 1998, 20,000 people were murdered in South Africa, and on average two women are raped every minute. Few criminals are caught; they are more likely to die 'resisting arrest'.

South Africa's economic development has depended on its mineral wealth, which provides almost two-thirds of export earnings. It has the world's largest reserves of gold, along with many other minerals such as platinum and manganese, as well as diamonds, coal, and iron. Diamond mining is controlled by the De Beers company which has also dominated the world diamond market. South Africa's manufacturing companies process these minerals, as well as agricultural produce, and produce a wide range of consumer goods, though many enterprises that flourished in response to sanctions now struggle to match international competition.

De Beers dominates the world diamond market

Agriculture still employs one-quarter of the workforce. The main crop is maize, most of which is still produced on white-owned farms. Agriculture was deregulated from 1996, which encouraged many farmers to shift to higher value crops, but smaller farmers, predominantly black, have suffered as they cannot afford the necessary investment. Land reform has been very slow. A 1994 law allows people to claim ancestral property that had been seized during the apartheid years. But by early 2000 only 7% of the 63,000 claims had been settled.

Like more advanced industrial economies, South Africa has a sophisticated service sector. This includes a major tourist industry that welcomed more than 1.4 million visitors in 1998—though many are deterred by the level of crime.

South Africa's new political era started when Nelson Mandela strode from prison in 1990. In the first multi-racial election in 1994 his once-banned African National Congress won 63% of the votes in the National Assembly, which duly elected him president. The National Party, the Afrikaaner party that had ruled under apartheid still got 20% of the vote. The main post-mortem on the apartheid years was through a Truth and Reconciliation Commission presided over by Bishop Desmond Tutu, which granted amnesties to many perpetrators of violence.

When Mandela retired, his successor, Thabo Mbeki, led the ANC to an even more decisive victory in the 1999 election, though falling just short of the two-thirds majority that would have enabled it to change the constitution. The only all-black party is the Zulu-nationalist Inkatha Freedom Party. This election also saw the National Party eclipsed by the new and more liberal Democratic Party, which should offer more coherent opposition. Disturbingly, despite efforts by the main parties to broaden their appeal, most people continued to vote on racial lines.

Spain

Spain has taken rapid economic and social strides but is threatened once more by terrorist violence

Land area: *505,000 sq. km.*
Population: *39 million—urban 77%*
Capital city: *Madrid, 5.2 million*
People: *Spanish, though with strong regional identities*
Language: *Spanish, Catalan, Galician, Basque*
Religion: *Roman Catholic*
Government: *Constitutional monarchy*
Life expectancy: *78 years*
GNP per capita: *$PPP 16,060*
Currency: *Peseta*
Major exports: *Cars, chemicals, fruit, vegetables*

Spain, Western Europe's second largest country, is dominated by the Meseta, the vast and often barren central plain that covers more than two-fifths of the territory. Most of the people who live on the Meseta are in its centre, in Madrid, which was established there for political reasons. Otherwise, the most densely populated areas are those that encircle the plain.

This dispersal of population contributes to strong regional identities. Though Spain is racially fairly homogenous, it has major groups, such as the 2 million Basques in the north and the 6 million Catalans in the north-east, who are determined to defend their distinctive language and culture.

In future, however, there are likely to be fewer Spaniards of any kind. The average fertility rate has fallen to only 1.1 children per woman of child bearing age, and after around 2010 the population will start to fall.

Spain used to be a country of emigration. And even in 1998 remittances from people overseas were still worth $2 billion. But in the past decade there have been far more immigrants. Spain has 700,000 legal immigrants. Most come from other EU countries, though the largest single group is from Morocco. In addition there are probably a similar number of undocumented immigrants.

These immigrants have been attracted by Spain's new era of prosperity. Even under the dictatorship of General Franco, Spain had a spurt of economic growth. This continued after his death in 1975, and especially after Spain joined the EU in 1986.

Only 7% of the workforce is engaged in farming, but the country is a major exporter of wine, fruit, vegetables, and olive oil. The rural population is shrinking fast, in some regions by 5% per year, and much of the land is turning to desert—left untended and subject to droughts and forest fires. Rural communities on the coast also have the option of fishing—Spain's 17,000 or more boats are the largest fleet in Europe—but fishing too seems to be in decline. Of these boats, the 2,000 deep sea vessels that fish in foreign waters take the bulk of the catch.

Rather more healthy is Spanish industry. The Basque country has long been a centre of heavy industry and machine tools. And Catalonia has thousands of small companies thriving in sectors such as textiles and shoes. But the most striking success in recent years has been the car industry, the third-largest in Europe, turning out around 3 million cars per year of which 80% are exported. All the companies are owned by foreign transnationals.

Spain exports 80% of its car production

Agriculture and industry are now eclipsed by services, which now account for more than 60% of GDP. Of these, tourism is one of the most important. More than 50 million people arrive each year, making this the world's second most popular destination, after France. Most visitors on package tours head for the Mediterranean beaches of the Costa Brava and the Costa del Sol.

Despite Spain's economic advance, and its 1998 participation in Economic Monetary Union, major problems persist. The most serious is unemployment, which has been falling but was still 15% in early 2000.

Spain's recent renaissance dates from the end of the dictatorship of General Francisco Franco who died in 1975. The first free elections for forty years were held in 1977, and in 1978 the country adopted a new constitution that established a constitutional monarchy. One of its most significant elements was devolution, with the creation of seventeen autonomous regions. Each was to have its own government and parliament and wield progressively more power. The regions to which most power is devolved are the Basque country, Catalonia, and Galicia, each of which has its own police force as well as its own tax system that controls more than 30% of income-tax revenue.

The successful transition to democracy owes a huge debt to King Juan Carlos—especially his role in resisting a 1981 coup attempt by right-wing army officers. But one of the most significant political figures, opening the country up both economically and socially, was Felipe González, whose centre-left Partido Socialista Obrero Español (PSOE) governed from 1982 to 1996.

González and the PSOE were replaced after the 1996 election by the centre-right Partido Popular, led by José Maria Aznar. In March 2000, Aznar was re-elected with an outright majority. Previously, governments had had to be formed with the support of regionally based parties; now in theory Aznar need not take them into account. However he has said he will now work with them in an informal alliance.

The most serious problem remains in the Basque country, where 38% of voters in 2000 chose parties that favour independence. The smallest of these parties is Herri Batisuna whose terrorist arm, ETA, has since 1969 killed more than 800 people. At the end of 1999, after a fourteen-month ceasefire, ETA resumed its bombing campaign—prompting widespread popular street demonstrations against political violence.

Sri Lanka

Despite fifteen years of civil war, Sri Lanka has maintained respectable standards of human development

Land area: *66,000 sq. km.*
Population: *19 million—urban 23%*
Capital city: *Colombo, 615,000*
People: *Sinhalese 74%, Tamil 18%, Moor 7%, Burgher, Malay, and Vedda 1%*
Language: *Sinhala 74%, Tamil 18%, English 8%*
Religion: *Buddhist 69%, Hindu 15%, Christian 8%, Muslim 8%*
Government: *Republic*
Life expectancy: *73 years*
GNP per capita: *$PPP 2,490*
Currency: *Sri Lankan rupee*
Major exports: *Textiles, garments, tea, gems, chemical and rubber products*

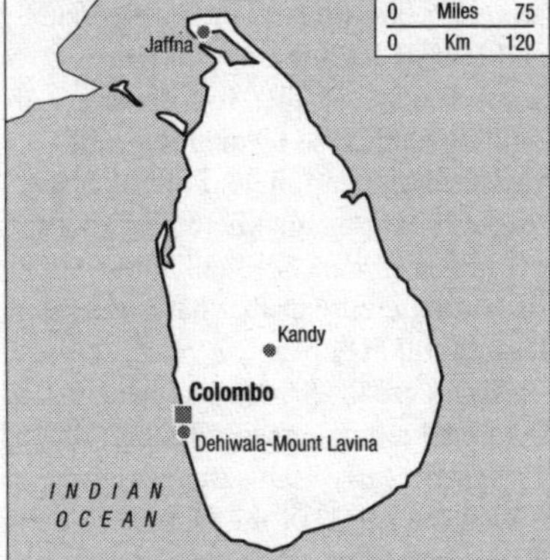

One-sixth of Sri Lanka consists of the Central Highlands in the south-centre. From these highlands a series of plains spread out, though rather than being flat they are traversed by a variety of ridges and valleys. Despite its relatively small size, Sri Lanka has distinct variations in rainfall, so there is a dry zone and a wet zone. The dry zone in the north and east relies for rainfall mostly on the annual monsoons. The wet zone is in the south-west. This is the heart of the country, with year-round rainfall and most of the cultivable land, as well as the bulk of industry and two-thirds of the people.

Three-quarters of the population are Sinhalese and Buddhist. But there are also significant minorities. The largest of these are the Tamils, which in turn are divided into two groups: half are the original 'Sri Lankan Tamils', who are generally better educated and live in the north of the island. The other half are 'Indian Tamils', descendants of people who came later during the colonial period to work on the tea plantations. Another, smaller, Tamil-speaking minority are the 'Moors', who are descendants of Arab traders. Sri Lanka's ethnic battles have primarily been between the Sinhalese and the Sri Lankan Tamils.

Despite years of conflict, in many respects Sri Lanka has been a human development success story. Successive governments have invested heavily in health and education. The results are impressive. Around 90% of the population are literate, and 93% have access to basic health facilities. Notably, Sri Lanka's successes have been shared equally between men and women. Nevertheless, unemployment remains high and around one-quarter of the population live below the poverty line. This has encouraged emigration. By the mid-1990s, around 9% of the population was working overseas—the majority being female domestic servants employed in the Middle East.

In 1977, the Sri Lankan government became the first in South Asia to liberalize and diversify its economy and pursue export-led growth. Since then, it has seen a rapid expansion of manufacturing industry which by 1997 was employing 16% of the labour force. The most dynamic industries have been garments and leather goods, which now account for about half of exports. But there are also other important industries, including food, chemicals, and rubber and petroleum products. Much of this was based on foreign investment, though this has slowed as a result of the ongoing conflict.

Agriculture remains important, employing around one-third of the labour force. Two-thirds of this is directed towards the domestic market, particularly the cultivation of rice, though one-quarter of the country's rice has to be imported. Sri Lanka's main agricultural exports—tea, rubber and, coconuts—are grown in the wet zone. Tea production is mostly on large plantations: Sri Lanka is the world's leading tea exporter. But rubber and coconuts, which are small-holder crops, have both stagnated as a result of low investment. A more buoyant source of export income in recent years has been the mining of gems, including sapphires and rubies, as well as semi-precious stones.

The world's leading tea exporter

It is paradoxical that such a relatively well-run country should be torn apart by a civil war. The roots seem to lie in the 1950s when the government changed the official language from English to Sinhala. Tamils argued that this and other measures discriminated against them. By the 1980s discontent had erupted into inter-communal violence as Sri Lankan Tamils embarked on a struggle for an independent Tamil homeland—Eelam, which is around one-third of the island in the north and east. Their armed group, which has around 4,000 fighters including many children, is the Liberation Tigers of Tamil Eelam (LTTE). In response, militant Sinhalese formed their own violent organization, and the security forces fought against both. For more than fifteen years Sri Lanka has suffered a civil war that has killed at least 50,000 people.

To its credit, Sri Lanka has remained a democracy. Through the 1980s and early 1990s the government was in the hands of the United National Party—whose leader Ranasingh Premadasa was assassinated by a Tamil suicide bomber in 1993. But the 1994 elections were won by a coalition group, the People's Alliance. The leading partner is the Sri Lanka Freedom Party whose leader Mrs Chandrika Kumaratunga was also elected president. Both were re-elected at the end of 1999.

Kumaratunga promised to bring peace and to negotiate with the Tigers' leader, Vellupillai Prabhakara. In February 2000 Norway tried to broker peace talks. But as yet the murders and bombings continue. By May 2000 the Tigers were close to taking the Jaffna peninsula.

The government responded to the crisis with emergency controls—introducing censorship, banning public meetings and establishing unlimited powers of arrest.

Sudan

Fighting continues between the Arabic north and the African south

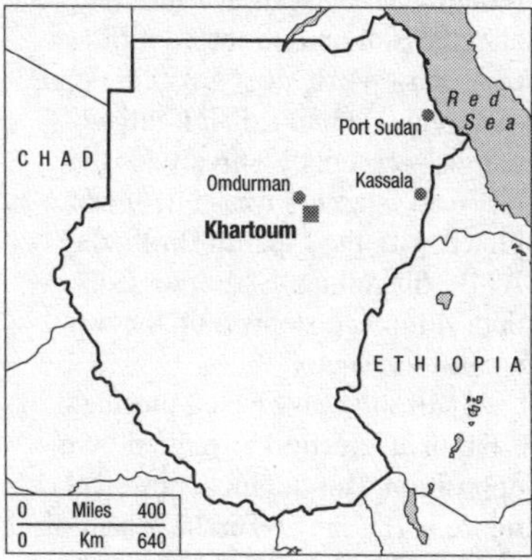

Land area: *2,506,000 sq. km.*
Population: *28 million—urban 33%*
Capital city: *Khartoum, 925,000*
People: *Black 52%, Arab 39%, Beja 6%, other 3%*
Language: *Arabic, Nubian, Ta Bedawie, many other languages*
Religion: *Sunni Muslim 70%, indigenous beliefs 25%, Christian 5%*
Government: *Republic*
Life expectancy: *55 years*
GNP per capita: *$PPP 1,360*
Currency: *Sudanese pound*
Major exports: *Sesame, cotton, livestock, groundnuts*

Sudan has three main geographical regions. The north, covering around one-third of the country, consists largely of an arid, rocky plain. The centre has low mountains and sandy desert. The more tropical south has extensive swamps and rainforests. One of the country's major features is the River Nile. The Blue Nile and the White Nile flow from the south, joining at Khartoum to form the Nile itself, which flows north into Egypt.

Sudan is ethnically very diverse, with more than a dozen major groups and hundreds of subgroups. The largest and politically the most dominant are the Sunni Muslim Arabs who live in the north and centre. Most of the other groups are black Africans who predominate in the south and are either Christians or animists. The southern region has around one-quarter of the population.

Sudan has a low level of human development. More than half the population are illiterate and only half the country's children enrol in primary school. Health standards too are very poor. Hospitals and clinics are primarily in the urban areas, while in the rural areas millions suffer from infectious diseases, particularly malaria and guinea worm. Poverty has been compounded by the long civil war. Since 1983, an estimated 1.9 million people have died in warfare. In 1998, around 4 million people were internally displaced, and 350,000 were refugees in neighbouring countries.

Sudan is heavily dependent on agriculture, which accounts for around half of GDP and employs two-thirds of the workforce. Sudan in theory could be a major agricultural producer. Most people are still working at the subsistence level, growing sorghum and millet, particularly in the south and also in parts of the centre and west. But Sudan also has a mechanized farming sector—the result of extensive government investment. Three-quarters of this is rain-fed, particularly in the area around the Blue Nile. The remainder of the mechanized sector relies on irrigation for food and cash crops. This includes the vast Gezira irrigation scheme south of Khartoum, between the White and Blue Niles, which waters the land of more than 100,000 tenant farmers. This was started in the colonial era for the production of long-staple cotton, which for decades was the country's leading export earner. More recently, however, cotton has been overtaken as an export crop by sesame seed.

Sudanese industry is limited, consisting largely of processing agricultural crops—refining sugar, for example, and producing cotton textiles. But industry generally has been restricted by low investment and by a shortage of skilled workers, since many Sudanese have emigrated to work in the Gulf. One of the most promising areas is oil. Large deposits were discovered in the south in the early 1980s but production and the laying of pipelines have been disrupted by rebel attacks.

Sudan's endemic civil war has its roots in the rebellion of a southern army corps in 1955 who were protesting at northern domination. A military coup in 1969, headed by Colonel Jafar al-Nimeiri, appeared to offer some respite and in 1972 the war stopped, following an agreement brokered by Ethiopia that granted the south cultural freedom and political autonomy.

A war that dates back to 1955

But in 1983 the war flared up again after the government rescinded this autonomy. Colonel John Garang led the rebellion of southern Sudanese People's Liberation Army (SPLA). Nimeiri turned to the Muslim Brotherhood for support, and in 1983, following his re-election, introduced Islamic sharia law. But following a crop failure and food riots in 1985 he was ousted in a bloodless military coup. A subsequent short-lived civilian government led by Sadiq el-Mahdi was replaced in 1989 by another Islamic-dominated military coup led by Brigadier Omar Hassan al-Bashir. He banned all political parties—except effectively for the National Islamic Front (NIF), which is linked with the Muslim Brotherhood. Al-Bashir ruthlessly suppressed opposition and stepped up the war against the south.

Al-Bashir was elected president in 1996 in an election boycotted by the opposition. But the most powerful figure is Hassan al-Turabi, leader of the NIF, which in 1999 was renamed the National Congress. In 1998, a new constitution legalized other parties and in 1999 al-Turabi was engaged in talks with both Nimeiri, who returned from exile, and with el-Mahdi, now a leading opposition figure. Meanwhile the war goes on.

The main peace broker in the Horn of Africa, the Intergovernmental Authority on Development (IGAD), early in 2000 seemed to have both sides agreed on a referendum to decide the country's future. Another initiative is being promoted by Libya and Egypt.

The combatants seem weary of the stalemate and could be prepared to talk. But it seems likely that they will step up the fighting in order to maximize their territory in advance of any settlement. The suffering continues, with the government denying relief supplies to rebel-controlled areas.

Suriname

Drug intrigues compound the problems of Suriname's fractious political system

Land area: *163,000 sq. km.*
Population: *413,000— urban 50%*
Capital city: *Paramaribo, 194,000*
People: *East Indians, 37%, creole 31%, Javanese 15%, Bosnegers 10%, other 7%*
Language: *Dutch, English, Sranang Tongo, Hindustani, Javanese*
Religion: *Hindu 27%, Muslim 20%, Roman Catholic 23%, Protestant 25%, indigenous beliefs 5%*
Government: *Republic*
Life expectancy: *70 years*
GNP per capita: *$PPP 3,400*
Currency: *Suriname guilder*
Major exports: *Alumina, aluminium, rice, bananas*

Suriname has a narrow, marshy coastal plain, but most of the country consists of a vast plateau along with ranges of mountains covered with dense tropical rainforests.

Suriname's complex ethnic mix reflects its colonial history. Today's Creole population are descendants of African slaves whom the Dutch brought to work on the sugar and coffee plantations. They were subsequently replaced by indentured workers from India and from Java—whose descendants now make up the majority of the population. Others include the Bosnegers, descendants of escaped slaves, and Amerindians.

Suriname is well endowed with natural resources. The most important of these is bauxite, which is mined by US- and South African-owned companies. All of this is processed within Suriname into alumina, and some into aluminium, taking advantage of cheap hydroelectric power at Afobaka, where the dam created one of the largest artificial lakes in the world.

Bauxite provides around three-quarters of export income. In addition, there are reserves of gold, nickel, and silver that have attracted the attention of Canadian companies.

Only a small proportion of GDP comes from agriculture, producing rice, fruit, and vegetables. But Suriname's vast tropical hardwood forests have drawn in foreign investment, notably from Asian logging companies, to the alarm of native people and many environmentalists.

Politics has in Suriname has frequently been marked by violence and overshadowed by the military. Following the 1996 National Assembly elections, the largest party was the pro-military National Democratische Partij, led by former military dictator, Desi Bouterse. Later the National Assembly elected Jules Wijdenbosch as president—at the head of a fractious five-party coalition.

Wijdenbosch has had a difficult time, with a collapsing currency whose value has been undermined by flows of drug money. In 1999, the Dutch government convicted Bouterse of cocaine smuggling and demanded his extradition—a difficult situation since Suriname relies on Dutch aid. In the face of widespread street protests in 1999, Wijdenbosch agreed he would step down after fresh elections.

Swaziland

Africa's longest surviving absolute monarchy faces labour unrest and AIDS

Land area: *17,000 sq. km.*
Population: *988,000—urban 33%*
Capital city: *Mbabane, 60,000*
People: *African 97%, European 3%*
Language: *Siswati, English*
Religion: *Christian 60%, indigenous beliefs 40%*
Government: *Monarchy*
Life expectancy: *60 years*
GNP per capita: *$PPP 3,580*
Currency: *Lilangeni*
Major exports: *Soft-drink concentrates, sugar, wood pulp, cotton yarn*

Swaziland can be divided into four regions from west to east. In the west is the Highveld, which rises to 1,400 metres and covers one-third of the country. This descends first to the Middleveld, and then the Lowveld, before reaching the Lubombo Mountains, which form the eastern border.

Almost all of the people are Swazi. Heavy investment in education has resulted in a 75% literacy level. Health standards are lower, with a relatively high infant mortality rate, and they are set to fall further still as a result of HIV/AIDS: in 1999, at least one-quarter of the population were carrying the virus.

Most economic activity is based directly or indirectly on agriculture. Landholdings are of two forms. Around 60% is Swazi National Land, held in trust by the king and used communally for rain-fed subsistence crops and livestock as well as for cotton. The rest is Title Deed Land, most of which is owned by corporations that irrigate it to grow sugar cane, citrus fruits and pineapples. These companies, like many of Swaziland's businesses, are in the hands of trusts controlled by the royal family.

Industrial activity is centred on processing agricultural goods. In 1986, Coca-Cola moved its concentrate plant from South Africa to Swaziland, responding to the pressure of sanctions as well as the opportunity for cheap sugar. Other similar companies have followed, and Swaziland's leading export is now soft-fruit concentrate.

Swaziland achieved independence in 1968 as a constitutional monarchy. This did not last. In 1973 King Sobhuza II suspended the constitution in what has been called the 'king's coup' and banned political activity. In 1986 his successor, King Mswati III, kept most of these restrictions in place and now rules as an absolute monarch. However, there is also some quasi-democratic representation, using the 'tinkhundla' system: members are elected to a house of assembly based on a show of hands.

The strongest organized opposition comes from the Swaziland Federation of Trade Unions, who have organized general strikes and have joined with the churches and other groups to form the Swaziland Democratic Alliance, which wants to see a return to a constitutional monarchy. Among their strongest cards will be alliances with trade unions in South Africa on whom Swaziland is heavily dependent for trade.

Sweden

Swedish social democracy has lost some of its gloss, but still has striking achievements

Land area: *450,000 sq. km.*
Population: *9 million—urban 83%*
Capital city: *Stockholm, 718,000*
People: *Swedish, Lapp (Sami)*
Language: *Swedish*
Religion: *Evangelical Lutheran 94%, other 6%*
Government: *Constitutional monarchy*
Life expectancy: *79 years*
GNP per capita: *\$PPP 19,480*
Currency: *Krona*
Major exports: *Manufactured goods, electrical machinery*

Sweden can be divided into three regions. The largest, in the north and centre, is Norrland, whose mountains and forests constitute around 60% of the country. In the far south is Götaland, which includes the Småland Highlands and, on the southern tip, the plains of Skåne. Between these, in the south-centre, is Svealand, a lowland area with numerous lakes.

Sweden's people until recent years were ethnically quite homogenous—the largest minorities being people of Finnish origin and small numbers of the reindeer-herding Sami in the north. From the 1970s, however, Sweden's liberal immigration and asylum policies welcomed people from further afield. By 1997, 1.7 million people, 19% of the population, were first- or second-generation immigrants. Of these one-third were from other Nordic countries; the largest numbers from elsewhere came from Yugoslavia, Iran, and Iraq.

Sweden's people enjoy one of the world's highest living standards. Between the 1930s and the 1970s, Sweden created an extensive welfare state which ensured that the benefits of economic growth were equitably distributed.

Some of the credit for this must go to a strong civil society, including well organized trade unions and a large number of voluntary organizations. Sweden has also created other institutions like the 'ombudsman', which many countries have since copied. By 1993, public-sector spending accounted for over 70% of GDP and employed one-third of the workforce. Most of this expenditure is based on local taxes spent by local governments.

Sweden's early industrialization had been based on raw materials like wood and iron ore, though it has neither coal nor oil and is heavily dependent on hydroelectric power. Minerals are still important: Sweden produces most of the EU's iron ore. But Sweden's investment in education also ensured that the country could move rapidly to higher levels of technology. In the internet age Sweden has the advantage that many of its people speak English well, and Sweden has one of the world's highest internet usage rates: almost 60% of the population are online. In early 2000 Stockholm had over 900 internet companies—the highest density in Europe.

This small country has also produced some of the world's leading manufacturing companies, including SKF, the world's largest producer of ball-bearings, and the Swiss-Swedish engineering group ABB. Some leading companies like Saab and Volvo have had their car divisions bought up by US companies, but Volvo and Scania are among the world's largest producers of trucks. And one of the most striking successes in recent years has been the telecommunications company Ericsson. As a result, Sweden has become a major trading country. In 1998, it exported 38% of its GDP. Remarkably, around 40% of the shares on the Stockholm stock exchange are controlled by one family, the Wallenbergs.

Sweden is also one of the world's most generous aid donors, giving more than 0.8% of GDP in official development assistance, one of the highest proportions in the world.

Sweden is a generous aid donor

Sweden's successful socio-economic model started to come under question in the 1970s and 1980s. Economic growth had slowed and could no longer support public expenditures. By the early 1990s the economy was deep in recession and unemployment had shot up to 8%. This forced the government to cut back on welfare spending. By the standards of other countries, these changes have been modest. Subsequently the economy has revived. Unemployment in 2000 was down to 5% and projected growth was around 3%.

For most of the period since the Second World War, Sweden has been governed by the Liberal Democratic Party (LDP), though often in co-operation with other parties. From 1969, the LDP was headed by Olaf Palme who in 1986 fell victim to one of the world's most unexpected assassinations.

He was replaced as prime minister by Ingvar Carlsson. By the 1991 election Sweden was deep in recession and the LDP lost heavily. Carlsson resigned and Carl Bildt took over as prime minister, heading a coalition led by his own Moderate (actually centre-right) Party along with the Centre, Liberal, and Christian Democrat Parties.

After the 1994 elections, the LDP returned, forming a minority government, but Carlsson resigned the following year to be replaced by Göron Persson. In the 1998 elections, the LDP lost ground and had to enter into an informal alliance with the Left Party (the former communists) and the Greens.

Though Sweden joined the EU in 1995, support is at best lukewarm. The LDP is divided; the Left Party questions membership of the EU and opposes Swedish membership of monetary union; the Greens are opposed to both. Meanwhile Persson continues with a pragmatic process of economic reform and gently squeezes social spending. But Sweden's decades of consensus are over, and political debates will sharpen.

Switzerland

Switzerland has joined neither the EU nor the UN, but could change its mind

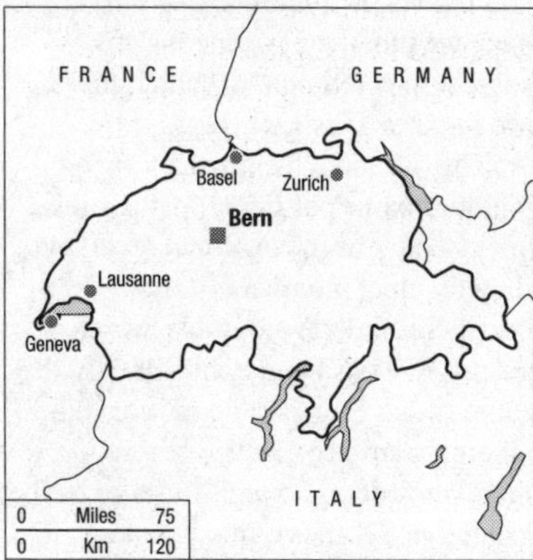

Land area: *41,000 sq. km.*
Population: *7 million—urban 62%*
Capital city: *Bern, 130,000*
People: *German 65%, French 18%, Italian 10%, Romansch 1%, other 6%*
Languages: *German 64%, French 19%, Italian 8%, Romansch 1%, other 9%*
Religion: *Roman Catholic 47%, Protestant 40%, other 5%, none 8%*
Government: *Republic*
Life expectancy: *79 years*
GNP per capita: *$PPP 26,620*
Currency: *Swiss franc*
Major exports: *Machinery, precision instruments*

Switzerland is one of Europe's most mountainous countries. More than two-thirds of its territory, to the south and east, is covered by the towering peaks of the Alps. Another eighth, running along the north-west border with France, is covered by the less dramatic Jura range. Lying between these, and occupying most of the rest of the country, is a plateau around 400 metres above sea level interspersed with hills. It is within this belt of land, stretching from Lake Geneva in the south-west to the Bodensee on the north-east border with Germany that most industrial and agricultural activity takes place, and where most people live.

Switzerland's population is formed by a conjunction of three European cultures: German, French, and Italian. A highly decentralized form of government, based on semi-autonomous states or 'cantons', has enabled these cultures to coexist and thrive. Switzerland thus has three official languages. The German-speaking majority live mostly in the north and east; the French in the south-west; and the Italian in the south-east. There is also a fourth, though not official, set of dialects—Romansch—which are also spoken in the cantons bordering on Italy.

Cultural diversity is further intensified by a large immigrant community, which makes up around 19% of the population. More than one-quarter are Italian, and another quarter, more recent arrivals, are from former Yugoslavia. These workers are very diverse: some are highly paid international business managers and bureaucrats; others are seasonal agricultural workers or hotel staff.

Poorly endowed with productive natural resources, Switzerland has relied for survival on the skills and ingenuity of its people. As with most richer countries, around two-thirds of the workforce is employed in service industries. In Switzerland, however, one of the most significant of these is banking: in 1994 Swiss banks managed more than $1.7 trillion and employed 120,000 people. Switzerland's banking secrecy laws have contributed to this success, though they have come under increasing criticism. In 1998, following accusations of collaboration with the Nazis in the Second World War, and of keeping the deposits of their victims, two banks agreed to pay $1.3 billion to settle Holocaust-related claims.

Industry in Switzerland has been weighted towards higher levels of technology in such areas as chemicals, pharmaceuticals, and the manufacture of precision instruments and watches. Engineering and food processing are also important.

The perennial strength of the Swiss franc hampers exports, but heavy investment in research has kept Switzerland at the technological leading edge. A notable achievement was that of the Swatch watch company in fending off the digital challenge from Japan. For a small country, Switzerland is also home to many multinationals, including CIBA, ABB, and Nestlé.

Swatch repels the Japanese challenge

Agriculture, whether growing crops on the plain or rearing livestock in the mountains, employs less than 5% of the workforce but is very productive and meets around 60% of local needs. It is also highly protected, and the expensive food produced encourages many Swiss to stock up in neighbouring countries. The beautiful Swiss countryside also draws in many tourists—over 11 million per year—though many are increasingly discouraged by the expense.

The most remarkable aspect of Switzerland, however, is its form of direct democracy. The central government is weak. First, because much of the power resides in the 23 cantons, each of which is responsible for education, hospitals, and taxation, and has its own judiciary. Second, because most vital decisions are subject to referenda, of which there are three or four each year.

This narrows the territory for national party politics. Most parties are stronger at the cantonal level, but they do elect members to the bicameral federal assembly which since 1959 has been controlled by the same broad four-party coalition. The assembly in turn elects a seven-member federal council to serve as the executive. Of these, one person is chosen to serve one year as president—a term of office so ephemeral that many Swiss are hard-pressed to name their head of state.

This decentralized system has produced stable if conservative government that has maintained Swiss neutrality and economic independence. A referendum in 1986 rejected joining the UN, even though the organization's European headquarters are in Geneva. The Swiss people have also resisted the EU, though views are divided. Broadly, urban dwellers and French-speakers tend to be in favour, while rural dwellers and German-speakers are more likely to be against.

A referendum in May 2000 suggested, however, that Switzerland was moving closer to the EU, when its citizens approved a series of bilateral agreements with the EU on such issues as taxation and the free movement of labour.

Syria

Hafez Assad's death marked the end of an era. His son may struggle to keep control

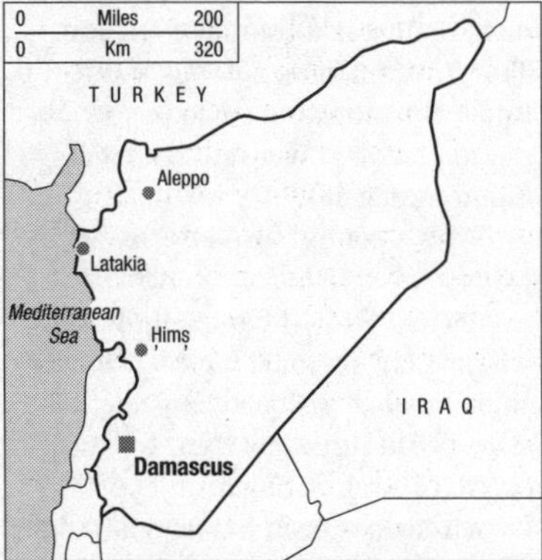

Land area: *185,000 sq. km.*
Population: *15 million—urban 54%*
Capital city: *Damascus, 1.8 million*
People: *Arab 90%, Kurds, Armenians, and others 10%*
Language: *Arabic*
Religion: *Sunni Muslim 74%, Alawi, Druze, and other Muslim sects 16%, Christian 10%*
Government: *Republic*
Life expectancy: *69 years*
GNP per capita: *$PPP 3,000*
Currency: *Syrian pound*
Major exports: *Oil, phosphates*

Syria has three main regions. One is a narrow fertile coastal strip that has year-round supplies of water. To the east of this is a mountainous zone with two ranges running parallel to the coast. The rest of the country is the Syrian Desert. Most people live in the section of land between Damascus in the south and the second city, Aleppo, near the Turkish border, though the most densely populated land is along the coast.

The population is mostly Arab and Muslim—split between the majority Sunni community and others, including the Alawi, a branch of the Shiah sect. Syria has some oil but it is not a wealthy country. The population is growing rapidly and the health system is poor. Education standards, however, are relatively high.

Agriculture is still an important part of the economy, employing around 25% of the labour force. Two-thirds of the cultivable land is in private hands and it is evenly distributed among small farmers, thanks to extensive land reform in the 1960s. Nevertheless, the government exerts a strong influence since it controls the prices of both inputs and food.

Farmers devote around two-thirds of the land to wheat and barley for local consumption, but more significant is cotton, which generates around half of agricultural GDP and provides around one-tenth of export earnings.

Some 80% of Syria's agriculture relies on the often erratic rainfall: the remaining irrigated land is mostly in the coastal strip. To expand the irrigated area the government is planning to construct a further series of dams.

Industry is also a major employer. The government has invested in heavy industries, but most activity nowadays is in lighter manufacturing such as cotton textiles, which employ one-third of the industrial workforce.

The government has tried to encourage greater private, and even foreign, investment, and since 1991 the proportion of the economy in private hands has risen from 35% to

70%. But liberalization has slowed in recent years. One major obstacle remains the state-controlled banking system. Even the government prefers to use banks elsewhere, particularly in neighbouring Lebanon.

Syria still depends heavily on oil, which provides around 60% of export income. Oil has only been extracted in quantity since the 1980s, nevertheless the reserves are far less than those in other countries, especially the Gulf, and could be exhausted within ten years or so, not merely reducing export income but also turning the country into a net importer. Production is controlled by the Syrian Petroleum Company, which is a joint venture with three foreign corporations.

Syria's oil will soon run out

Syria also has gas reserves which are being developed by foreign investors, Conoco and Elf Aquitaine, which are considering the construction of a pipeline to neighbouring Lebanon. The other major mineral export is phosphates. A further source of foreign exchange has been expatriate Syrian workers in the Gulf countries whose remittances are equivalent to 20% of export earnings.

Since 1963, the government of Syria has been the exclusive preserve of the socialist Ba'ath (Resurrection) Party, though the current regime dates from a coup in 1970 when a faction representing the minority Alawi sect seized control. In 1971 the coup's leader, Hafez al-Assad, was elected president, a post he held until his death in June 2000.

Although nominally a republic with a parliament and a council of ministers, Syria is in practice a dictatorship with the president exerting control through the army and the intelligence services. Military spending is heavy—11% of GDP.

The Assad family and other Alawis control the government but most of the business community is Sunni—a division that is a source of tension. The government is nervous about future liberalization since this would put too much power into the hands of Sunni merchants.

Syria's control also effectively extends over Lebanon. Syria sent in troops in 1976 to help quell the civil war and has retained a presence ever since in what has become a client state. Syria considers itself to be a centre of Arab nationalism and Damascus has been home to a number of dissident Palestinian groups. Syria has also been one of the most implacable opponents of Israel, with whom it has fought wars in 1967, 1973, and 1982.

Recently, however, Syria's attitude has been softening and it has been mending fences with former opponents. Syria joined the US-led coalition against Iraq in the Gulf War. Syria has also been engaged in US-sponsored peace negotiations with Israel over the return of the Golan Heights, a plateau in Syria that Israel seized in 1967.

Hafez Assad was succeeded by his son Bashar who was nominated by the People's Assembly and confirmed as president in a referendum in July 2000. Bashar is not as strong, and probably not as ruthless, as his father, and despite evident popular support, could struggle to deal with some of the political opposition his father successfully repressed.

Taiwan

Taiwan is the most financially robust of the Asian tigers, but its relationship with China remains precarious

Land area: *35,980 sq. km.*
Population: *22 million*
Capital city: *Taipei, 2.7 million*
People: *Taiwanese 84%, mainland Chinese 14%, aborigine 2%*
Language: *Mandarin Chinese, Taiwanese*
Religion: *Buddhist, Confucian, and Taoist 93%, Christian 5%, other 2%*
Government: *Republic*
Life expectancy: *77 years*
GNP per capita: *$PPP 16,500*
Currency: *New Taiwan dollar*
Major exports: *Machinery and electrical and electronic products*

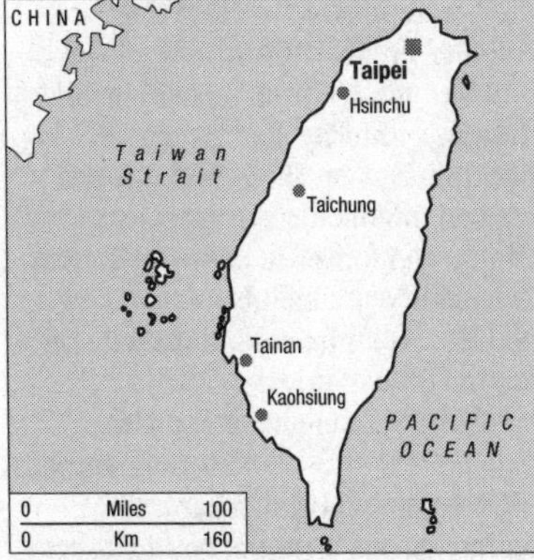

The eastern part of the island of Taiwan, around two-thirds of the territory, consists mostly of a series of mountain ranges running north to south that descend steeply to the eastern coast. To the west, they descend more gently to a broad coastal plain that is home to most of the population. The island is geologically active: in 1999 an earthquake killed 2,448 people.

Taiwan's original inhabitants were a diverse collection of Malayo-Polynesian groups. Subsequent waves of emigration from China, however, displaced most of these groups to the mountains and they now account for only around 2% of the population. Most people are descendants of the Chinese who had been arriving since the 17th century—and can still be divided in terms of dialect on the basis of the Chinese province from which they originated. A more recent addition, and the most powerful, however, are the descendants of the 2 million people who arrived following the 1949 communist revolution. At that point, this was equivalent to around one-third of Taiwan's population. These were largely the élite of the former regime, the industrialists and the professionals—probably the largest single movement of this social group in history. More recent still, but very much at the bottom of the social ladder, are the 300,000 or so immigrant workers who were drawn in by Taiwan's booming economy.

The basis for Taiwan's fairly equitable pattern of development was an extensive land reform over the period 1949-53. Most of the land on the fertile plains is still worked by small and very productive family farms that ensure the country is self-sufficient in rice, which is grown on around half the land, along with many other foods. Nowadays, however, agriculture accounts for only around 3% of GDP.

Taiwan's industrial development after 1949 benefited from considerable US aid. The initial emphasis was on import substitution, but from the 1960s the USA obliged the Taiwanese to open their economy and produce for export. This initiated a steady upward progression: in the 1960s, light assembly work and garments; in the 1970s, heavy industry; in the 1980s, TVs; and in the 1990s, computers.

Taiwan is now the world's third largest producer of information technology goods, mostly subcontracting for foreign brands—two-thirds of the monitors and the main circuit boards for the world's personal computers come from Taiwan. Meanwhile, Taiwanese companies have shifted assembly operations for TVs and VCRs to other countries, including China for which Taiwan is now one of the largest sources of investment.

Taiwan's industrial development is largely based on small producers—who account for around 80% of employment, and roughly half the economy. There is one company for every 18 people—the highest ratio in the world. Their effectiveness is based on extensive networking. Elsewhere, this might lead to corruption but this seems to have been less of a problem here. Taiwan did not suffer greatly in the Asian financial crisis, partly because its financial system is based on family loans and other unofficial sources, and because Taiwan has tight capital controls. It could not in any case get 'help' from the IMF, since it is not a member.

Taiwan has a company for every eighteen people

Taiwan would have a rosy economic future were it not for the looming threat from China. Since 1949, political life has been dominated by the question of the island's status. The Nationalists (the Kuomintang, or KMT) who fled the mainland and set up their government here have always asserted that the long-term aim is reunification—with the heroic assumption that they would rule the whole of China.

Until the 1970s this position, and Taiwan's security, had strong US backing. But by 1979 the USA had opened diplomatic relations with China, and loosened ties with Taiwan. Taiwan is not a member of the UN and has diplomatic relations with only around 30 countries.

The USA's engagement with Taiwan was also weakened by decades of a corrupt and authoritarian KMT regime. Since then, the political scene has been transformed. Taiwan is an open democracy, with direct elections for both parliament and the presidency.

In 1996 the presidential vote saw the re-election of the KMT's Lee Teng Hui who espouses reunification, but the elections in 2000, produced a dramatic change, with a victory for Chen Shui-ban of the Democratic Progressive Party which espouses formal independence. In practice, this will not make much difference: most Taiwanese prefer the ambiguous status quo—in which neither party achieves its objectives.

Moreover, now that he has achieved power, Chen has been taking a less strident line, saying that he will not push for a referendum on independence—which would only be declared if China attacked Taiwan. China seems to have been placated.

Tajikistan

Tajikistan has suffered constant war and political upheaval

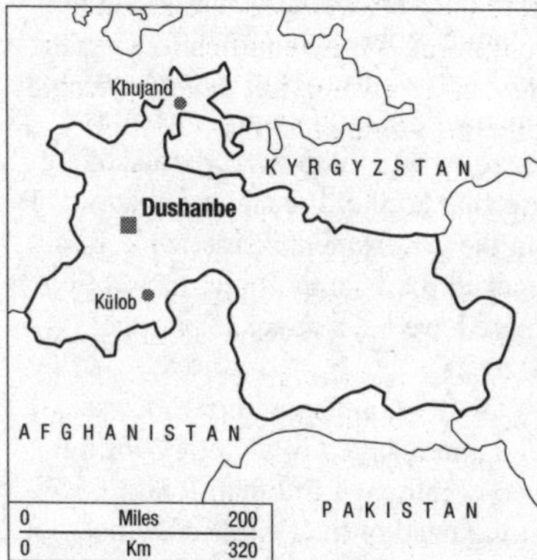

Land area: *143,000 sq. km.*
Population: *6 million—urban 32%*
Capital city: *Dushanbe, 582,000*
People: *Tajik 65%, Uzbek 25%, Russian 4%, other 6%*
Language: *Tajik, Russian*
Religion: *Muslim*
Government: *Republic*
Life expectancy: *69 years*
GNP per capita: *$PPP 920*
Currency: *Tajikistan rouble*
Major exports: *Aluminium. electricity, cotton*

Tajikistan is very mountainous. The country is largely a collection of valleys with rapidly-flowing rivers fed by melting snow and glaciers. More than half this landlocked country is 3,000 metres or more above sea level.

Tajikistan was a forced creation of the Soviet Union in 1929 that took little account of ethnic divisions. Tajiks make up two-thirds of the population but there is also a substantial Uzbek minority, in addition to Russians and numerous other smaller groups. Most Uzbeks live in the more industrialized northern region, Khujand, which is connected only tenuously to the rest of the country. The Tajiks, who are mostly Sunni Muslims, largely live in the rural areas in the foothills of the mountains and in small communities stretched out alongside the rivers and irrigation canals.

In the narrower valleys, the flat roof of one traditional house becomes the yard of the house higher up—heightening vulnerability to the earthquakes to which the region is prone.

This was always one of the poorest of the Soviet republics and a civil war since 1992 has further undermined human development. Some 700,000 people were internally displaced during the war, over 250,000 fled the country, and some 50,000 are thought to have died. In 1999, around 80% of the population lived below the poverty line.

Ironically, for a country with so many rivers, one of the scarcest commodities is clean drinking water. The country's water treatment plants are in a state of disrepair and water supplies are frequently contaminated. Infant mortality is high; in 1997 there was an outbreak of cholera.

Agriculture occupies around 60% of the workforce, though the principal crop is not wheat but cotton, which is one of the economic mainstays, accounting for 20% of exports. Cotton demands extensive irrigation from the rivers and canals, but run-off from heavily-used pesticides and fertilizers for cotton production has contaminated groundwater and rivers.

Farmers also rear livestock and grow cereals and a variety of other crops.

Tajikistan's dramatic terrain also contributes directly to its two other main exports. Many of its fast-flowing rivers have been harnessed for hydroelectric power. The largest dam, at Nurek, delivers 11 billion kilowatt hours per year, and a second is now under construction. Much of this electricity is sold to neighbouring countries and accounts for one-quarter of export earnings.

Abundant hydroelectric power is also ideal for aluminium smelters, which absorb 40% of electricity output—though all the aluminium oxide has to be imported. The Tursunzae smelter 65 kilometres west of the capital, Dushanbe, is one of the world's largest. But ageing equipment has contributed to a steady fall in output, and low world prices, together with the war, have discouraged fresh investment.

Fractured geography; fractious politics

Though it has no bauxite, Tajikistan does have rich deposits of other minerals, notably gold and silver, some of which are being extracted in co-operation with foreign mining companies.

However, economic development is seriously hampered by corruption which the European Bank for Reconstruction and Development reckons to be the worst in Central Asia. This include the trafficking of opium which is on its way from Afghanistan to Europe.

Tajikistan's fractured geography has contributed to its complex and fractious politics which aligns along not just ideological, but also religious and regional fault lines. Since independence in 1991, there has been a struggle for power between communists and Muslims and also secular democrats. Former communists effectively remained in power following independence, but Islamic groups embarked on a widespread armed struggle. Many fled the country and Islamic guerrillas established a base in Afghanistan. Around 25,000 Russian troops fought on the government's side while Iran backed the Islamic force. In addition there have been attacks from the Uzbeks.

In 1994, a disputed presidential election resulted in a victory for the neo-communist Imomali Rakhmanov at the head of his People's Democratic Party (PDP). But by 1997 Russia and Iran were keen to promote a long-term settlement and supported a UN-brokered peace deal. Rakhmanov agreed to share power with the other parties, which had come together as the United Tajik Opposition (UTO), and to hold presidential and parliamentary elections. The UTO, for its part, agreed to demobilize its 5,000-strong force.

Rakhmanov duly rigged the November 1998 election and was re-elected with an impressive 96% of the vote in a 98% turnout. Nevertheless, the UTO leader, Abdullo Nuri, decided to accept the result as the price of Islamic representation.

The February 2000 election to the lower house of the parliament was also flawed, giving the PDP two-thirds of the seats. Still, Tajikistan does at least now have a legal Islamic Party. Unfortunately, the Uzbeks could now shake this precarious peace.

Tanzania

Tanzania is politically stable, but development is slow and tarnished by corruption

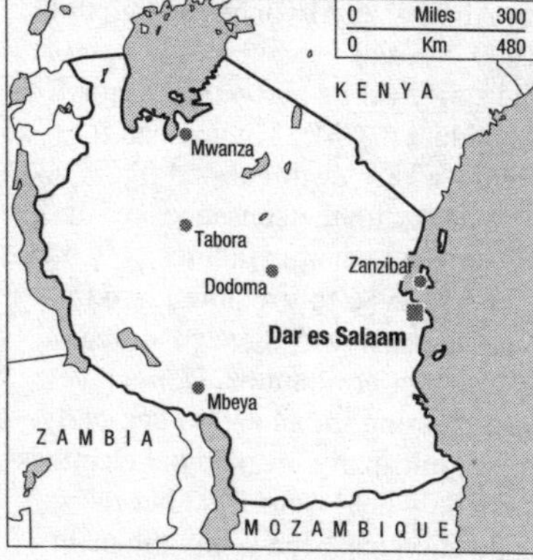

__Land area:__ 945,000 sq. km.
__Population:__ 32 million—urban 26%
__Capital city:__ Dar es Salaam, 1.4 million
__People:__ More than 100 African groups; Arab on Zanzibar
__Language:__ Kiswahili, English, Arabic, and many local languages
__Religion:__ Mainland: Christian 45%, Muslim 35%, indigenous beliefs 20%. Zanzibar: Muslim
__Government:__ Republic
__Life expectancy:__ 48 years
__GNP per capita:__ $PPP 490
__Currency:__ Tanzanian shilling
__Major exports:__ Coffee, manufactured goods, cashew nuts

Mainland Tanzania has a narrow, flat coastal plain which rises to the vast plateau that makes up most of the country. But there is also some spectacular scenery, including in the north-east Africa's highest mountain, Kilimanjaro, at 5,895 metres. Much of the land is assigned to national parks and game reserves. The republic also includes islands in the Indian Ocean; two of the largest of which make up Zanzibar.

Tanzanians can belong to any one of 120 or more ethnic groups. None of these holds a dominant position, but effective efforts at 'nation-building' after independence, which included the promotion of Kiswahili as the national language, helped Tanzania to avoid serious ethnic conflict. The same language is also spoken in Zanzibar, though the population here—around 1 million—has a strong Arab component and is almost entirely Muslim. Most Tanzanians are poor: around half are thought to be living below the poverty line. One-quarter of children are malnourished. Tanzanians do however have reasonable standards of education, a legacy of earlier socialist investment.

Most people live in the rural areas from subsistence agriculture though only 8% of the land is under cultivation; there are large fertile zones as yet untouched. The main food crops are maize, cassava, rice, sorghum, and beans. Most small-holders also grow one or more cash crops, including coffee, cotton, cashew nuts, and tobacco. Tea and sisal are the other main cash crops, though these are grown mostly on estates. In Zanzibar the main export crop is cloves. However, agricultural productivity is low and output is not increasing fast enough to have any real impact on poverty.

Most manufacturing is based on processing agricultural commodities and remains largely in state hands. Privatization has been slow, partly because of nationalist resistance but also because buyers will not take on inefficient enterprises. A promising future direction is the exploitation of minerals, which include gold and diamonds as well as iron ore, nickel, and phosphates. These have been attracting investment from Australian, Canadian, and South African companies.

Another area for development is tourism to the nature reserves and Africa's two largest game parks, as well as to the 'spice island' of Zanzibar. But annual tourist arrivals are only one-third of a million—far fewer than visit similar attractions in neighbouring Kenya.

Since 1986 Tanzania has been engaged in programmes of economic adjustment with the IMF, and it remains a favourite with aid donors—though even here aid funds have been falling. The private sector complains that it gets little support from government.

Another serious issue is corruption. Transparency International rates Tanzania as the world's seventh most corrupt country. In 1998 the government established a presidential commission to combat corruption but there has been little progress.

Julius Nyrere's influence

For the first quarter of a century after independence Tanzania was governed, first as prime minister and later as president, by Julius Nyerere. Nyerere was a hugely influential figure nationally and internationally, known to Tanzanians as Mwalimu (teacher). He was one of the strongest supporters in the 1970s and 1980s of liberation movements in South Africa and elsewhere. Nyrere's brand of African socialism had some social and political successes in Tanzania but also notable failures, including his attempts to concentrate scattered communities into villages and promote co-operative development of the land. When Nyerere retired in 1985, he was succeeded as president by Ali Hassan Mwinyi—though until 1990 Nyerere remained chairman of the single ruling party, the Chama Cha Mapiduzi (CCM). Mwinyi had to follow a very distinguished figure and also deal with the consequences of Nyerere's economic failures.

From 1986 this required him to sign up to an IMF-directed structural adjustment programme. Donors were also pressing for an end to one-party rule. Multi-party presidential elections were duly held from 1992 but the opposition has been weak: the main group is the Civic United Front (CUF). For the 1996 elections the ineffective Mwinyi was succeeded (with Nyerere's backing) by Benjamin Mkapa. Nyerere died in October 1999.

Semi-autonomous Zanzibar has representation in the mainland parliament, but it also has its own president and internal administration. There has long been tension with mainland Tanzania. The CUF on Zanzibar accuses the CCM of sacrificing Zanzibar to the mainland, while the CCM says the CUF has plans to dissolve the union.

The CUF has boycotted elections in Zanzibar since 1995 and there have been outbreaks of violence, arrests of opposition leaders, and allegations of police brutality. If the elections scheduled for October 2000 are not conciliatory Zanzibar could become the flashpoint of yet another African civil war.

Thailand

Never colonized, but economically dependent on foreign markets

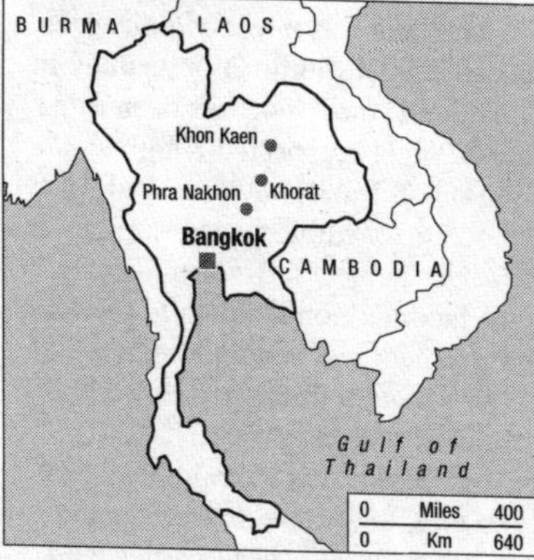

Land area: *513,000 sq. km.*
Population: *61 million—urban 21%*
Capital city: *Bangkok, 6 million*
People: *Thai 75%, Chinese 14%, other 11%*
Language: *Thai, English*
Religion: *Buddhism*
Government: *Constitutional monarchy*
Life expectancy: *55 years*
GNP per capita: *$PPP 5,840*
Currency: *Baht*
Major exports: *Food, machinery, manufactured goods*

Thailand's distinctive geographical shape extends over four main regions. In the far north are mountain ranges covered by forests of tropical hardwood, while the north-eastern area is much dryer—a barren plateau that makes up one-third of the country. The southern region, which stretches down the Malay peninsula, is mountainous with narrow coastal plains. But the core of Thailand, and the focus of most activity, is the central plain—a rich agricultural area criss-crossed with rivers and canals.

Thailand's people are relatively homogenous—held together by language, religion, and a deep respect for the monarchy. The majority of people speak Thai and almost all are Buddhist—most communities have ornate temples. Nevertheless, Thailand also has distinct ethnic groups. In the northern region these include the hill tribes and in the far south Malays, who are Muslims and have affinities with Malaysia. But the largest group of non-Thai origin, even if now mostly assimilated, are the Chinese who are the driving force in many commercial activities.

Thailand has made rapid progress in economic development but has been slower in aspects of human development. Literacy is high, but less than half of Thai children enrol in secondary school. As a result there are around 1 million child workers.

Although incomes have increased, 13% of people still live in poverty, The north-east in particular remains very poor. The financial crisis of 1997 heightened poverty, though not by as much as had been feared.

With high aspirations but low prospects, many unskilled workers have headed overseas. In the mid-1990s Thais were leaving at the rate of 140,000 per year, chiefly to Saudi Arabia, Brunei, and Singapore. Meanwhile, similar numbers were coming in from neighbouring Burma to work on construction sites and sugar mills or in the 'entertainment' industry.

Thailand's population is still predominantly rural and 60% of the labour force still work in agriculture, predominantly on small farms.

Thailand's rich and fertile land has enabled it to become a leading rice exporters, responsible for around one-quarter of the world's' rice trade.

Rapid economic growth has, however, taken its toll on the environment—particularly on the forests. Forest cover fell from over 50% in the mid-1960s to less than 20% by 1997.

In recent years the most dramatic development has been the hectic process of modernization and urbanization. In the 1960s the government opened up the economy and invested in infrastructure. This helped to expand exports, first of agricultural products and then of manufactured goods, starting with garments and later moving into higher technology items.

Most of the country's industrial activity is focused on the sprawling capital Bangkok which, with its environs, now accounts for more than half of the country's GDP—a rapid expansion that has also made the city a byword for pollution and traffic congestion. On the positive side Bangkok now boasts an overhead railway system. More worrying is that the city, built over a swamp, is sinking by five centimetres per year.

World-class traffic congestion

Thailand's leading source of foreign exchange is tourism. More than 8 million people visit each year, attracted to beach resorts such as Phuket and Samui, and the often raucous nightlife, as well as the more peaceful hills around Chiang Mai.

Thailand's boom came to a sudden halt in 1997 and triggered the Asian financial crisis. In 1996, exports had faltered and the currency came under attack. In July 1997, when the baht was floated it fell 30% against the dollar and the stock market dropped by 50%. Since then, the currency and economy have stabilized but unemployment is still high.

Thailand was never colonized. It became a constitutional monarchy in 1932, and since 1946 has been ruled by the highly respected King Bhumibol. It has, however, had many autocratic or military governments and has been subject to frequent coups. One landmark on the path to civilian government was a student uprising in 1973—though this was followed by a another brutal coup in 1976.

In 1992, it was the middle classes who took to the streets—protesting against military-backed parties, and this, along with an intervention by the king, opened the way to sustained civilian rule.

The economic collapse in 1997 brought down the government. This was replaced by a new seven-party coalition led by Chuan Leekpai of the Democratic Party. Like most other recent administrations, his government has been subject to splits and infighting, but he managed to steer Thailand away from the financial precipice. Efforts to clean up the political system seem to be bearing fruit. Many contests in the 2000 senate elections were duly rerun after candidates had been accused of corruption.

One concern in the years ahead is who will succeed King Bhumibol: whether the crown passes to his son or to one of his daughters, who are more popular, will be decided only after the king's death.

Togo

Togo has one of the world's longest-serving presidents, though not from choice

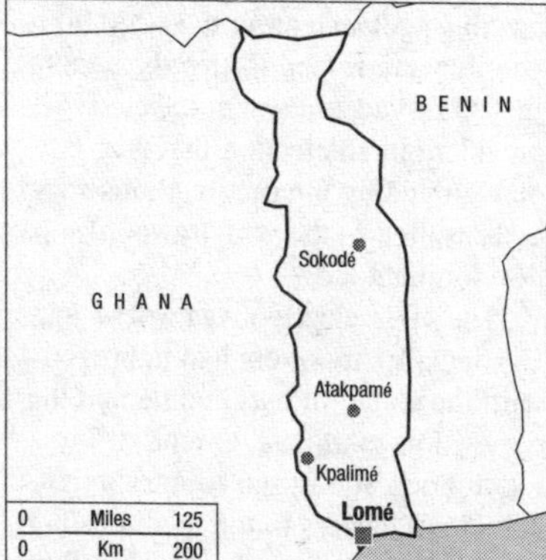

Land area: *57,000 sq. km.*
Population: *4 million—urban 32%*
Capital city: *Lomé, 700,000*
People: *Ewe, Mina, Kabre*
Language: *French, Ewe, Mina, Dagomba*
Religion: *Indigenous beliefs 70%, Christian 20%, Muslim 10%*
Government: *Republic*
Life expectancy: *49 years*
GNP per capita: *$PPP 1,390*
Currency: *CFA Franc*
Major exports: *Coffee, cotton,phosphates*

Within its elongated shape, Togo has a variety of geographical regions. Inland from the thin coastal belt with its series of lagoons there is a plateau region. This extends to the Togo Mountains, a chain that crosses the country from south-west to north-east. Beyond the mountains to the north-west there is another plateau drained by the River Oti.

Togo has more than 30 ethnic groups. The largest, who live mostly in the south are the Ewe, a group also to be found in Benin and Ghana. The population density is greatest in the south and continues to grow fairly rapidly—by more than 3% per year. This has put pressure on public services, particularly education. Togo has maintained higher educational standards than neighbouring Francophone countries but the system is deteriorating. Health services too are under strain and around one-fifth of children are malnourished. Togo is also afflicted by AIDS, which by the end of 1997 had killed around 130,000 people and orphaned more than 110,000 children. Services are particularly poor in the rural areas, where only 41% of people have access to safe water and 22% to sanitation.

Two-thirds of Togolese make their living from agriculture. Most are small-holders, growing such crops as cassava, millet, yams, and maize. In a normal year, Togo is self-sufficient in these crops, though it still needs to import rice. In the plateau regions and particularly in the north many people raise cattle and sheep.

Farmers can also supplement their incomes with a range of cash crops. In the mountains along the border with Ghana they grow cocoa and coffee, while to the east they grow cotton. Cotton has become particularly important and production, which takes place mostly on small farms, has more than doubled over the past decade, making this one of the country's leading export earners. However, the intensity of cotton production is raising fears of environmental damage.

Industrial activity is dominated by phosphates, of which Togo is one of the world's largest producers. Togo's deposits are extensive and compact, and conveniently located just 40 kilometres from the capital, Lomé, which is also the main port. The state-owned company that controls the industry makes a small profit, but the government is coming under increasing pressure from donors to open the industry up to private enterprise and has agreed to sell 40% of its stake.

Togo also has a small manufacturing sector. Much of this involves processing agricultural goods such as cotton, palm oil and coffee for export, but there are also other enterprises making cement, beer, and textiles for local consumption. Some of these companies are to be found in an export-processing zone which employs around 5,000 people, mostly in light manufacturing. However, activity in this zone as in many other parts of the economy has been severely affected by years of political turmoil.

Most Togolese have only known one ruler, Gnassingbe Eyadéma, who was appointed president following a military coup in 1967. Eyadéma, who is from the minority, northern Kabré group, headed a military government but later set up his own political party, the Rassemblement du peuple togolais (RPT), and in 1979 drew up a new constitution and held an election. Since the RPT was the only legal political party Eyadéma was duly elected.

Corpses washed up on the beaches

By 1991, with a wave of democracy sweeping across Africa, and following considerable donor pressure, Eyadéma was forced to hold a national conference which established an interim government that included members of opposition groups, most of whom are Ewe.

In 1992, this government came under attack from the army, provoking a nine-month general strike. In the ensuing violence more than 200,000 people were forced to flee the country. In 1993 Eyadéma was re-elected president in an election that was condemned by international observers and resulted in the withdrawal of most development aid.

The 1998 election was worse. Eyadéma's supporters had tampered with the electoral lists and denied the opposition candidate, Gilchrist Olympio (a son of the country's first president), access to the media. When it became clear that, despite this, the chief opposition candidate was winning, the paramilitary police seized the ballot boxes, the interior minister declared Eyadéma the winner, and Olympio fled into exile.

Following the election, repression was stepped up and in 1999 Amnesty International reported that hundreds of people were killed by the security forces. Corpses were washed up on the beaches of Togo and neighbouring Benin for days afterwards.

International mediation started in July 1999. Eyadéma agreed to the establishment of an electoral commission that will include opposition and international members. He promised not to stand in the next election.

But in early 2000 negotiations were bogged down and the government was still jailing journalists and student leaders, and facing yet more allegations of torture.

Tonga

One of the newest members of the UN, Tonga is dominated by its king

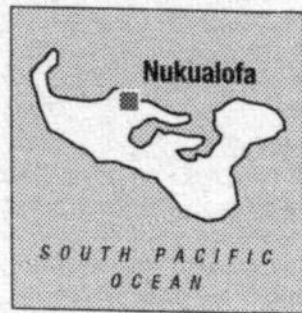

Tonga comprises an archipelago of more than 150 Pacific islands; some coral, some volcanic. Around two-thirds of the population live on the main island, Tongatapu. The islands are vulnerable to cyclones—a cyclone in early 2000 caused $4 million-worth of damage.

Tongans are ethnically fairly homogeneous and although they live in a lower-income country they enjoy good access to sanitation, clean water, and health care. Now they are starting to suffer from 'lifestyle diseases', including obesity and diabetes. They also have a high rate of literacy—close to 100%. Fertility remains high, but population growth has been slowed by high rates of emigration, particularly to New Zealand.

Most people still rely on agriculture, which accounts for around one-third of GDP. They grow food and a narrow range of cash crops—coconuts, squash pumpkins, vanilla, and melons. Tonga's foreign exchange income has become over-reliant on one commodity—squash pumpkins, which go primarily to Japan. So when the industry is hit by disease, or drought, or quota restrictions, the balance of payments suffers.

In the past, Tonga has benefited from foreign aid, but this is likely to dry up because Tonga, despite its protests of poverty, no longer qualifies as a 'least-developed country'. Its other main source of foreign exchange, migrant remittances from overseas workers, may also shrink because fewer people are leaving. So further progress will be difficult unless Tonga diversifies its economy.

Land area: *750 sq. km.*
Population: *99,000—urban 36%*
Capital city: *Nuku'alofa, 30,000*
People: *Polynesian*
Language: *Tongan, English*
Religion: *Christian*
Government: *Constitutional monarchy*
Life expectancy: *70 years*
GNP per capita: *$PPP 3,860*
Currency: *Pa'anga (Tongan dollar)*
Major exports: *Copra, squash, vanilla*

Tonga is effectively an absolute monarchy and the country is dominated by King Taufa'ahau Tupou IV, who has ruled since 1965. The king appoints the cabinet and the prime minister. Early in 2000, his cousin retired as prime minister and was replaced by his youngest son, Prince Ulukalala Lavaka Ata.

There is also a legislative assembly, the Fale Alea, but only nine of its 30 members are directly elected; the others include the king and his cabinet, as well as nine members elected by the traditional nobles.

There has been some pressure for greater democracy and there have been protests against the harassment of journalists. The People's Party, formed in 1994, has been campaigning for more accountability, and in the 1999 elections held five of the nine directly elected seats.

Tonga's international profile was raised in September 1999 when it became the 188th member of the UN, and claimed to be the first state to welcome the new millennium.

Trinidad and Tobago

Land area: 5,000 sq. km.
Population: 1.3 million—urban 73%
Capital city: Port of Spain, 600,000
People: Black 43%, East Indian 40%, mixed 14%, other 3%
Language: English, Hindi
Religion: Roman Catholic 32%, Hindu 24%, Protestant 28%, Muslim 6%, other 10%
Government: Parliamentary democracy
Life expectancy: 73 years
GNP per capita: $PPP 6,270
Currency: Trinidad and Tobago dollar
Major exports: Oil

The oil will soon run out so the country needs other sources of revenue and jobs

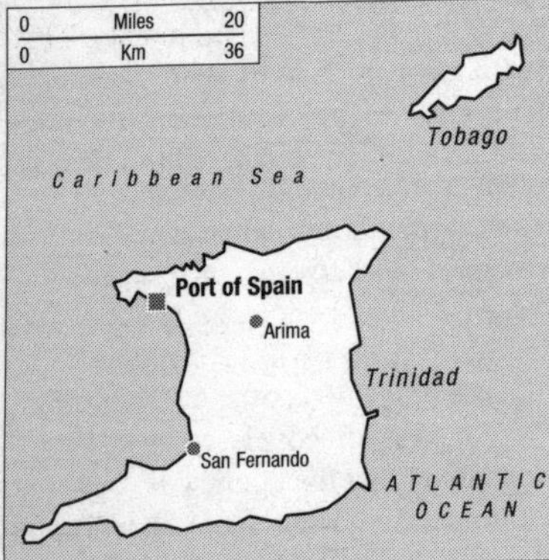

These two islands are the southernmost of the Caribbean chain. But they can also be considered as an extension of South America: Trinidad, which has 94% of the land area, is only 12 kilometres from the coast of Venezuela. Trinidad's northern range of mountains essentially continues the coastal range of the Andes, which surfaces again as the island of Tobago. The southern quarter of Trinidad is oil-bearing land and includes the pitch lake at La Brea, which is the world's largest natural source of asphalt.

Tobago is less industrially developed. Its chief geographical feature is its main ridge which slopes down to extensive coral reefs that are popular with divers.

The country is racially very diverse—a product of its sugar-producing past. The main groups are the blacks who are descendants of the original African slave labour force, and the East Indians who are descendants of the indentured Indian workers who largely replaced blacks on the plantations after the abolition of slavery. In addition, there are smaller European and Chinese communities. The people of Tobago have long felt dominated and neglected by Trinidad.

Sugar remained the mainstay of the economy for many years and the country is still a significant exporter. But since the middle of the 20th century economic life has largely been restructured around oil. Trinidad is a major offshore producer and also a refiner of crude oil imported from other countries in the region.

In the 1970s, the sharp rise in oil prices ushered in a boom with a sudden surge in income and government expenditure—transforming Trinidad and Tobago into one of the richest countries in the region. When the oil price collapsed again this hit the country hard. Between 1985 and 1989, real GDP fell by one-third and unemployment, which had been below 10%, had by 1987 risen to 22%.

During the 1970s Trinidad and Tobago had made efforts to diversify.

One of the focal points has been the Point Lisas industrial estate, which has used Trinidad's extensive reserves of natural gas as a raw material for petro-chemicals and fertilizers. Even so, by 1997 manufacturing still only accounted for about 8% of employment. Agriculture is another relatively small-scale employer, with 11%.

Two-thirds of the workforce are now employed in services, particularly the tourist industry which has become a major source of foreign exchange. But relatively few visitors spend much time in Trinidad which now suffers from high levels of crime, much of which is associated with drugs. The chief long-stay attraction is Tobago which has many unspoilt beaches as well as a variety of plants and wildlife in the protected rainforests.

Tourists head for Tobago

Recent years have seen an economic recovery. Between 1994 and 1998, unemployment fell from 18% to 14%. Low oil prices continued to undermine government income but by 1999 the energy sector accounted for only 21% of government revenues compared to 60% in 1975.

With oil reserves likely to last no more than ten years, the government is anxious to continue diversification into other sectors, including agribusiness and marine, financial, and information technology services.

Politics in Trinidad has usually been conducted along ethnic lines. There have also been disputes between the two islands which led in 1980 to the formation of the Tobago House of Assembly. For many years the dominant party was the People's National Movement (PNM), which has generally had the support of blacks as well as the Chinese, those of mixed race, and non-Hindu Indians. The PNM saw the country through independence and held power for decades afterwards, effectively excluding the Indian community. This pattern was broken in 1986 when the National Alliance for Reconstruction (NAR), a multi-racial coalition led by ANR Robinson, won 33 of the 36 seats in the house of representatives.

The NAR government's austerity measures proved unpopular and the coalition soon fell apart. In 1989, one of its factions formed a new party with largely Indian support—the United National Congress.

The low point came in 1990 when a Muslim group staged a coup, firebombing the police headquarters and storming the parliament chamber, holding Robinson and several ministers hostage. They were released when the rebels were granted an amnesty.

In the 1991 elections, the PNM regained power, only to lose it in 1995 when both the PNM and the United National Congress gained seventeen seats. The latter, led by Basdeo Panday, a former trade union official, formed the government, in coalition with the NAR which had won the remaining two seats. Panday is the first person of Indian extraction to become prime minister. One outcome of this election was greater autonomy for Tobago, which was given local responsibility for issues such as housing and education. In February 1997 the country had its first presidential election. This was won by former prime minister ANR Robinson.

Tunisia

Tunisians have traded political freedoms for economic stability

Land area: *164,000 sq. km.*
Population: *9 million—urban 64%*
Capital city: *Tunis, 674,000*
People: *Arab*
Language: *Arabic*
Religion: *Muslim*
Government: *Republic*
Life expectancy: *70 years*
GNP per capita: *$PPP 5,160*
Currency: *Tunisian dinar*
Major exports: *Textiles, food, petroleum products*

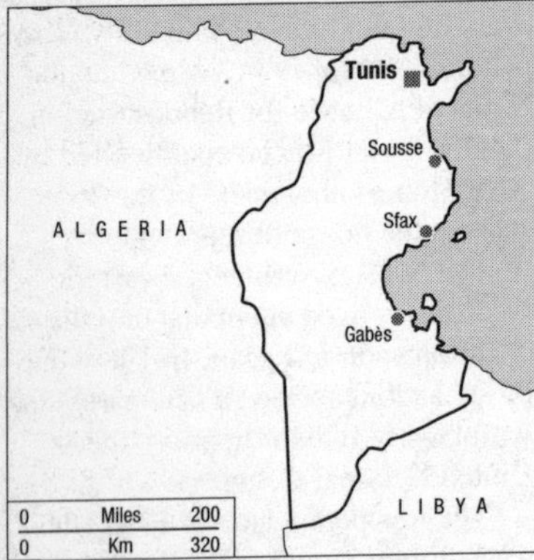

Tunisia can be divided into four main geographical regions. The northern one-third of the country consists of spurs of the Atlas Mountains but also includes fertile valleys and plains. These mountains descend further south to a broad plateau and further south still to a series of shallow salt lakes, known as shatts. Beyond these lies the Sahara Desert, which occupies around two-fifths of the territory.

Tunisians are almost entirely Arab, since the original Berber inhabitants have been assimilated. By African standards, they enjoy a relatively high standard of living and a low rate of population growth.

There is still some poverty, and unemployment is around 20%, but mindful of the potential for militant Islam among disaffected youth, the government has maintained food subsidies and largely free health services. Primary education is free and compulsory though literacy is still only 67%.

Tunisia's economy is broadly based. The country has successfully moved on from agriculture and from dependence on oil and phosphates and now has a number of manufacturing industries that in 1999 employed 18% of the workforce. Some of the fastest growth has been in textiles, which are now the leading export, though this industry is facing increasing competition from Asia.

Tunisia has been an oil producer since 1966 but reserves are dwindling and there have been few new discoveries. Phosphates too now make up a much smaller proportion of exports since they are used locally as raw material for fertilizers and chemicals.

One-fifth of the workforce is employed in agriculture. Most farms are fairly small and largely worked by hand. The main crop in the fertile northern plains is wheat, along with barley and vegetables, but harvests are vulnerable to erratic rainfall.

The drier parts of the country are used to grow dates and particularly olives, of which Tunisia is one of the largest producers. The main restriction is a lack of water since the country is already using around 80% of its potential for irrigation. A quarter of the land is forest, or used for grazing animals, but livestock raising too is vulnerable to drought.

Of the service industries, one of the most important is tourism. Tunisia's coastal resorts are favourite package-holiday destinations for Europeans. Tourism, with around 3 million visitors a year, accounts for 6% of GDP but revenues are fairly static. The government takes care to prevent tourists finding out about human rights abuses, and regularly bans the foreign press. The country's hotels and resorts will need considerable investment if they are to attract higher spending visitors.

Tunisia's political system is less diverse than its economy. Since independence in 1956, it has been ruled by the same party and has had only two presidents, neither of whom have been enthusiasts for political pluralism. Tunisia's first president was Habib Bourgiba, at the head of what was subsequently called the Parti socialiste destourien.

Only two presidents since 1956

Initially, Bourgiba was relatively progressive, promoting the rights of women, for example. But he grew increasingly autocratic, jailing opposition leaders and clamping down on the media. In 1975, he had himself elected president-for-life. The strongest opposition came from the underground Mouvement de la tendence Islamique (MTI). To combat the MTI, Bourgiba in 1986 appointed as interior minister, General Zine el-Abidine Ben Ali. He was so successful at crushing the MTI that in 1987 Bourgiba gratefully appointed him prime minister.

This was a mistake. Ben Ali had Bourgiba declared senile, removed him from office and in December 1987 assumed the presidency himself. At first Ben Ali seemed fairly liberal. He released hundreds of detainees and legalized opposition parties. He also renamed the party as the Rassemblement constitutionnel démocratique (RCD). In the 1989 elections, the RCD won most of the seats and Ben Ali was elected unopposed as president.

Ben Ali's enthusiasm for building consensus was short lived. By the early 1990s, he was again persecuting the MTI, by then renamed Hizb al-Nahda (party of the awakening), jailing hundreds of its members and driving others into exile. He also took control of other opposition parties, and restricted the press and trade unions.

In the 1994 elections, the RCD won almost every seat and in the presidential election Ben Ali was again elected unopposed, with 99% of the vote. To appear more democratic he subsequently decreed that minority parties would automatically get 20% of seats regardless of their share of the vote. The 1999 election produced a similar result.

State repression has spread beyond Islamic activists to include many secular groups, particularly human rights activists. Amnesty International reports hundreds of incidents of police intimidation, arbitrary arrest, and torture. While the opposition has largely been intimidated, the public reaction to Bourgiba's death and funeral in April 2000 suggested the potential for widespread unrest.

Turkey

Turkey is making peace with Greece and is now a candidate for the EU

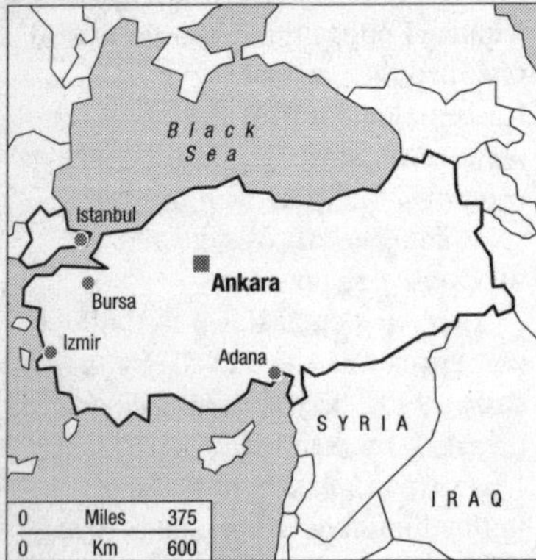

Land area: *779,000 sq. km.*
Population: *63 million—urban 73%*
Capital city: *Ankara, 2.8 million*
People: *Turkish 80%, Kurdish 20%*
Language: *Turkish, Kurdish, Arabic*
Religion: *Muslim*
Government: *Republic*
Life expectancy: *69 years*
GNP per capita: *$PPP 6,350*
Currency: *Turkish lira*
Major exports: *Garments, textiles, fruit, vegetables*

Turkey is predominantly mountainous. The lowlands are mostly confined to coastal areas around the Black Sea, the Aegean, and the Mediterranean. Turkey straddles the border between Europe and Asia—though its European part is quite small. The Asian part, known as Anatolia, has at its heart the central Anatolian plateau, which is encircled by mountains. Western Anatolia consists of long mountainous ridges and deep valley floors, though the highest mountains are in the east.

The majority of the population are Turkish and almost all are Sunni Muslim. Over recent decades Turkey has been industrializing rapidly and more than two-thirds of the population live in cities. But by the standards of other industrial countries, levels of human development are low. In 1997, adult literacy, for example, was only 83%, and significantly lower for women. And outside the cities, health services are poor. Until recently, many Turks were emigrating to the EU, particularly to Germany. The exodus has more or less ceased, but there are still some 2 million Turks in the EU, whose annual remittances are around $4.2 billion.

Within Turkey, there is also a significant minority of Kurds, who make up around one-fifth of the population. The Kurds are one of the world's largest ethnic groups without a state of their own, though eastern Anatolia, where most Turkish Kurds live, together with neighbouring regions of Iran and Iraq, is referred to as Kurdistan. The government of Turkey has long tried to repress Kurdish nationalism and since 1984 has been fighting the 3,000 guerrillas of the Kurdish Workers' Party in a war that has cost more than 30,000 lives.

With more than half the workforce employed in service industries, and one-quarter in industry, Turkey has characteristics of an advanced industrial economy. Many of the largest enterprises, including iron, steel, and chemicals, are run by the state. But the private sector has now become more significant, particularly in food processing, and in garments and textiles which make up 40% of exports. Turkey is also the world's second-largest exporter of pasta.

Tourism is also a major source of employment and income, bringing in around $7 billion per year. Most of the tourists on packaged holidays come from Germany and the UK.

Turkey's diverse landscape has sustained steady growth in agriculture which still employs 45% of the workforce. Although levels of technology are lower than in Western Europe, output has kept pace with population, so Turkey is largely self-sufficient in food, and has crops such as wheat, sugar beet, cotton, and tobacco, some of which are exported.

Turkey's recent political history, has followed an unsteady course. A series of weak coalition governments have been subject to military intervention: since 1945 there have been three military coups. The military intervened yet again after the 1995 election. At that point, the main centre-left and centre-right forces were split and the party with the largest proportion of votes—21%—was the pro-Islamic Welfare Party (RP). Following the election, the two main centre-right parties, True Path (DYP) and Motherland (Anap), briefly formed a coalition. But this rapidly collapsed and the leader of the DYP, a former prime minister, Tansu Ciller, formed a government with the RP, led by Necmettin Erbakan.

Weak governments and military coups

The prospect of Islamic influence in government alarmed the military, who in 1997 through the powerful National Security Council, forced Erbakan to resign in what was termed a 'soft coup'. A subsequent three-party coalition that included Anap and the DSP proved short lived. In 1999, therefore, Turkey had a further general election. This resulted in another coalition which had the DSP as the leading party, along with Anap and the right-wing Nationalist Action Party, (MHP).

The new government was led by the DSP's veteran survivor, and previous prime minister, Bulent Ecevit, whom the military had previously jailed and banned from politics.

Ecevit has a number of difficult issues to deal with. One is Turkey's relationship with Europe which has always been ambivalent. On the one hand, Turkey is strategically very important, and has been a key member of NATO, for which it was a missile launching pad in the Cold War. On the other hand, it has a poor record on human rights, particularly with respect to the Kurds. Added to this is the dispute with Greece over Cyprus.

These difficulties had made the EU nervous of inviting Turkey as a candidate for membership, but it finally did so in December 1999. However this invitation was conditional on making progress in human rights and on Turkey's resolving its various disputes with Greece—conditions which provoked popular discontent in Turkey.

Relations with Greece did improve in 1999 when each country helped the other to recover from earthquakes. But the Kurdish question remains unresolved, particularly the fate of the Kurdish leader Abdulla Ocalan, who has been captured and convicted and faces a death sentence.

Turkmenistan

An autocratic leader is spending scarce money on grandiose monuments

Land area: *488,000 sq. km.*
Population: *5 million—urban 45%*
Capital city: *Ashkhabad, 416,000*
People: *Turkmen 77%, Uzbek 9%, Russian 7%, Kazakh 2%, other 5%*
Language: *Turkmen 72%, Russian 12%, Uzbek 9%, other 7%*
Religion: *Muslim 89%, Eastern Orthodox 9%, unknown 2%*
Government: *Republic*
Life expectancy: *65 years*
GNP per capita: *$PPP 2,109*
Currency: *Manat*
Major exports: *Gas*

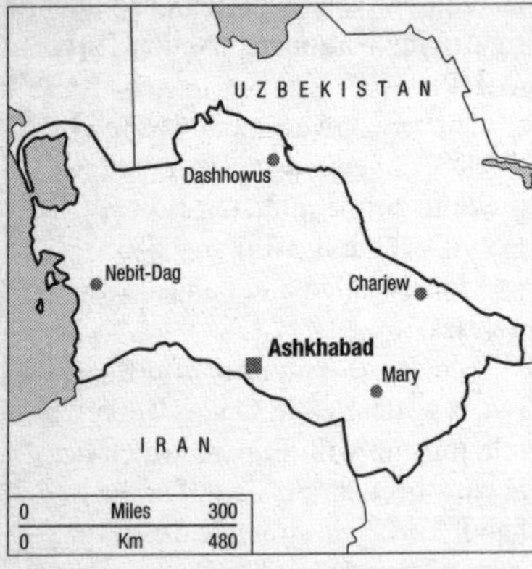

Turkmenistan is largely a vast, sandy desert, with some low mountains to the south. The country borders on the Caspian Sea, but the main rivers, which are along the northern and southern borders, flow into neighbouring countries to the east.

Turkmenistan does, however, have many canals to provide water for drinking and irrigation, including the Garagum canal, one of the world's longest, which takes water from the Amu Darya River on the eastern border to the capital, Ashkhabad, 1,400 kilometres to the south. The scale of the diversion has, however, created major ecological problems, including the drying up of the Aral Sea into which the Amu Darya flows.

The Turkmen, who are Sunni Muslims, were formerly a nomadic people. During the Soviet era much of their culture and lifestyle was repressed, and now they are mostly settled along the rivers and canals. Following the collapse of the Soviet Union, there were considerable population movements: between 1989 and 1995, many Russians left, while over 300,000 Turkmen arrived from other republics. Turkmenistan also has a substantial Uzbek minority living along the northern border.

The population grew swiftly over this period, though in recent years the birth rate has been falling. The population is fairly well educated though the quality of schooling has been slipping.

Agriculture, based on irrigation, employs around 40% of the workforce and makes up 20% of GDP. The largest crop is cotton, followed by wheat. But production has been falling. Farmers have little incentive to increase output. There has not been much progress in land reform and the state, which is the monopoly buyer, pays only around half of the world price for wheat and 14% of that for cotton.

Production is in any case fairly inefficient: much of the irrigation water in the canals evaporates before it can be used and excessive application of fertilizers for cotton has built up toxic residues in the soil.

In the past, weaknesses in agriculture have been compensated for by production of gas. The Garagum Desert in the east holds a huge basin of natural gas—over 2% of world reserves. During years of peak production, this has been responsible for most of the country's GDP and the bulk of export earnings. The main problem is to find pipeline routes to potential buyers.

Turkmenistan could supply huge markets, including Turkey and China. Unfortunately the neighbouring countries such as Azerbaijan, Iran, Russia, and Uzbekistan are also gas producers so are loathe to co-operate. On the other hand, proposals for a pipeline under the Caspian Sea to Azerbaijan run into environmental and other obstacles. Meanwhile, existing customers such as Ukraine and Georgia pay their bills late, if at all. All these disputes over transit and payment have led to a steep drop in income.

This creates problems elsewhere in the economy. Turkmenistan avoided economic liberalization and instead has been promoting a policy of import-substituting industrialization—using gas revenues for funds. The government has therefore been investing in food processing and textile manufacture, as well as in a cellulose plant and steel mills. But private investors are slower to spend, deterred by massive corruption and excessive bureaucracy.

Using gas funds to invest in industry

Gas revenue has also gone into construction. Much of this is for the gas industry itself, and also for the exploitation of oil. But there have also been a number of fairly grandiose projects, including a new international airport, a new marble presidential palace, and an enormous mosque.

All this activity has been directed by dictatorial president, and prime minister, Saparmurad Niyazov. He became leader of the Turkmen Communist Party in 1986 and tried to resist economic and political liberalization. Following independence in 1991 the party re-emerged as the Democratic Party, which is still the only legal political organization. The party itself does not have a heavy workload; it meets once or twice a year to rubber-stamp presidential decisions.

Niyazov has developed probably the world's most shameless personality cult. He has had himself proclaimed as 'Turkenbashi'—leader of the Turkmen, and one of his most striking monuments is a column topped by a revolving golden statue of himself. His heavyweight secret police, the KNB, have helped him ruthlessly to suppress all forms of dissent. There may be some covert opposition among the educated élite in Ashkabad but organized opposition groups are now in exile.

Though the economy remains sickly there is little sign of political change. Having held a rigged referendum in 1994, Niyazov was already due to stay in power until 2004. Then in early 2000 his dutiful parliament requested that he declare himself president-for-life. Niyazov was happy to oblige. If that life were to end, the succession remains very uncertain, since he has taken care to eliminate most potential rivals.

Uganda

Uganda's 'no-party' government offers a variation on one-party rule

Land area: *236,000 sq. km.*
Population: *21 million—urban 14%*
Capital city: *Kampala, 0.8 million*
People: *Baganda 17%, Karamojong 12%, Basogo 8%, Teso 8%, Langi 6%, Rwanda 6%, other 43%*
Language: *English, Luganda, Swahili, Bantu languages, Nilotic languages*
Religion: *Roman Catholic 33%, Protestant 33%, Muslim 16%, indigenous beliefs 18%*
Life expectancy: *40 years*
GNP per capita: *$PPP 1,170*
Currency: *Ugandan shilling*
Major exports: *Coffee, gold, fish, cotton*

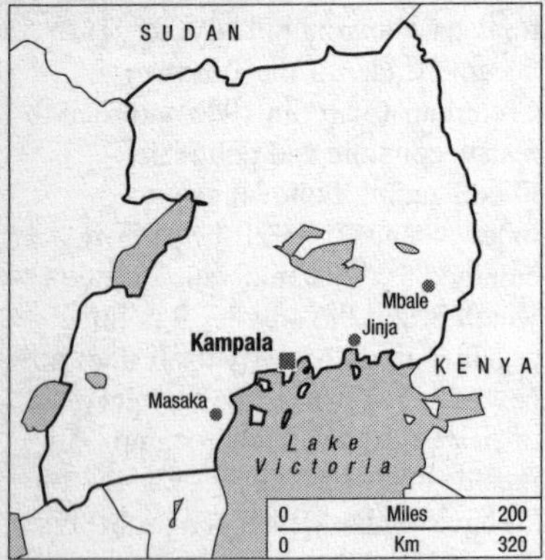

Uganda lies on the equator, but because of the altitude the climate is relatively mild. The country forms part of the East African Plateau, most of which lies between 1,000 and 2,000 metres. To the west the boundary is formed both by mountain ranges and by the Western Rift Valley which incorporates Lakes Edward and Albert. The eastern and north-eastern borders are also marked by mountains.

Most of the southern border runs across the world's second largest freshwater lake, Lake Victoria, which is shared with Kenya and Tanzania. Uganda's landscape shows great variety, from swampy river banks, to forests, to snowy peaks.

Uganda's population is also very diverse. It comprises dozens of major groups, but these can be divided into two main groups—the Bantu and the Nilotic. The Bantu, who live mostly in the south, make up around 70% of the population. The largest of these are the Ganda, also called the Baganda. The Nilotic group, mostly found in the north, include the Karamojong and the Teso. While the Bantu groups have provided most of the political élite, the Nilotic people have in the past dominated the armed forces.

Almost half of Ugandans live below the poverty line. However, the country does have one of Africa's most developed anti-poverty programmes, and poverty levels have been falling. The government's goal is to eliminate extreme poverty by 2017. This would be quite an achievement. Ugandans have one of the world's lowest life expectancies, a result partly of poor health services, but mainly of the AIDS epidemic which is the leading cause of death among adults. Uganda has been a pioneer in the fight against the disease, with a pervasive and frank information campaign.

More than 80% of the workforce depend on agriculture, generally working on small family farms growing basic food crops such as cassava, plantains, sweet potatoes, millet, and sorghum, mostly for their own consumption. They also grow a number of cash crops, notably coffee, which makes up around 70% of the country's export earnings.

Following independence in 1962, Uganda suffered decades of dictatorship and violence, much of it linked to rivalries between regions and ethnic groups. In 1971, the dictatorship of Milton Obote was overthrown by his chief-of-staff, General Idi Amin, whose reign of terror killed around 300,000 people and expelled 70,000 people of Asian origin. Amin was ousted in 1979 after an invasion by Tanzania. This resulted eventually in the return of Obote and a dubious election. But the violence and repression continued and one of the opposition parties, led by Yoweri Museveni, took up arms as a guerrilla National Resistance Army (NRA). In January 1986, the NRA seized Kampala and Obote fled.

Museveni was sworn in as president, representing the NRA's political arm, the National Resistance Movement (NRM). In an effort to subdue sectarianism, Museveni banned multi-party politics. Instead he introduced a 'movement' or 'no-party' system. Members of the constituent assembly instead have to be elected as independents, though in practice they have almost all been supporters of the NRM. In 1996, Museveni was elected president by a large majority.

A movement not a party

Museveni remained popular for a long period, largely because he ushered in political stability. He had also been rebuilding Uganda's wrecked economy, with the help of international donors who may have been disappointed by his lack of enthusiasm for democracy but were impressed by the fact that he was opening up the economy—removing many controls and welcoming private investment. Aid and stability produced steady economic growth, averaging around 7% annually over the period 1988-97. But growth subsequently slackened and donors have been withholding aid, concerned about corruption and rising expenditure on defence. Donors say corruption costs Uganda $200 million a year.

Museveni argues that he needs to spend on defence because he has to struggle against several rebel groups. The most serious, and the strangest, in the north, is the Lord's Resistance Army (LRA), led by Joseph Kony, who claims communication with the spirits, and has been killing thousands of people, kidnapping children to fight as soldiers, and generally wreaking havoc. Efforts to negotiate with, or crush, the LRA have come to nothing. Subsequently, another rebel group, the Allied Democratic Forces (ADF), started attacking towns in the west.

Museveni's military and economic problems have been compounded by his unsuccessful and costly intervention in the civil war in the neighbouring Democratic Republic of the Congo. Ostensibly, Museveni sent in 15,000 troops to protect Uganda by attacking ADF bases across the borders. In practice it looks as though he is more interested in overthrowing the Kabila government.

Meanwhile at home, the 'no-party' government is facing allegations of repression symptomatic of a one-party state. Even so, Museveni seems to remain popular, a referendum in July 2000 voted to retain his no-party system.

Ukraine

Ukraine sinks further into poverty, and could ultimately opt to unite with Russia

Land area: *604,000 sq. km.*
Population: *50 million—urban 72%*
Capital city: *Kiev, 2.6 million*
People: *Ukrainian 73%, Russian 22%, Jewish 1%, other 4%*
Language: *Ukrainian, Russian*
Religion: *Ukrainian Orthodox and others*
Government: *Republic*
Life expectancy: *69 years*
GNP per capita: *$PPP 2,190*
Currency: *Hryvna*
Major exports: *Metals, food, chemicals, machinery*

Ukraine consists almost entirely of gently rolling plains with the highest part in the west. The broad Dnieper River flows through the centre of the country, draining into the Black Sea in the south, north of the Crimean peninsula.

The majority of the population are ethnic Ukrainians, speaking a language closely related to Russian. Ukraine never existed as an independent country until the break-up of the Soviet Union, and its population distribution reflects its union with Russia. The population in the rural west is almost entirely Ukrainians while that in the more industrial east adjacent to Russia has a higher proportion of ethnic Russians. Since there are strong cultural and language links between the two communities, there is relatively little tension. Only in the Crimea, where around two-thirds of the population are ethnic Russians, are there separatist inclinations.

Ukraine's population shrank during the 1990s. Death rates rose as a result of declining standards of nutrition and health. Infectious diseases such as diphtheria, cholera, and TB surged, and health problems were compounded by alcoholism. In the early 1990s, falling numbers were offset to some extent by immigration from other former Soviet republics, particularly into the Crimea. Since then, however, the country has suffered net emigration.

Among the largest permanent departures have been of the Jews. Each year around one-tenth of Ukraine's 300,000 Jews head for Israel, Germany, or the USA. At the same time, there is steady labour migration to neighbouring countries, especially to the Czech Republic, where Ukrainians are prepared to work for desperately low wages.

This is a response to widespread poverty in Ukraine, where the GDP has fallen by more than 60% since independence. Poverty tends to be worst in the old smokestack, industrial, and coal mining areas of the east; people living in the rural west do at least have the option of farming their family plots.

Industry still employs more than one-fifth of the labour force—though it has gone into steep decline. Between 1990 and 1997, industrial output fell by more than two-thirds. Although some areas of heavy industry, such as steel or chemicals, have managed to sustain output, others have collapsed, particularly those related to defence and those producing low-quality consumer goods that cannot compete with imports.

Ukraine has a significant mining sector and is the world's fifth largest producer of iron ore. But its coal industry is rapidly disappearing and though it has deposits of oil and gas these remain under-developed. The power industry is still suffering from the effects of the 1986 disaster at Chernobyl—one of whose dangerous reactors was still working in 2000. Ukrainian industry remains almost entirely in state hands; only small retail enterprises have been privatized. Foreign investors have mostly stayed away, discouraged by an unpredictable legal system and corruption.

Agriculture, which also employs around one-fifth of the workforce, is in a similarly difficult situation. Ukraine is blessed with rich black soil—'chernozem'—and was considered the breadbasket of the Soviet Union. But output has collapsed since independence as a result both of the loss of its Soviet market and a general shortage of investment and inputs. Most land is still in the hands of collective farms, but half the output comes from the 14% of land that consists of smaller private plots.

Blessed with rich black soil

Ukraine was one of the final Soviet republics to declare its independence. Its first president was Leonid Kravchuk. A former communist, he somewhat belatedly declared himself in favour of independence and won the 1991 presidential election. But he had little appetite for economic reform and maintained most of the systems of price control and subsidy. In 1992, he appointed as prime minister the more reform-minded Leonid Kuchma. Kravchuk fell out with Kuchma and sacked him the following year, but in 1994 he conceded an early presidential election—which he lost to Kuchma.

Kuchma struggled with a parliament still dominated by communists. He managed to achieve a new constitution in 1996, which increased the power of the presidency. But his regime has been uninspiring, notable chiefly for enriching his family and friends, and for extensive political violence. Kuchma's initial support had come from the Russian-leaning east, as opposed to the more nationalist west, but he now says he wants a balanced relationship between east and west.

Kuchma was re-elected in 1999 after a ruthless campaign against the communist candidate. He corralled the state media to support him while harassing and censoring the rest of the press.

The only cause for optimism seems to be Kuchma's appointment in December 1999, under Western pressure, of Viktor Yushchenko as prime minister. He has set his sights on economic reform and has managed to renegotiate Ukraine's massive debt.

United Arab Emirates

One of the world's wealthiest countries that is a regional magnet for shoppers

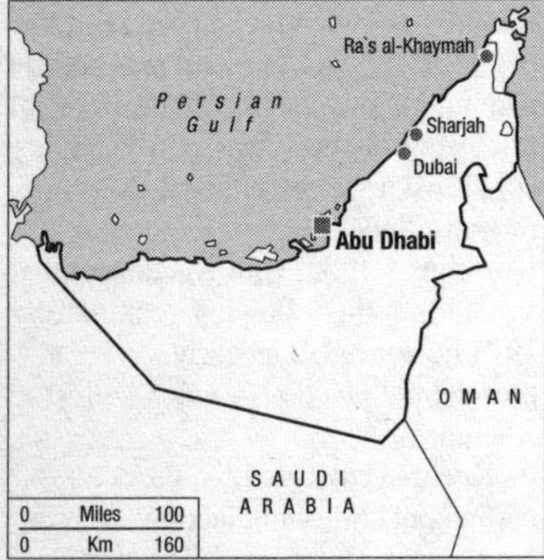

Land area: *84,000 sq. km.*
Population: *3 million—urban 85%*
Capital city: *Abu Dhabi , 670,000*
People: *Emiri 19%, other Arab and Iranian 23%, South Asian 50%, other 8%*
Language: *Arabic*
Religion: *Muslim*
Government: *Federation of monarchies*
Life expectancy: *75 years*
GNP per capita: *$PPP 19,720*
Currency: *Emirian dirham*
Major exports: *Oil, natural gas, re-exports, fish, dates*

Apart from the Al-Hajar mountains in the Musandam peninsula along the eastern border with Oman, the territory of the United Arab Emirates, which stretches south from the Persian Gulf, is flat, barren and low-lying—a mixture of sandy desert, gravel, and salt flats.

The UAE is a federation of seven sheikhdoms. By far the largest is Abu Dhabi, which covers three-quarters of the territory and includes the capital city. The six others lie east of Abu Dhabi, they are Dubai, Ajman, Sharjah, Umm al-Qaywayn, Ra's al-Khaymah on the Persian Gulf, and Al-Fujayrah, which faces the Gulf of Oman side.

Most people live on or near the coast. Only 13% are UAE citizens. They are mostly Sunni Muslims, though there are Shiah minorities in Sharjah and Dubai. The rest of the population are immigrant workers, chiefly from the Indian sub-continent. In an effort to reduce the imbalance, the government in 1999 stopped issuing new work permits and demanded of government-owned banks that between 1999 and 2006 they increase their proportion of nationals from 12% to 40%. The private sector is watching nervously, since even a national high-school graduate can command twice the salary of a qualified, experienced worker from India.

In the past, the people of this area made their living from subsistence agriculture and fishing, though with little good land or supplies of fresh water the agricultural prospects are limited. A combination of land reclamation and irrigation from underground aquifers allows farmers to grow dates for export and enables the UAE to be self-sufficient in fruit and vegetables. As a result of such efforts, total production increased six-fold during the 1990s. Nevertheless, most grains have to be imported.

The fortunes of the UAE changed forever in 1958 with the discovery of oil and gas in Abu Dhabi, and later in Dubai, where production started in 1969. Sharjah is the only other emirate with significant deposits. Abu

Dhabi's deposits are still substantial and could last one hundred years, though those in Dubai and elsewhere are running out more rapidly. But Abu Dhabi's wealth stems less from current oil income than from returns on its accumulated savings: in 1999, investments in foreign bonds and equity markets were thought to be worth $350 billion. Abu Dhabi also has substantial gas reserves which could last for another 150 years.

Both Abu Dhabi and Dubai have steadily been diversifying away from oil into such areas as refining and petro-chemicals. Dubai has done so more extensively. It has, for example, the world's largest single-site aluminium smelter and has a major duty-free zone at Jebel. This zone is used largely for small-scale local assembly, and as a distribution centre for other parts of the region: by the end of 1997, this was home to more than 1,300 international companies. The UAE's revenue from 're-exports' in 1998 was greater than that from oil and gas.

Tourism is another useful source of income, and there are around 2 mllion visitors to the UAE each year. Dubai's port, airport, and glittering array of hotels, restaurants, shops and brothels draw people from all over the region. In 1999, Dubai also announced that it was building a duty-free 'internet city'.

Building an internet city

Abu Dhabi now has similar ambitions and has been encouraging foreign investment. In 1996, the government established an Abu Dhabi Free Zone Authority to plan a huge new $3.3 billion financial centre on Saadiyat Island, where it has promised that investing companies need never pay any tax and can repatriate all their profits.

The UAE is a federation. The federal government deals with defence, for example, foreign policy, and immigration. But the federation is a weak one: only 30% of total UAE expenditures goes through the federal budget, and most of this is contributed by Abu Dhabi. The rest is spent by individual emirates who control their own natural resources and regulate local business. However there is a trend for greater federal responsibility: Dubai, for example, has now transferred its army to the federal defence structure—which means essentially that Abu Dhabi will pay.

Abu Dhabi's economic clout within the UAE is reflected in its political power. The rulers of the emirates meet as the Supreme Council and elect the president. Unsurprisingly, they choose the Emir of Abu Dhabi, who is Sheikh Zayed bin Sultan al-Nahayan. In 1996, he was elected for his sixth consecutive term. The Supreme Council also appoints the Council of Ministers. Legislative activity is handled by the forty-person Federal National Council, which is also appointed and has only advisory powers. The UAE has no political parties.

Doubts about the future succession for Abu Dhabi, and therefore for the UAE, were settled in 1999 when Sheikh Zayed, in his eighties and rather frail, summoned his elder sons to Geneva to announce that he would be succeeded by Crown Prince Kahlifa bin Zayed al-Nahayan, though subsequent succession would pass to a different line of the family.

United Kingdom

The UK is slowly edging towards closer integration with Europe.

Land area: 245,000 sq. km.
Population: 59 million—urban 89%
Capital city: London, 7 million
People: English, Scottish, Irish, Welsh, and ethnic minorities
Language: English, Welsh, Gaelic, Urdu, Hindi
Religion: Protestant, Roman Catholic, Muslim. Sikh, Hindu, Jewish
Government: Constitutional monarchy
Life expectancy: 77 years
GNP per capita: $PPP 20,640
Currency: Pound
Major exports: Manufactured goods, fuels, food

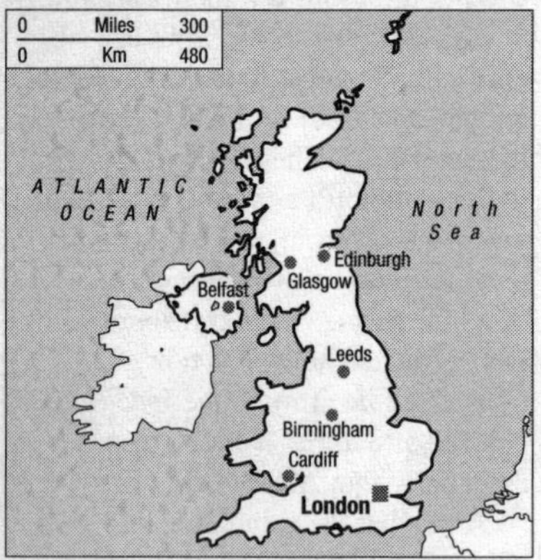

Scotland, England, and Wales, together with Northern Ireland make up the nation-state that is the United Kingdom (UK). Of the four, Scotland in the north is the most mountainous, though to the west Wales too has an often rugged landscape, and there are lower mountain ranges in England, mostly in the north. The lowlands and plains that make up around half the UK's territory have rich soil and a temperate climate that make for productive agriculture.

Around 80% of the population are English. The Scottish, Welsh, and Irish are smaller in number but tend to have stronger national identities, including their own languages—though these are spoken by only a small minority. The UK has also received immigrants from former colonies—in the 1950s and 1960s from the Caribbean, and later from Africa and South Asia. Ethnic minorities make up around 6% of the population; they are exposed to racism and are also generally poorer than white people. The UK has strong natural borders so illegal immigration is difficult, and the government has been taking an increasingly tough line on asylum.

The British still benefit from the egalitarian welfare state created after the Second World War, though health and education services have come under financial pressure. Wealth has become steadily more concentrated in London and the south of England—the per capita GDP in north-east England, Wales, and Northern Ireland is now one-third less than in greater London.

The UK was the cradle of the industrial revolution, but nowadays manufacturing industry accounts for only one-fifth of GDP. Some industries, such as coal, have virtually disappeared. British industry received an unexpected boost in the 1960s and 1970s from the discovery of oil and gas in the North Sea. Production has now declined, but the country is largely self-sufficient in oil. In recent years, the UK has been a magnet for multinationals seeking a loosely regulated labour market and a base in the EU, and has been getting around 10% of global investment.

Agriculture accounts for less than 2% of GDP but is highly productive and grows around two-thirds of national needs. The most serious setback was an outbreak of 'mad-cow' disease in the late 1990s that led to a ban on British beef exports. Fishing has also declined, but still meets most of local needs.

The UK has a very diverse service sector. This includes a leading global financial centre in the City of London which contributes $35 billion annually to overseas earnings. The UK is also the world's fifth most popular tourist destination. The tourist industry employs 2 million people, generating $80 billion annually and bringing in 25 million foreign visitors.

The UK is a constitutional monarchy ruled since 1952 by Queen Elizabeth II. For the past 50 years, British politics has been the preserve of two main parties: the pro-business Conservative Party and the trade-union backed Labour Party, with the party now called the Liberal Democrats some way behind.

Thatcher's legacy

The most radical government was the 1979-90 conservative administration of Margaret Thatcher, which shattered many areas of national consensus—privatizing state-owned industries and breaking the power of the trade unions. Though often bitterly opposed, many of these reforms are intact and 'Thatcherism' has been widely emulated elsewhere. Thatcher's popularity peaked with victory over Argentina in the Falklands War in 1982 but she eventually alienated too many people and in 1990 was replaced by John Major, who surprisingly won the 1994 general election. In 1997, however, with his party fatally split on its attitude to the EU, Major suffered a crushing electoral defeat.

The victor was Tony Blair, who had purged his party of its more divisive elements and created a New Labour Party to occupy the centre ground. One of his first challenges was Northern Ireland which for decades had been a battleground between Catholic and Protestant terrorists. In 1998, diplomacy seemed to prevail with the Good Friday Agreement that allowed for a new directly elected assembly. In 1999, both Wales and Scotland also acquired similar assemblies and a degree of devolved government.

Blair has benefited from a strong economy, and a weak opposition. Though he satisfied some supporters on the left by introducing such progressive measures as a minimum wage, he disappointed many others by initially holding back expenditure on health and education, and taking illiberal positions on immigration, drugs, and freedom of information.

With an election on the horizon in 2001, both main parties have started to resort to populist promises. Blair and New Labour seem likely to be elected to a second term, but one issue that could knock them off course is the decision on joining European Monetary Union, for which the policy is currently 'wait and see'. The UK joined the EU in 1972, but many people are wary of greater integration.

United States

The lone superpower, with a booming high-tech economy. But not everyone has gained and inequality is increasing

Land area: *9,364,000 sq. km.*
Population: *270 million—urban 77%*
Capital city: *Washington DC , 0.6 million*
People: *White 83%, black 12%, Asian 3%, Amerindian 1% (includes 11% Hispanic, of any race)*
Language: *English, Spanish*
Religion: *Protestant 56%, Roman Catholic 28%, other 6%, none 10%*
Government: *Republic*
Life expectancy: *77 years*
GNP per capita: *$PPP 29,340*
Currency: *Dollar*
Major exports: *Capital goods, automobiles, industrial supplies and materials, consumer goods, food*

Within its vast area, the USA has most types of landscape and climate—from tropical swamps in Florida, to the deserts of New Mexico, to the snow-capped peaks of the Rocky Mountains. The east of the country consists of the Atlantic coastal plain, which extends down from New England then broadens further south to include Florida and the Gulf coast. West of this plain are the Appalachian mountains, and then the vast areas of the prairies to the north and the Mississippi basin to the south.

West of the prairies are the Rocky Mountains and then a complex system of mountains and plateaux that stretches down to the Pacific coast. From north to south, the western landscape includes the forests of Washington state, through the beaches of California, to the semi-desert of Arizona in the south. The main land mass has 48 states. The remaining two are Alaska, which lies beyond Canada, and Hawaii in the Pacific Ocean.

The diversity of the US landscape is complemented by the ethnic diversity of its population. Most people are white—descendants of European immigration from the 17th century onwards. Added to these were millions of blacks who came mainly to the southern states as slaves. But the USA has always been a magnet for immigrants and today 9% of the population are foreign born. However the pattern of immigration shifted after legislative changes from the mid-1960s that removed an earlier racist bias and resulted in a dramatic increase in arrivals from Asia and Latin America. In 1998, of total legal arrivals of 0.7 million, the highest proportion came from Mexico (20%), China (5%), and India (5%). Millions more arrive illegally—there are probably around 6 million undocumented immigrants, half from Mexico.

The Immigration and Naturalization Service tries to control the borders with 7,000 staff. But this determination is undermined by thousands of enterprises only too happy to use illegal immigrants as cheap and exploitable labour.

The US population is generally mobile and dynamic, but it does suffer from persistent racial inequalities, most notably between black and white. The average income for black Americans is 20% lower than that for whites. The mortality rate for black infants is twice the rate of whites, and black adults are twice as likely to be unemployed and far more likely to be in jail. The prisons are also filling up—the USA has one-quarter of the world's prison population.

Hispanics are later arrivals, and they too tend to be poorer than whites. Many only speak Spanish, and some US communities are now effectively bilingual, but, like previous immigrants, by the second and third generation they will be using English.

From melting pot to salad bowl

The US population used to be called a melting pot; now it is thought of as a 'salad bowl' with discrete ingredients. Even so there is extensive inter-marriage. One-quarter of Hispanics who wed in the USA marry non-Hispanics. One-third of Asian-Americans marry non-Asians. Black and white are less likely to intermarry.

The USA has the world's largest and most diverse economy, built on a rich endowment of natural resources that include deposits of most important minerals, including copper, gold, aluminium, and coal. It is also a major oil producer, though the reserves are depleted and output has fallen. Much of US life is constructed around the automobile.

Another vital US resource has been its agricultural land. The USA produces two-fifths of the world's maize and around half its soybeans, and is also a major food exporter—accounting for around one-third of global exports of wheat. This vast output has been sustained despite a smaller farm labour force and a shrinking area of agricultural land. Most small farms have given way to agribusiness corporations.

Abundant natural resources, combined with an energetic immigrant population, and a large national market, have also made US industry dynamic and innovative. Major industries include steel, automobiles, chemicals, and aerospace. And although other countries have caught up in basic production, the USA has set the pace in more advanced industries such as electronics, telecommunications, and computers. For many years the world's largest company was General Motors; today it is the US software giant, Microsoft.

As in other advanced industrial countries, however, the USA's economy is now dominated by services. In 1997 only 2% of the labour force worked in agriculture, and 19% in manufacturing, with 6% in construction. Most of the rest were in trade or other kinds of service—around 20% work for the government.

Since it has a huge internal market, the USA does not need to depend heavily on exports of goods and services which are around only 12% of GDP—less than half the proportion for the EU, for example. Nevertheless its sheer size still makes it the world's largest exporter. The most important recent trade development was the signing in 1994 of the North

American Free Trade Agreement with Canada and Mexico. Even so, there is often strong resistance to free trade—US manufacturers, especially the steel industry, frequently protest at the 'dumping' of foreign goods.

The US economy has remained buoyant and in early 2000 unemployment was only around 4%. But not everyone has gained. Wages have risen slowly if at all, and inequality has increased. The richest one-fifth of US households get half the country's income, while the poorest fifth get less than 4%. More than 13% of the population live below the poverty line.

More than 13% of people live in poverty

Politics in the USA is based on competition between two main parties: the Democrats and the Republicans. While there is considerable overlap in terms of support and policy, historically the Democrats have represented working people, and ethnic minorities, and taken more liberal attitudes on civil rights and welfare. The Republicans have been more likely to represent big business and to assume socially conservative positions on gay rights or abortion, and will want to minimize the size of government.

Hovering around the government are thousands of interest groups with highly professional lobbying machinery. In recent years, one of the most significant influences has been the Christian Right—the USA has one of the highest rates of church going among the industrial countries.

The US government is based on a separation of powers between the executive (the President), the judiciary (the Supreme Court), and the legislature (the Congress). The Congress consists of a 100-seat upper house, the Senate, which has two senators for each of the 50 states, and a 435-seat lower house, the House of Representatives. Since this is a federal republic, individual states also wield considerable power through their governors and state legislatures.

This means, however that these bodies can frequently be at odds. Thus when the Democrat, Bill Clinton, was elected president in 1992, the Democrats were also in the majority in both houses. By the time he was re-elected for his second term in 1996, however, the Republicans had a majority in both houses. Congress was thus able to frustrate Clinton's efforts to reform the health care system, and in his second term it came close to impeaching him because of perjury and obstruction of justice relating to a sexual relationship with a White House intern, Monica Lewinsky.

Clinton also had considerable successes, notably a 1997 agreement with Congress to have a balanced budget by 2002. This was helped by a booming economy that boosted tax revenue, and the end of the Cold War meant that defence expenditure could be cut by more than 10%. Federal expenditure on welfare has also been cut now that welfare policy has been delegated to the states. With the stock market soaring to record highs, most voters prefer to ignore Clinton's personal failings and give him credit for economic success. Following the November 2000 election, he will be replaced either by his vice-president, Al Gore, or by the Republican candidate George W. Bush.

Uruguay

Uruguay had a reputation for prosperity and freedom that it is now trying to restore

Land area: *177,000 sq. km.*
Population: *3 million—urban 91%*
Capital city: *Montevideo, 1.3 million*
People: *White 88%, mestizo 8%, black 4%*
Language: *Spanish*
Religion: *Roman Catholic 66%, Protestant 2%, Jewish 2%, other 30%*
Government: *Republic*
Life expectancy: *74 years*
GNP per capita: *$PPP 9,480*
Currency: *Peso*
Major exports: *Wool, textiles, beef, rice*

Lodged between two much larger neighbours, Brazil and Argentina, Uruguay consists mostly of plateaux and rolling grasslands—the pampas—that are ideal for cattle raising. The highest parts of the country are in the hills of the Cuchilla Grande in the south-east. Another of Uruguay's natural advantages is its fresh, temperate climate, which, combined with long sandy beaches, makes this a popular holiday destination.

Uruguayans are largely of European origin, predominantly Spanish and Italian. The small black population has immigrated from Brazil. Uruguay has long been one of the most urbanized countries of Latin America. Income distribution has been fairly equitable and the country has a large middle class.

From the 1930s, Uruguay built up a comprehensive system of social welfare and by the late-1980s around one-quarter of the labour force was in government service. The welfare system has been eroded in recent years, and the social security system has been partly privatized. But Uruguayans still have high standards of health and education—even university education is free. By Latin American standards, this is also a relatively egalitarian country, and one of the few where inequality has not increased over the past decade. Most of the poor people live in the rural areas where many still lack safe water and sanitation.

Uruguay's wealth was built on the raising of cattle and sheep on the pampas. And although agriculture now accounts for only around one-tenth of GDP, and employs a similar proportion of the workforce, it still plays a central role in the economy since meat, wool, and hides make up around half the country's exports and also supply vital raw materials for industry. Uruguayans themselves are also serious meat eaters.

Most of the land is occupied by large ranches. Since the herd is largely disease-free, Uruguay has been very successful at selling meat to the USA and the EU. In recent years, it has also discovered a new market for wool in China. Most cereal output is for local consumption, but rice, which is chiefly grown in the department of Rocha on the southern coastal plain, is becoming an increasingly important export to Brazil.

Manufacturing and commerce are concentrated in Montevideo, which generates more than half the country's GDP. A high proportion of this is still in the public sector, which seems to have proved more efficient than in other countries. The state company ANAP refines petroleum, as well as producing alcohol and cement. Most manufacturing is for local consumption, but recently-planted forests of eucalyptus and pine have been supplying mills making pulp and paper for export.

The country's other major foreign-currency earner is tourism, mostly to the beaches around the exclusive up-market resort of Punta del Este to the east of Montevideo. More than 2 million visitors arrive each year, almost all of these from Argentina.

Argentines heading for the beach

Uruguay's trade links with its heavyweight neighbours have been further strengthened by the creation of Mercosur, a common market for the countries of the 'Southern Cone', whose secretariat is in Montevideo. There have also been suggestions of building a giant bridge from Buenos Aires across the River Plate which would promote even greater flows of trade and tourism.

Political power in Uruguay has traditionally alternated between the Partido Colorado and the Partido Nacional (also known as the 'Blancos'). This division does not correspond to any ideological divide; more a matter of personalities and history. People tend to vote for one party or the other based on family tradition. Such ideological divisions as do exist tend to be between factions within each of the parties.

The pattern of control by either the Colorados or the Blancos was broken in the 1970s. Left-wing groups, notably the Tupemaros urban guerrillas, established a strong presence and eventually provoked a coup by the military who ruled from 1973 to 1984 in a remarkably vicious fashion.

When democracy was restored, the Colorados, led by Julio María Sanguinetti, won the first presidential election in 1985. He was replaced in 1989 by Luis Albert Lacalle of the Blancos.

Throughout this period, however, a number of left-wing parties had steadily been building their support. So although Sanguinetti duly won the 1994 presidential election, the 1995 congressional elections produced a fairly even three-way split between the Colorados, the Blancos, and a left-wing coalition, the Frente Amplie. As a result, the Colorados and the Blancos for the first time were forced to enter into a coalition in order to form a government.

The Marxist candidate of the Frente Amplie almost won the presidential election in 1999, but he was defeated in the second round by Jorge Batlle, the Colorado candidate. Batlle is the latest in a long political dynasty. His father and grandfather were both presidents, and his great-uncle, Jose Batlle y Ordoñez, was one of the founders of Uruguay's welfare state.

Uzbekistan

Very dependent on cotton and gold, and making little progress to democracy

Land area: *447,000 sq. km.*
Population: *24 million—urban 42%*
Capital city: *Tashkent, 2.1 million*
People: *Uzbek 80%, Russian 6%, Tajik 5%, Kazakh 3% , other 6%*
Language: *Uzbek 74%, Russian 14%, Tajik 4%, other 8%*
Religion: *Muslim 88%, Eastern Orthodox 9%, other 3%*
Government: *Republic*
Life expectancy: *68 years*
GNP per capita: *$PPP 2,900*
Currency: *Som*
Major exports: *Cotton, gold*

Uzbekistan has some mountainous terrain in the east, and a few fertile oases, but around 80% of the territory is a sandy plain that merges in the south with the Kyzylkum Desert.

Most of the population are ethnic Uzbeks and live in the rural areas. Uzbeks are Sunni Muslims and tend to be more devout than those in neighbouring countries. Like other former Soviet Republics, Uzbekistan also has a substantial Russian minority. The Russians live mostly in Tashkent and other cities, though many have also left: over the period 1989-95 over half a million people emigrated. The next largest group, the Tajiks, are to be found in older cities like Samarkand.

The population is growing fairly rapidly, particularly among ethnic Uzbeks in the rural areas. Standards of health are poor, and recent years of economic crisis have caused health services to deteriorate further. Expenditure on education has also been falling, as has school enrolment. In 1995, almost half of households were receiving less than the minimum wage. Inequality has been rising steeply.

Housing has been privatized and more than 1 million people own formerly state-owned apartments.

Around 40% of the population work in private agriculture, though all farmers have to lease their land from the government. People are allocated small plots of land for lifetime use. These have helped maintain food production and account for around 80% of meat and milk production. They have the advantage of fertile land and a fairly mild climate, but since rainfall is light they rely heavily on irrigation.

The most important cash crop is cotton. Uzbekistan is the world's largest exporter of cotton, referred to locally as 'white gold'. Though most cotton producers are private or belong to co-operatives, they can sell only to the state—which in 1997 was paying only one-third of the world price so they had little incentive to increase efficiency or output. With so much of the land devoted to cotton, the country does not produce sufficient grain and is a substantial importer.

Heavy and inefficient use of water for cotton production has also drawn so much water from the country's two main rivers that the Aral Sea into which they drain has shrunk dramatically—by one-third between 1974 and 1995—with severe health and environmental damage in the surrounding areas.

Overuse of irrigation is drying up the Aral Sea

Industry too has been strongly connected with agriculture, notably through the Tashkent tractor factory. But the most lucrative industrial activity is gold mining which in recent years has helped to underpin the economy. Most of this takes place at the huge state-owned open-cast Muruntau mine. Uzbekistan is the world's ninth-largest producer of gold.

The government has declared in principle that it is moving more towards a market economy. However, progress has been slow. Unemployment is officially quite low but this is probably because enterprises are reluctant to restructure and to fire excess labour.

Rather than opening up to the outside world, Uzbekistan has pursued a strategy of import-substitution—borrowing from abroad to invest in heavy industry such as steel. With these debts hanging over the country, Uzbekistan is now even more dependent on exports of cotton and gold.

In 2000, the government again promised to increase privatization and even float the currency, which in the black market was worth around only one-sixth of its official rate.

Politics in Uzbekistan is dominated by the president, Islam Karimov, who is effectively the dictator of a police state. Karimov was the communist leader before the break-up of the Soviet Union. He opposed independence, but when it came he successfully had himself elected president in a 1991 vote generally assumed to have been rigged.

Uzbekistan does have a legislative body, the Supreme Assembly, but in practice this does little more than carry out presidential decisions. The two leading opposition parties are banned and their leaders have fled into exile.

The only effective opposition centres on Islamic groups. Mosques that were closed during Stalin's era have been allowed to reopen, but only under strict control. The clergy are regularly harassed by the police and by the national security service, the equivalent of the KGB—who have also used torture, illegal searches, and wiretaps. Karimov is particularly nervous about the prospect of an Islamic state appearing in neighbouring Tajikistan.

Nevertheless there have been glimmers of conciliation. In 1999, Karimov allowed Sheikh Mohammed Sadeq, an Islamic leader, to return from exile—hoping that he might neutralize the more radical groups.

For the presidential election in 2000 Karimov did at least take the trouble to arrange a contest, by setting up a token opponent, Abdulhafiz Jalalov. However, the state media largely ignored Jalalov and even he reportedly voted for Karimov, who received 92% of the vote.

Vanuatu

Vanuatu is still divided along colonial lines

Vanuatu comprises around eighty Pacific islands of either volcanic or coral origin, many of which are still covered by tropical rainforests. The country is vulnerable to natural disasters, including volcanic eruptions, earthquakes, and tidal waves.

Most of the population, who are called 'Ni Vanuatu', are of Melanesian extraction and have a pidgin-based lingua franca, Bislama, along with around 105 other languages.

Vanuatu's society remains divided by its strange colonial heritage. As the New Hebrides until 1980, the country was ruled jointly by the British and French—who had established their own schools and churches. As a result, the élite population tend to be either French-speaking Catholics, or English-speaking Protestants, with the latter in the majority.

The population as a whole is also fairly sharply divided between the 70% who live in scattered rural communities from subsistence or small-scale agriculture and the urban dwellers, most of whom work in services. The farmers grow food crops, such as taro and yams, as well as cash crops such as coconuts, cocoa, and squash for export. The cattle they raise also provide export income through beef sales.

Tourism, mostly from Australia and New Zealand, is an important source of income. Vanuatu has also been establishing itself as an offshore tax haven, and financial service companies contribute around one-tenth of GDP. In addition there is a small manufacturing sector, mostly involved in processing agricultural and forestry products.

After independence, the political parties organized themselves along language lines—though subsequently they have splintered. The main anglophone party is the Vanua'aku Party (VP), while the main francophone party is the Union des partis modérés (UMP).

The VP won the first election but subsequently split several times to create first the Melanesian Progressive Party (MPP) and later the National United Party. In the 1980s and 1990s Vanuatu was governed by a series of unstable coalitions.

After the 1998 elections, the VP leader, Donald Kalpokas, again took over as prime minister of a coalition government, but in November 1999 he was replaced by Barak Sope of the MPP after a dispute over the introduction of value-added tax. In 1999, John Bani was elected president by an electoral college made up of the parliament and the heads of regional councils.

Land area: *12,000 sq. km.*
Population: *190,000—urban 19%*
Capital city: *Port Vila, 30,000*
People: *Melanesian 94%, French 4%, others 2%*
Language: *English, French, Bislama*
Religion: *Christian*
Government: *Republic*
Life expectancy: *65 years*
GNP per capita: *$PPP 3,160*
Currency: *Vatu*
Major exports: *Copra, beef, cocoa*

Venezuela

Venezuela has seen a sharp increase in poverty, now its democracy is under threat

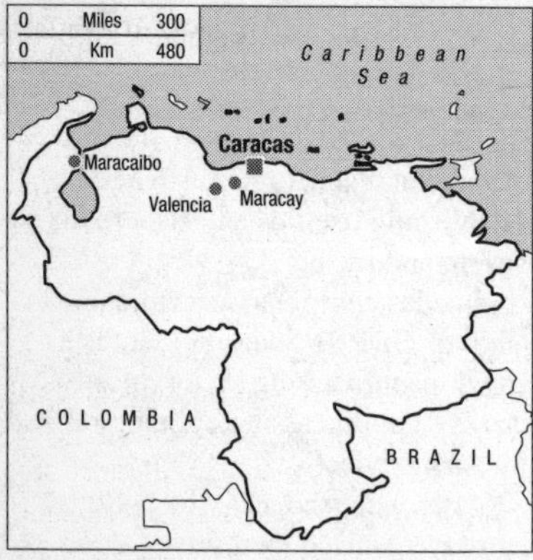

Land area: *912,000 sq. km.*
Population: *23 million—urban 86%*
Capital city: *Caracas—2.8 million*
People: *Mestizo 67%, white 21%, black 10%, Amerindian 2%*
Language: *Spanish*
Religion: *Roman Catholic*
Government: *Federal Republic*
Life expectancy: *72 years*
GNP per capita: *$PPP 8,190*
Currency: *Bolívar*
Major exports: *Oil, bauxite, aluminium, steel*

The central one-third of Venezuela consists of open grasslands, the 'llanos'. To the south-east, and along the borders with Guyana and Brazil, are the Guiana Highlands, an isolated area of heavily forested plateaux and low mountains.

Despite rapid population growth—since 1958 from 5 million to 23 million—Venezuela remains sparsely populated. The majority of people live in the north and north-west around the northern tip of the Andes, and within this area most are now concentrated in the cities that are home to 86% of the population. Caracas officially has less than 3 million people, though the real figure may be closer to 7 million.

In the past Venezuela has been one of the richer South American countries, with an extensive system of social security. But poverty has increased dramatically in recent years, especially in the 'ranchos', the slums that ring Caracas. Between 1975 and 1997, the proportion of people living on less than $2 per day increased from 33% to 67%.

At the same time, social services have crumbled. Schools are in poor shape as a result of underinvestment. And as poverty has increased, so enrolment and attendance have been dropping. The health system too is in crisis and many hospitals have closed.

Despite rising poverty levels Venezuela continues to attract immigrants who come across the porous and lawless border with Colombia to work as agricultural labourers or as illegal gold miners. There are thought to be around 2 million illegal immigrants—75% from Colombia.

Venezuela used to be an agricultural country—though only a small proportion of the land is suitable for arable farming. Nowadays, however, only around 11% of the labour force work in agriculture, many of them raising cattle, and more than 60% of food has to be imported.

Agriculture was pushed into the background after 1914 by the discovery of oil near Maracaibo in the north-west. Venezuela rapidly became the world's first major oil exporter. Even today, its proven reserves are the sixth largest in the world. Oil usually accounts for three-quarters of export income and nearly two-thirds of government revenue. In addition, Venezuela has large quantities of natural gas—the world's fifth largest reserves—as well as substantial reserves of bauxite, coal, iron ore, and gold.

Oil revenues accelerated Venezuela's economic and industrial development, much of which was in the government's hands. The government nationalized the oil industry in 1975 and subsequently invested heavily in other sectors such as steel, cement, and petro-chemicals. Unfortunately, abundant oil money, and the high exchange rates it sustained, reduced the incentive to establish a more broadly-based economy.

Public expenditure and investment have also fluctuated along with international oil prices—rising when prices are high, then crashing again.

Government spending crashes with the oil price

The worst crash was in the early 1980s when the country was hit by falling oil prices at a time of rising interest rates and the Latin American debt crisis. This triggered a recession from which Venezuela has never really recovered.

In recent decades Venezuela has usually been governed by one of two main political parties: the centre-left Democratic Action (AD) and the centre-right Independent Political Organization Committee (COPEI). But the political process has been deeply corrupt; elections have been fraudulent and the parties have lined their own pockets and distributed jobs to their friends.

Nowadays, presidential candidates have deemed it wise to break away from their own parties and stand under fresh colours. Hugo Chavez, a former military officer who organized a failed coup in the early 1990s, won the 1998 presidential elections on a populist platform. He organized a referendum to establish a constituent assembly to write a new constitution.

Chavez and his party won a landslide victory and then used the constitutional assembly to usurp the powers of the national parliament. In many ways, Chavez represents a return to the old-style caudillo, or strongman, politics, using government expenditure to win votes.

In the event, his first major task was to deal with one of the country's worst ever disasters in December 1999, when massive mudslides along the coast killed at least 30,000 people and made more than a quarter of a million homeless. Chavez blamed corrupt politicians and planners who had allowed shanty towns to mushroom on steep slopes.

With a new constitution that offered him the prospect of two six-year terms, and a higher oil price that allowed him to increase public spending a little, Chavez called an election in May 2000. He faced a stiffer challenge than he anticipated from a former supporter, Arias Cardenas who had no party of his own but was backed by some smaller parties. The election had to be postponed as the system was not ready but Chavez seems likely to win whenever it takes place.

Vietnam

Vietnam has partially liberalized its economy, but the Communist Party remains firmly in charge

Land area: *332,000 sq. km.*
Population: *78 million—urban 36%*
Capital city: *Hanoi, 2.1 million*
People: *Vietnamese 90%, Chinese 3%, other 7%*
Language: *Vietnamese, Chinese, English, French, Khmer, tribal languages*
Religion: *Buddhist, Taoist, Roman Catholic, indigenous beliefs*
Government: *Communist*
Life expectancy: *67 years*
GNP per capita: *$PPP 1,690*
Currency: *Dong*
Major exports: *Textiles, oil, rice, marine products, coffee, footwear*

Around two-thirds of Vietnam consists of the Annamite mountain chain, which snakes down the length of the country from north to south. The two main lowland areas are the Red River delta in the north, which includes Hanoi, and the much larger Mekong delta in the south, which includes Ho Chi Minh City. These two are linked by a narrow coastal plain.

Most of the population are ethnic Vietnamese who live in one of the two deltas. Also to be found there are many of the Khmer minority, and several million people of Chinese origin, chiefly in the urban areas. In the mountain areas, the ethnic composition is more complex, with more than 50 different groups.

Known collectively by the French term 'Montagnards', they live in small communities and have struggled to preserve their traditional lifestyles. Because of population pressure in the deltas where there are a number of natural hazards, the government has been resettling people in the uplands but has encountered considerable resistance. There are also many Vietnamese overseas: 750,000 people left after the end of the war, many for the USA.

The Vietnamese have had good standards of health and education but now that state subsidies have been removed, school attendance has dropped—and there has been an increase in the number of street children and child labourers. Poverty has certainly been reduced: between 1992 and 1998 the proportion living in poverty fell from 58% to 37%. However, there has also been a rise in inequality, and a widening gap between the cities and the countryside. Particularly poor are those in the central highlands and northern uplands. Around 40% of children are malnourished.

Two-thirds of people work in agriculture. Since 1989, most people have been working on their own account as households rather than as members of communes. Their principle crop, particularly in the deltas, is rice. Vietnam is now the world's second largest rice exporter. The main constraint is the lack of suitable land. Much of the additional land brought under cultivation in recent years, particularly in the highlands, has been used for cash crops such as tea, cotton, coffee, rubber, and sugar. Coffee has been a notable success: yields are high—by 1997 Vietnam was among the world's top five coffee exporters. Rubber too has done well.

Since 1986, Vietnam has undertaken a process of economic renovation—'doi moi'—with greater market forces and price incentives. This led to a rapid growth in industry, particularly in light manufacturing areas such as garments, toys, and footwear, as well as electronics. There is also a growing tourist industry, with around 2 million visitors per year.

Much of this expansion was driven by transnational companies tempted by the prospect of a high-quality labour force prepared to work for low wages. Investment accelerated after 1994 when the USA lifted its trade embargo, and by 1996 foreign direct investment accounted for one-third of GDP. Since then enthusiasm has waned. Vietnam has proved less economically liberal than investors had hoped, especially following the Asian financial crisis, which confirmed the government's doubts about exposure to foreign capital.

Foreign investors are disillusioned

As a result, privatization has proceeded very slowly. Central state-owned enterprises are responsible for around one-third of output. There are also locally-run state enterprises.

Vietnam has offshore oil deposits and is an oil exporter, but production has not been increasing sufficiently and the country could soon become an importer. It does, however, have plentiful supplies of coal, which it exports, and also much hydroelectric potential. Most rural communities rely on wood for fuel but the countryside has suffered from deforestation, both during the war and more recently as a result of illegal logging.

Over the period 1959-75, Vietnam was embroiled in one of the 20th century's major wars—referred to in Vietnam as the 'American War'. The communist forces of the north emerged victorious and since then the Communist Party has retained control. The 'doi moi' policy represented some slackening of socialist economic ideology. There were also some political shifts: the new constitution of 1992 no longer charged the government with 'building socialism' but established it more as a manager of the economy.

Nevertheless, the old guard of the Communist Party remains firmly in charge. In terms of economic policy the government is divided between the conservatives and the economic liberals, but both wings would probably put the brakes on economic reform if they felt this would loosen the party's political grip.

A major problem nowadays is corruption. In 1997, there was an outbreak of rural unrest in the northern province of Thai Binh in response to corruption among local officials, and since then the government has embarked on a major anti-corruption drive.

Virgin Islands (US)

One of the most popular US tourist destinations

Land area: *340 sq. km.*
Population: *118,000—urban 49%*
Capital city: *Charlotte Amalie*
People: *Black 80%, white 15%, other 5%*
Language: *English, Spanish, creole*
Religion: *Baptist 42%, Roman Catholic 34%, Episcopalian 17%, other 7%*
Government: *Dependency of the USA*
Life expectancy: *77 years*
GNP per capita: *$PPP $12,500*
Currency: *US dollar*
Major exports: *Refined petroleum products*

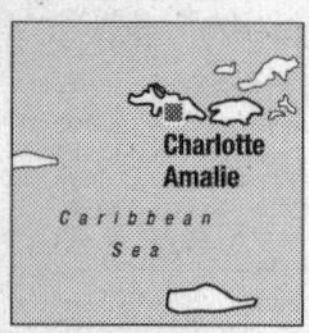

The US Virgin Islands in the Caribbean comprise three main islands: St Croix, St John, and St. Thomas, and more than 50 other islets or cays. The most southerly island, St Croix, is the largest. But the most developed is St John, which has the capital, Charlotte Amalie.

The islands' varied scenery includes rugged mountains, dense subtropical forests, and mangrove swamps, along with white, sandy beaches and coral reefs. The mild climate is also an attraction—though the islands are regularly hit by hurricanes.

The Virgin Islanders have a mixed African and European heritage. The Danes were in charge for a couple of centuries and they settled the country with African slaves to work on the sugar plantations.

But following more than eighty years of US ownership, the dominant culture is now American. The islands have one of the highest standards of living in the Caribbean and have also attracted immigrants from other Caribbean islands, particularly from Puerto Rico.

The main source of income is tourism, which employs around two-thirds of the workforce. More than 2 million visitors arrive each year, most of whom come from the USA, many on cruise ships, heading primarily for the beaches and the duty-free shopping.

On the agricultural front, sugar cane has given way to a wide range of fruit and vegetables grown for local consumption and to meet the demand from tourists.

The main industrial activity is oil refining, but there are also factories making pharmaceuticals and electronic goods which take advantage of duty-free entry into the USA.

The islands are an unincorporated territory of the USA. They send one member to the US House of Representatives, though he or she lacks full voting rights. The islanders also elect their own governor, as well as representatives to their fifteen-seat legislature.

Some of these seats are filled by representatives of the Democratic or Republican parties, but the majority tend to be taken by independents. In 1999, both the governor, Roy L. Schneider, and the Member of Congress, Donna Green, belonged to a local party, the Independent Citizens' Movement. There have at times been debates about the future constitution of the islands, though in 1993 the islanders voted in a referendum to retain the present status.

Western Sahara

Still waiting for a referendum on independence

Western Sahara's territory on the north-west coast of Africa is largely flat and almost entirely desert. The western two-thirds of the country is occupied by Moroccan troops, while the eastern third is controlled by the independence movement Polisario.

The Saharawi are a mixture of Arab, Berber, and black African descent. Three-quarters of the population, around 170,000 people, are now living in refugee camps in western Algeria. The camps are fairly well run; even so there appear to be serious health and nutritional problems. In recent years, the country has also been flooded with around 200,000 Moroccan settlers and more than 100,000 Moroccan soldiers.

In the past, the Saharawi have survived largely as nomadic herders, with a little agriculture along the coast. But this is an area of huge potential. In 1963, large phosphate deposits were discovered at Boucraa in the north. Total reserves have been estimated at 10 billion tons. In addition, there are rich coastal fishing grounds which are currently exploited by Spanish trawlers.

Western Sahara was a Spanish colony. An armed liberation movement, Polisario, was formed in 1973, but when Spain relinquished the territory in 1976 it handed the northern two-thirds to Morocco and the southern third to Mauritania—though the International Court of Justice said that the Saharawi were entitled to independence. Years of brutal warfare ensued with Polisario working from bases in Algeria. Mauritania eventually withdrew in 1976 and Morocco seized their portion too.

Land area: *266,000 sq. km.*
Population: *240,000, plus Moroccan settlers*
Capital city: *L'ayoune*
People: *Saharawi, Moroccan*
Language: *Arabic*
Religion: *Muslim*
Government: *Government in exile*
Life expectancy: *49 years*
GNP per capita: *Not available*
Currency: *Moroccan dirham*
Major exports: *Phosphates*

Polisario's guerrilla attacks did not shift Morocco, but their diplomatic offensive proved more successful. By the mid-1980s, more than 60 countries had recognized them as the legitimate government—with Muhammed Abdelaziz as president-in-exile. The real breakthrough, however, came in 1990, when the UN managed to achieve a peace plan that would lead to a UN-supervised referendum on independence based on a 1974 census. A ceasefire was declared in 1991.

Morocco's response has been to fill the country with settlers to swing the referendum their way—or at least to impede the process of voter registration with bogus claims. The UN mission now says that a vote is unlikely before 2002, if then. Morocco's new king, Mohammad VI, has made more placatory noises about autonomy, but given the rich phosphate prize, Morocco is unlikely to give up without a fight.

Yemen

Despite recent discoveries of oil, Yemen remains poor—and prone to violence

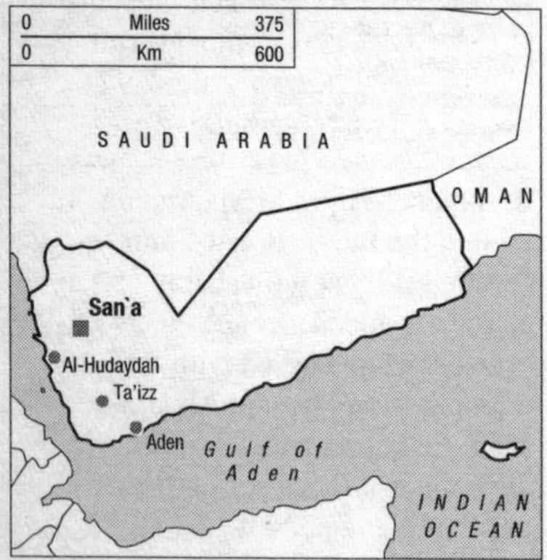

Land area: *528,000 sq. km.*
Population: *16 million—urban 36%*
Capital city: *San'a, 1.0 million*
People: *Arab*
Language: *Arabic*
Religion: *Muslim*
Government: *Republic*
Life expectancy: *58 years*
GNP per capita: *$PPP 740*
Currency: *Yemeni riyal*
Major exports: *Oil*

Yemen has three main regions. It has narrow desert coastal plains along both the Red Sea and the Gulf of Aden. These plains rise steeply to highlands that reach 1,500 metres. Then to the north the highlands descend to a desert area that covers half the country and merges with the 'empty quarter' of Saudi Arabia.

Almost everyone is Arab but the mountainous terrain has dispersed the population so there can be differences in dialects of Arabic, heightened by historical divisions between north and south. In the 1830s, the territory had been carved up between the Ottoman empire in the north and the British empire in the south. After independence, the government in the north remained more conservative while the government in the south pursued Soviet-style socialism that diluted some aspects of Islam—particularly the restrictions it imposed on women. The two countries united in 1990 but the social and political differences remain.

As a whole, Yemen is one of the world's poorest countries. Around 30% of people are poor. Only half have access to safe water, and less than one-third to effective sanitation. Literacy is low and around 30% of children are malnourished. Yemen also has a high annual population growth rate, around 3.7%.

Two-thirds of people rely on agriculture. Most of the country's rainfall is in the mountain areas, so farmers have had to build elaborate systems of terracing, growing basic subsistence crops such as sorghum and potatoes, as well as some cash crops, including fruit and high-quality 'mocha' coffee for export. But around one-third of agricultural production is of 'qat'—a plant whose chewable leaves contain a mild amphetamine. In addition, the mountains support large numbers of sheep and goats.

With little land to spare and few other opportunities for employment, more than 1 million Yemenis have left to work in richer neighbouring countries—though many were expelled from Saudi Arabia and Kuwait because of Yemen's tacit support for Iraq in the Gulf War.

Some respite from the country's

poverty came from the discovery of oil in the 1980s. By the mid-1990s, around 70% of government revenue was coming from oil. Yemen also has natural gas reserves, and there are plans to expand liquefaction plants to enable more gas to be exported.

The government is also attempting to capitalize on the country's strategic location by establishing a new Aden Free Zone. This will include a container port and an industrial estate, as well as a larger airport.

Another important source of foreign exchange has been tourism for the hardier travellers—around 80,000 of whom visit each year to explore the country's rich historical heritage. The industry has been badly hit by a spate of kidnapping of tourists by tribesmen wanting to draw attention to a lack of amenities. Although the tourists have rapidly been released unharmed, Yemen now has a reputation as an overly adventurous destination.

Adventure holidays in Yemen

Yemen's unification in 1990 was the culmination of a period of increasing cooperation between the Yemen Arab Republic in the north and the People's Democratic Republic of Yemen in the south. President Ali Abdullah Salih from the north—which had three-quarters of the total population—became president of a united Yemen, and his counterpart in the south, Ali Salim al-Bidh, became vice-president.

Unfortunately, unification coincided with the Gulf War, which forced more than 800,000 Yemeni migrant workers to return home—leading to unemployment and violent political unrest. Social services were also hit by the withdrawal of aid from Saudi Arabia and Kuwait.

Parliamentary elections in 1993 delivered a majority for Salih's General People's Congress—a mixture of military, tribes, and other groups. Al-Bidh's Yemeni Socialist Party came second—though with a majority in the south. An Islamic coalition, Islah ('gathering for Reform'), came third. People in the south, however, complained of harassment and 'internal colonization' and in 1994, with support from Saudi Arabia, they tried to secede. This caused a civil war, which Saleh's forces won after six months and 10,000 deaths.

Yemen looked for international aid and entered into agreements with the IMF that required it to liberalize the economy, but low oil prices and falling remittance income forced the government to cut many services and subsidies. In 1998, an increase in the price of staple foods resulted in riots in the main cities, and 50 deaths.

Even so, there was scarcely any opposition for the 1999 presidential election, largely because the Socialist Party boycotted it, and Islah decided to nominate Salih. Salih then had to get his supporters to nominate someone from his own party to stand against him. Unsurprisingly, he came out ahead, with 96% of the vote.

Meanwhile, much practical political power around the country remains dispersed among tribal leaders. They have official political control over certain areas and have ample arms—including ground-to-air missiles. Even more serious for the government is the prospect of violent opposition from Islamic dissidents.

Yugoslavia

The rump state continues in a state of siege—politically isolated, and with its economy in ruins

Land area: *102,000 sq. km.*
Population: *11 million*
Capital city: *Belgrade 1.1 million*
People: *Serbs 63%, Albanians 14%, Montenegrins 6%, Hungarians 4%, other 13%*
Language: *Serbo-Croatian, Albanian*
Religion: *Orthodox 65%, Muslim 19%,*
Government: *Republic*
Life expectancy: *74 years*
GNP per capita: *$PPP $2,280*
Currency: *Yugoslav dinar*
Major exports: *Manufactured goods, food, livestock*

Yugoslavia consists of two of the six republics of the former Federal Republic of Yugoslavia: Serbia and Montenegro. The larger is Serbia with 86% of the territory. This in turn has two provinces: Vojvodina, which has two-thirds of Serbia's territory, and consists in the north of low-lying fertile plains, through which flows the River Danube, and which rise to forested mountains in the centre and south. Further south still is Kosovo, which borders on Albania and Macedonia and consists of two inter-mountain basins. Montenegro lies to the west, bordering on the Adriatic and has high mountains and a narrow coastal plain.

The country is ethnically diverse, but the three main groups have been concentrated geographically—and even more so following the Kosovo War of 1999. Two-thirds are Serbians who are Eastern Orthodox Christians and are now almost entirely in Serbia. The next largest are the ethnic Albanians, most of whom are Sunni Muslims who now form almost all the population of Kosovo.

Montenegrins, who make up around two-thirds of the population of Montenegro, are related to Serbs in that they are also Eastern Orthodox, but in other ways are culturally distinct; the rest of Montenegro's population are mostly Albanian.

The fourth main group are Hungarians, who are in Vojvodina. In addition, there are more than 700,000 Serb refugees from neighbouring republics. Most people are well educated and health standards have been good, though the health system now has antiquated equipment.

Before the wars of the 1990s, Serbia formed the core of Yugoslavia and had a thriving economy based on diverse manufacturing industries—including chemicals, vehicles, furniture, and food processing. But the NATO bombing campaign of 1999 destroyed much of this. Agriculture was also doing fairly well. Even up to 1999, Yugoslavia had a food surplus. The chief crops are wheat and maize, along with a wide range of fruit and vegetables. Nowadays, a combination of warfare, sanctions, and economic mismanagement have savagely cut living standards. In 2000, probably around one-third of the workforce were unemployed.

Yugoslavia's political history since the mid-1980s has been dominated by one man, Slobodan Milosevic. He is a former communist leader who in 1989 was elected president of Serbia. He and the Serbs had resisted the break-up of Yugoslavia and supported Serb communities in other republics. By 1992, Serbia and Montenegro were the only republics left and declared themselves to be the Federal Republic of Yugoslavia, though as a result of Serb aggression in other republics the UN rejected its application for membership and imposed economic sanctions.

Dominated by Slobodan Milosevic

Milosevic was re-elected president of Serbia in 1992 and continued to support the Serbs in Bosnia who wanted to create a 'Greater Serbia'. In 1995, however, he took part in the negotiations in Dayton in the USA which ended the Bosnian War, and also ended UN sanctions against Yugoslavia. Having had two terms as Serbian president, Milosevic stood instead for the presidency of the federation, to which he was elected in 1997.

Meanwhile, matters were coming to a head in Kosovo. During the communist era, both Kosovo and Vojvodina had enjoyed considerable autonomy, but to suppress the Albanian community Milosevic had suspended Kosovo's autonomy and imposed rule from Belgrade. For years the resistance had largely been peaceful. But in 1997-8 a guerrilla movement, the Kosovo Liberation Army, stepped up its attacks on Serbian police. Milosevic responded with ferocious counter-attacks. Milosevic and the Kosovans attended a peace conference at Rambouillet in France. When this failed, NATO started to bomb Serbia, while Serbia drove hundreds of thousands of Albanians out of Kosovo.

The war ended after 72 days in June 1999 when Milosevic suddenly accepted the peace plan, which involved a heavy NATO presence in Kosovo and prospects of future autonomy. Most of the Albanians returned, but then it was the Serbians' turn to flee—180,000 to Serbia, 30,000 to Montenegro.

Early in 2000 Milosevic was attempting to shore up his position in Serbia by increasing the levels of repression and closing TV and radio stations. Thus far the opposition, whose best-known figure is Vuk Draskovic, has been too divided to offer a serious threat but discontent is mounting.

Meanwhile, Montenegro has been trying to distance itself from Serbia, both politically and economically. In 1999 it adopted the German mark as an official currency, and has sought closer ties with Croatia and Albania, as well as the EU. Its president, Milo Djukanovic, whose election in 1997 ousted Milosevic's protégé, wants Yugoslavia to be a looser federation. Independence would be difficult for Montenegro because the province is small, and one-third of the people are pro-Serb.

Zambia

Zambians suffer from low copper prices, HIV/AIDS, and an authoritarian government

Land area: *753,000 sq. km.*
Population: *10 million—urban 45%*
Capital city: *Lusaka, 1.0 million*
People: *Bemba, Tonga , and many others*
Language: *English, Bemba, Tonga, and about 70 other languages*
Religion: *Christian, Muslim, Hindu*
Government: *Republic*
Life expectancy: *44 years*
GNP per capita: *$PPP 860*
Currency: *Kwacha*
Major exports: *Copper, cobalt,, tobacco, lead*

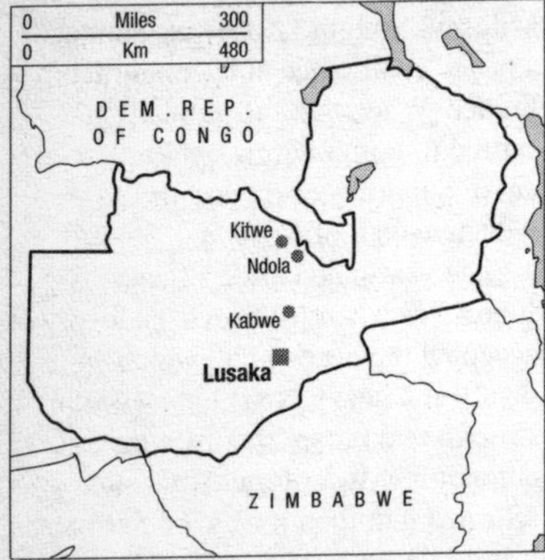

Most of Zambia consists of a plateau at around 1,200 metres above sea level. The highest point is in the Muchinga Mountains in the north-east. The territory is mostly open grasslands with occasional trees. The main river is the Zambezi, whose energies are tapped by the huge Kariba dam.

Zambians can belong to any of 70 or more ethnic groups, most of whom speak Bantu languages, though the official language is English. There are also small numbers of Europeans.

Two-thirds of Zambians live in poverty. In the past one of the more successful areas was education: more than 70% of children are enrolled in primary schools and adult literacy in 1997 was over 75%. Recently, however, with budget cuts and low and often late pay for teachers, and rising levels of poverty, educational standards have been falling.

Zambia had also made progress in health, but here too services have deteriorated in the past few years as a result of the IMF's structural adjustment programmes. Many people now have to pay 'user fees' for services once offered free. The under-five mortality rate, which in 1980 was 162 deaths per thousand live births, by 1997 had climbed to 202.

But the most alarming prospect is the spread of HIV/AIDS: at the end of 1997, officially, one-fifth of the population was HIV-positive, but the real proportion was almost certainly greater. By mid-1999 the Ministry of Health was warning that around half the population could die from the disease. Already, at least 20% of children have lost one or more parents, and more than two-thirds of households are now thought to be caring for one or more orphans. Since around half of Zambian children are already malnourished, prospects for these orphans are bleak.

Most people rely to some extent on agriculture. Zambia could be a major food producer: only around one-tenth of the land is arable though only about half of this is currently being worked. One of the main constraints for local food availability is the pattern of landholding. Much of the best land is held by large commercial farmers. While they do also grow the main food crop, maize, low prices have encouraged large farms to devote more land to tobacco, cotton, sugar, and flowers for the export market.

Meanwhile the subsistence farmers work on lower-quality communal land growing maize, sorghum, millet, and other basic crops, and in some cases cotton.

One of the most important sources of income and employment is copper, which provides 80% of export income. The 'copperbelt' is in the north-west of the country, bordering on the Democratic Republic of the Congo. This is the most industrialized part of Zambia, and also produces cobalt, coal, lead, and zinc. But mineral income has been much lower recently. This is partly a reflection of falling international prices but also of poor management and low investment by Zambia Consolidated Copper Mines, the main producer in which until early 2000 the government had a majority stake. The IMF had been pressing the government to sell its stake as a condition for future assistance, and to enable Zambia to qualify for debt relief.

Trouble in the copperbelt

After independence Zambia also invested heavily in manufacturing industry in areas such as food processing, chemicals, textiles, and tobacco. Initially most of this activity was in state hands, but in the past few years many enterprises have been sold off. Zambia could attract foreign investors but now faces stiff competition from neighbouring countries.

Zambia's initial decades of independence after 1964 were dominated by its first president, Dr Kenneth Kaunda. In 1972, Kaunda outlawed all political parties except his own United National Independence Party (UNIP). From then on, the most effective opposition came from the powerful Zambian Congress of Trade Unions, led by Frederick Chiluba. The economic situation deteriorated in the 1980s, and there were numerous strikes and also riots when the government, responding to IMF pressure, tried to reduce subsidies for maize. In 1990, after further unrest Kaunda finally agreed to permit other parties to organize.

Frederick Chiluba had by then created a new party, the Movement for Multiparty Democracy (MMD), and won the ensuing presidential election. Many people hoped that this would usher in a new open era in Zambian political life. Chiluba and the MMD have certainly liberalized the economy but they have had less appetite for democracy.

In 1996, Chiluba introduced a new constitution that prevented Kaunda from standing for election, so UNIP boycotted the election that year, giving Chiluba and the MMD an easy victory. In 1997, after the army attempted a coup, Chiluba declared a six-month state of emergency and temporarily imprisoned Dr Kaunda. Since then Chiluba and the MMD have been establishing many of the elements of a one-party state, and there have been increasing allegations of political repression and police brutality.

Zimbabwe

Facing a severe economic crisis, Zimbabwe's government has become increasingly authoritarian

Land area: 391,000 sq. km.
Population: 12 million—urban 34%
Capital city: Harare, 1.5 million
People: Shona 71%, Ndebele 16%, other African 11%, white 1%, other 1%
Language: English, Shona, Sindebele
Religion: Syncretic 50%, Christian 25%, indigenous 24%, other 1%
Government: Republic
Life expectancy: 44 years
GNP per capita: \$PPP 2,150
Currency: Zimbabwe dollar
Major exports: Tobacco, food, gold

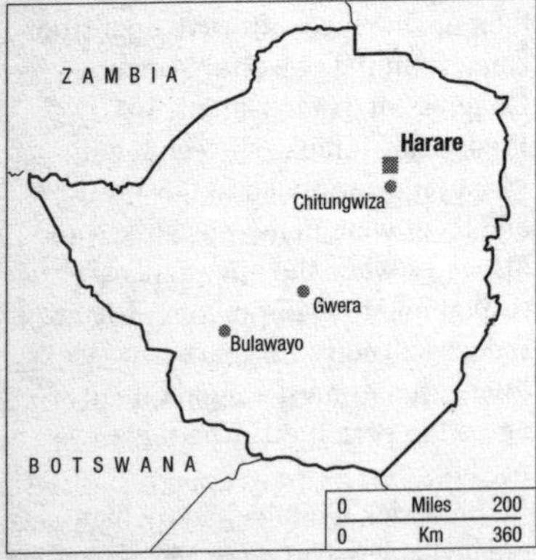

Zimbabwe's dominant topographical feature is the High Veld, a broad ridge around 1,500 metres above sea level that runs from south-west to north-east, and covers around one-quarter of the territory. The land drops on either side of this to the plateau of the Middle Veld, and then to the Low Veld, which reaches the frontiers at the Zambezi River in the north-west and the Limpopo in the south-east. Though it is in the tropics, Zimbabwe's elevation ensures a fairly mild climate.

The main population group are the Shona, who settled in the north and west of Zimbabwe more than 1,000 years ago and have primarily been farmers. The smaller Ndebele group arrived in the 19th century and lived initially as pastoralists in the south and east. With different forms of livelihood, the two coexisted fairly peaceably. More disruptive was the arrival from South Africa at the end of the 19th century of a small number of whites. Disappointed by not finding much gold to mine, instead they took the best land—the 'white highlands'—a seizure that rankles to this day.

When black majority rule was achieved in 1978, the government invested heavily in education and health. With free and compulsory primary education, enrolment ratios soon shot up to 100%. There was similar progress in health. Between 1980 and 1990, life expectancy rose from 54 to 58 years. Since then, things have slipped. Economic decline and falling commodity prices led to cuts in government expenditure, and fees were introduced for health and education services. Health has also been badly affected by the AIDS epidemic: by 1997, one-quarter of adults were HIV-positive and life expectancy had fallen to 44 years.

By the standards of Sub-Saharan Africa, Zimbabwe has a fairly diverse economy. Sanctions imposed during the final years of white rule in the 1970s had forced the country to develop its own manufacturing industry, including steel production.

Though output declined when price controls and protection were removed, even by 1997 manufacturing still made up 19% of GDP. Zimbabwe also has an important mining industry, particularly for gold, which makes up 10% of exports.

Agriculture remains central to the economy, accounting for more than a quarter of GDP and of employment. In years of good rainfall, Zimbabwe's farmers can even grow enough food to export, as well as producing cash crops such as sugar and cotton, and particularly tobacco, which is the major export earner.

Agriculture has always been overshadowed by questions of land distribution. After independence, the government, nervous of provoking 'white flight', left many of the large land-holdings intact. Whites make up less than 1% of the population but own one-third of arable land, employing around 350,000 workers—leaving black farmers to work the drier, lower-lying territory that is better suited to raising livestock.

Skewed patterns of land-holding

Unequal land distribution makes for a skewed distribution of income: in 1990, the top 10% of the population got 47% of income, and the bottom 10% only 1.8%.

When Zimbabwe achieved black majority rule in 1980, Robert Mugabe became prime minister at the head of the Zimbabwe African National Union-Popular Front (ZANU-PF). In 1985, the party was re-elected and in 1987 the parliament replaced the office of prime minister with that of an executive president. Since then, ZANU's dominance has been such that Mugabe and ZANU have won all subsequent assembly and presidential elections.

Mugabe also managed to amend the constitution fourteen more times—generally to augment his own autocratic power in what has become a one-party state controlled by patronage. In the early years he had some economic success, but recent years have been more difficult. Collapses in the prices of tobacco and gold, along with mismanagement, have undermined the economy. In 1999, inflation was running at 60% and unemployment was above 50%.

Widespread protests, food riots, extensive corruption, and involvement in the war in the Congo have made Mugabe increasingly unpopular. Early in 2000 a more effective opposition emerged as the Movement for Democratic Change, which has the backing of trade unions, churches, and others. In a shock result, Mugabe was finally defeated in February 2000 in another referendum designed to augment his powers.

The prospect of a powerful opposition, provoked an aggressive response. ZANU zealots started attacking and killing MDC members and Mugabe condoned the seizure of land by people claiming to be veterans of the civil war, who attacked and killed a number of white farmers. This drew international condemnation, notably from the UK, the former colonial power, which claimed that previous land reforms had generally enriched Mugabe's friends. Discontent was such that the MDC almost won the June 2000 parliamentary election, which was marred by widespread intimidation and violence.

Smaller countries

American Samoa

Pacific nation relying on the USA, tuna and tourism

People: *64,000, of whom 90% are Samoans, bilingual in Samoan and English. Life expectancy: 75 years*
Government: *Administered by the USA. Capital: Pago Pago*
Economy*: GNP per capita: $PPP 2,600. Main export: canned tuna*

American Samoa is a US territory in the South Pacific. It consists of three main, high volcanic islands and two atolls. Most people live on the main island of Tutuila, which also has a US naval base. More than 90% of the land is communally owned.

Although many Samoans have emigrated to the USA, there has been even more immigration from Asian countries such as Taiwan and South Korea and the population has been rising.

The territory is economically highly dependent on the USA, whose grants fund half the government budget. Around one-third of the workforce are employed by the government. Another one-third work in the two tuna canneries that produce the main export.

Tourism is a growing source of income. Plans to boost tourism by establishing a casino, were turned down in May 2000.

Although the US president is head of state, citizens elect their governor as well as members of the parliament, the Fono. In 1996 they chose a Democrat, Tauese Sunia, as governor. Though there have been threats to impeach him for corruption, he says he will stand for re-election in 2000.

Andorra

Distinctive co-principality between France and Spain

People: *65,000, speaking Catalan, Andorran, Spanish, and French. Life expectancy: 83 years*
Government: *Constitutional co-principality. Capital: Andorra la Vella*
Economy: *GNP per capita: $PPP 18,000. Main export: electricity*

Andorra is a tiny, mountainous country lodged in the eastern Pyrenees between France and Spain. Less than one-third of the population are native Andorrans. Most are Catalan Spanish, with some French, and the majority live in and around the capital, Andorra la Vella.

The main industry is tourism, which makes up over 80% of GDP. Millions are drawn each year to the spectacular scenery and the ski resorts. Duty-free shopping is also an attraction for the Spanish and French. Andorra has no currency of its own, using both the French franc and the Spanish peseta. It is also distinctive in that it has neither income nor valued-added tax, though the municipalities charge citizens $100 per year.

Andorra has a unique constitution. By tradition, the heads of state are two 'princes', the French president and the Bishop of Urgel in Spain. But this is largely a ceremonial arrangement. In 1993, Andorra adopted a new constitution that reduced the powers of the two princes and gave full sovereignty to the Andorrans, who elect a 28-member general council. The 1997 elections returned the Unión Liberal, with Marc Forné Molne as prime minister.

Anguilla

Politically lively British Caribbean dependency

People: *11,510, most of whom are black or mulatto. The language is English.*
Life expectancy: 76 years
Government: *Dependency of the UK.*
Capital: The Valley
Economy: *GNP per capita: $PPP 7,300.*
Main export: lobsters

Anguilla is a flat coral and limestone island in the eastern Caribbean. Most of its people are black or mulatto. The climate is dry and the soil is not very fertile so agriculture is limited. In the past, the main source of income has been fishing, but Anguillans nowadays rely more on remittances from migrants, luxury tourism, and more recently on financial services.

In 1969, Anguilla broke away from a self-governing federation with neighbouring St Kitts and Nevis—in a strange incident that required the dispatch of a squad of London policemen to restore order.

Subsequently, Anguilla again became a dependent territory with an 11-member house of assembly. The 1999 election returned Hubert Hughes as chief minister, but he has regularly quarrelled with the British government.

In early 2000, the island was plunged into a constitutional crisis when a combination of defections and boycotts meant that the House of Assembly could not manage a quorum. The governor ordered a new election for March 2000 which resulted in a victory for the conservative Anguilla National Alliance led by Osbourne Fleming.

Antigua and Barbuda

Tourist paradise tinged with crime and corruption

People: *67,000, most are black and English-speaking. Life expectancy: 75 years*
Government: *Constitutional monarchy.*
Capital: Saint John's
Economy: *GNP per capita: $PPP 9,440.*
Main exports: petroleum products and manufactures

Antigua is the larger and more populated island in this two-island state in the eastern Caribbean. Its most significant geographical features are its white, sandy beaches. It has a warm, dry climate.

The standard of living is high and most of the income comes from tourism: over 200,000 visitors arrive each year either on cruise ships, or to stay in the islands' exclusive resorts. Agriculture and manufacturing are mainly for local consumption and to supply the tourist industry.

The country has also become an offshore financial centre, and has more than 50 banks. Unfortunately, its lax regime has also made it an attractive money laundering centre for the Russian mafia and Colombian drugs barons.

Antigua's head of state is the British monarch, but for more than fifty years the country has been under the political sway of the Bird dynasty and the Antigua Labour Party (ALP), first Vere Bird, who died in 1999, and then his son Lester. The family has seldom been free of allegations of corruption. Even so, they and the ALP have consistently been re-elected, most recently in 1999, defeating the United Progressive Party.

Aruba

A rocky Caribbean dependency of the Netherlands

***People:** 94,000, ethnically diverse, speaking Dutch and Papiamento.*
Life expectancy: 75 years
***Government:** Dependency of the Netherlands. Capital: Oranjestad*
***Economy:** GNP per capita: $PPP 21,000.*
Main export: oil products

Aruba is a flat, rocky island in the Caribbean with few natural resources. Its people are a diverse ethnic mixture—with strains of Dutch, Amerindian, African, and Spanish. The majority are Roman Catholic. They have one of the highest standards of living in the Caribbean. Around one-quarter of the population are immigrants from the Netherlands, Venezuela, Colombia, and other Caribbean islands.

The chief industry is tourism, which in 1997 accounted for around 40% of GDP, but there is also a modest offshore financial services sector. In addition, the island refines some Venezuelan oil, so when the refinery was closed in 1985 this hit the island hard. However, it was reopened in 1993 which gave a strong boost to the economy.

Aruba was part of the Netherlands Antilles until 1986, when it was given 'status aparte', which involves having a Dutch governor but a locally elected assembly that deals with internal affairs. Earlier plans for eventual independence have now been shelved. The 1997 elections resulted in a two-party coalition government led by Jan Hendrik Eman of the Arubaanse Volkpartij.

Bermuda

Atlantic island of wealth that could become independent

***People:** 63,000, 60% black; white and other 40%. The language is English.*
Life expectancy: 77 years
***Government:** Dependency of the UK.*
Capital: Hamilton
***Economy:** GNP per capita: $PPP 29,000.*
Main export: pharmaceutical re-exports

Bermuda comprises one main coral-based island in the Atlantic. Bermudans enjoy a higher standard of living than their colonial masters in the UK. Two-thirds are black and the rest white; around one-quarter are foreign-born. There have been racial tensions, which broke out in riots in the 1970s, but conflict today is resolved through the political system.

Bermuda has little agriculture or manufacturing. The main source of income is tourism, which directly or indirectly employs more than half the population. The island receives more than half a million visitors per year, though it is facing competition from cheaper destinations. Another one-third of the workforce is employed in offshore finance and business services, particularly insurance.

Bermuda is a British colony, though internally self-governing. The 1998 elections were won by the black-based Progressive Labour Party, which, for the first time, defeated the white-based United Bermuda Party. This was partly because it had dropped its demands for higher income taxes and independence from the UK. Independence was rejected in a 1995 referendum, but the issue is likely to resurface.

British Virgin Islands

A dependency of the UK that prefers the US dollar

***People:** 19,000. Most are black, or mulatto with some whites and Asians.*
Language: English
***Government:** Dependency of the UK.*
Capital: Road Town
***Economy:** GNP per capita: $PPP 10,000.*
Main exports: rum, fish

There are thirty-six British Virgin Islands in the eastern Caribbean, but only sixteen are inhabited. The four main islands are Tortola, Anegada, Virgin Gorda, and Jost Van Dyke. The islands are hilly and have numerous lagoons and coral reefs.

The majority of Virgin Islanders live on Tortola. Some work in agriculture and fishing, but their main source of income nowadays is from tourists; some land-based, the others on yachts. Tourism accounts for around half of GDP.

Because of close economic links with the neighbouring US Virgin Islands the currency is the US dollar.

Since the mid-1980s the British Virgin Islands has had great success in building up an offshore financial services industry, and by 2000 had 300,000 companies registered locally. These include accountancy and legal firms, and banks and insurance companies,which are staffed by both a local and an expatriate work force.

As a dependent territory of the UK, the British Virgin Islands have an appointed governor and a fifteen-member legislative council. In the 1999 elections, the Virgin Islands Party retained control, with Ralph T. O'Neal as chief minister.

Cayman Islands

A congenial location for footloose international banks

***People:** 36,000, 50% of mixed ancestry, 25% black, 25% white. The language is English. Life expectancy: 68 years*
***Government:** Dependency of the UK.*
Capital: George Town
***Economy:** GNP per capita, $PPP $23,800.*
Main export: turtle products

These are three coral-based islands in the Caribbean, mostly flat and occasionally marshy, with white, sandy beaches and coral reefs. The islanders are on average far richer than their British colonial rulers—and pay no income tax. There are also many immigrant workers, who make up around half the workforce.

Tourism is the largest employer and provides three-quarters of foreign-exchange earnings. Around 400,000 people each year visit this up-market destination, the majority from the USA.

The Cayman Islands are also a major offshore financial centre and tax haven—with almost 600 registered banks and trust companies. The country is a favourite location for company registration—with 40,000 enterprises claiming this as home.

There is no pressure for independence. A British-appointed governor, who since April 1999 has been Peter Smith, has executive responsibility for many issues. The Cayman Islands also have a legislative assembly. This has been divided according to personalities or 'teams', though a party system is emerging. The 1996 elections made the National Team the largest grouping.

Christmas Island

Phosphates, crabs and tourism in the Indian ocean

People: *1,906, Chinese 70%, European 20%, Malay 10%. The language is English.*
Life expectancy: not available
Government: *Territory of Australia.*
Capital: The Settlement
Economy: *GNP per capita: not available.*
Main export: phosphates

Christmas Island in the Indian Ocean was left largely uninhabited until the discovery of phosphates at the end of the 19th century. Most of the subsequent mining work was done by immigrant labour, primarily from the Cocos Islands, Malaya and Singapore.

Since 1958 the island has been administered by Australia. In 1985, the island established its first local assembly and in 1994 the islanders voted overwhelmingly in a referendum against independence. Christmas Island now has a shire council as an electoral district within Australia's Northern Territory.

As the phosphate mines became exhausted, the Australian government transferred ownership to a private operator controlled by the unionized workforce, and a new lease was signed in 1998.

The government also started to invest in infrastructure in order to build up a tourist industry—including a casino, golf courses, and facilities for scuba diving. The island is well known for the migration of large numbers of red land crabs between October and January each year. A future possibility is to have a satellite launching station for the Asia Pacific Space Centre.

Cocos Islands

Australian dependency that aims for Australian wealth

People: *636, Cocos Malays, who are Muslim, and Europeans.*
Languages are Malay and English
Government: *Territory of Australia.*
Capital: West Island
Economy: *GNP per capita: not available.*
Main exports: Copra and coconuts

The Cocos Islands, officially called the Cocos (Keeling) Islands, comprise 2 main coral atolls in the eastern Indian Ocean. The only inhabited islands are Home Island and West Island.

Most of the Cocos Islander community, who are Muslims, are to be found on Home Island. They are descendants of people who were brought from Malaya, East Africa, and other countries to work on the coconut plantations.

Though there is some fishing and horticulture, their main source of income is still coconuts. Most of their work is organized by the Cocos Islands Co-operative Society, which supervises the production of copra and other activities.

Those on West Island are largely Australian government employees and their families.

The islands came under Australian control in 1955. In 1978, the Australian government purchased most of the land owned by the Clunies-Ross family and distributed it to the islanders. In 1984, the islanders voted to become a part of Australia, which committed itself to raising the islands' services and standards of living to mainland levels.

Cook Islands

Pacific islands steadily losing people to New Zealand

***People:** 22,000, of whom 80% are full Polynesian. Life expectancy: 71 years*
***Government:** Self-governing, in free association with New Zealand.*
Capital: Avarua
***Economy:** GNP per capita: $ PPP 4,000.*
Main exports: copra, fruit

The Cook Islands consist of fifteen islands and atolls scattered across 2 million square kilometres of the South Pacific Ocean.

Most Cook Islanders are of mixed Polynesian descent and speak Cook Islands Maori as well as English. More than half are on the island of Rarotonga. Many have also emigrated to New Zealand. Indeed more than half of all Cook Islanders live there.

Around one-fifth of the islanders depend on agriculture, growing food for local consumption and export. There is also a limited amount of industry, including the manufacture of clothing and footwear. However, most of the economy nowadays is based on tourism and financial services. There is also some income from migrant remittances.

The Cook Islands have full self-government in 'free association' with New Zealand, which deals with foreign affairs. The head of state is the British monarch. She and the New Zealand government are represented by a high commissioner, but most decisions are taken by the prime minister and the twenty-four-member parliament. In 2000, the prime minister was Dr Joseph Williams of the Cook Islands Party.

Dominica

Caribbean island heavily dependent on banana exports

***People:** 74,000, predominantly black and English-speaking. Life expectancy: 76 years*
***Government:** Republic. The president is elected by the legislature for a five-year term. Capital: Roseau*
***Economy:** GNP per capita: $PPP 3,940.*
Main export: bananas

Dominica is a volcanic island in the Caribbean with rich, fertile soil. Most people are of African or mixed descent and around 40% work on small farms, growing subsistence crops, as well as bananas for export to the EU, primarily the UK.

Dominica is highly dependent on preferential access to European banana markets, which provide more than 60% of export income. Other crops such as mangoes, grapefruits, avocados, and oranges do not offer such good returns.

Without a long-runway airport or extensive beaches, Dominica's tourist potential is limited. A better prospect is eco-tourism, which can capitalize on the rich fauna and wildlife.

For most of the period following independence in 1978, the government was in the hands of Dame Eugenia Charles and the conservative Dominica Freedom Party (DFP). She retired in 1995 and in elections later that year the DFP lost to the centre-left United Workers' Party.

In the 2000 election, the Dominican Labour Party won the most seats in the House of Assembly, and Rosie Douglas became prime minister at the head of a coalition with the DFP.

Faroe Islands

Fishing nation moving towards independence

***People:** 42,000, Faroese, who speak Faroese and Danish.*
Life expectancy: 78 years
***Government:** Dependency of Denmark.*
Capital: Tórshavn
***Economy:** GNP per capita: $PPP $16,300.*
Main export: fish

The Faroes are a group of seventeen rugged and largely treeless volcanic-based islands in the North Atlantic. Most Faroese live on the islands of Streymoy and Eysturoy.

The people are descendants of Viking settlers. The country's name means 'sheep islands' in old Norse, and raising sheep is still the main land-based activity, but the primary source of income is fishing, mainly for cod. Recently there have been some offshore oil discoveries. The islands also benefit from substantial subsidies from Denmark.

Since 1948, the Faroes have been a self-governing community within the kingdom of Denmark—though in order to protect their fishing interests they are not part of the EU. They have the oldest parliament in the world, the Løgting, founded more than 1,000 years ago.

Independence is on the agenda. In the 1998 elections, the leading parties were the Party for People's Government and the People's Party, whose leader Anfinn Kallsberg became prime minister. Most representatives support independence, which the Danish parliament has said it will grant—if and when the Faroese ask for it.

Falkland Islands

British territory claimed by Argentina as the Malvinas

***People:** 2,758, of British origin, speaking English.*
***Government:** Dependency of the UK.*
Capital: Stanley. Territory also claimed by Argentina as the Islas Malvinas
***Economy:** GNP per capita: not available.*
Main exports: wool, hides, mutton

The Falkland Islands consist of around 200 islands in the South Atlantic. This British dependency, is disputed with Argentina, which claims it as the Islas Malvinas. The main islands are East and West Falkland.

The population are of British extraction. They have a British-appointed governor but the islands are self-governing with their own executive and legislative councils. Most people make their living directly or indirectly from agriculture, predominantly sheep farming, though more recently there have been efforts to develop tourism and gain income from the sale of fishing licences to foreign trawlers. There are also good prospects for offshore oil.

The UK and Argentina had been trying to resolve their dispute when the Argentine military government invaded in 1982, provoking a war which ended when British troops reoccupied the islands. The UK maintains a military presence.

The islanders want to maintain the status quo—a view which the UK reluctantly has to support. However, there appeared to be a thaw in 1999 when talks were held in London between the islanders and Argentina's foreign minister.

Gibraltar

Spain and the UK still dispute the status of 'the rock'

People: *29,000, mostly of British and southern European descent.*
Life expectancy: 78 years
Government: *British dependency, though claimed by Spain. Capital: Gibraltar*
Economy: *Per capita income: $PPP 17,500. Main exports: mostly re-exports*

Gibraltar is a massive limestone and shale rock joined by a narrow isthmus to the coast of southern Spain. It holds a commanding position at the entrance to the Mediterranean.

Gibraltar's population reflects its long history as a British naval base: around two-thirds of the people are native Gibraltarians, of mixed British and southern European descent, while the rest are foreign workers.

The British military presence now accounts for only around one-tenth of Gibraltar's economy. More important are tourism, with more than 5 million visitors per year, and offshore financial services—the latest development being internet gambling.

Spain wants sovereignty over Gibraltar while the UK insists on respecting the wishes of the Gibraltarians who have steadfastly refused to unite with Spain. Gibraltarians have self-government in all areas but defence, and are British citizens.

In April 2000 Spain and the UK agreed on greater cooperation, but not on the long-term future. Independence seems unfeasible; integration into the UK unlikely; joint sovereignty plausible; a continuation of the status quo most likely.

Greenland

The world's largest island, but not very green

People: *56,000, more than 80% are Greenlanders, most of the rest are Danish.*
Life expectancy: 68 years
Government: *Dependency of Denmark. Capital: Nuuk.*
Economy: *GNP per capita, $PPP 16,100. Main export: fish*

Two-thirds of Greenland lies within the Arctic Circle and most of the territory is covered by an ice cap which at its centre is 8 kilometres thick and holds 10% of the world's total fresh water.

Greenlanders are mostly a mixture of the native Inuit and settlers from Scandinavia. Few pure Inuit remain. Traditionally they have survived by hunting seals, but this probably occupies only around one-fifth of the population. Today, more people make a living through fishing, mainly for shrimp. There has also been some zinc mining but this has now ceased, and left Greenland even more dependent on subsidies from Denmark.

Greenlanders are Danish citizens who elect two representatives to the Danish parliament—though Greenland withdrew from the EU in 1985 to protect its fishing interests. For internal affairs they have a Home Rule Parliament.

The 1999 elections resulted in a coalition between Siumit, a social democratic party that favours greater autonomy, and Atássut, a centre-right party that favours strong links with Denmark. Jonathan Motzfeldt of Siumit is prime minister.

Grenada

A spice island of strategic importance to the USA

People: *96,000, mostly black, speaking English or a French patois.*
Life expectancy: 72 years
Government: *Constitutional monarchy.*
Capital: St George's
Economy: *GNP per capita: $PPP 4,720.*
Main exports: nutmeg, mace

Grenada is a volcanic island with a rugged mountainous interior and an attractive coastline that has many secluded bays and beaches. Most Grenadans are black, while a minority are of mixed race.

The country's fertile soil and abundant rainfall allow around one-quarter of the population to make a living as small farmers. Apart from growing food crops, they also specialize in nutmeg, of which Grenada is the world's second largest producer. But the main source of foreign exchange nowadays is tourism. There are more than 100,000 annual stopover visitors, and twice as many again arrive on cruise ships.

Grenada, which achieved independence from the UK in 1974, has a history of political conflict. Turmoil in 1983 resulted in the killing of Prime Minister Maurice Bishop, and provoked an invasion by the USA which had been alarmed by Grenada's links with Cuba.

Democracy was restored, though it has been somewhat unstable. Elections in 1995 and 1999 were won by the conservative New National Party, headed by Keith Mitchell who has tried to improve relations with both Cuba and the USA.

Isle of Man

From buckets and spades to banking in the Irish Sea

People: *72,000, Manx and British.*
Life expectancy: 78 years
Government: *Dependency of the British Crown, rather than of the UK.*
Capital: Douglas
Economy: *GNP per capita, $PPP $13,100.*
Main exports: tweeds, kippers

The Isle of Man lies halfway between England and Ireland in the Irish Sea. The highest point is Snaefell, at 620 metres, but most of the territory is low-lying and used for agriculture.

Its people, the Manx, are of Celtic descent. Though health and welfare services are at least equal to those in the UK, the average per capita income is around one-third less.

Until recently, the island relied heavily on tourism. But with British holidaymakers heading further afield, tourism has been eclipsed by financial services. Companies have been attracted by tax rates lower than in the UK. By 1996, financial services accounted for 37% of GDP and 18% of employment.

The Isle of Man's economy has been very healthy, with growth of about 7 per cent combined with low inflation and zero unemployment.

The Isle of Man is not part of the UK; it is a crown dependency with a lieutenant-governor appointed by the British monarch. But it does have considerable autonomy, exercised through its parliament, the Tynwald. Politics is mostly consensual. The parliament elects a chief minister who in turn chooses a cabinet, but there are no political parties.

Kiribati

Small islands scattered over a vast area of ocean

People: *84,000, most of whom are Micronesians and Christians. Life expectancy: 60 years*
Government: *Republic, with a president elected by the legislature. Capital: Tarawa*
Economy: *Per capita income: $PPP 3,480. Main exports: copra, fish*

Kiribati consists of 33 islands or atolls spread over 3 million square kilometres of the Pacific. Since most of the territory is less than a metre or two above sea level, it would be an early victim of accelerated sea rise following global warming.

Its people, called the I-Kiribati, are mostly Micronesians and around one-third live on one atoll, Tarawa. Many I-Kiribati also work outside the islands, either elsewhere in the Pacific, particularly in Nauru, or as sailors on foreign, notably German, vessels.

There is little fertile soil, so agriculture is limited, though farmers do grow taro as well as breadfruit, bananas, and particularly coconuts. Most people earn their living from fishing. Kiribati's control over such a huge area of the Pacific gives it considerable fishing potential, particularly for tuna, both from its own boats and by selling licences to foreign fleets. Even so, the country is heavily dependent on aid.

Kiribati, formerly the Ellis Islands, gained its independence from the UK in 1979, and has a president, Teburoro Tito, who was re-elected in 1998, and a 39-member parliament. In 1999, Kiribati took its seat at the UN.

Liechtenstein

Commuters head for one of Europe's richest nations

People: *32,000, Alemani, though many people commute in from neighbouring countries. Life expectancy: 78 years*
Government: *Constitutional monarchy. Capital: Vaduz*
Economy: *GNP per capita: $PPP 23,000. Main export: machinery*

Liechtenstein is a tiny country between Austria and Switzerland. The western one-third lies along the valley of the River Rhine. The eastern two-thirds is mountainous, formed by the foothills of the Alps.

The people are descendants of the Alemani tribe and many people still speak the Alemani dialect, which is a variant of Swiss German.

Liechtenstein is closely linked with Switzerland, and uses the Swiss franc as its currency. There is some agriculture, primarily raising livestock. But more important are precision engineering factories, tourism, and the financial services industry. Attracted by Liechtenstein's low rates of corporate taxation, and secretive banks, more than 60,000 companies are registered there. These activities also give employment to people from neighbouring countries—every day more than one-third of the workforce commute across its borders.

Liechtenstein is a principality, with Prince Hans Adam as head of state. In 1997, elections to the single-chamber parliament gave a narrow overall majority to the conservative Patriotic Union Party, with Mario Frick returned as prime minister.

Marshall Islands

Reductions in US aid will have serious repercussions

***People:** 63,000, Micronesian, speaking English or Marshallese dialects.*
Life expectancy: 64 years
***Government:** Republic in free association with the USA. Capital: Majuro*
***Economy:** GNP per capita: $1,680.*
Main exports: fish, coconut oil

The Marshall Islands consist of thirty low-lying islands, along with hundreds of islets scattered across 2 million square kilometres of the Pacific. All are threatened by global warming. They include Bikini atoll, which was used as a US nuclear test site, and the largest, Kwajelein, which was a military testing range.

One-third of the population live in the slums of Majuro. Many Marshallese still suffer from diseases linked to radiation exposure, though they are entitled to compensation from a trust fund.

On the outer islands, most people survive through subsistence farming, fishing, and remittances from people working on other islands. Those on the larger islands have benefited from considerable US aid—$1 billion since 1986—but this is due to be phased out so there is now a period of painful adjustment. Tourism might provide an alternative but it is still on a small scale.

Since 1986, this has been an independent country in free association with the USA, which looks after defence and other matters. Politics is based on people more than parties. Since 1997, the president has been Imata Kabua.

Monaco

A minuscule, and not very democratic, city-state.

***People:** 47,000, of whom almost half are French; only 16% are Monegasque. Life expectancy: 78 years*
***Government:** Constitutional monarchy, ruled by the Grimaldi family.*
Capital: Monaco
***Economy:** Per capita GDP: $PPP $25,000*

Embedded in France's Mediterranean coast, and less than 2 square kilometres in surface area, Monaco is the smallest country in the UN, though landfill and reclamation from the sea have increased the area by 20% over the past fifty years. Monaco is highly dependent on France: the currency is the French franc and almost half its residents are French citizens attracted by lower taxes.

The primary industry is tourism—four-star and upwards. The casino in the Monte Carlo district is one attraction, and the largest employer, and the harbour is always packed with luxury yachts. Many banks and insurance companies find this a comfortable location. Monaco also has some industries, including pharmaceuticals and electronics. More than 25,000 people commute in each day from Italy and France.

Since 1949, Monaco's hereditary head of state has been Prince Rainier III—the latest in the line of succession of the Grimaldi family. There is a legislative national council, but executive power is in the hands of an unelected, and always French, minister of state whom the Prince chooses from a list presented to him by the French president.

Montserrat

Still suffering the effects of a disastrous volcanic eruption

People: *12,800, including refugees not yet returned. Black, with a few expatriates.*
Government: *Dependency of the UK. Capital: none, since Plymouth was destroyed*
Economy: *GNP per capita: not available. Main exports: light manufactures*

Montserrat is a volcanic, forest-covered island in the Eastern Caribbean. Its Soufrière Hills include a volcano that erupted catastrophically in 1997 laying waste to the south of the island, including the capital Plymouth.

At that point the population was around 12,000, which included the indigenous black population and white expatriates. Two-thirds of these were evacuated. Most expatriates have stayed away while the black population has been returning slowly. Some new houses have now been built and ash is being cleared from safer areas.

The main source of income has been tourism, along with some agriculture and light manufacturing. Since the eruption, the island has been heavily reliant on British aid, though there have been protests that this is inadequate. A plan for redevelopment of the north was agreed in 1999.

Montserrat is a UK dependency, with its own executive council and seven-member legislature. The 1996 election proved inconclusive. Two seats went to the new Movement for National Reconstruction whose leader David Brandt took over as chief minister in 1997.

Nauru

An island that has been almost entirely excavated

People: *10,000, Nauruan and other Pacific Islanders 26%. Most speak Nauruan or English. Life expectancy: 67 years*
Government: *Republic, with a president elected by the parliament*
Economy: *GNP per capita: $PPP 10,000. Main export: phosphates*

Nauru is a 21square-kilometre coral island, the centre of which had a plateau of phosphate rock allegedly formed by guano (bird droppings), leaving just a narrow coastal strip of fertile land.

Nauruans have grown wealthy with the income from phosphate exports. These have funded generous social services but also encouraged an unhealthy, sedentary lifestyle. Most of the mining is done by immigrants, from China and from neighbouring islands. Now that the deposits are virtually exhausted—likely to run out around 2005—Nauru has an uncertain future. The government has announced that over the next few years it will make cuts in services.

The government has embarked, with Australian assistance, on a twenty-year programme to repair the environmental damage. Most of this and other investment activity will have to be funded either from income from Nauru's overseas investments or from foreign aid.

Independent since 1968, Nauru has a twenty-member parliament that elects one member as president. In recent years, there have been a series of short-lived governments: the president is Rene Harris.

Niue

The largest uplifted coral island, linked to New Zealand

People: *1,800. Polynesian with some Europeans and others*
Government: *Self-governing, in free association with New Zealand. Capital: Alofi*
Economy: *GNP per capita: $1,200. Main exports: root crops, coconuts*

Though geographically part of the Cook Islands in the South Pacific, Niue is politically separate. This is the world's largest uplifted coral island.

Most people are Polynesian and speak their own Nieu language. They live predominantly from agriculture, working on family plantations, growing subsistence crops such as yams and taro, as well as cash crops, that include coconuts and passion fruit. The island also has a saw mill as well as some fruit processing factories.

Lacking local opportunities many people have migrated to New Zealand, where around 14,000 Niueans now live. Nieu's population has halved over the past thirty years.

The main exports are root crops, coconuts, honey and handicrafts. The island is heavily dependent on remittances, and aid from New Zealand, which at times has made up around two-thirds of GNP.

Since 1974, Niue has been a self-governing territory in free association with New Zealand, which appoints a high commissioner. The island has its own nine-member legislative assembly. Following the 1999 elections, Sani Lakatani of the Niue People's Party became prime minister.

Norfolk Island

Australian island settled by convicts and mutineers

People: *1,905, European and Polynesian. Around 30% were born on the Australian mainland and 23% in New Zealand*
Government: *External territory of Australia. Capital: Kingston*
Economy: *Main exports: agricultural products, postage stamps*

Norfolk Island is a volcanic island which lies north-west of New Zealand in the South Pacific. Though most of the land has now been cleared, the island still has many of its distinctive pine trees, and most of the coastline consists of cliffs. Originally a penal colony, Norfolk Island was later settled by descendants of mutineers from *The Bounty* who migrated from Pitcairn Island. Around 80% are citizens of Australia; most of the rest are citizens of New Zealand.

There is some agriculture, but the main source of income nowadays is tourism from Australia and New Zealand, with around 30,000 visitors per year.

Relations with Australia have at times been strained and there have been several efforts to clarify the island's status. It is not a dependent territory but an 'integral part of the Commonwealth of Australia'.

The Australian governor-general appoints an administrator, but the island has its own nine-member legislative assembly and raises its own taxes. In 1991, the islanders voted against any change in their constitutional status. Only since 1992 have they been able to vote in Australian federal elections.

Northern Mariana Islands

Offers duty-free entry to the USA for garment makers

People: *65,000, Chamorro, Carolinians and Asians, mostly Filipino and Chinese*
Government: *Self-governing commonwealth in political union with the USA. Capital: Saipan*
Economy: *Per capita income, $ PPP 9,300. Main export: garments*

The country consists of 22 volcanic or coral islands in the Pacific. The largest indigenous group are the Chamorro. They and other islanders are US citizens. But more than half the population are immigrant workers, particularly from the Philippines and more recently from China.

Few people work in agriculture. Many more now work in hotels and other parts of the tourist industry, which gets many visitors from Japan. The main employer, however, is a rapidly expanding foreign-owned garments industry which enjoys duty-free entry to the USA, and which by 2000 had 39 establishments employing more than 12,000 indigenous and foreign workers.

As a commonwealth of the USA, the islanders get substantial aid. They elect their own governor, who since 1998 has been the Republican Pedro P. Tenorio. The US federal government has been threatening to enforce higher labour standards and minimum wages and to exert greater control over immigration—which would effectively exclude many Asian workers. This alarms factory owners who fear losing their labour force, as local people prefer to work for the government which pays higher wages.

Palau

Probably the world's most intensively governed country

People: *19,000, Palauans speaking Palauan, English or other languages. Life expectancy: 71 years*
Government: *Republic in free association with the US. Capital: Koror*
Economy: *GNP per capita: $PPP $8,800. Main exports: shellfish, tuna*

Palau consists of more than 300 volcanic or coral islands in the Pacific, most of which are enclosed by a barrier reef. Palauans are Micronesians. More than half live on the island of Koror.

Many Palauans are still involved in subsistence agriculture and fishing, but the main sources of cash income are government employment and tourism. Around one-third of the workforce are employed by the government, which benefits from substantial US aid. There is also income from fishing licences sold to foreign fleets. Around 75,000 tourists visit each year.

Palau's emergence from the status of UN Trust Territory was a long and tortuous process—during which one president was assassinated—and was completed only when the country became independent in 1994 and joined the UN.

The national president is Kunio Nakamuro, but there is also a two-tier legislature, and a sixteen-member Council of Chiefs.

In addition there is an elected government and legislature in each of the country's sixteen component states, one of which has a population of just 100.

St Helena

A remote but strategic island in the South Atlantic

People: *7,000, of mixed European, African and Asian descent. English speaking*
Government: *Dependency of the UK Capital: Jamestown. Grouped with Ascension Island and Tristan da Cunha*
Economy: *Per capita GDP: $PPP 2,000. Main export: tuna*

St Helena is a mountainous island of volcanic origin, almost 2,000 kilometres from the coast of Angola, with a mild subtropical climate. Its remote but strategic location has in the past made this an important port of call for sailors and notably for aircrews during the Second World War. The most famous visitor was Napoleon Bonaparte, who was exiled here in 1815.

The island has few resources. Many people make a living from fishing, primarily for tuna, which is frozen for export. Agriculture is limited, though some farmers can grow maize, potatoes and other crops and raise some livestock. With few opportunities locally, many young people emigrate, some of whom have been going to the Falklands. To help them do so the islanders have requested automatic British citizenship, but this has been refused.

As a British dependency, St Helena has an appointed governor, but there is also a legislative council which includes twelve elected members. There have been pressures for greater autonomy. St Helena itself has other islands as dependencies, including Ascension Island and Tristan da Cunha.

St Kitts and Nevis

Two Caribbean islands that have stayed together—just

People: *41,000, black and English-speaking. Life expectancy: 70 years*
Government: *Federation under a constitutional monarchy. Capital: Basseterre.*
Economy: *Per capita income, $PPP 7,940. Main exports: machinery, food, electronics*

St Kitts (short for St Christopher) and Nevis is a federation of two volcanic islands in the eastern Caribbean. Three-quarters of the population live on St Kitts. Standards of human development are high—diseases are those of affluence rather than poverty.

On St Kitts, 40% of the workforce are employed by the sugar plantations which generate more than half of export income. But the government is concerned about over-dependence on one commodity and has encouraged diversification into small-scale manufacturing; in 1998, St Kitts had two electronics companies.

A second major source of income is tourism. The islands attract around 80,000 people each year, mostly fairly up-market, who occasionally stray from the beaches to visit historic sites. Nevis in particular has also become a centre for financial and business services: in 1998, it had more than 10,000 registered companies.

The 1997 and 2000 elections to the eleven-person National Assembly were won by the St Kitts-Nevis Labour Party with Dr Denzil Douglas as prime minister. Nevis is the richer of the two, and there has been some pressure for secession, but this was rejected in a 1998 referendum.

St Pierre and Miquelon

French fishing islands in the North Atlantic

***People:** 7,000, French, of Basque and Breton origin. Life expectancy: 77 years*
***Government:** Territorial collectivity of France, but self-government through a local assembly. Capital: Saint-Pierre*
***Economy:** GNP per capita: $PPP 11,000. Main exports: fish and fish products*

St. Pierre and Miquelon comprises two main islands off the southern coast of Newfoundland, Canada. The islands are fairly bleak and their chief importance are as a French presence in the North Atlantic, offering an opportunity to exploit the rich fishing grounds.

Most of the people are descendants of fishing communities who settled here from France. Their main activity is still fishing for cod. At times this has led to disputes with Canada, though these have now been settled with agreements on quotas. Even so, with the fishing industry in long-term decline, there are fewer opportunities and many of the islanders have been emigrating to Canada.

As they live in a territorial collectivity of France, the islanders are entitled to send a deputy to the French National Assembly. Locally, they have their own prefect, who since 1998 has been Rémi Thuau.

They also elect their own nineteen-member general council. The political parties correspond to those in metropolitan France. After the 1994 elections the most seats from constituencies on both islands went to local equivalents of Rassemblement pour la république.

San Marino

One of the world's smallest and oldest republics

***People:** 25,000, Sammarinese and Italian, speaking Italian. Life expectancy: 81 years*
***Government:** Republic. The joint heads of state are the elected captains-regent. Capital: San Marino*
***Economy:** Per capita income, $PPP 20,000. Main exports: stone, ceramics, textiles*

Enclosed within Italy, San Marino lies near the Adriatic coast on the slopes of Mount Titano. Although an independent republic, San Marino is necessarily linked in many ways to Italy, and a high proportion of residents are Italian.

Agriculture is still an important source of income, based on cereals and livestock. But the country also has a range of industries. The main one used to be stone quarrying. Legend has it that the state of San Marino was founded by a 4th-century stone-cutter.

Now that the quarries are mostly exhausted, manufacturing industry is devoted to a range of other products including ceramics, textiles, and electronics. San Marino has growing banking and tourist industries, with half a million visitors per year, and also does a good trade in postage stamps which provide around one-tenth of government revenue.

San Marino has an elected 60-member great and general council. The 1998 elections resulted in a coalition between the Christian Democrat and Socialist parties. The council chooses two of its members to serve for six-months as 'captains-regent' who are joint heads of state.

Seychelles

Tourist island where Heinz is the largest single employer

People: *79,000. Seychellois, a blend of Asians, Africans and Europeans. Life expectancy: 71 years. Languages are English, French and Creole*
Government: *Republic. Capital: Victoria*
Economy: *GNP per capita $PPP 10,530. Main export: canned tuna*

The Seychelles consists of over 100 islands in the Indian ocean, of which two-thirds are uninhabited. Most Seychellois, who for Africa have a high standard of living, are on the island of Mahé.

The mainstay of the economy is tourism, which employs around one-third of the labour force. Some 130,000 visitors arrived in 1999, mostly from Europe. The Seychelles has little agricultural land but has extensive fishing grounds and the tuna-fish cannery, majority-owned by Heinz, is the largest single employer and biggest export earner—though 40% of the workforce has to be imported.

Since a coup in 1977 politics in the Seychelles has been dominated by Albert René, who with his People's Progressive Front (SPPF) ran the country as a one-party socialist state until 1993 when he reverted to multi-party democracy and switched to a free-market development model.

René won the 1993 and 1998 presidential elections, and the SPPF won corresponding large majorities in the National Assembly. The main opposition party is the Seychelles National Party, led by Wavel Ramkalawan.

Tokelau

Three scattered atolls in the South Pacific

People: *1,500. Most are Polynesian, speaking Tokelauan and English*
Government: *Overseas dependency of New Zealand. No capital; there are centres for administration on each island*
Economy: *GNP per capita: $PPP 1,000. Main exports: stamps, handicrafts*

Tokelau consists of three widely separated atolls in the South Pacific—Atafu, Nukunonu, and Fakaofo. Each has a series of islets around a lagoon, which would be at risk from any rise in the sea level.

The people are of Polynesian origin. Most are Christian. They have some subsistence farming though the soil is thin and infertile. The main crops are coconuts, copra, breadfruit, papayas, and bananas. There is also some livestock raising and fishing, and a few people work in small enterprises producing handicrafts for export.

Tokelau also gains income from issuing licences for fishing in its waters and selling postage stamps, as well as from remittances from overseas workers. But the budget has to be balanced with substantial aid from New Zealand and elsewhere.

Tokelau is a dependent territory of New Zealand and has an appointed administrator. In addition there is an assembly, the General Fono, for which elections are held every three years.

However, there have been moves to change Tokelau's status to make it a self-governing territory in free association with New Zealand.

Turks and Caicos

Caribbean islands affected by drugs trafficking

People: *17,000, black and European, speaking English, with some illegal immigrants from Haiti*
Government: *Overseas dependency of the UK. Capital: Grand Turk*
Economy: *GNP per capita: $PPP 7,700. Main export: seafood*

The Turks and Caicos islands are two groups of about forty islands south of the Bahamas. Flat and sandy, the islands are surrounded by coral reefs. Only eight are inhabited.

Two-thirds of the residents are black, the 'belongers'. The rest are expatriates or illegal immigrants from Haiti. A few work in subsistence agriculture, but the main sources of income are fishing, tourism, including a Club Mediterranée, and financial services that cover more than 14,000 registered companies.

As a dependency of the UK, the islands have their own governor, as well as a local executive council and a 13-member legislative council. There are two political parties, the People's Democratic Movement (PDM) and the Progressive National Party (PNP). The PDM won the elections in 1995 and again in 1999, with Derek Taylor as chief minister.

Drugs are a problem. In 1985, three cabinet ministers were imprisoned for trafficking, and in 1996 the governor said that trafficking was still an issue, as was police corruption. Incensed, Taylor demanded his removal. In 1998, three tonnes of cocaine were seized from one boat.

Tuvalu

Owner of a valuable internet domain name—tv

People: *100,000, most are Polynesians. Life expectancy: 64 years*
Government: *Constitutional monarchy, Capital: Funafuti*
Economy: *Per capita income: $PPP 800. Main export: copra. Relies heavily on remittances from emigrant workers*

Though its name means 'eight together', Tuvalu actually comprises nine scattered Pacific islands and atolls. Most people make their living from fishing or from subsistence agriculture. The other main source of income is remittances from Tuvaluans working in the phosphate mines of Nauru, or as sailors on foreign ships.

The government gets 40% of its revenue from fishing licences from foreign vessels. But it has also made considerable sums from sales of stamps and coins, and more recently from selling access to its international telephone codes, initially for phone sex. Its internet domain name, 'tv', offers a prospective bonanza.

Tuvalu was formerly linked with Kiribati as the 'Gilbert' in the Gilbert and Ellis Islands colony. Its head of state is the British monarch represented by a local governor-general. The country has a 12-member directly-elected parliament, which, after the 1999 elections, chose Ionatana Ionatana as prime minister.

In 2000, Tuvalu was invited by the UN Security Council to become the UN's 189th member, though Chinese objections to Tuvalu's links with Taiwan could slow down its admission.

Vatican

A sovereign state in Rome, the headquarters of the Holy See

***People:** 1,000. Italians, Swiss, and many others, speaking Italian and Latin*
***Government:** Monarchical-sacerdotal. Head of state: Pope John Paul II*
***Economy:** Per capita income: not available. Currency is the Vatican lira. Main exports: stamps, religious mementos*

The Vatican is a 44-hectare enclave on the banks of the River Tiber in Rome. This is a territorial state which is the headquarters of the Holy See, the central government of the Roman Catholic Church.

The head of state is the Pope, but most of the temporal duties, including international relations, are the responsibility of the secretary of state, currently Cardinal Angelo Sodano. The Vatican City is administered by a governor.

Those who live and work within the Vatican become citizens. Some 3 thousand other workers commute in from Rome. Almost everything needed within the Vatican has to be imported. But the Vatican has its own diplomatic service, currency, radio station, and daily newspaper. The Swiss Guard are responsible for internal security.

The Roman Catholic Church derives its income from members' contributions, an extensive investment portfolio, and properties all over the world. These are administered by the Institute for Religious Works. In 1998, the Vatican's budget for income and expenditure was $183 million, of which $26 million was contributed by Catholic diocese around the world.

Wallis and Futuna

Pacific islands heavily dependent on French aid

***People:** 15,000. Polynesian, speaking Wallisian and French*
***Government:** Overseas territory of France. Capital: Mata-Utu*
***Economy:** Per capita GDP: $PPP 2,000. Main exports: taro and other crops. Relies heavily on French aid*

In addition to the islands of Wallis and Futuna the country includes the island of Alofi. These are formerly volcanic islands in the South Pacific. The people are mostly Polynesian, with a few French. The Roman Catholic Church has a strong influence.

Wallisians make their living from subsistence agriculture, growing taro, yams, bananas and other crops. The main cash crop is coconuts, grown for copra. They also fish for tuna. Everyone else works for the government. The country relies for survival on French aid.

With limited prospects at home, many people have emigrated, mainly to New Caledonia, and their remittances provide an important source of income.

The islanders send a deputy and a senator to the French National Assembly, but they also have their own territorial assembly. In addition to the equivalents of the parties in metropolitan France, there is also a local party, the Union locale populaire, though there is no pressure for independence. Wallis and Futuna also has a territorial council made up of three traditional kings and three other appointed members.

Indicator tables

Notes on indicator tables

These tables summarize economic and social data produced by the United Nations Development Programme (UNDP) and the World Bank. Full tables are available from these organizations in their annual reports—the UNDP *Human Development Report* and the World Bank *World Development Report*—and also on CDROM. Data unavailable from either of these sources is indicated as '..'.

Table 1. Income, poverty and structure of output

GNP $PPP—Gross national product per capita at purchasing power parity (PPP). For an explanation of PPP see page viii. While this gives some indication of the relative wealth of countries, it does not take into account the distribution of income: many Indians, for example, earn more than many Americans. Nor does it necessarily offer guidance to quality of life: people in Cuba, for example, may have a low income but good health services. Dissatisfaction with GNP as an indicator led to the creation of the UNDP human development index.

Distribution of income—The proportion of national income going to the highest and lowest 10% of income earners. The data are for the latest available years. Note that this refers to income; not to wealth or total assets. Contrasts in wealth can be much more marked, but more difficult to measure.

Poverty—The proportion of people below the international $1-per-day income poverty line. The data are for the latest available year, at 1985 prices. This is a measure of absolute income poverty. Around 1.3 billion people, one fifth of global population, live in absolute income poverty. There are other measures of poverty, thus 'human poverty' takes into account a lack not just of income but also of other essentials, such as basic services, though this is more difficult to estimate. Many countries, particularly the richer ones, also prefer to use relative measures of poverty, typically the proportion of households earning less than half the average national income.

HDI ranking—This is the human development index ranking produced annually by UNDP, based on a composite of indicators for income, health and education. In 2000, the ranking included 174 countries. This list is not exhaustive because it excludes non-UN member countries, such as dependencies, and also those countries for which there were insufficient data. Although the ranking was produced in 2000 it is based on data for earlier years.

Output as % of GDP—This shows the 'value added' by industry, agriculture, and services. This generally refers only to more organized business or government. In some countries, however, up to half the population work outside the 'formal sector' in unofficial employment in the 'informal sector', as street vendors, for example.

Table 2. Health and population

Life expectancy at birth—How long a newborn child can expect to live, on average. World average life expectancy in 1998 was 67 years.

Women have a biological advantage that should enable them to live six or seven years longer than men, so there are normally more women than men. Where there is severe discrimination against women that affects their health the difference can be far less. In Nepal the discrimination is so great that, on average, men outlive women.

Infant mortality—Out of every thousand live births, the number of children who die before their first birthday. This figure is sensitive to a wide range of social and economic conditions, so is one of the most basic indicators of development. The average for the richer countries is 12; for all developing countries it is 64.

Malnutrition—The proportion of children under five years old who weigh less than they should for their age. The data refer to the latest available year, between 1992 and 1997. Other indicators of malnutrition include stunting, which refers to low height for age, and deficiencies in important 'micronutrients' such as Vitamin A or iodine.

Total fertility rate—The number of children that a woman in each country on average bears throughout her life. A figure of 2.1 is the 'replacement rate' that would maintain a steady population. For many countries the rate is below this so their populations are set to fall if they do not replenish them through immigration.

Population growth—The average annual population growth over the period 1990-98. The world average was 1.6%. Total world population was 5.8 billion in 1998 and it is likely to rise to 7.0 billion by 2015.

Safe Water—The proportion of the population with reasonable access to safe drinking water, either treated surface water, or uncontaminated water from other sources such as springs or wells.

Sanitation—The proportion of the population with reasonable access to sanitary means of excreta and waste disposal.

Table 3. Education and communications

Adult illiteracy—The proportion of the population aged fifteen and above that cannot read a short, simple statement on their everyday life.

Education—Public expenditure on education, at all levels, as a proportion of GNP.

Primary enrolment—The proportion of children enrolled in primary school. This is the 'gross enrolment ratio', which is the number of children enrolled as a percentage of the number of children of primary school age. This ratio can rise above 100% because children outside this age group may also be enrolled; some may start early, others may repeat classes or start late.

Newspapers—Daily newspapers per thousand people.

Radios – Sets per thousand people.

TV— Sets per thousand people.

Telephones—Fixed lines per thousand people. Globally, there are three times as many fixed-line phones as there are mobile phones, though mobiles are rapidly catching up. Finland already has more mobiles than fixed lines.

Table 4. Other countries

Many countries do not produce sufficient internationally comparable data. This table collects some of the main available indicators.

Table1. Indicators for income, poverty, and structure of output

	GNP $PPP	Distribution of income		Poverty	HDI ranking	Output as % of GDP		
	per capita	Lowest 10%	Highest 10%	Proportion in	out of 174	Agriculture	Industry	Services
	1998	Share %	Share %	%	2000	1998	1998	1998
Albania	1,120	..	..	..	94	63	18	19
Algeria	4,380	2.8	26.8	..	107	12	47	41
Angola	840	..	..	..	160	14	54	32
Argentina	10,200	..	..	..	35	7	37	56
Armenia	2,260	..	..	..	93	41	36	23
Australia	20,130	2.5	24.8	..	4	3	26	77
Austria	22,740	4.4	19.3	..	16	1	30	68
Azerbaijan	1,820	..	..	..	90	19	44	36
Bangladesh	1,100	4.1	23.7	..	146	23	28	49
Belarus	4,850	3.4	22.6	..	57	14	44	42
Belgium	23,480	3.7	20.2	..	7	1	27	72
Benin	1,250	..	..	..	157	39	14	47
Bolivia	2,820	2.3	31.7	..	114	16	33	52
Botswana	8,310	..	..	33	122	4	46	51
Brazil	6,160	0.8	47.9	24	74	8	36	56
Bulgaria	4,010	3.3	24.7	3	60	23	26	50
Burkina Faso	1,020	2.2	39.5	..	172	32	28	40
Burma (Myanmar)	1,199	..	..	..	125	59	10	31
Burundi	620	..	..	..	170	49	19	32
Cambodia	1,240	..	..	..	136	51	15	34

Cameroon	1,810	..	..	..	134	42	22	36
Canada	24,050	2.8	23.8	..	1	..	..	..
Central African Republic	1,290	..	..	..	165	55	15	27
Chad	970	..	..	..	167	39	15	46
Chile	12,890	1.4	46.1	15	38	8	35	57
China	3,220	2.2	30.9	22	99	18	49	33
Colombia	7,500	1.0	46.9	7	68	13	38	49
Congo	1,430	..	..	..	139	12	50	39
Congo, Dem. Rep.	750	..	..	..	152	58	17	25
Costa Rica	6,620	1.3	34.7	19	48	14	22	64
Côte d'Ivoire	1,730	2.8	28.5	18	154	25	23	52
Croatia	4,895	..	..	..	49	..	..	..
Czech Republic	10,510	4.6	3.5	3	34	..	..	..
Denmark	23,830	3.6	20.5	..	15	..	..	..
Dominican Republic	4,700	1.6	39.6	20	87	12	33	56
Ecuador	4,630	2.3	31.6	30	91	12	34	54
Egypt	3,130	3.9	26.7	8	119	17	33	50
El Salvador	2,850	1.2	38.3	..	104	13	28	59
Eritrea	950	..	..	..	159	9	30	61
Estonia	5,240	2.2	26.2	6	46	5	27	67
Ethiopia	500	3.0	33.7	46	171	..	..	..
Finland	20,270	4.2	21.6	..	66	4	34	62
France	22,320	2.5	24.9	..	11	2	26	72
Georgia	1,960	..	..	..	70	32	23	45
Germany	20,810	3.7	22.6	..	14	1	..	44

Table1. Indicators for income, poverty, and structure of output

	GNP $PPP	Distribution of income		Poverty	HDI ranking	Output as % of GDP		
	per capita	Lowest 10%	Highest 10%	Proportion in	out of 174	Agriculture	Industry	Services
	1998	Share %	Share %	%	2000	1998	1998	1998
Ghana	1,610	3.6	26.1	..	129	37	25	38
Greece	13,010	..	..	..	25	..	..	..
Guatemala	4,070	0.6	46.6	53	54	21	19	60
Guinea	1,760	2.6,	32.0	26	120	22	35	42
Haiti	1,250	..	..	..	152	31	20	48
Honduras	2,140	1.2	42.1	47	113	23	30	47
Hungary	7,200	4.1	24.0	..	43	6	34	60
India	1,700	4.1	25.0	47	128	25	30	45
Indonesia	2,790	3.6	30.3	8	109	16	43	41
Iran	5,817	..	..	..	97	..	..	..
Ireland	18,340	2.5	27.4	..	18	..	..	..
Israel	17,310	2.8	26.9	..	23	..	..	..
Italy	20,200	2.9	23.7	..	19	3	31	66
Jamaica	3,210	2.4	31.9	4	83	7	35	58
Japan	23,180	..	..	..	9	..	..	..
Jordan	3,230	2.4	34.7	3	92	0.3	25	72
Kazakhstan	3,400	3.1	24.9	..	73	10	27	63
Kenya	1,130	1.8	34.9	50	138	29	16	55
Korea, South	12,270	..	..	..	31	6	43	51
Kuwait	25,314	..	..	..	36	..	..	..

Kyrgyzstan	2,200	2.7	26.2	19	98	46	24	30
Laos	1,300	4.2	26.4	..	140	52	21	27
Latvia	3,940	3.3	22.4	..	63	7	31	62
Lebanon	6,150	..	..	..	82	12	27	61
Lesotho	2,320	0.9	43.4	49	127	11	42	47
Lithuania	4,310	3.4	28.0	..	52	14	40	46
Macedonia	3,660	..	..	..	69	12	27	61
Madagascar	900	1.9	36.7	72	141	31	14	56
Malawi	730	..	..	..	163	39	19	41
Malaysia	6,990	1.9	37.9	4	61	12	48	40
Mali	720	1.8	40.4	..	165	45	21	34
Mauritania	1,660	2.3	29.9	31	147	24	30	45
Mexico	8,190	1.4	42.8	15	55	5	27	68
Moldova	1,500	2.7	25.8	7	102	31	35	34
Mongolia	1,520	2.9	24.5	..	117	33	28	40
Morocco	3,120	2.8	30.5	..	124	16	30	54
Mozambique	850	..	..	..	168	34	18	48
Namibia	4,950	..	..	..	125	10	34	56
Nepal	1,090	3.2	29.8	50	115	40	22	38
Netherlands	21,620	2.9	24.7	..	8	..	..	..
New Zealand	15,840	..	..	..	20	..	..	..
Nicaragua	1,790	1.6	39.8	44	116	34	22	44
Niger	830	0.8	35.4	62	173	41	17	42
Nigeria	820	1.3	31.4	31	151	32	41	27
Norway	24,290	4.1	21.2	..	2	2	32	66

Table1. Indicators for income, poverty, and structure of output

	GNP $PPP	Distribution of income		Poverty	HDI ranking	Output as % of GDP		
	per capita	Lowest 10%	Highest 10%	Proportion in	out of 174	Agriculture	Industry	Services
	1998	Share %	Share %	%	2000	1998	1998	1998
Pakistan	1,560	4.1	27.7	12	135	25	25	50
Panama	6,940	0.7	43.8	26	59	7	17	76
Papua New Guinea	2,700	1.7	40.5	..	133	28	36	36
Paraguay	3,650	0.7	46.6	..	81	25	22	53
Peru	4,420	1.6	35.4	..	80	7	38	55
Philippines	3,540	2.4	33.5	27	77	17	32	52
Poland	6,740	4.0	22.1	7	44	4	26	70
Portugal	14,380	..	..	..	28	..	..	..
Romania	3,970	3.7	22.7	18	64	15	36	48
Russia	3,950	1.4	37.4	..	62	9	42	49
Rwanda	690	4.2	24.2	46	164	34	23	43
Saudi Arabia	10,120	..	..	..	75	6	45	49
Senegal	1,710	1.0	42.3	54	155	17	23	59
Sierra Leone	390	0.5	43.6	..	174	44	24	32
Singapore	28,620	..	..	..	24	0	35	65
Slovakia	7,910	5.1	18.2	13	40	5	33	62
Slovenia	11,800	4.0	24.5	..	29	5	39	57
South Africa	6,990	1.1	45.9	24	103	4	38	57
Spain	16,060	2.8	25.2	..	21	3		
Sri Lanka	2,490	3.8	25.2	4	84	22	26	52

Sweden	19,480	3.7	20.1	..	6	..	..	..
Switzerland	26,620	2.9	28.6	..	13	..	..	..
Syria	3,000	..	..	..	111	..	..	..
Tajikistan	920	..	..	..	110	..	..	..
Tanzania	490	2.8	30.1	..	156	46	14	40
Thailand	5,840	2.5	37.1	..	76	11	40	49
Togo	1,390	..	..	..	145	42	21	37
Tunisia	5,160	2.3	30.7	4	101	14	28	58
Turkey	6,350	..	..	..	85	15	28	57
Turkmenistan	2,109	2.7	26.9	5	100	..	..	..
Uganda	1,170	2.6	31.2	69	158	43	18	39
Ukraine	2,190	1.4	36.8	..	78	12	40	48
United Kingdom	20,640	2.4	24.7	..	45	2	31	67
United States	29,340	1.5	28.5	..	10	2	27	71
Uruguay	9,480	..	..	..	39	8	27	64
Uzbekistan	2,900	..	..	..	106	28	30	42
Venezuela	8,190	1.5	35.6	12	65	4	43	52
Vietnam	1,690	3.5	29.0	..	108	26	31	43
Yemen	740	2.3	30.8	..	148	18	49	34
Zambia	860	1.6	39.2	85	153	16	30	55
Zimbabwe	2,150	1.8	46.9	41	130	18	24	58

Table 2. Indicators for health and population

	Life expectancy at birth Years, 1997		Infant mortality per '000 live births 1997	Malnutrition % children under 5 1992-97	Fertility rate per woman 1997	Population Annual growth % 1990-98	Safe water % access 1995	Sanitation % access 1995
	Males	Females						
Albania	69	75	26	..	2.5	0.3	76	58
Algeria	69	72	32	13	3.6	2.6	..	..
Angola	45	48	125	35	6.8	3.8	32	15
Argentina	70	77	22	2	2.6	1.5	65	75
Armenia	70	77	15	..	1.5	1.0	..	..
Australia	76	81	5	..	1.8	1.3	99	..
Austria	74	81	5	..	1.4	0.7	..	..
Azerbaijan	67	75	20	10	2.1	1.4		36
Bangladesh	58	58	75	56	3.2	1.9	84	35
Belarus	63	74	12	..	1.2	0.0	..	..
Belgium	73	80	6	..	1.6	0.3	..	..
Benin	52	55	88	29	5.8	3.3	72	24
Bolivia	60	63	66	8	4.4	2.7	70	41
Botswana	46	48	58	27	4.3	2.9	70	55
Brazil	63	71	34	6	2.3	1.6	69	67
Bulgaria	67	74	18	..	1.1	-0.8	..	..
Burkina Faso	44	45	99	33	6.6	2.7	..	..
Burma (Myanmar)	59	62	79	43	2.4	1.3	60	43
Burundi	41	44	119	38	6.3	2.7	58	48
Cambodia	53	55	103	38	4.6	3.1	13	..

Cameroon	55	58	52	..	5.3	3.2	41	40
Canada	76	82	6	..	1.6	1.4	99	95
Central African Republic	43	47	98	23	4.9	2.4	23	45
Chad	47	50	100	39	6.5	3.5	24	27
Chile	72	78	11	1	2.4	1.8	91	81
China	68	71	32	16	1.9	1.2	8.3	
Colombia	67	73	24	8	2.8	2.2	75	59
Congo	46	51	90	24	6.1	3.2	..	9
Congo, Dem. Rep.	49	52	92	34	6.4	3.6	..	..
Costa Rica	74	79	12	5	2.8	2.1	100	97
Côte d'Ivoire	46	47	87	24	5.1	3.1	72	51
Croatia	68	77	9	1	1.6	-0.6	63	61
Czech Republic	71	78	6	1	1.2	-0.1	..	..
Denmark	73	78	6	..	1.8	0.4	..	100
Dominican Republic	69	73	40	6	3.0	2.1	73	80
Ecuador	68	73	33	17	3.0	2.4	55	53
Egypt	65	68	51	15	3.2	2.3	84	70
El Salvador	67	73	32	11	3.2	2.4	53	77
Eritrea	49	52	62	44	5.8	3.0	7	..
Estonia	64	76	10	..	1.2	-1.2	..	..
Ethiopia	42	44	107	48	6.5	2.6	26	8
Finland	73	81	4	..	1.9	0.5	98	100
France	74	82	5	..	1.7	0.5	100	..
Georgia	69	77	17	..	1.5	-0.1	..	..
Germany	74	80	5	..	1.4	0.5	..	..

Table 2. Indicators for health and population

	Life expectancy at birth		Infant mortality	Malnutrition	Fertility rate	Population	Safe water	Sanitation
	Years, 1997		*per '000 live births*	*% children under 5*	*per woman*	*Annual growth %*	*% access*	*% access*
	Males	Females	*1997*	*1992-97*	*1997*	*1990-98*	*1995*	*1995*
Ghana	58	62	66	27	4.9	3.1	65	32
Greece	75	81	7	..	1.3	0.5	..	..
Guatemala	61	67	43	27	4.5	3.0	67	67
Guinea	46	47	110	24	5.5	3.0	55	14
Haiti	51	56	71	28	4.4	2.4	39	26
Honduras	67	72	36	18	4.3	3.3	77	82
Hungary	66	75	10	..	1.4	-0.3	..	..
India	62	64	71	53	3.3	2.0	85	16
Indonesia	63	67	47	34	2.8	1.9	65	55
Iran	69	70	32	16	2.8	1.9	90	81
Ireland	73	79	5	..	1.9	0.7	..	..
Israel	76	79	..	..	2.7	3.5	99	100
Italy	75	82	5	..	1.2	0.2	..	..
Jamaica	72	77	12	10	2.7	1.0	93	79
Japan	77	83	4	..	1.4	0.3	96	100
Jordan	69	73	29	10	4.2	5.2	98	98
Kazakhstan	60	70	24	8	2.0	-0.6	..	..
Kenya	51	53	74	23	4.7	3.1	45	45
Korea, South	69	76	9	..	1.7	1.1	83	100
Kuwait	74	80	12	11	2.9	-1.8	100	100

Kyrgyzstan	63	71	28	11	2.8	1.0	81	..
Laos	52	55	98	40	5.6	3.0	51	32
Latvia	64	75	15	..	1.1	-1.3	..	..
Lebanon	68	72	28	3	2.5	2.1	94	9'
Lesotho	55	57	93	16	4.8	2.6	62	..
Lithuania	66	77	10	..	1.4	-0.1	..	..
Macedonia	70	75	16	..	1.9	0.8	..	..
Madagascar	56	59	94	34	5.8	3.2	16	34
Malawi	43	43	133	30	6.4	3.1	60	64
Malaysia	70	75	11	20	3.2	2.8	89	94
Mali	49	52	118	40	6.6	3.2	48	37
Mauritania	52	55	92	23	5.5	3.2	64	32
Mexico	69	75	31	14	2.8	2.0	95	76
Moldova	63	70	20	..	1.6	-0.2	56	50
Mongolia	64	67	52	12	2.6	2.2	54	..
Morocco	65	69	51	10	3.1	2.1	57	68
Mozambique	44	47	135	26	5.3	2.6	24	23
Namibia	55	57	65	26	4.9	3.0	60	42
Nepal	58	57	83	47	4.4	2.8	59	23
Netherlands	75	81	5	..	1.5	0.7	99	100
New Zealand	75	80	7	..	1.9	1.7	90	..
Nicaragua	66	71	43	12	3.9	3.2	62	59
Niger	45	50	118	43	7.4	3.9	48	17
Nigeria	52	55	77	39	5.3	3.3	50	57
Norway	76	81	4	..	1.9	0.6	100	100

Table 2. Indicators for health and population

	Life expectancy at birth		Infant mortality	Malnutrition	Fertility rate	Population	Safe water	Sanitation
	Years, 1997		*per '000 live births*	*% children under 5*	*per woman*	*Annual growth %*	*% access*	*% access*
	Males	Females	*1997*	*1992-97*	*1997*	*1990-98*	*1995*	*1995*
Pakistan	61	63	95	38	5.0	2.8	62	39
Panama	72	76	21	6	2.6	2.0	84	90
Papua New Guinea	57	59	61	30	4.3	2.6	31	25
Paraguay	68	72	23	..	3.8	3.0	39	32
Peru	66	71	40	8	3.2	2.0	66	61
Philippines	67	70	35	30	3.6	2.6	83	77
Poland	69	77	10	..	1.5	0.2	..	..
Portugal	71	79	6	..	1.4	0.1	82	..
Romania	65	73	22	6	1.3	-0.5	62	44
Russia	61	73	17	3	1.3	-0.1	..	..
Rwanda	39	42	124	29	6.2	2.2	..	94
Saudi Arabia	69	72	21	..	5.9	3.9	93	86
Senegal	51	54	70	22	5.6	3.0	50	..
Sierra Leone	36	39	170	..	6.1	2.8	34	..
Singapore	73	79	4	..	1.7	2.2	100	100
Slovakia	69	77	9	..	1.4	0.3	..	51
Slovenia	71	79	5	..	1.3	-0.1	98	98
South Africa	62	68	48	9	2.8	2.3	59	53
Spain	75	82	5	..	1.1	0.2	..	97
Sri Lanka	71	75	14	38	2.2	1.4	70	75

Sweden	77	82	4	..	1.7	0.5	..	..
Switzerland	76	82	5	..	1.5	0.8	100	..
Syria	67	71	31	13	4.0	3.3	88	71
Tajikistan	66	71	30	..	3.5	2.0	69	62
Tanzania	47	49	85	31	5.5	3.3	49	86
Thailand	66	72	33	..	1.7	1.4	89	96
Togo	48	50	86	19	6.1	3.4	55	41
Tunisia	68	71	30	9	2.8	2.0	90	80
Turkey	67	72	40	10	2.5	1.8	..	..
Turkmenistan	62	69	40	..	3.0	3.6	60	60
Uganda	43	42	99	26	6.6	3.5	42	67
Ukraine	62	73	14	..	1.3	-0.5	55	49
United Kingdom	75	80	6	..	1.7	0.4	100	96
United States	73	79	7	1	2.0	1.1	73	..
Uruguay	70	78	16	4	2.4	0.8	89	61
Uzbekistan	66	72	..	19	3.3	2.3	57	18
Venezuela	70	76	21	5	3.0	2.5	79	72
Vietnam	66	71	29	45	2.4	2.3	47	60
Yemen	54	55	96	29	6.4	4.7	39	19
Zambia	43	43	113	24	5.6	3.1	53	51
Zimbabwe	51	54	69	16	3.8	2.6	77	66

Table 3. Indicators for education and communications

	Adult illiteracy rate %, 1997		Education % of GNP	Primary enrolment %	Newspapers per thousand	Radios per thousand	TV sets per thousand	Telephones per thousand
	Males	Females	1996	1996	1996	1996	1997	1997
Albania	..	..	3.1	102	34	235	161	23
Algeria	27	52	5.1	94	38	239	67	48
Angola	..	..	..	..	12	54	91	5
Argentina	3	4	3.5	..	123	677	289	191
Armenia	..	..	2.0	..	23	5	218	150
Australia	..	..	5.6	95	297	1,385	638	505
Austria	..	..	5.6	100	294	740	496	492
Azerbaijan	..	..	3.3	..	28	20	211	87
Bangladesh	50	73	2.9	..	9	50	7	3
Belarus	0	2	6.1	85	174	290	314	227
Belgium	..	..	3.2	98	160	792	510	468
Benin	52	79	3.2	63	2	108	91	6
Bolivia	9	23	5.6		55	672	115	69
Botswana	28	23	10.4	81	27	155	27	56
Brazil	16	16	5.5	90	40	435	316	107
Bulgaria	1	2	3.3	92	253	531	366	323
Burkina Faso	70	89	1.5	31	1	32	6	3
Burma (Myanmar)	11	21	1.2	..	10	89	7	5
Burundi	46	64	3.1	..	3	68	10	3
Cambodia	..	..	2.9	98	..	127	124	2

Cameroon	21	35	2.9	..	7	162	81	5
Canada	..	..	7.0	95	159	1,078	708	609
Central African Republic	44	70	..	..	2	84	5	3
Chad	..	..	2.4	46	0	249	2	1
Chile	5	5	3.1	88	99	354	233	180
China	9	25	2.3	102	..	195	270	56
Colombia	9	9	4.4	85	49	565	217	148
Congo	15	30	6.2	..	8	124	8	8
Congo, Dem. Rep.	..	..	..	54	3	98	43	1
Costa Rica	5	5	5.3	91	91	271	403	169
Côte d'Ivoire	49	66	5.0	55	16	157	61	9
Croatia	1	4	5.3	82	114	333	267	335
Czech Republic	..	..	5.4	91	256	806	447	318
Denmark	..	..	8.2	99	311	1,146	568	633
Dominican Republic	17	18	2.0	81	52	177	84	88
Ecuador	7	11	3.5	97	70	342	294	75
Egypt	35	60	4.8	93	38	316	127	56
El Salvador	20	26	2.2	78	48	461	250	56
Eritrea	..	..	1.8	30	..	101	11	6
Estonia	..	..	7.3	87	173	680	479	321
Ethiopia	59	71	4.0	28	2	194	5	3
Finland	..	..	7.6	99	455	1,385	534	556
France	..	..	61	100	218	943	606	575
Georgia	..	..	5.2	87	..	553	473	114
Germany	..	..	4.8	100	311	946	570	550

Table 3. Indicators for education and communications

	Adult illiteracy rate %, 1997		Education % of GNP	Primary enrolment %	Newspapers per thousand	Radios per thousand	TV sets per thousand	Telephones per thousand
	Males	Females	1996	1996	1996	1996	1997	1997
Ghana	23	43	..	..	14	238	109	6
Greece	2	5	3.0	90	153	477	466	516
Guatemala	26	41	1.7	..	31	73	126	41
Guinea	..	..	..	37	..	47	41	3
Haiti	52	57	..	..	3	55	5	8
Honduras	29	30	3.6	90	55	409	90	37
Hungary	1	1	4.7	97	189	697	436	304
India	33	61	3.4	..	..	105	69	19
Indonesia	9	20	1.4	97	23	155	134	25
Iran	19	34	4.0	90	24	237	148	107
Ireland	..	..	5.8	100	153	703	455	411
Israel	2	7	7.2	..	291	530	321	450
Italy	1	2	4.7	100	104	874	483	447
Jamaica	19	10	7.4	..	64	482	323	140
Japan	..	..	3.6	103	580	957	708	479
Jordan	8	18	7.3	..	45	287	43	70
Kazakhstan	..	..	4.7	..	30	384	234	108
Kenya	13	28	6.6	..	9	108	19	8
Korea, South	1	4	3.7	92	394	1,037	341	444
Kuwait	17	23	5.7	54	376	688	491	227

Kyrgyzstan	..	..	5.7	95	13	115	44	76
Laos	..	..	2.5	72	4	139	4	5
Latvia	0	1	6.5	90	246	699	592	302
Lebanon	9	22	2.5	76	141	892	354	179
Lesotho	29	7	7.0	70	7	48	24	10
Lithuania	0	1	5.6	..	92	292	377	283
Macedonia	..	..	5.6	95	19	184	252	204
Madagascar	..	..	1.9	61	4	192	45	3
Malawi	27	57	5.5	68	3	256	2	4
Malaysia	10	19	52	102	163	432	166	195
Mali	57	72	2.2	28	1	49	10	2
Mauritania	51	72	5.1	57	1	150	89	5
Mexico	8	12	4.9	101	97	324	251	96
Moldova	1	3	9.7	..	59	720	302	145
Mongolia	..	..	6.4	81	27	139	63	37
Morocco	41	67	5.3	74	26	241	160	50
Mozambique	43	75	..	40	3	39	4	4
Namibia	19	22	9.1	91	19	143	32	58
Nepal	44	79	2.8	..	11	37	4	8
Netherlands	..	..	5.2	99	305	963	541	564
New Zealand	..	..	7.3	100	223	1,027	501	486
Nicaragua	37	37	3.7	78	32	283	190	29
Niger	78	93	..	25	0	69	26	2
Nigeria	31	49	0.9	..	24	197	61	4
Norway	..	..	7.5	99	593	920	579	621

Table 3. Indicators for education and communications

	Adult illiteracy rate %, 1997		Education % of GNP	Primary enrollment %	Newspapers per thousand	Radios per thousand	TV sets per thousand	Telephones per thousand
	Males	Females	1996	1996	1996	1996	1997	1997
Pakistan	45	75	3.0	..	21	92	65	19
Panama	8	10	4.6	..	62	299	187	134
Papua New Guinea	..	..	..	..	15	91	24	11
Paraguay	6	9	3.9	91	50	182	101	43
Peru	6	16	2.9	91	43	271	143	68
Philippines	5	6	2.2	101	82	159	109	29
Poland	0	0	5.2	95	113	518	413	194
Portugal	6	12	5.5	104	75	306	523	402
Romania	1	3	3.6	95	..	317	226	167
Russia	0	1	4.1	93	105	344	390	183
Rwanda	29	44	..	..	0	102	..	3
Saudi Arabia	19	38	5.5	61	59	319	260	117
Senegal	55	75	3.5	58	5	141	41	13
Sierra Leone	..	..	..	..	5	251	20	4
Singapore	4	13	3.0	..	324	739	354	543
Slovakia	..	..	4.9	..	185	580	401	259
Slovenia	0	0	5.8	95	206	416	353	364
South Africa	15	17	7.9	..	30	316	125	107
Spain	2	4	4.9	105	99	328	506	403
Sri Lanka	6	12	3.4	..	29	210	91	17

Sweden	..	..	8.3	102	446	907	531	679
Switzerland	..	..	5.3	..	330	969	536	661
Syria	13	43	4.2	91	20	274	68	88
Tajikistan	1	2	2.2	..	20	..	281	38
Tanzania	18	38	..	48	4	278	21	3
Thailand	3	7	4.1	..	65	204	234	80
Togo	31	62	4.7	85	4	217	19	6
Tunisia	22	44	6.7	98	31	218	182	70
Turkey	8	26	2.2	96	111	178	286	250
Turkmenistan	..	..	..	..	..	96	175	78
Uganda	25	47	2.6	..	2	123	26	2
Ukraine	..	..	7.2	..	54	872	493	186
United Kingdom	..	..	5.4	100	332	1,445	641	540
United States	..	..	5.4	95	212	2,115	847	644
Uruguay	3	2	3.3	93	116	610	242	232
Uzbekistan	..	..	8.1	..	3	452	273	63
Venezuela	7	8	5.2	84	206	471	172	116
Vietnam	5	11	2.6	..	4	106	180	21
Yemen	36	79	6.5	52	15	64	273	13
Zambia	17	33	2.2	75	14	121	80	9
Zimbabwe	6	12	8.3	..	18	96	29	17

Table 4. Indicators for other countries

	Population density	Life expectancy	Infant mortality	Primary education	Adult illiteracy	With safe water	With safe sanitation	Human development
	per sq. km	Years	per '000	enrolment %	%	%	%	ranking of 174
	1998	1997	1997	1997	1997	1990-97	1990-97	1997
Afghanistan	40	45	..	..	67	..	..	..
American Samoa	315	75	..	..	..	..	..	..
Andorra	144	83	..	..	..	..	..	..
Antigua and Barbuda	152	75	17	..	..	..	96	38
Aruba	495	75	..	..	..	..	..	..
Bahamas	29	74	18	95	4	94	82	31
Bahrain	929	73	18	98	14	94	97	37
Barbados	618	76	11	97	..	100		29
Belize	10	75	35	100	..	83	57	83
Bermuda	1,260	77	..	..	..	..	..	..
Bhutan	16	61	87	13	..	58	70	145
Bosnia and Herzegovina	69	67	..	..	..	..	..	..
Brunei	60	76	8	88	10	..	..	25
Cape Verde	102	68	54	100	29	51	24	106
Cayman Islands	138	68	..	..	..	..	..	..
Channel Islands	478	78	..	..	..	..	..	..
Comoros	238	60	69	50	45	53	23	139
Cuba	101	76	7	100	4	47	66	58
Cyprus	82	78	8	..	4	100	97	26
Djibouti	28	50	111	32	..	90	55	157

Dominica	98	76	17	..	..	96	80	53
Equatorial Guinea	15	50	109	79	20	95	54	131
Faroe Islands	42	78	..	..	..	..	..	..
Fiji	45	73	20	100	8	77	92	61
French Guiana	2	77	..	..	..	..	..	..
French Polynesia	62	72	..	..	..	..	..	..
Gabon	5	52	85	..		67		124
Gambia	122	53	66	66	67	69	37	163
Greenland	0	68	..	..	..	..	..	..
Grenada	283	72	24	..	..	..	..	52
Guadeloupe	255	77	..	..	..	..	..	..
Guam	271	77	..	..	..	..	..	..
Guinea-Bissau	41	44	130	52	66	43	46	168
Guyana	4	64	59	93	2	91	88	99
Iceland	3	79	5	100	..	..	..	9
Iraq	51	58	94	75	..	91	75	125
Isle of Man	122	78	..	..	..	..	..	..
Kiribati	117	60	..	..	..	..	..	..
Korea, North	192	63	..	..	..	..	..	..
Liberia	31	47	..	..	52	..	..	..
Libya	3	70	22	100	24	97	98	65
Liechtenstein	200	78	..	..	..	..	..	..
Luxembourg	161	76	5	..	..	..	..	17
Maldives	874	67	53	..	8	60	44	93
Malta	1,180	77	9	100	4	..	..	32

Table 4. Indicators for other countries

	Population density	Life expectancy	Infant mortality	Primary education	Adult illiteracy	With safe water	With safe sanitation	Human development
	per sq. km	Years	per '000	enrolment %	%	%	%	ranking of 174
	1998	1997	1997	1997	1997	1990-97	1990-97	1997
Marshall Islands	310	64	..	..	9	..	..	..
Martinique	374	79	..	..	..	..	..	..
Mauritius	571	71	20	97	3	98		59
Mayotte	315	60	..	..	17	..	..	..
Micronesia.	155	67	..	..	..	..	..	..
Monaco	1,600	78	..	..	..	..	..	..
Netherlands Antilles	266	75	..	..	..	..	..	..
New Caledonia	11	73	..	..	4	..	..	..
Northern Mariana Islands	140		..	..	..	..	..	..
Oman	11	73	15	68	..	85	78	89
Palau	32	71	..	..	33	..	..	..
Palestine	411	71	..	..	..	..	..	..
Puerto Rico	435	75	..	..	7	..	..	..
Qatar	67	72	16	83	20	..	97	41
Réunion	275	75	..	..	14	..	..	..
St. Kitts and Nevis	113	70	30	..	..	100	..	51
St. Lucia	263	70	24	..	..	85	..	81
St. Vincent & Grenadines	290	73	18	..	..	89	98	75
Samoa	62	69	..	97	..	68	..	70
São Tomé and Príncipe	148	64	61	..	..	72	35	123

Seychelles	175	71	14	..	..	..	..	66
Solomon Islands	15	70	23	..	..	61	..	118
Somalia	14	47	..	..	..	..	..	..
Sudan	12	55	73	..	47	73	51	142
Suriname	3	70	24	100	..	..	..	64
Swaziland	57	60	66	95	23	50	59	113
Tonga	137	70	..	..	..	..	..	..
Trinidad and Tobago	257	73	15	100	2	97	79	46
United Arab Emirates	32	75	9	82	25	97	92	43
Vanuatu	15	65	39	71	..	77	28	116
Virgin Islands (US)	348	77	..	..	..	..	..	..